# Lecture Notes in Artificial Intelligence    7101

## Subseries of Lecture Notes in Computer Science

LNAI Series Editors

Randy Goebel
  *University of Alberta, Edmonton, Cano*
Yuzuru Tanaka
  *Hokkaido University, Sapporo, Japan*
Wolfgang Wahlster
  *DFKI and Saarland University, Saarbrücken, Germany*

LNAI Founding Series Editor

Joerg Siekmann
  *DFKI and Saarland University, Saarbrücken, Germany*

T0074183

Sabina Jeschke   Honghai Liu
Daniel Schilberg (Eds.)

# Intelligent Robotics and Applications

4th International Conference, ICIRA 2011
Aachen, Germany, December 6-8, 2011
Proceedings, Part I

 Springer

Series Editors

Randy Goebel, University of Alberta, Edmonton, Canada
Jörg Siekmann, University of Saarland, Saarbrücken, Germany
Wolfgang Wahlster, DFKI and University of Saarland, Saarbrücken, Germany

Volume Editors

Sabina Jeschke
RWTH Aachen University, IMA/ZLW & IFU
Dennewartstraße 27, 52068 Aachen, Germany
E-mail: jeschke.office@ima-zlw-ifu.rwth-aachen.de

Honghai Liu
University of Portsmouth, School of Creative Technologies
Intelligent Systems and Biomedical Robotics Group
Eldon Building, Winston Churchill Avenue, Portsmouth, PO1 2DJ, UK
E-mail: honghai.liu@port.ac.uk

Daniel Schilberg
RWTH Aachen University, IMA/ZLW & IFU
Dennewartstraße 27, 52068 Aachen, Germany
E-mail: daniel.schilberg@ima-zlw-ifu.rwth-aachen.de

ISSN 0302-9743              e-ISSN 1611-3349
ISBN 978-3-642-25485-7      e-ISBN 978-3-642-25486-4
DOI 10.1007/978-3-642-25486-4
Springer Heidelberg Dordrecht London New York

Library of Congress Control Number: 2011941364

CR Subject Classification (1998): I.4, I.5, I.2, I.2.10, H.4, C.2

LNCS Sublibrary: SL 7 – Artificial Intelligence

*Typesetting:* Camera-ready by author, data conversion by Scientific Publishing Services, Chennai, India

Printed on acid-free paper

Springer is part of Springer Science+Business Media (www.springer.com)

# Preface

Robots are increasingly being used for service duties, exploring inaccessible areas and for emergency and security tasks, besides their conventional application in industrial environments. The trend toward intelligent and autonomous systems is uninterrupted and poses new challenges for the interaction between humans and robots. Controlling robots is far beyond conventional programming specific tasks and cooperation between humans and robots becomes crucially important. As a result, the behavior of modern robots needs to be optimized toward these new challenges.

Against this background, the 4th International Conference on Intelligent Robotics and Applications picked "Improving Robot Behavior" as its central subject. Building on the success of the previous ICIRA conference series in Wuhan, China, Singapore and Shanghai, China, the renowned conference left Asia for the first time and took place between December 6–8, 2011 in Aachen, Germany. On the one hand, ICIRA 2011 aimed to strengthen the link between different disciplines developing and/or using robotics and its applications. On the other hand, it improved the connection between different perspectives on the field of robotics - from fundamental research to the industrial usage of robotics.

The response from the scientific community was great and after an extensive review 122 papers were selected for oral presentation at the conference. These high-quality papers from international authors cover a broad variety of topics, resembling the state of the art in robotic research. The papers accepted for the conference are presented in this volume of Springer's *Lecture Notes in Artificial Intelligence*. The volume is organized according to the conference sessions. The sessions cover a wide field of robotic research including topics such as "Robotics in Education", "Human–Robot-Interaction" and "Bio-inspired Robotics" as well as "Robotics Assembly Applications", "Parallel Kinematics" or "Multi-Robot Systems".

We would like to thank all authors and contributors who supported ICIRA 2011 and the organization team under the direction of Max Haberstroh and Ralph Kunze. Our special gratitude goes to the International Advisory Committee and Program Chairs for their help and guidance, as well as the many external reviewers who helped to maintain the high quality the conference demonstrated in the past three years. Our particular thanks goes to the keynote speakers Rüdiger Dillmann (KIT, Germany), Dennis Hong (Virginia Tech, USA) and Bradley Nelson (ETH Zürich, Switzerland) for their inspiring talks.

December 2011

Sabina Jeschke
Honghai Liu
Daniel Schilberg

# Conference Organization

## Conference Chair

Sabina Jeschke              RWTH Aachen University, Germany

## Conference Co-chair

Xiangyang Zhu           Shanghai Jiao Tong University, China

## Program Chairs

Ulrich Epple                RWTH Aachen University, Aachen
Stefan Kowalewski        RWTH Aachen University, Aachen

## Program Co-chairs

Honghai Liu                University of Portsmouth, UK
Jangmyung Lee          Pusan National University, Republic of Korea
Chun-Yi Su                Concordia University, Canada

## International Advisory Committee

Tamio Arai                University of Tokyo, Japan
Hegao Cai                Harbin Institute of Technology, China
Toshio Fukuda          Nagoya University, Japan
Klaus Henning          RWTH Aachen University, Germany
Huosheng Hu           Essex University, UK
Oussama Khatib         Stanford University, USA
Jurgen Leopold         Huazhong University of Science and
                                   Technology, China
Ming Li                  National Natural Science Foundation of China,
                                   China
Peter Luh                Connecticut University, USA
Jun Ni                   University of Michigan, USA
Nikhil R. Pal            Indian Statistical Institute, India
Grigory Panovko        Russian Academy of Science, Russia
Mohammad Siddique     Fayetteville State University, USA
Xinyu Shao             Huazhong University of Science and
                                   Technology, China
Shigeki Sugano         Waseda University, Japan
Michael Wang          Chinese University of Hong Kong, China

Kevin Warwick                  University of Reading, UK
Bogdan M. Wilamowski           Auburn University, USA
Ming Xie                       Nanyang Technological University, Singapore
Youlun Xiong                   Huazhong University of Science and
                                   Technology, China
Lotfi Zadeh                    California University of Berkeley, USA

## Conference Area Chairs

Andrew Adamatzky               University of the West of England, UK
Shamsudin H.M. Amin            Universiti Teknologi Malaysia, Malaysia
Nikos A. Aspragathos           University of Patras, Greece
Philippe Bidaud                Université Pierre and Marie Curie, France
Darwin G. Caldwell             Italian Institute of Technology, Italy
Jan-Olof Eklundh               Center for Autonomous Systems, Sweden
Ashraf M. Elnagar              University of Sharjah, United Arab Emirates
Hubert Gattringer              Johannes Kepler University Linz, Austria
Vladimir Golovko               Brest State Technical University,
                                   Republic of Belarus
Jwusheng Hu                    National Chiao Tung Universty, Taiwan
Karel Jezernik                 University of Maribor, Slovenia
Petko Kiriazov                 Bulgarian Academy of Sciences, Bulgaria
Heikki Koivo                   Helsinki University of Technology, Finland
Krzysztof Kozłowski            Poznan University of Technology, Poland
Maarja Kruusmaa                Tallinn University of Technology, Estonia
Dirk Lefeber                   Vrije Universiteit Brussel, Belgium
Yangmin Li                     University of Macau, Macau
Bruce MacDonald                University of Auckland, New Zealand
Eric T. Matson                 Purdue University, USA
Ivan Petrovic                  University of Zagreb, Croatia
Miguel A. Salichs              Universidad Carlos III de Madrid, Spain
Jim Torresen                   University of Oslo, Norway
Laszlo Vajta                   Budapest University of Technology and
                                   Economics, Hungary
Holger Voos                    University of Luxembourg, Luxembourg
Cees Witteveen                 Delft University of Technology,
                                   The Netherlands
Changjiu Zhou                  Singapore Polytechnic, Republic of Singapore

## Conference Special Session Chair

Naoyuki Kubota                 Tokyo Metropolitan University, Japan

# International Program Committee

Fakhreddine Ababsa, France
Ehsan Aboosaeedan, Iran
Sadek Crisóstomo Absi Alfaro, Brazil
Cihan Acar, Japan
Carlos Antonio Acosta Calderon,
  Singapore
Nitin Afzulpurkar, Thailand
Mojtaba Ahmadi, Canada
Andika Aji Wijaya, Malaysia
Otar Akanyeti, Italy
Berkant Akin, Turkey
Mohammad Al Janaideh, Jordan
Mohamed Al Marzouqi, UAE
Ahmed Al-Araji
Amna AlDahak, UAE
Khalid A.S. Al-Khateeb, Malaysia
Kaspar Althoefer, UK
Erdinç Altug, Turkey
Farshid Amirabdollahian, UK
Cecilio Angulo, Spain
Sherine Antoun, Australia
Silvia Appendino, Italy
Philippe S. Archambault, Canada
Kartik Ariyur, USA
Panagiotis Artemiadis, USA
Joonbum Bae, USA
Feng Bai, China
Subhasis Banerji, Singapore
Sven Behnke, Germany
Nicola Bellotto, UK
Cindy Bethel, USA
Richard J. Black, USA
Misel Brezak, Croatia
Elizabeth Broadbent, New Zealand
Magdalena Bugajska, USA
Darius Burschka, Germany
Qiao Cai, USA
Berk Calli, The Netherlands
Jiangtao Cao, China
Zhiqiang Cao, China
David Capson, Canada
Barbara Caputo, Switzerland
Guillaume Caron, France
Auat Cheein, Argentina

Xiaopeng Chen, China
Ian Chen, New Zealand
Zhaopeng Chen, Germany
Wenjie Chen, Singapore
Youhua Chen, USA
Dimitrios Chrysostomou, Greece
Xavier Clady, France
Burkhard Corves, Germany
Daniel Cox, USA
Jacob Crandall, UAE
Robert Cupec, Croatia
Boris Curk, Slovenia
Marija Dakulovic, Croatia
Konstantinos Dalamagkidis, Germany
Fadly Jashi Darsivan, Malaysia
Kamen Delchev, Bulgaria
Hua Deng, China
Ming Ding, Japan
Hao Ding, Germany
Can Ulas Dogruer, Turkey
Haiwei Dong, Japan
Zhenchun Du, China
Hadi ElDaou, Estonia
Martin Esser, Germany
Andrés Faíña, Spain
Yongchun Fang, China
Faezeh Farivar, Iran
Ehsan Fazl-Ersi, Canada
Ying Feng, Canada
Lucia Fernandez Cossio, Spain
Manuel Fernandez-Carmona, Spain
Kevin Fite, USA
Antonio Frisoli, Italy
Zhuang Fu, China
Velappa Gounder Ganapathy, Malaysia
Zhen Gao, Canada
Antonios Gasteratos, Greece
Yiannis Georgilas, UK
Hu Gong, China
Dongbing Gu, UK
Liwen Guan, China
Lei Guo, China
Alvaro Gutierrez, Spain
Norihiro Hagita, Japan

Hassan Haleh, Iran
Kenji Hashimoto, Japan
Mitsuhiro Hayashibe, France
Patrick Hénaff, France
Sophie Hennequin, France
Dominik Henrich, Germany
K.V. Hindriks, The Netherlands
Vesa Hölttä, Finland
Masaaki Honda, Japan
Tianjiang Hu, China
Yong'an Huang, China
Cong-Hui Huang, Taiwan
Mathias Hüsing, Germany
Detelina Ignatova, Bulgaria
Atsutoshi Ikeda, Japan
Akira Imada, Belarus
Mircea Ivanescu, Romania
Edouard Ivanjko, Croatia
Yumi Iwashita, Japan
Patric Jensfelt, Sweden
Seonghee Jeong, Japan
Li Jiang, China
Bahram Jozi, Australia
Takahiro Kagawa, Japan
Yasuhiro Kakinuma, Japan
Kaneko Kaneko, Japan
Pizzanu Kanongchaiyos, Thailand
Shigeyasu Kawaji, Japan
Eunyoung Kim, USA
Chyon Hae Kim, Japan
Balint Kiss, Hungary
Andreja Kitanov, Croatia
Bin Kong, China
Petar Kormushev, Italy
Akio Kosaka, USA
Volker Krueger, Denmark
Naoyuki Kubota, Japan
Chung-Hsien Kuo, Taiwan
Bela Lantos, Hungary
Kiju Lee, USA
Kristijan Lenac, Croatia
Gang Li, China
Kang Li, UK
Zhijun Li, China
Qinchuan Li, China
Bin Li, China

Feng-Li Lian, Taiwan
Geng Liang, China
Chyi-Yeu Lin, Taiwan
Wei Liu, China
Jindong Liu, UK
Jia Liu, China
Xin-Jun Liu, China
Bingbing Liu, Singapore
Benny Lo, UK
Yunjiang Lou, Macao
Leena Lulu, UAE
Dominic Maestas
Elmar Mair, Germany
Takafumi Matsumaru, Japan
Jouni Kalevi Mattila, Finland
Johannes Mayr, Austria
Abdul Md Mazid, Australia
Emanuele Menegatti, Italy
Qinhao Meng
Huasong Min, China
Lei Min, China
Seyed Mohamed Buhari Mohamed
   Ismail, Brunei Darussalam
Hyungpil Moon, Republic of Korea
Rainer Müller, Germany
Hyun Myung
Hiroyuki Nakamoto, Japan
Lazaros Nalpantidis, Greece
John Nassour, France
Andreas C. Nearchou, Greece
Samia Nefti-Meziani, UK
Duc Dung Nguyen, Republic of Korea
Hirotaka Osawa, Japan
Mohammadreza Asghari Oskoei, UK
Chee Khiang Pang, Singapore
Christopher Parlitz, Germany
Federica Pascucci, Italy
Fernando Lobo Pereira, Portugal
Anton Satria Prabuwono, Malaysia
Flavio Prieto, Colombia
Hong Qiao, China
Md. Jayedur Rashid, AASS, Sweden
Sushil Raut, India
Nilanjan Ray, Canada
Robert Richardson, UK
Roland Riepl, Austria

Jorge Rivera-Rovelo, México
Fabrizio Rocchi, Italy
Stephen Rock, USA
Andreja Rojko, Slovenia
Juha Röning, Finland
Anis Sahbani, France
Sébastien Saint-Aimé, France
Elsayed Sallam, Egypt
Marti Sanchez-Fibla, Spain
Ingrid Schjolberg, Norway
Kosuke Sekiyama, Japan
Naserodin Sepehry, Iran
Xinjun Sheng, China
Desire Sidibe, France
Ponnambalam Sivalinga G., Malaysia
Jorge Solis, Japan
Kai-Tai Song, Taiwan
Peter Staufer, Austria
Giovanni Stellin, Italy
Chun-Yi Su, Canada
Anan Suebsomran, Thailand
Jussi Suomela, Finland
Yoshiyuki Takahashi, Japan
Yuegang Tan, China
Li Tan, USA
Bo Tao, China
Kalevi Tervo, Finland
Ching-Hua Ting, Taiwan
Federico Tombari, Italy
Aksel Andreas Transeth, Norway
Nikos Tsourveloudis, Greece
Akira Utsumi, Japan
Kalyana Veluvolu, Republic of Korea
Ivanka Veneva, Bulgaria
Aihui Wang, Japan
Xiangke Wang, China
Hao Wang, China
Shuxin Wang, China

Furui Wang, USA
Guowu Wei, UK
Stephen Wood, USA
Hongtao Wu
Xiaojun Wu, Singapore
Xianbo Xiang, China
Elias Xidias, Greece
Rong Xiong, China
Caihua Xiong, China
Peter Xu, New Zealand
Xipeng Xu, China
Kai Xu, China
Jijie Xu, USA
Xin Xu, China
Guohua Xu, China
Bing Xu, China
Xinqing Yan, China
Wenyu Yang, China
Zhouping Yin, China
Masahiro Yokomichi, Japan
Kuu-Young Young, Taiwan
Hanafiah Yussof, Malaysia
Massimiliano Zecca, Japan
Jianguo Zhang, UK
Wenzeng Zhang, China
Xianmin Zhang, China
Xuguang Zhang, China
Yingqian Zhang, The Netherlands
Dingguo Zhang, China
Yanzheng Zhao, China
Xiaoguang Zhao, China
Yi Zhou, Singapore
Huiyu Zhou, UK
Chi Zhu, Japan
Limin Zhu, China
Chun Zhu, USA
Chungang Zhuang, China
Wei Zou, China

## Organizing Committee

Max Haberstroh
Ralph Kunze
Christian Tummel
Alicia Dröge
Claudia Capellmann

Katrin Ohmen
Richar Bosnic
Robert Glashagen
Larissa Müller
Kathrin Schoenefeld

# Table of Contents – Part I

## Progress in Indoor UAV

On the Way to a Real-Time On-Board Orthogonal SLAM for an Indoor
UAV .............................................................. 1
    *Mirco Alpen, Klaus Frick, and Joachim Horn*

Quadrocopter Localization Using RTK-GPS and Vision-Based
Trajectory Tracking ................................................. 12
    *Ulf Pilz, Willem Gropengießer, Florian Walder, Jonas Witt, and
    Herbert Werner*

Five-Axis Milling Simulation Based on B-rep Model .................. 22
    *Yongzhi Cheng, Caihua Xiong, Tao Ye, and Hongkai Cheng*

## Robotics Intelligence

Exploration Strategies for Building Compact Maps in Unbounded
Environments ...................................................... 33
    *Matthias Nieuwenhuisen, Dirk Schulz, and Sven Behnke*

The Basic Component of Computational Intelligence for KUKA KR C3
Robot ............................................................. 44
    *Tadeusz Szkodny*

An Experimental Comparison of Model-Free Control Methods in a
Nonlinear Manipulator.............................................. 53
    *Mateusz Przybyla, Rafal Madonski, Marta Kordasz, and
    Przemyslaw Herman*

## Industrial Robots

Research on Modular Design of Perpendicular Jointed Industrial
Robots ............................................................ 63
    *Lin Song and Suixian Yang*

Online Path Planning for Industrial Robots in Varying Environments
Using the Curve Shortening Flow Method ............................ 73
    *Marcel Huptych, Konrad Groh, and Sascha Röck*

Parallel-Populations Genetic Algorithm for the Optimization of Cubic
Polynomial Joint Trajectories for Industrial Robots.................. 83
    *Fares J. Abu-Dakka, Iyad F. Assad, Francisco Valero, and
    Vicente Mata*

# Robotics Assembly Applications

Integrative Path Planning and Motion Control for Handling Large
Components . . . . . . . . . . . . . . . . . . . . . . . . . . . . . . . . . . . . . . . . . . . . . . . . . . . . . .    93
  Rainer Müller, Martin Esser, and Markus Janssen

Automatic Configuration of Robot Systems – Upward and Downward
Integration . . . . . . . . . . . . . . . . . . . . . . . . . . . . . . . . . . . . . . . . . . . . . . . . . . . . . .    102
  Gunther Reinhart, Stefan Hüttner, and Stefan Krug

Process and Human Safety in Human-Robot-Interaction – A Hybrid
Assistance System for Welding Applications . . . . . . . . . . . . . . . . . . . . . . . .    112
  Carsten Thomas, Felix Busch, Bernd Kuhlenkoetter, and
  Jochen Deuse

Operation Simulation of a Robot for Space Applications . . . . . . . . . . . . . .    122
  Hui Li, Giuseppe Carbone, Marco Ceccarelli, and Qiang Huang

Re-grasping: Improving Capability for Multi-Arm-Robot-System by
Dynamic Reconfiguration . . . . . . . . . . . . . . . . . . . . . . . . . . . . . . . . . . . . . . . . .    132
  Burkhard Corves, Tom Mannheim, and Martin Riedel

A Parallel Kinematic Concept Targeting at More Accurate Assembly of
Aircraft Sections . . . . . . . . . . . . . . . . . . . . . . . . . . . . . . . . . . . . . . . . . . . . . . . . .    142
  Christian Löchte, Franz Dietrich, and Annika Raatz

Dimensional Synthesis of Parallel Manipulators Based on Direction-
Dependent Jacobian Indices . . . . . . . . . . . . . . . . . . . . . . . . . . . . . . . . . . . . . .    152
  Marwène Nefzi, Clément Gosselin, Martin Riedel,
  Mathias Hüsing, and Burkhard Corves

# Rehabilitation Robotics

EMG Classification for Application in Hierarchical FES System for
Lower Limb Movement Control . . . . . . . . . . . . . . . . . . . . . . . . . . . . . . . . . . . .    162
  Dingguo Zhang, Ying Wang, Xinpu Chen, and Fei Xu

Situated Learning of Visual Robot Behaviors . . . . . . . . . . . . . . . . . . . . . . . .    172
  Krishna Kumar Narayanan, Luis-Felipe Posada,
  Frank Hoffmann, and Torsten Bertram

Humanoid Motion Planning in the Goal Reaching Movement of
Anthropomorphic Upper Limb . . . . . . . . . . . . . . . . . . . . . . . . . . . . . . . . . . . .    183
  Wenbin Chen, Caihua Xiong, Ronglei Sun, and Xiaolin Huang

Human Sitting Posture Exposed to Horizontal Perturbation and
Implications to Robotic Wheelchairs . . . . . . . . . . . . . . . . . . . . . . . . . . . . . . .    192
  Karim A. Tahboub and Essameddin Badreddin

Automatic Circumference Measurement for Aiding in the Estimation of
Maximum Voluntary Contraction (MVC) in EMG Systems . . . . . . . . . . . .   202
    James A.R. Cannan and Huosheng Hu

Classification of the Action Surface EMG Signals Based on the Dirichlet
Process Mixtures Method . . . . . . . . . . . . . . . . . . . . . . . . . . . . . . . . . . . . . . . .   212
    Min Lei and Guang Meng

Displacement Estimation for Foot Rotation Axis Using a
Stewart-Platform-Type Assist Device . . . . . . . . . . . . . . . . . . . . . . . . . . . . . .   221
    Ming Ding, Tomohiro Iida, Hiroshi Takemura, and Hiroshi Mizoguchi

## Mechanisms and their Applications

Inverse Kinematics Solution of a Class of Hybrid Manipulators . . . . . . . . .   230
    Shahram Payandeh and Zhouming Tang

Stiffness Analysis of Clavel's DELTA Robot . . . . . . . . . . . . . . . . . . . . . . . .   240
    Martin Wahle and Burkhard Corves

Optimum Kinematic Design of a 3-DOF Parallel Kinematic Manipulator
with Actuation Redundancy . . . . . . . . . . . . . . . . . . . . . . . . . . . . . . . . . . . . . .   250
    Fugui Xie, Xin-Jun Liu, Xiang Chen, and Jinsong Wang

Integrated Structure and Control Design for a Flexible Planar
Manipulator . . . . . . . . . . . . . . . . . . . . . . . . . . . . . . . . . . . . . . . . . . . . . . . . . . .   260
    Yunjiang Lou, Yongsheng Zhang, Ruining Huang, and Zexiang Li

Effects of Clearance on Dynamics of Parallel Indexing Cam
Mechanism . . . . . . . . . . . . . . . . . . . . . . . . . . . . . . . . . . . . . . . . . . . . . . . . . . . .   270
    Zongyu Chang, Lixin Xu, Yuhu Yang, Zhongqiang Zheng, and
    Tongqing Pan

Design and Compliance Experiment Study of the Forging Simulator . . . .   281
    Pu Zhang, Zhenqiang Yao, Zhengchun Du, Hao Wang, and
    Haidong Yu

Design of Compliant Bistable Mechanism for Rear Trunk Lid of Cars . . .   291
    Shouyin Zhang and Guimin Chen

## Multi Robot Systems

DynaMOC: A Dynamic Overlapping Coalition-Based Multiagent
System for Coordination of Mobile Ad Hoc Devices . . . . . . . . . . . . . . . . . .   300
    Vitor A. Santos, Giovanni C. Barroso, Mario F. Aguilar,
    Antonio de B. Serra, and Jose M. Soares

Design of a High Performance Quad-Rotor Robot Based on a Layered
Real-Time System Architecture ..................................... 312
*Jonas Witt, Björn Annighöfer, Ole Falkenberg, and Uwe Weltin*

Simple Low Cost Autopilot System for UAVs ........................ 324
*S. Veera Ragavan, Velappa Ganapathy, and Chee Aiying*

A Marsupial Relationship in Robotics: A Survey ..................... 335
*Hamido Hourani, Philipp Wolters, Eckart Hauck, and Sabina Jeschke*

Multi-objective Robot Coalition Formation for Non-additive
Environments ..................................................... 346
*Manoj Agarwal, Lovekesh Vig, and Naveen Kumar*

Development of a Networked Multi-agent System Based on Real-Time
Ethernet .......................................................... 356
*Xiong Xu, Zhenhua Xiong, Jianhua Wu, and Xiangyang Zhu*

A Conceptual Agent-Based Planning Algorithm for the Production of
Carbon Fiber Reinforced Plastic Aircrafts by Using Mobile Production
Units .............................................................. 366
*Hamido Hourani, Philipp Wolters, Eckart Hauck,
Annika Raatz, and Sabina Jeschke*

## Robot Mechanism and Design

Trajectory Tracking and Vibration Control of Two Planar Rigid
Manipulators Moving a Flexible Object ............................ 376
*Balasubramanian Esakki, Rama B. Bhat, and Chun-Yi Su*

Concept and Design of the Modular Actuator System for the Humanoid
Robot MYON ...................................................... 388
*Torsten Siedel, Manfred Hild, and Mario Weidner*

Design of a Passive, Bidirectional Overrunning Clutch for Rotary Joints
of Autonomous Robots ............................................ 397
*Manfred Hild, Torsten Siedel, and Tim Geppert*

DeWaLoP-Monolithic Multi-module In-Pipe Robot System ............ 406
*Luis A. Mateos and Markus Vincze*

Design and Control of a Novel Visco-elastic Braking Mechanism Using
HMA .............................................................. 416
*Keith Gunura, Juanjo Bocanegra, and Fumiya Iida*

# Parallel Kinematics, Parallel Kinematics Machines and Parallel Robotics

Topological Design of Weakly-Coupled 3-Translation Parallel Robots
Based on Hybrid-Chain Limbs .................................... 426
    *Huiping Shen, Tingli Yang, Lvzhong Ma, and Shaobin Tao*

Working Space and Motion Analysis on a Novel Planar Parallel
Manipulator with Three Driving Sliders ........................... 436
    *Huiping Shen, Wei Wang, Changyu Xue, Jiaming Deng, and
    Zhenghua Ma*

Optimal Kinematic Design of a 2-DoF Translational Parallel
Manipulator with High Speed and High Precision ................... 445
    *Gang Zhang, PinKuan Liu, and Han Ding*

Modeling and Control of Cable Driven Parallel Manipulators with
Elastic Cables: Singular Perturbation Theory ...................... 455
    *Alaleh Vafaei, Mohammad A. Khosravi, and Hamid D. Taghirad*

CAD-2-SIM – Kinematic Modeling of Mechanisms Based on the
Sheth-Uicker Convention ......................................... 465
    *Bertold Bongardt*

# Handling and Manipulation

Non-rigid Object Trajectory Generation for Autonomous Robot
Handling........................................................ 478
    *Honghai Liu and Hua Lin*

Robotized Sewing of Fabrics Based on a Force Neural Network
Controller ...................................................... 486
    *Panagiotis N. Koustoumpardis and Nikos A. Aspragathos*

Dynamic Insertion of Bendable Flat Cables with Variation Based on
Shape Returning Points.......................................... 496
    *Yuuki Kataoka and Shinichi Hirai*

A Vision System for the Unfolding of Highly Non-rigid Objects on a
Table by One Manipulator ....................................... 509
    *Dimitra Triantafyllou and Nikos A. Aspragathos*

# Tangibility in Human-Machine Interaction

Optimizing Motion of Robotic Manipulators in Interaction with Human
Operators....................................................... 520
    *Hao Ding, Kurniawan Wijaya, Gunther Reißig, and Olaf Stursberg*

Haptic Display of Rigid Body Contact Using Generalized Penetration
Depth . . . . . . . . . . . . . . . . . . . . . . . . . . . . . . . . . . . . . . . . . . . . . . . . . . . . . . . . . . . .    532
   *Jun Wu, Dangxiao Wang, and Yuru Zhang*

Assistive Robots in Eldercare and Daily Living: Automation of
Individual Services for Senior Citizens . . . . . . . . . . . . . . . . . . . . . . . . . . . . . .    542
   *Alexander Mertens, Ulrich Reiser, Benedikt Brenken,
   Mathias Lüdtke, Martin Hägele, Alexander Verl,
   Christopher Brandl, and Christopher Schlick*

Key Factors for Freshmen Education Using MATLAB and LEGO
Mindstorms . . . . . . . . . . . . . . . . . . . . . . . . . . . . . . . . . . . . . . . . . . . . . . . . . . . . . . . .    553
   *Alexander Behrens, Linus Atorf, Dorian Schneider, and Til Aach*

## Navigation and Localization of Mobile Robot

Adaptive Dynamic Path Following Control of an Unicycle-Like Mobile
Robot . . . . . . . . . . . . . . . . . . . . . . . . . . . . . . . . . . . . . . . . . . . . . . . . . . . . . . . . . . . . .    563
   *Victor H. Andaluz, Flavio Roberti, Juan Marcos Toibero,
   Ricardo Carelli, and Bernardo Wagner*

A Study on Localization of the Mobile Robot Using Inertial Sensors
and Wheel Revolutions . . . . . . . . . . . . . . . . . . . . . . . . . . . . . . . . . . . . . . . . . . . . . .    575
   *Bong-Su Cho, Woosung Moon, Woo-Jin Seo, and Kwang-Ryul Baek*

Robust and Accurate Genetic Scan Matching Algorithm for Robotic
Navigation . . . . . . . . . . . . . . . . . . . . . . . . . . . . . . . . . . . . . . . . . . . . . . . . . . . . . . . . .    584
   *Kristijan Lenac, Enzo Mumolo, and Massimiliano Nolich*

Beacon Scheduling Algorithm for Localization of a Mobile Robot . . . . . . .    594
   *Jaehyun Park, Sunghee Choi, and Jangmyung Lee*

Position Estimation Using Time Difference of Flight of the Multi-coded
Ultrasonic . . . . . . . . . . . . . . . . . . . . . . . . . . . . . . . . . . . . . . . . . . . . . . . . . . . . . . . . .    604
   *Woo-Jin Seo, Bong-Su Cho, Woo-Sung Moon, and Kwang-Ryul Baek*

Detecting Free Space and Obstacles in Omnidirectional Images . . . . . . . .    610
   *Luis Felipe Posada, Krishna Kumar Narayanan,
   Frank Hoffmann, and Torsten Bertram*

A Composite Random Walk for Facing Environmental Uncertainty and
Reduced Perceptual Capabilities . . . . . . . . . . . . . . . . . . . . . . . . . . . . . . . . . . . .    620
   *C.A. Pina-Garcia, Dongbing Gu, and Huosheng Hu*

Motion Design for Service Robots . . . . . . . . . . . . . . . . . . . . . . . . . . . . . . . . . . .    630
   *Elias Xidias, Nikos A. Aspragathos, and Philip Azariadis*

**Author Index** . . . . . . . . . . . . . . . . . . . . . . . . . . . . . . . . . . . . . . . . . . . . . . . . . . . .    639

# Table of Contents – Part II

## A Body for the Brain: Embodied Intelligence in Bio-inspired Robotics

Biomechatronics for Embodied Intelligence of an Insectoid Robot . . . . . .    1
  *Axel Schneider, Jan Paskarbeit, Mattias Schäffersmann, and
  Josef Schmitz*

Novel Approaches for Bio-inspired Mechano-Sensors . . . . . . . . . . . . . . . . .    12
  *Alin Drimus and Arne Bilberg*

Helping a Bio-inspired Tactile Sensor System to Focus on the
Essential . . . . . . . . . . . . . . . . . . . . . . . . . . . . . . . . . . . . . . . . . . . . . . . . . . . .    24
  *Sven Hellbach, Marc Otto, and Volker Dürr*

Robust Dataglove Mapping for Recording Human Hand Postures . . . . . .    34
  *Jan Steffen, Jonathan Maycock, and Helge Ritter*

Software/Hardware Issues in Modelling Insect Brain Architecture . . . . . .    46
  *Paolo Arena, Luca Patané, Pietro Savio Termini,
  Alessandra Vitanza, and Roland Strauss*

Higher Brain Centers for Intelligent Motor Control in Insects . . . . . . . . . .    56
  *Roland Strauss, Tammo Krause, Christian Berg, and Bianca Zäpf*

An Insect-Inspired, Decentralized Memory for Robot Navigation . . . . . . .    65
  *Holk Cruse and Rüdiger Wehner*

Models of Visually Guided Routes in Ants: Embodiment Simplifies
Route Acquisition . . . . . . . . . . . . . . . . . . . . . . . . . . . . . . . . . . . . . . . . . . . . . .    75
  *Bart Baddeley, Paul Graham, Andrew Philippides, and
  Philip Husbands*

## Intelligent Visual Systems

Robust Object Tracking for Resource-Limited Hardware Systems . . . . . . .    85
  *Xiaoqin Zhang, Li Zhao, Shengyong Chen, and Lixin Gao*

Adaptive Rank Transform for Stereo Matching . . . . . . . . . . . . . . . . . . . . . .    95
  *Ge Zhao, Yingkui Du, and Yandong Tang*

Real Time Vision Based Multi-person Tracking for Mobile Robotics
and Intelligent Vehicles . . . . . . . . . . . . . . . . . . . . . . . . . . . . . . . . . . . . . . . . .    105
  *Dennis Mitzel, Georgios Floros, Patrick Sudowe,
  Benito van der Zander, and Bastian Leibe*

A Method for Wandering Trajectory Detection in Video Monitor . . . . . . .    116
  *Ruohong Huan, Zhehu Wang, Xiaomei Tang, and Yun Pan*

The Design of a Vision-Based Motion Performance System . . . . . . . . . . . .    125
  *Cheng Ren, Shuai Ye, and Xin Wang*

Window Function for EEG Power Density Estimation and Its
Application in SSVEP Based BCIs . . . . . . . . . . . . . . . . . . . . . . . . . . . . . . . .    135
  *Gan Huang, Jianjun Meng, Dingguo Zhang, and Xiangyang Zhu*

Efficient Multi-resolution Plane Segmentation of 3D Point Clouds . . . . . .    145
  *Bastian Oehler, Joerg Stueckler, Jochen Welle, Dirk Schulz, and
  Sven Behnke*

3D Body Pose Estimation Using an Adaptive Person Model for
Articulated ICP . . . . . . . . . . . . . . . . . . . . . . . . . . . . . . . . . . . . . . . . . . . . . .    157
  *David Droeschel and Sven Behnke*

## Self-optimising Production Systems

Artificial Cognition in Autonomous Assembly Planning Systems . . . . . . .    168
  *Christian Buescher, Marcel Mayer, Daniel Schilberg, and
  Sabina Jeschke*

Self-optimization as an Enabler for Flexible and Reconfigurable
Assembly Systems . . . . . . . . . . . . . . . . . . . . . . . . . . . . . . . . . . . . . . . . . . . .    179
  *Rainer Müller, Christian Brecher, Burkhard Corves, Martin Esser,
  Martin Riedel, Sebastian Haag, and Matthias Vette*

Flexible Assembly Robotics for Self-optimizing Production . . . . . . . . . . . .    189
  *Sebastian Haag, Nicolas Pyschny, and Christian Brecher*

Meta-modeling for Manufacturing Processes . . . . . . . . . . . . . . . . . . . . . . . .    199
  *Thomas Auerbach, Marion Beckers, Guido Buchholz,
  Urs Eppelt, Yves-Simon Gloy, Peter Fritz, Toufik Al Khawli,
  Stephan Kratz, Juliane Lose, Thomas Molitor, Axel Reßmann,
  Ulrich Thombansen, Dražen Veselovac, Konrad Willms,
  Thomas Gries, Walter Michaeli, Christian Hopmann, Uwe Reisgen,
  Robert Schmitt, and Fritz Klocke*

## Computational Intelligence

Control Architecture for Human Friendly Robots Based on Interacting
with Human. . . . . . . . . . . . . . . . . . . . . . . . . . . . . . . . . . . . . . . . . . . . . . . . . .    210
  *Hiroyuki Masuta, Eriko Hiwada, and Naoyuki Kubota*

Multi-modal Communication Interface for Elderly People in
Informationally Structured Space . . . . . . . . . . . . . . . . . . . . . . . . . . . . . . . .    220
  *Rikako Komatsu, Dalai Tang, Takenori Obo, and Naoyuki Kubota*

Motion Control Strategies for Humanoids Based on Ergonomics . . . . . . . .    229
    *Christian Schlette and Jürgen Rossmann*

Fuzzy Representations and Control for Domestic Service Robots
in Golog . . . . . . . . . . . . . . . . . . . . . . . . . . . . . . . . . . . . . . . . . . . . . . . . . . . . . . .    241
    *Stefan Schiffer, Alexander Ferrein, and Gerhard Lakemeyer*

## Robot Control Systems

Minimum Jerk-Based Control for a Three Dimensional Bipedal
Robot . . . . . . . . . . . . . . . . . . . . . . . . . . . . . . . . . . . . . . . . . . . . . . . . . . . . . . . . .    251
    *Amira Aloulou and Olfa Boubaker*

Development of a Smart Motion Control Card with an IEEE-1394
Interface . . . . . . . . . . . . . . . . . . . . . . . . . . . . . . . . . . . . . . . . . . . . . . . . . . . . . . .    263
    *Guo-Ying Gu, LiMin Zhu, and Ying Feng*

Control System by Observer for a Hyper-redundant Robot . . . . . . . . . . . .    275
    *Mircea Ivanescu, Nirvana Popescu, and Mihaela Florescu*

Towards a Multi-peclet Number Pollution Monitoring Algorithm . . . . . . .    287
    *John Oyekan, Dongbing Gu, and Huosheng Hu*

Self-balancing Controllable Robots in Education: A Practical Course
for Bachelor Students . . . . . . . . . . . . . . . . . . . . . . . . . . . . . . . . . . . . . . . . . . .    297
    *Paul Hänsch, John Schommer, and Stefan Kowalewski*

Intelligent Control Design in Robotics and Rehabilitation . . . . . . . . . . . . .    307
    *Petko Kiriazov, Gergana Nikolova, and Ivanka Veneva*

## Human-Robot Interaction

Behavior Based Approach for Robot Navigation and Chemical Anomaly
Tracking . . . . . . . . . . . . . . . . . . . . . . . . . . . . . . . . . . . . . . . . . . . . . . . . . . . . . . .    317
    *Sambit Bhattacharya, Bogdan Czejdo, Shubo Han, and
    Mohammad Siddique*

Detection of Lounging People with a Mobile Robot Companion . . . . . . . .    328
    *Michael Volkhardt, Steffen Müller, Christof Schröter, and
    Horst-Michael Groß*

Autonomous Control for Human-Robot Interaction on Complex Rough
Terrain . . . . . . . . . . . . . . . . . . . . . . . . . . . . . . . . . . . . . . . . . . . . . . . . . . . . . . . .    338
    *Mahmoud Mustafa and Alex Ramirez-Serrano*

A Modular Approach to Gesture Recognition for Interaction with a
Domestic Service Robot . . . . . . . . . . . . . . . . . . . . . . . . . . . . . . . . . . . . . . . . . .    348
    *Stefan Schiffer, Tobias Baumgartner, and Gerhard Lakemeyer*

Safety System and Navigation for Orthopaedic Robot (OTOROB) .....    358
  *Muralindran Mariappan, Thayabaren Ganesan,*
  *Vigneswaran Ramu, and Muhammad Iftikhar*

Approaching a Person in a Socially Acceptable Manner Using a Fast
Marching Planner .................................................    368
  *Jens Kessler, Christof Schroeter, and Horst-Michael Gross*

## Manipulators and Applications

Stiffness Identification for Serial Robot Manipulator Based on
Uncertainty Approach ............................................    378
  *Xiaoping Zhang, Wenyu Yang, Xuegang Cheng, and YuShan Chen*

Serial Comanipulation in Beating Heart Surgery Using a LWPR-Model
Based Predictive Force Control Approach .........................    389
  *Juan Manuel Florez, Delphine Bellot, Jérôme Szewczyk, and*
  *Guillaume Morel*

Application of Wavelet Networks to Adaptive Control of Robotic
Manipulators ...................................................    401
  *Hamid Reza Karimi*

Development of a Deep Ocean Master-Slave Electric Manipulator
Control System .................................................    412
  *Xiong Shen, GuoHua Xu, Kun Yu, Guoyuan Tang, and Xiaolong Xu*

Modelling of Flexible Link Manipulators ..........................    420
  *Clementina Mladenova*

An Outline for an Intelligent System Performing Peg-in-Hole Actions
with Flexible Objects............................................    430
  *Andreas Jordt, Andreas R. Fugl, Leon Bodenhagen,*
  *Morten Willatzen, Reinhard Koch, Henrik G. Petersen,*
  *Knud A. Andersen, Martin M. Olsen, and Norbert Krüger*

## Stability, Dynamics and Interpolation

Framework for Use of Generalized Force and Torque Data in
Transitional Levels of Autonomy .................................    442
  *Kyle Schroeder and Mitch Pryor*

A New Solution for Stability Prediction in Flexible Part Milling........    452
  *XiaoJian Zhang, Caihua Xiong, and Ye Ding*

A Practical Continuous-Curvature Bézier Transition Algorithm for
High-Speed Machining of Linear Tool Path ........................    465
  *Qingzhen Bi, Yuhan Wang, Limin Zhu, and Han Ding*

Design of a FPGA-Based NURBS Interpolator...................... 477
    *Huan Zhao, Limin Zhu, Zhenhua Xiong, and Han Ding*

Iso-scallop Trajectory Generation for the 5-Axis Machining of an
Impeller ........................................................ 487
    *Xubing Chen, Jinbo Wang, and Youlun Xiong*

## Evolutionary Robotics

Swarm Robot Flocking: An Empirical Study........................ 495
    *M. Fikret Ercan and Xiang Li*

Self-reconfiguration Path Planning Design for M-Lattice Robot Based
on Genetic Algorithm ........................................... 505
    *Enguang Guan, Zhuang Fu, Weixin Yan, Dongsheng Jiang, and
    Yanzheng Zhao*

Mobile Robot Controller Design by Evolutionary Multiobjective
Optimization in Multiagent Environments......................... 515
    *Yusuke Nojima and Hisao Ishibuchi*

Learning Intelligent Controllers for Path-Following Skills on Snake-Like
Robots ......................................................... 525
    *Francisco Javier Marín, Jorge Casillas, Manuel Mucientes,
    Aksel Andreas Transeth, Sigurd Aksnes Fjerdingen, and
    Ingrid Schjølberg*

## Bio-inspired Robotics

Modular Behavior Controller for Underwater Robot Teams:
A Biologically Inspired Concept for Advanced Tasks.................. 536
    *Dong-Uck Kong and Jinung An*

BioMotionBot - A New 3D Robotic Manipulandum with End-Point
Force Control................................................... 548
    *Volker Bartenbach, Klaus Wilging, Wolfgang Burger, and
    Thorsten Stein*

Adaptive Control Scheme with Parameter Adaptation - From Human
Motor Control to Humanoid Robot Locomotion Control .............. 558
    *Haiwei Dong and Zhiwei Luo*

Online Walking Gait Generation with Predefined Variable Height of
the Center of Mass ............................................. 569
    *Johannes Mayr, Hubert Gattringer, and Hartmut Bremer*

# Image-Processing Applications

Visual Control of a Remote Vehicle ................................ 579
    *David Sanchez-Benitez, Jesus M. de la Cruz, Gonzalo Pajares, and Dawei Gu*

Longitudinal and Lateral Control in Automated Highway Systems:
Their Past, Present and Future ................................... 589
    *Mohammad Alfraheed, Alicia Dröge, Max Klingender, Daniel Schilberg, and Sabina Jeschke*

Surface Defects Classification Using Artificial Neural Networks in
Vision Based Polishing Robot .................................... 599
    *Anton Satria Prabuwono, Adnan Rachmat Anom Besari, Ruzaidi Zamri, Md Dan Md Palil, and Taufik*

Efficient Skin Detection under Severe Illumination Changes
and Shadows ..................................................... 609
    *Bishesh Khanal and Désiré Sidibé*

Author Index ................................................... 619

# On the Way to a Real-Time On-Board Orthogonal SLAM for an Indoor UAV

Mirco Alpen, Klaus Frick, and Joachim Horn

Helmut-Schmidt-University / University of the Federal Armed Forces Hamburg,
Department of Electrical Engineering, Institute for Control Engineering,
P.O. Box 700822, D-22008 Hamburg, Germany

**Abstract.** Here we present the way to a real-time on-board SLAM (simultaneous localization and mapping) algorithm of a quadrotor using a laser range finder. Based on successfully implemented techniques for ground robots, we developed an orthogonal SLAM algorithm that merges a new scan into the global map without any iteration. This leads to a low requirement of computing power and computing time for the SLAM calculation. The algorithm delivers a 2D floor plan of the investigated area. All essential computations will be done on a microcontroller which is mounted on an industrial quadrotor. Due to the fact that all calculations including the SLAM algorithm will run on-board the robot is able to act autonomously in an unknown indoor environment.

To enable a robot to act autonomously several navigation controllers are needed. The basic ideas and the implementation are also part of this paper. Finally, it comprises the results of an autonomous indoor flight of the industrial quadrotor AR100B® of the AirRobot® Company equipped with a self constructed functional group.

## 1 Introduction

Mobile robots are used in areas that are too dangerous for humans or missions that are too time-consuming. A special task of mobile robots is exploring unknown environments. To operate autonomously in an unknown environment a mobile robot must be able to build a map and localize itself in it. This task is known as SLAM and several solutions for this problem have been proposed in the recent years. A general survey of the SLAM history is given by Durrent-Whyte and Bailey [1, 2].

Due to the fact that a lot of computing power is necessary for real-time SLAM, the implementation and validation of the different SLAM algorithms are mostly done on ground robots [3, 4]. To enable a small flight robot to operate in an unknown indoor environment, a ground station for the calculation of the SLAM algorithm is needed [5]. Therefore these robots can not act with full autonomy.

In general, the mapping of an indoor environment by a flying object is a 3D problem. With the assumption that the robot only acts with a constant altitude in a structured indoor environment like corridors, it can be reduced to a 2D problem. To get information about the robot's altitude, one can use an optical

S. Jeschke, H. Liu, and D. Schilberg (Eds.): ICIRA 2011, Part I, LNAI 7101, pp. 1–11, 2011.
© Springer-Verlag Berlin Heidelberg 2011

square for some laser beams along the yaw axis [5]. In this paper we assume a constant altitude during the flight.

In our work we focus on unknown indoor environments. Therefore the orthogonal SLAM [6] presented for the first time in 2006 is a useful way to build a floor plan with a low memory requirement. We assume that the environment can be represented by lines that are parallel or orthogonal. In our version of the orthogonal SLAM algorithm presented in 2010 [7] only one step of interation is needed to integrate a new scan into the global map. This allows an evaluation of the computing time without worst case assumptions and therefore a clear statement for the real-time behavior of the complete system. The used SLAM algorithm is briefly discussed in section 3.

GPS based navigation is often used in mobile robotics. But in indoor environments one can not ensure a GPS signal. Due to the ferromagnetic materials in working with magnetometer causes lots of problems, too. In our application the robot's navigation is based on a laser range finder which is the main sensor of the robot. In section 2 the used quadrotor and its functional group are described. The navigation techniques and the design and implementation of all needed controllers are presented in section 4.

The goal of our work is to build an on-board real-time SLAM algorithm for an indoor UAV. The results of the flight experiments in an underground parking presented in sections 4 and 5 show that all needed parts to reach this goal work sufficiently. Section 5 treats the experiment around the SLAM algorithm. At first the initial conditions are described and afterwards the results are presented.

## 2   Introductive System Description

The AR100B® quadrotor is by default equipped with an inertial measurement unit (IMU), compass, GPS, and a camera. The payload of this aerial vehicle is 0.4kg and the diameter is about 1m [8]. The definition of axes and angles in the body-fixed reference frame is shown in figure 1.

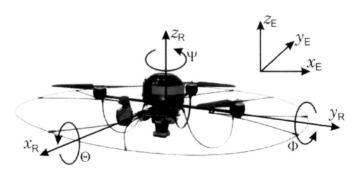

**Fig. 1.** Definition of the two reference frames

Because of the robot's varying orientation represented by the state $\Psi$ we need to establish the earth coordinate system. Body-fixed coordinates are denoted as $(x_R, y_R, z_R)$, earth coordinates as $(x_E, y_E, z_E)$.

We replaced the robot's camera by a functional group shown in figure 2. It is composed of a Hokuyo® laser range finder with an effective reach of 30m and a 16bit Infineon® microcontroller. Additionally a Gumstix Verdex pro® is part of the functional group. At the moment it is used just for preprocessing of the measurement data collected by the laser range finder but in the near future it will be used for on-board mission planing. All needed controllers and other time-critical functions are implemented on the microcontroller.

The 270 degree laser range finder is used with an angle resolution of 0.0184rad $\cong$ 1 degree and all required computations for autonomous flight and SLAM will run on this microcontroller. Optionally the functional group comprises a WLAN module to enable monitoring on a ground station. During our first experiments there were lot of interruptions in the data transmission particularly when the robot is in motion. Therefore we use a wired connection for some experiments to ensure data transmission without interruptions.

The weight of this functional group shown in figure 2 is 0.39kg and the power consumption is approximately 10W.

150mm

**Fig. 2.** Functional group with Hokuyo® laser range finder

The microcontroller of the functional group is connected with the quadrotor via RS232 to receive the current states of the robot (altitude, orientation) and transmit the corresponding actuating variables. To ensure safety and enable a manual operated mode at any time a hand held transmitter is embedded in the transmission line of the actuating variables.

## 3   SLAM Algorithm

The used SLAM algorithm was presented in 2010 [7]. Therefore this algorithm is only discussed briefly in this section. The basic idea is shown in figure 3.

One can see that our algorithm comprises five steps. Within the first step named 'Data preprocessing' erroneous measurements of the laser range finder are excluded and the scan values are transformed into the earth coordinates regarding the robot's orientation $\Psi$. During the second step lines are estimated based on the split and merge algorithm presented in [9]. Theses lines are checked for orthogonality within the third step. Extracted lines that are slightly non-orthogonal are changed to orthogonal. All other lines are neglected and will not be part of the global map.

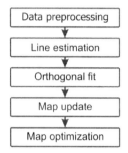

**Fig. 3.** Basic flowchart of SLAM algorithm

The fourth part of the SLAM algorithm is the most important one. The extracted lines of the current scan have to be integrated in the global map. To integrate the new lines successfully one has to estimate the robot's movement accurately. In our case this is done by just one step of iteration. As mentioned before the data processing is done considering the robot's orientation $\Psi$. Therefore the orthogonal lines are all parallel to one of the axes of the earth coordinates $x_E$ or $y_E$ fixed on the first scan and the calculation of the robot's movement can be divided in these two directions.

In the last part of the algorithm named 'Map optimization' double lines are merged to reduce the total number of lines in the global map. With this step computing time of the following map update and memory requirements are reduced.

## 4   Indoor Navigation

For our experiment we use the industrial quadrotor presented in section 2. This robot should follow a wall at it's left hand side with a constant velocity. The needed controllers for this kind of navigation are based on a formerly presented work about a nonlinear dynamic model of a quadrotor with onboard attitude control [10] shown in figure 4.

Figure 4 shows that our dynamic model has four degrees of freedom. Therefore four controllers are needed. The parts with index 'alt' are belonging to the robot's altitude, parts with index 'yaw' to the robot's orientation. The two corresponding controllers have been presented in [10], too. Both controllers are realized as proportional feedback loops. This quite simple controller design leads to a performance that is sufficient for our current work.

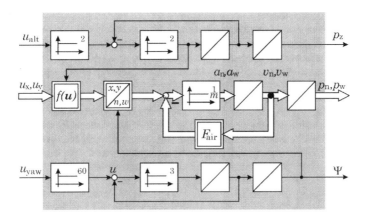

**Fig. 4.** MIMO model of the attitude controlled quadrotor [10]

In contrast to the former paper the robot's orientation is measured by the laser range finder in the following way: Due to the fact that we are in an indoor environment, we assume a straight wall on the left or the right hand side. The y-axis of the earth coordinates is parallel to this wall. The robot's orientation should be in y-direction of the earth coordinates. Therefore the minimum of the current set of scan values corresponding to this wall has to be on the x-axis of the earth coordinates.

The validation of the two following control loops is done by a flight experiment in an underground parking at our university. During the flight experiments the robot communicates with the ground station by wire. This cable is used to ensure the time-critical data recording of the functional group without interruption. Figure 5 shows the robot in the test environment.

**Fig. 5.** UAV in the test environment

*Position control*

The robot's position in the earth coordinates is controlled based on the laser range finder, too. In x-direction of the earth coordinates the distance between robot and wall has to be controlled. The corresponding plant model can roughly be described as a PT1 element in serial connection with an integrator. To get a sufficient phase margin it is reasonable to choose a PD controller. Because of the chosen accuracy of the laser range finder in contrast to the GPS, the parameters of the controller used for outdoor application presented in [10] had to be slightly changed due to the indoor conditions in our current work. Figure 6 shows the closed loop step response for the current controller.

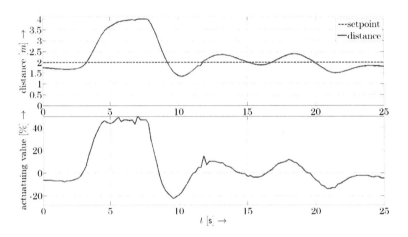

**Fig. 6.** Step response of the closed loop system

One can see that the step response of figure 6 shows some ripples. Due to the assumption of constant altitude and heading we assumed that there are no couplings between the different parts of the plant during the controller design. Effectively there is a small inaccuracy in the robot's orientation caused by measurement noise and disturbances like unevenness of the wall for example. This error in the heading leads to the errors in position control shown in figure 6.

One could think that the changing attitude of the robot has an influence to the measurement of the laser range finder, too. We have analyzed the interrelationship between the attitude angle caused by a actuating value $u_x$ and the error of the distance measurement $\Delta_{\text{dis}}$. The result is shown in figure 7.

Due to the indoor environment 60% of the maximum actuating value $u_x$ is a reasonable limit to ensure smooth movements of the robot. This limit leads to an attitude angle of approximately $10°$. Figure 7 shows that the corresponding measurement error is around 1.6%. In relation to the setpoint of 3m shown in figure 6 the maximum error of the distance measurement $\Delta_{\text{dis}}$ is 0.048m. Therefore it can be neglected in this control loop.

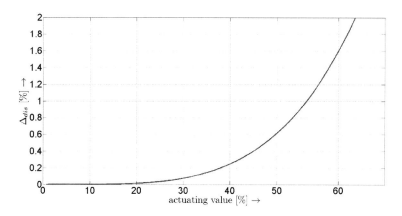

**Fig. 7.** Interrelationship between actuating value $u_x$ and distance

The second part of figure 6 shows that the controller uses a comparitively small part of the possible actuating values. This indicates that the controller is tuned conservatively. Thus, a smooth movement of the robot is ensured. This is an important point for the following design of the velocity controller, too.

*Velocity control*

To ensure a constant movement along a wall a velocity controller is needed. The used industrial quadrotor provides measurement data from the IMU with an update frequency of approximately 10Hz. This frequency is too low for an implementation of a Kalman filter based strapdown algorithm [11]. Therefore we use the measurement data of the laser range finder at the moment. With this measurement the control loop has long time stability but the short time stability of the strapdown algorithm is missing. This will lead to less accuracy in the performance of the controller. In the near future we will implement a strapdown algorithm based on an additional IMU placed on the functional group shown in figure 2.

At present, the velocity controller is realized by a proportional feedback loop. Due to comparatively small velocities of the robot moving in an indoor environment the air friction is small, too. Thus, the air friction is neglected in the first design of the controller. With this assumption the open loop transfer function composed of the proportional controller and the simplified plant includes an integrator and the steady state error is supposed to be zero. The current velocity is computed by the current and the former value of the laser range finder on the y-axes of the robot's body fixed coordinate system. Figure 6 shows the closed loop step response for the current controller.

Like the step response of the closed loop position control figure 8 shows some ripples, too. Furthermore one can see a steady state error. The ripples are caused by the same problems as mentioned in the paragraph before. The main reason for the steady state error might be the cable witch is used for the data recording of the functional group. The robot has to carry this cable and the payload of it depends on the altitude and the flight distance of the robot. In the near future the

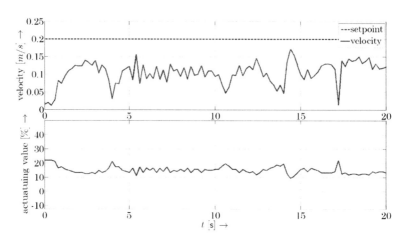

**Fig. 8.** Step response of the closed loop system

communication between robot and ground station will be realized by a wireless connection.

Due to the fact that our main focus is on the onboard SLAM algorithm, we presently accept the performance of the velocity controller. To ensure a collection of usable data for the SLAM algorithm, the robot must have a reasonable low velocity and has to move smoothly. Accurate approving of a given velocity is of minor importance.

The second part of figure 8 shows that the controller is tuned very conservative, too. Otherwise the robot would act with much more bumping and this would have a negative influence to the SLAM algorithm.

## 5   Experimental SLAM Results

The experiments for the SLAM algorithm have been done in the underground parking, too. In the right part of figure 5 one can see some piles which should be part of the map later on. On the left hand side we have a straight wall. Based on the presented controllers in section 4 the robot is able to move autonomously in the test area.

Right now the data collected by the laser range finder are processed on the ground. By changing the hardware of the functional group, we will have more computing power and the SLAM algorithm will be computed onboard. This will enable the robot to fly fully autonomously and to compute the whole SLAM algorithm on-board.

All presented controllers are implemented on the functional group. During the experiment the robot moves with a constant velocity of approximately 1m/s and a constant distance of approximately 3m along the straight wall on the left hand side of figure 5. The data of the laser range finder is collected with a frequency of 5Hz and transmitted to the ground station. Afterwards the collected data is processed in the SLAM algorithm. Due to the length of the underground parking the operating distance of the laser range finder was reduced to 15m to get a more challenging task. Figure 9 shows the result of the SLAM algorithm.

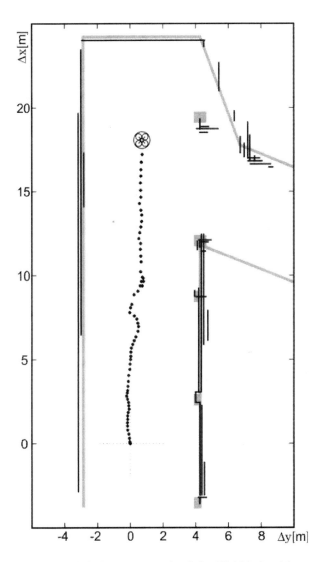

**Fig. 9.** Global map as result of the SLAM algorithm

The grey lines of figure 9 show the floor plan of the test environment. The black lines are the result of the SLAM algorithm. The robot's position estimated by the SLAM algorithm during the experiment is marked by the black dots. One can see that the limitation of operating distance ensures that the first third of the algorithm works without acknowledgment of the wall in $x$-direction at the end of the environment. In general there is a good accordance between the global map and the floor plan.

Some lines of the computed map in figure 9 are parallel and close to each other. As explained in section 3, the optimization reduces the total number of lines in the global map. If the threshold values for merging lines are too rough the comparitively fine structure of the pile would be omitted. Therefore some lines representing the same wall or feature of the map are remaining.

The resulting map in figure 9 shows some inaccuracy in the distances in $x$- and $y$-direction, too. This error probably arises because of the map optimization. Whenever two lines are merged, there is a shift and therefore errors concerning to the distances in a certain range are possible. But omitting the map optimization would lead to much more lines in the global map and a rising computation time in each step of the SLAM algorithm. A second reason might be the inaccuracy in the robot's orientation mentioned in section 4.

## 6  Conclusion

In this paper we have presented experimental results for indoor navigation with an industrial quadrotor and for a SLAM-algorithm based on extracting orthogonal lines from a set of data of a laser range finder. This line feature based algorithm has a comparatively small complexity and memory requirement and therefore is appropriate for embedded real time application. In contrast to most of the algorithms presented in the literature so far, only one step of iteration is needed to integrate a new scan into the global map, because the robot's orientation is available.

The validation of the presented controllers in section 4 shows that the robot is able to act autonomously in an unknown indoor environment based on the data collected by a laser range finder. Only the altitude is measured by a barometric sensor. In the near future, we will equip the robot with ultra sonic sensors to get more exact information about the altitude and the space above the robot.

Section 5 shows the result of the SLAM algorithm. To compute the SLAM algorithm the measurement data of the robot were sent to a ground station. To ensure the time-critical data recording of the functional group without interruption the robot communicates with the ground station by wire during the flight experiments. The offline computation leads to a good accordance between the global map and the floor plan.

By handing over more functions from the microcontroller to the Gumstix Verdex pro®, we will have a lot more of computing power. The analyses done so far ensure that in addition to all the controllers the SLAM algorithm will work with a frequency of 5Hz on this hardware. Realizing this, the robot will be able to map an unknown indoor environment fully autonomous.

In the near future we will use an additional IMU to implement a full strapdown algorithm for improvement of the velocity controller. Including the effects of rolling and pitching of the quadrotor might be helpful for this control loop, too.

# References

1. Durrant-Whyte, H., Bailey, T.: Simultaneous localization and mapping (SLAM): Part I The essential algorithms. IEEE, Robotics and Automation Magazine 13(2) (2006)
2. Bailey, T., Durrant-Whyte, H.: Simultaneous localization and mapping (SLAM): Part II State of the art. IEEE, Robotics and Automation Magazine 13(3) (2006)
3. Montemerlo, M., Thrun, S., Koller, D., Wegbreit, B.: FastSLAM: factored solution on the simultaneous localization and mapping problem. In: AAAI, Mobile Robot Competition and Exhibition, Edmonton, Canada (2002)
4. Eliazar, A., Parr, R.: DP-SLAM: fast, robust simultaneous localization and mapping without predetermind landmarks. In: 18th Int. Joint Conf. on Artificial Intelligence (IJCAI), pp. 1135–1142. Morgan-Kaufmann Publishers, Acapulco (2003)
5. Grzonka, S., Grisetti, G., Burgard, W.: Towards a navigation system for autonomous indoor flying. In: International Conference of Robotics and Automation (ICRA), Kobe, Japan (2009)
6. Nguyen, V., Harati, A., Martinelli, A., Seigwart, R.: Orthogonal SLAM - a step toward lightweight indoor autonomous navigation. In: IEEE/RSJ International Conference on Intelligent Robots and Systems (IROS), Beijing, China (2006)
7. Alpen, M., Willrodt, C., Frick, K., Horn, J.: On-board SLAM for indoor UAV using a laser range finder. In: SPIE Defence, Security and Sensing, Orlando, USA (2010)
8. N. N.: Operating Instructions AR100B. Airrobot, Arnsberg (2008)
9. Choi, Y.-H., Lee, T.-K., Oh, S.-Y.: A line feature based SLAM with low grade range sensors using geometric constrains and active exploration for mobile robot. Autonomous Robots 24(1) (January 2008)
10. Alpen, M., Frick, K., Horn, J.: Nonlinear modeling and position control of an industrial quadrotor with on-board attitude control. In: IEEE International Conference on Control and Automation (ICCA), Christchurch, New Zealand (2009)
11. Meister, O.: Integrierte Navigationssysteme: Sensordatenfusion, GPS und Inertiale Navigation. Oldenbourg, München, Germany (2007)

# Quadrocopter Localization Using RTK-GPS and Vision-Based Trajectory Tracking

Ulf Pilz[1], Willem Gropengießer[1], Florian Walder[1],
Jonas Witt[2], and Herbert Werner[1]

[1] Institute of Control Systems, Hamburg University of Technology,
Eissendorfer Str. 40, 21073 Hamburg, Germany
[2] Institute for Reliability Engineering, Hamburg University of Technology,
Eissendorfer Str. 40, 21073 Hamburg, Germany
{ulf.pilz,willem.gropengiesser,florian.walder,
jonas.witt,h.werner}@tu-harburg.de

**Abstract.** This paper presents a method for trajectory tracking control and waypoint navigation of a quadrocopter using a vision-based camera system and an exact method for outdoor positioning using the Real-Time Kinematic Global Positioning System (RTK-GPS). First a quadrocopter prototype developed at the university is introduced. Then localization results of a RTK-GPS are presented, which show that the precision of absolute position data for the aerial vehicle can be improved significantly compared to a standard GPS solution. Experimental results of a simple PID position control scheme are presented which is used to suppress position errors of a trajectory tracking controller. The main result of this paper is the development of a trajectory tracking scheme in three dimensions which can be used to navigate to several waypoints along a predefined path. Both position controller and trajectory tracking controller experiments are conducted using data gathered from a Wii Remote camera system.

**Keywords:** unmanned aerial vehicle (UAV), RTK-GPS, trajectory tracking, vision-based control.

## 1 Introduction

Quadrocopters are a popular experimental platform for unmanned aerial vehicle (UAV) research, because of their simplicity of construction, their ability for vertical take off and landing (VTOL) and their ease of maintenance. This is due to the reliance on fixed-pitch blades instead of complex mechanical control linkages for rotor actuation. The increased safety features are a further advantage compared to other VTOL capable UAVs. The size of the main rotor of a helicopter is bigger than the equivalent four rotors of a quadrocopter, relative to the size of the aircraft. This means that the kinetic energy of one rotor is smaller, hence the risk of damaging objects during a collision is reduced. A variety of applications can be tested for individual vehicles as well as multiple vehicle teams, which

S. Jeschke, H. Liu, and D. Schilberg (Eds.): ICIRA 2011, Part I, LNAI 7101, pp. 12–21, 2011.

includes surveillance, mobile sensor networks and search and rescue tasks [1], [2], [3], [4].

Modeling and attitude control of a quadrocopter is a problem which has been widely covered in the literature [1], [5], [6]. Position control of quadrocopters is mostly realized by an additional feedback loop an attitude controller. Besides the inertial measurement unit (IMU) which is used for attitude control, additional sensors like a vision-based system or a GPS sensor have to be installed on the quadrocopter to gather absolute position data. The combination of the inertial navigation system (INS) and GPS provides more accurate position data and has been covered in, e.g., [8]. The use of differential GPS (DGPS) for UAVs has been reported in [9], where one standard deviation uncertainty below 2m was achieved.

The main result of this paper is the design of a low-cost DGPS system for outdoor localization of the quadrocopter and the enhancement of a trajectory tracking control algorithm based on a vision based camera system. This is one step towards a fully autonomous UAV, which must be able to start, hover, navigate and land without interaction with a human pilot [7]. The trajectory tracking algorithm can be used to navigate to a landing platform, where camera-based autonomous hovering is applied.

This paper is organized as follows. Section 2 gives a short description of the quadrocopter. Section 3 presents the DGPS hardware and shows static experimental results of RTK-GPS. In Section 4 the position controller and the trajectory tracking controller are introduced. Conclusions are drawn in Section 5.

## 2    Characteristics of the Flight Platform

Fig. 1(a) shows a photo of the quadrocopter on a landing platform. This quadrocopter was used to verify the developed algorithm for trajectory tracking and position control. The coordinate system of the quadrocopter is shown in Fig. 1(b). The airframe orientation in space is given by a rotation matrix $R \in SO3$ from an earth-fixed initial frame $E$ to a body frame $B$.

### 2.1    Sensors and Hardware Equipment

The quadrocopter is equipped with a triaxial inertial sensor with magnetometer. The gyroscopes measure the angular rates of the roll angle ($\phi$), the pitch angle ($\theta$) and the yaw angle ($\psi$). The accelerometers give information about the translational accelerations in $x-$, $y-$ and $z$-direction and the magnetometer is able to determine the direction of the terrestrial magnetic field to fix a zero direction for the yaw angle. Since the measurement of the absolute position is error prone due to the integration of accelerations and angular rates, and hence due to the integration of the errors, a DGPS receiver is installed on the quadrocopter. Furthermore, a barometer is employed to detect the current altitude of the quadrocopter. The central computing device is based upon on an Intel Atom x86 which provides sufficient computational power to perform the calculations

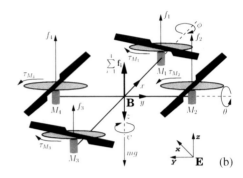

**Fig. 1.** Quadrocopter on a landing platform (a) and representation of the coordinate system of the quadrocopter (b)

necessary for the control algorithms. The main processor is also responsible for commanding the motor drivers which control the four brushless DC motors used for propulsion of the quadrocopter.

### 2.2 Software

The framework on which all software development takes place is the Executable Building Blocks Network (EBBN), especially designed for control and observation tasks for autonomous systems. In this application, EBBN is embedded in a Linux hosted board which is real-time capable because of the Xenomai extension. The EBBN configuration enables the user to develop modules which deliver the desired functionality. Different modules can be combined into a module list which is processed sequentially. Furthermore, the module lists run at different rates in parallel which form the process list.

## 3    Differential GPS

For an autonomous flight following a predefined trajectory and given waypoints, precise absolute position measurements are necessary. This section briefly describes which hardware equipment is used for acquiring the absolute position of the quadrocopter and results of static measurements are shown.

### 3.1    Real Time Kinematic GPS

In this work, a DGPS system is used, where a reference station whose position is exactly known, performs pseudorange measurements. These measurements are then broadcasted to the user who performs pseudorange corrections and computes a more accurate position compared to standard GPS. Since also the carrier-phase difference is measured and corrected with almost zero latency, the applied method of DGPS is called Real Time Kinematic GPS (RTK-GPS). The

GPS module which is used in this work is the μ-Blox LEA-6T connected via Universal Serial Bus (USB) to the main processor and a LEA-4T, which is assumed to act as a reference station whose exact position is known. Both GPS modules are able to output raw measurement data which is used to realize a RTK-GPS solution.

The raw measurement data provided by the GPS modules is processed by the Real-Time Kinematic Library (RTKLIB), see [10]. RTKLIB is an open source software collection which has been integrated into the EBBN framework. One important feature of RTKLIB is the ability to transmit correction data via TCP/IP. The correction signals needed for RTK-GPS are obtained in two ways: one possibility is to use an internet connection to receive data from the Federal Agency for Cartography and Geodesy which operates several reference stations throughout Germany. The other possibility is to use a movable reference station whose exact position has to be determined using an average of the received position data over time. For this method, no connection to the internet is necessary but a disadvantage is an increased position error.

### 3.2   Measurements

The results of static RTK-GPS measurements are shown in Fig. 2 and Fig. 3. In both Figures, the LEA-4T module acts as a reference station whose position is supposed to be known exactly and the LEA-6T is mounted on top of the quadrocopter.

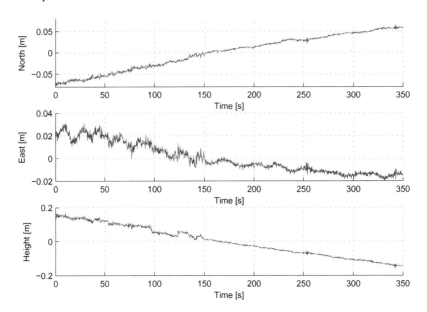

**Fig. 2.** Static RTK-GPS position measurement for $t = 350$s for x-, y- and z-axis

Fig. 2 shows the progress of the measured position data over time. One can see that the height of the measured position which corresponds to the z-axis provides the worst measurement with the greatest error. Still the difference between the maximum and minimum measured value for the height is at 0.3m, whereas for the x- and y-axis this difference is about 0.15m and 0.05m, respectively. For a trajectory based flight, the drift components which can be seen in Fig. 2 can not be canceled out. However, considering an outdoor trajectory flight with a range of several meters, this drift only accounts for a small error compared to the dynamic change of the position and hence is neglected.

In Fig. 3 a phase diagram of the x- and y-axis is presented. Furthermore, a circle denoting the two-sigma standard deviation is sketched. For the two-dimensional plot this deviation is about 0.08m. Including the z-axis, the three-dimensional deviation increases and is given by a ball with a radius of 0.2m. Table 1 summarizes these results.

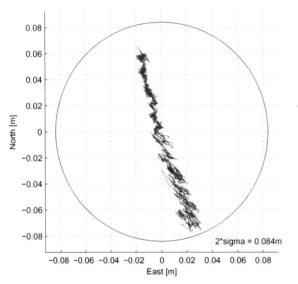

**Table 1.** Standard deviation

| Type | $2\sigma$ [m] |
|--------|---------|
| 2D | 0.0842 |
| 3D | 0.1983 |
| Height | 0.1794 |

**Fig. 3.** RTK-GPS position measurement as a 2D-plot

## 4    Position Control and Trajectory Tracking

An overview of the control structure used in this work is given in Fig. 4. The innermost loop is given by the attitude controller and the rotational model. The attitude controller is designed via mixed-sensitivity loop-shaping as a $\mathcal{H}_\infty$ MIMO controller, see [11]. The angles $\phi$, $\theta$ and $\psi$ are the inputs for the attitude controller whereas the outputs are given by the torques $M_\phi$, $M_\theta$ and $M_\psi$. The torques are generated by the brushless DC motors and act on the dynamic attitude model of the quadrocotper.

The middle loop is given by the position controller which is designed as a simple PID controller for each of the three translational axes and the position model. The inputs for the position controller are position errors in the body frame coordinates for all three axes, the outputs of the controller are the thrust $F_Z$ to influence the height of the quadrocopter and the desired pitch and roll angles which are inputs for the attitude controller. The thrust $F_Z$ is acting directly as an input to the dynamic position model of the quadrocopter, since a change in the height of the quadrocopter does not change its attitude.

The outermost loop is given by the trajectory tracking controller. The input of the trajectory controller consists of the actual position of the quadrocopter transformed into earth-fixed coordinates. Then the trajectory controller compares the actual position with the actual waypoint which has to be reached and generates a position error. The position error is transformed back into body-frame coordinates and handed over to the position controller. Furthermore, the yaw angle $\psi$ is also an output of the trajectory controller and acts directly as an input for the attitude controller since changes in the yaw angle do not influence the position of the quadrocopter.

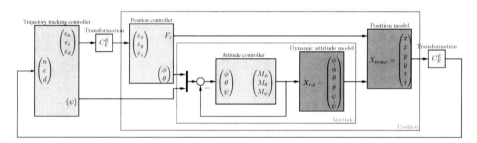

**Fig. 4.** Overview of the control structure

### 4.1 Position Controller

The position controller is realized as a PID controller with anti-windup compensation. Fig. 5 shows a block diagram of the controller. Note that for each component of the input vector a separate PID controller has to be designed. Due to the symmetric construction of the quadrocopter, the parameters of the PID controller for reference tracking in $x$- and $y$-direction are identical. The anti-windup compensation is necessary because of a limit in the roll and pitch angle which may lead to saturation of the PID controller.

Fig. 6 shows the results of a 0.1m reference step in $z$-direction applied to the quadrocopter helicopter. The position data is gathered using a camera extracted from a Wii Remote controller.

### 4.2 Trajectory Controller

The trajectory tracking controller closely follows the design performed in [2]. A major improvement is the extension to three dimensional space, whereas [2]

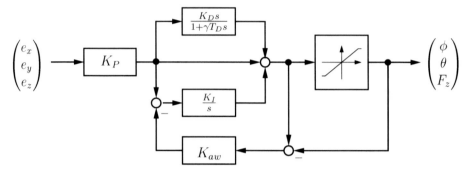

**Fig. 5.** Position controller structure including anti-windup compensation scheme

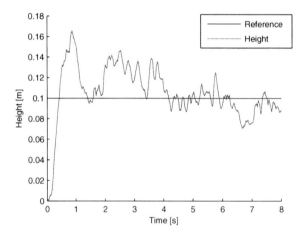

**Fig. 6.** Step response to a 0.1m reference step in z-direction

only considered vehicle paths in the x-y-plane. Another difference is given by the structure of the trajectory controller which generates desired reference positions for the position controller described in Section 4.1. The authors of [2] design the trajectory controller to generate reference attitudes which are processed by the attitude controller.

The trajectory is given as a sequence of $N$ waypoints $\vec{x}_i^{\,d} \in \mathbb{R}^3$, $i = 1, \ldots, N$ yaw angles $\psi_i^d$ and desired velocities $\vec{v}_i^{\,d}$, where the superscript $d$ indicates reference values. Fig. 7 shows the definition of a vehicle path. The segment $P_i$ of the path indicates the connection of the waypoints $i$ and $i + 1$. Along this segment, a coordinate system is defined for the trajectory to separate between a direction along the path and a direction perpendicular to the desired path. $\vec{t}_i$ decribes the unit vector along the path from $\vec{x}_i^{\,d}$ to $\vec{x}_{i+1}^{\,d}$, whereas $\vec{h}_i$ is given as the horizontal unit vector orthonormal to $\vec{t}_i$.

$$\vec{h}_i = \begin{pmatrix} 0 & -1 & 0 \\ 1 & 0 & 0 \\ 0 & 0 & 0 \end{pmatrix} \cdot \frac{\vec{t}_i}{\sqrt{t_{i,x}^2 + t_{i,y}^2}}. \tag{1}$$

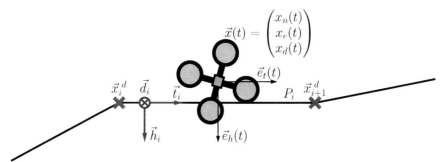

**Fig. 7.** Vehicle path definition, see [2]

In the special case where $\vec{t}_i$ points to a vertical direction, $\vec{h}_i$ is defined as $[1\ 0\ 0]^{\mathrm{T}}$. The direction of the unit vector $\vec{d}_i$ is given by the outer product of $\vec{t}_i$ and $\vec{h}_i$, such that

$$\vec{d}_i = \vec{t}_i \times \vec{h}_i. \tag{2}$$

The three unit vectors $\vec{t}_i$, $\vec{h}_i$ and $\vec{d}_i$ compose a basis along the path segment $P_i$. If the actual position $\vec{e}(t)$ and velocity $\vec{v}(t)$ of the quadrocopter are available, the position errors $e_h(t)$ and $e_d(t)$ orthogonal to the flying direction can be determined as

$$\vec{e}_h(t) = \left(\vec{x}_i^d - \vec{x}(t)\right) \cdot \vec{h}_i$$
$$\vec{e}_d(t) = \left(\vec{x}_i^d - \vec{x}(t)\right) \cdot \vec{d}_i. \tag{3}$$

Furthermore, the velocity errors $\dot{e}_h(t)$ and $\dot{e}_d(t)$ are calculated as

$$\dot{\vec{e}}_h(t) = -\vec{v}(t) \cdot \vec{h}_i$$
$$\dot{\vec{e}}_d(t) = -\vec{v}(t) \cdot \vec{d}_i. \tag{4}$$

Along the flight path, only the velocity error $\dot{e}_t(t)$ is determined as

$$\dot{\vec{e}}_t(t) = \vec{v}_i^d - \vec{v}(t) \cdot \vec{t}_i. \tag{5}$$

Note that only the velocity error $\dot{e}_t(t)$ depends on the desired velocity $\vec{v}_i^d$.

Now we are ready to transform the position and velocity errors into the body frame of the quadrocopter and use this error as an input for the position controller.

$$\vec{e}(t) = \left(\vec{e}_h(t) + K_D \dot{\vec{e}}_h(t)\right) \cdot \vec{h}_i + \left(\vec{e}_d(t) + K_D \dot{\vec{e}}_d(t)\right) \cdot \vec{d}_i + \dot{\vec{e}}_t(t) \cdot \vec{t}_i. \tag{6}$$

Fig. 8 shows the result of the trajectory tracking controller in an indoor environment. To gather absolute position data for the quadrocopter, a camera extracted from a Wii Remote controller was mounted on the quadrocopter facing downwards. For an exact description on how to use the Wii Remote camera on a quadrocopter we refer to [12] due to space limitations.

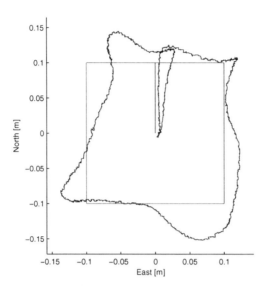

**Fig. 8.** Tracking a trajectory indoors using the Wii Remote camera

The trajectory tracking is shown for an area of about 0.2m×0.2m which is limited due to the horizontal field of view of the Wii Remote camera of approximately 45°. The maximal deviation from the predefined path is about 5cm. For outdoor applications, a larger area will be covered.

## 5    Conclusions and Future Research

Since many potential applications for rotorcrafts depend on the grade of their autonomy, this work is one step towards a fully autonomous quadrocopter. The main results of this work consist of the implementation of a trajectory tracking algorithm to follow a desired path and the improvement of the standard GPS system to get highly precise absolute position measurements. The trajectory tracking algorithm has been verified experimentally by tracking a path indoors with an position error of less than 5cm using vision-based position data. For outdoor use RTK-GPS measurements are used to generate the position of the quadrocopter. The $2\sigma$ standard deviations of three-dimensional RTK-GPS measurements are below 20cm which is adequate for most outdoor applications. A necessary extension to the work presented in this paper is to perform outdoor trajectory flights using RTK-GPS position measurements.

Future work will concentrate on obstacle and collision avoidance schemes for a group of quadrocopters. For this purpose, the experimental platform has to be extended by additional sensors like a stereo camera system. Furthermore, the software framework has to be configured to allow for changing mission scenarios. In this context, a search and rescue mission can comprise of a collective formation flight to a search region, where the formation breaks up to enter a search mode. This is necessary to cover the biggest possible area and to minimize search time. It will also be interesting to verify formation control algorithms which have already been tested in simulation [4].

# References

1. Hoffmann, G.M., Huang, H., Waslander, S.L., Tomlin, C.J.: Quadrotor Helicopter Flight Dynamics and Control: Theory and Experiment. In: AIAA Guidance, Navigation and Control Conference and Exhibit, Hilton Head, South Carolina (August 2007)
2. Hoffmann, G.M., Waslander, S.L., Tomlin, C.J.: Quadrotor Helicopter Trajectory Tracking Control. In: AIAA Guidance, Navigation and Control Conference and Exhibit, Honolulu, Hawaii (August 2008)
3. Sujit, P.B., Kingston, D., Beard, R.: Cooperative Forest Fire Monitoring Using Multiple UAVs. In: Proc. 46th IEEE Conference on Decision and Control, New Orleans, LA, USA, pp. 4875–4880 (December 2007)
4. Pilz, U., Popov, A.P., Werner, H.: Robust controller design for formation flight of quad-rotor helicopters. In: Proc. 48th IEEE Conference on Decision and Control, Shanghai, China, pp. 8322–8327 (December 2009)
5. Castillo, P., Lozano, R., Dzul, A.: Stabilization of a Mini Rotorcraft with Four Rotors. IEEE Control Systems Magazine 25(6), 45–55 (2005)
6. Bouabdallah, S., Siegwart, R.: Full Control of a Quadrotor. In: 2007 IEEE/RSJ International Conference on Intelligent Robots and Systems, San Diego, California, USA (October 2010)
7. Puls, T., Hein, A.: 3D Trajectory Control for Quadrocopter. In: 2010 IEEE/RSJ International Conference on Intelligent Robots and Systems, Taipei, Taiwan (October 2010)
8. Wendel, J., Trommer, G.F.: Tightly Coupled GPS/INS Integration for Missile Applications. Aerospace Science and Technology 8(7), 627–634 (2004)
9. Kim, J.-H., Sukkarieh, S., Wishart, S.: Real-Time Navigation, Guidance, and Control of a UAV Using Low-Cost Sensors. In: Yuta, S., Asama, H., Prassler, E., Tsubouchi, T., Thrun, S. (eds.) Field and Service Robotics, Springer Tracts in Advanced Robotics, vol. 24, pp. 299–309. Springer, Heidelberg (2006)
10. Takasu, T.: RTKLIB: An Open Source Program Package for GNSS Positioning, http://gpspp.sakura.ne.jp/rtklib/rtklib.htm
11. Falkenberg, O.: Robuste Lageregelung und GPS/INS-Integration eines autonomen Quadrokopters. Master's thesis, Institute for Reliability Engineering, Hamburg University of Technology (2010)
12. Wenzel, K.E., Rosset, P., Zell, A.: Low-Cost Visual Tracking of a Landing Place and Hovering Flight Control with a Microcontroller. Journal of Intelligent & Robotic Systems 57(1), 297–311 (2010)

# Five-Axis Milling Simulation Based on B-rep Model

Yongzhi Cheng[1,*], Caihua Xiong[1], Tao Ye[1], and Hongkai Cheng[2]

[1] State Key Laboratory of Digital Manufacturing Equipment and Technology,
School of Mechanical Science and Engineering,
Huazhong University of Science and Technology, Wuhan 430074, China
[2] Wuhan Ordnance NCO school, Wuhan 430075, China
hustcyz@163.com

**Abstract.** Formulating the swept volume by a cutter along its path plays an important role in volumetric simulation of five-axis machining. In some cases, the swept volume may experience self-intersection, which is a crucial issue and difficult to be solved. Based on B-rep model, this paper proposes an algorithm for formulating the swept volume for five-axis ball-end milling, including a method for solving the self-intersection. Simulation shows the proposed method can be robustly used for five-axis material remove simulation with large tool orientation changes, and calculating the material remove rate as well as evaluating machining precision.

**Keywords:** five-axis milling simulation, swept volume, self-intersection, B-rep model.

## 1 Introduction

In recent years, five-axis milling is widely used for machining complex surface. Compared with three-axis milling, five-axis milling has two additional rotation degrees which brings great challenge for material remove simulatiion. The basic principle of NC verification and simulation is, formulating tool swept volume along the NC trajectory, then carrying out boolean subtraction to remove the swept volume from the workpiece, finally obtaining the machined workpiece [1]. Therefore, formulating tool swept volume is essential for NC simulation.

Researchers have proposed many NC simulation methods which can be categorized into discrete simulation, solid-based simulation, and hybrid method. Discrete simulation regards the overall geometric outline of the individual cutter as tool swept volume, such as Z-buffer [2], dexel [3] and ray casting [4]. The advantage of discrete method is simple for calculating, but it has poor precision and costs a long time. Solid-based simulation generates a non-degenerate envelope surface to approximate tool swept volume. This method can simulate more precisely, however the swept

---

* Corresponding author.

S. Jeschke, H. Liu, and D. Schilberg (Eds.): ICIRA 2011, Part I, LNAI 7101, pp. 22–32, 2011.

volume is complex for calculating and self-intersection of swept profiles is always a difficult problem. So if it is convenient to generate swept volume and solve self-intersection, solid-based method is better than discrete method.

Many attempts have been made to generate tool swept volume, such as envelope theory [5], sweep differential equation [6], Jacobian rank deficiency method [7]. Chung et al. [8] presented a method to analytically compute envelope surface in a single valued form for a generalized tool in three-axis milling. Wang [4] proposed the envelope theory and used a moving frame to calculate the envelope surface for a flat-end cutter. Shang et al.[9] presented a detailed algorithm to approximate the swept volume for a generalized cutter in five-axis milling. Furthermore, Based on the tangency condition in envelope theory and the body velocity representation in spatial kinematics, LiMin Zhu et al. [10] proposed a closed-form solution of the swept envelope of a general rotary cutter moving along a general tool path. However, none of these methods has application for robust material remove simulation, and none of them is convenient for solving self-intersection.

B-rep model is widely used in solid modeling, because it supports most of the mathematical surface including Bezier surface, spline surface and NURBS surface, etc. ACIS is a powerful 3D modeling engine based on B-rep model, which utilizes open object-oriented C++ framework. Based on B-rep model and discrete modeling, this paper presents a hybrid method formulating tool swept volume for ball-end tool in five-axis milling, including solving self-intersection. The paper is organized as follows: In section 2, the geometry of ball-end tool is described in the moving frame. section 3 describes the process of swept profiles calculation and tool swept volume generation. In section 4, five-axis milling simulation is achieved by using ACIS and C++ programming, including obtaining the machining precision and material remove rate. In section 5, detecting and solving self-intersection are discussed.

## 2    Geometric Description of Ball-End Tool

A typical five-axis machine tool is composed of three translational motions and two rotational motions. Cutter location source file (CLSF) is generated by CAM software which describes the position and posture of cutting tool in discrete NC points. A moving frame $\{e_1, e_2, e_3\}$ is defined on every NC point to conveniently formulate tool geometry, where the origin is at the control point. The moving frame $\{e_1, e_2, e_3\}$ can be defined as [4]:

$$\vec{e_1} = \overrightarrow{A(t)}, \ \ \vec{e_2} = \overrightarrow{A(t)} \times \overrightarrow{A(t+1)}, \ \ \vec{e_3} = \overrightarrow{e1} \times \overrightarrow{e2} \tag{1}$$

Where $\overrightarrow{A(t)}$ is the current tool axes and $\overrightarrow{A(t+1)}$ is the next tool axes. If $\overrightarrow{A(t)}$ is parallel with $\overrightarrow{A(t+1)}$, the cutter posture has no change between two successive NC points, and that case is not in the consideration of five-axis milling. Figure.2. shows the geometric description of ball-end tool in the moving frame $\{e_1, e_2, e_3\}$.

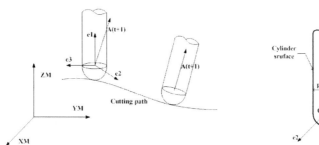
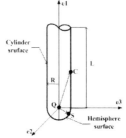

**Fig. 1.** Relationship between MCS and $\{e_1, e_2, e_3\}$

**Fig. 2.** Geometric description of ball-end tool

In Figure.2, R represents the radius of the ball-end tool. L represents the height of the cylinder. Q is the control point. C is a random point on cylinder surface and S is a random point on hemisphere surface. The projection length of $\overline{QC}$ on $\vec{e_1}$ is $k, k \in [0, L]$, and the angle between the projection of $\overline{QC}$ on $\vec{e_1}\vec{e_2}$ plane and $e_2$ is $\alpha, \alpha \in [0, 2\pi]$. The angle between $\overline{QS}$ and the opposite direction of $\vec{e_1}$ is $\beta, \beta \in [0, \frac{\pi}{2}]$, and the angle between the projection of $\overline{QS}$ on $\vec{e_2}\vec{e_3}$ plane and $e_2$ is $\gamma, \gamma \in [0, 2\pi]$.

The surfaces of ball-end tool can be divided into two parts which are cylinder surface $F_C$ and hemisphere surface $F_S$. Let $C_P(t)$ represent the coordinates of control point in MCS. As shown in figure.2, the mathematical expressions of $F_C$ and $F_S$ in MCS are as following:

$$^M F_C(\alpha, k, t) = C_P(t) + k\vec{e_1} + R\cos(\alpha)\vec{e_2} + R\sin(\alpha)\vec{e_3} \tag{2}$$

$$^M F_S(\beta, \alpha, t) = C_P(t) - R\sin(\beta)\vec{e_1} + R\sin(\beta)\cos(\alpha)\vec{e_2} + R\sin(\beta)\sin(\alpha)\vec{e_3} \tag{3}$$

The normal vector $\vec{N}$ of a point on surface $F(u, v)$ can be described as:

$$\vec{N}_{F(u,v)} = \frac{\dfrac{\partial F}{\partial u} \times \dfrac{\partial F}{\partial v}}{\left| \dfrac{\partial F}{\partial u} \times \dfrac{\partial F}{\partial v} \right|} \tag{4}$$

Applying Eq.(4) for Eqs.(2) and (3), The normal vector of a point C on cylinder surface and a point S on hemisphere surface are given as:

$$^M \vec{N(C)} = \cos(\alpha)\vec{e_2} + \sin(\alpha)\vec{e_3} \tag{5}$$

$$^M \vec{N(S)} = -\cos(\beta)\vec{e_1} + \sin(\beta)\cos(\gamma)\vec{e_2} + \sin(\beta)\sin(\gamma)\vec{e_3} \tag{6}$$

# 3     Tool Swept Volume Generation

Tool swept volume is defined as the set of spatial points occupied by the tool when moving along the cutting path. Supposing the cutting path is a continuous function of parameter $t \in [t_{\min}, t_{\max}]$, tool swept volume is given by[11]:

$$E(\Phi) = \{\bigcup \Phi(t) \mid t \in [t_{\min}, t_{\max}]\} \tag{7}$$

wherere $\Phi(t)$ represents the set of spatial points occupied by the tool at time $t$.

The boundary surface of a body describes the body without ambiguity. Hence, the description of tool swept volume can be simplied to the description of tool swept surfaces. According to the envelope theory, swept surface is constructed by the group of swept profiles, so swept profiles are tangent curves of swept surfaces and swept parent body. Supposing a point P is on swept profiles, P is necessary to satisfy the following:

$$\overrightarrow{V_P} \bullet \overrightarrow{N_P} = 0 \tag{8}$$

where $\overrightarrow{V_P}$ is the velocity vector of P on swept parent body and $\overrightarrow{N_P}$ is the normal vector of P on swept parent body.

## 3.1     Swept Profiles of Cylinder Surface

$\overrightarrow{V_E}$ is defined as the linear velocity of control point. $\overrightarrow{\omega}$ is supposed to be the tool rotational speed. Because ball-end tool is rotating body, $\overrightarrow{\omega}$ represents the angle from the current tool posture to the next tool posture without considering the tool rotation. So $\overrightarrow{V_E}$ and $\overrightarrow{\omega}$ can be obtained from CLSF and it is clear that $\overrightarrow{\omega}$ and $\overrightarrow{e_2}$ are in the same direction. In consideration of the vector operation relationships[12], the velocity $\overrightarrow{V(C)}$ of a point C on cylinder can be described in MCS as:

$$\overline{{}^M V(C)} = \overrightarrow{V_E} + \overrightarrow{\omega} \times \overrightarrow{QC} = \overrightarrow{V_E} + k(\overrightarrow{\omega} \times \overrightarrow{e1}) + R\sin(\alpha)(\overrightarrow{\omega} \times \overrightarrow{e3}) \tag{9}$$

Applying $\overline{{}^M V(C)}$ and $\overline{{}^M N(C)}$ to Eq.8, swept profiles of cylinder surface is given:

$$f_C(\alpha, k, t) = \sin(\alpha)(\overrightarrow{V_E} \bullet \overrightarrow{e3} - k|\overrightarrow{w}|) + \cos(\alpha)(\overrightarrow{V_E} \bullet \overrightarrow{e2}) = 0 \tag{10}$$

Eq.10 can be derived to:

$$\alpha = a\tan(-\frac{\overrightarrow{V_E} \bullet \overrightarrow{e2}}{\overrightarrow{V_E} \bullet \overrightarrow{e3} - k|\overrightarrow{\omega}|}) \qquad k \in [0, L] \tag{11}$$

In the range of $k$, take a group of samples $k_{1,2,3\ldots n} \in [0, L]$, where $k_1 = 0, k_n = L$.

Because $\alpha \in [0, 2\pi]$ and $a\tan(-\dfrac{\vec{V}_E \bullet \vec{e2}}{\vec{V}_E \bullet \vec{e3} - k|\vec{\omega}|}) \in [-\dfrac{\pi}{2}, \dfrac{\pi}{2}]$, it is obvious that one result of Eq.11 corresponds two values of parameter $\alpha$, which are both on the swept profiles. So the following formulas are given:

If $\quad a\tan(-\dfrac{\vec{V}_E \bullet \vec{e2}}{\vec{V}_E \bullet \vec{e3} - k|\vec{\omega}|}) \in [-\dfrac{\pi}{2}, 0]$

then $\quad \alpha_i = a\tan(-\dfrac{\vec{V}_E \bullet \vec{e2}}{\vec{V}_E \bullet \vec{e3} - k|\vec{\omega}|}) + \pi, \alpha_{ii} = \alpha_i + \pi$ $\qquad$ (12)

if $\quad a\tan(-\dfrac{\vec{V}_E \bullet \vec{e2}}{\vec{V}_E \bullet \vec{e3} - k|\vec{\omega}|}) \in [0, \dfrac{\pi}{2}]$

then $\quad \alpha_i = a\tan(-\dfrac{\vec{V}_E \bullet \vec{e2}}{\vec{V}_E \bullet \vec{e3} - k|\vec{\omega}|}), \alpha_{ii} = \alpha_i + \pi$ $\qquad$ (13)

Substituting $(k_i, \alpha_i), (k_i, \alpha_{ii})$ into Eq.2, Expressions of discrete sampling points $C(P)_i$ and $C(P)_{ii}$ in the MCS are as followings:

$$^M C(P)_i = C_P(t) + k\vec{e1} + R\cos(\alpha_i)\vec{e2} + R\sin(\alpha_i)\vec{e3} \qquad (14)$$

$$^M C(P)_{ii} = C_P(t) + k\vec{e1} + R\cos(\alpha_{ii})\vec{e2} + R\sin(\alpha_{ii})\vec{e3} \qquad (15)$$

Fitting splines through these discrete points, swept profiles of cylinder surface on one NC point can be constructed. Based on the above solutions, swept profiles of cylinder surface are generated on every NC point.

## 3.2     Swept Profiles of Hemisphere Surface

As the derivation for cylinder surface. The velocity $\vec{V(S)}$ of a point S on hemisphere surface can be described in MCS as:

$$^M\vec{V(S)} = \vec{V}_E + \vec{\omega} \times \vec{QS} = \vec{V}_E - R\cos(\beta)(\vec{\omega} \times \vec{e1}) + R\sin(\beta)\sin(\alpha)(\vec{\omega} \times \vec{e3}) \qquad (16)$$

Applying $\quad ^M\vec{V(S)} \bullet {}^M\vec{N(S)} = 0$, the swept profiles of hemisphere surface $f_s$ is given :

$$f_s(\beta, \gamma, t) = -\cos(\gamma)(\vec{V}_E \bullet \vec{e1}) + \sin(\beta)\cos(\gamma)(\vec{V}_E \bullet \vec{e2}) + \sin(\beta)\sin(\gamma)(\vec{V}_E \bullet \vec{e3}) = 0 \quad (17)$$

In Eq.17, applying the following transformations:

$$\begin{cases} X = \cos(\gamma)(\vec{V}_E \bullet \vec{e1}) \\ Y = \sin(\gamma)(\vec{V}_E \bullet \vec{e2}) \\ Z = \sin(\gamma)(\vec{V}_E \bullet \vec{e3}) \end{cases} \qquad (18)$$

Eq.17 is converted to:

$$-X + Y\cos(\beta) + Z\sin(\beta) = 0 \tag{19}$$

Applying $\sin^2(\beta) + \cos^2(\beta) = 1$   Eq.19 can be converted to:

$$(Y^2 + Z^2)\cos^2(\beta) - 2XY\cos(\beta) + (X^2 - Z^2) = 0 \tag{20}$$

Eq.20 is a quadratic equation of parameter $\cos(\beta)$. Defining:

$$a = Y^2 + Z^2, b = -2XY, c = X^2 - Z^2 \tag{21}$$

If there are real roots, Eq.20 must satisfy the condition $b^2 - 4ac \geq 0$, which is further derived to:

$$Y^2 + Z^2 - X^2 \geq 0 \tag{22}$$

From Eq.22, boundary condition of $\gamma$ is obtained:

$$\gamma_{\min} = a\sin(\frac{|\vec{V_E} \bullet \vec{e1}|}{\sqrt{(\vec{V_E} \bullet \vec{e1})^2 + (\vec{V_E} \bullet \vec{e2})^2 + (\vec{V_E} \bullet \vec{e3})^2}}) \tag{23}$$

If $\gamma \in [\gamma_{\min}, \pi/2]$, Eq.22 is satisfied and Eq.20 will have real roots. From Eq.20, the results of $\beta$ are given by:

$$\beta = a\cos(\frac{XY \pm |Z|\sqrt{Y^2 + Z^2 - X^2}}{Y^2 + Z^2}) \quad \text{where:} \quad \gamma \in [\gamma_{\min}, \pi/2] \tag{24}$$

In the range of $\gamma$, take a group of samples $\gamma_i, i = 1, 2, 3...n$, where $\gamma_1 = \gamma_{\min}$ $\gamma_n = \pi/2$.

Although there are two real roots solved in Eq.20, one of them is not satisfied with hemisphere surface equation. The satisfied real root is denoted as $(\gamma_i, \beta_i)$.

Because $a\cos(\frac{XY \pm |Z|\sqrt{Y^2 + Z^2 - X^2}}{Y^2 + Z^2}) \in [0, \pi]$ and $\beta \in [0, 2\pi]$, $\beta_i$ corresponds two values of $\beta$ which are both on the swept profiles. So following formulas given:

$$\beta_i = \beta_i, \beta_{ii} = \beta_i + \pi \tag{25}$$

Taking the groups $(\gamma_i, \beta_i)$ and $(\gamma_i, \beta_{ii})$ to hemisphere equation respectively, the corresponding points $S(P)_i$ and $S(P)_{ii}$ can be described in MCS as:

$$^M S(P)_i = C_P(t) - R\cos(\gamma_i)\vec{e1} + R\sin(\gamma_i)\cos(\beta_i)\vec{e2} + R\sin(\gamma_i)\sin(\beta_i)\vec{e3} \tag{26}$$

$$^M S(P)_{ii} = C_P(t) - R\cos(\gamma_i)\vec{e1} + R\sin(\gamma_i)\cos(\beta_{ii})\vec{e2} + R\sin(\gamma_i)\sin(\beta_{ii})\vec{e3} \tag{27}$$

Fitting spline through these discrete points, swept profile of hemisphere surface on one NC point is constructed. As above, swept profiles of hemisphere surface are generated on every NC point.

### 3.3     Formulating Tool Swept Volume

On every NC point, a complete tool swept profile is constructed by connecting swept profiles of cylinder surface and hemisphere surface. Tool swept surfaces are generated by applying skin method to these complete swept profiles in order. The space occupied by tool swept surfaces is tool swept volume.

## 4     Realization of Five-Axis Milling Simulation

Based on the above algorithm, five-axis milling simulation is realized using ACIS and C++ programing. After reading CLSF and completing tool parameters input where tool diameter is 12mm and tool height is 70mm, tool motions and worpiece are shown in Figure.3. Swept profiles are generated in every NC points which are shown in read curves in Figure.4. Blue area in Figure.5 represents tool swept volume generated by the swept profiles. Then carrying out boolean subtraction to remove tool swept volume from the workpiece, the machined workpiece is shown in Figure.6.

**Fig. 3.** Tool movement and workpiece          **Fig. 4.** Swept profiles

**Fig. 5.** Swept volume                    **Fig. 6.** The machined workpiece

In the process of milling simulation, every two adjacent swept profiles can also generate partial tool swept volume. With the advantage of ACIS, it is convenient to get the volume removed by the partial tool swept volume from workpiece. So, corresponding to the above tool swept volume, the material remove rate between every two successive NC points is shown in Table 1.

**Table 1.** Material remove rate (mm*mm*mm/second)

| Material remove rate | 64.51 | 99.21 | 132.62 | 165.31 | 192.12 | 211.96 | 222.44 | 223.28 | 213.06 | 190.91 |
|---|---|---|---|---|---|---|---|---|---|---|
| Cutting length (mm) | 5.19 | 5.24 | 5.28 | 5.25 | 5.19 | 5.14 | 5.09 | 5.04 | 5.01 | 5.14 |
| Material remove rate | 163.39 | 137.51 | 120.24 | 111.71 | 113.62 | 126.46 | 153.67 | 194.28 | 162.95 | |
| Cutting length (mm) | 5.32 | 5.47 | 5.53 | 5.59 | 5.65 | 5.66 | 5.65 | 5.62 | 3.74 | |

When the complete rough milling CLSF is read, rough milling simulation can be finished. The result is shown in Figure.7. Figure.8 shows the result of finish-milling simulation. The finish-milling surface is extracted and shown in yellow in Figure.9. In figure.10, design surface is shown in green compared with finish-milling surface. After calculating the difference between design surface and finish-milling surface on sampling points, the machining precision is obtained and shown in Table 2.

**Fig. 7.** Rough milling simulation

**Fig. 8.** Finish-milling simulation

**Fig. 9.** Finish-milling surface

**Fig. 10.** Finishing surface and design surface

**Table 2.** Machining precision on sampling points (mm)

(The positive number indicates missing cut; The negative number indicates over cut)

| -0.242 | -0.113 | -0.269 | -0.036 | -0.074 | -0.019 | 0.004 | -0.053 | -0.058 | -0.036 | -0.095 | -0.017 | 0.009 |
|---|---|---|---|---|---|---|---|---|---|---|---|---|
| -0.014 | 0.021 | -0.033 | -0.012 | -0.008 | -0.079 | -0.028 | -0.064 | -0.112 | -0.074 | -0.058 | -0.116 | |

## 5    Determining and Solving Self-intersection

In the process of swept volume generation, self-intersection of swept profiles is always a difficult problem to be solved. Self-intersection can lead to non-manifold boundary of swept volume, causing inconvenience for further analysis and application of swept volume. So solving self-intersection is very important and necessary. However, there is little research in swept volume field involving self-intersection. With regards to this, a convenient and reliable method for determining and solving self-intersection is proposed in this paper.

This method determines self-intersection by constructing surfaces using tool swept profiles [13]. Firstly, by using the method of through curve mesh for every complete swept profile, a surface is constructed by the swept profile on every NC point. Then, determining self-intersection by judging whether there is intersection among all the constructed surfaces. It is obvious that if two constructed surfaces intersect with each other, the corresponding swept profiles will also experience self-intersection when generating tool swept volume.

In the previous section, self-intersection will happen if tool parameters are increased. For example, Let tool diameter increase to 30mm and tool height increase to 100mm. As the previous section, swept profiles are generated which are shown in Figure.11 in red curves. The constructed surface are showen in Figure.12. By using ACIS fuction, it is convenient to determine whether there is intersection between two surfaces and obtain the intersecting curves.

**Fig. 11.** Swept profiles          **Fig. 12.** Generated Surface

Solving self-intersection is also a difficult problem in swept volume field. In this paper, a hybrid method of discrete modeling and swept volume method is proposed to solve self-intersection. After self-intersection determination, surfaces that experience intersecion are obtained. Firstly, if there are more than one successive swept profiles without self-intersecion, a partial swept volume is generated by using skin method through them. Then, discrete tool bodys are interpolated on both sides of the tool body whose swept profile experiences self-intersection or is not involved in any partial swept volume. At last, the final tool swept volume is the boolean union of all partial swept volume, all the tool body whose swept profile experiences self-intersection or is not involved in any partial swept volume, all the interpolated tool body, the first tool body and the last tool body. The final tool swept volume is shown in Figure.13.

**Fig. 13.** The final tool swept volume       **Fig. 14.** The result of machined surface

In Figure.13, the first tool body is in yellow, the last tool body is in purple, the tool body whose swept profile experiences self-intersection or is not involved in any partial swept volume is in green, the interpolated tool body is in red and the partial swept volume is in blue. The final tool swept volume is boolean union of all the body above. After removing the final tool swept volume from workpiece, The machined workpiece is shown in Figure.14. It can be seen that the machined surface is smooth. So the proposed method is convenient and reliable for determining and solving self-intersection for five-axis milling simulation.

## 6    Conclusions

Based on B-rep model, a method for generating tool swept volume for five-axis ball-end milling considering self-intersection has been presented in this paper. The method can be robustly used for five-axis material remove simulation and has satisfied results for solving self-intersecion. For further application of tool swept volume, machining precision is obtained and material remove rate is calculated. Although the method is applied to ball-end mlling, it is applicable for other types of rotary cutter. The proposed method may have various applications such as interference detection and cutting force prediction[14] for five-axis milling.

**Acknowledgement.** The work of this paper is partially supported by the National Key Basic Research Program (Grant No.2011CB706804), the National Natural Science Foundation of China (Grant No.50835004) and the National Funds for Distinguished Young Scientists of China (Grant No.51025518).

## References

1. Weinert, K., Du, S., Damm, P., Stautner, M.: Swept volume generation for the simulation of machining processes. International Journal of Machine Tools & Manufacture 44, 617–628 (2004)
2. Jerard, R.B., Hussaini, S.Z., Drysdale, R.L., Schaudt, B.: Approximate methods for simulation and verification of numerically controlled machining programs. The Visual Computer 5(6), 329–348 (1989)

3. Glaeser, G., Groller, E.: Efficient volume-generation during the simulation of NC-milling. In: Hege, H.-C., Polthier, K. (eds.) Mathematical Visualization, pp. 89–106. Springer, Heidelberg (1998)

4. Wang, W.P., Wang, K.K.: Geometric modeling for swept volume of moving solids. IEEE Computer Graphic Applications 6(12), 8–17 (1986)

5. Pottmann, H., Peternell, M.: Envelopes—computational theory and applications. In: Proceedings, Spring Conference on Computer Graphics and its Applications, Budmerice, Slovakia, pp. 3–23 (2000)

6. Blackmore, D., Leu, M.C., Wang, L.P.: The sweep-envelope differential equation algorithmand its application to NC-machining verification. Computer Aided Design 29(9), 629–637 (1997)

7. Abdel-Malek, K., Seaman, W., Yeh, H.J.: NC-verification of upto 5 axis machining processes using manifold stratification. ASME Journal of Manufacturing Science and Engineering 122, 1–11 (2000)

8. Chung, Y.C., Park, J.W., Shin, H.Y., Choi, B.K.: Modeling the surface swept by a generalized cutter for NC verification. Computer-Aided Des. 30(8), 587–594 (1998)

9. Du, S., Surmann, T., Webber, O., Weinert, K.: Formulating swept profiles for five-axis tool motions. International Journal of Machine Tools & Manufacture 45, 849–861 (2005)

10. Zhu, L., Zheng, G., Ding, H.: Formulating the swept envelope of rotary cutter undergoing general spatial motion for multi-axis NC machining. International Journal of Machine Tools & Manufacture 49, 199–202 (2009)

11. Chiou, C.-J., Lee, Y.-S.: A shape-generating approach for multi-axis machining G-buffer models. Computer Aided Design 31, 761–776 (1999)

12. Goldstein, H., Poole, C., Safko, J.: Classical Mechanics. Addison Wesley (2002)

13. Xu, Z.-Q., Ye, X.-Z., Chen, Z.-Y., Zhang, Y., Zhang, S.-Y.: Trimming self-intersections in swept volume solid modeling. Journal of Zhejiang University SCIENCE A (2007) ISSN 1673—565X (Print), ISSN 1862—1775

14. Boz, Y., Erdim, H., Lazoglu, I.: Modeling Cutting Forces for 5-Axis Machining of Sculptured Surfaces. In: International Conference on High Performance Cutting (CIRP HPC 2010, TR2010-114) (2010)

# Exploration Strategies for Building Compact Maps in Unbounded Environments

Matthias Nieuwenhuisen[1], Dirk Schulz[2], and Sven Behnke[1]

[1] Autonomous Intelligent Systems Group, University of Bonn, Germany
nieuwenh@ais.uni-bonn.de, behnke@cs.uni-bonn.de
[2] Fraunhofer Institute for Communication, Information Processing and Ergonomics
FKIE, Wachtberg, Germany
dirk.schulz@fkie.fraunhofer.de

**Abstract.** Exploration strategies are an important ingredient for map building with mobile robots. The traditional greedy exploration strategy is not directly applicable in unbounded outdoor environments, because it decides on the robot's actions solely based on the expected information gain and travel cost. As this value can be optimized by driving straight into unexplored space, this behavior often leads to degenerated maps. We propose two different techniques to regularize the value function of the exploration strategy, in order to explore compact areas in outdoor environments. We compare exploration speed and compactness of the maps with and without our extensions.

**Keywords:** Outdoor Exploration, Compact Map-Building.

## 1 Introduction

The autonomous exploration of unknown indoor and outdoor environments is an active research topic in mobile robotics. In the literature, solutions to special instances of the problem have been proposed over the last years. The overall goal of any exploration approach is to plan a robot's motion in such a way that a map of the robot's environment can be build efficiently, solely based on the robot's sensor data. Most of the approaches developed so far, decide on the robot's motions based on a trade-off between the expected information gain, e. g. the expected increase in newly observed area, and the cost of the exploration. In bounded spaces, like buildings or predetermined areas of interest, greedy motion strategies based on this idea exist that fully explore the environment with low (travel) costs (cf. [8], [6]). If the robot operates in a virtually unbounded outdoor environment, like it is the case e. g. in planetary exploration, it is generally not feasible to explore the whole reachable area. A strategy that greedily maximizes the information gain can lead to degenerated maps in this situation, as it is often possible to obtain a maximum of new information by stubbornly driving on a straight line away from the starting position. The resulting map cannot provide useful information about the local shape or the topology of the environment. For this reason, some additional means are required to constrain the robot's

S. Jeschke, H. Liu, and D. Schilberg (Eds.): ICIRA 2011, Part I, LNAI 7101, pp. 33–43, 2011.
© Springer-Verlag Berlin Heidelberg 2011

motion, while it explores an open outdoor environment. One simple possibility to achieve this is to artificially bound the area to explore, e. g. by manually defining a bounding polygon. This approach can lead to problems as the topology of the environment is a priori unknown, e. g. with concave inclusions. Although it is possible to reach all free space parts contained in the bounding polygon, it may require extensive exploration to discover a path in more complex scenarios.

In this article, we propose two different regularization techniques that – in combination with a greedy exploration strategy – allow to acquire *compact* maps of the environment. In the scope of this article, *compact* maps are maps with a width-to-height ratio close to one. We achieve this goal by introducing additional terms into the value function of the underlying decision-theoretic motion planner that decides on the robot's actions. The first regularization, called spiral exploration, biases the value function towards favoring motion commands that lead to a spiral exploration path, if possible. The second one, called distance-penalized exploration, directly penalizes motion commands that lead to maps with an unbalanced width-to-height ratio.

The remainder of the article is organized as follows: after discussing related work in the next section, we will briefly introduce the basics of greedy decision-theoretic exploration approaches in Section 3. Section 4.1 then introduces the spiral exploration extension, followed by Section 4.2 that explains the distance-penalized exploration technique. We present simulations in Section 5, where we evaluate the performance of both exploration approaches using experiments in environments of varying structure.

## 2   Related Work

A major element of exploration systems is to find optimal sensing positions where a robot can gather as much new information about the world as possible, also known as next best views. As the world is unknown a priori, strategies to estimate the next best positions are needed. A widely used approach in 2D exploration is to choose sensing positions at the frontier between known and unknown space and to weight them according to the travel costs to reach these positions [15]. Burgard, Moors, and Schneider described a strategy to coordinate frontier-based exploration in multi-robot systems [1]. González-Baños and Latombe use the maximal visible unexplored space at a scan position as an approximation of the art gallery problem [4]. Surmann, Nüchter, and Hertzberg applied this strategy in a 3D exploration system [12]. Pfaff et al. use virtual laser scans, simulated by 3D ray-casting, to calculate the expected information of scan positions to build a 2.5D world model [11]. Although our approach is similar to these techniques, as it uses a greedy exploration strategy, none of these works addresses the problem of building compact maps in unbounded environments. Several geometrical approaches for following motion patterns to cover unknown areas have been proposed for this purpose, e. g. Cao et al. [2] and Hert et al. [5]. They differ from our approach as their main objective is to cover a given bounding polygon completely. In these approaches, the expected information gain of scan positions is not evaluated. Moorehead [9] proposed a decision-theoretic exploration approach for planetary surfaces that uses additional metrics to guide the robot to areas of scientific interest, like dry waterbeds. In contrast to that, we are interested in maximizing the known area in a way that enables the robot to plan efficient paths afterward. Topological information is used by Morris et al. [10] to explore abandoned mines. We use an implicit selection of the next view positions, as this does not rely on any assumptions on the environment topology.

## 3   Greedy Exploration

The compact exploration strategies, we propose in this article, are an extension to the greedy exploration approach for autonomous map building. We briefly introduce this underlying approach first, following the notation used in [13].

The goal of greedy exploration is to control the robot's next measurement action in such a way that its uncertainty about the global state of the (static) world is minimized. Formally, this knowledge is represented by a probability distribution over possible world states that is called the robot's belief $b$. In the context of autonomous map building, the robot acquires information about the shape of the environment using, for example, laser range sensors. Here, the next action to be planned is a motion to a new location $u$, where a maximum of additional information about the shape of the environment is expected. This *information gain* can be expressed by the expected reduction of the entropy of the robot's belief after integrating a measurement at the new location $u$, i.e.

$$I_b(u) = H_b(x) - E_z\left[H_b(x'|z,u)\right],\tag{1}$$

where $H_b(x)$ denotes the entropy of the prior belief, and $E_z\left[H_b(x'|z,u)\right]$ is the expected conditional entropy of the belief after carrying out the motion and integrating a new sensor measurement $z$ obtained at the new location. A greedy exploration strategy is now a decision-theoretic approach to choose the action $\pi(b)$ with the best trade-off between information gain and expected travel cost using the value function

$$\pi(b) = \operatorname{argmax}_u \alpha I_b(u) + \int r(x,u)b(x)dx.\tag{2}$$

Here, $r(x,u)$ is the travel cost function and the factor $\alpha$ weighs the influence of gain and costs. Note that in the context of mapping, a probabilistic map representation, like occupancy probability grids [3] or multi-level surface maps [14], is generally used to represent the belief.

In order to achieve compact exploration, we add an extra cost term $C(b,u)$ to the value function $\pi(b)$ that penalizes motion commands which are likely to lead to non-compact maps. The resulting value function used is

$$\pi_C(b) = \operatorname{argmax}_u \alpha\left(\beta C(b,u) + I_b(u)\right) + \int r(x,u)b(x)dx.\tag{3}$$

The map representation of the belief allows to efficiently approximate the integral for the expected travel costs in Eq. 3 using value iteration (see [13] chapter 17 for details). $I_b(u)$ is generally determined by estimating the expected amount of newly explored area at the location reached after carrying out the motion command $u$. The new area can be estimated by determining the expected visibility polygon at a candidate view position and subtracting the already explored part of it. The expected visibility polygon can, for example, be computed using a ray sweep algorithm that treats unexplored space as free [4]. If the belief is represented by grid maps, virtual laser scans can alternatively be used. Beams are sent out from a candidate view position and followed through the grid. The estimation of yet unexplored space is reduced to counting the traversed explored and unexplored grid cells. As the simulation can mimic the characteristics of a real laser-range finder, the estimate is generally better than the one based on the visibility polygon.

It remains to describe, how we achieve an exploration behavior that leads to compact maps. For this purpose, we introduce two different utility or cost functions $C(b, u)$ for weighing candidate view positions $u$, each one leading to a different compact exploration behavior.

## 4   Compact Exploration Strategies

### 4.1   Spiral Exploration

In environments without obstacles, a simple exploration technique that leads to a compact map is to drive on a spiral path, with a radial distance between two turns that maximizes the information gain. In outdoor environments with a low to average obstacle density, a spiral trajectory approach can still be reasonable, although obstacles may occasionally block the robot's path. In such situations, the robot obviously needs to deviate from the spiral in a way that still leads to an efficient compact exploration. In order to achieve such a behavior, we implement $C(b, u)$ as a function that rewards motion commands leading to spiral trajectories. For this purpose, we keep track of the center of the map built so far, and we determine the angle $\theta$ between the radial vector $r$ that connects the center of the map with the robot's current position and the motion vector $v$ that connects the robot's current position with its intended scan position $u$. To achieve a spiral trajectory, $v$ should be kept orthogonal to $r$, because the motion direction is tangential to the map's border then. For this reason, we choose to reward considered scan positions with a value proportional to $|\sin(\theta)|$. This procedure is summarized as pseudo code in Algorithm 1. Integrated into the value function $\pi_C(b)$, the robot tends to explore the environment on a spiral path, but the robot starts to deviate from the spiral, if view points exist that, depending on the weighting constants $\alpha$ and $\beta$, lead to a sufficiently higher information gain with tolerable motion costs. This will for example happen, if an obstacle blocks the robot's path. To ensure a trajectory circling the convex hull of the map equally close in all directions, a floating center of the map is maintained during exploration by continuously computing its center of mass.

---

**Algorithm 1.** Compute_spiral_exploration_cost

    **Input**: map, scanPos, robotPos
1  com ← CenterOfMass (map)
2  robotToScan ← Normalize (scanPos - robotPos)
3  robotToCom ← Normalize (com - robotPos)
4  sinAngle ← sin (arccos (cosAngle))
5  **return** Abs (sin (arccos (cosAngle)))

---

### 4.2  Distance-Penalized Exploration

The spiral exploration strategy effectively leads to compact maps in environments known to have a low obstacle density like, e. g., in planetary exploration. However, with an increasing number of obstacles present in the environment, the spiral strategy tends to leave unexplored holes inside the convex hull of the already explored area. The information gain received by closing such holes is often small, compared to the costs of leaving the tangential exploration direction and the additional travel costs. In this section, we propose an exploration strategy that effectively avoids leaving such holes at the cost of a potentially lower exploration speed. As in the case of the spiral exploration strategy, this is achieved by introducing a cost term into the greedy value function, without explicitly considering to close exploration holes.

To mitigate the discrepancy between the lower information gain received at holes and the high information gain at the frontier to the unexplored space, we penalize view positions depending on their distance from the center of the map. We define the radius of a map as the maximum distance of an explored point from the center of the map. Every view point that potentially expands this radius is penalized. The penalty is proportional to the maximum difference between the current radius of the map and the potential new radius of the map after a range scan taken at this position has been integrated.

In the case of a balanced width-to-height ratio, expansions in every direction are equally penalized and the expected information gain dominates the calculation of the value function. Expansions in directions in which the map has not yet reached its maximum radius are not penalized, even if there are holes left. For this reason, holes inside the explored map have to provide a specific minimum gain to be chosen as an area to explore. Otherwise, the quality of the explored maps can decrease. Hence, the distance penalization criterion resembles our definition of a compact map. The computation of costs for distance-penalized view point selection is described in Algorithm 2.

## 5  Evaluation

We implemented both strategies for compact exploration in the context of a system for autonomously acquiring three-dimensional environment models using a 3D laser range scanner. All experiments used to get quantitative results are performed in Gazebo [7], the 3D simulation environment from the Player/Stage

---

**Algorithm 2.** Compute_distance_penalized_exp._cost

**Input**: map, maxRange, scanPos

1  com ← CenterOfMass (map)
2  direction ← Normalize (scanPos - com)
3  maxDistBefore ← 0
4  **foreach** exploredCell *in* map **do**
5  |    maxDistBefore ← Max (maxDistBefore, Distance (exploredCell,com))
6  **end**
7  maxDistAfter ← Distance (com, scanPos + direction * maxRange)
8  **if** maxDistAfter > maxDistBefore **then**
9  |    **return** 1 - α∗(maxDistAfter - maxDistBefore)
10 **else**
11 |    **return** 1
12 **end**

---

project. The 3D scanner simulated is a SICK LMS200 scanner, mounted on a turn-table in such a way that it continuously receives vertical 2D scans while it rotates. The horizontal angular resolution of the 3D scan was set to approximately 1 degree by adjusting the turn-table speed.

Following ideas of Triebel et al. [14], our system represents 3D models of the environment by multi-level surface maps, which are grid maps that can store multiple height values, called *surface patches*, representing surfaces at different heights, per cell. Each patch has a vertical extent and can therefore represent man-made structures like walls and floors with a memory complexity comparable to occupancy grid maps. As the traversable plane reachable by a robot in such a map is a 2-manifold, 2D planning algorithms can still be used.

Candidate view positions are determined with inverse ray-casting from up to 10.000 frontier points. To avoid candidate positions caused by very small frontiers, only clusters of five or more frontier points are considered during the ray-casting operation. From every considered frontier point, 100 beams are followed through the environment. As nearby candidate points are considered to gain a similar amount of information, only candidate points exceeding a distance threshold to neighboring points are added. For the information gain calculation, only patches not exceeding a distance threshold to the robot are considered. Due to the fixed angular distance between consecutive laser beams, the Cartesian distance of the endpoints hitting the ground plane exceed the size of the surface patches. Hence, they are not connected.

In the following, we compare the proposed compact exploration strategies with the plain greedy exploration strategy. As 3D range measurements are costly operations, in our setup the exploration speed is measured as the number of surface patches compared to the number of scans taken. The compactness of a map is the number of explored patches in comparison to the total number of grid cells in the map; this includes unexplored cells, because the size of the grid is chosen as the bounding rectangle of all laser scans.

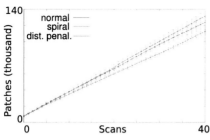
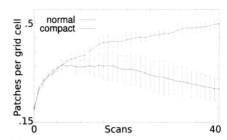

(a) Number of patches in the map for different exploration strategies

(b) Patches per grid cell for different exploration strategies

**Fig. 1.** In Experiment 1 the non-compact and compact strategies have nearly equal exploration speed, but the ratio of patches per grid cell is significantly higher when using the compact strategies

### 5.1  Experiment 1: Low Obstacle Density

In the first experiment, we chose an environment with a low obstacle density, in order to compare the maximum exploration speed of the strategies with and without the proposed extensions. The exploration is stopped after 40 3D scans. The trajectory of the non-compact exploration consists of nearly linear paths as these maximize the ratio between newly seen environment and travel costs. As the probability of a change of exploration direction caused by obstacles is low in this experiment, most of these changes are caused by the randomized sampling of candidate scan positions.

The spiral exploration strategy is able to gather compact maps comparable to the maps generated by the distance-penalized strategy. This is explained by the fact, that a spiral exploration extends the map uniformly in every direction without causing high travel costs, as long as the robot is not deflected by an obstacle. Therefore, the maximum distance of a patch to the center of the map is increasing. Figure 1 shows that the non-compact exploration exhibits a slightly higher exploration speed compared to the two compact strategies, which show no significant difference in exploration speed in maps with low obstacle density. During the first scans, there is no significant difference between the strategies, until the robot changes its exploration direction for the first time. The patches per grid cell-ratio decreases for the non-compact strategy then, because the number of occupied cells can only increase linearly with the distance traveled, while the total number of grid cells increases quadratically. This effect is typical for a non-compact strategy. For the compact strategies, the occupancy ratio continues to increase, because the robot's motions between measurements only have a small influence on the size of the bounding rectangle of the map during a compact expansion. This is also visible in a lower variance in the data averaged over several test runs.

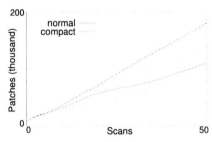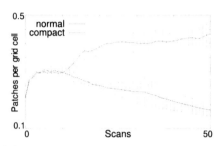

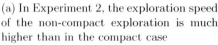

(a) In Experiment 2, the exploration speed of the non-compact exploration is much higher than in the compact case

(b) The non-compact strategy leads in Experiment 2 to sparse maps, the compact strategies strategies fills the map more homogeneously

**Fig. 2.** In an environment with a high density of small objects, the exploration speed of the compact strategies is lower than the speed without compact extensions, but the compactness is significantly higher

## 5.2  Experiment 2: High Obstacle Density

The purpose of the second and third experiment is to evaluate the exploration behavior of the strategies in an unbounded outdoor environment with a high obstacle density like, e.g., urban environments. We evaluated the strategies in two types of outdoor environments. The first one is an environment containing mainly smaller obstacles, i.e. obstacles that can be passed without long detours, while the second type of environment contains many elongated obstacles, which force the robot to drive longer detours. All the experiments are stopped after integrating 100 scans into the map.

Typical trajectories of the three strategies for Experiment 2 with the convex obstacles are shown in Figure 4a. The non-compact exploration strategy leaves the area where the obstacles are and moves into wide open space, leading to a degenerated map. This effect is typical for unconstrained greedy exploration. In order to maximize information gain, it tends to move away from obstacles, which occlude large portions of the scan. The proposed strategies, instead, direct the robot through passages between obstacles, in order to reach the goal of compact exploration.

In most cases, the distance-penalized strategy reached an exploration performance comparable to the spiral exploration strategy. For this reason, we combined the two compact strategies in Figure 2. Figure 2a shows that the non-compact exploration strategy is able to gather more new information per scan than the compact extensions. The effect is more pronounced than in Experiment 1, where the exploration speeds were nearly equal. This is explained by scan positions close to obstacles, which are avoided by the non-compact exploration strategy. The compact strategies tend to surround obstacles instead.

## 5.3    Experiment 3: Elongated Obstacles

The second type of outdoor environment, evaluated in Experiment 3, contains many elongated obstacles. These obstacles constrain the possible driving directions to the corridors between obstacles frequently. For the spiral exploration strategy, this can lead to problems, e. g. elongated obstacles orthogonal to the spiral direction force the robot to increase the exploration radius without being able to follow the spiral. After passing an obstacle, the robot follows the spiral again, now with the increased radius. This can lead to significant holes in the convex hull of the explored space and a less compact map.

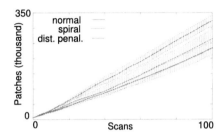
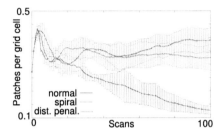

(a) In contrast to the experiments before, the exploration speed of the two compact strategies is not similar. The speed of the distance-penalized exploration is lower than the speed of the spiral exploration

(b) As the selection of motion commands is constrained by obstacles over long parts of the trajectory, spiral exploration leaves holes resulting in less compact maps

**Fig. 3.**  In environments with elongated obstacles, our proposed compact strategies perform differently. Compactness has to be traded-off against exploration speed.

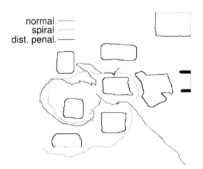
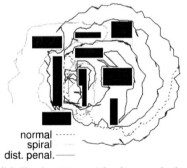

(a) Experiment 2. The edge length of obstacles is chosen to be small compared to the robot's sensing range here. Both compact strategies perform equally well.

(b) Exploration with elongated obstacles. The long obstacles force the spiral strategy to increase its exploration radius too fast.

**Fig. 4.**  Example trajectories of the exploration strategies

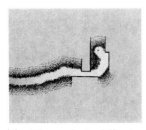
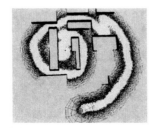
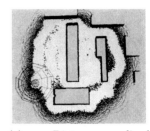

(a) The robot following the frontier-based exploration strategy leaves the area with obstacles quickly, leading to a map not suitable for navigation

(b) The area with obstacles is surrounded with the spiral exploration strategy, but unexplored enclosures are left in the case of elongated obstacles

(c)      Distance-penalized exploration resembles the compactness criterion, inducing compact maps in arbitrary environments

**Fig. 5.** Resulting maps of frontier-based exploration and our proposed strategies after 170 consecutive 3D scans. The green area is traversable, the gray area is unexplored.

Example trajectories for the two compact strategies are shown in Figure 4b, maps gathered with these strategies in Figure 5. The spiral exploration proceeds with a too large radius once it leaves the area where many obstacles are. As shown in Figure 3, the distance-penalized strategy achieves more compact maps in this type of environment, when compared to the spiral exploration strategy, at the cost of a slightly lower exploration speed.

## 6   Conclusions

In this article, we have shown that greedy exploration strategies, which only maximize the ratio between expected information gain and travel costs, are not directly applicable in unbounded outdoor environments, because they can lead to degenerated non-compact maps.

To produce compact maps that expand around a point of interest, additional control of the exploration is needed. For this purpose, we proposed two different extensions to greedy exploration strategies: spiral exploration and distance-penalized exploration. These regularizations extend the value function of a greedy strategy with an additional term rewarding sensing positions leading to more compact maps.

In simulation experiments, we compared the exploration speed between a greedy exploration strategy with and without these extensions resulting in the conclusion that the compact strategies are able to reach an exploration speed comparable to the plain greedy strategy in environments with a low to medium obstacle density. In environments with a high obstacle density, compactness has to be traded-off against exploration speed. Spiral exploration is suitable in environments where approximate spiral trajectories are possible. This is the case when the obstacles in the environment are nearly convex and small, compared to the sensing range. The distance-penalized exploration is able to produce maps that are compact, without relying on environmental characteristics, but possibly at a lower exploration speed. Hence, if the environment can be expected to contain obstacles relatively small compared to the measurement range a spiral shaped exploration should be performed. Otherwise, the distance-penalized exploration strategy leads to compact maps without prior knowledge about the area to explore.

# References

1. Burgard, W., Moors, M., Schneider, F.: Collaborative Exploration of Unknown Environments with Teams of Mobile Robots. In: Beetz, M., Hertzberg, J., Ghallab, M., Pollack, M.E. (eds.) Dagstuhl Seminar 2001. LNCS (LNAI), vol. 2466, pp. 52–70. Springer, Heidelberg (2002)
2. Cao, Z., Huang, Y., Hall, E.: Region Filling Operations with Random Obstacle Avoidance for Mobile Robots. Journal of Robotic systems 5(2) (1988)
3. Elfes, A.: Using Occupancy Grids for Mobile Robot Perception and Navigation. IEEE Computer 22, 46–57 (1989)
4. González-Baños, H.H., Latombe, J.C.: Navigation Strategies for Exploring Indoor Environments. Intl. J. of Robotics Research 21(10-11), 829–848 (2002)
5. Hert, S., Tiwari, S., Lumelsky, V.: A Terrain-covering Algorithm for an AUV. Autonomous Robots 3(2), 91–119 (1996)
6. Holz, D., Basilico, N., Amigoni, F., Behnke, S.: Evaluating the Efficiency of Frontier-based Exploration Strategies. In: Proceedings of ISR/ROBOTIK (2010)
7. Koenig, N., Howard, A.: Design and Use Paradigms for Gazebo, An Open-Source Multi-Robot Simulator. In: Proc. of IROS (2004)
8. Koenig, S., Tovey, C., Halliburton, W.: Greedy Mapping of Terrain. In: Proc. of ICRA (2001)
9. Moorehead, S.: Autonomous Surface Exploration for Mobile Robots. Ph.D. thesis, Carnegie Mellon University (2001)
10. Morris, A., Silver, D., Ferguson, D., Thayer, S.: Towards Topological Exploration of Abandoned Mines. In: Proceedings of ICRA, pp. 2117–2123 (2005)
11. Pfaff, P., Kümmerle, R., Joho, D., Stachniss, C., Triebel, R., Burgard, W.: Navigation in Combined Outdoor and Indoor Environments using Multi-Level Surface Maps. In: WS on Safe Navigation in Open and Dynamic Environments, IROS 2007 (2007)
12. Surmann, H., Nüchter, A., Hertzberg, J.: An Autonomous Mobile Robot with a 3D Laser Range Finder for 3D Exploration and Digitalization of Indoor Environments. Robotics and Autonomous Systems 45(3-4), 181–198 (2003)
13. Thrun, S., Burgard, W., Fox, D.: Probabilistic Robotics. MIT Press (2005)
14. Triebel, R., Pfaff, P., Burgard, W.: Multi-Level Surface Maps for Outdoor Terrain Mapping and Loop Closing. In: Proc. of IROS (2006)
15. Yamauchi, B.: A Frontier-based Approach for Autonomous Exploration. In: Proceedings of CIRA, pp. 146–151 (1997)

# The Basic Component of Computational Intelligence for KUKA KR C3 Robot

Tadeusz Szkodny

Silesian University of Technology, Institute of Automatic Control, Akademicka 16 St.
44-100 Gliwice, Poland
Tadeusz.Szkodny@polsl.pl

**Abstract.** In this paper the solution algorithm of inverse kinematics problem for KUKA KR C3 robot is presented. This algorithm may be a basic component of future computational intelligence for theses robots. The problem of computing the joint variables corresponding a specified location of end-effector is called inverse kinematics problem. This algorithm was implemented into the controller of the robot. It allowed controlling these robots by using the vision system, which specifies required location of the end-effector. This required location makes it possible for the end-effector to approach a manipulation object (observed by vision system) and pick it up. These robots are equipped with several manipulator which has 6 links joined by revolute joint. First the location of end-effector in relation to the base of the manipulator were described. Next the position workspace of this robot was illustrated. The example of solutions of the inverse kinematics problem and conclusions were presented in the end of this work. In this example are the multiple solutions for singular configurations of this manipulator.

**Keywords:** Kinematics, Manipulators, Mechanical System, Robot Kinematics.

## 1    Introduction

The KUKA KRC3 controllers allow for the movement programming using KRL (KUKA Robot Language). The following commends: PTP, LIN and CIRC can be applied to programming in Cartesian space. The aforementioned commands require a start and end locations definition. These points can be defined with the use of joint variables or robot global frame (ROBROOT). It is convenient for the end locations observed by a camera to define them with the use of global frame [1]. During such realization of movement implementation it occurs that a robot stops before reaching the border area. The entrapment results when the manipulator reaches a singular configuration or when the manipulator reaches the boundary surface of the workspace. It is robot's software fault, which prevents the correct cooperation of KUKA KR C3 robots with cameras.

The fault was eliminated with the use of solving inverse kinematics problem, which is presented in this paper. Manipulator singular configurations and workspace limitations were considered in this algorithm.

S. Jeschke, H. Liu, and D. Schilberg (Eds.): ICIRA 2011, Part I, LNAI 7101, pp. 44–52, 2011.

On the basis of the following algorithm the students of Silesian University of Automatic Control, Electronics and Computer Science Department in the Institute of Automatic Control, Robotics faculty, wrote a program *CKinematics KRC3* [2], which was implemented to a KUKA KR C3 robot controller. Moreover, the Ni1742 intelligent camera [3] was integrated with this controller. The robot can independently reach noticed manipulation objects without the necessity of preliminary reaching the manipulator to the object.

The implemented *CKinematics KRC3* program with integrated camera constitutes, in the future, the basis for the driver's independent software programming regardless of a robots' manufacturer.

In the second chapter a description of the manipulator's kinematics structure is presented, followed by the forward kinematics equations. The illustration of a robot's workspace is presented in chapter 3. An example of joint variables computations by means of the *CKinematics KRC3* program is shown in chapter fourth. In the last chapter the conclusions are presented.

## 2    Kinematics

Fig.1 illustrates the KUKA KR C3 manipulator. In this figure, manipulator's links are numbered. The base link 0 is fixed to ground and the other links 1-6 are movable. The last link with number 6 will be called an end-effector. The gripper, or other tool, is attached to this link. The neighboring links are connected by revolute joint. The co-ordinate systems (frames) $x_0 y_0 z_0$ - $x_6 y_6 z_6$ were associated with links according to a Denavit-Hartenberg notation [4-10]. The $x_7 y_7 z_7$ frame is associated with the gripper. Position and orientation of the links and tool are described by homogenous transform matrices. Matrix $A_i$ describes the position and orientation of the i-th link frame in relation to i-1-st. $T_6$ is a matrix, that describes the position and orientation of the end-effector frame in relation to the base link. Matrix $E$ describes the gripper frame in relation to the end-effector frame. Matrix $X$ describes the position and orientation of the gripper frame in relation to the base link. Matrix $A_i$ is described by (1) [7,9-12].

$$A_i = Rot(z, \theta_i) Trans(0, 0, \lambda_i) Trans(l_i, 0, 0) Rot(x, \alpha_i). \tag{1}$$

$\theta_i$, $\lambda_i$, $l_i$, $\alpha_i$ are Denavit-Hartenberg parameters. The values of these parameters are shown in Table 1. The range of variables $\theta_i$ were redefined and they are different than in technical documentation [13]. For further description of the kinematics $\theta_i'$ variables will be used: $S_i = \sin \theta_i'$, $C_i = \cos \theta_i'$, $S_{ij} = \sin \theta_{ij}'$, $C_{ij} = \cos \theta_{ij}'$, $\theta_{ij}' = \theta_i' + \theta_j'$ [8,12].

**Table 1.** Denavit-Hartenberg parameters

| Link | $l_i$ [mm] | $\lambda_i$ [mm] | $\alpha_i$ [°] | $\theta_i$ [°] |
|------|-----------|------------------|----------------|----------------|
| 1st | 100 | 350 | 90 | -90 ÷ +90 |
| 2nd | 265 | 0 | 0 | 0 ÷ +90 |
| 3rd | 0 | 0 | 90 | 0 ÷ +180 |
| 4th | 0 | 270 | -90 | -180 ÷ +180 |
| 5th | 0 | 0 | 90 | -90 ÷ +90 |
| 6th | 0 | 75 | 0 | -180 ÷ +180 |

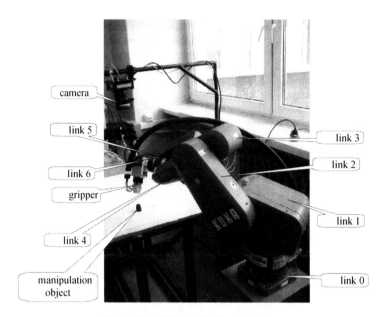

**Fig. 1.** The KUKA KRC3 manipulator

The matrix $\mathbf{T}_6$ is derived form (2) [11,12].

$$\mathbf{T}_6 = \mathbf{A}_1\mathbf{A}_2\mathbf{A}_3\mathbf{A}_4\mathbf{A}_5\mathbf{A}_6 =$$

$$= \begin{bmatrix} a_x & b_x & c_x & d_x \\ a_y & b_y & c_y & d_x \\ a_z & b_z & c_z & d_x \\ 0 & 0 & 0 & 1 \end{bmatrix} = \begin{bmatrix} c_1(-s_{23}(c_4c_5c_6 - s_4s_6) - c_{23}s_5c_6) + s_1(s_4c_5c_6 + c_4s_6) \\ s_1(-s_{23}(c_4c_5c_6 - s_4s_6) - c_{23}s_5c_6) - c_1(s_4c_5c_6 + c_4s_6) \\ c_{23}(c_4c_5c_6 - s_4s_6) - s_{23}s_5c_6 \\ 0 \end{bmatrix}$$

$$\begin{array}{cc} c_1(s_{23}(c_4c_5s_6 + s_4c_6) + c_{23}s_5s_6) + s_1(c_4c_6 - s_4c_5s_6) & c_1(c_{23}c_5 - s_{23}c_4s_5) + s_1s_4s_5 \\ s_1(s_{23}(c_4c_5s_6 + s_4c_6) + c_{23}s_5s_6) - c_1(c_4c_6 - s_4c_5s_6) & s_1(c_{23}c_5 - s_{23}c_4s_5) + c_1s_4s_5 \\ -c_{23}(c_4c_5s_6 + s_4c_6) + s_{23}s_5s_6 & c_{23}c_4s_5 + s_{23}c_5 \\ 0 & 0 \end{array}$$

$$\begin{array}{c} c_1(c_{23}(c_5\lambda_6 + \lambda_4) - s_{23}c_4s_5\lambda_6 - l_2s_2) + s_1s_4s_5\lambda_6 + l_1c_1 \\ s_1(c_{23}(c_5\lambda_6 + \lambda_4) - s_{23}c_4s_5\lambda_6 - l_2s_2) - c_1s_4s_5\lambda_6 + l_1s_1 \\ c_{23}c_4s_5\lambda_6 + s_{23}(c_5\lambda_6 + \lambda_4) + l_2c_2 + \lambda_1 \\ 1 \end{array} \end{bmatrix}. \qquad (2)$$

The matrices $\mathbf{E}$ and $\mathbf{E}^{-1}$ have following forms:

$$\mathbf{E} = \begin{bmatrix} 0 & 0 & -1 & l_7 \\ 1 & 0 & 0 & 0 \\ 0 & -1 & 0 & \lambda_7 \\ 0 & 0 & 0 & 1 \end{bmatrix}, \mathbf{E}^{-1} = \begin{bmatrix} 0 & 1 & 0 & 0 \\ 0 & 0 & -1 & \lambda_7 \\ -1 & 0 & 0 & l_7 \\ 0 & 0 & 0 & 1 \end{bmatrix}; \qquad (3)$$

where $\lambda_7 = 55mm$ and $l_7 = -120.5\ mm$ are the parameters of the gripper. The matrix $\mathbf{X}$ is obtained from (4).

$$X = T_6 E = \begin{bmatrix} b_x & -c_x & -a_x & d_x + l_7 a_x + \lambda_7 c_x \\ b_y & -c_y & -a_y & d_y + l_7 a_y + \lambda_7 c_y \\ b_z & -c_z & -a_z & d_z + l_7 a_z + \lambda_7 c_z \\ 0 & 0 & 0 & 1 \end{bmatrix}, \tag{4}$$

where $a_x \div d_z$ are the elements of the matrix $\mathbf{T}_6$.

Equation (4) allows to compute the position and orientation of the gripper's co-ordinates system $x_7 y_7 z_7$ in relation to the base link's co-ordinates system $x_0 y_0 z_0$ for the given joint variables $\theta_i{}'$. It is the forward kinematics problem of the manipulator.

The program *CKinematics KRC3* [2], which was implemented to a KUKA KR C3 robot controller, is calculating the joint variables $\theta_i{}'$ for the given matrix $\mathbf{X}_{req}$ [11,12]. After load the matrix $\mathbf{X}_{req}$ the program is computing the matrices $\mathbf{T}_{6req} = \mathbf{X}_{req} E^{-1}$. To test this program the user may load the value of link variables. For these variables the matrices $\mathbf{T}_{6req}$ from (2) is calculated.

## 3    Workspace

The workspace of the manipulator position depends on the first three elements of the position of a $O_5$ point in relation to the base frame $x_0 y_0 z_0$. This point is origin of

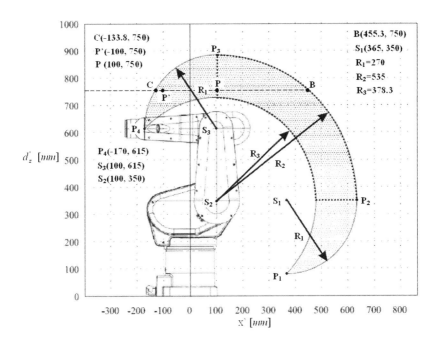

**Fig. 2.** The vertical section of the workspace

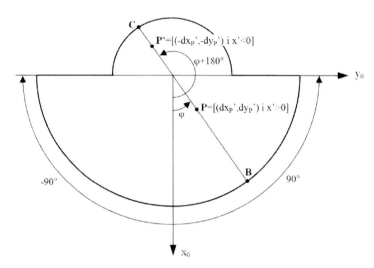

**Fig. 3.** The horizontal section of the workspace

frame associated to fifth link. This position depends only on the $\theta_1' \div \theta_3'$ variables. After taking these variables ranges under consideration, we obtain a description of position workspace. Fig.2 is an illustration of this workspace's vertical section with a $d_z'x'$ plane, which contains the $z_0$ axis. A co-ordinate $x' = \pm\sqrt{d_y'^2 + d_x'^2}$. $d_x', d_y', d_z'$ represents the first three elements of the $T_6'$ matrix's forth column. The matrix $T_6' = T_6 \cdot \text{Trans}(0,0,-\lambda_6)$.

The horizontal section of the workspace is illustrated on Fig.3. Values of the co-ordinates $x'$, belonging to the P and P' points, are opposite, i.e. $x_p' = -x_p' > 0$. For example, according to Fig.2 for $d_z' = 500mm$ the point P' is outside the vertical section of the workspace. However the appurtenance of the point P to the workspace is determined by an angle $\varphi = arctg2(d_y', d_x')$, illustrated on Fig.3. If $-90° \leq \varphi \leq 90°$, then the point P belongs to the workspace. If e.g. $\varphi = 100°$, then the point P is outside the workspace, despite that it belongs to the section in Fig.2.

In a case, when $d_z' = 750mm$ points P and P' belong to the section surface from Fig.2. In such a case the $O_5$ point of the manipulator can reach the points P and P' with the same value of the angle $\theta_1'$, and with different values of the $\theta_2'$ and $\theta_3'$ angles. If, for example, $\theta_1' = 0°$, then $\varphi = arctg2(0, d_x') = 0°$ for the point P. For the point P' $\varphi = arctg2(0, -d_x') = arctg2(0, d_x') + 180° = 180°$. Therefore points P and P', belonging to section in Fig.2, will be reachable for the manipulator point $O_5$ with any value of the angle $\varphi$. In such a case boundaries for the angle $\theta_1'$ do not pose any obstacles for reaching point P'.

The program *CKinematics KRC3* is checking if points P and P' belong to the vertical workspace section from Fig.2. Next is setting the variables $p$ and $pp$ to 0 or 1. For the point P belonging to this section $p=1$, otherwise $p=0$. Similarly if P' belongs to the section $pp=1$, otherwise $pp=0$. Next the angle $\varphi$ is computing and checking if this angle is from its range of changes. The range results from horizontal section illustrated on Fig.3. On the base this angle and values of variables $p$ and $pp$ program *CKinematics KRC3* is checking if given point $O_5$ of manipulator belongs to the workspace.

## 4    Example of Calculations

In the following chapter the example of testing calculations of the *CKinematics KRC3* program is presented. In this example of testing computations executed by *CKinematics KRC3* program the matrix $X_{req}$, described by (5a), was calculated for joint variables $\theta_1' = 0°, \theta_2' = 0°, \theta_3' = 0°, \theta_4' = 0°, \theta_5' = 0°, \theta_6' = 0°$.

$$X_{req} = \begin{bmatrix} 0 & -1 & 0 & 500 \\ -1 & 0 & 0 & 0 \\ 0 & 0 & -1 & 494.5 \\ 0 & 0 & 0 & 1 \end{bmatrix}. \tag{5a}$$

After loading matrix $X_{req}$ (5a) the program computed the matrix $T_{6req}$, joint variables and produced six sets of solutions. This matrix $T_{6req}$ is following:

$$T_{6req} = \begin{bmatrix} 0 & 0 & 1 & 445 \\ 0 & -1 & 0 & 0 \\ 1 & 0 & 0 & 615 \\ 0 & 0 & 0 & 1 \end{bmatrix}. \tag{5b}$$

Three sets $(\theta_1', \theta_2', \theta_3', \theta_4', \theta_5', \theta_6')$ are following:

$$-(0°, -91.0709°, 180°, 180°, 88.9291°, -180°) \tag{6a}$$

$$-(0°, -91.0709°, 180°, 180°, 88.9291°, 180°) \tag{6b}$$

$$-(0°, -91.0709°, 180°, 0°, -88.9291°, 0°) \tag{6c}$$

Additional three sets $(\theta_1', \theta_2', \theta_3', \theta_5', \theta_{46}')$ are:

$$-(0°, 0°, 0°, 0°, 0°) \tag{7a}$$

$$-(0°, 0°, 0°, 0°, -360°) \tag{7b}$$

$$-(0°, 0°, 0°, 0°, 360°) \tag{7c}$$

The sets (7) contains the sums $\theta_{46}' = \theta_4' + \theta_6'$. Therefore in every one of those sets the variables $\theta_4'$ and $\theta_6'$ can have any value. It means, that those sets describe an infinite number of solution sets $(\theta_1', \theta_2', \theta_3', \theta_4', \theta_5', \theta_6')$. The sets (6) contain–the variables in separate form. However, in the sets (6) the variable $\theta_2' = -91.0709°$

exceeds its range $[-90°, 0°]$. Therefore, the *CKinematics KRC3* program has omitted these sets.

This program computed the $\mathbf{T}_6$ matrices using (2) for the sets of solutions (7). In this calculations it was assumed that $\theta_4' = \theta_{46}'/2$ and $\theta_6' = \theta_{46}'/2$. It computed also $|\mathbf{T}_6 - \mathbf{T}_{6req}|$ for those sets. This computations proves, that an absolute value of difference between the elements of the $\mathbf{T}_6$ and $\mathbf{T}_{6req}$ matrices is not larger then $2.4 \cdot 10^{-16}$.

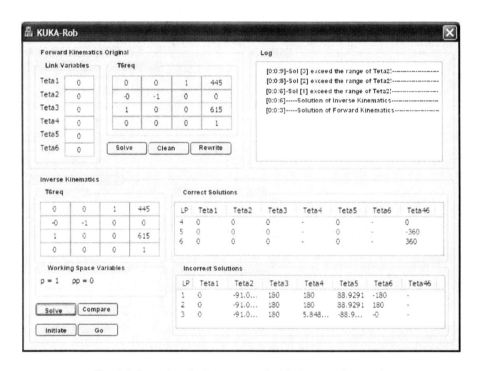

**Fig. 4.** Information display connected with the second example

Figure 4 shows information connected with computations of the matrix (5b), solutions (6) and (7). In the segment *Incorrect Solutions* the omitted solutions (1)-(3) described by sets (6) are shown, in which the variable $\theta_2'$ exceeds its range. Information about the exceeding are shown in the segment *Log* too. In the segment *Correct Solutions* the solutions (4)-(6) described by sets (7) are presented.

The choice of each of three solutions (7) and the use of *Initiate* and *Go* buttons resulted in the robot's movement from HOME position to the manipulator's position corresponding to these solutions. In the aforementioned solutions it was assumed that $\theta_4' = \theta_{46}'/2$ and $\theta_6' = \theta_{46}'/2$.

The robot did not move after programming movement, in KRL language by means programming in Cartesian space (without the use of *CKinematics KRC3*), from HOME position to the point described by the matrix (5a) within the global frame.

In the above example an absolute value of difference between the elements of the $T_6$ and $T_{6req}$ matrices is not larger then $1.4 \cdot 10^{-16}$. Such a small numerical error gives an evidence of a very good computations precision of this program.

# 5     Conclusions

The inverse kinematics algorithm problem solution discussed in this paper allowed for:

1)    Writing *CKinematics KRC3* program and its implementation to the KUKA KRC3 robot's controller.
2)    KUKA KRC3 Robot's movement control to the manipulation objects noticed by the Ni1742 intelligent camera without the necessity of the preliminary manipulator reaching to the object.
3)    The KUKA KRC3 robot reaching not one but all configurations corresponding to multiple solutions of the inverse kinematics problem.
4)    The elimination of software faults created by a KUKA KRC3 robot's manufacturer.

These faults result in the undesirable robot's entrapment while programming with the use of the global frame. The entrapment occurs at the moment of manipulator's reaching singular configurations or at the moment of reaching boundary surface of the workspace. Due to inverse kinematics problem solution algorithm, implemented to KUKA KRC3 robot's controller we can describe singular configurations. Then, we obtain infinite number of solutions for the $\theta_4'$ and $\theta_6'$ variables. It was assumed, for the robot's control, for the following configurations that $\theta_4' = \theta_{46}'/2$ and $\theta_6' = \theta_{46}'/2$. What is more, due to the analytical workspace locations description, illustrated in Fig.2 and 3, it is possible to check the manipulation object immersion noticed by a camera in this space before robot's movement.

The solution algorithm of inverse kinematics problem for IRB-1400 manipulator presented in [11,14], used in *CKinematics KRC3* program, can be applied to contemporary manipulators of the similar kinematic structure such as IRB manipulators series 1000, 2000, 3000, 4000, 6000; Fanuc manipulators M6, M16, M710, M10, M900; KUKA manipulators KR3, KR5, KR6, KR15, KR16; Mitsubishi manipulators RV-1a, RV-2A, RV-3S, RV-6S, RV12S and Adept manipulators s300, s650, s850, s1700. In case of KUKA KRC3 robot, after writing and implementing to the robots' controllers appropriate software (corresponding to *CKinematics KRC3* program), it is possible to integrated them with vision systems likewise. The vision systems integrated with robot's controller allow for the computer intelligence development of these robots independently from software faults-free, discussed above, designed by manufacturers.

# References

1. Tadeusiewicz, R.: Vision Systems of Industrial Robots. WNT, Warsaw (1992) (in Polish)
2. Kmiecik, M.: Solution Algorithm of Inverse Kinematics Problem for KUKA KRC3 Robot. M. Sc. Dissertation, Institute of Automatic Control, Faculty of Automatic Control, Electronic and Computer Science, Silesian University of Technology, Gliwice (2009); Poland, (in Polish)

3. Małek, D.: The External Communication of KUKA KRC3 Robot Controller. M. Sc. Dissertation, Institute of Automatic Control, Faculty of Automatic Control, Electronic and Computer Science, Silesian University of Technology, Gliwice (2009); Poland, (in Polish)
4. Paul, R.P.: Robot Manipulators: Mathematics, Programming and Control, Ch. 2. The MIT Press, Cambridge (1983)
5. Kozłowski, K., Dutkiewicz, P.: Modeling and Control of Robots, Ch.1. PWN, Warsaw (2003) (in Polish)
6. Jezierski, E.: Dynamics and Control of Robots, Ch. 2. WNT, Warsaw (2006) (in Polish)
7. Szkodny, T.: Modeling and Simulation of Industrial Robot Manipulator Motion, Ch. 2. Silesian University of Technology Publ. Company, Gliwice (2004); Poland, (in Polish)
8. Szkodny, T.: Kinematics of Industrial Robots, Ch.2,3,4. Silesian University of Technology Publ. Company, Gliwice (2009); Poland, (in Polish)
9. Szkodny, T.: Foundation of Robotics Problems Set, Ch.2. Silesian University of Technology Publ. Company, Gliwice (2010); Poland, (in Polish)
10. Szkodny, T.: Foundation of Robotics, Ch.3, 4. Silesian University of Technology Publ. Company, Gliwice (2011); Poland, (in Polish)
11. Szkodny, T.: Inverse Kinematics Problem of IRB, Fanuc, Mitsubishi, Adept and Kuka Series Manipulators. Int. Jorn. of Applied Mechanics and Engineering 15(3), 847–853 (2010)
12. Szkodny, T.: Kinematics of KUKA KRC3 Robots, vol. 2, pp. 357–368. Warsaw University of Technology Publ. Company, Warsaw (2010); Poland, (in Polish)
13. Technical Documentation of KUKA KR3 Robot: Operation Handbook
14. Szkodny, T.: Basic Component of Computational Intelligence for IRB-1400 Robots. In: Cyran, K.A., Kozielski, S., Peters, J.F., Stańczyk, U., Wakulicz-Deja, A. (eds.) Man-Machine Interactions, Part XI. AISC, vol. 59, pp. 637–646. Springer, Heidelberg (2009)

# An Experimental Comparison of Model-Free Control Methods in a Nonlinear Manipulator

Mateusz Przybyla, Rafal Madonski, Marta Kordasz, and Przemyslaw Herman

Chair of Control and Systems Engineering, Poznan University of Technology,
ul. Piotrowo 3A, 61-138, Poznan, Poland
{mateusz.przybyla,rafal.madonski,marta.kordasz}@doctorate.put.poznan.pl,
przemyslaw.herman@put.poznan.pl

**Abstract.** This paper presents an experimental comparison of various model-independent control strategies implemented on a system with unbalanced rotating mass. Proportional-Integral-Derivative (PID), Robust Tracking with Control Vector Constraints (RTCVC), and Active Disturbance Rejection Control (ADRC) are considered in this research. Although these control algorithms deal with parametric uncertainties, external disturbances, and nonlinear behavior of the system with different approaches, their common feature is that they do not need an explicit mathematical model of the physical process. Obtained results show that the ADRC achieved highest control performance in terms of position trajectory tracking of the manipulator link and energy efficiency. This work also confirms that the ADRC is a promising model-free control approach, which brings together what is best in both classic and modern control theories.

## 1 Introduction

In order to incorporate most of the modern control techniques (including robust, adaptive, and those based on neural networks; for examples see [3,8], a mathematical model of the system is required. Thus, the quality of control in above methods relies not only on the chosen control law, but also on the precision of assumed plant's model. Analytical descriptions are usually hard to define because of the systems nonlinearities, time-variance, high order dynamics, and imperfect plant data, especially in the presence of real environment phenomena, like heat effects, friction, and aging process.

The so-called model-free control methods, mostly appreciated by industry practitioners, are an alternative to the above techniques. In order to use them, user does not need to have an explicit mathematical representation of the considered system. The most common model-independent technique is a Proportional-Integral-Derivative controller (PID). In spite of its development over the years, PID remained relatively simple to understand and implement by the end-user, as well as was proven to be sufficient enough in most of the cases.

However, the PID method is not an all-purpose solution. There are many complex control systems where implementation of simple linear version of the

S. Jeschke, H. Liu, and D. Schilberg (Eds.): ICIRA 2011, Part I, LNAI 7101, pp. 53–62, 2011.
© Springer-Verlag Berlin Heidelberg 2011

controller results in poor performance. Additionally, the PID is mostly designed empirically and faulty tuning of proportional, integral, or derivative parts can cause some robustness issues, due to the possible effects of noise strengthening and phase lag. Finally, the lack of adaptive feature in PID often results in the need of retuning the controller every time the process dynamics change.

Some other model-free methods can be found in the literature. One example is a Robust Tracking with Control Vector Constraints (RTCVC), proposed in [2]. Other one is an Active Disturbance Rejection Control (ADRC), proposed in [4][1]. The former is easy to implement and is ideologically similar to sliding-mode controller. It generates continuous and constrained control signals that assure high quality of trajectory tracking, even in the presence of various disturbances. A practical application of RTCVC can be found in [1]. The latter deals with the occurred perturbations with an Extended State Observer (ESO), that estimates both internal and external disturbances (usually denoted as "total disturbance"), and cancels them out in the control signal. By the use of ADRC, the control of a nonlinear process is reduced to a disturbance-free cascade integrator form, as seen in [5], which can be further regulated using classical linear methods. Some practical implementations of ADRC can be found in [7].

Even though the PID, RTCVC, and ADRC are well-known methods in the literature, there is a lack of real environment comparison of these three model-free controllers. That is why this paper focuses on a case study which will be performed in order to verify the performance of the above techniques. The study will be conducted on a laboratory setup, which is a drive-link mechanical system (it will be denoted as PM1R), where the link mass is not evenly distributed around the axis of rotation. The uneven balance of the mass in the rigid link makes the manipulator a nontrivial nonlinear system.

Paper is organized as follows. Section 2 describes considered laboratory setup. It shows its electromechanical dynamics equation and justifies the use of model-free control algorithms. Next section focuses on the ideas, main goals, and design methods of proposed control laws. It describes each controller, its derivation and approach for dealing with the considered nonlinear and disturbed system. Section 4 consists of study preparation, where main assumptions of the experiment are made and the results of conducted tests with some comments on obtained outcomes can be found. Paper ends with concluding remarks in Section 5.

## 2  System Description

The PM1R's rotating link is driven with a DC motor with a reducing gear (Fig.1). Base of the system is fixed to the wall. The modular feature of PM1R allows the user to attach additional components to a link and thus modify the overall system dynamics (by changing its mass). Main electronic parts of the system consist of optical incremental angular position sensor, attached directly to the rotor, a DSP board, and a PC station.

---

[1] Earlier fundamental works of Jingqing Han, regarding ADRC, were in Chinese.

*Remark 1.* Model-free controllers, considered in this research, do not need a full mathematical description of the system, but for the sake of argument, a simplified version of it will be presented below.

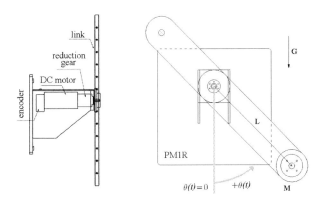

**Fig. 1.** Scheme of the PM1R system, with main electromechanical parts (left) and assumed plant's description (right)

A nonlinear dynamics model of the mechanical part is presented below:

$$J_l\ddot{\theta}(t) + f_l(\dot{\theta}(t)) + MGL\sin(\theta(t)) = \tau_l(t) - \tau_d(t), \tag{1}$$

where: $\theta(t)[rad]$ denotes the angular position of manipulator link (system output), $J_l[kgm^2]$, $M[kg]$, $L[m]$ are its moment of inertia, mass, and length respectively, $G[m/s^2]$ is the gravity acceleration, and $\tau_l(t)[Nm]$, $\tau_d(t)[Nm]$ are the driving and disturbance torques respectively. Function $f_l(\theta(t))[Nm]$ denotes the Coulomb friction model:

$$f_l(\theta(t)) = f_c sign(\dot{\theta}(t)) + b\dot{\theta}(t), \tag{2}$$

where: $f_c$ and $b$ are the friction parameters.

By adding an electric model to the equation (1), and assuming, that the armature induction of the motor can be neglected, we obtain the electromechanical model of the system[2]:

$$J\ddot{\theta}_m(t) + f(\dot{\theta}_m(t)) + \eta\tau_g(\eta\theta_m(t)) = k_I i(t) - \eta\tau_d(t), \tag{3}$$

where: $\theta_m(t)[rad]$, $\dot{\theta}_m(t)[rad/s]$, $\ddot{\theta}_m(t)[rad/s^2]$ denote the angular position of rotor, its speed and acceleration respectively, $\eta < 1$ is the gear transmission, $k_I[Nm/A]$ is the torque constant, and $\tau_g(\theta_m(t))[Nm]$ denotes the gravitational field influence.

---

[2] One can notice that the inaccuracy of parameters measurement and other nonlinear inconveniences such as friction saturation or gear backlash can significantly narrow the potential use of model-based control.

## 3    Model-Free Control Strategies

### 3.1    Proportional-Integral-Derivative

A continuous form of the PID controller (Fig.2) can be defined as:

$$u(t) = K_p e(t) + K_i \int_0^t e(t)dt - K_d \dot{\theta}(t), \qquad (4)$$

where: $u(t)[V]$ denotes the control signal, $K_p$ is the proportional gain, $K_i$ is the integral gain, $K_d$ is the derivative gain of the controller, and with $\theta_{ref}(t)[rad]$ denoting the reference position the tracking error of the manipulator's link is defined as $e(t) = \theta_{ref}(t) - \theta(t)$.

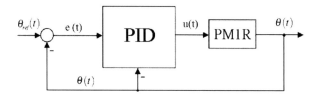

**Fig. 2.** A block diagram of PID control of the PM1R system

A key issue in PID is to select appropriate values of the controller gains, as each section is responsible for different type of dynamic reaction. This procedure should be accomplished in accordance to the system specifications and control requirements (e.g. settling time, convergence of tracking error, disturbance rejection, etc.).

The intuitiveness of PID, its relative level of robustness, implementation simplicity, and satisfactory performance, made it the most common controller used in industrial settings [6].

### 3.2    Robust Tracking with Control Vector Constraints

Proposed controller implicates that the desired position, velocity, and acceleration trajectories, are bounded functions of time. The definition of the generalized tracking error is assumed as:

$$r(t) = \dot{e}(t) + \Delta e(t), \qquad (5)$$

where: $\dot{e}(t) = \dot{\theta}_{ref}(t) - \dot{\theta}(t)$ is the velocity tracking error and $\Delta > 0$ denotes the constant coefficient.

The main idea of RTCVC (Fig.3) is to formulate a controller, that calculates the vector of control $u(t)$, which assures an asymptotic stability of the system. It can be proved, based on Lapyunov function, that this can be achieved by using a nonlinear controller defined as [2]:

$$u(t) = \begin{cases} \frac{u_{max}}{\|r(t)\|} r(t), & for \ \|r(t)\| \geq \epsilon, \\ \frac{u_{max}}{\epsilon} r(t), & for \ \|r(t)\| < \epsilon, \end{cases} \qquad (6)$$

where: $u_{max}[V]$ is the upper constraint of the control signal, $\|r(t)\|$ denotes an Euclidean norm of the tracking error, and $\epsilon > 0$ is the assumed linear control tunnel width.

Taking into account relation $\frac{r(t)}{\|r(t)\|} \leq 1$, the control value will not exceed the maximum value in all cases. Note, that in case of $\|r(t)\| < \epsilon$, the controller has a structure of Proportional-Derivative controller (PD), with proportional gain equals: $K_p = \frac{u_{max}\Delta}{\epsilon}$, and derivative gain equals: $K_d = \frac{u_{max}}{\epsilon}$. The most significant advantage of this type of controller is a guarantee of global and asymptotic stability of the system, for all types of desired trajectories, with respect to constraints of the control values. The ease of implementation of RTCVC depends on the fact that it requires only information about the degrees-of-freedom of controlled system, control constraints, as well as the initial values of positions and velocities of the process.

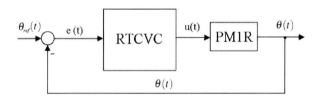

**Fig. 3.** A block diagram of RTCVC control of the PM1R system

## 3.3 Active Disturbance Rejection Control

The ADRC method consists of two key elements: an observer and a feedback controller (Fig.4). The observer can estimate and compensate the influences of internal and external disturbances in real time, and the controller is developed by improving the classic PID framework (see subsection 3.1).

With an intuitive algorithm and wide range of parameter adaptability, the ADRC is a method for solving nonlinearities, parameters uncertainties, external disturbances, and coupling issues. Let us consider PM1R system from (1-3) as a second order system, as seen below:

$$\dot{x}_1(t) = x_2(t), \qquad (7)$$
$$\dot{x}_2(t) = f(t, x_1(t), x_2(t), w) + bu(t), \qquad (8)$$
$$\theta(t) = x_1(t), \qquad (9)$$

where: $x_1(t)$, $x_2(t)$ are the state variables, $u(t)[V]$ is the input signal (control signal), $f(\cdot)$ is the "total disturbance", and $b$ is the system parameter.

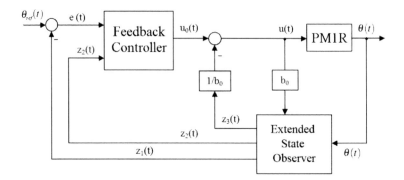

**Fig. 4.** A block diagram of ADRC control of the PM1R system

In the ADRC an assumption is made, that as long as the $f(t, x_1(t), x_2(t), w)$ is estimated closely by the ESO, analytical expression of the "total disturbance" (or its approximation) is not required.

The state space model from (7-9) is extended with an additional state $x_3(t)$, representing "total disturbance":

$$\dot{x}_1(t) = x_2(t), \tag{10}$$
$$\dot{x}_2(t) = x_3(t) + bu(t), \quad for \ x_3(t) = f(t, x_1(t), x_2(t), w), \tag{11}$$
$$\dot{x}_3(t) = h(t), \quad for \ h(t) = \dot{f}(t, x_1(t), x_2(t), w), \tag{12}$$
$$\theta(t) = x_1(t). \tag{13}$$

Now, all three states can be estimated with ESO, which is defined as:

$$\dot{z}_1(t) = z_2(t) - \beta_1 \hat{e}(t), \tag{14}$$
$$\dot{z}_2(t) = z_3(t) - \beta_2 \hat{e}(t) + b_0 u(t), \tag{15}$$
$$\dot{z}_3(t) = -\beta_3 \hat{e}(t), \tag{16}$$

where: $\beta_1$, $\beta_2$, $\beta_3$ are the observer gains, $z_1(t)$, $z_2(t)$, $z_3(t)$ are estimations of the states $x_1(t)$, $x_2(t)$, $x_3(t)$ respectively, $\hat{e}(t) = \theta(t) - z_1(t)$ is estimation error of the state $x_1(t)$, $b_0$ denotes the constant value, approximation of $b$ from equation (8).

In order to find the observer gains and simplify the tuning procedure a parametrization can be introduced, making the gains to be functions of just one design parameter - i.e. $\omega_o[rad/s]$:

$$\beta_1 = 3\omega_0, \ \beta_2 = 3\omega_0^2, \ \beta_3 = \omega_0^3, \tag{17}$$

where: $\omega_0[rad/s]$ is the observer's bandwidth.

Control signal in ADRC for the PM1R system is defined as:

$$u(t) = u_0(t) - \frac{z_3(t)}{b_0}, \tag{18}$$

where: $z_3(t)$ is the estimated "total disturbance" and $u_0(t)$ is the output signal from the feedback controller (e.g. PD).

## 4   The Experiment

Conducted tests provide an outlook on which of the considered controllers give most satisfying results in terms of error-in-time minimization of the position tracking. The study is divided into two parts:

  – test with base mass $(M)$,
  – test with additional mass $(M + m_{add})$.

First part focuses on the control performance of well-tuned algorithms. Second part demonstrates the position tracking efficiency in case of dealing with the same control task, but with artificially changed system dynamics (extra weight - $m_{add} = 150g$).

*Remark 2.* In order to study robustness of the applied controls no extra tuning is made for the second part of the experiment.

### 4.1   Study Preparation

The controllers are discretized using forward Euler method and implemented with sampling time set to $T_s = 0.01s$. To obtain an angular velocity[3] of the PM1R link a linear estimator is proposed:

$$G_{est}(s) = \frac{s}{sT_f + 1}, \tag{19}$$

where: $T_f = 0.025s$ is the filtering time constant[4]. The main goal in conducted experiment is to make the PM1R link $(\theta(t))$ follow a reference trajectory $(\theta_{ref}(t))$. For this particular test, a square reference signal with amplitude $A = \frac{\pi}{2}[rad]$ is designed. It is interesting to show the stabilization of the link in its inherently stable point $(\theta(t) = 0[rad]$, see Fig.1) and a point of maximum gravity influence $(\theta(t) = \frac{\pi}{2}[rad])$.

Since no information about the mathematical model of the system is assumed to be known, the control parameters for each of the applied controllers are chosen by using empirical or graphic techniques; see [2,5,9] for RTCVC, PID, and ADRC respectively.

The acquired PID parameters are shown below:

$$K_p = 100, K_i = 50, K_d = 8. \tag{20}$$

The RTCVC parameters need to be tuned very carefully because of its chattering phenomenon. Parameter $u_{max}$ was selected not to exceed the motors operating

---

[3] The angular velocity of the manipulator link is needed for the derivative parts of the considered controllers.
[4] Choosing a time constant is a compromise between level of noise filtering and phase lag effect.

voltage (i.e. $\pm 12[V]$). The tunnel width $\epsilon$ is decreased until chattering in the control signal remains acceptable. The RTCVC parameters are shown below:

$$u_{max} = 12V, \Delta = 15, \epsilon = 0.25. \tag{21}$$

For the ADRC method a simple linear PD controller is chosen. The observer is set to converge rapidly for all three states. The ADRC parameters are shown below:

$$K_p = 15, K_i = 0, K_d = 4, \omega_0 = 15rad/s, b_0 = 2. \tag{22}$$

*Remark 3.* The controller in ADRC has no integral part, i.e. $K_i = 0$. However, integral action still has influence by the use of a specific structure of the ESO [5].

### 4.2   Experimental Results

Results of conducted experiments are shown from Fig.5 to Fig.8, where Fig.5 and Fig.6 are the outcomes of test performed with unchanged dynamics (i.e. with its base mass), and Fig.7 and Fig.8 are the effects of control with changed system dynamics (i.e. with additional mass). Figures 5 and 7, by the presence of hardware saturation, do not show the control signals produced by each algorithm, but the actual voltage acting on the system. The chosen trajectory tested the behavior of the controllers in both the easiest and most challenging possible position of the PM1R system (i.e. $\theta(t) = 0[rad]$ and $\theta(t) = \frac{\pi}{2}[rad]$, see Fig.1).

It can be noticed that even if all of the control methods gave acceptable tracking efficiency, when tuned for the system with its base mass (Fig.5 and Fig.6), only ADRC delivered similar results when system was attached with extra weight (Fig.7 and Fig.8). The worst performance in terms of trajectory tracking was observed for the PID. The above comments are confirmed with the Integrated Squared Error (ISE) and Integrated Squared Control Signal (ISCS) indexes in Table 1.

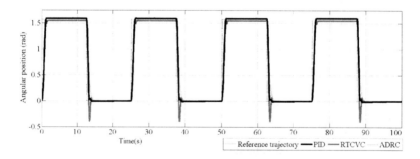

**Fig. 5.** The angular position of the manipulator link with its base mass

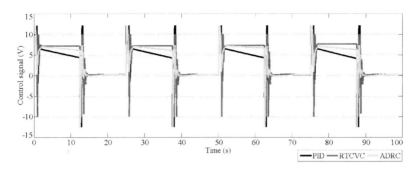

**Fig. 6.** Control signals for PID, RTCVC, and ADRC (link with its base mass)

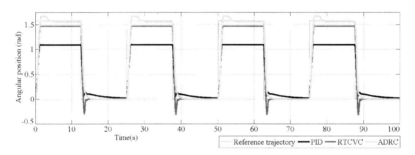

**Fig. 7.** The angular position of the manipulator link with additional mass

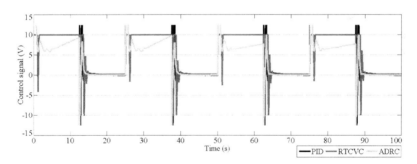

**Fig. 8.** Control signals for PID, RTCVC, and ADRC (link with additional mass)

**Table 1.** Control performance results using time domain ISE/ISCS indexes

| | ISE/ISCS | | | |
|---|---|---|---|---|
| Control method | $e(t)$ from Fig.5 | $u(t)$ from Fig.6 | $e(t)$ from Fig.7 | $u(t)$ from Fig.8 |
| PID | 0.5861509 | 4329.594 | 1.275845 | 20921.16 |
| RTCVC | 0.5372961 | 1277.553 | 0.6601092 | 2165.249 |
| ADRC | 0.5202689 | 1071.769 | 0.6322721 | 1405.971 |

# 5   Conclusions and Future Work

In this paper, three model-free control methods, i.e. PID, RTCVC, and ADRC, were tested on a system with unbalanced rotating mass. The observer-based ADRC proved to be the most effective solution in dealing with unique characteristics of the control process. It always kept higher precision of position tracking in the course of adjusting and had the highest energy efficiency (even after a significant change in system's dynamics and no extra retuning). Thanks to its structure, the ADRC has strong internal and external interference suppression, showing good robustness and adaptability. What is more, it is relatively simple, easy to implement and tune. The ADRC appears to be a promising alternative to widely-used PID, especially in solving certain process control problems in which an accurate model is difficult to obtain.

Authors would like to continue this research and compare other model-free controllers, as well as to use systems with more degrees of freedom. Since the kinematics of 1DOF mechanism can have a close-form solution, further investigation on systems with more complex structure seems to be justified.

# References

1. Dutkiewicz, P., Michalski, M., Michalek, M.: Robust tracking with control vector constraints. In: RoMoCo - Workshop on Robot Motion and Control, pp. 169–174 (2001)
2. Galicki, M.: Robust tracking of manipulators subject to control constraints, Poznan. Studies in Automation and Information Technology, vol. 25, pp. 83–94 (2000) (in Polish)
3. Gao, Y., Er, M.: Robust adaptive fuzzy neural control of robot manipulator. In: International Joint Conference on Neural Networks, Washington, pp. 2188–2193 (2001)
4. Gao, Z., Huang, Y., Han, J.: An alternative paradigm for control system design. In: IEEE Conf. on Control and Decision, Orlando, pp. 4578–4585 (2001)
5. Han, J.: From PID to Active Disturbance Rejection Control. IEEE Trans. on Industrial Electronics 56(3) (2009)
6. Levine, W.S.: The Control Handbook, pp. 198–201. CRC Press, New York (1996) access, www.books.google.com
7. Qing, Z., Gao, Z.: On practical applications of Active Disturbance Rejection Control. In: IEEE Proc. of CCC, Beijing, pp. 6095–6100 (2010)
8. Qu, Z., Dawson, D.M.: Robust tracking control of robot manipulators. IEEE Press (1996)
9. Toscano, R.: A simple robust PI/PID controller design via numerical optimization approach. Journal of Process Control 15 (2005)

# Research on Modular Design
# of Perpendicular Jointed Industrial Robots

Lin Song and Suixian Yang[*]

School of Manufacturing Science and Engineering, Sichuan University,
Chengdu 610065, P.R. China
{songlinsuper,yangsx}@163.com

**Abstract.** Modular design of industrial robots is one of the emergent topics in the area of robot design. In order to decrease the cost of robot fabrication and increase the efficiency of system developing, a modular design method of perpendicular joint industrial robot has been proposed by classifying it into three layer mechanical modules in this paper. The modular design theory, functional and structural features of the jointed-arm industrial robot were discussed in detail. Then, the division and definition of the modules were presented. After that, the first, second and third layer modules were defined. Based upon the analysis and classification of common industrial robot applications, a detailed library of the third layer is presented as well. As illustration, two modular robots have been constructed with the modules proposed in this paper.

**Keywords:** Modular Design, Industrial Robot, Perpendicular Jointed, Product Design.

## 1    Introduction

Since the industrial robot was proposed in the early 1960s, after decades of development, robots have become the most general solutions to automatic manufacture, and been extensively applied to industrial fields such as welding, assembly and material handling. Jointed-arm industrial robots, which are widely used in existing standard industrial robotic system, are advantageous in terms of compact mechanical structures, large workspaces, flexible actions, high generality, and relatively mature control theory. It is evident that the specifications of this kind of robots are competent for the requirements of most common industrial applications. However, a great variety of robot configurations are required to meet multiple functional demands. The trends of robot development are small quantity, short manufacturing period, and various series and specifications. Under these circumstances, modular design of industrial robots has become an emergent field in robotics research.

Around 1990s, the concept of the modular robotic system was proposed. Since then, researchers have paid their attentions to this area and several modular robotic

---

[*] Corresponding Author.

S. Jeschke, H. Liu, and D. Schilberg (Eds.): ICIRA 2011, Part I, LNAI 7101, pp. 63–72, 2011.
© Springer-Verlag Berlin Heidelberg 2011

systems have been developed. B. Benhabib and M. Q. Dai [1] developed a modular robot system consisting of several basic modular units, including 1-DOF main and end-effecter joints, and a variety of links and adapters. In order to meet the needs of the manufacturing industry, the structure of the drive units was similar to traditional industrial robots in modality, which limited the flexibility of the modular system to some extent. T. Matsumaru [2] developed a 3 DOF manipulatorassembled using three joint modules and optional link modules. G. Acaccia et al. [3] designed a library of robotic modules consisted of three types of joint modules and link modules. Based upon parametric design, the flexibility of the reconfiguration was extended by modules in different sizes, and the dynamic performance of the system was optimized for smaller modules which are needed at the end of the serial chain. To maximize reconfigurations of a robotic system and minimize number of elements of the module library, revolute joint module were created, which is assembled both in axial and in transversal configuration. Moreover, by integrating local processing unit into each joint to control the assembled robot in a distributed approach, the interface structure between two modules was dramatically simplified, which made the reconfiguration of the robot easier and quicker. Axiomatic design theory (ADT) was applied to ensure the rationale behind the definition and division of the modules by Z. M. Bi [4, 5]. K. Abdel-Malek and B. Paul [6] discussed the criteria for design of manipulator arms for a high stiffness-to-weight ratio. Z. M. Bi et al. [7] presented an automated method to build kinematic and dynamic models for assembling modular components of modular robotic systems which was applicable to any robotic configuration with serial, parallel, or hybrid structures. In order to meet the functional requirements of various manufacturing applications, Adaptive robotic system architecture (ARSA) was presented, which is characterized by the capability of the generation of more configuration and variants. The computational representation of ARSA was established as well by applying and extending the object indirect matrix (OIM). PowerCube [8] and its derived series, developed by SCHUNK, were the leading modular robotic system in practical products. Joint modules, which were equipped with motors, sensors and other necessary units, were combined into motion modules. A robotic system based on joint modular was proposed by L. Zhao and H. Yan [9, 10] which consisted of two kinds of modules: vertical module and horizontal module. By changing the sequence and the locations of these modules, the most familiar industrial robotic architectures, such as serial and SCARA robots, can be constructed to meet a variety of operational requirements. Z. M. Bi et al. [11] proposed a general architecture of modular manipulator systems. A systematic procedure has been presented to generate a mapping from modular design variables and the configuration description in terms of the D-H notation. G. Zhao et al. [12] involved in modular design of jointed-arm robot. A library consisted of five types of modules were designed, and the topological structure of modules were studied. Genetic algorithms (GA) and iteration algorithms (IA) [13, 14] were employed to determine and optimize robot performance, for example, the reachable workspace, the obstacle proximity, the dexterity of end-effecter and the expected number of involved module. IA was applied to resolve inverse kinematics and compute the reach ability in the work point in the space. Z. M. Bi and W. J. Zhang [15] investigated the concurrent optimal design of modular robotic configuration.

In summary, modular design of robots has attracted researchers' attentions and some creative achievements have been made. The architectures of modular robots have been developed to make the systems sufficient for all sorts of requirements. However, there were few attentions paid to modular design of robotic system for industrial applications. Some important issues are needed to be involved, such as dynamic performance and stiffness of the system, error at the end-effecter, simplification of the interface between two modules, design of integrated joints, the cost of fabrication and so on. For example, in order to allow the assembly of a wide variety of reconfiguration, a large number of link modules will be utilized which would lead to the stiffness of the robotic system relatively reduced and the error at the end of the serial chain amplified for the accumulation of the errors at each connection. Besides, more interfaces could be introduced for the increasing use of modules, which made the mechanical design more difficult, and inevitably, and thus a higher initial cost of the whole robot could be expected. In some other systems, in order to keep the library of the modules in a relatively small scale, highly integrated joint including motors, mechanical transmission, sensors, processors, and communication units was designed and acted as the main component of the system. In this case, the modular robots would suffer from some unavoidable mechanical limitations, such as higher overall mass and lower payload, due to the introduction of many additional parts and lower capability of sustaining strength for the complex mechanical structure. Because highly integrated joint are employed, the cost of each module for composition and reconfiguration would be extremely high. Therefore the economical benefit of the modular system will be weakened.

In this paper, an independent modular method which focuses on jointed-arm robot system is involved. To aim at economical manufacturing, an innovative modular design approach has been proposed. Based on the main structure of the jointed-arm industrial robot system and sacrificed part of its reconfigurability, the new system would be beneficial in terms of lower cost and better dynamic performance. This paper is organized as follows. Section II introduces modular division and its conceptional design. Subdivision and detailed design of execute modules are discussed in detail in section III. Conclusions and further work are derived at the end of the paper.

## 2    Modular Division and Conceptual Design

Division and definition of modules are important steps in the process of modular design. Based on the division and definition, the library of the modular system should support the construction of various configurations to meet a set of functional requirements. The completed robot should be characterized by stable performance, low cost, and easy maintenance. Furthermore, the flexibility and other factors related to the lifecycle of the robot system, such as manufacturing, assembly and after-sales maintenance should be also taken into consideration. Usually, modular robots are divided into several layers, and each layer consists of several modules. To simplify the system, it is necessary to keep the division layers and module scales in an appropriate level. Additionally, mechanical design of all modules should be standardized and uncomplicated.

First of all, the functional requirements and environmental conditions should be studied thoroughly by means of surveying market and application field of the system. Then, specifications of the robot will be determined, such as the number of axes, rated payload, maximum work range, speed and acceleration, positioning repeatability, protection classification and so on.

Based on the design method of industrial robots, the modular design theory, and the functional and structure features of the jointed-arm industrial robot, division and definition of the modules should be carried out according to the following criterions: (i) link module, with the study on mobility type and structure feature of each joint, introduction of redundant link modules should be avoided; (ii) independence of the modules, the mechanical independence, as well as functional integrality of the modules should be considered, which actually affect the subsequent process including detailed design, manufacturing, and assembly; (iii) driving unit, the disposal of motors and mechanical transmission should be studied carefully to improve the dynamic performance of the robot; (iv) interfaces, efficiency of reconfiguration is the main factor to ensure quick and easy integration of the modules, and high structural strength is another factor that should be take into account to ensures the system reliable in full payload; (v) the expansibility of the library, it is necessary to obtain some additional configurations to satisfying specific tasks in practice based on the existing modules.

According to the discussion above, the first layer of division and definition of our modular system is proposed, which consists of: (i) execute modules, (ii) drive modules, (iii) sensor modules, (iv) servo and control modules, (v) link and communication modules. The executive modules are the main components to construct mechanical structure of the robot. In details, executive module consists of the mechanical frame of the robot and some internal mechanism including transmission, decelerator, positioning, sealing, and buffering. The performances of the modular robot syatem, including structural stiffness, working range, and other dynamic behaviors, will  be determined by the design of execute modules directly.

## 3      Subdivision and Detailed Design of Execute Module

Based on functional analysis of the target product, the basic units obtained in foregoing step are merged to build series of modules according to a certain rule. The structural design should correspond to the result of functional analysis. The configuration of industrial robot is a decisive factor to the practical performance of the system. Therefore, structural analysis would play an important role in developing modular library. In this paper, subdivision and detailed design of execute modules are discussed in detail according to the functional requirement of the specific application, i.e. medium-size jointed-arm robots for general use with the load capacity from 30kg to 80kg.

With the survey of application field and customer requirement, a further division based on the second modular layer is conducted, which focuses the attention on concrete configurations and detailed information. The results of functional analysis of the second modular layer are listed in Table 1.

**Table 1.** Functional analysis of the second modular layer

| Module name | Functional analysis |
| --- | --- |
| Base frame | Determines the basic functions such as mounting, position of the rotating column, and additional mobility of the robot |
| Rotating column | Deploys axis 1 and 2, mainly relates to rotation angle, gyration radius, and effective working range |
| Link arm | Deploys axis 3, affect the workspace |
| Arm | Deploys axis 3 and 5, determines the effective working range |
| Wrist | Deploys axis 4 to 6, relates to the mobility types of these axes, determines the way in which the orientation of end-effecter is located |

According to the functional analysis above, several types of execute parts with different functions and structures are obtained by using the conjunctions of rotational joints to build up modular jointed-arm robots. Each part composing of transmission, decelerator and buffering can be equipped independently. For the second layer modules, according to their structural features, executive modules are divided into five modules including the base frame, rotating column, link arm, arm, and wrist. This kind of division reduces the number of elements involved in each configuration, consequently ensures the system a reliable stiffness and enables the formation of various configurations to meet multiple tasks. The modules with independent structure and integral function are economical in the subsequent production processes, such as detailed design, manufacturing, assembly, and maintenance.

According to the analysis above and classification of common industrial applications, a detailed library of the third layer is presented in Table 2 to Table 6.

**Table 2.** Subdivision and design notes of base frame

| Module type | | Configuration diagram | Design notes |
| --- | --- | --- | --- |
| I | Floor module | | Optimized for floor mounting. Expanded workspace and additional rotation angle, due to the higher position of rotating column. Capable of integrating with variety of communication cable and power supply lines. Larger volume and higher mass |
| II | Ceiling module | | Optimized for tilted and inverted mounting. Compact and simplified structure, in order to obtain a compromise among integration, volume and lightness |

**Table 2.** (*continued*)

| | | |
|---|---|---|
| III | Shelf module | Optimized for semi-shelf mounting. Simplified structure, low cost, and easy assembly. The lower base frame extends the flexibility of the downward reach |
| IV | Linear module | Optimized for linear-units mounting. Additional motion units, including linear motor and mechanical transmission are introduced. By connecting to Type I or Type II, an extra DOF is added to the robot |
| V | Gantry module | Optimized for gantry mounting. Linear movement is realized by equipping base frame with drive system |

**Table 3.** Subdivision and design notes of rotating column

| Module type | | Configuration diagram | Design notes |
|---|---|---|---|
| I | Coaxial module | | The shaft of the motor for rotating column and axis 1 are mounted on a common line. The transmission of the motion is easy to realize, which makes the module compact. In this situation, the distance between axis 1 and 2 is relatively longer, causing an increase in the minimum gyration radius and torque generated by rotating |
| II | Off-set module | | The shaft of the motor for rotating column and axis 1 are not mounted on a common line. Additional mechanical transmission should be equipped, and with a shorter distance between axis 1 and 2, the feature of the module is opposite to Type I. Furthermore, this deployment avoids the collision between motor and link arm, allowing a wider rotating range of axis 2 |
| III | Extended module | | Deployed in the same structure as Type I, in particular, by further increasing the distance of the two axis, the effective working range is distinctly extended |

**Table 3.** (*continued*)

| IV | Shelf module | | Based on the principle similar to Type III, but is optimized for semi-shelf mounting: the lower position of axis 2 extends the depth of the workspace and consequentially avoids the intrusion of the robot |
|----|-------------|--|-------------------------------------------------------------------------------------------------------------------------------------------------------------------------------------------------------------|
| V  | Gantry module | | In order to adapt to the gantry robot, the structure is simplified and the rotating joint is cancelled |

**Table 4.** Subdivision and design notes of link arm

| Module type | | Configuration diagram | Design notes |
|-------------|--|----------------------|--------------|
| I | Universal module | | A universal module. Can be apply to most application field |
| II | Extended module | Refers to Type I | Compared to Type I, the distance between axis 2 and 3 is extended and a slimmer structure is introduced, in order to reduce the overall mass and make the robot well suited to the requirement of long working range and low payload |

**Table 5.** Subdivision and design notes of arm

| Module type | | Configuration diagram | Design notes |
|-------------|--|----------------------|--------------|
| I | Universal module | | A universal module. To balance the force of the load, like most off-the-shelf robots, is equipped with drive and transmission system of the wrist |
| II | Extended module | | By connecting to Type I, the working range of the robot is increased |
| III | Extended module | Refers to Type II | Based on the principle similar to Type II, but is slimmer, in order to make the robot well suited to the requirement of long working range and low payload |

**Table 6.** Subdivision and design notes of wrist

| Module type | Configuration diagram | Design notes |
|---|---|---|
| I In-line module | | Similar to the common in-line wrists, while its internal mechanism is modified to ensure a quick and reliable connection to arm module. Can be apply to most application field |
| II Off-set module | | The off-set deployment is fitted for some special tasks |
| III Enhanced module | Refers to Type I | Deployed in the same structure as Type I. By improving its sealing ability and equipping with corrosion-resistant components, the module is capable of operating conditions involving greater mechanical and thermal stress |
| IV Compact module | Refers to Type I | Can be derived from Type I by optimizing the volume and mass, in order to make the robot well suited to the requirement of long working range and low payload |
| V Compact module | Refers to Type II | Can be derived from Type II by optimizing the volume and mass, in order to make the robot well suited to the requirement of long working range and low payload |

**Table 7.** Examples of the assembled execute modules

| Example I | | Example II | |
|---|---|---|---|
| | Consists of: base frame I, rotating column II, link arm I, arm I and II, wrist I Function: superior for the targeted applications such as medium to heavy material handling and metal processing | | Consists of: base frame I, rotating column II, link arm I, arm I and III, wrist IV Function: can be applied to application field with requirement of long working range and low payload such as small parts assembly, grinding and polishing |

The modular robotic system constructed with modules presented above will be in a relatively small scale and sufficient to most of the industrial applications. As regards some specific tasks, according to their requirements, new modules will be available by means of the variants which are based on the existing modules. A relatively lower cost of the whole modular library with the capability of further expanding could be expected by the approaches proposed in this paper.

The process of configuring a modular robot with modules presented in this paper includes two steps. Firstly, selecting the corresponding execute modules sequentially according to their functional requirements. Secondly, selecting or deploying drives, sensors, link modules and appropriate controlling strategy for the new configuration. As an illustration, two modular robots constructed with modules proposed above were shown in Table 7. By replacing some execute modules and adjusting the relative units, two configurations matched for different application fields were obtained.

# 4    Conclusions

The jointed-arm robot has peculiar benefits to many fields, and can be applied to a wide variety of industrial applications. Modular design of industrial robots should focus on easy realization and economical convenience with  specific kinematical structure. To achieve high efficiency and low cost, based on the design method of industrial robot and the modular design theory, criterions of the division and definition have been prposed in this paper. It has been presented that subdivision of the executive modules and the conceptual design of corresponding configurations have been implemented for a medium payload robot by taking into account the functional and structural features. The work presented in ths paper only took the mechanical module into consideration. Further work includes taking drive module and sensor module into consideration, invetigating the effect of the mechanical modules on the stiffness and workspace of the manipulator, and fabricating a prototype following the approach and modules presented in this paper.

**Acknowledgments.** This work was supported in part by the Natural Science Foundation of China under Grant 50975186 and project funded by MOST of China under Grant 2009GJF00009.

# References

1. Benhabib, B., Dai, M.Q.: Mechanical design of a modular robot for industrial applications. Journal of Manufacturing Systems 10(4), 297–306 (1991)
2. Matsumaru, T.: Design and control of the modular robot systems: TOMMS. In: IEEE International Conference on Robotics and Automation, Nagoya, Aichi, Japan, May 21-27, pp. 2125–2131 (1995)
3. Acaccia, G., Bruzzone, L., Razzoli, R.: A modular robotic system for industrial applications. Assembly Automation 28(2), 151–162 (2008)
4. Bi, Z.M.: On adaptive robot systems for manufacturing applications. Ph. D. thesis, Department of Mechanical Engineering, University of Saskatchewan, Saskatoon, Canada (2002)
5. Bi, Z.M., Lin, Y., Zhang, W.J.: The general architecture of adaptive robotic systems for manufacturing applications. Robotics and Computer-Integrated Manufacturing 26, 461–470 (2010)

6. Abdel-Malek, K., Paul, B.: Criteria for the design of manipulator arms for a high stiffness-to-weight ratio. Journal of Manufacturing Systems 17(3), 209–220 (1998)

7. Bi, Z.M., Gruver, W.A., Zhang, W.J., Lang, S.Y.T.: Automated modeling of modular robotic configurations. Robotics and Autonomous Systems 54, 1015–1025 (2006)

8. Schunk: Modular Robotics ( August 20, 2010),
   `http://www.schunk-modular-robotics.com/`

9. Zhao, L., Yan, H., Yu, J.: Modular industrial robot based on joint modular. Modular Machine Tool & Automatic Manufacturing Technique 9, 63–67 (2008)

10. Yan, H.: Researches on modular industrial robot design (In Chinese). Ph. D. thesis, Department of Mechanical Engineering, Zhejiang Univ., Hangzhou, China (2008)

11. Bi, Z.M., Zhang, W.J., Chen, I.-M., Lang, S.Y.T.: Automated generation of the D-H parameters for configuration design of modular manipulators. Robotics and Computer-Integrated manufacturing 23, 553–562 (2007)

12. Zhao, G., Wang, H., Liu, Y.: Research on configuration and kinematics of joint modular robots. Machinery Design & Manufacture 4, 178–180 (2010) (In Chinese)

13. Wei, Y., Zhao, J., Cai, H.: Task-based method for determining topology of reconfigurable modular robot. Chinese Journal of Mechanical Engineering 42, 93–97 (2006) (In Chinese)

14. Wei, Y., Zhu, Y., Zhao, J., Cai, H.: Reconfigurable robot system design based on flexible work. Journal of Jilin University (Engineering and Technology Edition) 38(2), 449–453 (2008) (In Chinese)

15. Bi, Z.M., Zhang, W.J.: Concurrent optimal design of modular robotic configuration. Journal of Robotic Systems 18(2), 77–87 (2011)

# Online Path Planning for Industrial Robots in Varying Environments Using the Curve Shortening Flow Method

Marcel Huptych[1], Konrad Groh[2], and Sascha Röck[1]

[1] Aalen University, Beethovenstr. 1, 73430 Aalen, Germany
[2] Institute for Control Engineering of Machine Tools and Manufacturing Units (ISW),
University of Stuttgart, Seidenstr. 36, 70174 Stuttgart, Germany
{Marcel.Huptych,Sascha.Roeck}@htw-aalen.de,
Konrad.Groh@isw.uni-stuttgart.de

**Abstract.** Handling tasks with robots which are interacting in a shared workspace provide a high risk of collision. A new approach, the so-called "Curve Shortening Flow Method", enables a collision-free path planning method for robots within a varying environment on basis of a workspace model. Thereby a global path planning method based on geometrical curvature flow is combined with the locally and reactively acting potential field method in order to describe the obstacles' influence, whereby the obstacles are modeled as a repulsive field, which displaces the robot's planned path. This path can be formulated as a time-dependant partial differential equation, which can be solved very efficiently using explicit numerical time integration. First results show that this online method is able to generate collision-free paths robustly in real-time.

**Keywords:** path planning, robot control, real-time, collision-free, curve shortening flow, potential field method.

## 1    Introduction

### 1.1    Problem

Cost-efficient realization of handling tasks has become one of the major demands within the field of production engineering. Referring to this request cycle times may be shortened enabling higher dynamics of processes and machines, installation spaces can be reduced by parallelization of the handling task or startup may be accelerated by minimizing the programming efforts.

Inevitably a minimized installation space leads to systems whose workspaces overlap themselves or are restricted by static or even moving obstacles. When, for example, several robots share the same workspace and the environment in the workspace is changing due to the operation, the robot trajectories can no longer be planned in advance without the risk of collision. Even with knowledge of the path of each end-effector a collision of arbitrary robot axes could be excluded just by enormous programming expense.

S. Jeschke, H. Liu, and D. Schilberg (Eds.): ICIRA 2011, Part I, LNAI 7101, pp. 73–82, 2011.
© Springer-Verlag Berlin Heidelberg 2011

With the "Curve Shortening Flow Method" a new algorithm, which adjusts the robot path on runtime by taking into account dynamic obstacles (see Fig. 1), is presented. Besides the safety-related benefits resulting from a collision-free motion a significant reduction of programming time can be achieved. The programming of the robot path can be reduced to its individual task without considering the other robots' paths.

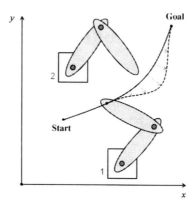

**Fig. 1.** Simplified operating principle of the Curve Shortening Flow Method: Robot 1 follows a given trajectory while robot 2 is approaching. In order to avoid a collision the path of robot 1 is adjusted online.

## 1.2    State of the Art

Trajectory planning is a field in automatization of industrial robots and autonomous systems researchers and engineers have been dealing with for years. A detailed overview can be found in [1], [2]. Thereby these algorithms can be classified into globally and local reactively working methods.

First global path planning methods using a discretization of the workspace go back to the Dijkstra algorithm [3], [4], which describes the problem as a search for the "cheapest" relation within a graph of nodes and cost-tainted edges. Further approaches which are also based upon workspace discretization are cell-decomposition methods. Although these algorithms are able to calculate global trajectories from a given start- to a given endpoint reliably they are not suitable for online applications due to their enormous computation effort. These methods are based on a static model of the environment whose adjustment to the current state of the workspace in every single cycle of the robot's control is too time-consuming.

Local reactively behaving planning algorithms are mainly applicable with autonomous systems within unknown dynamic environments. Due to its simplicity and computational efficiency the potential field method [5] has become a well-analyzed and –published method. Thereby the environment is modeled with repulsive force fields in the obstacles and an attracting force field in the destination. The motion aiming the goal is then deduced from the field's negative gradient which describes the direction of maximum potential decrease. This leads to the problem, that due to local minima, in which the robot can get stuck [6], [7], the reachability of the goal cannot be guaranteed. Even further developments of the potential field method [8], [9] do not provide the robustness that is needed for a secure robot trajectory planning.

In addition it is necessary to mention that path planning problems of robots can also be formulated in the robot's configuration space which is usually the case for industrial robots. Hereby the robot's position is not described with Cartesian coordinates of the workspace but with its joint angles. The collision-free motion of a whole kinematic chain can then be reduced to the motion of a single point [10] and obstacles are represented by domains of all possible configurations that would lead to a collision.

In summary it can be determined that no common algorithm provides an online-capable and at the same time robust path planning within a varying environment. Either the computation time is not acceptable for real-time planning or a robust and secure path to the goal cannot be guaranteed.

## 2    Curve Shortening Flow Method

### 2.1    Basic Principle

The mentioned shortcomings of common methods can be countered with a new algorithm which combines global and locally reactive path planning elements. This method, which we call the "Curve Shortening Flow Method", describes the profile of a trajectory $z$ from a starting point $A$ to a goal $B$ by combining geometrical curve flows with the well-known potential-field method. The former enables the evolution of a given initial path in order to shorten its length while the repulsive effect of obstacles on the path is modeled by virtual force fields. The basic principle of this new method will be at first explained in the x-y-plane (see Fig. 2) before discussing higher dimension problems in section 2.4.

Let an initial path $z_0$ between the starting point $A$ and the goal $B$ be given. If an obstacle is approaching (see Fig. 2 (a)) the path has to be adjusted without touching it. Therefore repulsive forces $f$ generated by the obstacles have a continuous effect along the path displacing it with a permanent safe distance to the obstacles. At the same time the curve flow causes curvature proportional forces against the repulsive forces of the obstacles along the path. As the obstacles vanish (see Fig. 2 (b)) these forces set the trajectory back to a state of minimum curvature respectively minimum curve length. Thereby these forces can be formulated as the product of curvature and the normal vector $kn$ along the path.

The optimal trajectory appears if all repulsive and resetting forces along the whole path are in balance.

This new method enables a path planning algorithm which is continually able to react on obstacles without knowing their paths in advance and guaranty a collision-free movement of the robot to its goal.

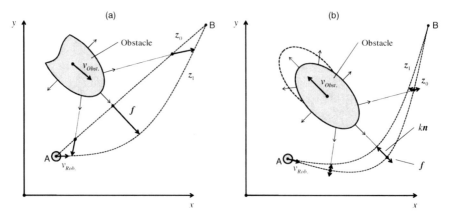

**Fig. 2.** (a) The obstacle is approaching and the initial path $z_0$ is displaced by the repulsive forces $f$. (b) The obstacle is diverging. The curvature-proportional forces $kn$ cause a reverse motion of the path towards a state of minimal length.

## 2.2    Equation

These above-mentioned characteristics can be achieved by mathematically formulating the path as a curvature flow curve given by the following partial differential equation [11]:

$$\dot{z}(p,t) = k\big(z(p,t)\big) \cdot n\big(z(p,t)\big) + \lambda \cdot t\big(z(p,t)\big) + f(z,h) \tag{1}$$

Thereby $z$ describes the trajectory as a planar parametric curve with coordinates $x$ and $y$ depending on the parameter $p$ and the time $t$.

$$z(p,t) = \begin{pmatrix} x(p,t) \\ y(p,t) \end{pmatrix} \tag{2}$$

$k$ is the curvature, $n$ the unified normal and $t$ the unified tangential vector in every point $p$ of the curve.

This formulation describes the evolution of $z(p,t)$ as an initial boundary value problem for (1). Thereby $z$ has to fulfill the initial conditions $z_0(p,0)$ as well as the boundary conditions $z(0,t) = A(t)$, which corresponds to the robot's position at the moment $t$, and $z(1,t) = B$ as fixed end point. By the vector $kn$ the path is forced to minimize its curvature and at the same time its length.

The repulsive effect of an obstacle $h = (x_h, y_h)^T$ in an arbitrary point $(x,y)^T$ on the curve is described by the vectors $f$ and depends on the distance to $z$:

$$f(x,y,h) = \rho\big(d(x,y,h)\big) \cdot \frac{\nabla d(x,y,h)}{|\nabla d(x,y,h)|}. \tag{3}$$

The repulsive effect is achieved by applying the unified gradient of a potential function $d$, which describes the minimal distance between trajectory and obstacle. Thereby the gradient ensures the "optimal" direction of avoidance and the weighting function $\rho$, which depends upon the potential function $d$ and decreases with increasing distance, provides a measure for the intensity of avoidance.

The tangential component $\lambda t$ serves, after a discretization of the curve, as control of the nodes' location on the curve and has no effect on the curve's shape. As, referring to the curve, the vector $kn$ always points in orthogonal direction and the force vector $f$ does not necessarily point parallel to $kn$ the component $\lambda t$ is needed to retain the nodes' location. Fig. 3 demonstrates the relation between the vectors.

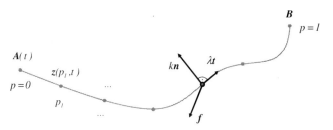

**Fig. 3.** Exemplary illustration of the relation between the vectors $f$, $\lambda t$ and $kn$ in one point on the curve

If these three vectors $f$, $\lambda t$ and $kn$ are in balance for all trajectory points $p$ then the equilibrium of the system and therefore the "optimal" trajectory is achieved.

## 2.3     Numerical Solution

A very important requirement on the algorithm is the numerically robust solution of the curve shortening flow equation (1). Written out this equation leads to a time-dependant and nonlinear $2^{nd}$ order partial differential equation:

$$\underbrace{\begin{pmatrix} \dot{x} \\ \dot{y} \end{pmatrix}}_{\dot{z}} = \underbrace{\frac{x'y'' - x''y'}{(x'^2 + y'^2)^2}}_{k} \cdot \underbrace{\begin{pmatrix} -y' \\ x' \end{pmatrix}}_{n} + \lambda(x, y) \cdot \underbrace{\begin{pmatrix} x' \\ y' \end{pmatrix}}_{t} + \underbrace{\begin{pmatrix} f_x \\ f_y \end{pmatrix}}_{f} \tag{4}$$

The local derivations of $x$ and $y$ $(x', x'', y', y'')$ can be discretized with the first and second order central differences, which leads to a system of ordinary differential equations. Thus this system can be solved very efficiently concerning computation time by using explicit numerical time integration. Every time step provides a new curve, which is displaced towards the before-mentioned equilibrium.

Thereby the Runge-Kutta method of $4^{th}$ order fulfils the necessary requirements on a time integration method for solving this system. These requirements are on one hand time-efficiency and -determinism for real-time control by explicitly evaluating the calculation and on the other hand monotonic solution behavior within the stability region of the method. The latter of them is urgently necessary as each new solution has to provide a trajectory "better", meaning closer to the equilibrium, than the last one.

Another important characteristic of the curve shortening flow method is its ability to robustly enable extreme deformations of the curve, like for example the multiple loops in the fictive scenario shown in Fig. 4.

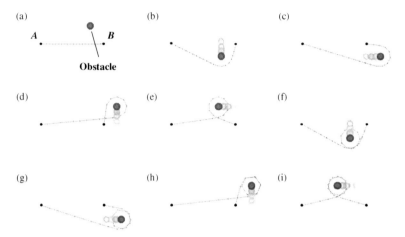

**Fig. 4.** Fictive scenario that demonstrates the robustness of the curve shortening flow method. With the aid of a punctual obstacle it is possible to generate multiple loops.

A problem the evolution of the trajectory by numerical time integration suffers from is the phenomenon that the initially equidistant nodes converge in regions of high curvature caused by steady shift in normal direction and get stuck after a couple of time steps. This "freezing-effect" can be derived from the use of difference quotients to compute the curvature which in this case always results in zero, a apparent static state (see Fig. 5).

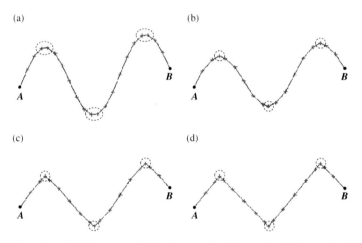

**Fig. 5.** Evolution of an initial curve suffering from collapsing nodes: Without the influence of an obstacle a given initial curve (a) aspires to a straight line connecting **A** and **B**. In (b) the nodes around the three turning points collapse and get stuck at these positions (c). The curve shortening flow forces all the rest of the nodes to straight lines between these stuck nodes (d).

This problem is avoided by adding the tangential component $\lambda t$ to the curve shortening flow equation (1). The sign of $\lambda$ is derived from the difference of each node's distance to its two neighbors. Hereby it is possible to keep the nodes permanently equidistant on the curve and eliminate the possibility of collapsing without having an influence on the trajectory's shape.

## 2.4    Extension to Three Dimensions

To make the algorithm suitable for common robot kinematics with more than two degrees of freedom the Curve Shortening Flow Method was in a first step adapted for three dimensions with $z(p,t) = (x(p,t), y(p,t), z(p,t))^T$. The curve shortening flow for space curves $\dot{z} = kn$ was considered in [12]. Whereas the vectors $f$ and $t$ of equation (4) can easily be generalized to $f = (f_x, f_y, f_z)^T$ and $t = (x', y', z')^T$, the curvature term $kn$ is slightly more complicated.

Space curves have more than one normal vector. A typical choice is associating a Frenet frame, which consists of the tangent vector $t$, the normal vector $n$ and a binormal vector $b$, to each point of the curve. Looking at the Frenet-Serret formulas it is possible to derive the corresponding curvature term for three dimensions:

$$\underbrace{\begin{pmatrix} \dot{x} \\ \dot{y} \\ \dot{z} \end{pmatrix}}_{\dot{z}} = \frac{1}{|z'|^4} \underbrace{\begin{pmatrix} x''(y'^2 + z'^2) - x'(y'y'' + z'z'') \\ y''(x'^2 + z'^2) - y'(x'x'' + z'z'') \\ z''(x'^2 + y'^2) - z'(x'x'' + y'y'') \end{pmatrix}}_{curvature\ term} + \lambda(x,y,z) \cdot \underbrace{\begin{pmatrix} x' \\ y' \\ z' \end{pmatrix}}_{t} + \underbrace{\begin{pmatrix} f_x \\ f_y \\ f_z \end{pmatrix}}_{f} \quad (5)$$

For solving the Curve Shortening Flow equation for space curves (5) the similar numerical solution as for the planar case is used (see section 2.3).

## 3    Results

The Curve Shortening Flow Method has been implemented and validated for the simulation of a planar handling task. The visualization is shown in Fig. 6.

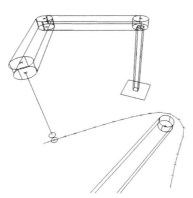

**Fig. 6.** Modeling of a Pick-And-Place task for a 2-DOF robot whose path can be crossed by a second manipulator. The Curve Shortening Flow Method continuously adjusts this path in such way that the second manipulator is steadily circumnavigated in order to avoid a collision.

Following the example mentioned in the introduction (see Fig. 1) a Pick-And-Place task of a 2-DOF robot has been modeled. The robot's path can be crossed by a second manipulator which is regarded as an obstacle. The Curve Shortening Flow Method hereby adjusts the path of the robot continuously so that the second manipulator is steadily circumnavigated and a collision is avoided.

To demonstrate the method's efficiency performance characteristics of different scenarios have been recorded. Subject of the measurements was always the required time for the calculation of one time step as this is the major criterion whether an algorithm is applicable to be run on a real-time control. This calculation time was analyzed while varying the number of obstacles and nodes the curve was discretized with (see Fig. 7).

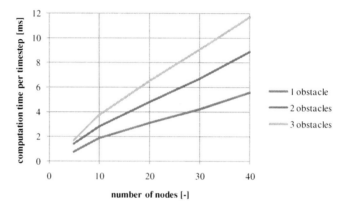

**Fig. 7.** Efficiency of the Curve Shortening Flow Method: The calculation time increases linearly – with the number of nodes as well as with the number of obstacles

For the discussed examples with one obstacle and a discretization of 20 nodes (see Fig. 5) calculation times of below 3ms per time step could be achieved. Furthermore the analysis shows that the computation time increases linearly with both discretization nodes and obstacles.

These results prove the capability of the Curve Shortening Flow Method to be used within a real-time robot control and its advantages over common methods. On the one hand the non-optimized algorithm already achieves calculation times in the region of modern controls and on the other hand the computational effort for solving higher dimensional problems grows only linearly with the number of degrees of freedom.

Furthermore the Curve Shortening Flow Method for space curves was implemented for scenarios with multiple punctual obstacles (see Fig. 8). Compared to the planar case the behavior of the curve has improved as it cannot be endlessly displaced by the obstacles. Due to one more degree of freedom the Curve Shortening Flow for space curves is able to "jump" over punctual obstacles and generate shorter optimal paths.

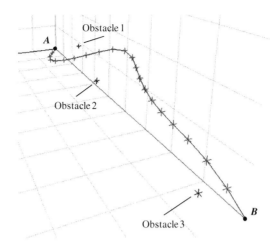

**Fig. 8.** Curve Shortening Flow Method for space curves with three obstacles

# 4        Summary and Outlook

In this paper a new path planning method for industrial robots is introduced. The method is based on the combination of a global and a local path planning principle. The so-called Curve Shortening Flow Method enables the implementation of a very efficient and robust algorithm for dynamically adjusting paths at runtime. Fields of application for this algorithm are for example handling tasks with robots, which share the same work space or whose work space is disturbed by other moving obstacles that carry a high potential for collisions. The Curve Shortening Flow Method enables a collision-free path planning on basis of a parallelly running real-time model of the environment. Thereby a global path planning element based on geometrical curve flows is combined with the locally reactive potential field method in order to describe obstacles. Obstacles are modeled by repulsive force fields which displace the robot's path. This path can be formulated as a partial differential equation, which after spatial discretization can be solved very efficiently by numerical time integration. First simulative results with planar and space curves prove the functionality of this new method and also its ability to be used within a real-time application.

The use of the Curve Shortening Flow Method is independent from the space the problem is formulated in. Path planning problems with industrial robots are usually solved in the robot's configuration space. Here the motion of the robot's whole kinematic chain is reduced to the motion of a single point. Obstacles are modeled as regions of all forbidden configurations that would lead to a collision with the obstacle [5]. Therefore the Curve Shortening Flow Method is very suitable for trajectory planning of robots in the configuration space which exemplarily was already shown by the authors for a 2-DOF robot [13].

In further steps the Curve Shortening Flow Method will be extended up to six dimensions to enable trajectory planning in the configuration space for kinematics of industrially relevant six-axis robots. Also modeling geometries of complex obstacles will be part of this project. The basis for whose necessary real-time distance calculation will be provided by the Closest Feature Algorithm by Lin Canny [14].

Furthermore the verification of the algorithm's numerical robustness respectively the stability limits of the numerical time integration are a major aspect of the future work on this project. Thereby common methods like stability identification using the spectral radius of the evaluation's transition matrix will be applied.

**Acknowledgments.** The authors Marcel Huptych, Konrad Groh and Sascha Röck would like to thank the German Research Foundation (DFG) for financial support of the project within the Cluster of Excellence in Simulation Technology (EXC 310/1) and the Graduate School for Advanced Manufacturing Engineering (GSC 262) at the University of Stuttgart.

# References

1. LaValle, S.M.: Planning Algorithms. Cambridge University Press, Cambridge (2006)
2. Hwang, Y.K., Ahuja, N.: Gross Motion Planning - A Survey. ACM Comput. Surv. 24, 219–291 (1992)
3. Dijkstra, E.W.: A Note On Two Problems In Connection With Graphs. Numerische Mathematik (1959)
4. Hart, P.E., Nilsson, N.J., Raphael, B.: A Formal Basis For The Heuristic Determination Of Minimum Cost Paths. IEEE Trans. On Systems Science And Cybernetics 4, 100–107 (1968)
5. Khatib, O.: Real-Time Obstacle Avoidance For Manipulators And Mobile Robots. In: Proceedings of The IEEE International Conference on Robotics And Automation, St. Louis, Missouri, pp. 500–505. IEEE, New York (1985)
6. Koren, Y., Borenstein, J.: Potential Field Methods and Their Inherent Limitations For Mobile Robot Navigation. In: Proceedings of The IEEE International Conference on Robotics and Automation, Sacramento (1991)
7. Koditschek, D.E.: Exact Robot Navigation By Means Of Potential Functions: Some Topological Considerations. In: IEEE International Conference on Robotics and Automation, Raleigh, NC, pp. 1–6 (1987)
8. Borenstein, J., Koren, Y.: The Vector Field Histogram – Fast Obstacle-Avoidance For Mobile Robots. IEEE Journal of Robotics and Automation (1991)
9. Connolly, C.I., Burns, J.B., Weiss, R.: Path Planning Using Laplace's Equation. In: Proc. IEEE Int. Conf. Robot. Automation, Cincinnati, OH, vol. 1, pp. 2102–2106 (1991)
10. Lozano Pérez, T.: Spatial Planning: A Configuration Space Approach. IEEE Transactions on Computers (1983)
11. Chou, K.S., Zhu, X.-P.: The Curve Shortening Problem. Chapman&Hall/CRC (2001)
12. Altschuler, S.J.: Singularities of The Curve Shrinking Flow For Space Curves. J. Differential Geometry 34, 491–514 (1991)
13. Groh, K., Röck, S.: A contribution to collision-free trajectory planning for handling systems in varying environments. Journal of Production Engineering, Research & Development (2009)
14. Lin, M.C.: Efficient Collision Detection for Animation and Robotics. PhD thesis, Department of Electrical Engineering and Computer Science, University of California, Berkeley (1993)

# Parallel-Populations Genetic Algorithm for the Optimization of Cubic Polynomial Joint Trajectories for Industrial Robots

Fares J. Abu-Dakka[1], Iyad F. Assad[2], Francisco Valero[1], and Vicente Mata[1]

[1] Technology Research Center of Vehicles, Polytechnic University of Valencia, Valencia, 46022, Spain

[2] Computer Center, Birzeit University, Ramallah, Palestine

{fares.abudakka,iyadassad}@gmail.com

{fvalero,vmata}@mcm.upv.es

**Abstract.** In this paper a parallel-populations genetic algorithm procedure is presented for the obtainment of minimum-time trajectories for industrial robots. This algorithm is fed in first place by a sequence of configurations then cubic spline functions are used for the construction of joint trajectories for industrial robots. The algorithm is subjected to two types of constraints: (1) Physical constraints on joint velocities, accelerations, and jerk. (2) Dynamic constraints on torque, power, and energy. Comparison examples are used to evaluate the method with different combinations of crossover and mutation.

**Keywords:** Industrial robots, Trajectory planning, Genetic algorithm, Obstacle avoidance.

## 1 Introduction

In the last decades, industrial robots have been used widely in automatic production lines. They are, in general, highly nonlinear, coupled, multivariable systems with nonlinear constraints. For this reason, the indirect method for trajectory planning is often used. Indirect method is divided into two stages: path planning and then trajectory adjustment. Path planning concerns of the obtainment of the free collision path between initial and final configurations of the manipulator considering kinematic and geometric constraints. A trajectory can be adjusted to a given path by optimizing the temporal evolution of the robot configurations.

In order to maximize the speed of operation that affects the productivity in industrial situations, it is necessary to minimize the total traveling time of the robot. More research works have been carried out to get minimum time trajectories [1]-[5]. The early trajectory planning models [6],[7] used a nonlinear programming approach to solve the trajectory planning problem in either gripper or joint space. These models suffer from the deficiency that the manipulator dynamics are not considered.

In this paper, cubic spline functions have been used for constructing joint trajectories for industrial robots. Algebraic splines are widely employed for path

S. Jeschke, H. Liu, and D. Schilberg (Eds.): ICIRA 2011, Part I, LNAI 7101, pp. 83–92, 2011.

planning, cubic splines [7], quartic splines [8], and quintic splines [9]. The first formalization of finding the optimal curve by interpolating a sequence of nodes in the joint space can be found in [7]. This sequence of nodes are obtained in base of a discrete set of positions of the end-effector of the robot. In [10] the same algorithm is presented, but the trajectories are expressed by means of cubic B-splines. The authors in [11] modified the optimization algorithm proposed by [7] to deal with dynamic constraints. In [12], the authors resolved the [7] algorithm using genetic algorithms. In [9], a new trajectory planning technique is presented, which assumed that the geometric path is given in the form of sequence of via points in the operating space of the robot. In that case, only kinematic constrains are considered. A Sequential Quadratic Programming (SQP) method for optimal motion planning problem for PUMA560 robot manipulator is used [15], where the robot dynamics are considered. In the other hand, some authors used harmonic functions to interpolate a sequence of configurations construction a trajectory for industrial robots [13], [14].

The methods that are used in the literatures such as sequential unconstrained minimization technique (SUMT) [1]-[5], sequential quadratic programming (SQP) [15], interval analysis [16], [9] and numerical iterative procedure [17] to deal with the complex instances (obstacles environment) have some notable drawbacks: (1) they may fail to find the optimal path , (2) they have limited capabilities when handling cases where the limits of maximum acceleration and maximum deceleration along the solution curve are no longer met and (3) singular points or critical points of robot configuration may exist. To overcome the above drawbacks, the evolutionary algorithms can be used [18]. The advantages of evolutionary techniques are (1) Population based search, so more lucky to avoid local minima. (2) No need of any auxiliary information like gradients, derivatives, etc. (3) Complex and multimodal problems can be solved for global optimality. (4) Problem independent nature, i.e. Suitable for all types of problems [19]. In, [20], a general method using B-splines for computing optimal motion, using an evolutionary algorithm, of an industrial robot manipulator in the presence of fixed and oscillating obstacles.

In this paper, two parallel-populations genetic algorithms procedures will be introduced. The first algorithm PGA1 will resolve the cubic polynomial joint trajectory formulation introduced by [7], where only kinematic constraints are considered. A comparison will be made with the genetic algorithm procedure proposed by [12]. Moreover, this procedure will modify the algorithm to include dynamic constraints, such as, torques, power, and energy consumption.

The second algorithm PGA2 will resolve the clamped cubic spline algorithm, where only velocities are zeros at the initial and final configuration of the robot. The algorithm will consider the kinematic and dynamic constraints.

## 2   Formulation of Cubic Polynomial Joint Trajectory

The philosophy of splining is to use low order polynomials to interpolate from grid point to grid point. This is ideally suited when one has control of the grid locations and the values of data being interpolated. As this control is dominated, the relative accuracy can be controlled by changing the overall space between the grid points.

Cubic splines are the lowest order polynomial endowed with inflection points. If one would think about interpolating a set of data points using parabolic functions without inflection points, the interpolation would be meaningless.

The formulation of the cubic spline is based on the n joint vectors ($n$ configurations) that construct the joint trajectory. Joint vectors are denoted as $q_i^j$ which represents the position of the joint $i$ with respect to configuration $j$. The cubic polynomial trajectory is then constructed for each joint to fit the joint sequence $q_i^0, q_i^1, \cdots, q_i^n$. Let $t_0 < t_1 < \cdots < t_{n-2} < t_{n-1} < t_n$ be an ordered time sequence, at time $t = t_j$ the joint position will be $q_i^j$ . Let $q_i^j(t)$ be a cubic polynomial function defined on the time interval $[t_j, t_{j+1}]$; $0 \le j \le n - 1$. The problem of trajectory interpolation is to spline $Q_i(t)$, for $i = 1, 2, \cdots, n - 1$, together such that the required displacement, velocity and acceleration are satisfied; and the displacement, velocity and acceleration are continuous on the entire time interval $[t_1, t_n]$. Given that $Q_i(t)$ is cubic and represents the joint position, let $Q_i'(t)$ and $Q_i''(t)$ are the joint velocity and acceleration between $q_i$ and $q_{i+1}$.

## 2.1   PGA1 Formulation

The border conditions in this case are $\dot{q}_1 = \dot{q}_n = \ddot{q}_1 = \ddot{q}_n = 0$

$$Q_i(t) = \frac{Q_i''(t_i)}{6h_i}(t_{i+1} - t)^3 + \frac{Q_i''(t_{i+1})}{6h_i}(t - t_i)^3 \tag{1}$$
$$+ \left[\frac{q_{i+1}}{h_i} - \frac{h_i Q_i''(t_{i+1})}{6}\right](t - t_i) + \left[\frac{q_i}{h_i} - \frac{h_i Q_i''(t_i)}{6}\right](t_{i+1} - t)$$

where $i = 1, 2, \cdots, n - 1$, $h_i = t_{i+1} - t_i$

$$Q_i'(t) = \frac{-Q_i''(t_i)}{2h_i}(t_{i+1} - t)^2 + \frac{Q_i''(t_{i+1})}{2h_j}(t - t_i)^2 \tag{2}$$
$$+ \left(\frac{q_{i+1}}{h_i} - \frac{h_i Q_i''(t_{i+1})}{6}\right) - \left(\frac{q_i}{h_i} - \frac{h_i Q_i''(t_i)}{6}\right)$$

$$Q_i''(t) = \frac{t_{i+1} - t}{h_i}Q_i''(t_i) + \frac{(t - t_i)}{h_i}Q_i''(t_{i-1}) \tag{3}$$

The two extra knots $q_2$ and $q_{i-1}$ are not fixed and are used to add two new equations to the system in such a way that it can be solved. The joint positions of these two knots are

$$q_2 = q_1 + h_1\dot{q}_1 + \frac{h_1^2}{3}\ddot{q}_1 + \frac{h_1^2}{6}Q_1''(t_2) \tag{4}$$

$$q_{n-1} = q_n - h_{n-1}\dot{q}_n + \frac{h_{n-1}^2}{3}\ddot{q}_n + \frac{h_{n-1}^2}{6}Q_{n-2}''(t_{n-1}) \tag{5}$$

Using a continuity conditions on velocities and accelerations, a system of $n-2$ linear equations solving for unknowns $Q_i''(t_i)$'s is derived as [7]:

$$A \begin{bmatrix} Q_2''(t_2) \\ Q_3''(t_3) \\ \vdots \\ Q_{n-1}''(t_{n-1}) \end{bmatrix} = Y \tag{6}$$

where matrices $A$ and $Y$ are given by:

$$A = \begin{bmatrix} a_{11} & a_{12} \\ a_{21} & a_{22} & a_{23} \\ & a_{32} & a_{33} & a_{34} \\ & & & \vdots \\ & & & a_{n-3,n-4} & a_{n-3,n-3} & a_{n-3,n-2} \\ & & & & a_{n-2,n-3} & a_{n-2,n-2} \end{bmatrix}, Y = \begin{bmatrix} y_1 \\ y_2 \\ y_i \\ \vdots \\ y_{n-3} \\ y_{n-2} \end{bmatrix} \tag{7}$$

The Values of $a_{ij}$ and $y_i$ are in the appendix.

A unique solution is guaranteed once matrix $A$ is nonsingular.

## 2.2   PGA2 Formulation

In the clamped cubic spline the border conditions will be $\dot{q}_1 = \dot{q}_n = 0$.

$$\begin{aligned} Q_i(t) &= a_i + b_i(t - t_i) + c_i(t - t_i)^2 + d_i(t - t_i)^3 \\ Q_i'(t) &= b_i + 2c_i(t - t_i) + 3d_i(t - t_i)^2 \\ Q_i''(t) &= 2c_i + 6d_i(t - t_i) \end{aligned} \tag{8}$$

where $i = 1, 2, \cdots, n-1$, $h_i = t_{i+1} - t_i$. A system of $n-2$ linear equations will be solved as following:

$$A \begin{bmatrix} c_1 \\ c_2 \\ \vdots \\ c_{n-1} \end{bmatrix} = Y \tag{9}$$

where

$$A = \begin{bmatrix} 3h_1 & h_1 \\ h_1 & 2(h_1 + h_2) & h_1 \\ & h_2 & 2(h_2 + h_3) & h_3 & & 0 \\ & & & \vdots \\ & 0 & & & h_{n-2} & 2(h_{n-2} + hn - 1) & h_{n-1} \\ & & & & & h_{n-1} & 2h_{n-1} \end{bmatrix} \tag{10}$$

and, matrix $Y$ is given by:

$$Y = \begin{bmatrix} \frac{3}{h_1}(a_2 - a_1) - 3\dot{q}_1 \\ \frac{3}{h_2}(a_3 - a_2) - \frac{3}{h_1}(a_2 - a_1) \\ \vdots \\ \frac{3}{h_{n-2}}(a_{n-1} - a_{n-2}) - \frac{3}{h_{n-3}}(a_{n-2} - a_{n-3}) \\ 3\dot{q}_{n-1} - \frac{3}{h_{n-1}}(a_n - a_{n-1}) \end{bmatrix} \tag{11}$$

## 3   Optimization Technique Using GA

The objective in this optimization procedure is to determine a set of optimum values of time intervals $t_1, t_2, \cdots, t_{n-1}$. A genetic algorithm procedure with parallel populations with migration technique has been implemented to optimize the time intervals needed to move the robot through a sequence of configurations [21].

This GA has multiple, independent populations. Each population evolves using steady-state genetic algorithm, but at each generation, some individuals migrate from one population to another. The migration algorithm is deterministic stepping-stone; each population migrates a fixed number of its best individuals to its neighbor. The master population is updated each generation with best individual from each population. The Steady State Genetic Algorithm (SSGA) uses overlapping populations. This means, the ability to specify how much of the population should be replaced in each generation. Newly generated offspring are added to the population, and then the worst individuals are destroyed.

***Objective Function***

$$Minimize \sum_{i=1}^{n-1} h_i \tag{12}$$

subjected to

1. Kinematic constraints

$$\begin{cases} \text{Joint Positions:} & \left| q_i^j(t) \right| \le q_i^{max} & i = 1, \cdots, n-1 \\ \text{Joint Velocities:} & \left| \dot{q}_i^j(t) \right| \le \dot{q}_i^{max} & i = 1, \cdots, n-1 \\ \text{Joint Accelerations:} & \left| \ddot{q}_i^j(t) \right| \le \ddot{q}_i^{max} & i = 1, \cdots, n-1 \\ \text{Joint Jerks:} & \left| \dddot{q}_i^j(t) \right| \le \dddot{q}_i^{max} & i = 1, \cdots, n-1 \end{cases} \tag{13}$$

2. Dynamic constraints

$$\begin{cases} \text{Joint Torques: } | \tau_i(t) | \le \tau_i^{max} & i = 1, \cdots, n-1 \\ \text{Joint Power: } | P_i(t)| \le P_i^{max} & i = 1, \cdots, n-1 \\ \text{Joint Energy: } | E_i(t)| \le E_i^{max} & i = 1, \cdots, n-1 \end{cases} \tag{14}$$

**_Chromosome._** The chromosome consists of set of genes. Each gene contains a real number represents the time interval. Number of genes depends on the fed path.

The value of each gene is selected randomly from $\left[t_j^{\min}, t_j^{\max}\right]$. The value of $t_j^{\max}$ will change in each generation depending on the new generated offsprings.

**_Selection._** A roulette-wheel selection method is applied.

**_Crossover._** The crossover operator defines the procedure for generating a child from two selected parents. The new child will be calculated as follows:

$$a_i = (mom_i + dad_i)/2$$
$$child_i = a_i \cdot dad_i + (1 - a_i) \cdot mom_i \tag{15}$$

**_Mutation._** In this procedure, an offspring will be selected randomly then the algorithm will select a random set of genes in each chromosome for the mutation.

$$gene_j = gene_j + RV\left(t_j^{\min}, t_j^{\max}\right)\left[RV(t_j^{\min}, t_j^{\max}) - RV(t_j^{\min}, t_j^{\max})\right] \tag{16}$$

where $RV$ = Random Value (between $t_j^{\min}$ and $t_j^{\max}$).

## 4   Application Examples

C++ programs have been written and executed using a computer with Intel Xeon CPU E5440 @ 2.83 GHz, 8 GB of RAM. For GA, the MIT GA Library [22] are used and adapted to the problem.

### 4.1   Example 1: Comparison with [7] and [12]

In this example, PUMA560 robot is used. For more details about the example characteristics; refer to [7], [12].

In this example, only kinematic constraints are considered and resolved using PGA1 & PGA2. Many combination of crossover and mutation rates are done to find the best combination that gives the minimum time.

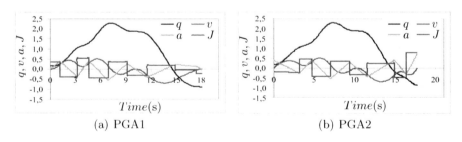

(a) PGA1                              (b) PGA2

**Fig. 1.** Joint 1: $q$=Positions [rad], $v$=Velocities [rad/s], $a$=Accelerations [rad/s$^2$], and $J$=Jerks [rad/s$^3$]

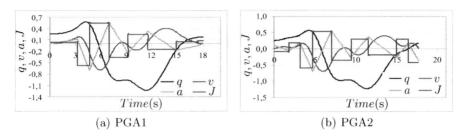

(a) PGA1                                (b) PGA2

**Fig. 2.** Joint 2: $q$=Positions [rad], $v$=Velocities [rad/s], $a$=Accelerations [rad/s$^2$], and $J$=Jerks [rad/s$^3$]

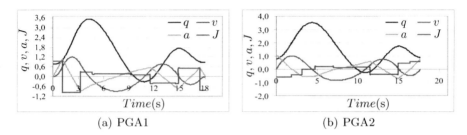

(a) PGA1                                (b) PGA2

**Fig. 3.** Joint 3: $q$=Positions [rad], $v$=Velocities [rad/s], $a$=Accelerations [rad/s$^2$], and $J$=Jerks [rad/s$^3$]

**Table 1.** Minimum time when $p_c = 0.95$ with different values of $p_m$

|  |  | Mutation |  |  |  |  |  |
|---|---|---|---|---|---|---|---|
|  |  | 0.001 | 0.01 | 0.05 | 0.1 | 0.2 | 0.3 | 0.4 |
|  | [12] | 20.156 | 19.880 | 18.211 | 18.226 | 18.929 | 18.957 | 19.062 |
| Time (sec.) | PGA1 | 19.159 | 19.578 | 18.010 | 18.205 | 18.121 | 18.039 | 18.162 |
|  | PGA2 | 18.091 | 17.726 | 17.706 | 17.971 | 17.896 | 17.897 | 17.931 |
| Average Comp. Time(s) |  | 1128 | 1714 | 6339 | 9857 | 19267 | 29625 | 45192 |

In Figures (1-3), the smoothness of the joint position and velocity curves can be noticed. Moreover, the motion doesn't violate the kinematic limits.

Observing the results in Table(1), the minimum time found for PGA1 is 18.01 s. and for PGA2 is 17.706 s. at $p_c = 0.95$ and $p_m = 0.05$, while the minimum time obtained by [12] is 18.211, and by [7] is 18.451. Besides, the rest of results in Table(1) are better than the [12] results. In addition, the results obtained when $p_c = 0.35$, 0.65 and $p_m = 0.01$ and 0.05 are 18.112 and 18.191 for PGA1, 18.087 and 18.009 for PGA2 respectively, which are better than [12] results 18.356 and 18.258.

## 4.2   Example 2: With Dynamic Constraints

In this example, only dynamic constraints are considered and solved using PGA1 with $P_c = 0.95$ and $P_m = 0.05$. The sequence of configurations used is the same one used in the previous example. The robot parameters and dynamic limits are extracted from [15]. The minimum time is found to be 5.2187 seconds.

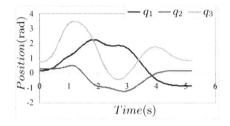

**Fig. 4.** Joint Position in Joints 1, 2, 3

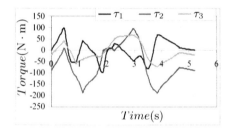

**Fig. 5.** Joint Velocity in Joints 1, 2, 3

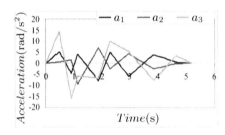

**Fig. 6.** Joint Acceleration in Joints 1, 2, 3

**Fig. 7.** Joint Torque in Joints 1, 2, 3

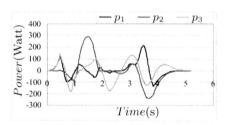

**Fig. 8.** Joint Power in Joints 1, 2, 3

Observing Figures (4-8), the motion doesn't violate the constraints. Moreover, it can be considered that the execution time achieved is reasonable, since the robots actuators saturation are achieved, obtaining a high performance.

## 5   Conclusions

A parallel-populations genetic algorithm procedure with migration technique has been developed to find the minimum trajectory time of a manipulator with cubic spline trajectories with different end conditions. The presented algorithm has been validated and evaluated by comparing the results with the results of other works of other authors. The minimum time values obtained using the introduced procedure are better than the values presented by [7] and [12].

Moreover, the presented algorithm is capable to solve the minimum time trajectory problems with dynamic constraints as seen in example 2.

In further work, it will be interesting to apply the presenting parallel-populations genetic algorithm procedure to trajectories with different interpolation functions, such as: $5^{th}$-order B-splines, harmonic, etc.

# References

1. Saramago, S.F.P., Steffen Jr., V.: Optimization of the trajectory planning of robot manipulators taking into account the dynamics of the system. Mechanism and Machine Theory 33(7), 883–894 (1998)
2. Saramago, S.F.P., Steffen Jr., V.: Dynamic optimization for the trajectory planning of robot manipulators in the presence of obstacles. J. Brazilian Soc. Mech. Sci. 21(3), 1–17 (1999)
3. Saramago, S.F.P., Steffen Jr., V.: Optimal trajectory planning of robot manipulators in the presence of moving obstacles. Mechanism and Machine Theory 35(8), 1079–1094 (2000)
4. Saramago, S.F.P., Steffen Jr., V.: Trajectory modeling of robot manipulators in the presence of obstacles. J. Optim. Theory Appl. 110(1), 17–34 (2001)
5. Saramago, S.F.P., Ceccareli, M.: An optimum robot path planning with payload constraints. Robotica 20, 395–404 (2002)
6. Luh, J.Y.S., Lin, C.-S.: Optimal path planning for mechanical manipulators. ASME J. DYN. Syst. Meas. Contr. 102, 142–151 (1981)
7. Lin, C.-S., Chang, P.R., Luh, J.Y.S.: Formulation and optimization of cubic polynomial joint trajectories for industrial manipulators. IEEE Trans. Automat. Contr. AC-28(12), 1066–1074 (1983)
8. Thompson, M., Patel, R.: Formulation of joint trajectories for industrial robots using B-splines. IEEE Trans. Indus. Electr. 34, 192–199 (1987)
9. Gasparetto, A., Zanotto, V.: A new method for smooth trajectory planning of robot manipulators. Mechanism and Machine Theory 42, 455–471 (2007)
10. Wang, C.H., Horng, J.G.: Constrained minimum-time path planning for robot manipulators via virtual knots of the cubic B-Spline functions. IEEE Trans. Automat. Contr. 35(35), 573–577 (1990)
11. Jamhour, E., André, P.J.: Planning smooth trajectories along parametric paths. Mathematics and Computers in Simulation 41, 615–626 (1996)
12. Tse, K.-M., Wang, C.-H.: Evolutionary Optimization of Cubic Polynomial Joint Trajectories for Industrial Robots. In: IEEE International Conference on Systems, Man, and Cybernetics, San Diego, CA, USA, vol. 4, pp. 3272–3276 (1998)
13. Rubio, F.J., Valero, F.J., Suñer, J.L., Mata, V.: Simultaneous algorithm to solve the trajectory planning problem. Mechanism and Machine Theory 44, 1910–1922 (2009)
14. Rubio, F.J., Valero, F.J., Suñer, J.L.: The simultaneous algorithm and the best interpolation function for trajectory planning. Industrial Robot: An International Journal 37(5), 441–451 (2010)

15. Chettibi, T., Lehtihet, H.E., Haddad, M., Hanchi, S.: Minimum cost trajectory planning for industrial robots. European Journal of Mechanics A/Solids 23, 703–715 (2004)
16. Aurelio, P.: Global minimum-jerk trajectory planning of robot manipulators. IEEE Trans. Indus. Electr. 47(1), 140–149 (2000)
17. Elnagar, A., Hussein, A.: On optimal constrained trajectory planning in 3D environments. Robot. Auton. Syst. 33(44), 195–206 (2000)
18. Ata, A.A., Myo, R.T.: Optimal Point-to-Point Trajectory Tracking of Redundant Manipulators using Generalized Pattern Search. International Journal of Advanced Robotic Systems 2(3), 239–244 (2005)
19. Saravanan, R., Ramabalan, S.: Evolutionary Minimum Cost Trajectory Planning for Industrial Robots. International Journal of Advanced Robotic Systems 52, 45–77 (2008)
20. Saravanan, R., Ramabalan, S., Balamurugan, C., Subash, A.: Evolutionary Trajectory Planning for an Industrial Robot. International Journal of Automation and Computing 7(2), 190–198 (2010)
21. Abu-Dakka, F.: Trajectory Planning for Industrial Robot Using Genetic Algorithms. Doctorate Thesis, Departamento Ingeniería Mecánica y de Materiales, Universidad Politécnica de Valencia. Valencia, Spain (2011)
22. Wall, M.: GAlib: A C++ Library of Genetic Algorithm Components. MIT, Cambridge (1996), http://lancet.mit.edu/ga

# Appendix

The Values of $a_{ij}$ and $y_i$ in the (7).

$$a_{11} = 3h_1 + 2h_2 + \frac{h_1^2}{h_2}, \qquad a_{12} = h_2, \qquad a_{21} = h_2 - \frac{h_1^2}{h_2}$$

$$a_{22} = 2(h_2 + h_3)$$

$$a_{23} = h_3$$

$$a_{32} = h_3$$

$$a_{33} = 2(h_3 + h_4)$$

$$a_{34} = h_4$$

$$a_{n-3,n-4} = h_{n-3}$$

$$a_{n-3,n-3} = 2(h_{n-3} + hn - 2)$$

$$a_{n-3,n-2} = h_{n-2} - \frac{h_{n-1}^2}{h_{n-2}}$$

$$a_{n-2,n-3} = h_{n-2}$$

$$a_{n-2,n-2} = 3h_{n-1} + 2h_{n-2} + \frac{h_{n-1}^2}{h_{n-2}}$$

$$y_1 = 6\left(\frac{q_3}{h_2} + \frac{q_1}{h_1}\right) - 6\left(\frac{1}{h_1} + \frac{1}{h_2}\right)\left(q_1 + h_1\dot{q}_1 + \frac{h_1^2}{3}\ddot{q}_1\right) - h_1\ddot{q}_1$$

$$y_2 = \frac{6}{h_2}\left(q_1 + h_1\dot{q}_1 + \frac{h_1^2}{3}\ddot{q}_1\right) + \frac{6q_4}{h_3} - 6\left(\frac{1}{h_2} + \frac{1}{h_3}\right)q_3$$

$$y_i = 6\left(\frac{q_{i+1} - q_i}{h_i} - \frac{q_i - q_{i-1}}{h_{i-1}}\right)$$

$$y_{n-3} = \frac{6}{h_{n-2}}\left(q_n - h_{n-1}\dot{q}_n + \frac{h_{n-1}^2}{3}\ddot{q}_n\right) - 6\left(\frac{1}{h_{n-2}} + \frac{1}{h_{n-3}}\right)q_{n-2} + \frac{6q_{n-3}}{h_{n-3}}$$

$$y_{n-2} = -6\left(\frac{1}{h_{n-1}} + \frac{1}{h_{n-2}}\right)\left(q_n - h_{n-1}\dot{q}_n + \frac{h_{n-1}^2}{3}\ddot{q}_n\right) + 6\left(\frac{q_n}{h_{n-1}} + \frac{q_{n-2}}{h_{n-2}}\right) - h_{n-1}\ddot{q}_n$$

# Integrative Path Planning and Motion Control for Handling Large Components

Rainer Müller, Martin Esser, and Markus Janssen

Laboratory for Machine Tools and Production Engineering (WZL),
Chair of Assembly Systems, RWTH Aachen University
Steinbachstr. 19, 52074 Aachen, Germany
{r.mueller,m.esser,m.janssen}@wzl.rwth-aachen.de

**Abstract.** For handling large components a large workspace and high precision are required. In order to simplify the path planning for automated handling systems, this task can be divided into global, regional and local motions. Accordingly, different types of robots are used to fulfill the kinematic requirements. An integrative path planning and motion control concept has been developed, which simplifies the commissioning of handling systems consisting of different robots. It combines the tasks of path planning and motion control by an integrative approach, as the motion data of a simulation tool is directly used for controlling the real robots. An overlying control module coordinates and distributes the data to the robots. This modular control concept facilitates the flexibility which is needed to build up a reconfigurable robot system for customized handling of large components.

**Keywords:** path planning, motion control, robotic assembly application, integrative production.

## 1 Introduction

There has been a fundamental change in the conditions governing the manufacturing industry in recent years. Progressive globalization, rapid technological development and changes in the availability of resources at reasonable costs are responsible for increasing complexity and dynamics in the industry and the industrial environment [1, 2]. The consequences are a further reduction of product life cycles, a sustained increase in the variety of products and constant pressure to cut manufacturing costs [3]. Assembly systems and processes are particularly exposed to these pressures, as they add a large part of the value in the manufacturing process.

## 2 Motivation

Progressive development in the field of industrial robotics has led to a variety of new applications in recent years, saving jobs in high-wage countries by increasing the level of automation. Traditional demands on handling systems are currently undergoing

S. Jeschke, H. Liu, and D. Schilberg (Eds.): ICIRA 2011, Part I, LNAI 7101, pp. 93–101, 2011.
© Springer-Verlag Berlin Heidelberg 2011

change. In the past, higher load capacity and speed as well as greater precision have been demanded. However, priorities are increasingly shifting towards customized production and flexible solutions to component-dependent problems. Currently available handling systems frequently cannot fulfill these demands and complex tasks [4].

Against this background, one current problem is the handling of large components, some of which have no intrinsic rigidity. Such components are used in aerospace systems, shipbuilding, wind turbine construction and the production of solar panels. The trend is predominantly discernable in aircraft construction, where large shell elements in carbon-fiber reinforced plastics are being used for aircraft fuselages [5]. High precision and a large workspace are required. A single robot is usually not capable of moving the component without exposing it to any forces. Large jigs are therefore used, rendering the system very inflexible and expensive [6].

Cooperating robots represent a more versatile approach to the problem described as inflexible jigs can be replaced when the component is gripped and supported at different points by several robots [7].

## 3      Path Planning and Motion Control for Robots

Before a robot can be used in an application, its motion has to be planned and programmed. During path planning the geometry of a robot motion is determined through different motion types. In general, the motion types can be distinguished in point-to-point (PTP), multi-point (MP) and continuous path (CP) interpolation. The robot trajectory results from combining and linking several segments to the path. PTP interpolation is used for rapid movements between two points. As the interpolation is done for each joint of the robot, the resulting geometrical curve is hardly predictable and of secondary interest. In a MP interpolation the path is described by several points between initial and final point. The robot moves between via points in the motion type PTP. The resulting trajectory is more predictable than a PTP motion, but its geometry is not defined exactly. When a robot has to move on a straight line, on a circle or a smooth curve (spline), the trajectory has to be described by a mathematical equation. These motion types are summarized as CP interpolation.

Path planning and programming of cooperating robots can be a complex and time-consuming task. In order not to stop a producing assembly station, this task is nowadays usually done in an offline simulation tool, where a virtual production cell is modeled and virtual robots are programmed. Before the programs can be transferred to the real robot controllers and used in a production cell, they have to be adapted in the real environment because of geometrical deviations and tolerances of the equipment.

One present way to simplify programming is to derive the robot motions from the path of the handled component. The trajectory of each robot can be calculated from the gripping point at the object that has to be handled. The transformation of the objects' basis to each gripping point is considered constant during the motion and the resulting trajectory describes the movement of the tool center point (TCP) of each robot. In a final step the TCP-trajectory is transformed to the motion control of the servo drives by the inverse kinematic of each robot. For synchronization and coordination one robot is in control and the other robots follow, which is known as 'master-slave-principle' [8].

Derived from the master-slave-principle, robot manufacturers use different hardware concepts for their cooperating robots (Fig. 1).

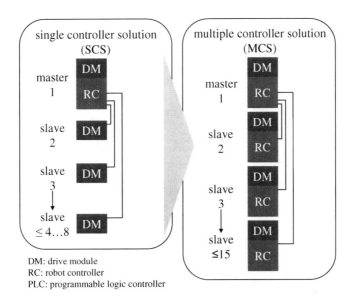

**Fig. 1.** Hardware concepts for cooperating robots

As the coordination is controlled by a master robot, all calculations and transformation can be executed on the master controller. In this 'single controller solution' only additional drive modules are required for additional robots, which reduces costs when the robot system needs to be expanded [9]. Furthermore, synchronization between the robots is very easy and guarantees high accuracy [10]. As a disadvantage of this concept one can say that all robots are dependant of the master robot and that the number of robots is limited from four (e.g. ABB) to eight (e.g. Motoman) due to controller capacity [9, 11]. In order to overcome this disadvantage, other robot manufacturers like KUKA use a 'multiple controller solution', where every robot retains its own controller. As the calculations and transformations are shared on several controllers, much more robots can be coordinated. But similar to the single controller solution, all robot controllers need a master for synchronization. The communication between master and slaves is done via high-speed local network (Ethernet), which causes a large amount of data traffic and limits this concept to 15 robots presently [8].

## 4     Integrative Path Planning and Control Concept

For the handling of large components a large workspace as well as high precision is required. In the case of objects which have no intrinsic rigidity also the application of forces can be necessary to form the object into a specific shape. To fulfill these requirements, the path planning task can be divided into a three-level procedure (Fig. 2). At first a global motion has to be planned to cover a large workspace and to prepare the robot system for the next step, a regional motion to position the handled object. Finally a local motion may be necessary to compensate geometrical deviations e.g. by applying forces to the object. This layout leads to a handling system consisting of different types of robots for different movements, e.g. gantries for global, vertical articulated arms for regional and tools for local motions.

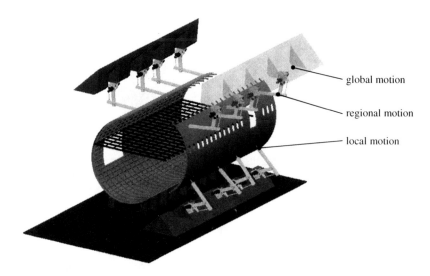

**Fig. 2.** Global, regional and local path planning for large components

In order to provide interoperability between different robots, a modular control system for coordination and synchronization has been developed as the main contribution to the solution of controlling the heterogeneous system. The control system comprises a robot simulation tool for path planning, a central control module for coordination and several handling modules with one robot controller each. In other modular concepts programming of the different robot types is done iteratively and separately for each robot, until a suitable motion has been found. In contrast to this multi-level programming the motion of all robot types is planned in one central module, which guarantees a consistent movement of the complete handling system. This control architecture enhances the flexibility and reconfigurability of existing solutions as no dependencies between the regional robots exist, which is a basic requirement for easy reconfiguration. Furthermore an integrative approach of path planning and motion control had been developed, which combines the tasks of path planning and trajectory generation in one tool. That means that the trajectories which are generated during simulation, are directly used for controlling the robots. This motion control of each robot corresponds to a multi-point interpolation (see chapter 3), where the initial, via and final points are given by the simulation data. This strategy for trajectory generation implies that the virtual environment has to be modeled in very high accuracy and that the motion data has to be transferred to the robot controllers very fast (ideally real-time). This approach replaces the efforts for adjusting the robot programs in the real environment and simplifies the commissioning of robot applications significantly, which is an important advantage, especially for frequently changing tasks.

Starting point of the path planning is the motion path of the handling object which is provided by the user or the handling task. On the basis of the object trajectory a suitable system configuration, i.e. the type, number and base position of appropriate robots, can be determined. The resulting trajectories can be checked for collisions and reachability in the virtual environment. Monitoring and adaptation of the trajectories is done manually offline. This avoids inconsistent solutions of the multi-level controller and a collision or deadlock of the handling system.

After a suitable movement has been determined, the motion data is exported from the simulation tool to a leading control module. In order to achieve smooth robot motions, it is essential to generate accurate nominal values in a fast interpolation step.

In the next step the motion data is distributed from the leading control module to the kinematic modules via real time bus system. On each robot controller a simple program is running and awaiting instructions from the leading control module. This program can cope with all possible motions, instructions and signals that might occur, and thus does not need to be adapted when a task changes.

In this approach each robot is being considered as a mechatronic module incorporating all responsibilities needed to execute a task. This approach facilitates a maximum of reconfigurability, scalability and exchangeability so that it can be applied to robots of different manufacturers and furthermore to special handling units with a standard controller. An overlying control module is used to coordinate the complete handling system. In contrast to existing control concepts for cooperating robots, this leading control module replaces the master robot and leads to equality between all robots, which is a basic requirement for the modular approach and unrestricted reconfiguration. The workpiece that is handled serves as a virtual master.

In this concept the data of the offline programmed motion is directly used for task execution without adapting, e.g. by online teaching. This approach extremely simplifies the programming of cooperating robots but requires a high accuracy of the virtual environment. This can only be guaranteed by a holistic identification of the assembly cell after reconfiguration [12].

# 5    Implementation

The concept of integrative path planning and motion control was developed and implemented on a demonstrator. A 3D robot simulation tool 'Easy-Rob' is used as a virtual environment for path planning, simulation-based programming and trajectory generation of the handling system [13]. Furthermore, a task-specific configuration can be determined and checked for collisions and reachability within this tool. In contrast to conventional simulation tools of robot manufacturers, where an executable robot program is created offline and transferred to the robot controller, in this approach the data of each robot TCP is being transferred. This facilitates independency of any specific robot language and allows interoperability between different robot manufacturers. These capabilities are being be validated in current research. Easy-Rob had been selected, because it provides an open software interface, which is vital for data exchange with the control module. The simulation tool runs on a PC which is connected to the central control module via TCP/IP Ethernet for transferring the trajectories of the handling modules.

The control system of the handling modules are supplied by 'B&R Automation' [14]. Each kinematic unit consists of its own control cabinet with standard components to provide basic robot capabilities for kinematic calculation. Coordination and synchronization is done by a superordinated controller in a separate control cabinet. The kinematic modules are connected to the central controller via 'Powerlink', an interface with real-time capabilities.

The challenge of this path planning and control concept is to guarantee an efficient and safe communication between distributed control systems. Consistent motion data between the simulation tool and the robot controller is required to achieve smooth robot movements. One critical factor is the data transfers from the simulation tool via TCP/IP Ethernet to the controller. First analysis show, that the central controller receives data in a cycle time of about 12 ms. In current examinations the signal flow, beginning at the trajectory generation in Easy-Rob and ending at the converter of each drive, is being analyzed in order to improve the performance of the control system. Further tasks in the field of communication are safety issues, as an error or emergency stop in one handling module has to be recognized by the central controller, which then has to stop the other robots quickly. In order to continue work after an emergency stop, the simulation systems has to be stopped and updated before new motion data is being transferred to the central controller.

For handling large scale objects with cooperating robots, simple handling units have been developed which enhance the flexibility and reconfigurability of existing solutions by a consistent modular approach. In order to allow easy reconfiguration by a worker without any mechanical support, the handling modules are designed light-weight and less massive than conventional industrial robots. Further reduction of weight is obtained by a simplified drive concept, as not all six joints of the kinematic modules are actuated by a servo drive but remain passive. Due to the low weight the assembly arms can be rearranged by a worker for each task, so that an automated handling system can be configured even for small series. The handling modules for regional motions are integrated into an existing modular assembly system which consists of an industrial robot and surrounding modular assembly processes (Fig. 3).

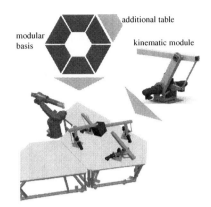

**Fig. 3.** Design of the demonstrator

However, small robots can provide high precision, but only a small workspace especially when they have to handle an object collaboratively and may hinder each other. In the future, the system will be enhanced by attaching the handling modules to a gantry in order to expand the workspace and to handle larger components.

This handling system provides more degrees of reconfigurability than a system with conventional robots. This fact has to be considered in the control system for the assembly platform. As the number and position of the arms can be varied for each handling task, the current system configuration has to be identified and considered for the control of the robots.

## 6 Application

The objective is the implementation of a platform concept which can be easily configured to new tasks in a production environment where large components are handled. One test application of the referenced assembly platform is stringer installation in aircraft production (Fig. 4). In this case, challenges arise predominantly from the spherical curvature of the shell components and the accompanying differently sized stringers. A further difficulty is that the stringers, which are up to 20 m long, are flexible and therefore have to be supported by additional grippers.

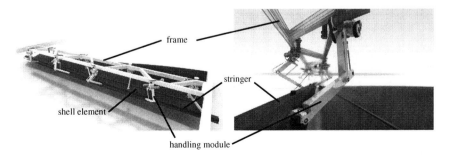

**Fig. 4.** A possible configuration for the stringer handling

In a cooperative handling the stringer can be passed on to another kinematic unit before it leaves the workspace of a kinematic unit. Thus, large workspace can be covered by relatively small handling units. This transfer of components usually cannot be achieved cost-effectively by conventional industrial robots, due to the high number of required kinematic units.

Compared to conventional solutions, this new handling concept also offers potential to other sectors in the industry. The new technology is particularly suitable for handling flexible components which can only be manipulated by gripping at several points. Possible examples are the assembly of wind turbine components or rail wagons.

# 7     Summary and Outlook

Path planning for large components can be divided into global, regional and local motions to achieve a large workspace as well as high precision of a handling system. An integrative path planning and control concept has been developed, which simplifies the commissioning of cooperating robots by combining the tasks of programming and trajectory generation in an offline simulation tool. This implies a high accuracy of the virtual environment. For this purpose, a measurement system will be added to the concept to make alignment needless during set-up of the handling modules, by adapting the control program automatically and therefore reduce set-up time.

The high level of flexibility, which is necessary for the handling of large components, is obtained by a modular structure of the multi robot application, where all robots are treated as mechatronic objects and are being coordinated by a central control module. The control concept in combination with simple kinematic units facilitates an easy reconfiguration of the handling system, so that it can be adapted to the requirements of different tasks and processes. Defining the handling object as the master of a motion makes it possible to compensate deviations of the workpiece directly by an inline measurement system. This approach replaces re-teaching of the robots to achieve high position accuracy and simplifies programming of the handling system.

# References

1. Möller, N.: Bestimmung der Wirtschaftlichkeit wandlungsfähiger Produktionssysteme. In: Forschungsbericht IWB, vol. 212 (2008)
2. Müller, R., et al.: Montagetechnik und –organisation. Apprimus Verlag, Aachen (2009)
3. Lotter, B.: Montage in der industriellen Produktion. Ein Handbuch für die Praxis. Springer, Berlin (2006)
4. Nyhuis, P.: Wandlungsfähige Produktionssysteme. Heute die Industrie von morgen gestalten Garbsen, PZH, Produktionstechn. Zentrum (2008)
5. Licha, A.: Flexible Montageautomatisierung zur Komplettmontage flächenhafter Produktstrukturen durch kooperierende Industrieroboter. Meisenbach, Bamberg (2003)

6.  Wollnack, J., Stepanek, P.: Form correction, positioning and orientation guidance for a flexible and automated assembly of large components. wt Werkstattstechnik online 94, 414–421 (2004)
7.  Feldmann, K., Ziegler, C., Michl, M.: Motion control for cooperating robots in the field of assembly automation - Simplified programming of multi-robot systems. wt werkstattstechnik online 97, 713 (2007)
8.  Schulze, J.: Production robots are becoming versatile team players. KUKA Press Release (2006)
9.  Bredin, C.: Team-mates – ABB MultiMove functionality heralds a new era in robot applications. ABB Review 1/2005.9
10. Stoddard, K., et al.: Method and control system for controlling a plurality of robots. Patent No.: US 6,804,580 B1 (October 12, 2004)
11. Motoman, DX100 Robot Controller Specifications (July 14, 2010), http://www.motoman.com/datasheets/DX100%20Controller.pdf
12. Müller, R., Esser, M., Janßen, C., Vette, M.: System-Identifikation für Montagezellen – Erhöhte Genauigkeit und bedarfsgerechte Rekonfiguration. wt Werkstattstechnik online 100 9, S687–S691 (2010) ISSN 1436-4980
13. Easy-Rob 3D Robot Simulation Tool, http://www.easy-rob.com
14. Bernecker + Rainer Industrie Elektronik Ges.m.b.H., http://www.br-automation.com

# Automatic Configuration of Robot Systems – Upward and Downward Integration<sup></sup>

Gunther Reinhart, Stefan Hüttner, and Stefan Krug

Institute for Machine Tools and Industrial Management (*iwb*)
Technische Universität München (TUM), Boltzmannstraße 15, 85748 Garching, Germany
Stefan.Huettner@iwb.tum.de

**Abstract.** This paper covers the automatic configuration of robot systems under consideration of its upward integration into higher automation levels and the downward integration of peripheral devices into the robot control. First the use of automatic configuration in current production environments is examined, followed by an analysis of the paradigm shift in automation technology. Subsequently approaches for machine readable functional descriptions of industrial equipment are outlined.

**Keywords:** Robot, Reconfiguration, Plug & Produce.

## 1 Introduction

Production technology holds a central role in the economies of developed countries and accounts for a decisive proportion of public wealth, but the continuing progress of economical globalization increases the competitive pressures (cf. [1]). Especially in markets for high quality products, companies are facing a steadily rising demand for customisation. This and the increasingly fast technological development induce shorter product lifecycles. Thus manufacturers of e. g. end-user products demand more flexible and changeable production systems from their respective production technology suppliers. Their goal is to reuse equipment for multiple products or different product generations and thereby to lower overall investment to optimize profitability and competitiveness. Contrary to this, the usual investment planning for robot systems demands its amortisation within the first application. Future approaches have to take the whole life-cycle into account (cf. [2]).

To lay the foundations for an automatic configuration, certain challenges arise. The information interfaces connecting the modules, like bus systems, are often vendor-specific and heterogeneous – even within industrial branches. Furthermore centralized data management in the projection phase is the current state of the art. Existing widely

---

<sup>*</sup> The authors would like to express their gratitude towards the German Federal Ministry for Education and Research (BMBF) and the Project Management Agency Karlsruhe (PTKA) for the funding of the research project plawamo (Planning, Design and Operation of Changeable Assembly Systems). The results presented in this paper would not have been possible without their support.

S. Jeschke, H. Liu, and D. Schilberg (Eds.): ICIRA 2011, Part I, LNAI 7101, pp. 102–111, 2011.
© Springer-Verlag Berlin Heidelberg 2011

used programming languages are usually proprietary and vendor specific. Therefore the benefits of modularization cannot be utilized to the extent technologically possible and economically profitable.

## 2     Scope of the Paper

This paper covers the automatic configuration of robot systems and focuses on the upward integration of these systems into PLC-controlled production units and the downward integration of e. g. sensors and tools into the robot control (cf. Figure 1).

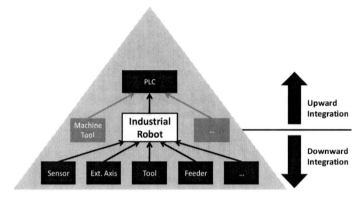

**Fig. 1.** Considered Integration Directions

Generally the configuration of robot systems is a mechatronic challenge. This implies that interfaces of mechanics, electrics and information technology have to be taken into account. Especially the mechanic and electronic interfaces of current robots are partly standardized and therefore can enable easy modularization. (cf. e. g. [3]). However, the modularization of mechanic and electronic components is often not reflected by the architecture of the robot control.

Thus to enable automatic configuration (Plug & Produce) the existing deficits of robot systems will be identified and new solutions for the domains of modularization and functional descriptions will be presented.

## 3     Existing Approaches

Existing approaches can be categorized into upward configuration to integrate robots into superior controls and downward configuration integrating different peripheral devices into the robot control.

**Upward Configuration:** Within the research project OSACA (Open System Architecture for Controls within Automation Systems) a software reference architecture was developed which allows an easier connection of controls (numeric control, robot control, programmable logic controller). Thus a vendor independent development of software modules is enabled and the integration effort for reconfiguration of different controls is reduced. [4]

The aim of the research project SIARAS (Skill-based Inspection and Assembly for Reconfigurable Automation Systems) was exploration and development of a formal description language for the characterization of the abilities of a production cell and the requirements of the production processes. By means of a so-called "skill server" an automatic comparison between the abilities of the devices and the production requirements is conducted. This can reduce the necessary development effort for reconfiguration. [5-7]

**Downward Configuration:** An additional communication layer was developed and integrated into the communication model in the research project PAPAS (Plug-And-Play Antriebs- und Steuerungskonzepte für die Produktion von morgen). This enables the integration of different devices and information about their respective device profiles to be integrated into a bus system within a specific PAPAS-application. However, this modification of the classic layer model of communication has to be integrated in all connected devices and furthermore in the cell control. Programming with "classic" programming methods is subsequently restricted. [8-9]

XIRP (XML Interface für Roboter und Peripherie) is an XML-based protocol which has been published by the VDMA (Verband Deutscher Maschinen- und Anlagenbauer). It was predominantly developed to simplify the integration of image processing systems into a robot by means of standardization. [10-11].

SMErobot developed on the basis of XIRP and PAPAS a new cell control and a programming environment, which enables the provision of the functionalities of connected devices. Thereby a cell control is mandatory since the robot is also considered as a device with certain functionalities. [12-15]

New approaches for automatic reconfiguration for robot cells and their equipment on the one hand, controls and Manufacturing Execution Systems (MES) on the other hand have already been presented by the authors of this paper. They introduced a five-step-model for reconfiguration (cf. Figure 2), built and examined different realistic setups and introduced different solutions for automatic configuration of an Industrial Ethernet based field bus system. [16]

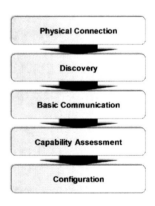

**Fig. 2.** Steps in Plug and Produce Network Integration

# 4     Conceptual Design

The conceptual design defines fundamentals necessary for the automatic configuration of industrial robots for upward and downward integration. For this purpose, three important aspects will be examined: (1) The necessity for changeable production systems denotes a paradigm shift from centralized (Top-Down) to decentralized (Bottom-Up) data management. (2) This decentralization induces requests regarding modularization and thus requirements for the used devices. (3) Within the Bottom-Up approach the requirements and functions of the devices have to be described in a machine readable form.

## 4.1    Paradigm Shift

On the one hand the term configuration can be used for the retooling of production systems. This usually addresses the flexibility of the system, hence its ability to be adjusted along previously defined flexibility bands (e. g. work piece size, tools, etc.). On the other hand configuration constitutes the overall setup of a production system, thus the (re-)combination of e.g. machines, tools, robots, etc. and their respective interaction including communication and control. For the latter changeability in contrast to flexibility denominates a transformation of a production system, which was not a priori planned and considered in the production system's design phase. [17]

Robot controls are usually designed to allow an easy and user-friendly retooling process. This follows logically from the fact that most of these processes are executed by personnel from the shop floor, which in most cases have no expert knowledge in robot controls. In the case of a major change of the robot cell, e.g. the addition of external axis or a camera system for quality control, the configuration process has to be done by experts, for example specialised system integrators.

Both contemplated fields of configuration will be examined within this paper, though the overall setup will be focussed, since the challenges in this area are more complex and attained solutions therefore can be easily derived for changeover and retooling. The configuration of a control system, e.g. for a robot, can in principle be done in two distinct ways:

All information necessary for the configuration is collected within a central hub (Top-Down). This hub is frequently a projecting tool for the used control system. Necessary information about specific requirements or functionalities of the modules that need to be configured must be included within this hub. This is normally done manually and requires expert knowledge both about the system constituting the hub as well as regarding the modules which should be configured. The configuration data is created centrally and delivered to all modules. Until today, this is the standard method for system configuration (cf. [18]).

However, the need for changeable robot systems requires new methodologies to enable easy and automatic configuration. The authors propound a decentralized approach for information provision (Bottom-Up). Each module stores information about its configuration requirements and specific functionality in machine readable form. For configuration this information must be collected and analysed to derive the necessary configuration data, which then can be transferred to all modules. Contrary to the Top-Down approach, the automation of the configuration process can be easier achieved and since the necessary information is provided by the respective manufacturer of each module, the requirements regarding expert knowledge in the configuration process can be decisively reduced. Furthermore the Bottom-Up approach is better suited for changing a robot system beyond its flexibility capabilities, since the new setup is to a far extent automatically recognized and configured.

## 4.2    Characteristics of Modules

A mandatory requirement of an automatic configurable system is the functional modularization of its components. This means that all components (mechanical, electrical and software), which are needed to execute a specific function, are combined in one module. Such a module may have multiple functions and different interfaces to the environment (cf. Figure 3). Typical interface types are hardware interfaces e.g. for force transmission, electrical interfaces for power supply and software interfaces for data exchange. Here only the primary function of the interface is considered in its classification. Thus e.g. the plug of an electrical interface is not considered to be a hardware interface.

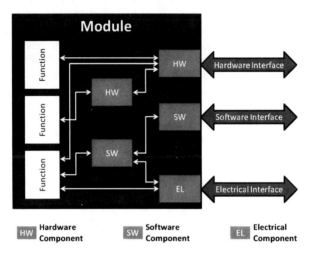

**Fig. 3.** Schematic Module Structure

With reference to the scope of this paper only software interfaces will be discussed. Since decentralized control architectures, which support the modularization approach, become more and more established many devices already fulfil the requirements of functional modularization (cf. [19]).

At the example of a pneumatic gripper, which is connected to a robot via a bus system, the functions would be open and close. The hardware components are represented by the gripper itself and the mechanical part of the valve. The electrical component is the electrical part of the valve. The software component would be the bus module which converts the bus signals to a signal for the valve.

To enable devices for automatic configuration as shown in the abovementioned approach, they have to be augmented with data and certain communication abilities. This includes the storage of device specific information on the one hand and the ability to procure this information via the network on the other hand. Since there is a multitude of devices available in the market, not all have the required capabilities to conduct the task. Especially within downward integration the capabilities are highly diverse and a classification is therefore reasonable. Three categories of devices (cf. Figure 4) can be distinguished:

(1) Complex devices with sufficient information processing capabilities and an integrated bus interface
(2) Standard devices with small information processing capabilities and an integrated bus interface
(3) Simple devices with no or little information processing capabilities and no integrated bus interface

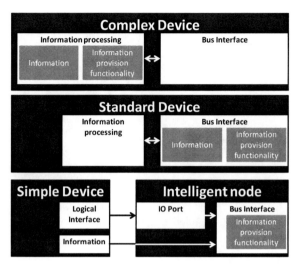

**Fig. 4.** Three Categories of Devices

**(1) Complex Devices:** In case of the use of complex devices, which have extensive information processing capabilities, e.g. an own PLC, the provision of information and its functionality can be integrated into the existing logical processing units. This has been experimentally validated at the example of a two-axis positioner equipped with an own control PLC (cf. [16]).

**(2) Standard Devices:** Standard devices usually work on a micro controller basis. This controller manages the software-sided execution of the functions and the communication with the bus interface. The ability of the controller to integrate Plug & Produce functionality is not assured. Thus, other means have to be found to integrate the necessary capability. The processing unit of the bus interface, which manages the real time data transfer and connects the interface, to e.g. the micro controller, usually has sufficient performance reserves. Hence the functionalities were adapted and integrated into the software structure of the interface's processing unit. Figure 5 shows two Industrial Ethernet based interface boards where this approach was put into practice. For this purpose standard products were used, partly extended by additional memory.

**(3) Simple Devices:** Beside the complex and standard devices, low cost sensors and actuators with no information processing capabilities, such as reed contact sensors or pneumatic valves, are frequently used in robotic applications. These components do not have an own bus interface, but are usually connected by direct wiring to the robot via I/O bus modules. Since it is not economic to equip each of these sensors or actuators with an extra processing unit – the price for a bus interface would exceed the device price by far – alternative solutions are necessary to economically enable Plug & Produce functionality for these devices.

One feasible approach is to equip the simple devices with common low cost flash memory chips (as used for example in USB memory sticks) and connect multiple devices to an intelligent I/O field bus node. This node has a bus interface and the ability of information provision. The information of the different devices can be collected and pre-processed in this intelligent node. Then the information can be allocated for automatic configuration.

**Fig. 5.** Two Industrial Ethernet based Interface Boards enabled with Plug & Produce Functionality (Manufacturers: left – IXXAT Automation GmbH; right – SYSTEC electronic GmbH)

### 4.3 Function Modelling

The modules which need to be integrated into the setup (upward or downward) have to make their functionalities available to the superior system (e.g. robot or PLC). Thereby the function modelling for upward and downward integration has in a first step been separated to meet the specific requirements.

**Function Modelling for Downward Integration (Robot Control):** There are several aspects that need to be taken into account to describe device functions for robot controls:

- Robot specific programming languages
- Robot specific restrictions on data types
- Sequential control, in contrast to PLCs' and usual devices' cyclic controls
- Setup depending addressing (IO-mapping) – Adaption of functions may be required due to setup

Current robot controls are based on a multitude of vendor-specific proprietary programming languages. To assure transferability of the proposed solution, a vendor-independent description language has to be identified. Robot manufacturer independent offline programming environments already use their own description languages for application programs and functions. Also the Industrial Robot Language (IRL) [20] provides a universal description for application-level functions. Although it has not become established within commercial robot controls, it is well suited for function modelling, since it can be converted into robot specific languages by means of post processors. The latter also applies to offline programming description languages.

With these languages a sufficient description of the device functions is possible. To consider all abovementioned aspects these functions have to be augmented with (1) setup information and (2) data about the robot system. By means of (3) information about the robot language the modelled functions can be processed to an arbitrary robot specific programming language (cf. Figure 6).

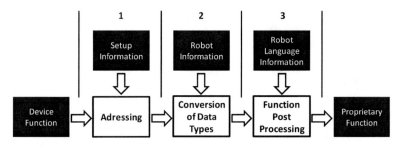

**Fig. 6.** Course of the Transformation of Vendor-Independent Function Descriptions to Proprietary Robot Functions

**Function Modelling for Upward Integration (PLC):** To integrate devices, e.g. a robot, into a more comprehensive production cell, the respective controls have to communicate with other devices controls, e.g. PLCs. Like in the case of downward integration discussed above, the robot's functionalities have to be made available to the other control systems in the cell to enable effective programming and productive operation. Some approaches for the description of industrial devices like the Electronic Device Description Language (EDDL) and Field Device Tool / Device Type manager (FDT/DTM) have been developed in recent years. [21]

In case of PLCs there are also the standardized programming languages defined in ISO IEC 61131-3, which can be utilized to provide functionalities as function blocks for the programmer [22]. This has been experimentally validated in a setup consisting of different PLC controls. One of the experimental setups allows the remote control of signal lamps via predefined function blocks. These function blocks are provided by one PLC (to which the lamps are connected via analogue I/Os) and can be accessed by any other control connected and configured to the network. The programmer is no longer required to know about the real input/output signal exchange executed by the controls via the bus system. More complicated approaches for e.g. machine tools can be accomplished in a comparable way. Even though this approach is feasible and based on established technologies it cannot provide full Plug & Produce functionality. Further device information is required to enable automatic configuration and function integration, which can either be stored in manufacturer specific way or by enhancing common description languages like EDDL.

# 5    Experimental Setup

The presented results have been developed and tested in a experimental setup with a KUKA Robot, a 2-axis-positioner (equipped with a PLC-control) and a device, representing the interface of a welding unit (equipped with a simple bus interface). POWERLINK, an Ethernet based real time bus system, was used for communication (cf. Figure7). Experiments with the described setup showed, that configuration time was reduced to a few minutes.

**Fig. 7.** Experimental Setup

# 6    Conclusions and Outlook

The focus of this paper was to examine areas which need to be addressed to achieve a fully automated configuration (Plug & Produce) of a robot system, both upward and downward. First the deficits of current projection methods have been discussed, namely the central data management and the consequential necessity for manual data integration. Here an alternative Bottom-Up approach was presented, which is more suited for changeable production systems. Regarding the modularisation of robotic systems a classification of devices concerning their communication and control performance was introduced. For all identified categories of devices solutions to implement Plug & Produce functionalities were presented. Finally the function modelling for upward and downward integration was addressed. Current description languages both in the fields of robotics and PLCs were identified. A solution for function modelling and its adaption to different robot controls has been demonstrated.

Based on these results further development will be directed to the identification of a unified function modelling language, which can be used both for robots and PLCs. The automatic integration of modelled functions into different programming environments will be further examined and tested.

## References

1. Hoffmann, H., Reinhart, G., Zäh, M.-F. (eds.): Proceedings of the Münchener Kolloquium – Innovationen für die Produktion, Munich, Germany, October 6. Utz, Munich (2010)
2. Hägele, M., Skordas, T., Sagert, S., Bischoff, R., Brogardh, T., Dresselhaus, M.: White paper – Industrial Robot Automation: EURON – European Robotics Network (2005)
3. Deutsches Institut für Normung (ed.): DIN 11593: Automatische Wechselsysteme für Endeffektoren. Beuth Verlag GmbH, Berlin (1996)
4. N.N.: OSACA - Open System Architecture for Controls within Automation Systems – OSACA I & II Final Report (1996)

5. Bengel, M., Pflüger, M.: Cell-Controller für rekonfigurierbare Produktionsanlagen – Durchgängige Prozesskette von Benutzereingabe bis Maschinenebene. In: Robotik 2008 Leistungsstand, Anwendungen, Visionen, Trends, Munich, Germany, June 11-12. VDI-Verlag, Düsseldorf (2008)

6. Haage, M., Nilsson, A., Nugues, P.: Assisting Industrial Robot Setup and Instruction. In: 5th International Conference on Informatics in Control, Automation and Robotics (ICINCO 2008), Funchal, Madeira, Portugal, pp. 263–270. INSTICC Press, Setúbal (2008)

7. Research Project SIARAS, http://www.ipa.fraunhofer.de/index.php?id=90

8. Plank, G., Reintsema, D., Grunwald, G., Otter, M., Kurze, M., Löhning, M., Reiner, M., Zimmermann, U., Schreiber, G., Weiss, M., Bischoff, R., Fellhauer, B., Notheis, T., Barklage, T.: PAPAS - Plug and Play Antriebs- und Steuerungskonzepte für die Produktion von Morgen – Forschung für die Produktion von morgen Schlüsselkomponente Handhabungstechnik, Final Report (2006)

9. Grunwald, G., Plank, G., Reintsema, D., Zimmermann, U.: Communication, Configuration, Application – The three layer concept for Plug-and-Produce. In: 5th International Conference on Informatics in Control, Automation and Robotics (ICINCO 2008), Funchal, Madeira, Portugal, May 11-15, pp. 255–262. INSTICC Press, Setúbal (2008)

10. Sagert, S.: Neue VDMA-Einheitsblätter. VDMA Nachrichten 11, 30 (2006)

11. VDMA-Einheitsblatt 66430-1 – XML-basiertes Kommunikationsprotokoll für Industrieroboter und prozessorgestützte Peripheriegeräte (XIRP). Beuth, Berlin (2006)

12. Verl, A., Naumann, M.: Kleine Losgrößen im Griff – Flexible Steuerungsarchitekturen für Automatisierungssysteme (2008), http://www.elektrotechnik.vogel.de

13. Naumann, M., Wegener, K., Schraft, R.D., Lachello, L.: Robot Cell Integration by Means of Application-P'n'P. In: VDI (ed.) Proceedings of the Joint Conference on Robotics, VDI-Berichte, pp. 93–100. VDI, Düsseldorf (2006)

14. Naumann, M., Wegener, K., Schraft, R.D.: Control Architecture for Robot Cells to Enable Plug'n'Produce. In: International Conference on Robotics and Automation (ICRA 2007), Rome, Italy, April 10-14, pp. 287–292 (2007)

15. Verl, A., Naumann, M.: Plug'n'Produce-Steuerungsarchitektur für Roboterzellen. wt-Werkstattstechnik online 5, 384–390 (2008)

16. Reinhart, G., Krug, S., Hüttner, S., Mari, Z., Riedelbauch, F., Schlögel, M.: Automatic Configuration (Plug & Produce) of Industrial Ethernet Networks. In: Cardoso, J.R. (ed.) 9th IEEE/IAS International Conference on Industry Applications (INDUSCON 2010), Sao Paulo, Brazil, November 8-10, pp. 1–6 (2010)

17. Nyhuis, P., Reinhart, G., Abele, E. (eds.): Wandlungsfähige Produktionssysteme - Heute die Industrie von morgen gestalten. PZH Produktionstechnisches Zentrum GmbH, Garbsen (2008)

18. Dietrich, D., Thomesse, J.: Fieldbus systems and their applications 2003. In: Proceedings from the 5th IFAC International Conference on Fieldbus Systems and their Applications, Aveiro, Portugal, July 7-9, Elsevier, Oxford (2003)

19. Swanson, D.-C.: Signal processing for intelligent sensor systems. Marcel Dekker, New York (2000)

20. Deutsches Institut für Normung (ed.): DIN 66312 Industrieroboter - Programmiersprache - Industrial Robot Language (IRL). Beuth, Berlin (1996)

21. Kastner, W., Kastner-Masilko, F.: EDDL inside FDT/DTM. In: Proceedings, September 22-24, pp. 365–368. Institution of Electrical and Electronics Engineers, Piscataway (2004)

22. Deutsches Institut für Normung (ed.): DIN 61131-3 Speicherprogrammierbare Steuerungen; Teil 3: Programmiersprachen. Beuth, Berlin (1992)

# Process and Human Safety in Human-Robot-Interaction – A Hybrid Assistance System for Welding Applications

Carsten Thomas[1], Felix Busch[2], Bernd Kuhlenkoetter[1], and Jochen Deuse[2]

[1] TU Dortmund, Industrial Robotics and Production Automation, Leonhard-Euler-Str. 2,
44227 Dortmund, Germany
[2] TU Dortmund, Chair of Industrial Engineering, Leonhard-Euler-Str. 5,
44227 Dortmund, Germany
{carsten3.thomas,felix.busch,bernd.kuhlenkoetter,
jochen.deuse}@tu-dortmund.de

**Abstract.** The paper focuses on work and process safety in robot assisted welding operations and discusses technical means to ensure a safe and ergonomic human-robot-interaction with overlapping workspaces. It discusses the development of a multi-robot assistance system to reduce labour-intensive manual handling of heavy parts in welding of tubular and framework constructions. The research is part of the project "rorarob" [1],[2],[3] and is supported by a demonstrator at TU Dortmund University. Parts of the research are contemporaneous published in [4].

**Keywords:** Process Safety, Human Safety, Multi Robot Assistance System, Human-Robot-Interaction (HRI), Welding.

## 1 Introduction

The welding of tubular and framework constructions has to be done in several industries and is widely spread in small and medium-sized businesses. In comparison to mass production, where a high degree of automation is used, assemblies in small batches are normally welded manually. This is based on high investment costs for automated systems and efforts like programming tasks. But the manual done welding operations and additional handling tasks are very labour-intensive and followed by high physical strain on the employees due to heavy weights. Other consequences are high tolerances of the assemblies and a sequential production with long lead times. The employee has to change his position during the entire welding process, because of the heavy weight of the assembly, which cannot be moved and positioned manually. Currently, the welding of pipe sections and frames is done with simple tools and help of cranes. In addition to welding operations, the worker performs several other tasks like handling and positioning of parts, preparing the welding seam or changing his personal safety equipment. Due to restrictions of the workplace and heavy and bulky parts, the worker is restricted in his welding operations. As a result,

S. Jeschke, H. Liu, and D. Schilberg (Eds.): ICIRA 2011, Part I, LNAI 7101, pp. 112–121, 2011.

the welder follows the welding seam by bending and twisting his corpus with the geometry of the assembly. Thus, the ergonomic aspects and requirements of welding tasks regarding the geometric arrangement of the parts are often contrary.

The welding process forces the worker to stay in a defined position and a high level of concentration to achieve a high welding quality. Periods of rest are necessary several times during the process because of high physical loads. Moreover, the required operations for handling and attachment of parts before welding are time consuming and extend lead times significantly.

To reduce the described problems in actual welding tasks the research project "rorarob", performed at the TU Dortmund University [1],[2],[3] together with partners from the machine building industry, aims at developing a robot-based assistance system for welding applications, which combines the advantages of humans and robots in a hybrid system. The robots handle the parts, which are joined to an assembly, and the worker focuses directly on the welding task. Humans can work very flexible and are able to decide in unforeseeable situations. In comparison to humans robots can handle heavy parts in good accuracy and without any fatigue.

The conflict between the requirements of the welding process regarding the geometric arrangement of the parts and ergonomic aspects is one key issue of the research. By integrating a digital human model (DHM) into an offline simulation software for robots the path planning of humans and robots can be done prospectively and ergonomically optimised. Furthermore, the robot-based system enables to eliminate the time required for handling and thus reduce the process time by up to 50 % (referring to the reference parts used for test scenarios).

But a direct collaboration with overlapping workspaces, i.e. without dedicated separating devices, puts substantial requirements on work safety and particularly on monitoring the workspace (e.g. continuous position monitoring). New safety controllers for robots and technical advancements in sensor technology allow establishing overlapped workspaces with a direct collaboration in a hybrid system.

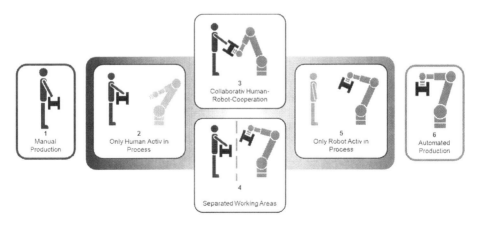

**Fig. 1.** Modes of human-robot-interactions [5],[6]

Figure 1 shows different modes of human-robot-interaction between an absolute manual production (1) and a fully automated production (6). The different types of human-robot-interaction are described below:

- Mode 2: Human and robot are working in one workspace. In this process step the robot is activated, but standing still in a defined position.
- Mode 3: Human and robot working actively together. The speed of the robot is limited to 250 mm/s, the worker has to be protected from shear and crush zones.
- Mode 4: Human and robot are working at the same time together in different parts of the workspace, a contact between both is not allowed.
- Mode 5: Only the robot is active in this process step, the human is waiting in a safety distance to the robot.

Even the combination of different modes is possible; e. g. mode 3 and 4.

Additionally to human safety a strategy to guarantee process safety is necessary to secure a high accuracy and quality of the products. Influences on the quality of welded assemblies are based on welding distortion following by heat in combination with an inadequate fixation. Other sources of inaccuracy in welding with a robot-based assistance system can be deviations during the clamping step or inaccuracies of the kinematic chains of robots. The position and orientation of the handling robots and even of gripped parts has to be checked during the operation and analysed continuously. Out of the gathered data, the welding sequence can be optimised regarding quality. [5],[6]

## 2    State of the Art in Human-Robot-Interaction (HRI) and Legal Requirements for Industrial Application

The industry requires new automated and flexible production systems that directly integrate the human workforce. This implies further development and adaptation of the current robot systems, especially with regards to current safety guidelines. In the past a separation between humans and automatic working machines (e. g. robot systems) has been mandatory. Fences or other spatial separation had to be installed. Entering the robot cell consequently leads to an emergency stop. The application of modern sensors and new add-ons for robot controllers now enable applications with overlapping workspaces for human and robots with non-separating protection devices.

Several research activities in this field of robot-based assistance systems are taking place. The general aim is to combine the different skills of humans and robots. Humans are very flexible and able to react to external influences like tolerances or process variations. They are able to handle complex geometries and are not fixed in their position. In comparison to humans, robots can handle high payloads, are very accurate and do not fatigue. By combining the advantages of humans and robots, these hybrid systems are adaptable to a variety of industrial applications. This leads to several research activities in the field of human-robot interaction (HRI):

In the project "LiSA" a horizontal joint arm robot on mobile units for assistance operations in laboratories has been developed [7]. Orientation in laboratories, environments for voice control, safe concepts with driveway monitoring and force damping bumpers with the detection of collisions were included. "ASSISTOR" built up local and mobile robot-based assistance systems [8]. The mobile robot arm is teachable by using playback operations for assistance or welding tasks. Fields of research has been the human-machine-interaction, the mobility and the assistance functionality. Other systems for a direct human-robot-interaction focus on small robots (e.g. SCARA robots) for assembly tasks [9]. To guarantee the work safety, laser scanner, safety mats and safety robot controllers are used. The systems are developed for low weights and forces as well as partly for high mobility. Following by these parameters the handling potential and the accuracy are limited. Also the use of a single robot arm restricts the possibilities. In "RAAS" developed by ZHAW in Zurich (Switzerland) a single robot is used to handle and position sub-assemblies for welding [10]. The robot positions the part and the human operator performs the welding task. The robot and human use the same working area, but the robot does not move during the welding process. DLR develops a lightweight robot especially for a direct human-robot-interaction with a kinematic similar to the human arm. The weight of this robot arm is nearly as same as his payload [11].

But the fundamentals for direct human-robot cooperation do not exist only from a pure engineering perspective. Also the existing standards and guidelines have been adapted and do now allow simultaneous cooperation of humans and robots in overlapping workspaces. The current development of new security concepts enables to reduce strict separation between humans and robots, but ensure high safety standards anyway [12],[13].

The most important requirement for the use of industrial robots in overlapping workspaces is that both partners must not in any way be injured or damaged. In the past, this requirement has been achieved through strict safety guidelines and elaborated safety systems around the robot cell. The standards EN 775 and ISO 10218:1992 required a strict separation of workers and robots to avoid collisions and accidents and guarantee a high work safety. For this reason, simultaneous collaboration between humans and robots was almost impossible. The old standard EN 775 has now been replaced by the current standards DIN EN ISO 10218-1:2006 and draft ISO 10218-2:2008 [14],[15]. The new standards allow hybrid systems with overlapping workspaces under specific restrictions, e.g. a reduced speed of 250 mm/s or a maximum dynamic power of 80 W when using a robot in collaboration with a human. With this adaptation, it is possible to realise a mixture between manual and fully automated systems to take advantage of the strengths of each partner, human and robot [9].

## 3    Human Safety and Ergonomics

In comparison to the state of the art, especially other research projects, the innovative approach in the project "rorarob" is the user-friendly positioning and handling of parts by a robotic assistance system in a manual done welding process. The challenge is to develop a multi-robot system with a direct human robot collaboration which is suitable for industrial applications especially in small and medium size businesses. For the realisation different technical solutions available on the market have to be integrated into a new holistic safety system for overlapping workspaces.

### 3.1    Workspace Monitoring

The described application, handling of heavy parts in a welding process, requires high loads and ranges of the robots used. But large robots indicate heavy and fast moving components with high velocities and thus a high kinetic energy. Consequently, a collision between humans and robots needs to be excluded at any time during the process.

For continuous monitoring of the shared workspace, various sensor systems are available on the market. Examples are laser scanner (e.g. Sick) and safe camera systems (e.g. Pilz SafetyEye [16]). Additionally to systems that monitor the area human and robot work in, safe robot controllers are required to guarantee a safe operation at all times. All leading manufacturers of robots, like Kuka, ABB, Fanuc, offer safety controls for different robot models. These systems are redundant, which means that two independent systems control each other and cause a stop in case of a conflict. The challenge is to combine sensor systems for monitoring and safe controller architectures of robots to a holistic safety system that permits a safe collaboration with humans.

For the planned multi-robot assistance system an overlapping working area is necessary for using the different skills of humans and robots at one time in the same operation (e.g. welding to parts together).

The developed safety concept is tested together with industry partners within a demonstrator build-up at TU Dortmund University. The system uses the SafetyEye by Pilz as monitoring system. The system outputs digital signals in the event of a warning or protection zone violation. These signals are used to activate monitoring functions of the robot controller to have an influence on the program of the robot, such as the reduction of speed or an emergency stop.

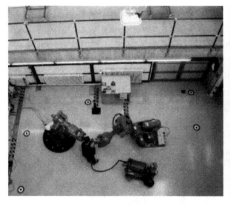 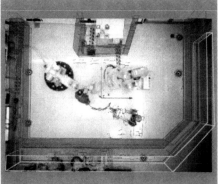

**Fig. 2.** Example of a secured area using Pilz SafetyEye [5],[6]

The system detects variations (e.g. movements) in different defined areas. These areas can be categorised in two steps: By detecting an object in the warning zone the movement of the robots slows down (< 250 mm/s). In the detection zone the robot system stops directly, because an unsafe state is reached. In the described welding process with movements of human and robot in one overlapping workspace especially the prevention of shear and crush zones is important. With the help of the camera system, the different operation modes described in Figure 1 can be defined by different configuration modes of the safety system (e.g. Figure 2).

## 3.2   Ergonomics

The design and planning of the hybrid robot cell is done by an offline programming system. The offline programming software used in the described project is FAMOS, a software solution especially for small and medium sized businesses, developed by carat robotic innovation GmbH [17]. The software is able to simulate single- und multi-robot applications in a virtual workspace environment and is going to be extended by a digital human model (DHM) for simulating hybrid robot cells (Figure 3). The approach in this project is to use a character animation system developed for video games to implement a DHM into the existing solution. In this case, EmotionFX by MGD [18] is used. The main tasks of the implemented DHM are: collision avoidance during the path planning and evaluation of the ergonomic conditions.

To prevent human from possible injuries due to direct contact between the two partners, path planning must prospectively consider movements of the worker during the welding process. With a DHM in the offline programming system, it is possible to match the path planning of the two handling robots with human movements to realise a safe and ergonomic collaboration. Additionally to the prevention of immediate risks such as collisions, the long-time preservation of the workers' health is a key issue in the research project.

**Fig. 3.** Simulated hybrid robot cell in FAMOS [5],[6],[17]

During a manual, non-assisted welding process, the employee has to change his position depending on the position of the joint. Therefore, the employee is forced to bend and twist during operation. Moreover, the required operations for handling and attachment of the parts before welding are time consuming and extend the lead time significantly. The welding process forces the worker to stay in a defined position. In consequence, the physical load on the employee is significantly high. As a result, periods of rest are necessary several times during the process. At the industrial partner's facility a wide range of postures were observed during the welding process [19]. The employee has to stretch and work overhead, bent over or kneel down to reach low joint positions. The conflict between the requirements of the welding process regarding the geometric arrangement of the parts and ergonomic aspects is one key issue of the project "rorarob". The physical load on the employee should be kept to a minimum during the entire welding process. The flexibility of the robot system allows to adapt the manufacturing cell and especially the handling operations directly to the employee. The offline simulation software allows coordinating the trajectories of the human and the robot in a way that minimises the physical load on the human body. To evaluate the ergonomic conditions within the assembly system a standardised assessment procedure is performed. Normally, these assessment procedures are designed for an in-house analysis of existing work systems in the shop floor. One of these methods is the Owako Work Analysis System (OWAS) [20]. [21], which is utilised in the offline programming system.

The underlying evaluation methodology of OWAS is mainly based on the observation of body postures. A body posture can be described by joint positions of the human model and their conversion into a so called posture code. The OWAS method has 252 possible posture and load combinations divided into four back postures, three arm postures and seven leg postures with three load dimensions. The postures are automatically identified during the simulation and labelled by an individual posture code.

Joint coordinates and motion data can be easily extracted from the human simulation. Thus, it is possible to obtain information on the posture type and the time spent in this posture out of the analysed motion sequence. The aim is to analyse systematically the time duration of each posture that occurs during the whole motion sequence and evaluate the resulting load on the musculoskeletal system for back, arms and legs.

The result of the OWAS evaluation is a colour code divided into four categories (red, orange, yellow and green). The classification stands for the level of risk for injuries on the musculoskeletal system and indicates the need and urgency for corrective actions regarding the movements of the human body in the analysed configuration, e.g. the current path planning for the robot-assisted welding process.

The implemented algorithm identifies each posture, calculates the time spent in each posture and finally returns the colour code for each posture and the entire simulated work task. [4]

Based on the virtually planned and simulated robot cell, a demonstrator at TU Dortmund University is built up. The prototype is able to weld two reference assemblies. In several test scenarios, the multi-robot application, the offline pre-planned processes, the safety concept and the human-robot interaction can be tested and further developed. Especially the development of a reliable safety concept for a real-time workspace monitoring is a key factor for the industrial implementation of the system.

## 4      Process Safety

Next to the human safety and ergonomic working conditions a high quality of the assembly has to be guaranteed for industrial usability of the planned assistances system. The quality standard has to be as high as in current manual welding applications and if possible be increased by using a robot-based assistance system.

The sources of inaccuracy in a multi-robot assistance system for welding tasks can be: inaccuracy of the welding process itself, the connection between the work piece and the effector, inaccuracy of the work piece and inaccuracy of the robots.

Steel distorts due to heat impact during welding result in inaccuracies of the welded assembly. Another source can be an incorrect position of the work piece before or during the gripping process. Consequently the work piece is not in the planned position relatively to the robot. Position errors can although be caused by incorrect geometries of work pieces, which partly have high tolerances. Furthermore inaccuracy can also result from the kinematic chain of industrial robots, which is not totally stiff, especially at joints.

To increase the quality of the welded assembly, a two way strategy is followed. The first part is the possibility for the worker to weld in a process-optimised sequence of the welding seams. In current welding applications the sequence is predetermined by restrictions like fixation or additional handling processes. A reorientation during welding operation is normally not done because of additional time and effort. In comparison, an assistance system built up with robots allows several reorientations of the partly welded assembly without any additional effort for the worker. Thus, the welding task can be made in a process optimised sequence for better product accuracy.

The second part is the integration of a strategy to avoid inaccuracy by measuring and finally compensate it. Next to a force/torque sensor, position and orientation deviations will be inspected by an optical coordinate measurement system. The used measuring system K610 of Nikon Metrology NV detects the position of infrared LEDs by means of linear CCD cameras. Through triangulation, the 3D position of each LED is calculated. At least three LEDs can build up a coordinate system and orientations can be measured. Based on measurements during the validation of the project, the process and welding sequence can be optimised. First measurements are planned to analyse the position and orientation of the robots during their motion, to described kinematic chain inaccuracies. Afterwards the measurement will be done during the handling process with combined parts.

## 5      Conclusion

Aim of the research project is the development of a robot-based assistance system for welding applications which combines the flexibility of humans and the benefits of industrial robots. A safety concept for process and human safety is developed and integrated into a demonstrator at TU Dortmund University. The process safety is secured by a detailed measuring of inaccuracies followed by different compensation strategies. The human safety in welding processes with overlapping workspaces is guaranteed by building up a holistic safety system. The regulations of the draft guidelines for human-robot-interactions define the different possibilities and limitations for a collaborative human-robot-interaction for robot-based assistance systems in welding tasks and for other industrial applications. For an industrially usable solution, the proposed speed of 250 mm/s given by this guideline will be analysed in the next project steps regarding safe operation.

# References

1. Thomas, C., Busch, F., Kuhlenkoetter, B., Deuse, J.: Safe and Ergonomic Collaboration of Humans and Robots for Welding of Assemblies. In: Proc. of 3rd CIRP Conference on Assembly Technologies and Systems (CATS) 2010, Trondheim (Norway), June 01-03. Responsive, customer demand driven, adaptive assembly, pp. 121–125 (2010)
2. Thomas, C., Kuhlenkoetter, B.: Sichere und kollaborierende Mensch-Roboter-Interaktion – Entwicklung eines roboter-gestuetzten Assistenzsystems fuer das Handling im Schweißprozess. In: Internationales Forum Mechatronik (IFM) 2010 Conference, Winterthur (Switzerland), November 03-04 (2010)
3. Federal Ministry for Economy and Technology (March 15, 2011) http://www.autonomik.de
4. Thomas, C., Busch, F., Kuhlenkoetter, B., Deuse, J.: Ensuring Human Safety with Offline Simulation and Real-time Workspace Surveillance to Develope a Hybrid Robot Assistance System for Welding of Assemblies. In: Proceedings of 4 th International Conference on Changeable, Agile, Reconfigurable and Virtual Production (CARV), Montreal (Canada), October 02- 05 (2011)
5. Thomas, C., Busch, F., Kuhlenkötter, B., Deuse, J.: Ensuring Human Safety with Real-time Workspace Surveillance in Human-Robot Interaction. In: VDI-Berichte 2143 - Automation 2011, Baden-Baden (Germany), June 28-29, pp. 259–262 (2011)
6. Thomas, C., Kuhlenkoetter, B., Busch, F., Deuse, J.: Mensch-Roboter-Kooperation, atp edn., August 7, vol. 53, pp. 54–61. Oldenbourg Industrieverlag, Jahrgang (2011)
7. Fritzsche, M., Schulenburg, E., Elkmann, N., Girstl, A., Stiene, S., Teutsch, C.: Safe Human-Robot Interaction in a Life Science Environment. In: Proc. of the IEEE International Workshop on Safety Security and Rescue Robotics (2007)
8. Schraft, R.D., Helms, E., Hans, M., Thiemermann, S.: Man-Machine-Interaction and Co-Operation for Mobile and Assisting Robots. In: Proceedings of EIS (2004)
9. Reinhart, G., Roesel, W.: Interactive Robot-assistant in Production Environments – Safety Aspects in Human-Robot Co-operation. Zeitschrift fuer wirtschaftlichen Fabrikbetrieb Jahrgang 105, 80–83 (2010)
10. Hueppi, R., Grueninger, R., Nielsen, E.: Effizienter Robotereinsatz schon bei kleineren und mittleren Serien. In: Proceedings ifm 2006 Mechatronic-Cluster ClusterlandOberoesterreich GmbH, Linz (2006)
11. Albu-Schaeffer, A., Haddadin, S., Ott, C., Stemmer, A., Wimkoeck, T., Hirzinger, G.: The DLR lightweight robot: design and control concepts for robots in human environments. Industrial Robot: An international Journal 34(5), 376–385 (2007)

12. Beumelburg, K.: Faehigkeitsorientierte Montageablaufplanung in der direkten Mensch-Roboter-Kooperation. Dissertation, Institut fuer industrielle Fertigung und Fabrikbetrieb, Universitaet Stuttgart (2005)
13. Thiemermann, S.: Direkte Mensch-Roboter-Kooperation in der Kleinteilemontage mit einem SCARA-Roboter. Dissertation, Institut fuer industrielle Fertigung und Fabrikbetrieb, Universitaet Stuttgart (2005)
14. DIN EN ISO 10218, Teil 1: Industrieroboter – Sicherheitsanforderungen – Teil 1: Roboter. Beuth Verlag, Berlin (2006)
15. DIN EN ISO 10218, Teil 2: Industrieroboter – Sicherheitsanforderungen – Teil 2: Robotersystem und Integration. BeuthVerlag, Berlin (2008)
16. (March 11, 2011), http://www.pilz.de/products/sensors/camera/f/safetyeye/index.en.jsp
17. (March 15, 2011), http://www.carat-robotic.de
18. (March 11, 2011), http://www.mysticgd.com
19. Busch, F., Deuse, J.: Ergonomische Bewertung von manuellen Schweißarbeitsplaetzen mittels Automotive Assembly Work Sheet (AAWS). In: 57. Arbeitswissenschaftlicher Kongress, Gesellschaft fuer Arbeitswissenschaft, March 23-25, pp. 585–588. GfA-Press, Chemnitz, Germany (2011)
20. Mattila, M.: Analysis of working postures in hammering tasks on building construction sites using the computerized OWAS method. Applied Ergonomics 24(6), 405 (1993)
21. Ismail, A.R., Yeo, M.L., Haniff, M.H.M., Zulkifli, R., Deros, B.M., Makhtar, N.K.: Assessment of Postural Loading among the Assembly Operators: A Case Study at Malaysian Automotive Industry. European Journal of Scientific Research 30(2), 224–235 (2009)

# Operation Simulation of a Robot
# for Space Applications

Hui Li[1], Giuseppe Carbone[2], Marco Ceccarelli[2], and Qiang Huang[1]

[1] School of Mechatronical Engineering,
Beijing Institute of Technology, Haidian District, Beijing, 100081, China
{lihui2011,qhuang}@bit.edu.cn
[2] LARM: Labarotory of Robotics and Mechatronics,
University of Cassino, Via Di Biasio 43, 03043, Cassino (Fr), Italy
{carbone,ceccarelli}@unicas.it

**Abstract.** In this paper we have outlined design considerations and design solutions for a structure of a chameleon-like robot for assembling, service and repairing of space stations. Requirements and characteristics are discussed with the aim to define design problems and operation features that give motivation for a biomimetic inspiration to chameleons. Simulation in space station has been done to validate the feasibility of the proposed chameleon-like robot.

**Keywords:** Chameleon-like, space application.

## 1 Introduction

According to the International Federation of Robotics (IFR), "a service robot is a robot which operates semi or fully autonomously to perform services useful to the wellbeing of human and equipment, excluding manufacturing operations". Therefore, a service action can be understood as a complex set of operations that can achieve goals with a variety of aspects, in manipulation and transportation but also in dealing with interactions with environment and human beings as users or operators or assisted person [1].

Since a decade service robots have addressed great attention for developing new robotic systems for new applications even in no technical areas. Typical robots are already developed for medical care, space exploration, demining operation, surveillance, entertainment, museum guide and many other applications. In some cases results are even already available in the market. A considerable literature is available not only on technical issues but it is not reported in the paper for space limits.

Specific activity has been developed in the past for possible designs of robots in space applications, but only few robotic arms have been applied so far, for example Canadarm2 and Robonaut [2,3,4,5]. Plans for large orbital stations have motivated a renewed interest in developing human-like robots and other structures, as the recent programs of national space stations, like US, China, Europe, and Russia [6,7,8].

S. Jeschke, H. Liu, and D. Schilberg (Eds.): ICIRA 2011, Part I, LNAI 7101, pp. 122–131, 2011.

Canadarm and Robonaut are all well designed, but they can be considered too complicated, and cannot work on all of places outside space station.

In this paper, problems for designing a structure for a service robot in applications for orbital stations are approached by analyzing peculiarities of the application with the aim to propose a reliable solution with reduced DOFs and flexibly features. Simulation has been carried out to validate the proposed chameleon-like design solution.

## 2   A Space Service Robot

The ISS is an internationally developed research facility that is being assembled in low Earth orbit, as shown in Fig. 1(a). On-orbit construction of the station began in 1998 and is scheduled for completion by late 2011. The station is expected to remain in operation until at least 2015, and likely 2020. The ISS serves as a research laboratory that has a microgravity environment in which crews may conduct experiments in biology, chemistry, human biology, physics, astronomy and meteorology [9,10].

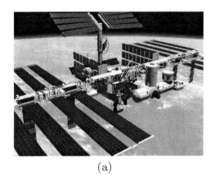
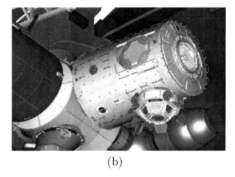

(a)                                          (b)

**Fig. 1.** The international space station: (a) The whole international space station; (b) A segment of the international space station

Because ISS is still under construction, and some other space stations will be constructed, there are too much assembling, repairing and monitoring work for the astronauts to do. Because of radiation, space debris, upper atmospheric drag and spacecraft electrostatic charging, the space station can be broken in any place. In addition, too much work is expected, and the space environment is very dangerous for astronauts, therefore space robots are urgently needed to be developed to assist or replace astronauts.

The application of a service robot in a space orbital station can be characterized and constrained by environment characteristics and operation tasks. The space environment is characterized by the following aspects:

## Low Gravity

The condition of low gravity acting on the robot makes motion easier but also very sensitive to be effected by unexpected actions, even if of small magnitude.

## Strong Radiation

Radiation from the sun, can be dangerous and even affecting the operation of actuators and electronic devices.

## Drastic Temperature Change

Temperature changes drastically and temperature difference of an object between the sunny side and on the shady side is large. Temperature control device should be added on the robot to make the robot survive in the drastic temperature changes, and large temperature difference environment.

## Lack of Energy Source

In orbital stations, energy source is very limited and therefore energy consumption must be kept at the lowest level as possible.

## Hard to Transport Things

In order to make the transportation of the space service robot to space station easier, the robot should be as light and small as possible.

Similarly, operation tasks of space service robot in orbital stations can be characterized by specific aspects as the following:

## Autonomy

A robot helps or cooperates with the astronauts to in the assembling, repairing and monitoring. The robot should work even without astronauts.

## Full Mobility

A robot should work on any place of the space station.

The peculiarities of the space environment and its constraints require novel solutions for a space robot with capability of service operations within the outside structure of a space station. A biomimetic inspiration for design architectures and motion strategies can be obtained by looking at chameleon animals. In Fig. 1(b), there are hundreds of handrails and beams outside the international space station. The environment outside the space station is very similar to the living environment of the chameleon. Chameleons move slowly but firmly in intricate environments, with reduced mobility structures. They have legs that they use also as arms with an extremity with two fingers only. Those two fingers show a very powerful structure with a large mobility in grasping handrails or in contacting surface as a foot. In general, a chameleon moves slowly with the aim to achieve safe and reliable postures during its motions, likewise it is needed in space stations by astronauts. This gives also the possibility to reduce the power that is needed for the movement and operation, by concentrating the force requirements in the extremity for attaching the surface of handrail along it moves. Thus, a chameleon has legs with reduced size with respect to the body transport.

A new structure has been thought as inspired by chameleon animals to get compact, light, and reliable structure for a service robot in space with reduced DOFs. The proposal has been investigated as in the scheme of Fig. 2 [11,12].

A chameleon-like robot is composed of one trunk and three legs. Each leg has four DOFs and is composed of one ball joint and one normal rotary joint. In order to ensure that chameleon-like robot has good mobile performance, a kind of foot/hand is designed on each leg extremity with four DOFs and it can grasp the handrails and beams. The foot/hand can ensure that chameleon-like robot can move and work almost the entire places outside space station. In addition the robot leg can also be folded to reduce its volume, as shown in Fig. 2 (b).

Summarizing, a chameleon-like robot for space service operations can be characterized by having legs with reduced size and motion power but with the possibility to be used as arms, and by being equipped with a hand/foot extremity with only two powerful fingers that can be adjusted to grasp handrails during walking actions. A chameleon-like robot can help astronauts in the assembling, repairing and monitoring. In addition, the robot is small, light and highly reliable with suitable mechanism design.

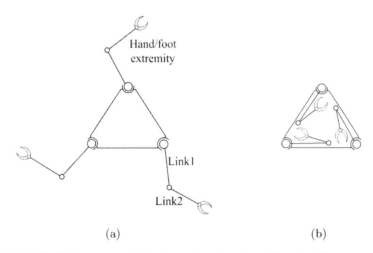

(a)                                                        (b)

**Fig. 2.** A sketch of the proposed structure of a chameleon-like robot for space applications: (a) Full stretched configuration; (b) Folded configuration

## 3   Adams Model

The models of chameleon-like robot in ADAMS are shown in Fig. 3 and Fig. 4. The CAD model of chameleon-like robot is shown in Fig. 3. The CAD model of the hand of robot is shown in Fig. 4. The dimensions of the chameleon-like robot and hand of the robot are listed in Table  1.

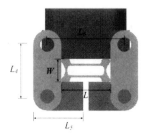

**Fig. 3.** CAD model of chameleon-like Robot

**Fig. 4.** CAD model of chameleon-like Robot

**Table 1.** The Parameters of foot/hand

| Parameter | Meaning | Value |
|:---:|:---:|:---:|
| $L1$ | length of first link of the chameleon-like robot | $250mm$ |
| $L2$ | length of second link of the chameleon-like robot | $200mm$ |
| $L3$ | length of trunk side of the chameleon-like robot | $500mm$ |
| $L4$ | length of the first phalange | $35.9mm$ |
| $L5$ | length of the second phalange | $54.95mm$ |
| $L6$ | length of the palm | $15.9mm$ |
| $L$ | width of the handrail | $34.95mm$ |
| $W$ | length of the palm | $15.9mm$ |

Working environment of chameleon-like robot is shown in Fig. 5. Chameleon-like robot can move to most places outside space station by grasping the handrails like the astronaut.

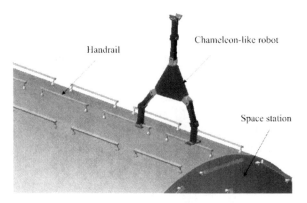

**Fig. 5.** Working environment of chameleon-like robot

## 4  Simulation Results

The chameleon-like robot has two moving modes, namely one is the revolving mode, and the other is the walking mode. In the revolving mode, the legs grasp the handrails in turns, and the trunk of the robot rotates when the robot moves. In the walking mode, the robot moves only by two legs, the two legs grasp the handrails in turns, and the third leg does not to participate to the walking, and it can do some other tasks.

In simulation, the chameleon-like robot moves straight by grasping the handrails like astronauts do. Because the robot walks straight, only four joints of the robot move in the simulation. In order to validate the performance of the robot, torques for the joints, velocity and acceleration of robot trunk, and the contact forces between the foot/hand and handrails are measured, as shown in Fig. 6.

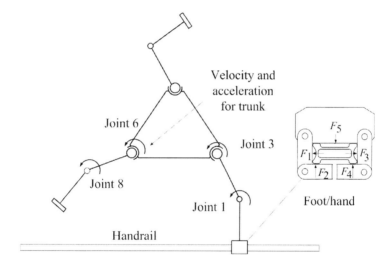

**Fig. 6.** A sketch of the chameleon-like robot

As shown in Fig. 7, gait of robot straight movement on the handrails can be summarized as following:

1) The leg A moves up and forward, as shown in Fig. 7(a) and Fig. 7(b), then moves down and grasps the handrail again, as shown in Fig. 7(c).
2) The leg B moves up and forward, as shown in Fig. 7(d), then moves down and grasps the handrail again, as shown in Fig. 7(e).
3) The leg A moves up and forward again, as shown in Fig. 7(f) and Fig. 7(g), then moves down and grasps the handrail again, as shown in Fig. 7(h).

The robot trunk can be moved while legs A leg B move. After the three steps, the robot can move from on handrail to another handrail.

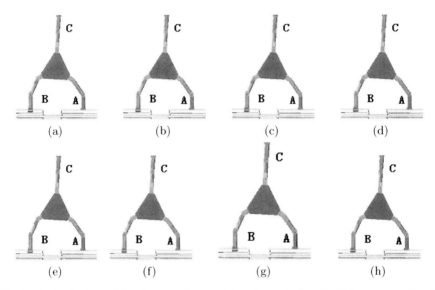

**Fig. 7.** A simulation with robot moving straight along the handrails by means of walking mode

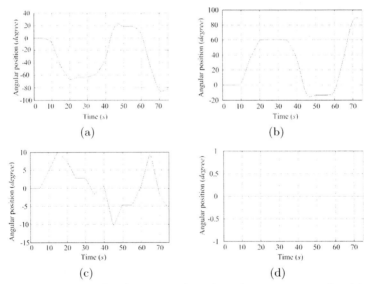

**Fig. 8.** Angular positions for the joints when the robot moves straight: (a) Angular position for the first joint; (b) Angular position for the second joint; (c) Angular position for the third joint; (d) Angular position for the fourth joint

The angular position of the joints when the robot moves straight, are shown in Fig. 8. In order to simply the kinematics and control, joint 8 is kept at a constant value. The maximum valves of accelerations of the joints' movements are limited to 2.5 $degree/s^2$.

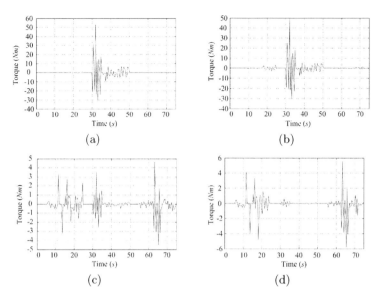

**Fig. 9.** Torques of the joints when the robot moves straight: (a) Torque for the first joint; (b) Torque for the second joint; (c) Torque for the third joint; (d) Torque for the fourth joint

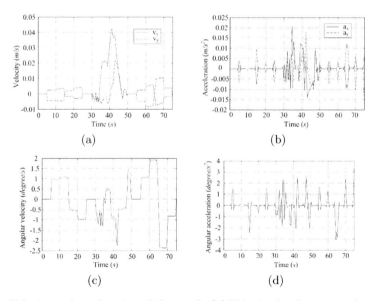

**Fig. 10.** Velocity and acceleration of the trunk: (a) Velocity for the center of trunk; (b) Acceleration for center of trunk; (c) Angular velocity for trunk; (d) Angular acceleration for trunk

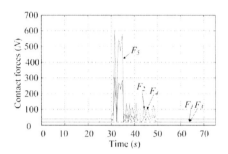

**Fig. 11.** Contact forces for hand A

Therefore, the movements of the joint, which is shown in Fig. 8, are very smooth to reduce the driving torques. In Fig. 9, the largest driving torque is $54Nm$, and is can easily got by a motor and reducer system.

In Fig. 10, velocity and angular velocity of the robot trunk are very smooth. The largest acceleration is $0.022m/s^2$, and the largest angular acceleration is $3degree/s^2$. Therefore, the movement of the trunk is smooth.

The contact forces between the hands and the handrails are shown in Fig. 11 and 12. The handrails can support $200lbs$ ($889N$) load in any direction [13]. In Fig. 11 and 12, the largest contact force is about $610N$, and it is much smaller than the largest force which the handrail can support. Therefore, by grasping the handrail, the foot/hand can hold the position of robot body and react to forces and torques exerted while walking.

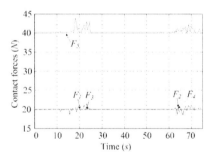

**Fig. 12.** Contact forces for hand B

## 5    Conclusion

In this paper, a new kind of service robot for space application is presented by using simulation results to show characteristic operation features and its feasibility for use in orbital space station. The simulation shows the effectiveness of the proposed chameleon-like robot with suitable motion ranges, reasonable torques and contact forces.

# References

1. Ceccarelli, M.: New challenging applications for service robots: problems and experiments. In: Proceeding of IARP Workshop on Service Robotics and NanoRobotics, invited paper No.2 Beijing (2009)
2. MD Robotics.: Mobile Servicing System - Data Sheet. MD Robotics, Brampton, Ontario, Canada (2002)
3. Ambrose, R.O., Aldridge, H., Scott Askew, R., Burridge, R.R., Bluethmann, W., Diftler, M., Lovchik, C., Magruder, D., Rehnmark, F.: Robonaut: NASA's Space Humanoid. IEEE Intelligent Systems and their Applications 15, 57–63 (2000)
4. Bluethmann, W., Ambrose, R., Diftler, R., Askew, S., Huber, E., Goza, M., Rehnmark, F., Lovchik, C., Magruder, D.: Robonaut, A robot designed to work with humans in space. Autonomous Robots, 179–198 (2003)
5. Ambrose, R.O., Savely, R.T., Michael, S.S, Difiler, M.A., Spain, I., Radford, N.: Mobile Manipulation using NASA's Robonaut. In: Proceedings of the 2004 IEEE International Conference on Robotics and Automation, pp. 2104–2109 (2004)
6. Hirzinger, G., Brunner, B., Lampariello, R., Landzettel, K., Schott, J., Steinmetz, B.-M.: Advances in orbital robotics. In: Proceedings of the 2000 IEEE international Conference on Robotics and Automation, San Francisco, Albuquerque, New Mexico, pp. 898–907 (2000)
7. Hirzinger, G., Sporer, N., Schedl, M., Butterfass, J., Grebenstein, M.: Robotics and mechatronics in aerospace. In: Proceedings of 7th International Workshop on Advanced Motion Control, pp.19–27 (2002)
8. Stieber, M.F., Trudel, C.P., Hunter, D.G.: Robotic systems for the International Space Station. In: Proceedings of the IEEE International Conference on Robotics and Automation, pp. 3068–3073 (1997)
9. Uri, J.J., Cooley, V.: International Space Station - a unique place for research. In: Proceedings of IEEE Aerospace Conference, vol. 1, pp. I-91–100 (2003)
10. Gibbs, G., Sachdev, S.: Canada and the international space station program: overview and status. Acta Astronautica 51(2), 591–600 (2002)
11. Li, H., Ceccarelli, M., Huang, Q., Carbone, G.: A Chameleon-Like Service Robot for Space Station. In: International Workshop on Bio-Inspired Robots, Nantes, France (2011)
12. Li, H., Ceccarelli, M., Huang, Q., Carbone, G.: Problems and Requirements for a Chameleon-Like Service Robot in Space Station. In: Proceeding of 2011 IEEE/ASME International Conference on Advanced Intelligent Mechatronics (AIM 2011), Budapest, Hungary, July 4-6, pp. 463–468 (2011)
13. Mission Operations Directorate, Training Division: EVA Tool Catalog. NASA Doc. No. JSC-20466, Prepared by R.C. Trevino and R.K. Fullerton (1985)

# Re-grasping: Improving Capability
# for Multi-Arm-Robot-System by Dynamic Reconfiguration

Burkhard Corves, Tom Mannheim, and Martin Riedel

Department of Mechanism Theory and Dynamics of Machines (IGM)
RWTH Aachen University, Aachen, Germany
{corves,mannheim,riedel}@igm.rwth-aachen.de

**Abstract.** In previous works a novel flexible and versatile handling concept, called PARAGRIP(Parallel Gripping), was introduced. This concept is based ona reconfigurable architecture with a modular and alterable layout. The robot system is able to handle objects with six DOF by forming a parallel kinematic structure including several robotic arms and the object itself. As many kinematic parameters, like the grasp- and base-points of the arms as well as the arm combination can be designed freely, the handling system offers a fast and economic possibility to adapt the performances to the requirements of the task. This adaption can proceed before or even during manipulation. The latter is realized by dynamic re-grasping, where the object is passed from one arm to the next, if more than three arms are available in the layout.

This Paper deals with the question how an optimal configuration set can be planned automatically, if the robot layout offers the possibility of dynamic re-grasping. It shows the benefits and the challenges as well as the strategies of the planning process and the realization. The focus of this paper is how to manage the complexity of this numerousness of configuration possibilities and choose the optimal one within the shortest computation time.

**Keywords:** parallel manipulator, reconfigurable robot, dynamic re-grasping, PARAGRIP.

## 1   Introduction

In recent years, manufacturing industry is governed by fundamental changes with regard to the conditions, like progressive globalization and rapid technological development as well as changes in the resources situation [1, 2]. Classical demands in handling systems are currently undergoing change. The priorities are increasingly shifting from higher load capacity, greater precision and higher speeds in the past towards customized production and flexible solutions to component-dependent problems. Often currently available handling systems cannot fulfill the new demands of complex and frequently changed assembly tasks.[3] Applications with frequently challenging manipulation tasks can often be found in small series like e.g. in aerospace-, ship-building- or wind energy industries, where large-scaled components have to be

S. Jeschke, H. Liu, and D. Schilberg (Eds.): ICIRA 2011, Part I, LNAI 7101, pp. 132–141, 2011.
© Springer-Verlag Berlin Heidelberg 2011

assembled. Here a versatile, flexible and scalable handling system is needed for automatic assembly in an economic way. A classical industrial robot with a single large customized gripper is not an appropriate and flexible solution for these kinds of automation tasks.

A more versatile approach is to use co-operating robots, as the object can be gripped and supported at different points by several robots depending on the requirements of the object [4]. The major disadvantage of this concept is the high number of actuators, e.g. 18 actuators for 3 robots to perform 6 DOF object motion. Thus this concept leads to high costs and complex control architecture. Another disadvantage of common industrial robots is the long set-up time when rearranging, because they are not design to be mobile and they need to be calibrated carefully after relocation. The common way to handle large-scaled components nowadays is a rough manipulation via an under slung crane and multiple workers to control the precise position and orientation by pushing and pulling the part to its correct destination. This manual method is quite simple but has many disadvantages due to the lack of automation, like e.g. poor efficiency, long cycle-time and limited economy as well as often low accuracy and low repeatability.

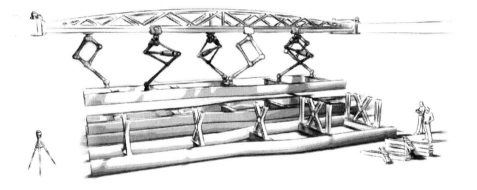

**Fig. 1.** Design c concept of the novel handling system PARAGRIP

A novel handling concept, called PARAGRIP (Parallel Gripping), is a feasible approach to enable economic automation in small series. Its new handling principle comes along with a high potential of flexibility, versatility and changeability, which are some of the key requirements to handle frequently changing large-scaled components efficiently [2, 6, 7]. The novel reconfigurable handling system is shown in **fig. 1** and features a comparable handling performance as co-operating robots, but with a reduced overall number of actuators and a tailor-made and mobile arm design.

## 2    Handling Concept

The key idea of the handling concept is to generate closed-loop kinematic chains formed by the object and the arms similar to the architecture of a parallel robot,

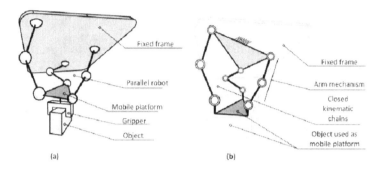

**Fig. 2.** (a) classical parallel robot structure, (b) idea of new handling system

illustrated in **fig. 2**. Manipulating an object with three arms in six-dimensional Cartesianspace requires two main actuators per arm and six in total. Compared to cooperating robots the overall number of drives can be reduced when the arms are meant to work together. This drive configuration leads to an under actuated single arm design with less drives than required to meet the mobility number of the arm. Hence, the combination of the arms to manipulate objects is the fundamental of this handling principle.

With the idea of several arms working together in a closed kinematic chain the robot system provides the same kinetostatic performance as a parallel manipulator. Its capability is defined by the parameters of the closed loop structure, generated by the combination of arms. Hence, the single arm can be developed specifically to feature a more lightweight and mobile design in comparison to a regular industrial robot. Several kinematic parameters, e.g. dimensions of the moving platform, can be changed every time the system is grasping or re-grasping an object. A temporary jointed connection between the arms and the object can transfer forces in all directions and integrates the object completely into the robot structure. In comparison to mechanical handling systems imitating hands [7] the object is not clamped or clutched to handle, but is connected to the wrist using adhesive forces. The possibility to locate the contact points on the surface of the handling part automatically eliminates the need for a customized gripper for each object and task. Hence, this approach enables the system to manipulate objects of different shapes and sizes without any mechanical reconstruction. The grasp process, using the under actuated arm, is investigated in detail in [13].

## 3    Robot Architecture

The system consists of several arms, featuring six DOF, respectively. The arms can be controlled independent from each other. At the distal ends of the arms contactelements, e.g. vacuum cups or electro magnets etc., ensure the arms stay in connection with the object. The system needs six main actuators to perform the handling task. For 3D grasping one additional drive is required for each arm. While object manipulation these smaller drives can either be disconnected, driven passively or support the motion. Each arm mechanism is designed as a five-bar-linkage with a parallelogram arrangement, a pivot revolute joint fixed to the frame and a three DOF spherical wrist joint, similar to the one mentioned in [10].This leads to a design with proximal located drives to reduce the inertia while dynamic movements. A first prototype is realized to demonstrate the functionality of the novel concept. It is shown in **fig. 3**. The detailed architecture of this robot, as well as the kinematics and dynamics are discussed within the work of the dimensional synthesis [11].

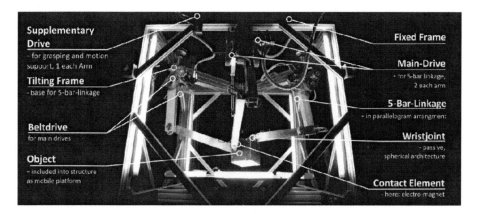

**Fig. 3.** First Prototype of PARAGRIP, here with three arm layout

## 4    Reconfiguration

Reconfiguration means adapting the handling system to the desired task by specifically adjusting some kinematic parameters. To fulfill the requirements on flexibility and economy, it is necessary that the reconfiguration of the handling system is fast and easy. In case of the presented system there are three fundamental possibilities to reconfigure. The first possibility deals with the variation of kinematic parameters, like link length inside one robot arm, joint position on the object and base point position. This influences workspace and performance criteria, e.g. payload, stiffness and accuracy. The second one is to achieve reconfiguration by varying modules with different functions, e.g. modules with measurement, joining or balancing units. The last possibility is to scale the system, in this case scaling doesn't mean to change the size but means to change the number of involved arms. When using simultaneous more than three arms to manipulate an object the system becomes highly redundant. This enables to increase the load capacity of the robot system, but raises also the control effort. The combination of these three possibilities generates the base of an alterable robot system.

In a previous work [8] the influence of the first possibility was investigated. In this case the arm is seen as a module with fixed lengths inside the robot arm. Thus changing kinematic parameters can simply be realized by varying the grasp- or base point positions as well as the arm combination. Modifying these parameters means to define the dimension of the fixed and moving platform, which leads to variations in the kinematic parameter, illustrated in **fig. 4**.

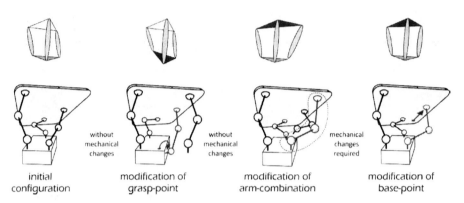

Fig. 4. Possibilities of reconfiguring fixed and mobile platform

As mentioned before the object is integrated into the kinematic structure as the moving platform. Thus changing grasp points means to alter the kinematic parameters of this platform. This action has major influence on the orientation workspace. In **fig. 5** the rotational workspaces for different grasp points are shown, the rotations are defined about the Euler angles $\varphi$, $\theta$, $\psi$ (z, y', z''). In all three cases the handling object is a cube, the position is in the center of the translational[1] workspace.

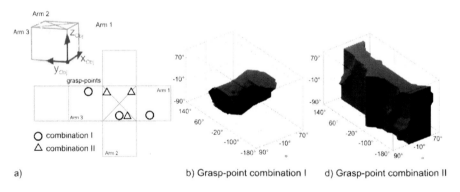

Fig. 5. Different grasp point combinations and their related rotational Workspace

The base points are representing the dimensions of the fixed platform. Changing these dimensions can be done by moving the mobile designed arms to different positions at the frame or using a different arm combination. Relocation of the arms has primary influences on the shape of the translational workspace as shown in **fig. 6**.

---

[1] Translational Workspace means the capability to move an object with constant orientation.

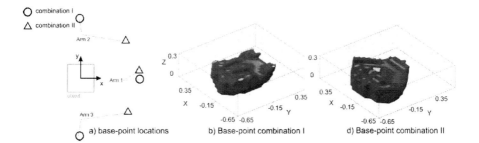

Fig. 6. Three Base point combinations and their related translational workspace

# 5    Re-grasp Planning

If the layout of the handling system consists of more arms than needed to handle an object- in this case: more than three- it is possible to change the configuration even during continuous object manipulating by passing the object through the arms. This means shifting between the different workspaces, like those illustrated in fig. 5-6. This feature offers the possibility to adjust the shape and size of the workspace depending on the desired handling situation. In contrast to re-grasping with humanoid hands [9], where friction contact is needed, all reachable grasp point can be used, if they are not engaged with a different arm. This kind of reconfiguration enables new motion possibilities, as the rotational and translational workspace can be extended and redesigned while moving the object. Free and continuous object rotations with more than 360° about any axis in space become possible. **Fig 7** shows a simple turn-around-motion with a 180° object rotation.

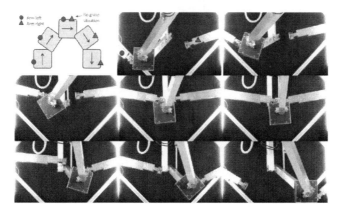

Fig. 7. 180° object rotation with dynamic re-grasping

In **fig. 8** the desired object motion, illustrated as the red arrow, is larger than the translational workspace of any three arm combination. Slices of the workspaces at ground level are illustrated as colored, transparent areas. With the help of re-grasping five times this sample task can be performed, when eight arms are located at the displayed positions A1-A8.

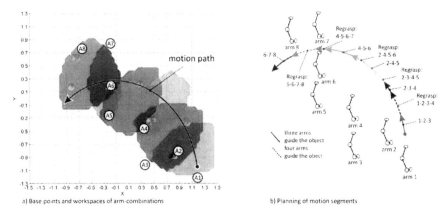

a) Base points and workspaces of arm-combinations            b) Planning of motion segments

**Fig. 8.** Desired motion task with re-grasping

The almost infinite configuration possibilities enabled byre-grasping, turn a manual planning into a very challenging and inefficient operation for a non-skilled user. The demand for a quick, user-friendly and economic reconfiguration of the system does also include the planning process. An automatic layout planning tool needs to optimize re-grasp motions as well.

Equation 1 is meant to clarify the complexity of a configuration planning process by calculating the theoretic number of possible configuration sets. This value can be used to estimate the computation effort of the algorithm. Here the given parameters are: **n** the total number of arms in this layout, **h** the number of arms needed to manipulate an object, **m** the number of sample steps, which are computed during motion and **g** the number of grasp points on the object. The result **C** is the total number of theoretical configuration sets:

$$C = \left( \frac{g!}{(g-h)!} \frac{n!}{h!(n-h!)} \right) \left( (g-h)h \right)^{(m-1)} \tag{1}$$

In an easy example a 10 seconds motion should be performed. The object to handle is a cube with nine possible grasp points on each side, which means 54 grasp possibilities for one single arm in total. The robot layout features four arms where three of these are needed for object manipulation. The sample step size for planning and motion calculation is 0.1 seconds, which leads to$m=100$ time steps at a ten second motion. Equation (1) calculates a number of $1.14 \times 10^{222}$ theoretic possible configuration sets to perform this motion task, only by customizing these few parameters. It is obvious that computing all possible combinations and evaluating their performance is unfeasible. A fast pre-selection algorithm can reduce the number of possible solution sets by separating theoretic and realistic sets. The pre-selection algorithm is realized in three main steps. The first step scans the orientation of the surfaces. If any grasp point surface is showing in a prohibited direction, which would violate the permissible joint angles, it is rejected. In the second step the distance between grasp- and base point is analyzed and compared with the motion range of arm, respectively. In the last step all critical joint angles are computed, to ensure the point is inside the workspace.

The third step only executes if the point passes the first two checks, which saves approximately 30% of computation, in comparison with only a single phase preselection. As simplified illustrated in **fig.9** the pre-selection scans a given number of motions points.

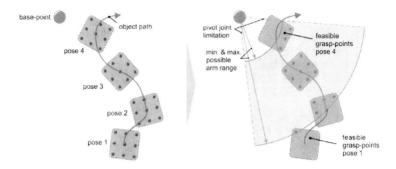

**Fig. 9.** Preselection of grasp-points

To compute the number of possible solution sets left after preselecting, a "regular" case can be approximated. If only one side of the cube is accessible for each arm the total set of solutions is shrank to $3.26x10^{145}$.This number is still far away from any realistic and computable solution set. Hence, some boundary conditions have to be specified or added to constrain the field of solutions.

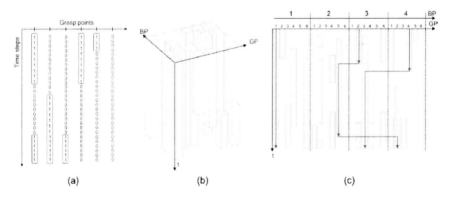

**Fig. 10.** (a) recognization as segments for one arm,(b) segments for four arms, (c) computed configuration set

In **fig. 10(a)**the path planning matrix is shown for an object with only six grasp points. The ones are standing for reachable points. A satisfying approach to downsize the field of solutions is to recognize serial points as segments, which are illustrated in the figure using black lined boxes. This method allows the planning tool to change the configuration of the arm combination only at a specific position of the segment, e.g. at the end of the segment. By computing the minimum time needed to re-grasp, the segments which are shorter than this, can be rejected. In our case this deterministic approach proved as practical. Another approach is to use the Random Rapid Tree method (RRT) or Probabilistic Roadmap Method (PRM)presented in [14], the gain of performance has to be investigated. These methods have more implementation effort.

After those steps of merging hundred motion points to just a few motion segments, the field of solutions is limited to a manageable size, which can be evaluated by a search algorithm. The task of the search algorithm is to find three completely independent ways through the segments to the end of the motion without violating the boundary conditions. Three boundary conditions are defined as follows: Only one segment per base point (BP) can be used at the same time, only one reconfiguration operation at the same time and the minimum distance between the grasp points (GPs) shouldn't be smaller than the diameter of the wrist joint, to avoid a collision. In **fig 10(c)** one solution is illustrated. Here the red vertical arrows are representing the correlation of base- and grasp point. The horizontal ones are marking the configuration changes. In this example the system is re-grasping three times. In a first step the costs of a solution is defined by the overall number of re-grasp operations. Because the remaining re-grasp operations cannot be estimated there is no heuristic available. Thus only uninformed search algorithms can be considered. Because of its completeness and space efficiency the iterative deepening depth-first search (DFID) is a suitable algorithm to solve this problem[10]. The depth of the algorithm matches the number of re-grasp operations in our case. The algorithms first goal is to minimize the number of re-grasp operations. In case the algorithm finds more than one solution set, the sets are compared and optimized regarding to a user given performance criteria, e.g. maximal drive torque, maximum accuracy or maximum stiffness. These kinetostatic criteria as well as the algorithms used for optimizing the configuration parameters can be derived from the approach of a dimensional synthesis of parallel manipulators, as presented in [11, 12].The algorithm solves the above mentioned scenario at a 2.66 GHz CPU in less than 4 seconds.

## 6    Conclusion

In this paper a novel flexible and versatile handling concept, called PARAGRIP (Parallel Gripping), was presented which can be used to manipulate large-scaled components automatically in small series. Here, optimized reconfiguration of kinematic parameters is the key for an economic application. The dynamic reconfiguration by re-grasping offers new possibilities to perform even high complex motions on the one hand, but also comes with new challenges in the fields of computations and planning. To manage the new design parameter efficiently an optimization tool was developed using different methods to reduce computation time.

**Acknowledgements.** As parts of this work are within the scope of the cluster of excellence "integrative production technology for high-wage countries (EXC 128)", the authors thank the German Research Foundation for its support. This project is part of the sub-category "ICD D-3.2: Flexible Assembly for Self optimising Automation" is realized in collaboration with the Laboratory for Machine Tools and Production Engineering at RWTH Aachen University.

# References

1. Möller, N.: Bestimmung der Wirtschaftlichkeit wandlungsfähiger Produktionssysteme. Forschungsbericht IWB, Band 212 (2008)
2. Müller, R., Riedel, M., Vette, M., Corves, B., Esser, M., Hüsing, M.: Reconfigurable Self-Optimising Handling System. In: Ratchev, S. (ed.) IPAS 2010. IFIP AICT, vol. 315, pp. 255–262. Springer, Heidelberg (2010) ISBN 978-3-642-11597-4
3. Nyhuis, P.: Wandlungsfähige Produktionssysteme. Heute die Industrie von morgen gestalten. Garbsen, PZH, Produktionstechnisches Zentrum (2008)
4. Feldmann, K., Ziegler, C., Michl, M.: Bewegungssteuerung für kooperiende Industrieroboter in der Montageautomatisierung. wtwerkstattstechnik online, Jg 97(9), S.713 (2007)
5. Nefzi, M., Riedel, M., Corves, B.: Development and design of a multi-fingered gripper for dexterous manipulation. In: Proceedings of the 4th IFAC-Symposium on Mechatronic Systems, Heidelberg (2006)
6. Riedel, M., Nefzi, M., Huesing, M., Corves, B.: An adjustable gripper as a reconfigurable robot with a parallel structure. In: Proceedings of the Second International Workshop on Fundamental Issues and Future Research Directions for Parallel Mechanisms and Manipulators, pp. 253–260 (2008)
7. Lee, J.-J., Tsai, L.-W.: Structural Synthesis of Multi-Fingered Hands. Journal of Mechnical Design 124, 272–276 (2002)
8. Riedel, M., Mannheim, T., Corves, B.: and versatility in automated handling process with an alterable parallel manipulator. Accepted at DECT2011/MECH 47929, Proceedings of the 35th Mechanisms and Robotics Conference (2011)
9. Roa, M.A., Suárez, R.: Regrasp planning for discrete objects. In: Proceedings of 2009 IEEE International Symposium on Assembly and Manufacturing, Suwon, Korea (2009)
10. Korf, R.E.: Depth-First Iterative-Deepening: An Optimal Admissible Tree Search. Artificial Intelligence 27, 97–109 (1985)
11. Riedel, M., Nefzi, M., Corves, B.: Performance Analysis and Dimensional Synthesis of a Six DOF Reconfigurable Parallel Manipulator. In: Proceedings of the IFToMM Symposium on Mechanism Design for Robotics, Mexico City (2010)
12. Nefzi, M., Riedel, M., Corves, B.: Towards an Automated and Optimal Design of Parallel Manipulators. In: Arreguin, J.M.R. (ed.) Automation and Robotics, pp. 143–156. I-Tech, Wien (2008) ISBN 978-3-902613-41-7
13. Riedel, M., Nefzi, M., Corves, B.: Grasp planning for a reconfigurable parallel robot with an underactuated arm structure. Mechnaical Science, 33–42 (2010) ISSN: 2191-9151, 2191-916X.-1
14. LaValle, S.: Planning Algorithms, Ch. 5, Cambridge, pp. 228–248 (2006) ISBN 9780521862059

# A Parallel Kinematic Concept Targeting at More Accurate Assembly of Aircraft Sections

Christian Löchte, Franz Dietrich, and Annika Raatz

TU Braunschweig, Institute of Machine Tools and Production Technology (IWF),
Langer Kamp 19b, 38106 Braunschweig, Germany
{c.loechte,f.dietrich,a.raatz}@tu-bs.de
http://www.iwf.tu-bs.de/

**Abstract.** This article is concerned with the kinematics for flexible and precise assembly systems for big and heavy parts, e.g. parts of plane fuselages or wings. The hypothesis of this article is that the common 3-PPPS Tripod (which is a current industrial solution to the problem) may be replaced by a 6-SPS parallel kinematic. In difference to many other parallel kinematic machines, the part which has to be assembled is used *itself* as the end effector platform in this concept. On the part and on the floor, there is a generic grid of fixation points, which gives the possibility for (re)configuration and adaption to suit particular requirements.

This article compares the transmission of drive errors in order to evaluate the transmission of alignment increments. This criterion is used for an optimization that searches for a kinematic configuration that outperforms the Tripod systems. It is shown that there is a considerable number of configurations which are superior to the Tripod system. Based on these insights, it is concluded that there is potential for the improvement of current systems through multi-objective optimization.

**Keywords:** Precision Assembly of Aircraft Fuselages, Stewart Platform, Kinematic Analysis, Jacobian.

## 1 Introduction

The upcoming production of aircrafts made of carbon fibre reinforced plastics (CFRP) demands for the revision of many common production technologies. For example, if the fuselage shall use CFRP, it is, with respect to the minimization of the weight, advantageous to minimize the number of flanges between the sections. Hence, the sections become bigger and their assembly will have to deal with bigger parts. At the same time, the accuracy of the alignment prior to fixation must be preserved or even increased. It is straight forward to conclude, that, for the assembly of such (still imaginary) designs, the requirements for the assembly automation will be subject of substantial changes. Under these premises, it is worth to review and analyse the optimality of current solutions.

This article investigates the kinematics that are used for the alignment of huge parts, e.g. fuselage sections or wing sections. Especially, this article focuses on the accuracy achieveable, which is represented by the transmission of

S. Jeschke, H. Liu, and D. Schilberg (Eds.): ICIRA 2011, Part I, LNAI 7101, pp. 142–151, 2011.

increments of the actuators. In a benchmark, the 3-$\underline{P}$PPS Tripod[1], which is used currently in industry for such tasks [2], is compared to a 6-S$\underline{P}$S Hexapod (Stewart Platform). This article proposes to use the part to be aligned *itself* as the end effector platform. Spoken in expressions of the community of parallel kinematic researchers, the *part* is the end effector platform of the kinematic. In this way, the parallel kinematic is established in an ad-hoc manner, and the mechanical infrastructure is kept at a minimum. Actuators could be reused flexibly for multiple assembly situations, and eventually more simple measurement systems could be employed. Redundant actuation, e.g. for the compensation of elasticities can be added. Then, the need for specialized bulky frames could be reduced for the sake of more flexibility, better accessibility and lower invest for infrastructure. However, there are many challenges related to such a proposal. For example, the set-up and the geometrical calibration of the system has to be quick and simple for the user. Also, the fixation points of the kinematics have to be chosen wisely (this article proposes a generic grid for this purpose).

The hypothesis of this article states, that this newly proposed kinematic outperforms the current Tripod system in terms of accuracy. The following sections are organised along the investigation of this aspect: **Section 2** draws the scenario in more detail, **Section 3** explains the kinematics. **Section 4** discusses suitable performance indices and **Section 5** outlines the optimization task. **Section 6** shows and discusses numerical results that are related to the hypothesis stated.

## 1.1   Related Work

The optimal choice of the structure and the parameters of kinematics, especially for parallel kinematics, has received profound attention in the past. The optimization of parallel kinematics is complex, due to many criteria, which are relevant for the success of a particular realization. For this reason, multi-objective optimization is widely recommended [1,3,11,13], but shows some difficulties regarding the choice of objective weights. In contrast, genetic algorithms are able to find a set of superior compromises whereas the incompatibility of the dimensions of the criteria remains preserved [8,10,9]. Such sophisticated optimization is beyond the scope of the present article and will be involved in future work.

Research on the kinematic for the assembly of huge lightweight parts is treated recently by [5]. There, many kinematic chains grip a part and form a parallel kinematic structure (see the demonstrator PARAGRIP). Due to their complexity, each kinematic chain can be considered a robot itself. Though related, due to the production of CFRP-aircrafts, the concept proposed in the present article aims at a complementary scenario: It is intended for the accurate assembly of big, heavy parts (e.g. sections of the fuselage), whereas PARAGRIP is optimized for bulky lightweight structures that require redundant kinematics to support the flexible workpieces (e.g. CFRP wing surface covers). In this sense, the two concepts complement each other.

---

[1] P: prismatic joint, S: spherical joint, $\underline{P}$ : actuated prismatic joint.

Literature about tripod kinematics for the assembly of aircraft parts can be found in [12,7]. There, the authors are mainly interested in the dynamic model and the trajectory planning for the assembly of wings on fuselages.

## 2    Scenario and Concepts

In the assembly scenario investigated, the assembly of two sections of an aircraft fuselage is considered. The outer hull of these sections are tube-styled with a length of 8 m and a diameter of 4 m. One of the sections is rigged in a fixed frame and cannot be moved. The second section is moveable and has to be aligned relatively to the fixed section in order to be assembled in the right way. A predefined frame of the moveable section, the Tool Center Point (*TCP*), has to be aligned to a second frame, called *FIX*, which is located on the fixed section of the fuselage. The following analysis refers to the alignment at this point as the assembly situation. The further research will try to find an optimized kinematic structure to perform best in this point and to meet the narrow tolerances. It is clear, that this is a major simplification of the reality, but it serves the investigation of the question, whether there is room for further improvement of the current solutions at all.

For this assembly scenario, a 6-SPS structure with 6 dof (Hexapod) is proposed, as shown in fig. 1b. In the left hand side, the immoveable tube is fixed in its rig. In the right, the moveable section is abstracted by a tube. This tube is connected either to the floor or to the walls via six legs with linear actuators. There are many fixation points on the part and on the floor. These fixation points provide the possibility for the (re)configuration of the structure by choosing different fixation points. The grid of joint candidates is indicated by holes in the floor and on the wall. Rails with holes on the moveable tube indicate the other joint candidates to which the legs may be attached.

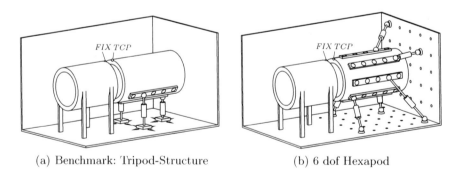

(a) Benchmark: Tripod-Structure          (b) 6 dof Hexapod

**Fig. 1.** Outline of the kinematic structures analysed

To make sure, that the proposed structure can keep up in terms of performance with conventional solutions, it is compared with a 6 dof 3-PPPS, as shown in

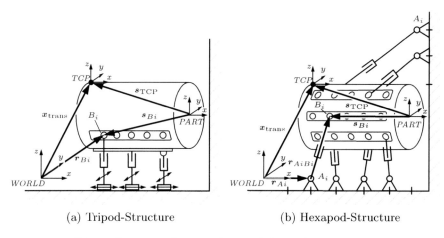

(a) Tripod-Structure                    (b) Hexapod-Structure

**Fig. 2.** Frames and vector chains of the analysed structures

fig. 1a. In [12] this structure is also introduced and discussed as an alignment system for wing assembly.

In the following section the kinematic description of these two conceptual structures is discussed and a quality criteria is found to compare them in a proper way.

## 3   Kinematic Modelling

For the description of the scenarios mentioned above, three coordinate system are introduced (see fig. 2): *WORLD*, *PART* and *TCP*. *PART* and *TCP* are attached to the part. The point of interest, i.e. where the posture alignment system must reach given tolerances, is denoted by $\boldsymbol{x}$.

$$\boldsymbol{x} = \left[\boldsymbol{x}_{\text{trans}}^T, \boldsymbol{x}_{\text{rot}}^T\right]^T = \left[X, Y, Z, \psi, \vartheta, \varphi\right]^T \tag{1}$$

The tolerances of $\boldsymbol{x}$ may be specified by $\Delta\boldsymbol{x}$ as a vector. Alternatively (and more practical), the tolerance may be specified by $(\Delta x, \Delta\phi)$, which represents the maximum tolerable spatial and angular displacement, respectively.

For the analysis of the assembly structures the inverse kinematic model (IKP) and the analytical Jacobian $\boldsymbol{J}_a$ are required. Both rely on the closed chain of vectors, as displayed in figs. 2a and 2b (Tripod, Hexapod). The drive coordinates are stored in $\boldsymbol{q} = [\ldots, q_i, \ldots]$, where $i = 1 \ldots 6$ (Hexapod), $i = 1 \ldots 9$ (Tripod). $A_n$ indicates the $n$-th joint on the floor. $B_n$ is the $n$-th joint on the part, which is connected to $A_n$ via $\boldsymbol{r}_{AnBn}$.

### 3.1   Tripod

$B_n$ are the joints on the part, which are represented by the vectors $\boldsymbol{r}_{Bn}$ ($n = 1 \ldots 3$, indicates the three kinematic chains that support the part). Since $\boldsymbol{r}_{Bn}$

contains the drive coordinates of the $n$-th support, the vector of drive coordinates $q$ is written as:

$$\boldsymbol{r}_{Bn} = \begin{bmatrix} q_{xn}, q_{yn}, q_{zn} \end{bmatrix}^T = \begin{bmatrix} q_{3n-2}, q_{3n-1}, q_{3n} \end{bmatrix}^T \qquad n = 1 \ldots 3 \qquad (2)$$

$$\boldsymbol{q} = \begin{bmatrix} q_{x1}, q_{y1}, q_{z1} \; q_{x2}, q_{y2}, q_{z2} \; q_{x3}, q_{y3}, q_{z3} \end{bmatrix}^T \qquad (3)$$

Based on these definitions, the closed chains of vectors are written as:

$$\boldsymbol{r}_{Bn} = \boldsymbol{x}_{\text{trans}} - \boldsymbol{K} * (-\boldsymbol{s}_{Bn} + \boldsymbol{s}_{TCP}). \qquad (4)$$

$$\boldsymbol{f}_n(\boldsymbol{x}, \boldsymbol{r}_{Bn}) = \begin{bmatrix} f_{3n-2} \\ f_{3n-1} \\ f_{3n} \end{bmatrix} = \boldsymbol{x}_{\text{trans}} - \boldsymbol{K} * (-\boldsymbol{s}_{Bn} + \boldsymbol{s}_{TCP}) - \boldsymbol{r}_{Bn} = 0. \qquad (5)$$

$\boldsymbol{s}_{Bi}, \boldsymbol{s}_{TCP}$     : Position Vectors of Bi and TCP w.r.t. $PART$
$\boldsymbol{K} = \boldsymbol{K}(\boldsymbol{x}_{\text{rot}})$     : Rotation Matrix $WORLD{\to}PART$

Equation (5) expands to nine equations, which means that the kinematic system is over-determined by three dimensions (the part is considered as a rigid body). In the present article, only 6 dof out of 9 are considered to be actuated, in order to resolve problems related to non-squared Jacobian matrices. Whenever applicable, the best combination of 6 actuated drives is used here ("best" in the sense of a given optimization task).

## 3.2   Hexapod

The vector chain of eq. (6) describes the relationship of $TCP$ and $WORLD$ of the Hexapod. At the Hexapod, the index $n$ is equivalent to $i$, since the $n$-th kinematic chain corresponds to the $i$-th drive coordinate. The vector $\boldsymbol{r}_{AiBi}$ points from the base joint $A_i$ to the corresponding $B_i$ along the $i$-th actuated leg. Its length is equal to the $i$-th drive coordinate: $||\boldsymbol{r}_{AiBi}||_2 = q_i$. This relationship is used to obtain the inverse kinematics[2]:

$$\boldsymbol{x}_{\text{trans}} = \boldsymbol{r}_{Ai} + \boldsymbol{r}_{AiBi} + \boldsymbol{K} * (-\boldsymbol{s}_{Bi} + \boldsymbol{s}_{TCP}) \qquad (6)$$

$$(\boldsymbol{r}_{AiBi})^2 = (\boldsymbol{x}_{\text{trans}} - \boldsymbol{r}_{Ai} - \boldsymbol{K} * (-\boldsymbol{s}_{Bi} + \boldsymbol{s}_{TCP}))^2 \qquad (7)$$

$$q_i = \sqrt{(\boldsymbol{x}_{\text{trans}} - \boldsymbol{r}_{Ai} - \boldsymbol{K} * (-\boldsymbol{s}_{Bi} + \boldsymbol{s}_{TCP}))^2} \qquad (8)$$

$$f_i(\boldsymbol{x}, \boldsymbol{q}) = (\boldsymbol{x}_{\text{trans}} - \boldsymbol{r}_{Ai} - \boldsymbol{K} * (-\boldsymbol{s}_{Bi} + \boldsymbol{s}_{TCP}))^2 - q_i^2 = 0 \qquad (9)$$

## 3.3   Jacobian Matrices

The analysis of the kinematics and the dynamics of parallel kinematic machines relies mostly on the Jacobian $\boldsymbol{J}_a$:

$$\dot{\boldsymbol{x}} = \boldsymbol{J}_a \dot{\boldsymbol{q}} \qquad (10)$$

---

[2] $\boldsymbol{\alpha}^2 = \boldsymbol{\alpha}^T \cdot \boldsymbol{\alpha}$, where $\boldsymbol{\alpha} = [\ldots, \alpha_k, \ldots]^T$.

Differentiation of eqs. (5) and (9) yields the Jacobian $\boldsymbol{J}_a$ for the Tripod and the Hexapod, respectively [6]:

$$\frac{d\boldsymbol{f}(\boldsymbol{x},\boldsymbol{q})}{dt} = \frac{\partial \boldsymbol{f}(\boldsymbol{x},\boldsymbol{q})}{\partial \boldsymbol{x}^T}\dot{\boldsymbol{x}} + \frac{\partial \boldsymbol{f}(\boldsymbol{x},\boldsymbol{q})}{\partial \boldsymbol{q}^T}\dot{\boldsymbol{q}} = \boldsymbol{0} \tag{11}$$

$$\dot{\boldsymbol{x}} = -\underbrace{\left(\frac{\partial \boldsymbol{f}(\boldsymbol{x},\boldsymbol{q})}{\partial \boldsymbol{x}^T}\right)^{-1}}_{\boldsymbol{J}_{\mathrm{DKP}}} \underbrace{\frac{\partial \boldsymbol{f}(\boldsymbol{x},\boldsymbol{q})}{\partial \boldsymbol{q}^T}}_{\boldsymbol{J}_{\mathrm{IKP}}} \dot{\boldsymbol{q}}, \qquad (\text{if } \boldsymbol{J}_{\mathrm{DKP}}^{-1} \text{ exists}) \tag{12}$$

$$\boldsymbol{J}_a = -\boldsymbol{J}_{\mathrm{DKP}}^{-1}\,\boldsymbol{J}_{\mathrm{IKP}} \tag{13}$$

## 4   Criteria for the Benchmark of Kinematics

$\boldsymbol{J}_a$ transforms a hyper-sphere in joint space $\dot{\boldsymbol{q}}$ into a hyper ellipsoid in carte-sian space $\dot{\boldsymbol{x}}$. Many authors have proposed to optimize the kinematics towards isotropy, which means that the inverse of the condition number of $\boldsymbol{J}_a$ shall be $\kappa^{-1} = 1$ (Stronger anisotropy in $\boldsymbol{J}_a$ results in stronger deformation of the hyper ellipsoid). However, the present article is interested in the transmission of small-est possible increments of a drive $\varDelta q$. These two criteria have been considered as equivalent [4], misleadingly. Since the input increments $\varDelta q$ form a hyper cube in input space, not a hyper sphere, the output $\varDelta \boldsymbol{x}$ is a deformed hyper cube, not a hyper sphere. In the result, serious numerical mistakes are caused [9,10].

Each of the drives may have a smallest increment $\varDelta q$, which contributes to the increment vector $\varDelta \boldsymbol{q} = [\mu_1 \varDelta q, \ldots, \mu_n \varDelta q]$, $\mu_i = \pm 1$. The spatial output increment that results from $\varDelta \boldsymbol{q}$ is stated as:

$$\varDelta \boldsymbol{x} = \boldsymbol{J}_{a,\mathrm{trans}}\varDelta \boldsymbol{q} \tag{14a}$$

$$\varDelta \boldsymbol{\phi} = \boldsymbol{J}_{a,\mathrm{rot}}\varDelta \boldsymbol{q} \tag{14b}$$

The transmission ratio of the input hyper cube of interest is obtained via nor-malization by the increment $\varDelta q$ and maximization over the $\mu_i$

$$\varDelta \hat{x}_{\max} = \max_{\mu_i} \frac{||\boldsymbol{J}_{a,\mathrm{trans}}\varDelta \boldsymbol{q}||_2}{\varDelta q}, \qquad \varDelta q \neq 0 \tag{15a}$$

$$\varDelta \hat{\phi}_{\max} = \max_{\mu_i} \frac{||\boldsymbol{J}_{a,\mathrm{rot}}\varDelta \boldsymbol{q}||_2}{\varDelta q}, \qquad \varDelta q \neq 0 \tag{15b}$$

The translational and rotational degrees are stated separately, in order to main-tain the physical meaning of the norm operator $||\cdot||_2$. Following the proposal in [10], the transmission of translational errors and the transmission of rotational errors are treated as two individual performance criteria. In a later stage of the kinematic optimization, this gives a more realistic impression of a particular candidate. For reason of simplification, this paper focuses on the transmission of input increments towards the translational degrees of freedom as stated in eq. (15a).

# 5  Optimization Algorithm

In the present benchmark, the criterion mentioned in eq. (15a) shall be optimized, in order to improve the transmission of minimum increments of the kinematic for assembly. Based on eq. (15a), the optimization problem is stated as:

$$\min_{B,x,\Delta q} \left( \Delta \hat{x}_{max} \right) \qquad \text{Tripod} \qquad (16a)$$

$$\min_{A,B,x,\Delta q} \left( \Delta \hat{x}_{max} \right) \qquad \text{Hexapod} \qquad (16b)$$

$$A = \left[ \ldots, r_{Ai}, \ldots \right], \qquad r_{Ai} \in \{\text{set of base joint candidates}\}$$
$$B = \left[ \ldots, r_{Bi}, \ldots \right], \qquad r_{Ai} \in \{\text{set of platform joint candidates}\}$$

In consideration of the Hexapod, the joint index is $i = 1\ldots6$. At the Tripod, $i = 1\ldots3$. For the present benchmark, the set of candidates for base joints is concatenated from a raster of points of $5 \times 6$ on the floor and $5 \times 5$ on the wall (cf. fig. 1b) . For the Hexapod, the set of candidates of platform joints consists of $5 \times 8$ points across the outer surface of the fuselage section. The Tripod may only be attached to points on the lower side of the fuselage, due to its constraint to operate from ground level (cf. fig. 1a). Hence, there are only $5 \times 3$ candidates for platform joints to choose from.

The definitions above result in $\binom{55}{6} \cdot \binom{40}{6} = 1.13 \cdot 10^{14}$ combinations for the Hexapod and $\binom{15}{3} = 455$ combinations for the Tripod. Consequently, *all* combinations of the Tripod can be computed and analysed easily[3]. For the Hexapod, not all (theoretically possible) combinations can be analysed, due to excessive time consumption. Hence, a simple random optimization algorithm is used to gain the insights sought: In each iteration, 6 base joints and 6 platform joints are chosen randomly. For this candidate, collision of legs with the fuselage is checked by computing the angles enclosed by the leg vectors and the fuselage normal vector at the respective platform joint[4]. If one of these angles is below $90°$, leg collision is detected and this candidate is skipped. Our computations showed, that only $\approx 0.25\%$ of the configurations tested pass this plausibility check.

---

[3] Computation time: $< 10\,\text{s}$ on a $2 \times 3.5\,\text{GHz}$ Windows 7 System running non-optimized code in MATLAB.

[4] Fuselage normal vector: Identity vector, which points normal to the fuselage surface inwards.

## 6    Numerical Results, Benchmark and Discussion

After testing $5 \cdot 10^8$ candidates, the results following can be stated: The minimum values found are:

$$\min_{B, x, \Delta q} \left( \Delta \hat{x}_{\max} \right) = 5.754 \qquad \text{Tripod} \qquad (17)$$

$$\min_{A, B, x, \Delta q} \left( \Delta \hat{x}_{\max} \right) = 3.341 \qquad \text{Hexapod} \qquad (18)$$

Figure 3 shows a variety of the best 20 solutions found by this algorithm.

It is not sufficient to be interested in the *one* optimal solution in the sense of eq. (16a) or eq. (16b). This is due to the fact that many other requirements

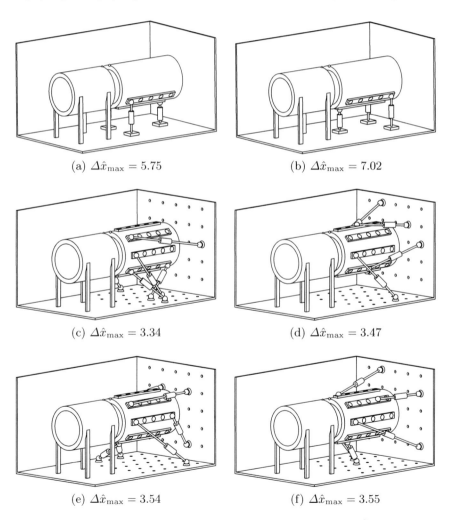

(a) $\Delta \hat{x}_{\max} = 5.75$

(b) $\Delta \hat{x}_{\max} = 7.02$

(c) $\Delta \hat{x}_{\max} = 3.34$

(d) $\Delta \hat{x}_{\max} = 3.47$

(e) $\Delta \hat{x}_{\max} = 3.54$

(f) $\Delta \hat{x}_{\max} = 3.55$

**Fig. 3.** Some of the best performance indices ($\Delta q = 10^{-3}$ m)

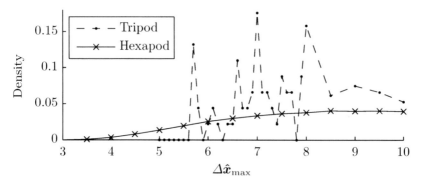

**Fig. 4.** Statistical distribution of the solutions w.r.t. eq. (16b)

and criteria will influence the choice of the kinematics in practice. Since this multi-objective optimization is beyond the scope of this article, it is of interest how many combinations in a certain range of the performance criterion can be obtained. The probability density function of $\min(\Delta \hat{x}_{max})$, computed from random choices of $\boldsymbol{A}, \boldsymbol{B}$, gives some valuable insight to this aspect. Figure 4 shows the probability density function for both, the Tripod and the Hexapod. It displays that there is a considerable amount of candidates of the Hexapod available, which perform better than the best combination of the Tripod. The percentage of candidates that is similar to the Tripod or better ($\Delta \hat{x}_{max} < 6.0$) has been estimated to 2.25%, based on the data presented in fig. 4. Hence, it can be concluded, that it is worth to take a closer look at kinematic optimization of assembly systems for aircraft fuselages.

## 7    Conclusion

The present article is concerned with the benchmark of well-established 3-<u>PPP</u>S kinematics for the assembly of big workpieces versus a 6-S<u>P</u>S Hexapod structure. This is of interest, for example, for the improvement of the accurate assembly of fuselage sections. In this context, criteria for the assessment of the transmission of drive increments are discussed and a suitable measure is proposed. A scenario is designed, in which comparability for both kinematics is stressed. For both kinematics, the performance indices are computed for a wide range of candidates, and some of the best solutions for each concept are presented.

It can be stated, that the well-established 3-<u>PPP</u>S structure is *not at all* an optimum in the sense of error transmission. Improvements of $\approx 40\%$ can be expected from the benchmark carried out. Hence, review and optimization of the kinematics is recommendable and promises potential for substantial improvement.

In the future, multi-objective optimization shall take place, in order to find practical compromises. Even if such optimizations have been investigated for parallel kinematic machines in general [9], the specialties of the application in aircraft production impose special requirements on this task. This will require specialized treatment in the future in order to improve common solutions, which are now in practice.

# References

1. Arsenault, M., Boudreau, R.: The synthesis of a general planar parallel manipulator platform with prismatic joints for optimal stiffness. In: Proceedings of the 11th World Congress in Mechanism and Machine Science, Tianjin (China), pp. 1633–1641 (2004)
2. Broetje Automation: Final assembly - joining processes meeting the highest demands, http://www.claas-fertigungstechnik.com/cft-ba/generator/cft-ba/de/applications/finalassem/start,lang=de_DE.html, (checked April 21, 2011)
3. Ceccarelli, M.: An optimum design of parallel manipulators - formulation and experimental validation. In: Proceedings of the 1st International Colloquium of the Collaborative Research Center 562, Braunschweig. pp. 47–63 (2002)
4. Chedmail, P.: Optimization of Multi-DOF Mechanisms. Springer, Heidelberg (2001)
5. Corves, B., Riedel, M., Nefzi, M.: Performance analysis and dimensional synthesis of a six dof reconfigurable parallel manipulator. In: IFToMM Symposium on Mechanism Design for Robotics, SMDR 2010 (2010)
6. Gosselin, C., Angeles, J.: Singularity analysis of closed-loop kinematic chains. IEEE Transactions on Robotics and Automation 6(3), 281–290 (1990)
7. Guo, Z., Jiang, J., Ke, Y.: Stiffness of postural alignment system based on 3-axis actuators for large aircraft components. Chinese Journal of Mechanical Engineering (English Edition) 23(4), 524–531 (2010)
8. Kirchner, J.: Mehrkriterielle Optimierung von Parallelkinematiken. Ph.D. thesis, Technische Universität Chemnitz (2001)
9. Krefft, M.: Aufgabenangepasste Optimierung von Parallelstrukturen für Maschinen in der Produktionstechnik. Ph.D. thesis, Fakultät für Maschinenbau, TU Braunschweig, Vulkan Verlag (2006)
10. Krefft, M., Hesselbach, J.: The dynamic optimization of PKM. In: Advances in Robot Kinematics (ARK) - Mechanisms and Motion, pp. 339–348. Springer, Berlin (2006)
11. Ottaviano, E., Ceccarelli, M.: Optimum design of parallel manipulators for workspace and singularity performances. In: Proceedings of the Workshop on Fundamental Issues and Future Research Directions for Parallel Mechanisms and Manipulators, Quebec City (Kanada), pp. 98–105 (2002)
12. Zhang, B., Yao, B.G., Ke, Y.L.: A novel posture alignment system for aircraft wing assembly. J. Zhejiang Univ. Sci. A 10(11), 1624–1630 (2009)
13. Zhang, D., Xu, Z., Mechefske, C.K., Xi, F.: Design optimization of parallel kinematic toolheads with genetic algorithms. In: Proceedings of the 2nd NCG Application Conference on Parallel Kinematic Machines, Chemnitz, pp. 941–956 (2002)

# Dimensional Synthesis of Parallel Manipulators Based on Direction-Dependent Jacobian Indices

Marwène Nefzi[1], Clément Gosselin[2], Martin Riedel[1],
Mathias Hüsing[1], and Burkhard Corves[1]

[1] Department of Mechanism Theory and Dynamics of Machines, Aachen, Germany
[2] Laboratoire de robotique de l'université de Laval, Canada

**Abstract.** This work proposes direction-dependent Jacobian indices
that allow tackling the performance evaluation and dimensional synthesis
of parallel manipulators. These indices characterize the kinetostatic capabilities of a manipulator along and about each direction of the Cartesian
space and are more likely to help the designer to achieve an assessment of
different geometries without having to resort to predefined trajectories.
We shed light on these indices by considering a 2-dof parallel manipulator whose modeling is relatively straightforward. The generic example
of a five-bar manipulator allows establishing a geometric interpretation
of the proposed indices and helps to develop a better understanding of
their use within the scope of dimensional synthesis, the main goal being the derivation of kinetostatic indices that are valid for n-dof parallel
manipulators.

**Keywords:** Dimensional synthesis, parallel manipulators, performance
evaluation, kinetostatic performance indices.

## 1 Introduction

When dealing with parallel manipulators, designers have often to cope with the
determination of the approximate lengths of the links that build up the mechanical architecture opted for. This task is termed as dimensional synthesis and
must be carried out at an early stage of the design process. It is decisive for a
successful design, as it affects all subsequent stages such as structural dimensioning, the selection of adequate actuators etc. Although it is an active research
area, the performance evaluation and dimensional synthesis of parallel manipulators are not well defined. Many approaches are based on indices that stem from
numerics such as the determinant, condition number, singular value decomposition, infinity norm etc., see also [10] and [14]. Instead of these indices that may
mix up different units, this work proposes direction-dependent indices that are
more adequate to evaluate the capabilities of parallel manipulators. To this end,
a five-bar mechanism is considered. This generic example is relatively straightforward and allows developing a better understanding of direction-dependent
kinetostatic indices, the main goal being the derivation of kinetostatic indices
that are valid for n-dof parallel manipulators, see also [6], [8], [11] and [12].

S. Jeschke, H. Liu, and D. Schilberg (Eds.): ICIRA 2011, Part I, LNAI 7101, pp. 152–161, 2011.
© Springer-Verlag Berlin Heidelberg 2011

In the first section, typical design requirements are defined. In the second section, performance evaluation is tackled and direction-dependent Jacobian indices are derived. Based on these indices, dimensional synthesis is addressed.

## 2    Typical Design Requirements

Usually, the starting point of dimensional synthesis is a specifications list. Apart from the workspace, the end-effector accuracy and maximal achievable velocities play a key role in customizing a manipulator to a given task. Furthermore, process and inertia forces should be taken into account as they are decisive for performing high-speed trajectories and the selection of adequate actuators. Let us consider the following task of designing a 2-dof parallel manipulator whose workspace must be a rectangle of $1 \times 0.5 \ m^2$ above a line at y= 0.5 m. The manipulator end effector should also be capable of performing velocities of $\dot{x}_d = \dot{y}_d = 1 \frac{m}{s}$ along each direction and of withstanding process and inertia forces of $F_{x_d} = F_{y_d} = 100$ N.

Aside from these demands (performance requirements that must be satisfied), the designer may also be interested in:

– a large amplification of the actuator capabilities,
– a homogeneous distribution of the kinetostatic performance of a manipulator,
– equal kinetostatic characteristics along and about each direction of the Cartesian space, as long as the designer does not aim at favoring certain directions and
– a manipulator whose workspace complies with the specified one as closely as possible in order not to resort to costly actuators featuring large strokes.

Once the manipulator requirements to be considered have been determined, one may tackle the performance evaluation of the mechanical architecture opted for.

## 3    Workspace and Kinetostatic Performance Evaluation

The most obvious manipulator characteristic is the workspace. The determination of its boundaries can be achieved either numerically or graphically, see also [3] , [4] and [7]. Thereafter, the workspace can be characterized by different indices such as its area/volume, a ratio between this area/volume and the installation space or the space occupied by the manipulator links over the whole workspace etc. **Figure 1(a)** depicts the resulting workspace boundaries of a five-bar linkage featuring the following dimensions $\rho_{min} = 0.5 \, m$, $\rho_{max} = \sqrt{2} \, m$ and $L = 1 \, m$, see **Figure 1(b)** for the used nomenclature.

Once the workspace boundaries are known, one may evaluate the manipulator kinetostatic performance. According to [1, chap. 8], these characteristics are understood as the capabilities of a robot to achieve a certain end-effector velocity and to withstand thereby definite wrenches under the constraint that the actuator velocities and forces are bounded. Accordingly, if a manipulator is

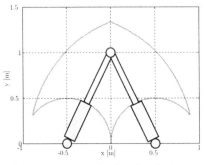
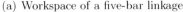

(a) Workspace of a five-bar linkage

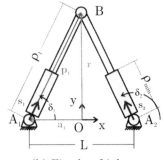

(b) Five-bar Linkage

**Fig. 1.** A five-bar linkage and its workspace

capable to achieve higher end-effector velocities or requires lower actuator velocities and forces to perform a prescribed trajectory, then it is said to have better
kinetostatic capabilities. In the broader sense, accuracy is also considered as a
kinetostatic performance, since the underlying equation is similar to the velocity
equation. Apart from the considered pose, these capabilities highly depend on
the manipulator geometry. More precisely, they depend on the amplification of
the actuator capabilities by the kinematic chains underlying the manipulator.
Clearly, the higher the transmission ratios between the actuators and the end-
effector are throughout the workspace, the better the kinetostatic capabilities
will be for any trajectory.

Instead of partially inspecting the manipulator workspace by means of predefined trajectories and the resulting actuator velocities and forces, direction-
dependent Jacobian indices were proposed in [2] and [8] in order to evaluate
the performance of a given manipulator. In contrast to the well-known indices
as determinant, condition number and norm that aim at characterizing the manipulator by means of a single index, direction-dependent indices do not mix
different physical units and allow the quantification of the adequacy of a manipulator for any number of trajectories. This, in turn, enables an assessment
of different manipulator geometries at an early stage of the design process. Furthermore, these indices can be computed throughout the desired workspace. The
value distribution provides global information about the kinetostatic capabilities.
Prior to this performance evaluation, the underlying equations are revisited.

**Position and Jacobian Analysis of the Manipulator:** Referring to Figure
1(b), a vector loop equation can be written as:

$$\mathbf{p}_i = -\mathbf{a}_i + \mathbf{r} \text{ , for } i = 1, 2 \tag{1}$$

where $\mathbf{p}_i$ is the vector pointing from $A_i$ to B, $\mathbf{a}_i$ is the position vector of $A_i$ and
$\mathbf{r}$ is the position vector of B. Differentiating equation (1) with respect to time
leads to the following equation:

$$\begin{pmatrix} \dot{\rho}_1 \\ \dot{\rho}_2 \end{pmatrix} = \begin{pmatrix} \mathbf{s}_1^T \\ \mathbf{s}_2^T \end{pmatrix} \begin{pmatrix} \dot{x} \\ \dot{y} \end{pmatrix} = \begin{pmatrix} s_{1x} & s_{1y} \\ s_{2x} & s_{2y} \end{pmatrix} \begin{pmatrix} \dot{x} \\ \dot{y} \end{pmatrix} \tag{2}$$

where $\mathbf{s}_i$ is a unit vector along the $i$-th leg, $\dot{\rho}_i = \mathbf{p}_i \cdot \mathbf{s}_i$ is the velocity of the actuator in the $i$-th leg and $\dot{x}/\dot{y}$ is the end-effector velocity along the $x/y$-direction. In a more compact way, equation (2) can be written as:

$$\dot{\rho} = \mathbf{J}_p \dot{\chi} \tag{3}$$

where the end-effector velocity vector $\dot{\chi}$ is related to the actuator velocity vector $\dot{\rho}$ by the Jacobian $\mathbf{J}_p$. A relationship between a wrench $\mathbf{F}$ acting on the platform and the actuator forces $\boldsymbol{\tau}$ can be determined by means of the principle of virtual work $\delta\boldsymbol{\rho}^T\boldsymbol{\tau} = \delta\boldsymbol{\chi}^T\mathbf{F}$ , see also [5] and [13]. The resulting equation is:

$$\boldsymbol{\tau} = \mathbf{J}_p^{-T}\mathbf{F} \tag{4}$$

where $\mathbf{J}_p^{-T}$ is the transpose of the Jacobian inverse. For the mechanism at hand, it can be written as:

$$\mathbf{J}_p^{-T} = \begin{pmatrix} \dfrac{s_{2y}}{s_{1x}\,s_{2y}-s_{1y}\,s_{2x}} & -\dfrac{s_{2x}}{s_{1x}\,s_{2y}-s_{1y}\,s_{2x}} \\[2ex] -\dfrac{s_{1y}}{s_{1x}\,s_{2y}-s_{1y}\,s_{2x}} & \dfrac{s_{1x}}{s_{1x}\,s_{2y}-s_{1y}\,s_{2x}} \end{pmatrix} \tag{5}$$

Equations (3 and 4) allow finding out the actuator velocities and forces for any end-effector velocity. The Jacobian $\mathbf{J}_p$ is a function of the end-effector position and the geometric parameters of the manipulator. In order to asses different geometries over a prescribed workspace, it is therefore plausible to resort to this matrix. Classical indices strive for the evaluation of a geometry by a single index as the Jacobian determinant, condition number or norm. In the following, direction-dependent indices are proposed.

**Direction-Dependent Kinetostatic Performance Indices:** Based on equations (3 and 4), one may identify that the limiting factor for higher end-effector velocities are the actuator capabilities. If different manipulator geometries have to be assessed and the same actuators are to be used, the most appropriate geometry is the one, whose Jacobian components feature the lowest absolute values. More precisely, if the manipulator has to perform a line along the x-axis with the velocity $\dot{x}_E$ and to additionally withstand forces $F_{x_E}$ only along this direction, the maximal actuator velocity $\dot{\rho}_{max}$ and force $\tau_{max}$ are:

$$\dot{\rho}_{max} = \max\left(|s_{1x}\dot{x}_E|,|s_{2x}\dot{x}_E|\right)$$
$$\tau_{max} = \max\left(\left|\frac{s_{2y}}{s_{1x}\,s_{2y}-s_{1y}\,s_{2x}}F_{x_E}\right|,\left|-\frac{s_{1y}}{s_{1x}\,s_{2y}-s_{1y}\,s_{2x}}F_{x_E}\right|\right) \tag{6}$$

Similarly, if the manipulator has to perform a line along the y-axis with the velocity $\dot{y}_E$ and to additionally withstand forces $F_{y_E}$ only along this direction, the maximal actuator velocity $\dot{\rho}_{max}$ and force $\tau_{max}$ are:

$$\dot{\rho}_{max} = \max\left(|s_{1y}\dot{y}_E|,|s_{2y}\dot{y}_E|\right)$$
$$\tau_{max} = \max\left(\left|-\frac{s_{2x}}{s_{1x}\,s_{2y}-s_{1y}\,s_{2x}}F_{y_E}\right|,\left|\frac{s_{1x}}{s_{1x}\,s_{2y}-s_{1y}\,s_{2x}}F_{y_E}\right|\right) \tag{7}$$

For a 2-dof manipulator, motions and forces are expected along both directions. Hence, the resulting actuator velocities and forces depend on the manipulator kinetostatic capabilities along each direction to a different extent. As manipulators should be versatile and the trajectories to be performed cannot be completely known at this stage of the design process, direction-dependent indices are more appropriate. In addition to this consideration, one may assume that the end-effector velocities and forces acting on the manipulator are normed to unity. In this way, one ends up with the following velocity transmission indices along the $x/y$-direction for a 2-dof manipulator and along the $j$-th direction for a $n$-dof manipulator:

$$
\begin{array}{cc}
\text{2-dof manipulator} & \text{$n$-dof manipulator} \\
\hline
\mathcal{H}_{v_1} = \max\left(|s_{1x}|, |s_{2x}|\right) & \\
\mathcal{H}_{v_2} = \max\left(|s_{1y}|, |s_{2y}|\right) & \mathcal{H}_{v_j} = \max_i |\mathbf{J}_{p_{ij}}|
\end{array}
\tag{8}
$$

In equation (8), the corresponding indices for a $n$-dof manipulator are also given. The index $i = 1 \cdots n$ refers to the $i$-th actuator and the index $j = 1 \cdots n$ refers to the $j$-th direction.

Similarily, the following force transmission indices are obtained along the $x/y$-direction for a 2-dof manipulator and along the $j$-th direction for a $n$-dof manipulator:

$$
\begin{array}{cc}
\text{2-dof manipulator} & \text{$n$-dof manipulator} \\
\hline
\mathcal{H}_{f_1} = \max\left(\left|\frac{s_{2y}}{s_{1x}\,s_{2y} - s_{1y}\,s_{2x}}\right|, \left|-\frac{s_{1y}}{s_{1x}\,s_{2y} - s_{1y}\,s_{2x}}\right|\right) & \\
\mathcal{H}_{f_2} = \max\left(\left|-\frac{s_{2x}}{s_{1x}\,s_{2y} - s_{1y}\,s_{2x}}\right|, \left|\frac{s_{1x}}{s_{1x}\,s_{2y} - s_{1y}\,s_{2x}}\right|\right) & \mathcal{H}_{f_j} = \max_i \left|\left(\mathbf{J}_p^{-T}\right)_{ij}\right|
\end{array}
\tag{9}
$$

**Figure 2** depicts the value distribution of the derived indices over the workspace of a five-bar linkage, the geometry of which has been introduced in Section 3. Due to the symmetry of the chosen manipulator geometry, the index $\mathcal{H}_{v_1}$ is minimal along the x-axis and at positions distant from points $A_{1,2}$. In these positions, the manipulator legs are less sensitive to motions along the x-direction. The index $\mathcal{H}_{v_2}$ features large values in these positions, as the mechanism is more sensitive to displacements along the y-direction. Large values of this index are also expected in the edge regions, as one leg is almost parallel to the y-axis. On the other hand, $\mathcal{H}_{f_1}$ is minimal for positions near to point O, since both actuator forces are almost parallel to the x-axis and equally contribute to withstanding forces along this direction. $\mathcal{H}_{f_2}$ is minimal along the y-axis since the legs are almost parallel to this axis. Comparing the value distribution of $\mathcal{H}_{f_1}$ and $\mathcal{H}_{f_2}$ leads to the conclusion that the geometry opted for is more appropriate to support forces along the y-direction and to perform higher end-effector velocities along the x-direction. The last statement has however to be mitigated as higher end-effector velocities also imply larger inertia forces along this direction.

In order to develop a deeper understanding of these indices, a geometric interpretation is given in the next subsection.

**Geometric Interpretation of the Derived Performance Indices:** A geometric interpretation of the derived indices is straightforward when the Jacobian components are expressed by means of angles. To this end, $\cos(\delta_1), \sin(\delta_1), \cos(\delta_2)$

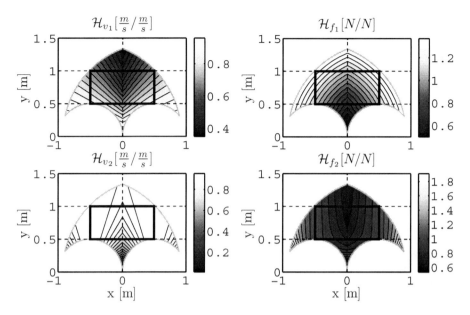

**Fig. 2.** Value distribution of the derived kinetostatic indices

and $\sin(\delta_2)$ are substituted for $s_{1x}, s_{1y}, s_{2x}$ and $s_{2y}$. Equation (2) can then be written as:

$$\begin{pmatrix} \dot{\rho}_1 \\ \dot{\rho}_2 \end{pmatrix} = \begin{pmatrix} \cos(\delta_1)\sin(\delta_1) \\ \cos(\delta_2)\sin(\delta_2) \end{pmatrix} \begin{pmatrix} \dot{x} \\ \dot{y} \end{pmatrix} \tag{10}$$

The velocity performance indices can then be expressed in terms of the angles $\delta_1$ and $\delta_2$:

$$\begin{aligned} \mathcal{H}_{v_1} &= \max\left(|\cos(\delta_1)|, |\cos(\delta_2)|\right) \\ \mathcal{H}_{v_2} &= \max\left(|\sin(\delta_1)|, |\sin(\delta_2)|\right) \end{aligned} \tag{11}$$

Similarly, equation (5) can be written as:

$$\begin{pmatrix} \tau_1 \\ \tau_2 \end{pmatrix} = \begin{pmatrix} \dfrac{\sin(\delta_2)}{\sin(\delta_2-\delta_1)} & -\dfrac{\cos(\delta_2)}{\sin(\delta_2-\delta_1)} \\ -\dfrac{\sin(\delta_1)}{\sin(\delta_2-\delta_1)} & \dfrac{\cos(\delta_1)}{\sin(\delta_2-\delta_1)} \end{pmatrix} \begin{pmatrix} F_1 \\ F_2 \end{pmatrix} \tag{12}$$

The corresponding force performance indices become:

$$\begin{aligned} \mathcal{H}_{f_1} &= \max\left(\left|\frac{\sin(\delta_2)}{\sin(\delta_2-\delta_1)}\right|, \left|-\frac{\sin(\delta_1)}{\sin(\delta_2-\delta_1)}\right|\right) \\ \mathcal{H}_{f_2} &= \max\left(\left|-\frac{\cos(\delta_2)}{\sin(\delta_2-\delta_1)}\right|, \left|\frac{\cos(\delta_1)}{\sin(\delta_2-\delta_1)}\right|\right) \end{aligned} \tag{13}$$

**Figure 3** represents the dependency of the indices $\mathcal{H}_{v_1}$, $\mathcal{H}_{v_2}$, $\mathcal{H}_{f_1}$ and $\mathcal{H}_{f_2}$ on the angles $\delta_1$ and $\delta_2$. The computation of these indices was made under the assumption that: $0 < \delta_1 < \delta_2$, so that the two legs always intersect. Although it is unrealistic, the actuator lengths vary from 0 to $\infty$. This assumption allows a large variation of the angles $\delta_1$ and $\delta_2$. Figure 3 highlights that:

- $\mathcal{H}_{f_1}$ is minimal for $\delta_1 = 0°$ and $\delta_2 = 180°$. In this manipulator configuration, both actuators are directed to the x-axis and equally withstand to a force along this axis.
- As opposed to $\mathcal{H}_{f_1}$, $\mathcal{H}_{f_2}$ is minimal when the actuators are directed to the y-axis. $\delta_1$ and $\delta_2$ are then close to 90°.
- On the other hand, $\mathcal{H}_{v_1}$ is minimal when $\delta_1$ and $\delta_2$ are close to 90°. In this configuration, the manipulator is less sensitive to motions along the x-direction. Hence, the actuator velocities do not need to be large to perform a velocity along this direction.
- In contrast to $\mathcal{H}_{v_1}$, $\mathcal{H}_{v_2}$ is minimal when $\delta_1 = 0/180°$ and $\delta_2 = 0/180°$. In these configurations, an end-effector velocity along the y-direction implies the lowest actuator velocities.

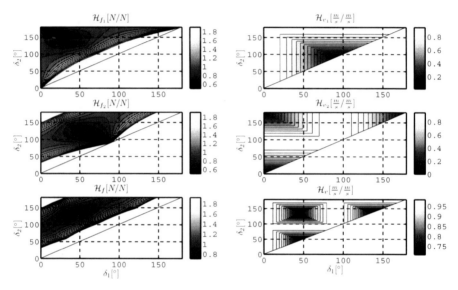

**Fig. 3.** Value distribution of the indices in terms of the joint variables $\delta_1$ and $\delta_2$

The diagrams of $\mathcal{H}_f = \max(|\mathcal{H}_{f_1}|, |\mathcal{H}_{f_2}|)$ and $\mathcal{H}_v = \max(|\mathcal{H}_{v_1}|, |\mathcal{H}_{v_2}|)$ points out that a configuration of $\delta_1 = 45°$ and $\delta_2 = 135°$ minimizes velocities and forces in both actuators and along both directions. This configuration corresponds to a single end-effector pose within the workspace. Hence, minimizing $\mathcal{H}_f$ and $\mathcal{H}_v$ leads to a manipulator whose workspace degenerates to a single pose. For this reason, it is necessary to consider value ranges for each performance index as a design goal rather than a single value.

The geometric interpretation of the derived kinetostatic indices makes clear that these indices are geometrically interpretable. Optimizing them may therefore lead to an appropriate manipulator geometry that minimizes the actuator velocities and forces required to perform different trajectories.

## 4    Dimensional Synthesis

Dimensional synthesis usually starts off with the choice of design variables. As the workspace depends on the minimal and maximal leg length, it is necessary to consider $\rho_{min}$ and $\rho_{max}$. Their variations will guarantee that the demanded workspace is met. Furthermore, the parameter $L$ affects the manipulator kinetostatic performance and should also be included in the design parameters. Hence, one ends up with the following design parameter vector $\boldsymbol{\pi} = (\rho_{min}, \rho_{max}, L)^T$. For simplicity of exposition, the y-coordinates of points $A_{1,2}$ are not taken into account, even though they affect the manipulator kinetostatic capabilities.

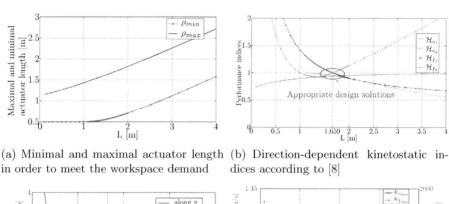

(a) Minimal and maximal actuator length in order to meet the workspace demand

(b) Direction-dependent kinetostatic indices according to [8]

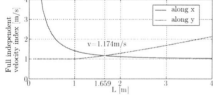
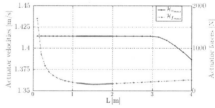

(c) Full independent velocity index according to [7]

(d) Maximum required actuator velocities and forces to perform the demands

**Fig. 4.** Parameter variation

Once the design parameters have been determined, a variation may be carried out in order to find out appropriate design solutions. As the Jacobian does not depend on $\rho_{min}$ and $\rho_{max}$, the kinetostatic capabilities of the manipulator do not depend on these parameters. Hence, one may first find out what should be the minimal and maximal leg lengths in order to meet the workspace requirement. These lengths correspond to the distance between points $A_{1,2}$ and the nearst/most distant edge of the prescribed rectangular workspace. Then, an adequate $L$ can be found to maximize the manipulator kinetostatic capabilities. **Figure 4(a)** shows that there exists for each $L$ a combination of $\rho_{min}$ and $\rho_{max}$ so that the prescribed workspace is met.

**Figure 4(b)** depicts the maximum values of the performance indices over the workspace: $\max_{\mathcal{W}_d}(\mathcal{H}_{v_1})$, $\max_{\mathcal{W}_d}(\mathcal{H}_{v_2})$, $\max_{\mathcal{W}_d}(\mathcal{H}_{f_1})$ and $\max_{\mathcal{W}_d}(\mathcal{H}_{f_2})$. These extrema correspond to the "worst" case for each $L$ over the workspace. For simplicity of exposition, $\max_{\mathcal{W}_d}$ is omitted in the following. Figure 4(b) underlines that:

- the manipulator velocity and force perfomance criteria are conflicting and
- the wishes of equally improving the kinetostatic capabilities along each direction may be contradictory. In contrast to $\mathcal{H}_{v_1}$ and $\mathcal{H}_{f_2}$, $\mathcal{H}_{v_2}$ and $\mathcal{H}_{f_1}$ decrease with increasing $L$.
- Finally, there does not exist one single design solution that minimizes all performance indices to the same extent but rather a set of solutions that trades off these indices against each other. This set will be termed as a set of appropriate solutions.

Clearly, the designer's experience plays a key role in taking the decision of which performance criteria should be favored and selecting the final design solution. In the case of a five-bar manipulator, this task is relatively straightforward since all appropriate solutions are very close to each other. Hence, the selection of any solution from this set does not require large trade-offs. For parallel robots with a larger number of degrees of freedom, this task may be more crucial, see also [6], [8], [9], [11] and [12]. **Figure 4(c)** depicts the full independent velocity index as defined in [7]. This index is a measure of the maximal reachable end-effector velocity along each direction, the actuator velocities being normed to unity i.e. $1\frac{m}{s}$. Whereas the maximal velocity along the x-direction rapidly decreases with increasing $L$ and bottoms out at $1\frac{m}{s}$, the maximal velocity along the y-direction gradually rises from $1\frac{m}{s}$. The difference of the increase/decrease rate of these indices is due to the position of the prescribed workspace above a line at $y = 0.5\,m$. According to Figure 4(c), the designer may opt for $L = 1.659\,m$ since this solution minimizes the maximal reachable end-effector velocity along each direction. This choice is in accordance with Figure 4(b). The latter however provides more information about the manipulator characteristics. By means of **Figure 4(d)**, the designer is able to select adequate actuators. For the chosen $L$, it is possible to read off the required maximum actuator velocities and forces: $\mathcal{H}_{vmax} = \, , \mathcal{H}_{fmax}$ in order to meet the demands of Section 2.

## 5    Conclusion

Although this generic example is relatively straightforward, one may retain that an improvement of the kinetostatic performance of parallel manipulators should preferably be performed by means of direction-dependent indices that provide a better insight into the manipulator characteristics. Furthermore, it is possible to divide the design process into three stages. First, direction-dependent indices are optimized over the demanded workspace, which has to be feasible by the manipulator. Second, one may identify some design parameters that affect only the workspace. These parameters could help to meet the wish of matching the workspace as closely as possible. This is always the case for manipulators that feature only prismatic actuators. Third, the dimensioning of the manipulator links, actuated and passive joints can be performed. This approach has already been applied to different parallel manipulators: to a 3 dof parallel robot in [6], to a 5 dof parallel robot in [8] and to a reconfigurable 6 dof parallel robot in [12] and [11].

# References

1. Angeles, J.: Fundamentals of Robotic Mechanical Systems. Springer, Heidelberg (2007)
2. Cardou, P., Bouchard, S., Gosselin, C.: Kinematic-sensitivity indices for dimensionally nonhomogeneous jacobian matrices. IEEE Transactions on Robotics 26(1), 166–173 (2010)
3. Ceccarelli, M.: Fundamentals of Mechanics of Robotic Manipulation. Kluwer Academic Publishers (2004)
4. Gosselin, C.: Determination of the workspace of 6-dof parallel manipulators. ASME Journal of Mechanical Design 112(3), 331–336 (1990)
5. Gosselin, C.: Parallel computational algorithms for the kinematics and dynamics of planar and spatial parallel manipulators. Transactions of ASME, Journal of Dynamic Systems, Measurement and Control 118(1), 22–28 (1996)
6. Hüsing, M., Riedel, M., Nefzi, M., Corves, B.: Vorgehensweise bei der Entwicklung von maßgeschneiderten Handhabungsgeräten in kleinen und mittleren Unternehmen - von der Idee bis zur Umsetzung. In: Bewegungstechnik 2010, VDI-Berichte 2116, pp. 191–205. VDI Verlag, Düsseldorf (2010)
7. Merle, J.-P.: Parallel Robots, 2nd edn. Solid Mechanics and Its Applications. Springer, Dordrecht (2006)
8. Nefzi, M.: Analysis and Optimisation of 4UPS - 1UPU Parallel Robots. PhD thesis, RWTH Aachen (2010)
9. Nefzi, M., Riedel, M., Corves, B.: Development and design of a multi-fingered gripper for dexterous manipulation. In: 4th IFAC Symposium on Mechatronic Systems, Wiesloch/Heidelberg, Germany, vol. 4(1) (2006)
10. Neugebauer, R.: Parallelkinematische Maschinen. Springer, Heidelberg (2006)
11. Riedel, M., Nefzi, M., Corves, B.: Grasp planning for a reconfigurable parallel robot with an underactuated arm structure. Mechanical sciences 1, 33–42 (2010)
12. Riedel, M., Nefzi, M., Corves, B.: Performance analysis and dimensional synthesis of a six dof reconfigurable parallel manipulator. In: IFToMM Symposium on Mechanism Design for Robotics (2010)
13. Tsai, L.-W.: Robot Analysis: The Mechanics of Serial and Parallel Manipulators. John Wiley and Sons, Inc. (March 1999)
14. Yoshikawa, T.: Manipulability of robotic mechanisms. The International Journal of Robotics Research 4(2), 3–9 (1985)

# EMG Classification for Application in Hierarchical FES System for Lower Limb Movement Control

Dingguo Zhang*, Ying Wang, Xinpu Chen, and Fei Xu

State Key Laboratory of Mechanical System and Vibration,
Institute of Robotics, School of Mechanical Engineering,
Shanghai Jiao Tong University, China
dgzhang@sjtu.edu.cn
http://www.robot.sjtu.edu.cn

**Abstract.** This paper proposes a functional electrical stimulation (FES) system based on electromyogram (EMG) classification, which aims to serve for the hemiplegia or incomplete paralyzed patients. This is a hierarchical system and the controller contains three levels. This work focuses on EMG signal processing in order to get the motion intention. Autoregressive (AR) feature, time domain statistics (TDS), and discriminant fourier feature (FC) are adopted as the EMG features. Linear discriminant analysis (LDA) and quadratic discriminant analysis (QDA) are used as the classifier. The performances of motion recognition are compared on three subjects. We find the FC feature generally has the best performance. Preliminary FES experiment is conducted on a healthy subject.

**Keywords:** functional electrical stimulation, electromyogram (EMG), feature extraction, classification, hemiplegia.

## 1 Introduction

Electromyogram (EMG) signal is a good control source for functional electrical stimulation (FES) application. Many researchers have already adopted EMG as a trigger of biofeedback for FES system design, and some encouraging results are achieved [1]. Generally, there are two prerequisite conditions for the feasibility of EMG controlled FES system: the residual (weak) EMG signals can be detected [2], or the EMG from the healthy side can be used [3]. In this work, we aim to design an advanced FES control system to restore movements of lower limbs for hemiplegia or incomplete paralyzed patients. The pioneer work was conducted by D. Graupe et al., where the EMG of upper body is used to provide the control pattern for lower limb [4]. Later, G. Hefftner et al. made further improvement on EMG pattern recognition in similar control scheme as [4], where autoregressive (AR) method is the kernel for EMG discrimination [5]. W. Yu et al. have

---

* Corresponding author.

S. Jeschke, H. Liu, and D. Schilberg (Eds.): ICIRA 2011, Part I, LNAI 7101, pp. 162–171, 2011.
© Springer-Verlag Berlin Heidelberg 2011

proposed EMG classification based FES control system for hemiplegia patients, where artificial neural work is used to classify the EMG from healthy limb in order to get the desired intention [6]. However, the classification accuracy of EMG signals in previous work still has much space to improve. Moreover, nearly all the previous research only focus on the switching control from EMG signals, which cannot guarantee a smooth and continuous performance during the full motion. Especially, the misclassification is significant during motion transition.

In order to address these problems, a hierarchical FES control system is proposed, which combines switching control and continuous control together. The system has three levels, and this work focuses on the control component of upper level, i.e. motion intention recognition from EMG.

## 2    System Structure

The architecture of the proposed FES system for hemiplegia and incomplete paralyzed patients is shown in Fig. 1. The hierarchical controller is composed of three levels, which is inspired by the work in [7]. The high level serves as a switching controller, which has two components: motion intention recognition and control method selection. Motion intention recognition is automatically obtained via EMG signal processing. In this work, four types of motions (sitting up, standing up, standing still and walking) can be recognized. Control method selection is set by the users, which provides the lower level control with different control options.

The middle level serves as a feedforward controller and it has two components. Stimulation pattern generator can provide the electrical stimulation patterns for muscles. These stimulation patterns are acquired from EMG pattern on the concerned muscles of healthy subjects during a specific movement such as walking. These patterns are stored in advance. Similarly, the reference generator aims to generate the desired control objective such as desired trajectory, joint angle (angular velocity), torque etc. These references can set the standard for the FES system and evaluate if the control performance is satisfactory. The middle level is triggered by the intention recognized from upper level.

Although the lower level is named as smooth control, actually it is a typical feedback control. The error between reference and actual data from sensors is the input, and the low level provides online tuning in combination of the feedforward control from middle level. The control method can be selected in the upper level. There are various FES control methods available [8]. For simple and practical criteria, three control methods, position (PID) control, force (impedance) control and hybrid (position+impedance) control, may be used. The lower level can guarantee a continuous control, and it will solve the problems facing in a pure switching control system.

Only the first step, motion intention recognition based on EMG, will be investigated in detail in this paper.

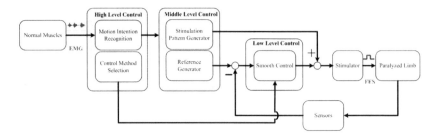

**Fig. 1.** Block diagram of hierarchical FES control system for lower limb

# 3   EMG Signal Processing

The motion intention can be achieved from EMG, and it is an active research topic especially for prosthetic limb control [9]. Here, we summarize the classical methods or algorithms for EMG recognition, and compare their performance with ours.

## 3.1   EMG Acquisition

Three healthy subjects (ZJ, LZZ, YYC) participated in the EMG measurement experiment. Mega (ME6000) EMG system with a band-pass filter of bandwidth 8-500 Hz and a 14 bit A/D converter is used. Six channels of EMG signals are acquired from six muscle groups of right leg as shown in Fig. 2. The targeted muscles are rectus femoris, vastus group, biceps femoris, and semimembranosus

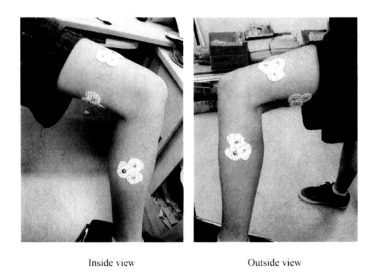

Inside view                     Outside view

**Fig. 2.** Placement of EMG electrodes on one leg of a subject

in the thigh; gastrocnemius and soleus in the shank. The sampling frequency is 1000 Hz, which can satisfy the requirement to obtain sufficient information, because the most relevant information is contained in EMG signal with frequency ranged from 20 to 500 Hz. The targeted skin areas are cleaned beforehand with alcohol. For one muscle, three surface Ag/AgCl disc electrodes are attached at a distance of 2 cm (one is the reference electrode, the other two is a pair of bipolar electrodes).

The subjects perform four types of movements: sitting down, standing up, stillness (standing quietly and keeping body balance), and walking, respectively. The state transition is shown in Fig. 3. Every type of motion will be performed 60 times. The EMG signal acquired during the first 30 times will be used as training data, and that of the last 30 times as testing data. The data during the initial stage of 200ms will be sampled for feature extraction and classification.

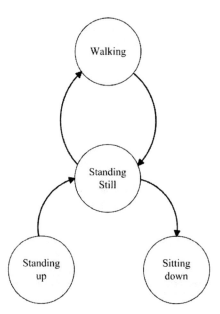

**Fig. 3.** State transition diagram for lower limb motion

## 3.2 Algorithms

The EMG signal processing for motion intention recognition mainly has two procedures: feature extraction and classification. According to the survey on previous research, autoregressive (AR) feature and time domain statistics (TDS) features of EMG are used widely and well recognized. Discriminant fourier feature (FC) as a kind of EMG feature is proposed in our previous work for hand motion recognition, which shows superior performance [10]. Linear discriminant analysis (LDA) and quadratic discriminant analysis (QDA) are two popular classification methods. The brief introduction of these algorithms is given as follows.

**TDS Features:** TDS features have several different representations including mean absolute value, zero crossing, slope sign changes and waveform length.

*Mean absolute value* is given by

$$\overline{X} = \frac{1}{N} \sum_{i=1}^{N} | x_i |$$
(1)

where $\overline{X}$ is a signal segment of EMG, $N$ is the sample length of the signal segment, $x_i$ is the $i$-th sample of the signal segment.

*Zero crossing* counts the number of times the waveform crosses zero. A threshold is needed to reduce the undesired crossing caused by noise. Given two consecutive samples $x_i$ and $x_{i+1}$, the zero crossing number is increased by one if

$$x_i x_{i+1} \leq 0, and \mid x_i - x_{i+1} \mid \geq \varepsilon_z$$
(2)

*Slope sign changes* are incremented by one if

$$(x_{i+1} - x_i)(x_i - x_{i-1}) \geq \varepsilon_s$$
(3)

where $x_i$, $x_i$, and $x_{i+1}$ are three consecutive samples, $\varepsilon_s$ is a specified threshold.

*Waveform length* is the cumulative length of the waveform over the time segment, which describes the complexity of the signal. It is defined as

$$l = \sum_{i=1}^{N} | \Delta x_i |$$
(4)

where $\Delta x_i = x_i - x_{i-1}$.

**AR Features:** EMG signal can be viewed as a stationary Gaussian process during a short time interval (0.1-0.2s), so EMG time series can be represented by a AR model:

$$x_n = \sum_{i=1}^{k} a_i x_{n-1} + \sigma_n$$
(5)

where $x_n$ is the EMG signal in time series, $k$ is the order of the AR model ($k = 4$ in this work), $a_i$ is the estimate of the AR coefficients, and $\sigma_n$ is the white noise. There are some mature technology available to obtain the coefficients such as LMS and sequential least square.

**FC Features:** The discrete cosine transform is employed for converting the Fourier spectrum of EMG signal to meaningful cepstral features, because it can decorrelate features and compress spectral information. The FC technique can be summarized as:

(1) Calculate the energy spectrum using the discrete Fourier transform

$$X[k] = \sum_{n=0}^{N-1} x[n] exp^{-j\frac{2\pi}{N}nk}, k = 0, 1, ..., N - 1.$$
(6)

(2) Calculate FC coefficients from the nonlinear magnitude of the Fourier-spectrum transform directly using discrete cosine transform

$$FC_i = \sum_{k=0}^{N-1} Y_k cos(\frac{(k+1/2)(i-1)\pi}{N}), i = 0, 1, ..., N. \tag{7}$$

where $x(n)$ is the EMG data. $Y_k = f(|X[k]|)$ is a nonlinear transformation (e.g. logarithm of magnitude) of $|X[k]|$ that is the magnitude of Fourier coefficients, and $N$ is the number of FC coefficients. More details can be found in [10].

After obtaining FC coefficients, separability criterion is used to remove the redundant features and keep the most discriminatory FC coefficients for constructing discriminant FC features. The post-processing method is needed to reduce the feature dimension and improve recognition accuracy, otherwise it will make the following classifier too complex and requires large storage for the training set.

Fisher linear discriminant (FLD) is adopted to reduce the dimension before QDA classification in this work, because this way can place the covariance matrix singularity of QDA.

**LDA and QDA Classifier**

Given an input feature vector $y$ for classifiers, the Bayes decision rule shows that the minimum error decision is based on the posterior probability of class membership $p(\omega_i \mid y)$ as

$$p(\omega_i \mid y) = p(\omega_i)\frac{p(y \mid \omega_i)}{p(y)} \tag{8}$$

where $p(y \mid \omega_i)$ is the class-conditional probability density function (PDF), $p(\omega_i)$ is the prior probability, $p(y)$ is the unconditional PDF, and $\omega_i$ denotes the $i$-th class, $i = 1, 2, \ldots, C$.

The discriminant function $g_i(y)$ is defined as $\log[p(\omega_i)p(y \mid \omega_i)]$. The class label of $y$ is $\omega_i$, if $g_i(y) > g_j(y)$ for all $j \neq i$. The general assumption is that all class-conditional PDFs follow normal distributions

$$p(y \mid \omega_i) = \frac{1}{(2\pi)^{\frac{P}{2}}|\Sigma_i|^{\frac{1}{2}}}\exp\{-\frac{1}{2}(y-\mu_i)^T\Sigma_i^{-1}(y-\mu_i)\} \tag{9}$$

with mean $\mu_i$ and covariance matrix $\Sigma_i$ for each class, $P$ is the dimension of the input feature vector. It shows that the discriminant function constructs pairwise linear decision surfaces if all covariances $\Sigma_i$ are equal to a pooled within-class scatter matrix $\hat{\Sigma}_W$. It is called LDA. When covariances $\Sigma_i$ are assumed to be different, the decision boundaries are hyperquadric surfaces, and this is called QDA.

## 4   Results of Intention Recognition

The methods of feature extraction classification are presented in the previous section. This section will evaluate the performance of these methods. Each complete EMG processing must contain feature extraction and classification. Three methods of feature extraction (AR, TDS, FC) and two methods of classification (LDA,

QDA) are fully combined in order to compare their performance and find the best combination. There are six combinations: FC+LDA, FC(FLD)+QDA, AR+LDA, AR(FLD)+QDA, TDS+LDA, TDS(FLD)+QDA. Note that FLD is used before QDA in order to reduce the feature dimension. Here, the dimension of AR and DFC feature vector is 42 (7*6), and that of TDS is 24. The average classification accuracy of 4 types of motions is evaluated by the six combinations for the three subjects (ZJ, LZZ, YYC). The results are shown in Table I. The best result in each row is emphasized by bold font. Since only four movements are involved, the classification accuracy for all the method combination is very good. However, there is still some slight difference. In general, FC feature shows the best performance. TDS features outperform AR features. It is different from the case of upper limb in our previous work [10], where AR features outperform FC features.

**Table 1.** Average classification accuracy for three subjects

| Subjects | FC +LDA | FC(FLD) +QDA | AR +LDA | AR(FLD) +QDA | TDS +LDA | TDS(FLD) +QDA |
|----------|---------|--------------|---------|--------------|----------|---------------|
| ZJ       | 95.83   | 95.83        | 95.83   | 94.17        | 96.67    | **97.50**     |
| LZZ      | **98.33** | 97.50      | 92.50   | 90.00        | 96.67    | 95.83         |
| YYC      | 97.50   | **99.17**    | 94.17   | 94.17        | 92.50    | 90.83         |
| Mean     | 97.22   | **97.50**    | 94.17   | 92.78        | 95.20    | 94.72         |

The average classification accuracy of each motion for the three subjects is shown in Table II. For each movement, FC features show the best performance.

**Table 2.** Average classification accuracy for four types of movements

| Subjects | FC +LDA | FC(FLD) +QDA | AR +LDA | AR(FLD) +QDA | TDS +LDA | TDS(FLD) +QDA |
|----------|---------|--------------|---------|--------------|----------|---------------|
| Walking       | 96.67   | 98.89      | **100** | 100     | 98.75 | 97.22 |
| Standing up    | 95.56   | **95.56**  | 87.78   | 86.67   | 92.04 | 91.94 |
| Sitting down   | **96.67** | 95.56    | 88.89   | 84.44   | 90.01 | 89.72 |
| Standing still | 100     | 100        | 100     | 100     | 100   | 100   |
| Mean           | 97.23   | **97.50**  | 94.17   | 92.78   | 95.20 | 94.72 |

We further test the performance of combined feature (TDS+FC), and LDA classifier is adopted. The classification accuracy is shown in Table III. The result is also satisfactory.

**Table 3.** Average classification accuracy of four types of motions on each subject based on combined features

| Feature Combination | ZJ | LZZ | YYC | Mean |
|---------------------|-----|-------|-----|-------|
| (TDS+FC)+LDA        | 100 | 99.17 | 100 | 99.27 |

## 5    Preliminary FES Experiments

Preliminary experiments were performed on a healthy subject as shown in Fig. 4. EMG signal is acquired from right leg. Electrical pulse is generated by a commercial stimulator (Compex Motion II, Switzerland), and delivered to left leg that is viewed as a paralyzed limb. The control scheme is simplified in current work. It only contains two components (motion intention recognition and stimulation pattern generator) shown in Fig. 1. Obviously, this is an open loop control system. The motion intention recognition is accomplished in the previous section. The stimulation pattern is set according to the EMG pattern measured from healthy subjects. During experiments, the motion intention can be acquired accurately, but the open loop control cannot make the left leg work as the normal one, and the movements are awkward. In a healthy person, there are at least 9 muscle groups involved for one leg during walking movement, but the current level of surface FES technique cannot provide accurate stimulation for each muscle group in practice. It is the inherent limitation of surface FES technology, which cannot be broken through in a short term. In fact, this is just one factor hindering the success of FES application, and there are some other challenges [8]. It is why most surface FES commercial products are not successful and popular in the market at present.

**Fig. 4.** FES experiment on a healthy subject

## 6    Conclusion and Future Work

In this work, a hierarchical FES control system for hemiplegia is proposed, which has three levels for controller. In this scheme, the switching control and continuous control is combined together. The important component of the controller, motion recognition via EMG, is studied. Four states of lower limb, standing up, sitting down, walking and standing still are recognized. Several kinds of feature extraction and classification methods are introduced. The EMG features used include AR, TDS, and FC. The classification methods used here are LDA and QDA. The performances are compared on three healthy subjects. We find the FC feature outperforms the other features in general. In future, more types of motion should be added for the motion recognition. For example, the gait pattern (i.e. heel contact, toe off, single support, double support) should be recognized during a single walking cycle. We also have done the rudimental FES experiment on a healthy subject. The current version of the controller is a kind of open loop control scheme, so the performance of FES experiment is not good. In future, we will study and construct the other components of the controller, and finalize the whole control system design as we proposed. Correspondingly, more FES experiments will be conducted.

**Acknowledgement.** The authors would like to thank the volunteers for participating in the experiments. This work is supported by Research Project of State Key Laboratory of Mechanical System and Vibration (No.MSVMS201112), and National Natural Science Foundation of China (No.51075265).

# References

1. Kannenberg, A., Mileusnic, M.: Functional electrical stimulation and EMG triggered electrotherapy in motor rehabilitation after stroke: An analysis of scientific literature, Literature Survey, Otto Bock HealthCare (2009)
2. Futami, R., Seki, K., Kawanishi, T., Sugiyama, T., Cikajlo, I., Handa, Y.: Application of local EMG-driven FES to incompletely paralyzed lower extremities. In: 10th Annual Conference of the International FES Society, Montreal, Canada (July 2005)
3. Giuffrida, J.P., Crago, P.E.: Reciprocal EMG control of elbow extension by FES. IEEE Trans. Neural Syst. Rehab. Eng. 9, 338–345 (2001)
4. Graupe, D., Kohn, K.H., Kralj, A., Basseas, S.: Patient controlled electrical stimulation via EMG signature discrimination for providing certain paraplegics with primitive walking functions. J. Biomed. Eng. 5, 220–226 (1983)
5. Hefftner, G., Zucchini, W., Jaros, G.: The electromyogram (EMG) as a control signal for functional neuromuscular stimulation-part I: autoregressive modeling as a means of EMG signature discrimination. IEEE Trans. Biomedical Engineering 35, 230–237 (1988)
6. Yu, W., Yamaguchi, H., Yokoi, H., Maruishi, M., Manoa, Y., Kakazu, Y.: EMG automatic switch for FES control for hemiplegics using artificial neural network. Robotics and Autonomous Systems 40, 213–224 (2002)
7. Varol, H.A., Sup, F., Goldfarb, M.: Multiclass real-time intent recognition of a powered lower limb prosthesis. IEEE Trans. Biomedical Engineering 57, 542–551 (2010)

8. Zhang, D.G., Tan, H.G., Widjaja, F., Ang, W.T.: Functional electrical stimulation in rehabilitation engineering: A survey. In: International Convention on Rehabilitation Engineering & Assistive Technology (i-CREATe), Singapore, pp. 221–226 (April 2007)
9. Zecca, M., Micera, S., Carrozza, M.C., Dario, P.: Control of multifunctional prosthetic hands by processing the electromyographic signal. Crit. Rev. Biomed. Eng. 30, 459–485 (2002)
10. Chen, X.P., Zhu, X.Y., Zhang, D.G.: Use of the discriminant Fourier-derived cepstrum with feature-level post-processing for surface EMG signal classification. Physiological Measurement 30(12), 1399–1413 (2009)

# Situated Learning of Visual Robot Behaviors

Krishna Kumar Narayanan, Luis-Felipe Posada,
Frank Hoffmann, and Torsten Bertram

Institute of Control Theory and Systems Engineering, Technische Universität
Dortmund, 44227, Dortmund, Germany
krishna.narayanan@tu-dortmund.de

**Abstract.** This paper proposes a new robot learning framework to acquire scenario specific autonomous behaviors by demonstration. We extract visual features from the demonstrated behavior examples in an indoor environment and transfer it onto an underlying set of scenario aware robot behaviors. Demonstrations are performed using an omnidirectional camera as training instances in different indoor scenarios are registered. The features that distinguish the environment are identified and are used to classify the traversing scenarios. Once the scenario is identified, a behavior model trained by means of artificial neural network pertaining to the specific scenario is learned. The generalization ability of the behavior model is evaluated for seen and unseen data. As a comparison, the behaviors attained using a monolithic general purpose model and its generalization ability against the former is evaluated. The experimental results on the mobile robot indicate the acquired behavior is robust and generalizes meaningful actions beyond the specifics presented during training.

**Keywords:** visual navigation, learning from demonstration, situated learning, behavior based robotics.

## 1 Introduction

Learning visual robot navigation in an indoor environment calls for a sound design of robot behaviors that are robust to the variations of geometry and appearance of the environment. One approach is to generate a 3d model of local environment using laser scanners and perform a semantic classification [6]. However, such an approach is prone to ignore information in the image, that might be useful to improve the navigational capabilities of the robot. A vision system in contrast to proximity sensors is able to distinguish between objects such as obstacles, walls or doors based on appearance. An alternate approach would be to identify the relevant features that best generalize the relationship between the visual perceptions and actions across the whole spectrum of available scenarios. Such monolithic model is hugely prone to ambiguities and errors due to the immense variation in the appearance and shape of the environment. This dependency of the behavior on the environment is described as *situatedness* of the

S. Jeschke, H. Liu, and D. Schilberg (Eds.): ICIRA 2011, Part I, LNAI 7101, pp. 172–182, 2011.
© Springer-Verlag Berlin Heidelberg 2011

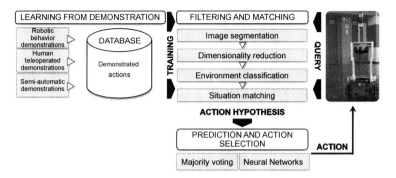

**Fig. 1.** Robot navigation learning framework

robot [7]. This observation motivates our contribution where visual features relevant to individual scenarios are automatically generated, identified and learned to generate a multiple model autonomous navigation behavior. We propose a new robot learning architecture (Fig. 1) in which a robot behavior is learned from teleoperated demonstrations. The proposed framework is also equally applicable to pure human examples or demonstrations based on another sensor modality such as sonar or laser. Learning from Demonstration (LfD) seeks to extend the capabilities of the robot through observation of a task demonstrated by a teacher without the need for explicit programming [2]. In mobile robot navigation it allows to attain behavior policy with a novel sensor modality by observing demonstrations of the desired behavior demonstrated by a human or already existing policies. In order to realize *think the way you act* paradigm of behavior based control [7], we need a good understanding of the underlying network of communicating behaviors emerging from interactions between the robot and its surroundings. One way to model this emergence is to modularize the global behavior policy into sub-behavior control agents. In our case, the demonstrations are performed manually by teleoperating the robot in different scenarios. Human interaction with the environment is more intuitive because of the inherent situational awareness to look ahead and foresee obstacles in executing motor decisions. This rules out a need for a centralized planner to fuse the individual sub-policies, but to learn scenario specific behavior emergence. We propose a two level matching architecture, where first a classification of the traversing scenario using the gathered spatial information is performed. In the case of omnidirectional vision, the classification relies on the distribution and the shape of segmented free space in the image. In the second level, the entire scenario is modeled by means of an artificial neural network (ANN). In a multiple scenario environment, it is apparent that the decisions in separate scenarios depend on different aspects, e.g. obstacle avoidance relies on the angular distribution of the local free space, whereas corridor following relies on the robots lateral and angular displacement with respect to the parallel corridor walls. Thus, within each scenario the relevant subset of features that best generalizes unseen validation data are extracted using a separate feature selection relying on a wrapper approach (forward chaining) [5]. This mapping between the geometric feature set and robot action is learned and the training data are cross-validated for both bias and unseen data. To establish a benchmark to the multiple model navigation scheme, we investigate and analyze also the approach by modeling the entire training set spanning all the scenarios using ANN.

### 1.1  Related Work

Computer vision systems for imitation learning has conceptually taken its inspiration from biology where parsing of the visual sensory information has lead to perform multitude of household tasks to mobile navigation [10,14]. Subsequently, the core of LfD research is involved with the breakdown of a generalized sensory-action policy into learning multiple task dependent policies or consequently learning movement primitives as sequences of actions or temporal behaviors [13]. The authors of [9] use a second person LfD for learning a single behavior fusion policy as a combination of multiple behavioral primitives. The attained behaviors are limited by the selection of a suitable decision space to cover all the control policies and pertain to a single demonstrated domain. Addressing similar problem was proposed by the authors of [1] who use inverse reinforcement learning to extract an unknown reward function given observed, expert behavior demonstration for autonomous helicopter acrobats. Our approach is different from [9] in that the separate fusion policies in individual domains are learned by identifying the relevant features that best predict the corresponding robot action. This way the dimensionality of the problem is simplified and has a constrained space of solutions thereby making it less sensitive to abrupt changes in the environment. By relying on semi-automatic demonstration behavior, compared to pure human or kinesthetic demonstrations [3,9], ambiguity and noise in demonstration process is reduced without the need of a expert demonstrator with a proficient domain knowledge [1]. The contribution is also an extension of our previous work [8] by improving the scenario classification through a shape analysis and also establish the effectiveness of situated learning against monolithic model.

## 2   Behavior Representative Features

In our case, the training data is generated by a semi automatic behavior fusion of obstacle avoidance and corridor following behaviors. The demonstration is performed by a human teacher who controls the robots turn rate with a joystick whereas similar to cruise control the translational velocity is automatically controlled based on the distance to the sonar detected nearest obstacle. This allows to execute more knowledgeable and intuitive motor decisions compared to fully automated behaviors [8]. A total of 3231 examples are recorded in three typical indoor office environment namely corridor, open room and cluttered office spaces (Fig. 2). Each environment differs in texture and appearance of the floor as well as the geometry and locations of walls and obstacles. The demonstration

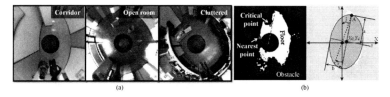

**Fig. 2.** (a) Training scenarios and (b) Visual features

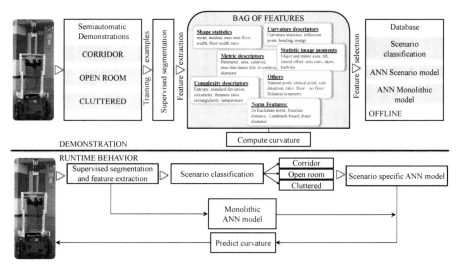

**Fig. 3.** Feature matching architecture

is performed on the Pioneer 3DX mobile robot equipped with an omnidirectional camera with a hyperbolic mirror and a vertical field of view of 75°. Segmentation of the omnidirectional image into floor and non-floor regions is performed using the supervised mixture of experts segmentation scheme proposed by the authors of [12]. The segmented image presents itself as a similarity map with every pixel value representing the probability of it being a floor or an obstacle. By scanning radially through the map, two determinant points namely, the closest obstacle point in the robots frontal field $[-90°, 90°]$ and a closest point in a defined critical zone of $[-30°, 30°]$ are identified. For both the points, we register the inverse of the radial distance $(r_{min}, r_c)$ and angular position $(\theta_{min}, \theta_c)$ thereby capturing the proximity and the direction of the corresponding obstacle. Additionally the nearest safe traversable free floor direction to the front of the robot that extends beyond a distance D is also registered. Further computational shape analysis on the segmented image is performed to extract boundary-based and region-based descriptors. The requirement of shape analysis is to uniquely characterize the shape using a shape descriptor vector that is invariant to translation, scale and rotation [4]. After binarizing the image numerous features arising from shape statistics (mean, median, max & min width of the floorand their ratio), metric

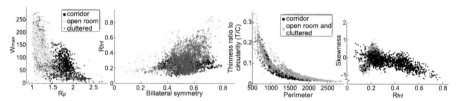

**Fig. 4.** Scatter plot depicting the distribution of selected few features across the different scenarios

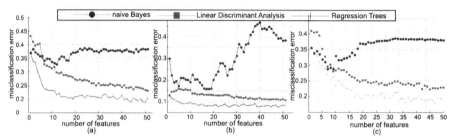

**Fig. 5.** Forward chaining results for scenario classification. (a) 3 classes ,(b) 2 classes: C vs. others, (c) 2 classes: O vs. L.

descriptors (perimeter, area, centroid, max and min distance to centroid, mean distance to the boundary, diameter), curvature-based shape descriptors (curvature statistics, inflection point, bending energy), statistical image moments, simple complexity descriptors (multi-scale entropy, multi-scale standard deviation, circularity, thinness ratio, Area to perimeter ratio, rectangularity, temperature of contour) and bilateral symmetry are extracted [4]. Additional norm features that quantify shape sizes based on the planar shape representations from extremity landmark points of the shape are also computed. Hence, the initial feature set is composed of fifty one features altogether.

## 3    Modeling Situatedness

The proposed two staged matching architecture (Fig. 3) accounts for situatedness of the behavior by first classifying the scenario and then select action on the basis of the specific model. The robot demonstrations are performed in corridor, open room and cluttered environment and are labeled as C, O and L respectively.

### 3.1    Scenario Classification

As a prerogative to any classification problem, the most distinctive features are identified through a wrapper approach (Forward chaining) by convolving it with three established classifiers namely naive Bayes (NB), linear discriminant analysis (LDA) and regression trees (RT). We employ a minimal-redundancy-maximal-relevance ($mRMR$) feature selection technique [11] to identify the features that demonstrate a strong dependency on the target class and at the same

**Table 1.** Features for scenario classification

| Features | 3 way classification (C vs. others) | O vs. L |
|---|:---:|:---:|
| Ratio of the principle major and minor axis | x | - |
| Billateral symmetry | x | x |
| Floor-no-floor ratio | x | - |
| Ratio of floor in the front to the sides | - | x |
| Semi-major axis | x | - |
| Thinness circularity ratio | x | x |
| Maximum floor width | x | - |
| Mean floor width | x | x |
| Critical distance | x | x |
| Perimeter | x | x |
| Skewness | x | - |
| Kurtosis | - | x |
| X-coordinate of the mid pt of $W_{max}$ | x | x |
| Minimum distance of centroid to the boundary | - | x |
| X-coordinate of elliptical centroid | - | x |

time exhibit minimal redundancy. The final feature set is selected by picking the features that deem themselves as relevant across all the considered classifiers. From Fig. 5(a) one can see that RT outperform both LDA and NB achieving a classification accuracy of 80%. In order to improve the performance, a two tier classification is proposed where first, the cluttered and openroom examples are grouped together under a single label and classified against the corridor examples. This achieves a maximum of 93% accuracy. This relative spike in the performance can be attributed to the similarity of open room and cluttered data shown in the scatterplot Fig. 4. If the query is not a corridor, a secondary classification is carried out against the open room and cluttered examples. Fig. 5(c) shows the corresponding feature selection performance which achieves 82% accuracy thereby achieving considerable improvement compared to a single shot 3 class classification. Table 1 shows the list of selected features for classification. The selected features are again validated using a *5-fold cross validation*, where the performance of the classifier against unseen data is tested. Table 2 shows that RT outperforms the other two schemes with an accuracy in the range of 77 − 92%. The table also shows the bias errors arising out of tests where the entire data is shown in training phase and is cross validated against its own model. RT dominates the scheme by achieving a high accuracy of 99% for corridor and 96% for openroom and cluttered examples.

### 3.2   Scenario Modeling

In this level, the perception-action relationship for every scenario is represented by multiple ANNs. The most characteristic features for every scenario is identified using forward chaining (Table 3). Unlike classification, here in regression the

**Table 2.** Scenario Classification: Cross validation

| Classifier | Misclassification error | | | | | |
| | all 3 classes | | C vs. others | | O vs. L | |
| | CV | Bias | CV | Bias | CV | Bias |
|---|---|---|---|---|---|---|
| NB | 0.28 | 0.27 | 0.15 | 0.12 | 0.28 | 0.24 |
| LDA | 0.29 | 0.27 | 0.11 | 0.11 | 0.28 | 0.26 |
| RT | 0.23 | 0.05 | 0.08 | 0.01 | 0.18 | 0.04 |

**Table 3.** Selected features for individual scenarios

| Feature | C | O | L | O and L | all |
|---|---|---|---|---|---|
| X-coordinate of elliptical centroid | x | - | - | x | - |
| Y-coordinate of elliptical centroid | - | - | x | x | - |
| Orientation error (beta) | x | - | - | - | - |
| Floor-no-floor ratio | x | x | - | - | - |
| Nearest distance | x | - | - | x | x |
| Nearest angle | - | x | - | x | - |
| Bilateral symmetry | x | x | x | x | x |
| Next Safe free floor direction | x | - | - | - | - |
| Ratio of the principle major and minor axis | x | x | x | x | x |
| Critical distance | x | - | - | - | - |
| Critical angle | x | - | x | x | x |
| Semi major axis | - | - | x | x | - |
| Semi minor axis | x | x | - | x | - |
| Multiscale entropy | - | x | - | - | - |
| X-coordinate of the mid pt of $W_{max}$ | - | x | x | - | - |
| Kurtosis | - | - | x | - | x |
| Area-perimeter ratio | - | - | x | - | - |
| Maximum floor width $W_{max}$ | - | - | - | x | x |
| Thinness circularity ratio | - | - | - | - | x |
| Rectangularity | - | x | x | - | x |

mean squared generalization error ($mse$) is minimized here. Multilayer feed forward network is trained with Levenberg-Marquardt backpropagation algorithm. A *hold-out validation* with 60% of the data used for training, 20% for validation and remaining 20% for testing is performed. The training, validation, testing $mse$ and its corresponding normalised mean squared error ($nmse$) between the predictied output and the true curvature for the different ANN models are listed in Table 4. The $nmse$ interprets the residual variance of the predicted output by dividing the prediction by the variance of the target. As we can observe, corridor and open room model generalize the best achieving a considerable improvement in the residual variance of the prediction by almost 35%. The generalization of cluttered room examples is marginally inferior to corridor or open room mainly attributed to the large variance of the data. In order to improve the quality of the model, we group the open room and cluttered examples together and identify the most characteristic examples (Table 3). The $nmse$ also sees an improvment

**Table 4.** Intrascenario cross-validation

| Scenario | Training mse $\times 10^{-3}[\circ/cm]^2$ | Validation mse $\times 10^{-3}[\circ/cm]^2$ | Testing mse $\times 10^{-3}[\circ/cm]^2$ | nmse mse | Bias | # neurons |
|---|---|---|---|---|---|---|
| C | 6.7 | 8.3 | 6.1 | 0.65 | 6.9 | 8 |
| O | 12 | 14 | 10 | 0.73 | 14.3 | 8 |
| L | 9.7 | 7.7 | 7.6 | 0.85 | 8.6 | 6 |
| O and L | 9.9 | 10 | 9.7 | 0.8 | 10.5 | 10 |
| Monolithic | 11.1 | 11.4 | 8.5 | 0.87 | 10.7 | 8 |

**Table 5.** Interscenario cross-validation

| Training | C | C | L | L | O | O | C | O&L |
|---|---|---|---|---|---|---|---|---|
| Testing | O | L | C | O | L | C | O&L | C |
| mse $\times 10^{-3}[\circ/cm]^2$ | 13 | 14.4 | 13.5 | 11.2 | 10.7 | 19.7 | 21 | 12.3 |

of 5% compared to pure cluttered model nevertheless marginally inferior to open room model. Selected features for a complete monolithic model are also listed in the table. The corresponding validation errors in Table 4 concur to the effectiveness of a situated modeling as monolithic model finds difficult to generalize against unseen examples. An interscenario cross-validation tests the ability of the learner to generalize to potentially different scenario. From Table 5, one can observe that the generalization error between fundamentally different data is relatively larger than the intrascenario validation (Table 4). The difficulty of corridor model to generalize open room and cluttered examples can be coupled to the potential difference in the geometry of the traversing environment. Open room and cluttered demonstrations are mainly dominated by obstacle avoidance behavior thus finding it hard to generalize against more consistent corridor examples. Generalization error between open room and cluttered examples is higher than their intrascenario bias errors, but still better than generalizing corridor examples. An improvement in the generalization capability can be seen when open room and cluttered examples are grouped together and tested against corridor examples. From the results, one can conclude that a 2-scenario modeling (corridor and the rest) performs marginally better than a 3-scenario modeling mainly due to the lack of distinction between open room and cluttered room example. The performance of the proposed architecture on the robot would establish both the validity of the classification algorithm and the false positive rate of the ANN models to predict the right curvature.

## 4    Experimental Results

The visual navigation scheme with three scenario models (C,O and L), two scenario models (C and rest) and a monolithic ANN model are experimented on a Pioneer 3DX mobile robot in different indoor environments. The robustness of the visual navigation from demonstration was assessed by allowing the robot to wander in different environments for a duration of 45 minutes with frequent restarts and randomized initial poses. Two such proof of concept scenarios are presented here. Fig. 6(top) shows the generalization capability of the different schemes for a prototypical obstacle avoidance scenario in an unseen corridor for which no training instances exist. Note the two open doors further down the corridor requiring the robot to adapt accordingly to the changed geometry. Both the two model and three model schemes circumnavigate the obstacles and traverse the corridor successfully. The apparent difference in the trajectory and the scenario classification in the initial stages of both the schemes is attributed to the presence of an open door at the start of the run suggesting more free floor on the left and correspondingly a different geometry. During the test run with three models the door was closed manually in the middle of the run, thus reverting the classification back to corridor after the initial misclassification. The two open doors down the corridor blocks the free space of the corridor thus altering the geometry. This change in geometry is rightly picked up by the scenario classification scheme, where the classification switches from corridor thus deploying the open room and cluttered ANN models for prediction. Both the schemes complete the test successfully in comparison to the monolithic model which failed at crossing door blocked narrow passage further establishing the conclusions from the training data cross validation (Table 4). Fig. 6(bottom) shows another scenario

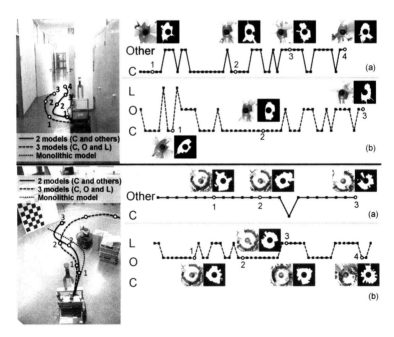

**Fig. 6.** (Top)Untrained corridor with ANN. (Bottom)Cluttered scenario with ANN. Exhibited at the featured nodes are the acquired omnidirectional image and its corresponding segmentation. (a) Two ANN models: corridor and other (open room and cluttered) and (b) three ANN models: corridor, open room and cluttered.

previously unseen, cluttered with boards and obstacles thus exhibiting a mix of open room and cluttered room geometries. Both the schemes avoid the obstacles with the two model scheme getting very close to the boards but eventually avoids it. Supported by a robust scenario classification scheme, the three model scheme successfully avoids all the obstacles with a safe distance. The monolithic ANN model in contrast struggles to avoid the obstacles repeatedly thereby establishing the lack of flexibility of a general purpose model. Further experiments are conducted in seen corridor and foyer environments with the modeled learning consistently performing better than its monolithic counterpart.

## 5  Conclusions

Navigational behaviors in autonomous robots are highly environment dependent. Hence we presented a new framework for acquiring visual robotic navigational behaviors from demonstration examples. The relevant features in individual indoor scenarios are extracted that best reflect the relationship between the visual perception and the performed action. Furthermore, artificial neural networks are employed to model the individual scenarios and their generalization capability is compared against a monolithic general purpose model. We explore the difference in generalization performance of the discussed multimodal scheme by grouping open room and cluttered room examples together and comparing it with a clearly partitioned 3 model scheme. Exhaustive tests are performed to confirm the accuracy and the robustness of the models at every level. Experimental results are performed with all the three schemes and the results demonstrate the ability of the learned scenario specific ANN models in unknown scenarios. The results also establishes the difficulty of the monolithic behavior model to generalize to both known and unknown examples.

## References

1. Abbeel, P., Coates, A., Ng, A.Y.: Autonomous helicopter aerobatics through apprenticeship learning. I. J. Robotic Res. 29(13), 1608–1639 (2010)
2. Argall, B., Chernova, S., Veloso, M., Browning, B.: A survey of robot learning from demonstration. Robotics and Autonomous Systems 57(5), 469–483 (2009)
3. Calinon, S.: Robot Programming by Demonstration: A Probabilistic Approach. EPFL/CRC Press (2009)
4. da Fontoura Costa, L., Cesar Jr., R.M.: Shape Classification and Analysis: Theory and Practice, 2nd edn. CRC Press, Inc., Boca Raton (2009)
5. Kohavi, R., John, G.: Wrappers for feature subset selection. Artificial Intelligence 97(1-2), 273–324 (1997)
6. Martínez Mozos, O., Stachniss, C., Burgard, W.: Supervised learning of places from range data using adaboost. In: ICRA, pp. 1742–1747 (2005)
7. Mataric, M.J.: Learning in behavior-based multi-robot systems: Policies, models, and other agents. Cognitive Systems Research 2, 81–93 (2001)
8. Narayanan, K.K., Posada, L.F., Hoffmann, F., Bertram, T.: Scenario and context specific visual robot behavior learning. In: IEEE Int. Conf. Robotics and Automation (ICRA), pp. 439–444 (May 2011)

9. Nicolescu, M., Jenkins, O., Olenderski, A., Fritzinger, E.: Learning behavior fusion from demonstration. Interaction Studies Journal, Special Issue on Robot and Human Interactive Communication (2007)
10. Pardowitz, M., Knoop, S., Dillmann, R., Zollner, R.D.: Incremental learning of tasks from user demonstrations, past experiences, and vocal comments. IEEE Transactions on Systems, Man, and Cybernetics, Part B 37(2), 322–332 (2007)
11. Peng, H., Long, F., Ding, C.: Feature selection based on mutual information: Criteria of max-dependency, max-relevance, and min-redundancy. IEEE Transactions on Pattern Analysis and Machine Intelligence 27, 1226–1238 (2005)
12. Posada, L.F., Narayanan, K.K., Hoffmann, F., Bertram, T.: Floor segmentation of omnidirectional images for mobile robot visual navigation. In: Proc. of IEEE/RSJ Intl. Conference on Intelligent Robots and Systems, IROS (2010)
13. Schaal, S.: Is imitation learning the route to humanoid robots? Trends in Cognitive Sciences (6), 233–242 (1999)
14. Sofman, B., Lin, E., Bagnell, J., Vandapel, N., Stentz, A.: Improving robot navigation through self-supervised online learning. In: Proceedings of Robotics: Science and Systems, Philadelphia, USA (2006)

# Humanoid Motion Planning in the Goal Reaching Movement of Anthropomorphic Upper Limb

Wenbin Chen[1,*], Caihua Xiong[1], Ronglei Sun[1], and Xiaolin Huang[2]

[1] State Key Lab of Digital Manufacturing Equipment and Technology
Institute of Rehabilitation and Medical Robotics
Huazhong University of Science and Technology, Wuhan 430074, China
wbchen@smail.hust.edu.cn
[2] Department of Rehabilitation Medicine, Tongji Hospital
Tongji Medical College of Huazhong University of Science and Technology,
Wuhan 430030, China

**Abstract.** The anthropomorphic limb, such as, full size prosthetic upper limbs and exoskeleton rehabilitation robot, etc. moving human like motion during the reaching movements is important for safe and ergonomic consideration. This study is toward planning the humanoid motion of the hand of anthropomorphic limbs in the goal reaching movement with high curved trajectory. The proposed method treats the configuration of hand as element in the $SE(3)$, and uses local coordinate chart mapping on cotangent space between group structure and manifold structure. The wrench on $se^*(3)$ which drives the hand to target configuration is derived from the force one form based on the defined conservative potential field. In order to guarantee the curvature of trajectory and bell-shaped velocity profile, the repulsive potential field is used to derive the repulsive wrench. The result trajectory and corresponding velocity profile are basically consistent with the human hand motion in the goal reaching movement.

**Keywords:** anthropomorphic limb, humanoid motion planning, $SE(3)$, $se^*(3)$.

## 1 Introduction

A reaching movement toward a target in three-dimensional (3D) space during the activities of daily living, such as drinking, combing, etc. generally requires reaching the target position with orientation matching. The hand orientation adjustment by the center nervous system is natural and inherent. Due to the redundancy of human limb, these movements define a highly redundant task at the geometric, kinematic, and dynamic levels of control [6]. These unconstrained movements are not straight but rather following highly curved trajectory[10]. The velocity profile along the trajectory during the reaching movement is bell-shaped and single-peaked[5].

In a long time the two-thirds power law [15] was used to describe the relation between the radius of the curvature of the trajectory and the tangential velocity, although it was unsuccessful in explaining unconstrained three-dimensional (3D)

---

* Corresponding author.

S. Jeschke, H. Liu, and D. Schilberg (Eds.): ICIRA 2011, Part I, LNAI 7101, pp. 183–191, 2011.
© Springer-Verlag Berlin Heidelberg 2011

movements. Upon this issue, a curvature planning strategy based on internal force field for 3D pointing movement was proposed[10]. Recently, a new power law[12], called by 3D power law, originally proposed to describe the scribbling movements was proved to be better consistently with the 3D complex tracing movement[8].

Modeling the appropriate computational approach approximating to the empirical behavioral data were particular useful for planning movement of the anthropomorphic upper limbs. Most existing models [13; 3; 8; 10] were mainly toward reproducing the trajectory for the point-to-point movement while ignoring the hand orientation during the goal reaching movement. The trajectory planning was represented by an optimal problem on minimizing the cost function related to the configuration difference between the initial and target point[14]. This strategy only considered the geometry profile and the temporal feature can not be reproduced. Considering that some geometrical feature were inherent in the human hand movement, some studies have tried to plan the human arm movement under the frame work of affine geometry and Riemannian manifold[3; 2]. However, these models assumed a separate processing for the spatial and temporal dynamics of motion and predicted identical path trajectories for different speeds.

While none of the existing models provides a satisfactory solution , which is consistent with spatio-temporal feature of human motion, for simultaneously planning the position and orientation trajectory during the reaching movement with high curved trajectory. In this study we extend the curvature planning model proposed by Petreska et al[10] to the Lie group, i.e. SE(3), and our model can simultaneously reproduce the position and orientation trajectory of hand with similar spatio-temporal feature of human motion. We propose a new strategy for generating force field which guarantee the curvature of trajectory to approximate that of human motion. The force field does not need to provide in advance, which overcomes the difficulty on selecting appropriate repulsive force vector in[10].

## 2    Method

### 2.1    Twists and Wrenches

If the element $A \in SE(3)$ is parameterized by a local coordinate chart $\varphi = \left( \varphi^1, \varphi^2, \varphi^3, \varphi^4, \varphi^5, \varphi^6 \right)$, then the point $A \in SE(3)$ is given by

$$A(\varphi) = Trans_x(\varphi^4) \cdot Trans_y(\varphi^5) \cdot Trans_z(\varphi^6) \cdot Rot_y(\varphi^1) \cdot Rot_z(\varphi^2) \cdot Rot_x(\varphi^3) \quad (1)$$

If we denote the smooth manifold consisting of the element of the $SE(3)$ by $\Psi$, then Eq.(1) gives a mapping from the local coordinate chart of $\Psi$ to $SE(3)$ , $\Psi = \left\{ (A, \varphi) \middle| \varphi : A \rightarrow \varphi(A) \in \mathfrak{R}^6 \right\}$. Because the Lie group $SE(3)$ has inherent manifold structure, the tangent vector field respect to the coordinate basis $E_i = \partial(\cdot)/\partial\varphi^i$ at a point $A$ on the manifold $\Psi$ is given by

$$T_A \Psi = V\big|_A = \sum_{i=1}^{6} \frac{d\varphi^i}{dt} E_i \big|_A \quad (2)$$

The component and the coordinate basis of the force one-form $F$ for a conservative system are given by $\partial\Phi/\partial\varphi^i$ and $d\varphi^i$ respectively. The force one-form can be expressed by linear combination of coordinate basis:

$$F = -\sum_{i=1}^{6}\frac{\partial\Phi}{\partial\varphi^i}d\varphi^i = -\sum_{i=1}^{6}F_i d\varphi^i \tag{3}$$

The two basis satisfy $\langle d\varphi^i, E_j\rangle = \delta^i_j$, where $\delta^i_j$ is the *Kronecker Delta*. Thus the component of force one-form $F$ respect to the basis $d\varphi^i$ is given by

$$F_i = \langle F, E_i\rangle \tag{4}$$

On the other hand, the $SE(3)$ has inherent group structure, we can give the left invariant vector field on the tangent space $TSE(3)$ and the force one-form on the cotangent space $T^*SE(3)$, respectively.

$$V = \sum_{i=1}^{6}V^i\hat{L}_i \tag{5}$$

$$F = \sum_{i=1}^{6}W_i\hat{\lambda}^i \tag{6}$$

where $\hat{L}_i$ is the left invariant basis of $TSE(3)$ at a point $A \in SE(3)$ and $\hat{\lambda}^i$ is the basis of $T^*SE(3)$. They are also satisfies $\langle \hat{\lambda}^i, \hat{L}_j\rangle = \delta^i_j$. The components $W_i$ form the wrench on $se^*(3)$ and the components $V^i$ form twist on $se(3)$. Since the motion planning in this study is executed on the $SE(3)$, the twist motion of the end-effector of the anthropomorphic upper limbs is caused by the wrench corresponding to the force one-form in the conservative system. So the relationship between the component of force one-form, $\partial\Phi/\partial\varphi^i$, and the wrench, $W^i$, is needed to establish. In fact, it can be achieved by expressing the basis of force one-form in terms of the basis of $T^*SE(3)$. Thus according to coordinate notation in Eq.(1), we can let $F = \hat{\lambda}^i$ in Eq.(6), use Eq.(4) and $E_i = \partial A/\partial\varphi^i$ to write the component of the wrench as:

$$\begin{pmatrix}W_1 & \cdots & W_6\end{pmatrix}^T = -\left(N^{-1}\right)^T\left(\frac{\partial\Phi}{\partial\varphi^1} \quad \cdots \quad \frac{\partial\Phi}{\partial\varphi^6}\right)^T \tag{7}$$

where $N$ is the mapping matrix from $\hat{\lambda}_i$ to $d\varphi^i$ related to the local coordinate chart at a point on the manifold[16].

## 2.2    Second Order Kinematic Model

As shown in Fig. 1(a), the force one-form directed from current point toward the target, is called by target attractive force denoted by $\mathbf{F}_a$. The force one-form from the initial point $A_0 \in SE(3)$ toward current point, is called by co-pull force $\mathbf{F}_c$. Our humanoid motion planning method is governed by a second order kinematic model on $SE(3)$, this model represent the dynamic twist motion of hand of the anthropomorphic upper limb under the action of on-line corrected wrench considering the resultant effect of target attractive potential and human trunk interference avoiding potential.

$$\mathbf{M} \cdot \nabla_{\mathbf{V}} \mathbf{V} + \kappa \cdot \mathbf{V} = \mu \cdot \tilde{\mathbf{F}}(\mathbf{A}_0, \mathbf{A}_f(t), \mathbf{A}(t)) \tag{8}$$

where $\nabla_{\mathbf{V}} \mathbf{V}$ is the acceleration of the hand on $TTSE(3)$ [17; 16], which is compatible with the kinematic connection. The $\tilde{\mathbf{F}}(\mathbf{A}_0, \mathbf{A}_f(t), \mathbf{A}(t))$ is the generalized wrench acting on the hand which is related to initial point, current point and target point. This wrench drives the hand from its current configuration $\mathbf{A}(t)$ to the target configuration $\mathbf{A}(f)$. The scalar $\kappa$ and $\mu$ in Eq.(8) are constant scaling factor, in which the $\kappa \in \mathbb{R}^+$ act as damping coefficient and the term $\kappa \cdot \mathbf{V}$ prevents the system from oscillating too importantly, the $\mu \in \mathbb{R}^+$ act as modulator of the amplitude of the velocity and increasing $\mu$ will result in higher speed and shorten the movement duration. The role of the terms and scalers in the model (8) is something like the term of model F2REACH model in[10] but our model is more general and is specially defined in the framework of Lie Group. The dynamic trajectory of hand orientation is also considered, which is more practical useful especially in the orientation required reaching task. The F2REACH model needs a target attractive force and a repulsive force field that is linear combination of two predefined constant repulsive force. The coefficient of the linear combination is relative to the distance between current position and the target position. The key in F2REACH model is to select two appropriate constant repulsive forces in advance, but it is not a simple work to make the proper selection. In our work, we give a more practical method to determine the online corrected wrench acting on the hand to drive it from initial configuration to the target configuration.

Recall that the conservative potential field can be defined by the distance metric on $SE(3)$, thus we can define two potential fields, i.e., $\Phi_a$ consisting of target point $\mathbf{A}_f(t) = (\mathbf{R}_f(t), \mathbf{P}_f(t))$ and current point $\mathbf{A}(t) = (\mathbf{R}(t), \mathbf{P}(t))$, $\Phi_c$ consisting of $A(t)$ and initial point $\mathbf{A}_0(t) = (\mathbf{R}_0(t), \mathbf{P}_0(t))$, respectively.

$$\Phi_a(\mathbf{A}_f, \mathbf{A}) = \sqrt{\varepsilon_1 \left\| \mathbf{P}_f - \mathbf{P} \right\|^2 + \varepsilon_2 \left\| \log(\mathbf{R}^{-1}\mathbf{R}_f) \right\|^2 + 1} \tag{9}$$

$$\Phi_c(\mathbf{A}, \mathbf{A}_0) = \sqrt{\varepsilon_1 \left\| \mathbf{P} - \mathbf{P}_0 \right\|^2 + \varepsilon_2 \left\| \log(\mathbf{R}_0^{-1}\mathbf{R}) \right\|^2 + 1} \tag{10}$$

where $\varepsilon_1$ and $\varepsilon_2$ are the constant scaling factor, and the parameterization of $A(t) \in SE(3)$ is according to the notation in Eq.(1). Thus the target attractive force one-form, $\mathbf{F}_a$, and the co-pull force one-form, $\mathbf{F}_c$, can be obtained according to Eq.(3). Because the basis of these two force one-form are with respect to the same point on $T^* SE(3)$, we can do the linear algebra operation between their components. During the hand moving toward the target, the amplitude of force one-form $\mathbf{F}_a$ is decreasing, while the amplitude of co-force one-form $\mathbf{F}_c$ is increasing. The amplitude of target attractive force one-form can be scaled to have the bell-shape profile by:

$$\mathbf{F}'_a\big|_{\mathbf{A}(t)} = -\|\mathbf{F}_c\| \cdot \mathbf{F}_a \qquad (11)$$

where the operator $\|\bullet\|$ is the Euclidean length of the vector consisting of the component with respect to the basis of the force one-form.

In order to generate the movement curvature consistent with the 3D power law[11; 12], an avoiding potential field related to the distance between hand and surface of human trunk is used[1]. This avoiding potential field is used to construct the repulsive force to generate the movement curvature. The resultant force one-form acting on the hand is given by:

$$\mathbf{F}\big|_{\mathbf{A}(t)} = \sum_{i=1}^{6}\left(\sigma\frac{\partial\Phi_r}{\partial\varphi^i} - \|\mathbf{F}_c\|\frac{\partial\Phi_a}{\partial\varphi^i}\right)d\varphi^i \qquad (12)$$

where $\sigma < 1$ is the scaling factor and $\Phi_r$ is the avoiding potential field. Substituting the basis of force one-form $d\varphi^i$ for the basis $\hat{\lambda}_i$ of the $T^*SE(3)$, the vector field in the cotangent space $T^*_{A(t)}SE(3)$ is given by

$$\mathbf{F}\big|_{\mathbf{A}(t)} = \sum_{i,j=1}^{6}\left(\frac{\partial\Phi_r}{\partial\varphi^i} - \|\mathbf{F}_c\|\frac{\partial\Phi_a}{\partial\varphi^i}\right)\cdot\mathbf{N}_{ij}^{-1}\cdot\hat{\lambda}_j \triangleq \sum_{i=1}^{6}W^i(t)\hat{\lambda}_i \qquad (13)$$

where $\mathbf{N}_{ij}^{-1} = (\mathbf{N}^{-1})_{ij}$. Because the basis $\hat{\lambda}_i$ of force one-form is dual to the left invariant basis $\hat{L}_i$ of the tangent space $TSE(3)$, the component $W^i$ is the generalized force acting on the origin of the hand frame with respect to the hand frame. We referred the vector pair $\{\boldsymbol{\tau}(t), \mathbf{f}(t)\}$:

$$\boldsymbol{\tau}(t) = [W^1(t),\ W^2(t),\ W^3(t)]^T,\quad \mathbf{f}(t) = [W^4(t),\ W^5(t),\ W^6(t)]^T$$

as the wrench $\tilde{\mathbf{F}}$ where the $\boldsymbol{\tau}(t)$ act as moment and $\mathbf{f}(t)$ act as force. The hand undergoing twist motion toward the target is driven by the time-varying wrench. The solution of second order differential motion equation (8) is the expected trajectory of hand in the conservative system constructed by $\mathbf{A}_0$, $\mathbf{A}$ and $\mathbf{A}_f$. Here the geometrical integration method [9] is used to compute the dynamic trajectory. The real time performance of our method seriously depends on the efficiency of algorithm of geometrical integration.

## 3     Numerical Simulation

Here, we give one example on goal reaching movement with high curved trajectory to illustrate the proposed method. The geometry size of the anthropomorphic upper limb and scaling factor of the distance metric in Eq.(9) and Eq.(10) are listed in Table 1.

The constant factors $\kappa$ and $\mu$ in Eq.(8) are set to be 10 and 5, respectively. The initial configuration $\mathbf{A}_0$ of hand corresponding to the rest arm posture and target configuration $\mathbf{A}_f$ of hand corresponding to the arm configuration touching contra lateral shoulder of are set to be:

$$\mathbf{A}_0 = \begin{bmatrix} -0.2680 & -0.9167 & -0.2964 & 0.0065 \\ 0.9581 & -0.2858 & 0.0176 & -0.3003 \\ -0.1008 & -0.2793 & 0.9549 & -0.6758 \\ 0 & 0 & 0 & 1 \end{bmatrix}$$

$$\mathbf{A}_f = \begin{bmatrix} -0.4860 & 0.2233 & 0.8450 & 0.0149 \\ -0.3821 & 0.8152 & -0.4352 & 0.1662 \\ -0.7860 & -0.5343 & -0.3108 & -0.0155 \\ 0 & 0 & 0 & 1 \end{bmatrix}$$

where the unit of the position is meter. The high curved trajectory from different views are shown in Fig. 1(b) In order to validate the predicted trajectory on how much is consistent with the real trajectory, five experimental trails under predefined protocol were done. To eliminate the influence of body size and trunk movement on the final validation, we do not directly record the configuration of hand ,but only record the joint angles of the upper extremity of subjects and the hand configuration were computed through forward kinematics of anthropomorphic upper limb using recorded joint angles. The experiment procedure for measuring joint angles of upper extremity refer to the work in [4]. The comparison about the trajectory profile and velocity profile are shown in Fig. 2 and Fig. 3. The planned trajectory matches the experimental results well. The angular and linear velocity both have bell-shape profile with single peak and also match the velocity profile of real hand.

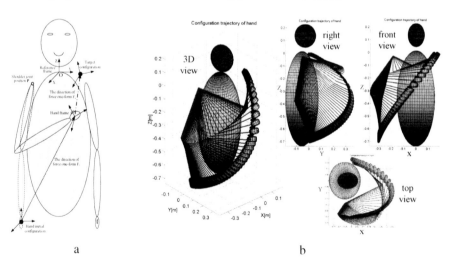

a                                    b

**Fig. 1.** a) The hand configuration during reaching movement from initial position to the target position. b) The trajectory of the hand of the anthropomorphic upper limb toward the target from initial configuration.

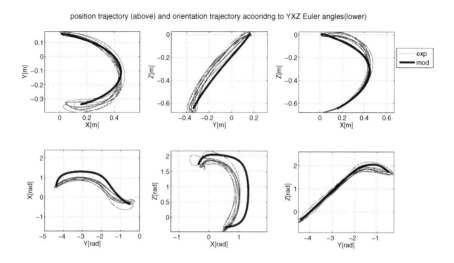

**Fig. 2.** The comparison between trajectory planned by the model (thick line in blue color) and trajectories measured from 5 experimental trials (thin line in red color). Upper three figures are the position trajectories in three planes(X-Y,Y-Z,X-Z) respectively and lower three figures are the orientation trajectories around three axis in YXZ Euler angles (Y-X, X-Z,Y-Z) respectively.

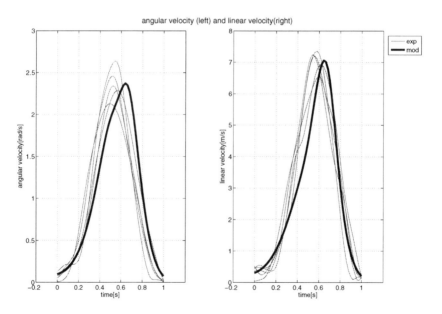

**Fig. 3.** The comparison of normalized velocity between the planned trajectory and experimental trajectory

**Table 1.** Geometry size of the anthropomorphic upper limb and the distance metric factor

| Limb size | Scaling factor of the distance metric in Eq.(9) and Eq.(10) |
|-----------|-----------------------------------------------------------|
| $L_u$ : 368mm | $\varepsilon_1$ : 1 |
| $L_f$ : 290mm | $\varepsilon_2$ : 1.3 |
| $P_s$ : $(-60,-188,-26)^T$ | |

## 4     Discussion and Conclusion

The bell-shaped velocity profiles on the angular and linear aspects, together with high curvature along the trajectory, are preserved. The spatio-temporal features of the position and orientation trajectory of human hand during the goal reaching movement are successfully reproduced. Since our method describes the dynamics from the geometrical aspect, the motion planning strategy can explain the modulating relationship, i.e., 3D power law, between velocity and curvature along the trajectory. In order to generate the motion curvature, we used the superquadric surface approximate to human trunk shape to generate the repulsive force. This strategy has the physical meaning and reflects how the center nervous system avoids the human body during self-reaching movement.

The model proposed has better ability to reproduce spatio-temporal feature of the position and orientation trajectory in the high curved humanoid motion, and it obviously can reproduce patio-temporal feature in the straight humanoid motion, which not like most methods[7; 3] only work well in straight or pse-straight point-to-point movement. The traditional methods such as interpolating method usually require giving boundary condition to determine model parameters for each task in advance, which are not suit for the tasks with possible changing target randomly, such as the human hand motion. Since our model employs the target attractive potential force, it can guarantee the motion converging to the target with variable configuration. As stated above, the real time performance of the second order kinematic equation is dependent on the performance of geometrical integration algorithm, which may limit its real time application.

However, the method proposed in this paper has the potential on the motion control of anthropomorphic limb, such as, exoskeleton rehabilitation robot and full size prosthetic upper limb. It is also helpful to understand the mechanism of the center nervous system on how to modulate the hand motion during goal reaching and grasping movement. The inversed kinematics of the redundant anthropomorphic limb, which is important to determine the arm configuration, is not represented here for limited page space.

**Acknowledgments.** This work was supported by the National Science Fund for Distinguished Young Scholars of China under Grant 51025518, the "863" Hi-Tech Research and Development Program of China under Grant 2008AA040202, the National Natural Science Foundation of China under Grant 50875100 and the Fundamental Research Funds for the Central Universities under Grant 2010MS093. Correspondence should be addressed to wbchen@smail.hust.edu.cn.

# References

1. Badawy, A., McInnes, C.R.: Small spacecraft formation using potential functions. Acta Astronautica 65(11-12), 1783–1788 (2009)
2. Biess, A., Flash, T., et al.: Riemannian geometric approach to human arm dynamics, movement optimization, and invariance. Physical Review E 83(3), 1–11 (2011)
3. Biess, A., Liebermann, D.G., et al.: A Computational Model for Redundant Human Three-Dimensional Pointing Movements: Integration of Independent Spatial and Temporal Motor Plans Simplifies Movement Dynamics. The Journal of Neuroscience 27(48), 13045–13064 (2007)
4. Chen, W.B., Xiong, C.H., et al.: Kinematic analysis and dexterity evaluation of upper extremity in activities of daily living. Gait & Posture 32(4), 475–481 (2010)
5. Flash, T., Hogan, N.: The coordination of arm movements: an experimentally confirmed mathematical model. The Journal of Neuroscience 5(7), 1688–1703 (1985)
6. Guigon, E., Baraduc, P., et al.: Computational motor control: redundancy and invariance. Journal of Neurophysiology 97(1), 331 (2007)
7. Kang, T., He, J., et al.: Determining natural arm configuration along a reaching trajectory. Experimental Brain Research 167(3), 352–361 (2005)
8. Maoz, U., Berthoz, A., et al.: Complex Unconstrained Three-Dimensional Hand Movement and Constant Equi-Affine Speed. Journal of Neurophysiology 101(2), 1002–1015 (2009)
9. Park, J., Chung, W.K.: Geometric integration on Euclidean group with application to articulated multibody systems. IEEE Transactions on Robotics 21(5), 850–863 (2005)
10. Petreska, B., Billard, A.: Movement curvature planning through force field internal models. Biological Cybernetics 100(5), 331–350 (2009)
11. Pollick, F., Flash, T., et al.: Three-dimensional movements at constant affine velocity (1997)
12. Pollick, F.E., Maoz, U., et al.: Three-dimensional arm movements at constant equi-affine speed. Cortex 45(3), 325–339 (2009)
13. Todorov, E., Jordan, M.I.: Optimal feedback control as a theory of motor coordination. Nature neuroscience 5(11), 1226–1235 (2002)
14. Torres, E.B., Zipser, D.: Simultaneous control of hand displacements and rotations in orientation-matching experiments. Journal of Applied Physiology 96(5), 1978–1987 (2004)
15. Viviani, P., Terzuolo, C.: Trajectory determines movement dynamics. Neuroscience 7(2), 431–437 (1982)
16. Zefran, M., Kumar, V.: A geometrical approach to the study of the Cartesian stiffness matrix. Journal of Mechanical Design 124, 30–38 (2002)
17. Zefran, M., Kumar, V., et al.: On the generation of smooth three-dimensional rigid body motions. IEEE Transactions on Robotics and Automation 14(4), 576–589 (1998)

# Human Sitting Posture Exposed to Horizontal Perturbation and Implications to Robotic Wheelchairs

Karim A. Tahboub and Essameddin Badreddin

Automation Laboratory, Institute of Computer Engineering, Heidelberg University,
B6, 26, 68131 Mannheim, Germany
{karim.tahboub,badreddin}@ziti.uni-heidelberg.de

**Abstract.** In this article human sitting posture exposed to perturbations through the vibration of seat is analyzed and modeled. Motor control aspects related to sitting such as muscle activation patterns due to horizontal perturbations are addressed. Further, this analysis is augmented by presenting results of vibration studies performed on sitting posture where frequency response measures as apparent mass and transmissibility functions are introduced. A biomechanics and control model is proposed on the basis of both physiological and vibration experimental studies. Finally, the implications of the findings to robotic wheelchair control are discussed and suggestions are made to enhance user's comfort and feeling of safety.

**Keywords:** Robotic Wheelchair, Sitting Posture, Horizontal Vibration, Biomechanics Model, Comfort.

## 1 . Introduction

Maintenance and stability of sitting posture on a robotic wheelchair is a subject that has been rarely addressed. Although sitting seems to be a straightforward task for healthy humans, it resembles a challenge to patients with limited sensorimotor abilities. Patients sitting on wheelchairs face extra challenges due to the translation and rotation of the wheelchair as its motion acts as a destabilizing disturbance to sitting posture. Even if users can overcome such a disturbance, the required attentional investment adds a burden and leads to a feeling of discomfort and insecurity. In this contribution, the problem of sitting posture is addressed and its different aspects are tackled. Section 2 discusses the biomechanics of sitting posture and presents results of physiological studies performed to analyze its sensorimotor aspects. On the other side, vibration analysis techniques applying to seated posture and introduced in Section 3. An analytical biomechanics and control model is presented in Section 4. Through such a model, the effects of horizontal perturbation on the seated body are predicted. Finally, some preliminary concepts how to apply the presented conclusions to robotic wheelchairs, with the aim of improving user's feeling of comfort and safety are introduced in Section 5.

S. Jeschke, H. Liu, and D. Schilberg (Eds.): ICIRA 2011, Part I, LNAI 7101, pp. 192–201, 2011.
© Springer-Verlag Berlin Heidelberg 2011

## 2    Biomechanics and Motor Control of Sitting Posture

Depending on the location of the upper body center of gravity (CG) with respect to the ischial tuberosities (sitting bones), three sitting postures were defined by Schoberth [1] as shown in Fig. 1. In the middle position, the CG lies above the sitting bones and the feet carry about one fourth of the body weight. In the anterior position, the CG is anterior to the sitting bones and more than one fourth of the body weight is carried by the feed.   The third is the posterior position that is reached by a simultaneous extension rotation of the pelvis and kyphosis (outward curvature) of the spine to move the CG to become posterior to the ischial tuberosities. In this position, less weight is supported by the feet and, at the same time, an extra load is added on the muscles and discs. The trunk, represented as an inverted pendulum, is inherently unstable causing a major problem for people with spinal cord injuries [2]. Thus, trunk muscles must play a major role in maintaining upright sitting posture.

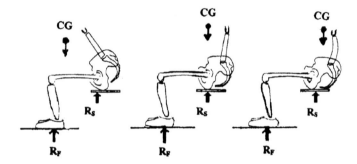

**Fig. 1.** Three sitting postures (from the left: anterior position, middle position, and posterior position) according to Schoberth [1]

Forssberg and Hirschfeld [3] were the first to examine sitting postural responses and to describe corresponding muscle activation. For this, they adopted the surface perturbation paradigm proposed by Nashner [4] which he devised to investigate standing posture. In this paradigm, healthy and patient subjects stand on a movable support surface (platform) and are asked to keep upright posture which is disturbed by moving the movable platform with different amplitudes, frequencies, and along different axis. Subject's reaction is measured by recording the kinematic displacement of different body segment through a visual tracking system and by measuring body-platform reaction forces (including force distribution and center of pressure) through force sensors imbedded in the platform (force platform).

Forssberg and Hirschfeld [3] reported that trunk muscles play a major role in stabilizing upright sitting posture when disturbed by platform translation. For example, a forward platform translation (causing a backward tilt of the upper body) evoked postural adjustments with consistent muscle activation patterns in all subjects where ventral (abdominal) muscles were activated first (60-80 ms) after the onset of the platform movement. They noticed as well that the threshold for postural adjustments are higher during sitting than during standing and higher for forward sway perturbation than for backward sway perturbations. The complexity of the muscle activation pattern and its independence of muscle stretch made them suggest that the responses are, in contrast to reflexes, centrally generated. Further they highlighted the importance of coactivation of antagonist muscles to produce stability by increasing the stiffness of the trunk. On the sensory side, they concluded that the vestibular system plays a minor role compared to proprioception (rotation of pelvis and hip movement) and cutaneous receptors that measure the distribution of the pressure under various parts of the buttock and thigh.

In another study, Zedka, Kumar, and Naryan [5] investigated the role of vision and expectation of rotational perturbation on the muscle response. They found that visual feedback in slow perturbations was not significant for the EMG magnitude and that expectation does not have a significant role.

Preuss and Fung [6] demonstrated in a comparative experimental study that trunk displacement in sitting posture due to a horizontal surface perturbation is significantly larger than that in standing posture. Recently, Massani et al. [2] measured and compared the activity of trunk muscles prior and after horizontal perturbations to sitting postures. They found that tonic activity is low but still above resting levels by about 1-3% of the maximum voluntary contraction (MVC) for the abdominal muscles and 4-6% for the back muscles. Phasic responses are found to be, inline with previous reported studies, highly direction-dependent.

Although sitting seems to be easier than standing (due to lower CG, larger base support, and less number of joints), patients with stroke still exhibit some disability in trunk function and in maintaining sitting posture [7]. This disability is explained by body scheme miss-representation and loss of force in the trunk musculature.

## 3     Vibrational Analysis of Sitting Posture

There have been numerous studies since the early 1950s related to sitting postures exposed to vertical vibration with relevance to the design of vehicle seating and suspension systems [8]. The results of these studies have been summarized in ISO 5982 [9]. More recently, some studies to measure the dynamic response of sitting postures to horizontal (fore-aft and lateral) vibration have been conducted; see [10] for a review.  In a typical experiment, a subject sits on a rigid seat that is randomly vibrated through an external actuator. The applied force together with the acceleration of the driving point and the acceleration of head and sometimes trunk are measured.  Different seat-back scenarios are tested; these include the existence/nonexistence of seat back and the angle of inclination of posture. Arm configuration can vary as well including placing them on the chair arms, crossing them on the trunk, or placing them in parallel on the thighs. These experimental-setup variations make the comparison of results of different studies more difficult.

The biodynamic response to horizontal and vertical vibration obtained through these experiments is usually expressed by two measures: the apparent mass characterizing the driving point impedance and vibration transmissibility featuring end-point characteristic. Apparent mass $M(f)$ is defined as the ratio of the force $F(f)$ to the acceleration $a(f)$ at the driving point at frequency $f$ [11]:

$$M(f) = \frac{F(f)}{a(f)} \tag{1}$$

or equivalently as [12]:

$$M(j\omega) = \frac{S_{\ddot{x}F}}{S_{\ddot{x}}} \tag{2}$$

where $M(j\omega)$ is the complex apparent mass response as a function of the circular frequency $\omega$, $S_{\ddot{x}F}$ is the cross-spectral density of acceleration and force measured at the driving point, and $S_{\ddot{x}}$ is the auto spectral density of the seat acceleration. On the other hand, vibration transmissibility $H(f)$ is defined for example as [8]:

$$H(f) = \frac{\ddot{x}_{head}}{\ddot{x}_{seat}} \tag{3}$$

where $\ddot{x}_{head}$ is the acceleration of head along the x-direction whereas $\ddot{x}_{seat}$ is the acceleration of the seat along the same direction.

Hinz et al. [8] gave a brief summary of a range of studies in terms of the apparent mass peak frequency. For vertical vibration, the main resonance peak was found to be approximately 4-5 Hz and partially a secondary resonance was between 8-13 Hz. For vibration in the lateral direction, they noticed inconsistency in observed modes of apparent mass where some studies reported the first mode at 0.7 Hz and a second one at 2-2.5 Hz. Other studies indicated 1 Hz for the first mode and 1-3 Hz for the second mode. They noted also that the apparent mass in this direction is influenced by the backseat contact, the sitting posture, foot support, and thigh contact. The same notes hold for the fore-aft direction where the first mode was about 0.7 Hz and the second mode was at around 2 Hz.

Rakheja et al. [10] performed a synthesis study to identify the most probable ranges of biodynamic responses (from selected experimental results of different research groups) of the human body to whole-body vibration. For example, Fig. 2 shows the idealized ranges of apparent mass magnitude and phase responses of a body seated without a back support under vibration along the fore-aft direction. Two peak frequencies at about 0.7 Hz and 2.5 Hz are evident from Fig. 2. Fig. 3 shows the response of a body seated with a vertical back support under vibration along the fore-aft direction as well. Here, the effect of back support is clear in the peak apparent mass magnitude and the corresponding peak frequency, which exceed those measured without seat back. Finally, different studies demonstrated dependence of apparent mass response on the amplitude of vibration excitation [8, 11].

# 4    Biomechanics and Control Model

Experimental results give insight into biodynamic response of seated human body exposed to whole-body vibration but fall short to explain the mechanisms behind the observed response. A biomechanics model is sought to depict experimental results while taking the body structure into account. Based on such a model, it would be possible to clarify the measured response and to predict the behavior of the body under different conditions. Several research groups have proposed different mathematical models for human seated posture behavior. Some models try to merely fit measured dynamic response [9]. Others assume lumped-parameter models with different number of body segments connected by springs and dampers, for example [13, 14, 15]. Unfortunately, all proposed models, which the authors are aware of, assume inert biomechanics that is not subject to any active or reactive control through the muscles. Although such models can be justified in the vertical direction by assuming that the controlled response play a minor role, active and reactive control must be considered to explain response to horizontal vibration as explained in Section 2.

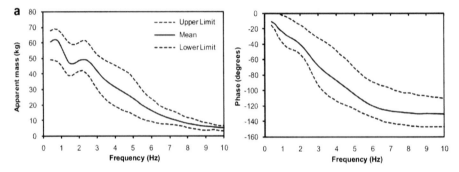

**Fig. 2.** Idealized range of apparent mass magnitude response of a body seated without a back support under vibration along the fore-aft direction [10]

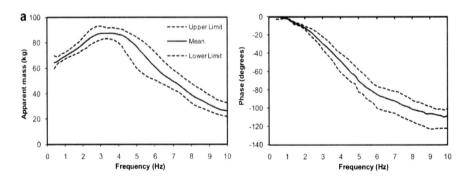

**Fig. 3.** Idealized range of apparent mass magnitude response of a body seated with a back support under vibration along the fore-aft direction [10]

Hereafter, a simplified planar two-degree-of-freedom biomechanics model for a human in a free sitting posture is presented. The two degrees of freedom correspond to the angular motion of the trunk with respect to the thighs about the hip joint ( $\theta_2$ ) and to the angular motion of the head with respect to the trunk about the neck joint

($\theta_3$). As shown in Fig. 4, the lower body is assumed to rest stationary on the seat that moves in the sagittal plane (translation along the x-direction and rotation about the hip joint with an angle $\theta_1$). Joint stiffness and damping elements are not included in the model as their contribution is considered in the control model as explained in the sequel. The mass distribution of body segments is represented by the corresponding centers of gravity located at a distance $l_i$ from the center of rotation and at angle $\phi_i$ from the segment's center line as shown in Fig. 4. The reaction forces between the body and the seat are represented by two vertical forces $F_F$ and $F_B$ and one tangential shear force $F_s$. Further, the participating muscles apply net joint torques of $T_t$ and $T_h$. For the purpose of this work, it is assumed that the seat remains horizontal without tilt ($\theta_1 = 0$). Applying Lagrange's method yields the following nonlinear biomechanics model:

$$(m_2 l_2 \cos(\theta_2 + \phi_2) + m_3 L_2 \cos(\theta_2))\ddot{x} + (I_2 + m_2 l_2^2 + m_3 L_2^2)\ddot{\theta}_2 + m_3 L_2 l_3 \cos(-\theta_3 - \phi_3)(\ddot{\theta}_2 + \ddot{\theta}_3)$$
$$+ m_3 L_2 l_3 \sin(-\theta_3 - \phi_3)\dot{\theta}_2^2 - M_2 l_2 \sin(\theta_2 + \phi_2) - M_3 L_2 \sin(\theta_2) = T_t - T_h \tag{4}$$

$$m_3 l_3 \cos(\theta_2 + \theta_3 + \phi_3)\ddot{x} + m_3 L_2 l_3 \cos(-\theta_3 - \phi_3)\ddot{\theta}_2 + (I_3 + m_3 l_3^2)(\ddot{\theta}_2 + \ddot{\theta}_3)$$
$$- m_3 L_2 l_3 \sin(-\theta_3 - \phi_3)\dot{\theta}_2^2 - M_3 l_3 \sin(\theta_2 + \theta_3 + \phi_3) = T_h \tag{5}$$

where $I_i$ is the mass moment of inertia of body segment $i$ about its center of mass, $m_i$ and $M_i$ are the mass and weight of body segment $i$, and $L_2$ is the distance between the two joints. Joints angular position and velocity (proprioceptive signals), the

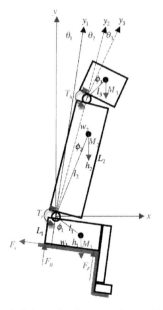

| Parameter | Value | Unit |
|---|---|---|
| $m_2$ | 35.82 | $kg$ |
| $m_3$ | 4.86 | $kg$ |
| $I_2$ | 2.3 | $kg.m^2$ |
| $I_3$ | 0.12 | $kg.m^2$ |
| $l_2$ | 0.1885 | $m$ |
| $l_3$ | 0.159 | $m$ |
| $L_2$ | 0.504 | $m$ |
| $\phi_2$ | 0 | $rad$ |
| $\phi_3$ | 0 | $rad$ |

**Fig. 4.** Schematic diagram of seated human without seatback with anthropometric parameters

reaction forces $F_F$, $F_B$, and $F_s$ (cutaneous signals) together with head translational acceleration components and angular velocity (vestibular signals) are all derived analytically as the output equations complementing the above model but not shown here for space limitations.

The voluntary active control of the trunk and head (imposing a desired body posture) as well as the reactive disturbance rejection in seated posture are assumed to be analogous to those in standing posture. Standing posture control is relatively a well-understood problem as it has been under analytical investigation in the past few decades [16, 17]. The role of proprioception and the vestibular sensor has been shown to be instrumental in explicitly estimating external disturbances and isolating them from self-induced effects and thus enabling for rejecting (compensating for) these disturbances [16, 18]. Based on a previous study where a biologically-inspired postural control scheme is proposed for a humanoid [18], a simple disturbance-rejection and robust tracking controller is proposed. In general, the controller should reflect the dynamic coupling between the two joints and thus be formed as a multi-input multi-output controller. However, it is assumed here that the coupling effects are not significant (low speed voluntary motion) and thus can be considered as joint disturbances. Hence, independent joint controllers can be employed. Such a controller is then composed of an internal loop (state feedback: affecting damping and natural frequency) and an external loop (error integral control: achieving robust tracking). Such a control scheme is capable of implicitly rejecting a class of disturbances acting on the process [18]. Thus, the muscle torque at the hip joint, for example, becomes:

$$T_t = k_{ti} \int (\theta_{2,desired} - \theta_2)dt - k_{tp}\theta_2 - k_{td}\dot{\theta}_2 \qquad (6)$$

where $k_{ti}$, $k_{tp}$, and $k_{td}$ are respectively the integral, proportional, and derivative control gains for the hip joint and $\theta_{2,desired}$ is the desired joint angle to be tracked. The proportional and derivative control gains can be considered as reflecting both the passive connecting elements at the joints together with the active control effort. These gains are found based on body-segment mass-distribution parameters (based on anthropometric data assuming a total mass of 60 kg and a height of 1.75 m) by choosing appropriate damping ratio, natural frequency, and tracking-error exponential frequency that approximately produce the observed response reported in experimental studies.

Apparent-mass and seat-head acceleration transmissibility functions corresponding to fore-aft vibration are shown in Fig. 5. They are computed based on the linearized dynamics of the model shown in Fig. 4   and the given closed-loop control law (Eq. 6). Although, it is theoretically possible to find numerical values for damping ratios and natural frequencies to better fit the average of reported experimental results given in Ref. [10], realistic values are adopted here. For the head segment these values are: $\omega_n = 2.0Hz$, $\zeta = 1$, and tracking time constant of 0.05 second whereas for the trunk segment the values are: $\omega_n = 0.7Hz$, $\zeta = 1.5$, and tracking time constant of 0.2 second. The shown results (Fig. 5) fall within the acceptable range observed in different studies. As mentioned before, it is difficult to compare results of different experiments due to the variability of posture (location of arms and feet, inclination of seat back). Transmissibility function of seat vibration to the head (Fig. 5) shows a considerable magnification of transmitted vibration at frequencies around the peak frequency of 3 Hz. Such a magnification is a source of discomfort to the seated subject.

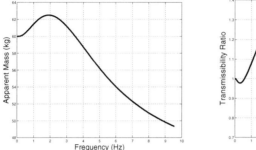 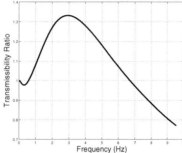

**Fig. 5.** Apparent mass magnitude response and seat-head transmissibility ratio of a body seated without a back support under vibration along the fore-aft direction

## 5      Implications to Robotic Wheelchairs

Powered and robotic wheelchairs are thought as assistive devices for humans with reduced mobility and/or neurological disorders.   Thus dynamic characteristics of such wheelchairs are reflected as user's acceptance, comfort, and feeling of safety. Different ergonomic design factors (e.g. dimensions, seating, interface modalities, and suspension) have been already considered in several studies.

Unlike vertical vibrations, horizontal seat acceleration that is considered in details in this study is paired with wheelchair motion. All daily-life wheelchair maneuvers include accelerating and decelerating longitudinal and lateral components.   Fig. 6 shows the longitudinal velocity component corresponding to the wheelchair trajectory show in the same figure where a healthy young subject drove the wheelchair through a joystick from point (0,0) through the room and back. Although the maximum speed is limited to 0.7 m/sec, the longitudinal velocity fluctuates considerably depending on the task and the subject's performance.

The wheelchair horizontal acceleration corresponding to the above trajectory acts as a disturbance to the posture of the seated person and is transmitted to the different body segments with variable intensities. It is proposed here to improve the user's comfort by limiting the trajectory acceleration (equivalent to perturbations) in the frequency range where transmissibility is high. Given the functions obtained through the biomechanics and control sitting posture model (Fig. 4), this implies applying a trajectory notch filter around the 3-Hz frequency. Discomfort is usually correlated with jerk. But here the wheelchair user has to react to posture-destabilizing acceleration disturbances leading to discomfort.

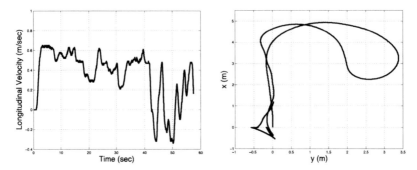

**Fig. 6.** Robotic wheelchair longitudinal velocity and space trajectory

Wheelchairs are usually used by persons with impaired sensorimotor abilities and not by healthy subjects. It is expected, as well, that corresponding dynamic responses of patient subjects might differ from those of healthy subjects. All studies discussed in Section 3 correspond to healthy subjects and thus cannot serve as basis for designing the proposed notch filter. On the other hand, clinical biomechanics studies presented in Section 4 concentrated on muscle activation patterns and do not provide useful frequency response measures. Thus it is advisable to conduct relevant sitting posture vibration analysis experiments, including apparent mass and transmissibility functions, for patients with different sensorimotor impairments and to propose matching notch filters.

Finally, it is to be noted that attentional investment in posture control significantly increases for subjects with postural control impairments [19]. So the impact of minimizing harmful (with high transmissibility ratio) trajectory acceleration components on the comfort of these subjects is high.

## 6    Conclusions

Horizontal acceleration components of robotic wheelchair trajectories act as a source of disturbance to the sitting posture of a person using the wheelchair. Vibration studies with healthy subjects show that transmissibility of vibration to the upper body part has a peak at a low frequency (2-3 Hz) of the seat fore-aft acceleration. Thus it is proposed to employ a notch filter that minimizes the seat acceleration around the peak frequency. Further, it is recommended to experimentally study the corresponding frequency response of seated subjects with sensorimotor impairments.

## References

1. Harrison, D., Harrison, S., Croft, A., Harrison, D., Troyanovich, S.: Sitting Biomechanics Part I: Review of the Literature. Journal of Manipulative and Physiological Therapeutics 22, 594–609 (1999)
2. Masani, K., Sin, V., Vette, A., Thrasher, T., Kawashima, N., Morris, A., Preuss, R., Popovic, M.: Postural reactions of the trunk muscles to multi-directional perturbations in sitting. Clinical Biomechanics 24, 176–182 (2009)

3. Forssbergand, H., Hirschfeld, H.: Postural adjustments in sitting humans following external perturbations: muscle activity and kinematics. Experimental Brain Research 97, 515–527 (1994)
4. Nashner, L.: Adapting Reflexes Controlling the Human Posture. Experimental Brain Research 26, 59–72 (1976)
5. Zedka, M., Kumar, S., Narayan, Y.: Electromyographic response of the trunk muscles to postural perturbation in sitting subjects. Journal of Electromyography and Kinesiology 8, 3–10 (1998)
6. Preuss, R., Fung, J.: Musculature and biomechanics of the trunk in the maintenance of upright posture. Journal of Electromyography and Kinesiology 18, 815–828 (2008)
7. Genthon, N., Vuillerme, N., Monnet, J.P., Petit, C., Rougier, P.: Biomechanical assessment of the sitting posture maintenance in patients with stroke. Clinical Biomechanics 22, 1024–1029 (2007)
8. Hinz, B., Bluethner, R., Menzel, G., Ruetzel, S., Seidel, H., Woelfel, H.: Apparent mass of seated men - determination with single- and multi-axis excitations at different magnitudes. J. Sound and Vibration 298, 788–809 (2006)
9. International Organization for Standardization ISO 5982, Mechanical vibration and shock-range of idealized values to characterizeseated-body biodynamic response under vertical vibration (2001)
10. Rakheja, S., Dong, R.G., Patra, S., Boileau, P.E., Marcotte, P., Warren, C.: Biodynamics of the human body under whole-body vibration: synthesis of the reported data. International Journal of Industrial Ergonomics 40, 710–732 (2010)
11. Mansfield, N.J.: Impedance methods (apparent mass, driving point mechanical impedance and absorbed power) for assessment of the biomechanical response of the seated person to whole-body vibration. Industrial Health 43, 378–389 (2005)
12. Wang, W., Rakheja, S., Boileau, P.E.: Effects of sitting posture on biodynamic response of seated occupants under vertical vibratio. International Journal of Industrial Ergonomics 34, 289–306 (2004)
13. Matsumoto, Y., Griffin, M.: Modeling the dynamic mechanisms associated with the principal resonance of the seated human body. Clinical Biomechanics 16(Supplement No. 1), 31–44 (2001)
14. Kim, T., Kim, U., Yoon, Y.: Development of a biomechanical model of the human body in a sitting posture with vibration transsmissibility in the vertical direction. International Journal of Industrial Ergonomics 35, 817–829 (2005)
15. Liang, C., Chiang, C.: A study on biodynamic models of seated human subjects exposed to vertical vibration. International Journal of Industrial Ergonomics 36, 869–890 (2006)
16. Mergner, T.: A neurological view on reactive human stance control. Annual Reviews in Control 34, 177–198 (2010)
17. MacNeilage, P., Ganesan, N., Angelaki, D.: Computational approaches to spatial orientation: from transfer functions to dynamic Bayesian inference. J. Neurophysiol 100, 2981–2996 (2008)
18. Tahboub, K.: Biologically-inspired humanoid postural control. Journal of Physiology – Paris 103, 195–210 (2009)
19. Roerdink, M., Hlavackova, P., Vuillerme, N.: Center-of-pressure regularity as a marker for attentional investment in postural control: A comparison between sitting and standing postures. Human Movement Science (in press, 2011)

# Automatic Circumference Measurement for Aiding in the Estimation of Maximum Voluntary Contraction (MVC) in EMG Systems

James A.R. Cannan and Huosheng Hu

University of Essex,
Wivenhoe Park, Colchester, Essex CO4 3SQ, United Kingdom
Jarcan@essex.ac.uk
http://www.essex.ac.uk/csee/

**Abstract.** Maximum Voluntary Contraction(MVC) is frequently used in human machine muscle interfaces, especially the ones using Electromyography(EMG) and Acousticmyography(AMG). In some cases MVC alone is enough to adapt a system from one user to another, which could potentially create a simple system that any user could instantly use with minimal training and calibration. This research work evaluates the usefulness of automating circumference measurement for estimating MVC thereby reducing the need for training and calibration. A preliminary implementation of a circumference measuring armband is presented to demonstrate the feasibility and performance of this technology.

**Keywords:** Human Machine Interfaces(HMI), Electromyography (EMG), Acousticmyography (AMG), Circumference, Maximum Voluntary Contraction (MVC), Bionics, Auto Calibration.

## 1 Introduction

Bionic muscle interfaces such as electromyography(EMG),which measure the electrical properties of our muscles, have been a popular research topic for the last few decades. They show much potential for naturally interfacing the complexity of our body movements with everyday electronics, and have influenced the development of many devices, including prothesis [1], exoskeletons[2], and electrical devices[3]. This technology however has never really reached the general population, as the complexity and discrepancies between users prevents the development of standards for compensating for the multitude of different body compositions. The development of portable, reliable and adaptable technology is the next step forward.

A simple electrode bracelet that anyone can use, with ideally little or no training or adjustments would be a very beneficial system for people. At the moment steps towards this idea are slowly being taken, with the wireless armband already in development [4]. The majority of EMG systems are stuck in laboratories, when they should be utilized to enhance our everyday lives. One of

S. Jeschke, H. Liu, and D. Schilberg (Eds.): ICIRA 2011, Part I, LNAI 7101, pp. 202–211, 2011.
© Springer-Verlag Berlin Heidelberg 2011

the biggest issues with muscle interfacing, is that everyone has different types of muscles with varying shapes and sizes and so, we require some level of identification to incorporate these differences into the signal processing to compensate for discrepancies.

A system which uses amplitude based features like Root Mean Squared (RMS), Mean Absolute Value (MAV), or any averaging function, is often combined with thresholding techniques. It is these thresholds that need to be adapted from one user to another. This is usually done by establishing the users Maximum Voluntary Contraction (MVC), which can then be used to normalize the EMG signal. MVC is useful for determining activation thresholds, and for simple signal segmentation. Adjusting to an acceptable level of MVC helps determine a more comfortable activation threshold for individual users. A system where one person has to apply intense force to pass the threshold and where others barely have to flex their muscles, makes the system unresponsive to user requirements. Being able to adjust to half the users maximum strength enables a system to find a comfortable level, making the system more user friendly.

Currently there are no methods for automatically estimating MVC before the user begins movement, which means every user is required to calibrate a new system. In this paper, we examine a novel approach that automatically calibrates a system by estimating MVC from forearm circumference. Our aim is to create a system that is instantly compatible with almost any user with minimal need for calibration and training, which is similar to Saponas et al [5]. The system takes a small step towards making bionic muscle interfaces, not only including EMG but also Acousticmyography(AMG), easier to use. Our system is primarily beneficial to systems that purely require Maximum Voluntary Contraction(MVC) for calibration.

The rest of the paper is organized as follows. Section 2 presents some background about bionic muscle interfaces and maximum voluntary contraction (MVC). In Section 3, the design of an automatic circumference armband is described and a preliminary functional prototype is presented. Experimental results are given in Section 4 to show the feasibility and performance of the developed armband. Section 5 presents a brief discussion of this research. Finally, a brief conclusion and future work is presented in Section 6.

## 2    Background

Bionic muscle interfaces come in two popular forms: Electromyography(EMG)[6] and Acousticmyography (AMG)[7]. EMG is the monitoring of very small electrical signals produced during the activation process for controlling our muscles, and is usually monitored through differential or double differential electrodes. The signal is only a few millivolts in amplitude and needs to be amplified close to 1000 times to be usable. The frequency spectrum, which compared to most bionic signals is quite large, ranges from 0-500hz.

AMG measures the very small acoustical signal, or sounds, that our muscles make, and also needs to be amplified considerably. It does not use electrodes but instead uses microphones and accelerometer's which are usually designed for monitoring low frequency signals, as AMG reside mostly in the 0-50hz frequency band. There are a number of considerations that need to be taken into account when using EMG, for example electrode position, electrode contact, temperature, fatigue, noise, body composition and physiology. Every person is different, every reading is different, and by beginning to stabilize some of the unknown variables, and incorporating or considering these values in calculations, it is likely to increase accuracy or at least stabilize results.

A circumference armband should be able to roughly estimate the MVC by automatically measuring the circumference of the forearm, this is viable as there is a correlation between muscle size and muscle strength. Attempting to measure forearm size can be used in various fields of research. It has primary interest within the medical and health industries but could also importantly be used in area's of wearable robotics. Detecting human physiological characteristic is likely to become a more important field in the future, when an increased number of wearable devices will be available, making automatic adaption or calibration a very useful feature.

The feasibility of this research comes from a number of sources that prove muscle and grip strength is positively correlated to some anthropometric variables, such as forearm circumference, size, volume, and cross-sectional area [8][9][10][11]. Figure 1 from Anakwe et al demonstrates the linear relationship between grip strength and forearm circumference of men, but on the other hand reveals the limited relationship in women. However, with additional compensations like body fat percentage, the correlation might be improved.

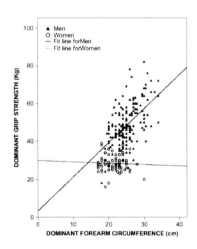

**Fig. 1.** The relationship between dominant grip strength and dominant forearm circumference for 250 subjects with lines of best fit applied for both sexes [9]

There are circumstances where the larger muscle is not always the stronger muscle, as there are three important factors that contribute towards muscle strength: physiological strength, neurological strength and mechanical strength. Physiological strength involves factors of muscle size, neurological strength relates to the strength of the signal that tells your muscles to contract, and mechanical strength is how efficiently your muscles and bones work together as levers. In addition there are two types of voluntary muscle fibers, slow twitch and fast twitch. Slow twitch fibers generate little force but operate for long periods of time, while fast twitch fibers are powerful but tire rapidly. Depending on which muscle fibers you have can influence your strength.

Maximum Voluntary Contraction (MVC) is the maximum ability to contract ones muscles. Logically when related to the MVC of forearm muscles, grip strength becomes a good predictor, as forearm muscles control the majority of hand motions. Hou et al [12] were able to relate hand grip force with EMG MVC levels, which demonstrate the relationship between MVC and hand grip strength. However, they show varying ranges of accuracy is produced at different levels of MVC, with the most accurate results produced in the mid range of 30-50%.

A system estimating MVC could be beneficial to a number of research projects [13][14] [15] in cases where thresholds could be automatically adapted, or added to adapt to a wider population. Thresholds that are averaged over a group work reasonably well for the majority, but there are always outliers for whom the system fails. Having technology that automatically detects human characteristics and adjusts accordingly would be very beneficial to the user.

Estimating MVC from forearm circumference may work for a large portion of the population, but it assumes that you are healthy and have no debilitating muscle related problems. Hand strength can diminish with conditions like carpal tunnel syndrome, nerve tendon or any neuromuscular disorders. In which case the system can easily be calibrated using the MVC amplitude of the EMG signal. There are certain issues with measuring MVC through automatic circumference measurements, like fatigue for example. circumference doesn't vary considerably over the day however your MVC may. This is why circumference can only be used to estimate MVC for aiding in the adjustment of thresholds.

## 3   Design of Automatic Circumference Armband

As a preliminary functional prototype, the automatic circumference armband was built from relatively easy to obtain materials, plus a couple of custom made parts. It is intended to be used specifically on the forearm where a large amount of closely compacted and overlapping muscles occur, as this is where the most complex EMG and AMG signal resides, and hence the greatest need for stability. The basic structure of the armband can been seen in the original design in figure 2.

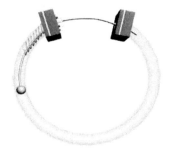

**Fig. 2.** Circumference Band Model

The circumference armband is made from springs, elastic, tubing, barbed fittings, steel wire, braided cable sleeve, nonconductive wire, and custom made Acrylic connectors, all of which are depicted in figure 3. The armband was designed to operate on a wide range of body shapes, allowing the system to be easily adapted or constructed to almost any part of the body with just a few alterations.

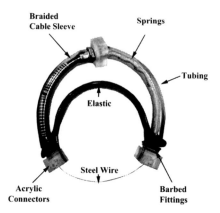

**Fig. 3.** Circumference Band

The prototype is able to measuring varying circumferences from a minimum of 120mm, small enough for a young child, and a maximum of 280mm, big enough for the average adult. This gives the armband an adjustable circumference of 160mm. A picture of the armband on a model arm is shown in figure 4. It can fit quite comfortably on the wrist and midforearm on almost any individual, but begins to get restrictive on the upper forearm. Additional length would be possible with an increase in cable length, tubing and number of springs. However measuring size is directly proportional to the size of the armband, therefore the greater the adjustable length the larger the size of the arm band.

**Fig. 4.** Circumference Band on forearm

This armband is able to detect circumference by taking advantage of the resistance properties of metallic wire. A resistance is produced when an electric current flows through the wire, and the moving electrons collide with the atoms of the wire. This makes it more difficult for the current to flow, and causes resistance. The longer the wire the greater the chance of collision hence the increase in resistance. Similarly the greater the thickness of the wire the more room there is for the current to flow, reducing the frequency of collisions and therefore reducing the resistance of the wire. There are potential factors that may influence wire readings, the wire length, thickness, temperature, resistance, materials, and the voltage applied. Most of these can be kept constant, or easily compensated for with the correct hardware. The armband has a sturdy structure which minimizes any big differences in readings, but does not entirely remove the effect of motion.

**Fig. 5.** Basic operational flow chart

The readings from the armband are passed into a OPA277 operational amplifier and amplified to a usable level. The resulting signal is passed into a 10bit ADC of a 16f877a microcontroller and transmitted to a computer, where the data could be graphical represented. In theory with a 10bit ADC the circumference armband could detect close to 1 millimeter movements. Sufficient for most applications.

## 4    Experimental Results and Analysis

Initial tests showed that the armband was uncomfortable when reaching close to maximum range, and was a little difficult to put on. This could easily be fixed by extending the armbands measuring capabilities. Cable rubbing on the

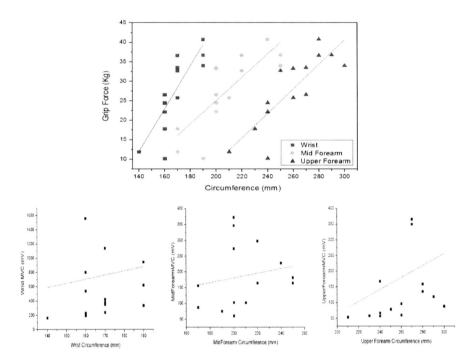

**Fig. 6.** TOP: Grip Force VS Circumference chart, BOTTOM: Wrist, Mid Forearm and Upper Forearm VS MVC

interior of the plastic tubing was another drawback to the design, consequently fluid motion was not always possible, although the effect was reduced by coving the wire with a braided cable sleeve. The size of the overall system along with cables was not a mechanical limitation but more an esthetic one. The size and weight could be significantly reduced by altering the dimensions of a few of the parts, however further redesigns may be required to fully optimize the hardware.

During movement i.e. putting on the armband, there is some recording noise, however, as soon as the wearer stops moving the device, it quickly stabilizes. When the circumference armband worked correctly the signal was relatively clean, a linear relationship between circumference and a wire resistance was easily observable. During certain intense movements the armband readings did vary slightly, but mostly due to the size and weight of this prototype. Miniaturizing the design would improve resilience. Overall the design fulfilled its purpose, and was able to automatically estimate the circumference.

A preliminary study was performed assessing the relationship of forearm circumference with force and MVC. Wrist, mid-forearm and upper forearm circumference measurement were taken from 14 subjects aging between 24 and 60. Three EMG electrodes were placed on the inside of the forearm at the same locations as the circumference measurements. Participants were asked to grip a force sensor as hard as they could for a short period of time. The Hardware used for this experiment includes Biometrics EMG electrodes, Dynamometer, and EMG acquiring hardware. Early results did show promise. Strong relationships were observed when comparing wrist, mid forearm and upper forearm circumference to force, but were weaker when compared and MVC data. The upper forearm preformed the best with wrist and mid forearm results not as strong or accurate, but still potentially usable.The preliminary results are shown in figure 6. This confirms the usefulness of automating circumference measurements for aiding in the estimation of MVC thresholds. The wrist and mid forearm relationships were not as strong as the upper forearm when comparing MVC, with more participants a greater relationship may be observed. Considering there is such a strong relationship between forearm circumference and force but not as strong for EMG MVC, it is likely that more compensationary measurements may be needed.The electrode's position is likely to vary slightly between individuals, which may have caused some of the error.

## 5    Discussion

It is possible that there are too many factors that contribute towards estimating MVC, circumference certainly plays a role, but perhaps not significantly enough to be used alone. MVC is often used for adjusting thresholds, considering only an estimation is needed to slightly increase or decrease thresholds, automatic circumference measuring could provide an acceptable way to estimate thresholds, or at least be combined with 1 or 2 other measures, for example body fat percentage which might enhance reliability. The further away the monitoring electrode or microphone is from the source, the greater the reduction of MVC Amplitude[16]. Therefore higher body fat percentages increase the distance of monitoring devices from muscles which in turn effects the MVC amplitude. With obesity on the rise, detection of body fat percentage would be a useful parameter for increasing the stability of results.

Bioelectric impedance(BI) shows promise for improving results, it measures the resistance between the skin and electrodes. Monitors are not uncommon, and come in varying shapes and sizes but usually provide the same functionality, i.e. measuring body fat. The problem with these monitors is the lack of confirmed standards, as all do not produce accurate results. The other big issue is that they usually require additional height, weight and gender details which contradicts the main principal of this research, which is automatic detection for improving muscle interfaces. By ignoring height, weight and gender you are likely to get an error in your calculations, whether or not this is significant enough to effect an estimation is as yet unknown and will require further research. Bioelectric impedance has also been shown to estimate muscle volume[17] which might provide a useful addition or alternative to circumference measurement, but whether this can be all done within a small surface area, for example on a wrist band, will have to be evaluated.

Using muscle circumference to estimate MVC thresholds could be an initial step, it would be possible to use the average EMG signal over time to fine tune readings. This would also begin to help compensate for fatigue. All EMG systems have cross user interfacing issues, no one system has been able to adapt to every user faultlessly[4], but there have been instances of relatively good cross user implementations, with results in the region of 90%[18]. It is possible that signal processing alone is able to establish a reasonable level of cross user operability, however, adding body compositional information could improve results further.

By adding more automatic training parameters, it would be possible to break down the population into segments, with each population group having there own settings, and therefore potentially simplifying some of the cross user interoperability issues. The circumference armband is therefore not limited to simple thresholding techniques, but could benefit systems using machine learning and pattern recognition, by automatically differentiating which user group is using the device, and automatically tuning the settings. With simple programming the system could have the bonus of being able to detect when a user was attempting to put on or take off the armband, meaning the system could reduce its operation while the user is adjusting it. Once the system is removed the springs compress the armband to its minimum circumference, verifying the likelihood that the device has been removed and could switch off after a few minutes of inactive operation.

## 6   Conclusion and Future Work

Using Anthropometric variables is an unusual way for improving muscle based interfaces, and provides a new area to be investigated. This is the first known instance of using automatic circumference measuring for attempting to aid in the adjustment of MVC thresholds. In this research the designed armband is able to measure the forearm circumference of a large portion of the population, from a minimum of 120mm to a maximum of 280mm, with close to 1mm accuracy. The circumference armband is by no means a complete solution for fully automating a muscle interfacing system, but it is certainly a step in the right direction. Further properties may have to be incorporated before it becomes reliable enough to be usable on a variety of body compositions.

The current version of the circumference armband is a first prototype, it was designed to evaluate the effectiveness of circumference measurability. A number of problems were identified with the armband and with improvements the design could be more elegant. The addition of non-conductive springs would have reduced the armband dimensions, with smaller tubing and fitting further reducing the size. Evaluating the usefulness of the circumference band design as well as its purpose will determine what level of research will be allocated in the future to follow the concept. Other approaches are being analyzed and evaluated to determine an optimized design for portable applications.

**Acknowledgments.** This research is funded by EPSRC Studentship EP/P504910/1.

# References

1. http://www.touchbionics.com/i-LIMB i-Limb
2. http://www.cyberdyne.jp/english/robotsuithal/index.html
   HAL Exoskeleton
3. Kim, J., Mastnik, S., Andre, E.: EMG-based Hand Gesture Recognition for Real-time Biosignal Interfacing. In: IUI 2008 (2008)
4. Scott Saponas, T., Tan, D.S., Morris, D., Balakrishnan, R.: Demonstrating the feasibility of using forearm electromyography for muscle-computer interfaces. In: CHI 2008 (2008)
5. Scott Saponas, T., Tan, D.S., Morris, D., Turner, J., Landay, J.A.: Making Muscle-Computer Interfaces More Practical (2010)
6. Konrad, P.: ABC of EMG - Electromyography background
7. GRASS, Acoustic Myography, AMG (2004)
8. Aoi, W., Naito, Y., Yoshikawa, T.: Exercise and functional foods (2006)
9. Anakwe, R.E., Huntley, J.S., Mceachan, J.E.: Grip Strength And Forearm Circumference In A Healthy Population (2006)
10. Fraser, A., Vallow, J., Preston, A., Cooper, R.G.: Predicting 'normal' grip strength for rheumatoid arthritis patients (1999)
11. Gunther, C.M., Burger, A., Rickert, M., Crispin, A., Schulz, C.U.: Grip strength in healthy caucasian adults: reference values (2008)
12. Hou, W., Jiang, Y., Zheng, J., Zheng, X., Peng, C., Xu, R.: Chongqing Univ., Chongqing. Handgrip Force Estimation Based on a Method Using Surface Electromyography (sEMG) of Extensor Carpi Radialis Longus (2007)
13. Guerreiro, T.J.V., Jorge, J.A.P.: Emg As A Daily Wearable Interface (2006)
14. Benko, H., Scott Saponas, T., Morris, D., Tan, D.: Enhancing Input On and Above the Interactive Surface with Muscle Sensing ITS (2009)
15. Costanza, E., Inverso, S.A., Allen, R., Maes, P.: Intimate interfaces in action: assessing the usability and subtlety of emg-based motionless gestures. In: CHI 2007 (2007)
16. Baars, H., Jollenbeck, T., Humburg, H., Schroder, J.: Surface-electromyography: Skin And Subcutaneous Fat Tissue Attenuate Amplitude And Frequency Parameters (2006)
17. Miyatani, M., Kanehisa, H., Masuo, Y., Ito, M., Fukunaga, T.: Validity of estimating limb muscle volume by bioelectrical impedance (2001)
18. Xiang, C., Lantz, V., Kong-Qiao, W., Zhang-Yan, Z., Xu, Z., Ji-Hai, Y.: Feasibility of Building Robust Surface Electromyography-based Hand Gesture Interfaces (2009)

# Classification of the Action Surface EMG Signals Based on the Dirichlet Process Mixtures Method

Min Lei and Guang Meng

Institute of Vibration, Shock and Noise, State Key Laboratory of Mechanical System and
Vibration, Shanghai Jiao Tong University, Shanghai 2000240, P.R. China
leimin@sjtu.edu.cn

**Abstract.** This paper proposes a new classification method based on Dirichlet
process mixtures(DPM) to investigate the classification of the four actions from
the action surface EMG(ASEMG) signals. This method first builds a
classification model of the data by using the multinomial logit model (MNL).
Then a classifier is given by using the classification information of training
data. For the features of ASEMG, we use a combined method of the empirical
mode decomposition(EMD), Largest Lyapunov exponent and Linear
discriminant analysis(LDA) dimension reduction. The highest average
classification accuracy rates are over 90%. The results indicate that this
classification method could be applied the classification of the ASEMG signals.

**Keywords:** Dirichlet process mixture, the action Surface EMG(ASEMG)
signal, empirical mode decomposition(EMD), Largest Lyapunov exponent,
Linear discriminant analysis(LDA).

## 1    Introduction

The theory of Dirichlet Process (DP) mixture model can be traced back to
Antoniak(1974)[1]. This model uses Dirichlet process priors introduced by
Ferguson(1973) [2]to provide a flexible Bayesian solution for removing some of the
limitations of current parametric finite mixture models. A Dirichlet process $D$ is a
distribution over distributions. It comprises a baseline $G_0$ and scale parameter $\alpha$, i.e.
$D(G_0, \alpha)$. The distributions sampled from a Dirichlet process are discrete almost
surely based on the Polya urn scheme by Blackwell and MacQueen(1973)[3]. Thus,
the Bayesian solution based on Dirichlet process priors supports data-adaptive
estimations.

Though this theory has been known for a long time, its practical applications begin
since the nineties of the last century. With the development of MCMC techniques, the
DP mixture models have recently attracted wide attention and are now used in many
fields, such as genomics, data mining, oral health analysis, image classification, and
so on[4-12]. In this paper, we consider Dirichlet process mixture model as a classifier
for the action surface EMG signal classification. To our knowledge, this method has
not received attention in the ASEMG analysis. For feature inputs of the DPM
classifier, this paper use a combined method of the empirical mode decomposition

S. Jeschke, H. Liu, and D. Schilberg (Eds.): ICIRA 2011, Part I, LNAI 7101, pp. 212–220, 2011.

(EMD)[13], Largest Lyapunov exponent (LLE)[14-16] and linear discriminant analysis (LDA)[17-18] dimension reduction to give the feature vectors of the ASEMG signal of the forearm different movements from the normal subjects.

The rest of the article is organized as follows. In Section 2 we describe the DP mixture model, and the feature extraction strategy. The methods are illustrated with the forearm actions of two healthy subjects in Section 3. We conclude with additional comments and discussion in Section 4.

## 2     Methods

### 2.1     Dirichlet Process Mixture Model

Consider a set of the given data $x_i$, $i=1,\ldots, n$, where $x_i$ is a vector of $k$ dimension. The corresponding type variable $y_i=j$, $i=1,\ldots, n$, $j \in [1, J]$. $J$ is the number of data types. In other words, if $y_i$ is the $j$-th category, $y_i=j$. In general, the distribution of the data $x_i$ is unknown. If one assumes that it is a simple distribution, it will result in poor classification results. In this paper, we assume that the data $x$ come from a Dirichlet process. And a Dirichlet process mixture model is introduced as a classifier of the ASEMG signals. The model builds as follows[7]:

$$
\begin{aligned}
y_i, x_{i1}, x_{i2}, \cdots, x_{ik} | \theta_i \ &\sim \ F(\theta_i) \\
\theta_i | G \ &\sim \ G \\
G \ &\sim \ DP(G_0, \gamma) \\
G_0 \ &= \ \theta_0
\end{aligned} \tag{1}
$$

where $F(\theta_i)$ is defined as a multinomial logit (MNL) model, i.e. the following form:

$$
P(y_i = j | x_i, \alpha, \beta) = \frac{\exp(\alpha_j + x_i \beta_j)}{\sum_{j'=1}^{J} \exp(\alpha_{j'} + x_i \beta_{j'})} \tag{2}
$$

$$
x_{il} \sim N(\mu_l, o_l^2)
$$

This model estimates the joint distribution of $y$ and $x$ so that the class probabilities based on this model is generative. The joint distribution $P(y, x) = P(x)P(y|x)$. That is, it is equal to the product of the marginal distribution $P(x)$ and the conditional distribution $P(y|x)$. The parameters $\theta_i$, $\theta=(\mu, \sigma, \alpha, \beta)$, are assumed to be independent under the prior with distribution $G$. $G$ denotes a distribution with a Dirichlet process $DP(G_0, \gamma)$, where $G_0$ is a base distribution and $\gamma$ is a positive scaling parameter that controls the number of components in the mixture. The parameters of $G_0$ are defined as follows:

$$
\begin{aligned}
\mu_l \ &\sim \ N(0, \mu_{l0}^2) \\
\log(\sigma_l^2) \ &\sim \ N(0, \sigma_{l0}^2) \\
\alpha_j | \tau \ &\sim \ N(0, \tau^2) \\
\beta_{jl} | v \ &\sim \ N(0, v^2)
\end{aligned} \tag{3}
$$

Here, the parameters $\mu = (\mu_1, \mu_2, \ldots, \mu_k)$ and $\sigma = (\sigma_1, \sigma_2, \ldots, \sigma_k)$ are the means and standard deviations of covariates for the data $x$. That is, $\mu_l$ is the mean of the $l$-th dimension of the data $x$. $\sigma_l$ is the standard deviation of the $l$-th dimension of the data $x$. $x_{il}$ has the Gaussian distribution with $\mu_l$ and $\sigma_l$. The $j$ represents the $j$-th class for the data $x_i$, i.e. $j \in [1, J]$, where $J$ is the number of classes. $\alpha = (\alpha_1, \alpha_2, \ldots, \alpha_J)$ and $\beta_{k \times J} = (\beta_1, \beta_2, \ldots, \beta_J)^T$ are the parameters of the multinomial logit (MNL) model.

Since the observations are assumed to be exchangeable, according to the Polya urn scheme[3, 12], by integrating over $G$, the conditional distribution of $\theta_i$ becomes

$$\theta_i | \theta_{-i} \sim \frac{1}{n-1+\gamma} \sum_{j \neq i} \delta(\theta_j) + \frac{\gamma}{n-1+\gamma} G_0 \tag{4}$$

where $\delta(\theta_j)$ is the distribution concentrated at $\theta_j$. $n$ is the number of the observations. In order to estimate posterior predictive probabilities, the Markov chain Monte Carlo (MCMC) algorithms are used to simulate samples from the posterior distribution. Based on these probabilities, we can give the posterior predictive probability of class variable $y'$ for a new data $x'$ by the following forms:

$$P(y' = j | x') = \frac{P(y' = j, x')}{P(x')}$$

$$P(y' = j, x') = \frac{1}{S} \sum_{s=1}^{S} P(y' = j, x' | G_0, \theta^{(s)}) \tag{5}$$

$$P(x') = \frac{1}{S} \sum_{s=1}^{S} P(x' | G_0, \theta^{(s)})$$

where S is the iteration number of the MCMC algorithms, $\theta^{(s)}$ represents the set of parameters obtained at iteration s. The Gibbs sampling algorithm with auxiliary parameters proposed by Neal(2000) is applied to draw the samples from the posterior distribution of Dirichlet process mixtures. The details of this algorithm can be referred to the literature[12].

For all models, this paper runs 100 MCMC iterations to sample from the posterior distributions. The initial 20 samples are discarded and the rest are used for classification.

## 2.2     Feature Extraction

In order to obtain the feature values of the ASEMG signals during forearm movements, this paper first uses the empirical mode decomposition (EMD)[13] to decompose the given data into 8 levels time series. Then for each level time series, its Largest Lyapunov exponent (LLE) is estimated by using Kantz's algorithm [14-16]. Thus, we can give 32-dimension features of the Largest Lyapunov exponents for the four-channel ASEMG signals. Furthermore, in order to avoid too much computation, the linear discriminant analysis (LDA) method [17-18] is used to reduce the feature dimension and keep as much classification information as possible.

**Empirical Mode Decomposition (EMD)[13]**

The Empirical Mode Decomposition (EMD) is an adaptive time–frequency data analysis method with a posteriori-defined basis based on and derived from the data. The main idea of EMD is to decompose a time series into a number of different simple intrinsic oscillatory modes $h_1,...,h_N$ and a residue $r$. Each intrinsic oscillatory mode is defined as an intrinsic mode function (IMF) that is symmetric with respect to the local zero mean and have the same numbers of zero crossings and extremes. Thus, the intrinsic oscillatory modes can be identified by their characteristic time scales in the time series empirically [13].

First, all the local extrema are identified. Then, all the local maxima are connected by a cubic spline line as the upper envelope. All the local minima are connected by another cubic spline line forming the lower envelope of the time series. The upper and lower envelopes should cover all the time series between them. Their mean value is given as a running mean $m_1(t)$. And the first component $h_1(t)$ can be yielded by the difference between the data and $m_1(t)$,

$$h_1(t) = x(t) - m_1(t) \qquad (6)$$

The $h_1$ is an IMF if it satisfies the conditions: (i) $h_1(t)$ eliminate riding waves. (ii) It displays symmetry of the wave profiles with respect to zero. (iii) The number of extreme and the number of zero-crossings are the same, or only differ by one. Repeating the step of the decomposition, we can get a number of $h$ until the residual signal can not be spilt again.

**Largest Lyapunov Exponent (LLE)**

The Lyapunov exponents are a measure that characterizes the rate of convergence or divergence of the nearby trajectories in phase space $X$ with respect to time. Let $X_r$ is a reference point in this embedding space, $X_p$ is a very close point to $X_r$. The distance between $X_p$ and $X_r$ ($\Delta_0 = \| X_p - X_r \|$) is considered as a small perturbation. After $l$ time steps ahead, the distance will grow exponentially to $\Delta_l = \| X_{p+l} - X_{r+l} \| \approx \Delta_0 e^{\lambda l}$, then $\lambda$ is the largest Lyapunov exponent. In order to avoid fluctuations around the general exponential growth, the average value can be computed by a robust consistent and unbiased estimator as follows[14-16].

$$X(\Delta_l) = \left\langle \ln\left( \frac{1}{U_l} \sum_{X_p \in U_l} \left| X_{r+l} - X_{p+l} \right| \right) \right\rangle \qquad (7)$$

If $X(\Delta_l)$ has a linear growth trend, the largest Lyapunov exponent can be given by the slope within its linear range. Thus this exponent gives the average information of the divergence of the distance $\Delta_0$ in time $l$. Here, the formula (7) is implemented in the algorithm introduced by Kantz [14].

**Linear Discriminant Analysis (LDA)**

Linear discriminant analysis is a well-known method for feature extraction and dimension reduction[17-18]. The aim of LDA tries to find an optimal transformation by which the original data in high-dimensional space is transformed to a much lower dimensional space. That is, the maximum discrimination can be achieved by minimizing the within-class distance and maximizing the between-class distance simultaneously. The optimal transformation is readily computed by applying the eigen-decomposition to the scatter matrices.

In the basic formulation, LDA first computes the between-class covariance matrix $S_b$ and the within-class covariance matrix $S_w$. $S_b$ is the covariance matrix of class means and represents the separation of the class means. $S_w$ is equal to the sum of covariance matrices computed for each class separately so that $S_w^{-1}$ captures the compactness of each class. Then finds eigenvectors of matrix $T=S_w^{-1}S_b$. Here, $T$ captures both the compactness of each class and the separation of the class means. The rows of the transform matrix $W$ is formed by the eigenvectors corresponding to largest eigenvalues of $T$. Thus, the original ones $x$ is transformed simply into new discriminative features y, i. e. $y = Wx$.

LDA has been applied successfully in various fields, such as face recognition, text classification, micro-array data analysis. This paper uses LDA to reduce the 32-dimension features based on EMD and Lyapunov methods to 5-dimension features for the ASEMG signals.

# 3    Materials

The data to be analyzed are obtained from the ME6000 EMG system (Mega Electronics Ltd., Kuopio, Finland). The corresponding skin areas were cleaned with alcohol cotton balls to reduce skin impedance. The 100 sets of the ASEMG signals are collected at 1000 Hz from each of four different postures: finger flexion, finger tension, forearm supination and forearm pronation for two normal subjects. The ASEMG data were acquired from flexor carpi ulnaris, flexor digitorum supercifialis, extensor carpi radials and extensor carpi ulnaris of 4 channels. Our previous work has revealed the nonlinear mechanism underlying ASEMG[19]. The result showed that the ASEMG is not period or quasi-period but certain deterministic nonlinear signal because its LLE based on equation (7) is a positive value. Here, we use the LLE values in all scales based on EMD method as the characteristics of the ASEMG signals. The dimension of the LLE feature vector would be too high. The feature reduction technique has been applied in the sEMG classification [20]. In order to avoid muscle fatigue, all movements are sampled by four times in one day for each subject. For evaluation of the classification accuracy, the 50 sets of data were randomly selected from 100 sets of data as a training set, the rest for the test set. And this paper applies the randomly selected data 10 times for each subject.

## 4    Analysis and Results

For the ASEMG data recorded in our experiments, we first apply the EMD method in Section 2 to decompose each channel data into 8-level time series. The LLE value of each level time series is estimated by using the algorithm of Kantz. Thus, we can form a 32-dimension LLE vector for every ASEMG signal. Next, the LDA method is used to reduce the 32-dimension vector into a 5-dimension vector. Figure 1 shows the 32-dimension LLE vectors of 50 sets of the ASEMG signals for four movements of subject 1. The features of four movements have more overlap so that it is difficult to give a good recognition rate of these movements. The characteristics of the corresponding dimension reduction are given in Figure 2. By comparing Figure 1 and Figure 2, we can see that the reduced dimensional data have more significant differences between every movement.

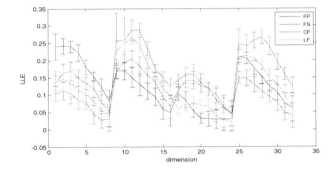

**Fig. 1.** The 32-dimension LLE vectors of four movements for subject 1

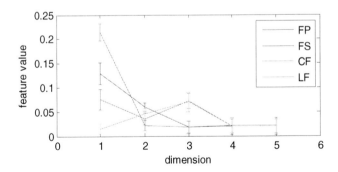

**Fig. 2.** The 5-dimension feature vectors of LDA reducing dimension of the 50 set ASEMG signals for four movements of subject 1

Then, the DPM classification method introduced by this paper is applied to give the classes of the ASEMG signals based on the 5-dimension vector. This method is based on data-driven. That is, $\theta_0$ is given by using the raw data. Therefore, unlike the method of Shahbaba et al.[7], our approach can avoid that it can sometimes cluster to only one class. This paper chooses 100 MCMC iterations to sample from the posterior distributions without the initial 20 samples. For each subject, the classification accuracy rates are given based on 10 times the test data that were randomly selected from 100 sets of data in Table 1 and Table 2. It can be found that the recognition rate of each randomly selected data is not the same. The results show that the 10-time selections can be equivalent to do 10 experiments for each people. The average rates are over 90%.

**Table 1.** The classification accuracy rates of the 50 randomly selected test data of four movements for subject 1 by 10-time selections by using DPM

| Selected times | FP | FS | CF | LF | Average rate |
|---|---|---|---|---|---|
| 1 | 0.92 | 0.98 | 0.90 | 0.84 | 0.91 |
| 2 | 0.96 | 0.96 | 0.74 | 0.98 | 0.91 |
| 3 | 0.92 | 0.98 | 0.86 | 1.00 | 0.94 |
| 4 | 0.98 | 0.96 | 0.70 | 1.00 | 0.91 |
| 5 | 0.72 | 0.96 | 0.80 | 0.98 | 0.865 |
| 6 | 0.90 | 1.00 | 0.76 | 0.98 | 0.91 |
| 7 | 0.78 | 0.96 | 0.82 | 1.00 | 0.89 |
| 8 | 0.90 | 0.94 | 0.90 | 0.94 | 0.92 |
| 9 | 0.82 | 0.88 | 0.88 | 0.88 | 0.865 |
| 10 | 0.86 | 1.00 | 0.88 | 1.00 | 0.935 |
| mean±std | 0.876±0.0815 | 0.962±0.0346 | 0.824±0.0717 | 0.96±0.0566 | 0.9055±0.0255 |

**Table 2.** The classification accuracy rates of the 50 randomly selected test data of four movements for subject 2 by 10-time selections by using DPM

| Selected times | FP | FS | CF | LF | Average rate |
|---|---|---|---|---|---|
| 1 | 0.92 | 0.88 | 0.92 | 0.98 | 0.925 |
| 2 | 0.88 | 0.88 | 0.88 | 0.90 | 0.885 |
| 3 | 0.86 | 0.84 | 0.92 | 0.96 | 0.895 |
| 4 | 0.84 | 0.92 | 0.94 | 0.90 | 0.90 |
| 5 | 0.86 | 0.86 | 0.94 | 0.94 | 0.90 |
| 6 | 0.88 | 0.82 | 0.92 | 0.94 | 0.89 |
| 7 | 0.84 | 0.90 | 0.92 | 0.96 | 0.905 |
| 8 | 0.94 | 0.82 | 0.94 | 0.84 | 0.885 |
| 9 | 0.96 | 0.98 | 0.92 | 0.84 | 0.925 |
| 10 | 0.90 | 0.86 | 0.92 | 0.98 | 0.915 |
| mean±std | 0.888±0.0413 | 0.876±0.0488 | 0.922±0.0175 | 0.924±0.0523 | 0.9025±0.015 |

Meanwhile, in order to compare the performance of DPM, this paper also uses three other classifiers, such as Fuzzy classification, Bayes classification and BP neural network. The average recognition results of four movements can be seen in Table 3 and Table 4 for the 10-time selected data the two subjects. The results show that the rates of the DPM method are higher than those of the other three methods. The DPM method can be applied as a classifier for the ASEMG signal classification.

**Table 3.** The classification accuracy rates of the four classifiers for subject 1

| Selected times | Fuzzy | Bayes | BP | DPM |
|---|---|---|---|---|
| 1 | 0.81 | 0.915 | 0.875 | 0.91 |
| 2 | 0.775 | 0.81 | 0.895 | 0.91 |
| 3 | 0.745 | 0.635 | 0.855 | 0.94 |
| 4 | 0.895 | 0.94 | 0.95 | 0.91 |
| 5 | 0.885 | 0.685 | 0.91 | 0.865 |
| 6 | 0.905 | 0.945 | 0.905 | 0.91 |
| 7 | 0.76 | 0.93 | 0.89 | 0.89 |
| 8 | 0.79 | 0.25 | 0.905 | 0.92 |
| 9 | 0.91 | 0.94 | 0.89 | 0.865 |
| 10 | 0.875 | 0.25 | 0.90 | 0.935 |
| mean±std | 0.835±0.0651 | 0.73±0.2763 | 0.8975±0.0246 | 0.9055±0.0255 |

**Table 4.** The classification accuracy rates of the four classifiers for subject 2

| Selected times | Fuzzy | Bayes | BP | DPM |
|---|---|---|---|---|
| 1 | 0.89 | 0.905 | 0.89 | 0.925 |
| 2 | 0.895 | 0.72 | 0.885 | 0.885 |
| 3 | 0.905 | 0.92 | 0.88 | 0.895 |
| 4 | 0.855 | 0.90 | 0.89 | 0.90 |
| 5 | 0.85 | 0.88 | 0.86 | 0.90 |
| 6 | 0.875 | 0.92 | 0.85 | 0.89 |
| 7 | 0.87 | 0.92 | 0.87 | 0.905 |
| 8 | 0.855 | 0.915 | 0.87 | 0.885 |
| 9 | 0.88 | 0.92 | 0.875 | 0.925 |
| 10 | 0.90 | 0.925 | 0.84 | 0.915 |
| mean±std | 0.8775±0.0199 | 0.895±0.0621 | 0.8710±0.0168 | 0.9025±0.015 |

# 5    Conclusions

A new classification method based on Dirichlet process mixtures(DPM) is introduced to identify the four movements of the action surface EMG(ASEMG) signals from the forearm of the normal subjects. This classification model is built by using the multinomial logit model (MNL) as a classifier. Then this classifier is given by using the information of training data. The 5-dimension features of ASEMG are given by using a combined method of the empirical mode decomposition(EMD), Largest Lyapunov exponent and Linear discriminant analysis (LDA) dimension reduction. The average classification rates are over 90%. The results indicate that the DPM classification method introduced by this paper could be applied the classification of the ASEMG signals.

**Acknowledgments.** This work is supported by the National Natural Science Foundation of China (No. 10872125), Science Fund for Creative Research Groups of the National Natural Science Foundation of China(No. 50821003), State Key Lab of Mechanical System and Vibration□Project supported by the Research Fund of State Key Lab of MSV, China (Grant No. MSV-MS-2010-08) and Science and Technology Commission of Shanghai Municipality (No.06ZR14042).

# References

1. Antoniak, C.E.: Mixture of Dirichlet process with applications to Bayesian nonparametric problems. Annals of Statistics 273(5281), 1152–1174 (1974)
2. Ferguson, T.S.: A Bayesian analysis of some nonparamteric problems. Annas of Statistics 1, 209–230 (1973)
3. Blackwell, D., MacQueen, J.B.: Ferguson distributions via Polya urn scheme. Annals of Statistics 1, 353–355 (1973)
4. Escobar, M.D., West, M.: Bayesian density estimation and inference using mixtures. J. Amer. Stat. Assoc. 90, 577 (1995)
5. MacEachern, S.N., Müller, P.: Estimating mixture of Dirichlet process models. J. Comput. Graph. Stat. 7, 223–238 (1998)
6. Shahbaba, B., Gentles, A.J., Beyene, J., Plevritis, S.K., Greenwood, C.M.T.: A Bayesian nonparametric method for model evaluation application to genetic studies. J. Nonparam. Stat. 21(3), 379–396 (2009)
7. Shahbaba, B., Neal, R.M.: Nonlinear models using Dirichlet process mixtures. J. Mach. Learn. Res. 10, 1829–1850 (2009)
8. Jara, A., García-Zattera, M.J., Lesaffre, E.: A dirichlet process mixture model for the analysis of correlated binary responses. Computational Statistics & Data Analysis 51, 5402–5415 (2007)
9. Jackson, E., Davy, M., Doucet, A., Fitzgerald, W.J.: Bayesian unsupervised signal classification by dirichlet process mixtures of Gaussian processes. In: The 2007 IEEE International Conference on Acoustics, Speech and Signal Processing, pp. III-1077 - III-1080 (2007)
10. Xue, Y., Liao, X.J., Carin, L., Krishnapuram, B.: Multi-Task learning of classification with dirichlet process priors. Journal of Machine Learning Research 8, 35–63 (2007)
11. Silva, A.: A dirichlet process mixture model for brain MRI tissue classification. Medical Image Analysis 11, 169–182 (2007)
12. Neal, R.M.: Markov chain sampling methods for Dirichlet process mixture models. Journal of Computational and Graphical Statistics 9, 249–265 (2000)
13. Huang, N.E., Shen, Z., Long, S.R., et al.: The empirical mode decomposition method and the Hilbert spectrum for non-stationary time series analysis. Proc. Roy. Soc. London 454A, 903–995 (1998)
14. Kantz, H.: A robust method to estimate the maximal Lyapunov exponent of a time series. Phys. Lett. A 185, 77–87 (1994)
15. Hegger, R., Kantz, H., Schreiber, T.: Practical implementation of nonlinear time series methods: The TISEAN package. CHAOS 9, 413–440 (1999)
16. Hegger, R., Kantz, H., Schreiber, T.: Nonlinear Time Series Analysis, http://www.mpipks-dresden.mpg.de/~tisean/TISEAN_2.1/index.html
17. Belhumeur, P., Hespanha, J., Kriegman, D.: Eigenfaces vs. fisherfaces: recognition using class specific linear projection. IEEE Transaction on Pattern Recogntion and Machine Intelligence 19(7), 711–720 (1997)
18. Franc, V., Hlavac, V.: Statistical Pattern Recognition Toolbox (STPRtool), http://cmp.felk.cvut.cz/cmp/software/stprtool/
19. Lei, M., Wang, Z.Z., Feng, Z.J.: Detecting nonlinearity of action surface EMG signal. Physics Letters A 290, 297–303 (2001)
20. Chen, X.P., Zhu, X.Y., Zhang, D.G.: Use of the discriminant Fourier-derived cepstrum with feature-level post-processing for surface electromyographic signal classification. Physiol. Meas. 30, 1399–1413 (2009)

# Displacement Estimation for Foot Rotation Axis Using a Stewart-Platform-Type Assist Device

Ming Ding[1], Tomohiro Iida[2], Hiroshi Takemura[2], and Hiroshi Mizoguchi[2]

[1] RIKEN-TRI collaboration Center for Human-Interactive Robot Research,
RIKEN (The Institute of Physical and Chemical Research)
2271-130, Anagahora, Shimoshidami, Moriyama-ku, Nagoya, Aichi 463-0003, Japan
mingding@nagoya.riken.jp
http://rtc.nagoya.riken.jp/
[2] Department of Mechanical Engineering, Faculty of Science and Technology,
Tokyo University of Science.
2641 Yamazaki, Noda, Chiba, 278-8510, Japan
{takemura,hm}@rs.noda.tus.ac.jp
http://www.rs.noda.tus.ac.jp/brlab

**Abstract.** In this research, we developed a novel ankle-foot assist device for stroke rehabilitation and walking assistant purpose. A Stewart platform mechanism is used, which can adapt to the displacement of the rotation axis of human foot. With using six potentiometer assembled cylinders, the posture of human foot can be controlled/measured in all 6-DOF direction by controlling/measuring the lengths of all cylinders. A calculating method is also proposed, to estimate the instantaneous rotation axis of ankle-foot motion. It can make foot motion assistant more accurate and comfortable. In this paper, we describe the structure and the control/estimation method of this assist device. Some initial results of experiments will show the validity of this device and the rotation axis estimation method.

**Keywords:** Ankle-foot device, Stroke rehabilitation, Parallel link mechanism, Instantaneous rotation axis.

## 1 Introduction

Stroke is one of the most frequent causes of death in the world. One in six people worldwide will have a stroke in their lifetime. Stroke attacks about 15 million people and about 6 million people die of stroke each year [1]. Stroke rehabilitation is a main therapeutic approach, which can maximize motor performance and minimize functional deficits of patient. With the rehabilitation and physiotherapy, brain and nerve of patient can be treated by self-reorganization or plasticity. In hospital, rehabilitation and physiotherapy are always done with the assistant of one or more physiotherapists through repeating the exercises many times. However, in order to reduce the workload of doctors and therapists and improve the quality of life, robotics technology has been used widely and widely in recent years.

S. Jeschke, H. Liu, and D. Schilberg (Eds.): ICIRA 2011, Part I, LNAI 7101, pp. 221–229, 2011.

With the development of robotics technology, many kinds of orthosis and assist device have be developed for rehabilitation and power-assist by controlling position and motion of human joints [2,3,4,5]. Other applications are for load reduction in factory and motion support for people with disability. Ankle-foot assist device is a device which is to correct or address the motion between ankle and foot. In the design of ankle-foot assist device, one most important thing is to find a way to control the movement of ankle joint naturally and correctly. However, it is still difficult since our human has a very complex ankle joint structure.

For the past several decades, many researches have been carried out to analyze the change of the rotation axis of ankle joint. Many kinds of optical and mechanical devices were used in these researchs [6,7]. Ankle joint is responsible for 3-DOF rotation motion of the foot, up-and-down, side-to-side and medial-to-lateral. Even for dorsiflexion and plantarflexion, there are two different axes to respond them with approximately 20 to 30 [deg] between them. The rotation axis of foot always changes during the movement. Including the joints of foot, a large number of rotation axes are exist in ankle and foot. Individual measurement of all these axes is very difficult [8]. However, most of orthosis and assist devices still fixed the rotation axis of ankle joint for using motors or bearings.

In order to realize more effective and comfortable assistant in foot motion, device must be able to change its rotation axis during the movement. And the rotation axis also have to be estimated by the device for adapting the individual differences. By knowing the rotation axis, the movement and force (moment) of ankle joint can be controlled more correctly.

In this research, taking into account the displacement of rotation axis, a novel ankle-foot assist device is developed, which has a Stewart Platform mechanism. Six potentiometer assembled cylinders are used to control and measure the posture of foot in all 6-DOF direction by changing the air pressure. In this paper, the structure of this first prototype and the control/measurement methods are described. Using measured lengths of all cylinders, this device can also estimate the instantaneous rotation axis of ankle joint, which may be used for more validity motion control in stroke rehabilitation. Some experiments also have been carried out to estimate the posture and the rotation axis of subjects' foot. The results show the validity of the rotation axis estimation method of this device.

## 2   Stewart-Platform-Type Ankle-Foot Assist Device

Figure 1(a) shows the developed Stewart-platform-type ankle-foot assist device. Six potentiometer assembled cylinders (Fig. 1(b)) are mounted between two plates fixed on leg and foot (Leg Plate and Foot Plate) by ball-joints. Two cylinders ($C_3, C_4$) are mounted behind the heel, and other four cylinders ($C_1, C_2, C_5, C_6$) are mounted on both two side of foot. For easy to ware and fix it on the foot, we assembled a shoe on the foot plate. The motion of ankle joint can be controlled and measured by controlling and measuring the lengths of cylinders.

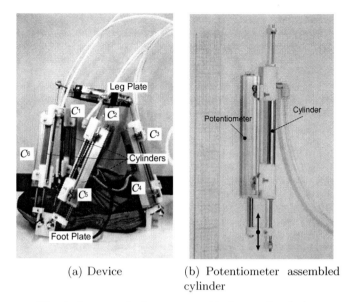

(a) Device

(b) Potentiometer assembled cylinder

**Fig. 1.** Stewart-platform-type ankle-foot assist device

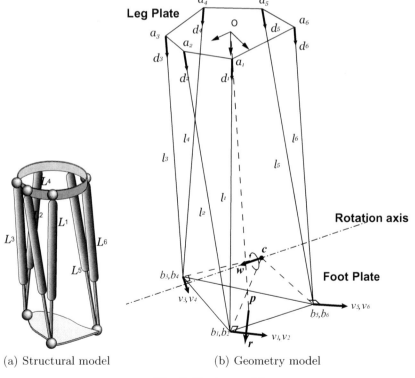

(a) Structural model

(b) Geometry model

**Fig. 2.** Device model

Figure 2 shows the model of our assist device. $o$ is the center of Leg Plate, which is the original point of the system, $o = [0, 0, 0]^T$. $AB$ are the mounted position of cylinders in Leg Plate and Foot Plate, $A = [a_1, \cdots, a_6] \in R^{3 \times 6}$ and $B = [b_1, \cdots, b_6] \in R^{3 \times 6}$. The center of Foot Plate is $p \in R^{3 \times 1}$ and the rotation of Foot Plate is $r \in R^{3 \times 1}$. The posture of Foot Plate $P$ (position $p$ and rotation $r$) is defined as a generalized position, $P = [p^T, r^T]^T \in R^{6 \times 1}$.

Potentiometers are set by the cylinders to measure the displacements $\Delta l = [\Delta l_1, \cdots, \Delta l_6]^T$ as shown in Fig. 1(b). The length of all cylinders $l = [l_1, \cdots, l_6]^T$ between mounted positions $A$ and $B$ are calculated as follows:

$$l = l_0 + \Delta l, \tag{1}$$

where $l_0 = [l_{10}, \cdots, l_{60}]^T$ is the pre-measured initial length of cylinders.

### 2.1   Control the Posture (Inverse Kinematics)

It is an inverse kinematics problem to calculate and control the lengths of cylinders.

From a desired foot posture $P$, the mounted position $B$ is calculated as follows:

$$B = H_{(P)} B^0, \tag{2}$$

where $B^0$ ($\in R^{3 \times 6}$) is the initial local position, while $P = 0$. $H_{(P)}$ is the homogeneous transform matrix.

$$H_{(P)} = R_{(r)} T_p = R_{(r1)} R_{(r2)} R_{(r3)} T_p. \tag{3}$$

where $R_{r_i}$ is the rotation matrix and $T_p$ is the transform matrix. The length of cylinders $l = [l_1, \cdots, l_6]^T$ is the distance from $A$ to $B$.

$$l_i = \|b_i - a_i\|, \quad (i = 1, \cdots, 6) \tag{4}$$

Control all cylinders to the length $l$, we can control the Foot Plate and human foot to the desired posture $P$.

### 2.2   Measure the Posture (Forward Kinematics)

From measured length of cylinders $l$, the posture of Foot Plate $P$ can also be estimated. In robotics, it is a forward kinematic problem. However, it is a difficult problem to solve this forward kinematic problem due to the structure between cylinders in the Stewart platform mechanism. In order to solve this problem, several method had been proposed[9,10]. In this research, we used a searching algorithm by calculating and renewing the Jacobian matrix.

Foot Plate is moved by all six cylinders. There is a linear relation between the velocity of Foot Plate $\dot{P}$ and the velocity of cylinders $\dot{l}$.

$$\dot{P} = J\dot{l} \tag{5}$$

where $J$ is the Jacobian matrix, which is calculated as follows[11]:

$$J = \begin{bmatrix} (\boldsymbol{b}_1 \times \boldsymbol{d}_1)^T, & \boldsymbol{d}_1^T \\ (\boldsymbol{b}_2 \times \boldsymbol{d}_2)^T, & \boldsymbol{d}_2^T \\ \vdots & \vdots \\ (\boldsymbol{b}_6 \times \boldsymbol{d}_6)^T, & \boldsymbol{d}_6^T \end{bmatrix}^{-1} \tag{6}$$

$\boldsymbol{d}_i \in \boldsymbol{R}^{3 \times 1}$ is the direction of each cylinder, which is calculated as:

$$\boldsymbol{d}_i = \frac{\boldsymbol{b}_i - \boldsymbol{a}_i}{\|\boldsymbol{b}_i - \boldsymbol{a}_i\|}. \tag{7}$$

$\boldsymbol{a}_i$ is pre-measured mounted position in Leg Plate and $\boldsymbol{b}_i$ is calculated in (2).

Between two measurement, if the time $\Delta t$ is small enough, it can be approximated as:

$$\dot{\boldsymbol{P}} \approx \Delta \boldsymbol{P}, \dot{\boldsymbol{l}} \approx \Delta \boldsymbol{l} \quad \Rightarrow \quad \Delta \boldsymbol{P} \approx \boldsymbol{J} \Delta \boldsymbol{l}. \tag{8}$$

Using this equation, next search posture $\boldsymbol{P}_{n+1}$ can be renewed from present search posture $\boldsymbol{P}_n$ using (8) as follows:

$$\boldsymbol{P}_{n+1} = \boldsymbol{P}_n + \boldsymbol{J}_n(\boldsymbol{l} - \boldsymbol{l}_n), \tag{9}$$

where $\boldsymbol{J}_n$ and $\boldsymbol{l}_n$ are present Jacobian matrix and present length of cylinders, which are calculated from $\boldsymbol{P}_n$ in (6) and (4). $\boldsymbol{l}$ is the measured correct length of cylinders (target value).

From a initial posture of Foot Plate $\boldsymbol{P}_0$ (e.g. $\boldsymbol{P}_0 = [0, \cdots, 0]^T$), if $\boldsymbol{l}_n$ is close to $\boldsymbol{l}$ almost completely, search will be stopped and $\boldsymbol{P}_n$ will be used as the correct posture of Foot Plate, $\boldsymbol{P}_n \Rightarrow \boldsymbol{P}$.

## 3   Rotation Axis Estimation of Ankle Joint

### 3.1   Ankle Joint

Ankle joint has a very complex structure, which is responsible for up-and-down, side-to-side and medial-to-lateral motion of foot as shown Fig. 3(a). Ankle joint what we generally called is not a singular joint, which actually includes two different joints, the true ankle joint and the subtalar joint, as shown Fig. 3(b). True ankle joint is made up of three bones: tibia, fibula and talus. It makes up-and-down motion of foot. Under the true ankle joint, there is an other joint which is called as subtalar joint. It is responsible for the side-to-side motion of foot. Motion of ankle joint is the motion of both these two joints. And including the joints in foot, there are about eight axes in ankle and foot [8]. Only from the posture of foot, it is difficult to be analyzed to know the status of all axes. All these axes also displaced during the movement due to the irregular shape and contact face of bones. Several special devices have be developed for getting the location of these axes [6,7].

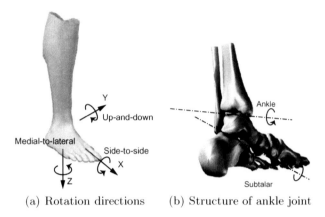

(a) Rotation directions     (b) Structure of ankle joint

**Fig. 3.** Rotation and joints of ankle

## 3.2 Rotation Axis Estimation

If we consider the foot as one rigid, there is only one instantaneous rotation axis in each moment. Using our ankle-foot device, a following method is proposed to estimate the instantaneous axis. Rotation axis of Foot Plate is a directed line segment. The direction and position of it are estimated separately.

### Direction of Rotation Axis

At time $t$ and $t+1$, the foot posture $P_t, P_{t+1}$ can be calculated by solving the forward kinematics problem that described in previous chapter and the mounted position $B_t, B_{t+1}$ can be calculated in (2). Comparing $B_t$ and $B_{t+1}$, the velocities of all mounted points $V_t = [v_{t1}, \cdots, v_{t6}]$ can be estimated approximately as follows:

$$V_t \approx (B_{t+1} - B_t)/\Delta t, \tag{10}$$

where $\Delta t$ is the time between two measurement.

The singular value decomposition of $V$ is:

$$[U \ \Sigma \ W^*] = \mathtt{svd}(V_t) \tag{11}$$

where $U$ and $W$ are the left and right singular matrix of $V$, $U \in R^{3\times3}$, $W \in R^{6\times6}$. $\Sigma = \mathtt{sig}(\lambda_1, \lambda_2, \lambda_3) \in R^{3\times6}$ is the diagonal matrix with the singular values on the diagonal. Foot plate is considered as a rigid body, which make all velocities $V$ are arranging in one plane, $\lambda_3 \approx 0$. The direction of rotation axis $\omega$ can be calculated by calculating the normal vectors as follows:

$$\omega = (\lambda_1 u_1) \times (\lambda_1 u_2) \tag{12}$$

where $u_1, u_2$ are the first and second singular vector in $U$.

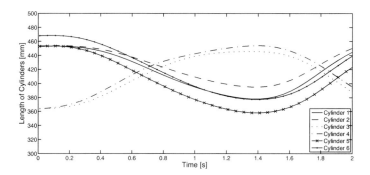

**Fig. 4.** Measured lengths of cylinders

## Position of Rotation Axis

Let $c$ be a point on the rotation axis. All line from $c$ to the mounted points $B$ are perpendicular to the velocities $V$.

$$
\begin{cases}
\boldsymbol{\omega} \times (\boldsymbol{b}_1 - \boldsymbol{c}) = \boldsymbol{v}_1 \\
\quad\vdots \qquad\qquad \vdots \\
\boldsymbol{\omega} \times (\boldsymbol{b}_6 - \boldsymbol{c}) = \boldsymbol{v}_6
\end{cases}
\tag{13}
$$

Solving this equation by $c$ can get one point in rotation axis as follows:

$$
\boldsymbol{c} =
\begin{bmatrix}
\boldsymbol{\omega} \times \\
\vdots \\
\boldsymbol{\omega} \times
\end{bmatrix}^{+}
\begin{bmatrix}
\boldsymbol{v}_1 - \boldsymbol{\omega} \times \boldsymbol{b}_1 \\
\vdots \\
\boldsymbol{v}_6 - \boldsymbol{\omega} \times \boldsymbol{b}_6
\end{bmatrix}
\tag{14}
$$

where $[\ ]^{+}$ is the pseudo-inverse matrix; $\boldsymbol{w} \times \in \boldsymbol{R}^{3 \times 3}$ is the wedge product of $\boldsymbol{w}$. Instantaneous rotation axis $f_t$ in time $t$ is defined with $\boldsymbol{c}$ and $\boldsymbol{\omega}$ as:

$$
f_t = \boldsymbol{c} + k\boldsymbol{\omega}, k \in \boldsymbol{R}^{1 \times 1}.
\tag{15}
$$

## 4    Experiment and Result

Some experiments were carried out to verify the practical effectiveness of the ankle-foot assist device and the control and measurement method. The length of cylinders is measured and calculated when subjects move their foot. Using the measured data, the posture of subjects' foot and the instantaneous rotation axis are estimated for each measure point.

As an example, figure 4 shows estimated length of cylinders in two seconds of one trail, while a subject rotated his foot up and down. When the foot moves down, the cylinders $(C_3, C_4)$ were shortened and other cylinders $(C_1, C_2, C_5, C_6)$ were extended. The displacement of each cylinder is about 100 [mm].

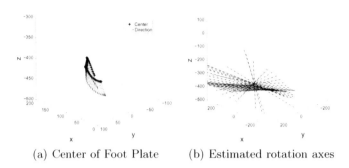

(a) Center of Foot Plate        (b) Estimated rotation axes

**Fig. 5.** Change of rotation axis

Figure 5(a) shows the estimated posture of Foot Plate. When subject rotated his foot up and down, the displacement of Foot Plate was about 72.9 [mm] and the rotation of foot was about 50.3 [deg]. Figure 5 shows the change of instantaneous axis in the movement. The position of rotation axis displacement was moved about 17.6 [mm], and the direction of it was changed about 13.4 [deg]. Even subject only wanted to move his foot up and down, the rotation axis of human foot still had a very large change. These changes have to be take into consideration in control and support of human foot motion.

## 5    Conclusions

In order to control and measure the ankle-foot motion, we developed a novel ankle-foot assist device. It may be used for rehabilitation and walking assistant. In consideration of the displacement of the rotation axis of foot, a Stewart platform mechanism is used. Six potentiometer assembled cylinders are mounted between Leg and Foot Plates. A control/estimation method was also proposed by using this device. The foot posture of foot in all 6-DOF direction is controlled and measured in inverse and forward kinematics. Based on the measured foot posture, instantaneous rotation axis of ankle-foot joint was also estimated, which can made the motion control more accurate. From the result of experiments, the change of rotation axis was estimated, which shown the validity of this device and the proposed method. In the future, we need to develop a method to create personal model of ankle-foot joint from the estimated data and using the model data to control the human motion more accurate and comfortable to test the effectiveness in rehabilitation and walking assistant.

**Acknowledgments.** A part of this work was supported by Grant-in-Aid for Young Scientists (B) (23700782) of Japan Society for the Promotion of Science(JSPS).

# References

1. World Stroke Organization, http://www.world-stroke.org
2. Farris, R., Quintero, H., Withrow, T., Goldfarb, M.: Design and simulation of a joint-coupled orthosis for regulating fes-aided gait. In: 2009 IEEE International Conference on Robotics and Automation (ICRA 2009), Kobe International Conference Center, Kobe, Japan, May 12-17, pp. 1916–1922 (2009)
3. Krebs, H.I., Celestino, J., Williams, D., Ferraro, M., Volpe, B., Hogan, N.: A wrist extension for mit-manus. In: Advances in Rehabilitation Robotics, pp. 377–390 (2004)
4. Lee, S., Sankai, Y.: Power assist control for walking aid with hal-3 based on emg and impedance adjustment around knee joint. In: IEEE/RSJ International Conference Intelligent Robots and Systems, pp. 1499–1504 (2002)
5. Roy, A., Krebs, H.I., Patterson, S.L., Judkins, T.N., Khanna, I., Forrester, L.W., Macko, R.M., Hogan, N.: Measurement of human ankle stiffness using the anklebot. In: The 2007 IEEE 10th International Conference on Rehabilitation Robotics, June 12-15, pp. 358–363 (2007)
6. Wright, D.G., Desai, S.M., Henderson, W.H.: Action of the subtalar and ankle-joint complex during the stance phase of walking. Journal of Bone and Joint Surgery 46, 361–382 (1964)
7. Lundberg, A., Svensson, O.K., Nemeth, G., Selvik, G.: The axis of rotation of the ankle joint. The Journal of Bone and Joint Surgery 71(B), 94–99 (1989)
8. Hicks, J.H.: The mechanics of the foot: I. the joints. Journal of Anatomy 87, 345–357 (1953)
9. Ku, D.M.: Forward kinematic analysis of a 6–3 type stewart platform mechanism. Process of the institution of Mechanical Engineers 214, 233–241 (2000)
10. Alrashidi, M., Yldz, İ., Alrashdan, K., Esat, İ.: Evaluating elbow joint kinematics with the stewart platform mechanism. WIT Transactions on Biomedicine and Health 13, 181–189 (2009)
11. Advani, S.: The Kinematic Design of Flight Simulator Motion-Bases. Doctoral dissertation, Faculty of Aerospace Engineering, Delft University of Technology (1998)

# Inverse Kinematics Solution of a Class of Hybrid Manipulators

Shahram Payandeh and Zhouming Tang

Experimental Robotics Laboratory
Simon Fraser University
8888 University Drive, Burnaby
British Columbia, Canada, V5A 1S6

**Abstract.** Hybrid manipulators are defined as a kinematic configuration which combines two classes of kinematic chains, namely parallel and serial which can offer a design with six degrees of freedom. These configurations offer mechanical advantages where it is possible to locate most of the actuation and transmission systems away from the floating and distal parts of the manipulator. In this paper we present the kinematic modeling and solution of spherical-parallel and serial manipulator. We present both forward and inverse kinematic solutions and demonstrate the solution methodology through a numerical example.

**Keywords:** hybrid manipulator, spherical-parallel configuration, kinematic modeling, inverse kinematics solution.

## 1 Introduction

Hybrid manipulators take advantage of the best features of parallel and serial robot configurations. Parallel robots can offer structural rigidity while reducing the total floating mass of the manipulator where attachment of the serial robot can offer larger workspace. Hybrid robots have great advantages in the applications requiring high accuracy and dexterous workspace, such as in medical surgery [1] , [2] and components manufacturing [3]. In this paper we propose kinematic modeling and inverse solutions for a configuration of the hybrid manipulator defined in [4], [5] and [6]. This configuration combines a 3DOF spherical-parallel manipulator located at the fixed-base to its mobile platform where a 3DOF serial robot configuration is attached.

Tanio [7] presented a hybrid (parallel-serial) manipulator which is composed of two serially connected parallel mechanisms where each mechanism has 3DOF. Four closed-form solutions for both forward and inverse kinematics of this manipulator are presented. Geometrical properties are utilized to obtain forward kinematic solutions, while algebraic approach is implemented to obtain inverse kinematic solutions. A hybrid manipulator proposed by Romdhane [8] is composed of serial connection of parallel platforms. Eight closed-form solutions are obtained through the forward kinematic analysis. [9] proposed quaternion base

S. Jeschke, H. Liu, and D. Schilberg (Eds.): ICIRA 2011, Part I, LNAI 7101, pp. 230–239, 2011.

forward kinematic solutions of two sequentially connected 3-UPU parallel mechanisms. The first 3-UPU mechanism constitutes with middle platform and fixed base, while the second rotational 3-UPU mechanism is compose of middle platform and end platform. By applying unit quaternion transformation, 8 closed-form solutions are obtained. [3] introduces the design and analysis of a new modular hybrid parallel-serial manipulator. The proposed hybrid configuration consists of a 3-DOF planar parallel platform and a 3-DOF serial robotic arm. The forward kinematic analysis of the planar parallel mechanism is carried out by utilizing the geometric properties while the product-of-exponentials formulation approach is adopted to perform the forward kinematic analysis of the serial mechanism which resulted in four real solutions. Based on their proposed modeling approach, the inverse kinematic analysis is accomplished based on algebraic method. Ceccarelli [2] presented a hybrid manipulator which consists of a spatial parallel manipulator with 3-DOF and a telescopic serial manipulator with 2-DOF. Three Euler parameters are introduced to perform the kinematic analysis of the spatial parallel manipulator, while an angle between the telescopic arm and the mobile platform and a distance variable at the prismatic joint are introduced to characterize the kinematic model of the telescopic serial manipulator. In this paper, we propose an approach for modeling and inverse kinematic solution for a class of hybrid manipulator. Section 2 presents an overview of the the main kinematic structure of the hybrid manipulator and its kinematic modeling framework. Section 3 presents the inverse kinematic solution followed by section 4 which presents a numerical example.

## 2    Overview of Kinematic Configuration and Modeling

Figures 1.a and 1.b show the basic configuration of the proposed class of hybrid manipulator. The supporting spherical-parallel mechanism is composed by three identical kinematic branches each of which has three revolute joints. $J_{11} - J_{13}$ represent of the base joint, passive joint and platform joint of the first kinematic chain respectively where all the branches are connected to the mobile platform. The center of the mobile platform moves along the geodesic paths on a sphere having a fixed redial distance about point O. A link $l_1$ is connected to the moving platform which is also the base of the serial manipulator. Link $l_2$ is the exterior link of the serial robot connected to the wrist mechanism. The two intersecting joint axes at the distal end of $l_2$ is defined as the wrist of the manipulator.

The kinematic modeling of the supporting spherical 3-DOF parallel manipulators has been extensively studied in the literature, e.g. see [10]. The axis of the first revolute joint as $U_i$ ($i = 1, 2, 3$) and the third revolute joint connected to the moving platform as $V_i$. Let us define the second joint axis of each branch as $W_i$ (Figure 2). The second joint axis and Here we present an overview of the basic kinematic modeling and solution needed for the whole hybrid structure. In this configuration, we define the following basic geometrical relationship $U_i \cdot W_i = \cos(\alpha_1)$ and $W_i \cdot V_i = \cos(\alpha_2)$ where we have selected $\alpha_1 = \alpha_2 = 90°$. This definition also results in the following kinematic constraint:

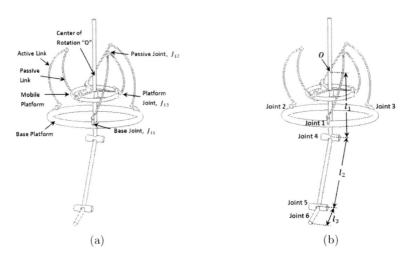

(a)                                          (b)

**Fig. 1.** The kinematic configuration of the manipulator: (a): Kinematic model of the hybrid parallel/serial manipulator; (b): Joint and link configuration of hybrid parallel/serial manipulator

$W_i \cdot V_i = 0$; $U_i \cdot W_i = 0$. As a result we also have: $U_1 \perp U_2 \perp U_3$ and $V_1 \perp V_2 \perp V_3$ which corresponds to $\gamma_1 = \gamma_2 = 90°$. We also define $\beta_1$ as the angle between $U_i$ and the normal axis of the base plane, and $\beta_2$ is defined as the angle between $V_i$ and the normal axis of the mobile platform plane. We also have the following relationship between the angles $\beta_i$ and $\gamma_i$ as [11]: $\sin(\beta_i) = \frac{2\sqrt{3}}{3}\sin(\frac{\gamma_i}{2})$ which results in $\beta_1 = \beta_2 = 55°$.

In the kinematic model, a based frame $\{B\}$ is assigned with respect to $U_i$ axes. A mobile platform coordinate frame $\{PCF\}$ is defined with respect to $V_i$ axes. Figure 3.a depicts the frame assignment of the frame $\{B\}$ and $\{PCF\}$, where $X_b$, $Y_b$ and $Z_b$ are the axes of the frame $\{B\}$ respectively; $X_p$, $Y_p$ and $Z_p$ are the axes of the $\{PCF\}$ respectively. A fixed world coordinate frame $\{WCF\}$ is also defined as shown in Figure 3.b, where the Z axis of $\{WCF\}$, $Z_w$, is pointing upwards and is normal to the base plane and the Y axis of $\{WCF\}$, $Y_w$, is pointing towards the opposite direction of $\boldsymbol{a}$ (i.e. the projection vector of $Y_b$ to the base plane). Figure 3 also depicts the reference or kinematic home configuration of the manipulator. At this configuration, $Z_b$ and $Z_p$ are coincide and make $180°$ angle with the axis $W_2$. The axes of base frame $\{B\}$ are defined with respect to the reference configuration as $X_b = U_2 = [1, 0, 0]^T$; $Y_b = U_3 = [0, 1, 0]^T$; $Z_b = U_1 = [0, 0, 1]^T$. The relationship between $V_i$ and base frame can be written as $V_i = \mathbf{R}[X_b, Y_b, Z_b]^T$ where $\mathbf{R}$ is defined by $Z - Y - X$ Euler angles $(\mathbf{R}_z(\phi_1), \mathbf{R}_y(\phi_2), \mathbf{R}_x(\phi_3))$ [12]:

$$V_1 = \begin{bmatrix} c\phi_1 c\phi_2 \\ s\phi_1 c\phi_2 \\ -s\phi_2 \end{bmatrix}, V_2 = \begin{bmatrix} c\phi_1 s\phi_2 s\phi_3 - s\phi_1 c\phi_3 \\ s\phi_1 s\phi_2 s\phi_3 + c\phi_1 c\phi_3 \\ c\phi_2 s\phi_3 \end{bmatrix}, V_3 = \begin{bmatrix} c\phi_1 s\phi_2 c\phi_3 + s\phi_1 s\phi_3 \\ s\phi_1 s\phi_2 c\phi_3 - c\phi_1 s\phi_3 \\ c\phi_2 c\phi_3 \end{bmatrix}.$$

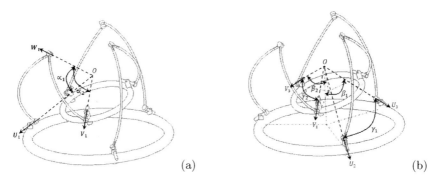

**Fig. 2.** Geometric parameters of spherical parallel mechanism: (a): $\alpha_1$, $\alpha_2$ (b): $\beta_1$, $\beta_2$, $\gamma_1$, $\gamma_2$

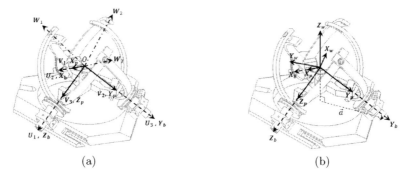

**Fig. 3.** The reference configuration and frame assignments: (a): the assignments of the base frame and platform frame (b): the assignment of the world frame

The set of $W_i$ axes are defined based on the reference configuration as: $W_1 = \left[ s\theta_1, -c\theta_1, 0 \right]^T$, $W_2 = \left[ 0, s\theta_2, -c\theta_2 \right]^T$, and $W_3 = \left[ -c\theta_3, 0, s\theta_3 \right]^T$, where, $\theta_1$, $\theta_2$ and $\theta_3$ are the joint variables of the spherical platform.

Substituting expressions for $W_i$ and $V_i$ in the constraint equation $W_i \cdot V_i = 0$ will lead to three equations with three unknowns, $\phi_1$, $\phi_2$ and $\phi_3$, which are used in the definition of $\mathbf{R}$. This results in the eight possible orientations of $\{PCF\}$ with respect to the base frame. Among these eight solutions, four solutions are nontrivial while the rest of four solutions are trivial. It has been shown that the first solution, $\mathbf{R}_1$, of the four nontrivial solutions is the only correct solution [13].

$\mathbf{R}_1$ is then used as a part of the forward kinematics of the serial part of the robot. To reduce the complexity of kinematic mapping from $\{PCF\}$ to frame $\{4\}$ (first joint of the serial link) and to solve the orientation of $\{4\}$ in inverse kinematic solution section, an intermediate at $\{p'\}$ which coincides with the origin of frame $\{PCF\}$. Referring to Figure 4, $Z_{p'}$ axis is chosen to be pointing towards the opposite direction of $Z_4$ axis of $\{4\}$ while $X_{p'}$ axis is chosen so that it not only aligns with $X_4$ axis when $\theta_4$ is equal to $0°$ but also makes an $180°$ angle with $X_4$ axis.

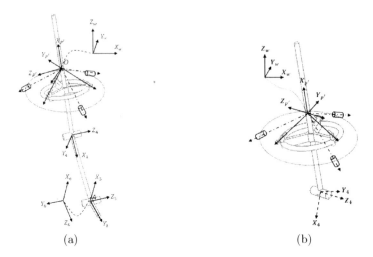

(a)                                             (b)

**Fig. 4.** The kinematic configuration of the manipulator: (a): The serial mechanism configuration of the hybrid manipulator; (b): Frame assignment for solving the orientation of frame $\{4\}$

The transformation between the coordinate frame of the first serial joint $\{4\}$ with respect to the $\{WCF\}$ can be formulated as follow [14]:

$$\substack{w\\4}T = T_1 \; \substack{p\\p'}T \; \substack{p'\\4}T, \tag{1}$$

where, $T_1$ is the homogeneous transformation from $\{WCF\}$ to $\{PCF\}$ of the parallel spherical mechanism corresponding to the first nontrivial orientation solution $\mathbf{R}_1$. The forward kinematic relationship given solution for $T_1$ is written as:

$$\substack{w\\6}T = T_1 \; \substack{p\\p'}T \; \substack{p'\\4}T \; \substack{4\\5}T \; \substack{5\\6}T. \tag{2}$$

## 3   Inverse Kinematics Solution

In this section we present an approach for solving inverse kinematics problem for the proposed class of hybrid manipulator. We present a solution for a given position and orientation of the reference frame $\{4\}$ with respect to $\{WCF\}$ which results in a solution for the first three joints ($\theta_1, \theta_2$ and $\theta_3$) of the parallel spherical part of the manipulator. Giving $\substack{w\\4}T$ and $\substack{w\\6}T$, the solutions for $\theta_4$ and the last two joints ($\theta_5$ and $\theta_6$) are then can be determined.

Figure 5(a) demonstrates a conceptual diagram of our solution approach for determining the solution for $\theta_4$. In this figure, sphere 1 is centered at $O$ having the radius equal to the first link of serial part $l_1$. The second sphere is centered at the origin of the wrist coordinate frame $\{A\}$ having a radius of $l_2$. The intersection circle between the two spheres, $RO'$, is centered at $O'$. The plane OBAC, which intersects the circle $RO'$ at point $B$ and $C$, is defined by origins of frames $\{4\}$,

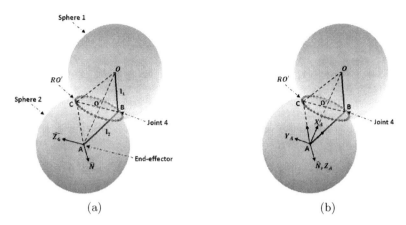

**Fig. 5.** The kinematic configuration of the manipulator: (a): Conceptual visualization for solving the two possible positions of frame {4}; (b): Conceptual visualization for determining the valid position of joint 4

{5} and the center of rotation $O$. We define the unit vector $\widehat{N}$ which is also normal to this plane.

For a particular orientation of the plane OBAC, point $B$ and $C$ are the two possible locations of the origin of coordinate frame {4}. Given the finite limits for $\theta_4$, it can be seen that the solution configuration associated for example with the position $C$ is unattainable. We also note that $\boldsymbol{OO'}$ perpendicular to the plane of circle $RO'$. Any rotation of the mobile platform will result the plane OBAC rotate about the axis $AO$. As a result, the origin of frame {4} (e.g. point $B$) will travel along the circumference of the circle $RO'$: $\angle OBA = cos^{-1}(\frac{|OB|^2+|BA|^2-|OA|^2}{2|OB||BA|})$ where we can compute:

$$\theta_4 = -(180° - \angle OBA). \tag{3}$$

The two sphere can now be defined in terms of the position of the origin of of the frame {4} (i.e. $[^wP_{x_4}, {}^wP_{y_4}, {}^wP_{z_4}]^T \rightarrow {}^wP_{x_4}^2 + {}^wP_{y_4}^2 + {}^wP_{z_4}^2 = l_1^2$ and $(^wP_{x_4} - {}^wP_{x_6})^2 + (^wP_{y_4} - {}^wP_{y_6})^2 + (^wP_{z_4} - {}^wP_{z_6})^2 = l_2^2$). The normal vector $\widehat{N}$ to the plane OBAC can also be defined as: $\widehat{N} = \frac{AO}{|AO|} \times \widehat{Z}_6$ or $\widehat{N} \cdot \frac{OB}{|OB|} = 0$ where: $\boldsymbol{OB} = [^wP_{x_4}, {}^wP_{y_4}, {}^wP_{z_4}]^T = [- {}^wP_{x_6}, - {}^wP_{y_6}, - {}^wP_{z_6}]^T$.

In order to determine the valid position for the origin of the frame {4}, i.e. point $B$, frame {A} is assigned to coincide with the origin of the end-effector $A$ as shown in Figure 5(b). In particular, the Z axis of frame {A} ($Z_A$), is aligned with $\widehat{N}$ and the X axis of frame {A} ($X_A$), is defined to be pointing towards $O$. Giving the position and orientation of the end-effector with respect to {WCF}, the orientation matrix of frame {A} can be defined as $\widehat{Z}_A = \widehat{N}$, $\widehat{X}_A = [\frac{-{}^wP_{x_6}}{|AO|}, \frac{-{}^wP_{y_6}}{|AO|}, \frac{-{}^wP_{z_6}}{|AO|}]^T$ and $\widehat{Y}_A = \widehat{Z}_A \times \widehat{X}_A$.

The position of point $B$ and $C$ uniquely define the unit vector $\hat{AB}$ and $\hat{AC}$ respectively as depicted in Figure 5. Unit vectors pointing from point $A$ to the two possible positions for the origin of the frame $\{4\}$ are defined as:

$$\hat{Sol_1} = [\frac{^wP_{x4_1} - {}^wP_{x6}}{|l_2|}, \frac{^wP_{y4_1} - {}^wP_{y6}}{|l_2|}, \frac{^wP_{z4_1} - {}^wP_{z6}}{|l_2|}]^T,$$

$$\hat{Sol_2} = [\frac{^wP_{x4_2} - {}^wP_{x6}}{|l_2|}, \frac{^wP_{y4_2} - {}^wP_{y6}}{|l_2|}, \frac{^wP_{z4_2} - {}^wP_{z6}}{|l_2|}]^T,$$

$$(4)$$

In addition to the position of the origin of $\{4\}$, the orientation of $\{4\}$ with respect to $\{WCF\}$, i.e. $^w_4\mathbf{R}$, is required in order to determine three spherical parallel joint angles. The expression for $^w_{p'}R$ can be developed based on the position of the origin of frame $\{4\}$, (i.e. $\{^w_4P\}$, and the vector $\hat{N}$. Specifically, $X_{p'}$ can be determined based on the position of $\{4\}$; $Z_{p'}$ can be determined based on the vector $\hat{N}$; $Y_{p'}$ can be determined by taking the cross product of aforementioned two unit vectors, or: $\hat{X}_{p'} = [\frac{-{}^wP_{x4}}{|l_1|}, \frac{-{}^wP_{y4}}{|l_1|}, \frac{-{}^wP_{z4}}{|l_1|}]^T$, $\hat{Z}_{p'} = -\hat{N}$ and $\hat{Y}_{p'} = \hat{Z}_{p'} \times \hat{X}_{p'}$.

Having determined the orientation of $\{p'\}$ frame with respect to $\{WCF\}$, the orientation of frame associated with $\{4\}$ with respect to $\{WCF\}$ can be obtained as:

$$^w_4\mathbf{R} = {}^w_{p'}\mathbf{R} \, {}^{p'}_4\mathbf{R}$$

The homogeneous transformation between frames $\{WCF\}$ and $\{PCF\}$ can be obtained by equation as:

$$T = {}^w_{p'}T \, {}^{p'}_p T$$

From the kinematic constraint $W_i \cdot V_i = 0$ and $U_i \cdot W_i = 0$ we can obtain the solutions for $\theta_i(i = 1, 2, 3)$ [15]. The results are as follow:

$$\theta_1 = atan2(V_{1y}, V_{1x}); \theta_2 = atan2(V_{2z}, V_{2y}); \theta_3 = atan2(V_{3x}, V_{3z}) \qquad (5)$$

where, $V_{ix}$ and $V_{iy}$ are the x and y component of $V_i$. Lastly, having $^w_4T$ and $^w_6T$, the values for $\theta_5$ and $\theta_6$ can be determined through equation (1). $^4_6T$ is defined as equation (2), the solution can be written as:

$$\theta_5 = atan2(-{}^4_6T(1,1), {}^4_6T(2,1)); \quad \theta_6 = atan2(-{}^4_6T(3,1), -{}^4_6T(3,2)) \qquad (6)$$

$$^4_6T = [^w_4T]^{-1} \, {}^w_6T$$

Where, $^4_6T(1,1)$, the entry for the first row and the first column of $^4_6T$, represents the projection of $X_6$ to $X_4$.

## 4    A Numerical Example

In this section, we present a numerical example for solution of the inverse kinematic of hybrid manipulator shown in Figure 6. A set of forward kinematic solutions will then be used to verify the solution to the inverse kinematics. The dimensions of the robot is given as: $d_1 = 55mm$, $d_2 = 40mm$, $d_3 = 28mm$, $l_1 = 146$ and $l_2 = 128mm$ and the following joint limits: $\theta_1 = (0°, 90°)$ , $\theta_2 = (0°, 90°)$ , $\theta_3 = (0°, 90°)$, $\theta_4 = (-120°, 0°)$, $\theta_5 = (-160°, 0°)$ and $\theta_6 = (0°, 360°)$.

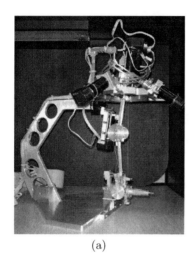
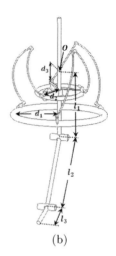

(a)                                             (b)

**Fig. 6.** (a): A prototype of a hybrid manipulator; (b): Kinematic dimension for the case study example

Given the position of the end-effector, $l_1$, $l_2$, the value of joint 4 can be determined based on equation (3),

$$\theta_4 = -(180° - \angle OBA) = -60.13° \tag{7}$$

where, $|OA| = \sqrt{40.49^2 + (-131.14)^2 + (-192.93)^2} = 237.30$; $|OB| = 146$; $|AB| = 128$; $\angle OBA = 119.87°$.

The position of $\{4\}$ is determined geometrically by solving $^wP_{X_4}, ^wP_{Y_4}$ and $^wP_{Z_4}$. By substituting the position information of the end-effector and the orientation information of $Z_6$, the normal to the plane OBAC (i.e $\hat{N}$) can be determined as:

$$\hat{N} = [-0.11, -0.97, 0.15]^T. \tag{8}$$

Two possible solutions of the position of the origin of $\{4\}$ can be defined as:

$$^wP_{4_1} = [-121.23, 1.13, -81.35]^T; \quad ^wP_{4_2} = [-2.23, -21.76, -144.35]^T \tag{9}$$

In order to determine the valid position of joint 4, the numerical value of frame $\{A\}$ is required to be solved. Substituting equation (8) and the position information of the end-effector, the numerical result of frame $\{A\}$ can be obtained as shown:

$$\hat{X}_A = [-0.13, -0.57, -0.81]^T; \hat{Y}_A = [-0.81, -0.40, 0.41]^T; \hat{Z}_A = [-0.56, 0.71, -0.40]^T. \tag{10}$$

The two possible solutions of the position of $\{4\}$ are used in equation (4) to solve for $\hat{Sol}_1$ and $\hat{Sol}_2$:

$$\hat{Sol}_1 = [-0.54, -0.69, -0.46]^T; \hat{Sol}_2 = [0.33, -0.26, -0.91]^T. \tag{11}$$

By taking the inner product of these two vectors with $Y_A$, one is able to determine that $\hat{Sol}_2$ is in fact $\hat{AB}$, and $^{W'}P_{4_2}$ is the valid solution of the position of $\{4\}$, or:

$$PROJ_1 = \hat{Sol}_1 \cdot \hat{Y}_A = 0.53; \quad PROJ_2 = \hat{Sol}_2 \cdot \hat{Y}_A = -0.53.$$

With the position information of $\{4\}$, the orientation of $\{4\}$ with respect to $\{WCF\}$ can be computed. In particular given $^{w}P_{4_2}$ the solution of $^{w}_{p'}R$ can be determined. The solution of $^{w}_{4}R$ can be determined as:

$$^{w}_{4}R = \begin{bmatrix} -0.86 & 0.47 & -0.11 \\ 0.02 & -0.18 & -0.97 \\ -0.50 & -0.86 & 0.15 \end{bmatrix} \tag{12}$$

Having solved the orientation of frame 4 with respect to $\{w\}$, the solution for matrix $\mathbf{R}$ can be obtained:

$$\mathbf{R} = \begin{bmatrix} 0.82 & -0.37 & 0.42 \\ 0.48 & 0.87 & -0.13 \\ -0.30 & 0.32 & 0.89 \end{bmatrix} \tag{13}$$

Having determined the orientation of the $\{PCF\}$ with respect $\{WCF\}$, the three spherical joints angles can be solved as:

$$\begin{bmatrix} \theta_1 \\ \theta_2 \\ \theta_3 \end{bmatrix} = \begin{bmatrix} 30.15° \\ 20.07° \\ 25.25° \end{bmatrix} \tag{14}$$

Having solved for the joint 1 to 4, the two wrist joints, joint 5 and 6, can be determined:

$$\begin{bmatrix} \theta_5 \\ \theta_6 \end{bmatrix} = \begin{bmatrix} -50.36° \\ 120° \end{bmatrix} \tag{15}$$

## 5    Discussion and Conclusion

This paper present the kinematic modeling and solution of a novel 6-DOF hybrid manipulator. A partially algebraic and partially geometric inverse kinematics solution has been described in detail. It consists of three sets of dependent solutions: the position and orientation of the joint 4, the three spherical parallel actuator joint variables and the two wrist joint variables. We have also demonstrated the inverse kinematics solution through a numerical example.

# References

1. Lum, M.J., Rosen, J., Sinanan, M.N., Hannaford, B.: Optimization of a spherical mechanism for a minimally invasive surgical robot: theoretical and experimental approaches. IEEE Trans. Biomed. Eng. 53(7), 1440–1445 (2006)
2. Ceccarelli, M., Ottaviano, E., Carbone, G.: A Study of Feasibility for a Novel Parallel-serial Manipulator. Journal of Robotics and Mechatronics 14, 304–312 (2002)
3. Yang, G., Chen, I., Yeo, S.H., Lin, W.: Design and Analysis of a Modular Hybrid Parallel-Serial Manipulator for Robotised Deburring Applications. In: Smart Devices and Machines for Advanced Manufacturing. Springer, London (2008)
4. Li, T., Payandeh, S.: On Design of Spherical Parallel Mechanisms for Application to Laparoscopic Surgery. Robotica 20(02), 133–138 (2002)
5. Payandeh, S., Li, T., Van Der Wall, H.: Devices for positioning implements about fixed points, United States Patent 6997866
6. Tang, Z., Payandeh, S.: Modeling and Experimental Studies of a Novel 6-DOF Haptic Device. In: Kappers, A.M.L., van Erp, J.B.F., Bergmann Tiest, W.M., van der Helm, F.C.T. (eds.) EuroHaptics 2010. LNCS, vol. 6191, pp. 73–80. Springer, Heidelberg (2010)
7. Tanev, T.K.: Kinematics of a hybrid (parallel-serial) robot manipulator. Mechanism and Machine Theory 35, 1183–1196 (2000)
8. Romdhane, L.: Design and analysis of a hybrid seria-parallel manipulator. Mechanism and Machine Theory 34, 1037–1055 (1999)
9. Zheng, X.Z., Bin, H.Z., Luo, Y.G.: Kinematic analysis of a hybrid serial-parallel manipulator. International Journal on Advanced Manufacturing Technology 23, 925–930 (2004)
10. Gosselin, C.M., Gagne, M.: A Closed-Form Solution for the Direct Kinematics of a Special Class of Spherical Three-Degree-Of-Freedom Parallel Manipulators. In: Computational Kinematics, pp. 231–240. Kluwer Publishing (1995)
11. Craver, W.M.: Structural analysis and design of three-degree-of-freedom robotic should module. Masters thesis, the University of Texas at Austin (1989)
12. Bai, S., Hansen, M.R., Andersen, T.O.: Modeling of a special class of spherical parallel manipulators with Euler parameters. Robotica 27, 1–10 (2009)
13. Kong, X., Gosselin, C.: Forward Displacement Analysis of a Quadratic Spherical Parallel Manipulator: The Agile Eye. In: Proc. of the ASME Inter. Design Eng. Technical Conf., Paper DETC2009-87467
14. Craig, J.J.: Introduction to robotics mechanics and control, 3rd edn. Pearson Prentice Hall, Upper Saddle River (2005)
15. Ma, A., Payandeh, S.: Analysis and Experimentation of a 4-DOF Haptic Device. In: Proceedings of IEEE Haptics Symposium, Reno, Nevada, USA, pp. 351–356 (March 2008)
16. Bonev, I.A., Chablat, D., Wenger, P.: Working and assembly modes of the agile eye. In: IEEE International Conference on Robotics and Automation, pp. 2317–2322 (2006)

# Stiffness Analysis of Clavel's DELTA Robot

Martin Wahle and Burkhard Corves

Department of Mechanism Theory and Machine Dynamics, RWTH Aachen,
Eilfschornsteinstr. 18,
52062 Aachen, Germany
{Wahle,Corves}@igm.rwth-aachen.de

**Abstract.** This work deals with the structural stiffness properties of the spatial 3-DOF DELTA robot. Firstly, the kinematic model is presented. Based on the kinematic model a static model is derived. The static model is able to map all relevant constraint forces of the parallel structure. Based on this relationship the stiffness matrix of the DELTA robot can be deduced. As a result, the overall stiffness properties and the different stiffness contributors are presented for an exemplary structure.

**Keywords:** Kinematics, static model, structural stiffness.

## 1    Introduction

Due to numerous advantages compared to serial structures parallel robots have gained increasing attention among researchers and also within industry applications. Parallel structures feature high positioning accuracy as well as high stiffness capability as closed kinematic loops are utilized. Furthermore, the moving mass compared to serial robots is small, which makes it possible to perform motions with high dynamic effects [1].

One common example for parallel structures is the Stewart-Gough platform which was already presented in 1966. It holds six degrees of freedom and its main application was the translational and rotational positioning of a flight-simulator [2].

In 1988, Clavel proposed a structure for a spatial, 3-DOF parallel structure for positioning applications. As the dynamic properties of the structure are very advantageous it became a successful tool in industry applications, especially for pick-and-place tasks [3,4].

In this paper a method to determine the stiffness contributors of the DELTA structure is presented. First of all, the solution for the inverse kinematic problem is presented. Based on the kinematic model and while utilizing the basic relationships for static equilibrium a force transmission model is derived. Subsequently, the stiffness matrix can be deduced from the force transmission model.

The compliance throughout the workspace is presented for a representative structure. Also, the different stiffness contributors are quantified regarding this exemplary case.

S. Jeschke, H. Liu, and D. Schilberg (Eds.): ICIRA 2011, Part I, LNAI 7101, pp. 240–249, 2011.
© Springer-Verlag Berlin Heidelberg 2011

## 2    Inverse Kinematics

The calculation of the inverse kinematics starts with the vector loop equation for each kinematic chain:

$$p = l_{1i} + l_{2i} + a_i - b_i \ . \tag{1}$$

We assume that all joint coordinates of the base frame as well as all joint coordinates of the end-effector lie on circles with radii $a$ and $b$ but have the same angular allocations. In this case, transformation matrices from the global reference frame into the leg-sided reference frames can be introduced [5]:

$$^iT_0 = \begin{pmatrix} \cos\alpha_i & \sin\alpha_i & 0 \\ -\sin\alpha_i & \cos\alpha_i & 0 \\ 0 & 0 & 1 \end{pmatrix} \ . \tag{2}$$

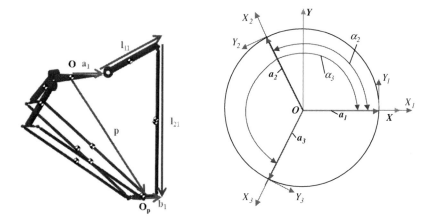

**Fig. 1.** Principal structure of the DELTA robot with vector loop visualization (left side). Definition of local reference frames for each kinematic chain (right side) [6].

At this point a new auxiliary vector $^ir_i$ can be calculated:

$$^ir_i = -{}^ia_i + {}^ip + {}^ib_i = \begin{pmatrix} -a+b \\ 0 \\ 0 \end{pmatrix} + {}^iT_0 \cdot p \ . \tag{3}$$

During the inverse kinematic calculation the end-effector position vector $p$ is known. The vector $^ir_i$ can also be expressed with:

$$^{i}\boldsymbol{r}_{i} = {}^{i}\boldsymbol{l}_{1i} + {}^{i}\boldsymbol{l}_{2i} = \begin{pmatrix} l_{1} \cdot \cos(\varphi_{1i}) \\ 0 \\ l_{1} \cdot \sin(\varphi_{1i}) \end{pmatrix} + \begin{pmatrix} l_{2} \cdot \sin(\varphi_{3i}) \cdot \cos(\varphi_{1i} + \varphi_{2i}) \\ l_{2} \cdot \cos(\varphi_{3i}) \\ l_{2} \cdot \sin(\varphi_{3i}) \cdot \sin(\varphi_{1i} + \varphi_{2i}) \end{pmatrix}. \tag{4}$$

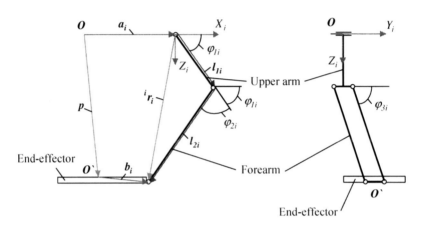

**Fig. 2.** Vector and angle definitions within the local reference frame of kinematic chain i (left side). Definition of angle $\varphi_{3i}$ in y-z-plane of local reference frame i.

While evaluating the second component equations (3) and (4) lead to the equation for angle $\varphi_{3i}$:

$$\varphi_{3i} = \cos^{-1}\left( \frac{-x \cdot \sin \alpha_{i} + y \cdot \cos \alpha_{i}}{l_{2}} \right). \tag{5}$$

The second auxiliary variable $\varphi_{2i}$ can now be computed with the help of the magnitude of vector $^{i}\boldsymbol{r}_{i}$:

$$\varphi_{2i} = \cos^{-1}\left( \frac{{}^{i}r_{i,x}{}^{2} + {}^{i}r_{i,y}{}^{2} + {}^{i}r_{i,z}{}^{2} - l_{1}^{2} - l_{2}^{2}}{2 \cdot l_{1} \cdot l_{2} \cdot \sin(\varphi_{3i})} \right). \tag{6}$$

The actuation angles $\varphi_{1i}$, which are the final results of the inverse kinematic calculations are also resulting from the evaluation of equations (3) and (4):

$$\tan(\varphi_{1i}) = -\frac{-l_{1} \cdot {}^{i}r_{i,z} - l_{2} \cdot \sin \varphi_{3i} \cdot \cos \varphi_{2i} \cdot {}^{i}r_{i,z} + l_{2} \cdot \sin \varphi_{3i} \cdot \sin \varphi_{2i} \cdot {}^{i}r_{i,x}}{l_{1} \cdot {}^{i}r_{i,x} + l_{2} \cdot \sin \varphi_{3i} \cdot \sin \varphi_{2i} \cdot {}^{i}r_{i,z} + l_{2} \cdot \sin \varphi_{3i} \cdot \cos \varphi_{2i} \cdot {}^{i}r_{i,x}}. \tag{7}$$

## 3    Static Force Transmission

As the stiffness influences of all relevant components should be covered with the stiffness model the static model needs to map the force transmission throughout the entire structure. The derivation of the static force transmission model starts with the equilibrium of the end-effector:

$$F_{P,ext} + \sum_i F_i = 0 \,,$$

$$r_{P,ext} \times F_{P,ext} + \sum_i b_i \times F_i = 0 \,. \tag{8}$$

The forces $F_i$ are acting in the ball joints that connect the forearm rods to the end-effector. Assuming that the external wrenches on the rods are just exerted from the ball joints the force directions of $F_i$ are equal to the rod directions $s_i$:

$$F_i = F_i \cdot s_i \,. \tag{9}$$

The direction of the forearm rods (two rods within one forearm pair are always parallel) is computed with the relationship:

$$s_i = {}^iT_0^T \cdot \left( {}^i r_i - l_1 \begin{pmatrix} \cos \varphi_{1i} \\ 0 \\ \sin \varphi_{1i} \end{pmatrix} \right). \tag{10}$$

The static equilibrium for each arm is evaluated analogously to equation (8). External forces are just exerted on the platform. For each arm six further equations can be derived which result in the reaction forces and moments at the revolute joint of the arm. The torque about the motion axis is equal to the actuation torque required to compensate the pre-defined external wrenches acting on the end-effector.
The following linear relationship can be defined:

$$J_P \cdot F_{int} = F_{ext} \,. \tag{11}$$

The internal forces / torques vector as well as the external wrenches vector hold 24 entries. The square matrix $J_P$ displays the position-dependent coefficients of the system of linear equations. The internal forces $F_{int}$ vector consists of the components:

$$F_{int} = \left( F_1 \quad .. \quad F_6 \quad F_{R,1}{}^T \quad F_{R,2}{}^T \quad F_{R,3}{}^T \quad M_{R,1}{}^T \quad M_{R,2}{}^T \quad M_{R,3}{}^T \right)^T \,. \tag{12}$$

For static considerations the external wrenches are just exerted on the end-effector. Hence, the external forces vector holds zero entries for the part corresponding to the arm equilibriums:

$$F_{ext} = \begin{pmatrix} -F_{P,ext} \\ -r_{P,ext} \times F_{P,ext} \\ 0_{18 \times 1} \end{pmatrix}. \tag{13}$$

The final Jacobean of the DELTA-robot can be computed with the 24 x 24 matrix:

$$J_P = \begin{pmatrix} s_1 & s_1 & s_2 & s_2 & s_3 & s_3 & \\ b_1 \times s_1 & b_2 \times s_1 & b_3 \times s_2 & b_4 \times s_2 & b_5 \times s_3 & b_6 \times s_3 & 0_{6 \times 18} \\ -s_1 & -s_1 & 0_{3 \times 1} & 0_{3 \times 1} & 0_{3 \times 1} & 0_{3 \times 1} & \\ 0_{3 \times 1} & 0_{3 \times 1} & -s_2 & -s_2 & 0_{3 \times 1} & 0_{3 \times 1} & \\ 0_{3 \times 1} & 0_{3 \times 1} & 0_{3 \times 1} & 0_{3 \times 1} & -s_3 & -s_3 & \\ -r_1 \times s_1 & -r_2 \times s_1 & 0_{3 \times 1} & 0_{3 \times 1} & 0_{3 \times 1} & 0_{3 \times 1} & I_{18 \times 18} \\ 0_{3 \times 1} & 0_{3 \times 1} & -r_3 \times s_2 & -r_4 \times s_2 & 0_{3 \times 1} & 0_{3 \times 1} & \\ 0_{3 \times 1} & 0_{3 \times 1} & 0_{3 \times 1} & 0_{3 \times 1} & -r_5 \times s_3 & -r_6 \times s_3 & \end{pmatrix}. \tag{14}$$

## 4    Stiffness Model

As the upper-arm bearing reaction forces calculated by model (11) are measured in the global reference frame a transformation of the result vector has to be performed.

This is due to the fact that for further stiffness transformations the forces must point in directions for which stiffness properties are known.

Hence, the required local X-axis needs to point in upper arm direction to map the longitudinal extension stiffness as well as the torsional stiffness about the upper arm axis. Furthermore, the Y-axis has to be orientated in joint revolute axis direction. This force component is linked to the lateral shear stiffness and the bending stiffness of the upper arm about the actuation axis. The corresponding Z-axis maps the shear stiffness and the bending stiffness about the axis perpendicular to the revolute joint direction. In order to solve the problem as presented in equation (11) the Jacobean of the system needs to be transformed.

The transformation matrix for each upper-arm reference frame can be calculated with:

$$^{i'}T_0 = \begin{pmatrix} \cos(-\varphi_{li}) & 0 & -\sin(-\varphi_{li}) \\ 0 & 1 & 0 \\ \sin(-\varphi_{li}) & 0 & \cos(-\varphi_{li}) \end{pmatrix} \cdot {}^0T_i^T. \tag{15}$$

As the forearm forces are pointing in extension stiffness direction the first six components of the Jacobean are maintained. The entire transformation matrix is computed with:

$$
T_{ov} = \begin{pmatrix}
I_{6\times6} & 0_{3\times3} & 0_{3\times3} & 0_{3\times3} & 0_{3\times3} & 0_{3\times3} & 0_{3\times3} \\
0_{3\times3} & {}^{1'}T_0 & 0_{3\times3} & 0_{3\times3} & 0_{3\times3} & 0_{3\times3} & 0_{3\times3} \\
0_{3\times3} & 0_{3\times3} & {}^{2'}T_0 & 0_{3\times3} & 0_{3\times3} & 0_{3\times3} & 0_{3\times3} \\
0_{3\times3} & 0_{3\times3} & 0_{3\times3} & {}^{3'}T_0 & 0_{3\times3} & 0_{3\times3} & 0_{3\times3} \\
0_{3\times3} & 0_{3\times3} & 0_{3\times3} & 0_{3\times3} & {}^{1'}T_0 & 0_{3\times3} & 0_{3\times3} \\
0_{3\times3} & 0_{3\times3} & 0_{3\times3} & 0_{3\times3} & 0_{3\times3} & {}^{2'}T_0 & 0_{3\times3} \\
0_{3\times3} & 0_{3\times3} & 0_{3\times3} & 0_{3\times3} & 0_{3\times3} & 0_{3\times3} & {}^{3'}T_0
\end{pmatrix}.
\tag{16}
$$

The new Jacobean which can be used for the stiffness calculation is given by:

$$
J_{P,N} = J_P \cdot T_{ov}^{-1}.
\tag{17}
$$

For parallel structures the stiffness at the end-effector can be computed by transforming a diagonal stiffness matrix with the Jacobean of the system. The diagonal stiffness matrix describes the elasticity properties in actuation directions. As the force transmission model also maps the constraint force transmission the stiffness effects in the constraint directions can also be modeled. The final end-effector stiffness matrix can be obtained with:

$$
K_P = J_{P,N} \cdot K_{diag} \cdot J_{P,N}{}^T.
\tag{18}
$$

As the definition of the Jacobean is altered the calculation is differing from the derivation in [7]. In our case the system's Jacobean is defined with the force transmission whereas it is commonly defined as velocity transmission matrix into the actuation space.

Displacements of the end-effector caused by external wrenches can now be computed with the relationship:

$$
x_e = K_P{}^{-1} \cdot F_{ext}.
\tag{19}
$$

## 4.1    Relevant Structural Stiffness Effects

The first six entries of the diagonal stiffness matrix $K_{diag}$ are corresponding to the extension stiffness of the forearm rods. Fig. 3 presents the resulting elasticity effects, $K_4$ belongs to the forearms.

$K_1$ results from the bending stiffness of the upper arms about the Y-axis as well as the torsional stiffness of the gearbox unit. Both stiffness effects are located in a serial connection which is reducing the overall resulting stiffness $K_1$ (about the Y-axis).

Accordingly, $K_2$ represents the elasticity effect resulting from the upper arm transverse bending stiffness about the Z-axis as well as the tilt stiffness of the gearbox unit. $K_3$ displays the resulting stiffness from the serial connection of the torsional upper arm stiffness as well as the tilt stiffness of the gearbox unit about the X-axis which is commonly equal to the previously mentioned tilt stiffness about the Z-axis.

The stiffness properties of the upper arms and forearms are resulting from the geometry setup (tab. 1) and can be obtained using the standard equations for linear deflections [8].

Shear stiffness effects were also considered but are of no relevance for the overall deflection behavior.

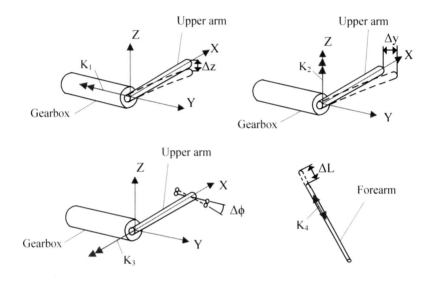

**Fig. 3.** Visualization of relevant stiffness effects

**Table 1.** Relevant geometry and stiffness characteristics of an exemplary DELTA structure

| Property | Value |
|---|---|
| Diameter forearm | 20 mm |
| Wall thickness forearm | 1 mm |
| Diameter upper arm | 50 mm |
| Wall thickness upper arm | 2 mm |
| | |
| Gearbox unit torsional stiffness | $10^8$ Nmm |
| Gearbox unit tilt stiffness | $30^8$ Nmm |

## 5     Results

En exemplary structure with the geometry parameters presented in tab. 2 is analyzed. The values are not resulting from a structural geometry optimization. Hence, the stiffness characteristics within the selected workspace might be impractical. Yet, the calculation possibilities should be outlined.

**Table 2.** Geometry and workspace parameters of an exemplary DELTA structure

| Property | Value [mm] |
|---|---|
| Base plate joint radius | 200 |
| End-effector joint radius | 120 |
| Length upper arm | 500 |
| Length forearm | 1000 |
| Joint offsets | 160 |
| | |
| Workspace height | 500-1000 |
| Workspace radius | 800 |

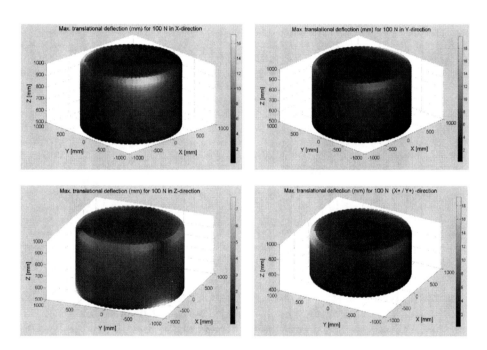

**Fig. 4.** Different visualizations of stiffness calculations. Results for the translational deflection are presented for standardized 100 N wrenches at end-effector in X, Y, Z-directions and load in combined X-Y-direction (under 45 degree).

It can be observed that the stiffness characteristics are strongly depending on the analyzed position. Approaching the workspace borders the behavior declines progressively. Furthermore, the elasticity is depending on the direction of the applied external force. For DELTA structures the stiffness in Z-direction is commonly higher than in X- and Y-directions.

As the highest deflections occur at the workspace borders it makes sense to analyze the upper and lower Z-plane of the workspace cylinder. Fig. 5 presents the corresponding results for external loads in Z- and X-direction.

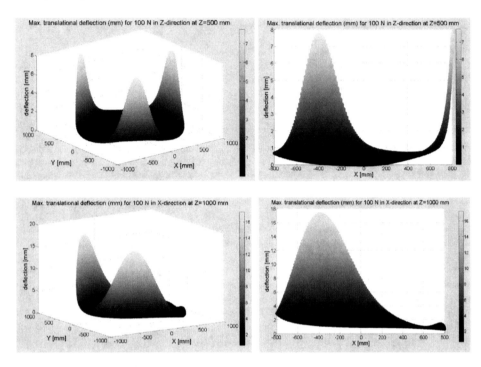

**Fig. 5.** Analysis of Z=500 mm plane for external wrench in Z-direction (upper part) and Z=1000 mm plane for 100 N external load in X-direction (lower part)

The presented results are corresponding to the effect of all structural elasticities simultaneously. For stiffness optimization tasks it might be of interest to determine which elasticity has the biggest impact on the overall translational deflection. Again, the stiffness is depending on the direction of the external loads.

The analysis is performed with a reference load pointing in a pre-defined direction. Afterwards, all stiffness values except one are set to infinity to contemplate the influence of one isolated component elasticity. The ratio of the maximum deflection and the sum of all separated stiffness analysis deflections equals the influence percentage of one elasticity contributor.

For the exemplary structure it could be observed that the percentage distributions for reference loads in X- and Y-direction are equal.

For loads in X- and Y-directions the transverse bending stiffness of the upper arms has the biggest impact on the overall elasticity. In contrast to that the torsional stiffness of the upper arm is most relevant for wrenches pointing in Z-direction.

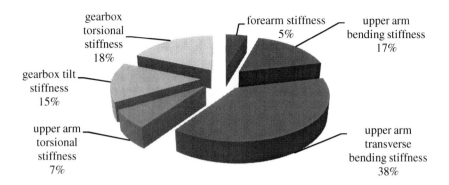

**Fig. 6.** Elasticity contributors to maximum deflection for reference load in X- and Y-direction

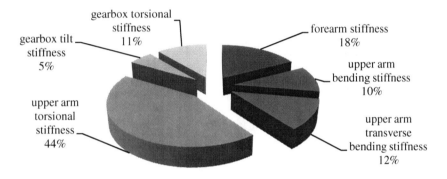

**Fig. 7.** Elasticity contributors to maximum deflection for reference load in Z-direction

# References

1. Merlet, J.-P.: Parallel Robots. Springer, Heidelberg (2006), 978-1402041327
2. Stewart, D.: A Platform with Six Degrees of Freedom, UK Institution of Mechanical Engineers Proceedings, Vol. 180(15), Pt. 1 (1965)
3. Clavel, R.: Device for the Movement and Positioning of an Element in Space, US Patent No. 4976582 (December 11, 1990)
4. Clavel, R.: Delta, a fast robot with parallel geometry. In: Proceedings of 18th International Symposium on Industrial Robots, pp. 91–100 (1988)
5. Tsai, L.-W.: Robot Analysis: The Mechanics of Serial and Parallel Manipulators. John Wiley & Sons (1999) 978-0471325932
6. Nefzi, M.: Kinematics and Dynamics of Robots, Exercise RWTH Aachen, Germany: Vector-based kinematic calculations for parallel robots, not published (2010)
7. Gosselin, C.: Stiffness Mapping for Parallel Manipulators. IEEETransactions on Robotics and Automation 6(3), 377–382 (1990)
8. Timoshenko, S.: Strength of Materials: Elementary Theory and Problems. CBS Publishers & Distributors (2004) 978-8123910307

# Optimum Kinematic Design of a 3-DOF Parallel Kinematic Manipulator with Actuation Redundancy

Fugui Xie, Xin-Jun Liu[*], Xiang Chen, and Jinsong Wang

The State Key Laboratory of Tribology & Institute of Manufacturing Engineering, Department of Precision Instruments and Mechanology, Tsinghua University, Beijing 100084, China
xinjunliu@mail.tsinghua.edu.cn

**Abstract.** Design of a parallel kinematic manipulator (PKM) with actuation redundancy is one of the main issues in the field. In this paper, the *local minimized transmission index* (LMTI) is proposed as the motion/force transmissibility evaluation criterion for such a manipulator. The optimum kinematic design of the 4-PSS-PU PKM with actuation redundancy is then carried out based on this index and the optimized parameters are given. For the purpose of comparison, the transmission performance of the 3-PSS-PU PKM without redundant actuation is analyzed. Performance comparison shows that the motion/force transmissibility and orientation capability have been improved greatly by the introduction of actuation redundancy. The LMTI proposed here can be applied into the optimum kinematic design of other parallel manipulators with actuation redundancy.

**Keywords:** Motion/force transmissibility, Parallel kinematic manipulator, Actuation redundancy, Optimum kinematic design.

## 1    Introduction

After the success has been made by the Sprint Z3 tool head, parallel mechanisms with two rotational degrees of freedom (DOFs) and a translational DOF have been intensively investigated in the field of parallel kinematic manipulators (PKMs). The 3-PSS-PU (P, S and U represent prismatic, spherical and universal joints, respectively, and P denotes the prismatic joint is active) PKM is one of them. But, the orientation capability of this manipulator is not so satisfactory for practical application due to singularity. As is well known, the most feasible method for dealing with singularity-free workspace enlargement is using actuation or kinematic redundancy [1-3]. Actuation redundancy means that the mobility of a manipulator is less than the number of its actuated joints, while kinematic redundancy means that the mobility is greater than the DOFs needed to set an arbitrary pose of the mobile platform [2, 4, 5]. Recently, redundant actuation of robotic manipulators and machine tools has become a field drawing active research for its advantages, such as decreasing or eliminating singularity, increasing workspace, stiffness and

---

[*] Corresponding author.

S. Jeschke, H. Liu, and D. Schilberg (Eds.): ICIRA 2011, Part I, LNAI 7101, pp. 250–259, 2011.

manipulability [6], improving transmission properties [7]. Actuation redundancy is used to eliminate singularity and improve the orientation ability of the Eclipse in Ref. [8]. For such reasons, the 4-$\underline{P}$SS-PU PKM generated by introducing actuation redundancy to the 3-$\underline{P}$SS-PU PKM should have better orientation capability theoretically. In this paper, the optimum kinematic design of the 4-$\underline{P}$SS-PU PKM will be introduced and the performance comparison will also be presented consequently.

Optimum kinematic design is always an important and challenging subject in designing PKMs due to the closed-loop structures. This problem becomes more complex due to the introduction of redundancy to non-redundant PKMs. Generally, there are two issues involved: performance evaluation and dimension synthesis. Dimension synthesis is to determine the link lengths of PKMs, which is the destination of optimum kinematic design. Due to the fact that PKMs have the advantages of high stiffness, high velocity, and high load/weight ratio, for some applications, they are or should be good for motion/force transmission. For such a reason, researchers did some contribution to such kind of performance evaluation of a PKM. For example, a transmission index considering only the transmissibility to the output was defined for the 3-DOF SPM by Takeda et al. [9]. Based on the virtual coefficient of screw theory, Chen et al. [10] proposed a *generalized transmission index* to evaluate the output transmissibility in one limb of a non-redundant PKM. A *local transmission index* (LTI) based on the transmission angle was proposed by Wang et al. [11] to evaluate the motion/force transmissibility of PKMs, which is limited in the domain of planar or decoupled PKMs without redundancy. Thereafter, to evaluate the motion/force transmissibility of all non-redundant PKMs, Wang et al. [12] updated the definition of LTI based on the concept of reciprocal product of screw theory, and both the input and output motion/force transmissibility were taken into consideration. To the best of our knowledge, the research on the evaluation of motion/force transmissibility of redundant PKMs has not been reported yet, and the majority of current contributions focus only on the field of non-redundant PKMs in terms of optimum kinematic design. Based on the previous outcomes in the non-redundant area, this paper will suggest a new index to evaluate the motion/force transmissibility of the PKMs with actuation redundancy. This index will be used in the optimum design of the redundant 4-$\underline{P}$SS-PU PKM.

## 2    Mechanism Description and Inverse Kinematics

The CAD model and kinematic scheme of the 4-$\underline{P}$SS-PU parallel manipulator with actuation redundancy are presented in Fig. 1 (a) and (b), respectively. The mobile platform is connected to the base through four identical $\underline{P}$SS limbs and a PU limb (P, S and U represent prismatic, spherical and universal joints, respectively, and $\underline{P}$ denotes the prismatic joint is active). Since a PSS limb has no kinematic constraint to the mobile platform and only the PU limb limits its output, the DOF of the manipulator is then the mobility of the PU limb. So, DOFs of the PKM are two orientational DOFs about the $x$- and $y$-axis and a translational DOF along the $z$-axis. The radii of the mobile platform and the base are $R_1$ and $R_3$, respectively. The link length is $R_2$, i.e., $P_i S_i = R_2$, $i = 1, 2, 3, 4$.

Since all inputs are along the $z$-axis, the kinematic design and dimensional synthesis can neglect the translation along the $z$-axis for the analysis result in Refs. [11, 13]. For the manipulator, the orientation ability is the main performance for the optimum design. Here, the *Tilt-and-Torsion* (T&T) angles are used to describe the orientation of the manipulator. As shown in Fig. 2, the vector $\boldsymbol{H}$ represents the unit normal vector of the mobile platform, and $\varphi$ and $\theta$ are the *azimuth angle* and the complement of the *tilt angle*, respectively.

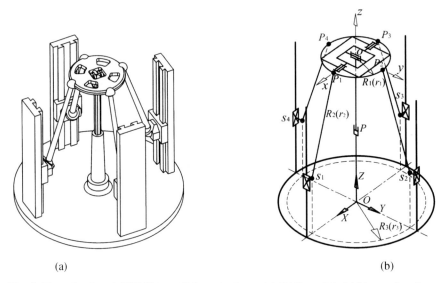

(a)                                           (b)

**Fig. 1.** The redundant 4-PSS-PU parallel manipulator: (a) CAD model; (b) kinematic scheme

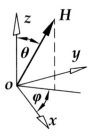

**Fig. 2.** The orientation description of the manipulator

Under this description, the rotation matrix can be derived as

$$R(\varphi,\theta) = \begin{bmatrix} \cos^2\varphi\cos\theta+\sin^2\varphi & \sin\varphi\cos\varphi(\cos\theta-1) & \cos\varphi\sin\theta \\ \sin\varphi\cos\varphi(\cos\theta-1) & \sin^2\varphi\cos\theta+\cos^2\varphi & \sin\varphi\sin\theta \\ -\cos\varphi\sin\theta & -\sin\varphi\sin\theta & \cos\theta \end{bmatrix}. \tag{1}$$

The coordinate frames are established as shown in Fig. 1(b), where, $\mathfrak{R} : O\text{-}XYZ$ is the global frame, $\mathfrak{R}' : o\text{-}xyz$ is a mobile frame, and the mobile frame $\mathfrak{R}'$ is fixed to the platform of the manipulator.

When the output $(z, \varphi, \theta)$ is given, the positions of the active sliders along the $z$-axis can be easily derived as

$$s_1 = z - R_1 \cos\varphi\sin\theta - \sqrt{R_2^2 - \left(R_1 \cos^2\varphi\cos\theta + R_1 \sin^2\varphi - R_3\right)^2 - R_1^2 \sin^2\varphi\cos^2\varphi\left(\cos\theta - 1\right)^2} , \quad (2)$$

$$s_2 = z - R_1 \sin\varphi\sin\theta - \sqrt{R_2^2 - \left(R_1 \sin^2\varphi\cos\theta + R_1 \cos^2\varphi - R_3\right)^2 - R_1^2 \sin^2\varphi\cos^2\varphi\left(\cos\theta - 1\right)^2} , \quad (3)$$

$$s_3 = z + R_1 \cos\varphi\sin\theta - \sqrt{R_2^2 - \left(R_1 \cos^2\varphi\cos\theta + R_1 \sin^2\varphi - R_3\right)^2 - R_1^2 \sin^2\varphi\cos^2\varphi\left(\cos\theta - 1\right)^2} , \quad (4)$$

$$s_4 = z + R_1 \sin\varphi\sin\theta - \sqrt{R_2^2 - \left(R_1 \sin^2\varphi\cos\theta + R_1 \cos^2\varphi - R_3\right)^2 - R_1^2 \sin^2\varphi\cos^2\varphi\left(\cos\theta - 1\right)^2} . \quad (5)$$

# 3    Optimum Kinematic Design

## 3.1    Indices Definition

For the manipulators with actuation redundancy, there exists mutual interference among the input actuators, and it is difficult to predict the force distribution among these mutual interference actuators in advance [14, 15]. However, this problem can be addressed by removing the $r$ actuation-redundancy actuators from the $k$ mutual interference actuators (for the 4-PSS-PU PKM, $r=1$ and $k=4$), and $q$ non-redundant manipulators will be generated, $q = C_k^r$. According to the definition of *local transmission index* (LTI) [12], there is an LTI value for each manipulator with respect to the designated position and orientation, denoted by $\kappa_i$ $(i = 1, 2, ..., q)$, and one of the $q$ non-redundant manipulators can transmit motion/force better than others. Take the LTI value of this manipulator as the *local minimized transmission index* (LMTI) of the redundant PKM. The LMTI can be expressed as

$$\mathbb{M} = \max\left\{\kappa_1, \kappa_2, ..., \kappa_q\right\}, \quad q = C_k^r . \quad (6)$$

This index reflects the minimum motion/force transmission performance in a designated pose of the actuation-redundancy manipulators. The larger value of LMTI indicates that the more efficient motion/force transmission would take place.

For the purpose of obtaining a high-speed and high-quality motion/force transmission, the most widely accepted range for the transmission angle is $(45°, 135°)$ [16]. Therefore, the corresponding LMTI limit will be

$$\mathbb{M} > \sin(\pi/4) \quad \text{or} \quad \mathbb{M} > 0.7 . \quad (7)$$

Obviously, LMTI is independent of any coordinate frame and has distinct physical significance.

With the constraint of $M > 0.7$, a good-transmission workspace described by the *tilt-and-torsion* angles, i.e., $(\varphi, \theta)$, can be identified, and there exists a maximal circular area $\varpi$ defined by $0 \leq \varphi \leq 2\pi$ and $0 \leq \theta \leq \theta_{max}$ within this workspace. Take $\theta_{max}$ as the *good-transmission orientational capability* (GTOC) of the PKM, that is

$$W_{GTOC} = \theta_{max}. \tag{8}$$

To reflect the transmission performance of the redundant PKM over a considered workspace, the *global transmission index* (GTI) over the workspace $\varpi$ is defined as

$$\Gamma_{\varpi} = \frac{\iint_{\varpi} M \, d\varphi d\theta}{\iint_{\varpi} d\varphi d\theta}. \tag{9}$$

### 3.2    Normalization of the Geometric Parameters

For the mechanism presented in Fig. 1, there are three parameters $R_1$, $R_2$ and $R_3$. Let

$$D = (R_1 + R_2 + R_3) / 3 \tag{10}$$

and three normalized parameters can be generated as

$$r_i = R_i / D, (i = 1, 2, 3), \tag{11}$$

then, there is

$$r_1 + r_2 + r_3 = 3. \tag{12}$$

To make the mechanism be assembled and be sure of having workspace, two geometric constraint equations of the normalized parameters can be derived as

$$r_1 + r_2 > r_3 \text{ and } r_1 \leq r_3. \tag{13}$$

By using Eqs. (12) and (13), the *parameter design space* of the 4-PSS-PU PKM can be determined as shown in Fig. 3.

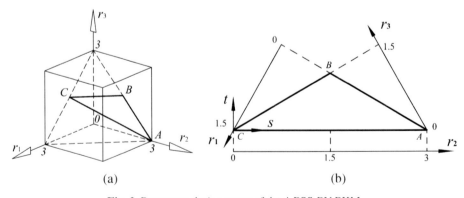

(a)                              (b)

**Fig. 3.** Parameter *design space* of the 4-PSS-PU PKM

The mapping function between $(s, t)$ and $(r_1, r_2, r_3)$ can be expressed as

$$\begin{cases} s = r_2 \\ t = \sqrt{3} - \dfrac{2\sqrt{3}}{3} r_1 - \dfrac{\sqrt{3}}{3} r_2 \end{cases} \text{and} \begin{cases} r_2 = s \\ r_1 = \dfrac{3 - s - \sqrt{3}t}{2} \\ r_3 = 3 - r_1 - r_2 \end{cases}. \tag{14}$$

Especially, by using Eq. (14), one may plot the performance atlas in Fig. 3(b) if the performance index of a manipulator with $r_1$, $r_2$ and $r_3$ is known.

### 3.3    Optimum Kinematic Design

Optimum kinematic design of the 4-PSS-PU PKM can be implemented by using the process proposed in Ref. [13], which can be described as following.

**Step 1:** Generation of the performance atlases.
According to the definitions of GTOC and GTI introduced in Section 3.1, the performance atlases in the *parameter design space* can be generated by using Eq. (14) as shown in Figs. 4 and 5.

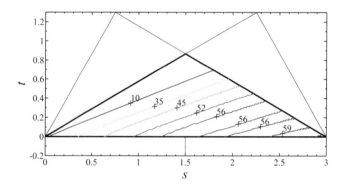

**Fig. 4.** Atlas of the good-transmission orientational capability

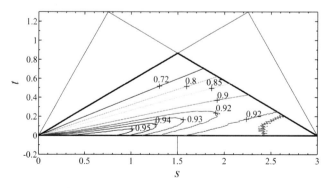

**Fig. 5.** Atlas of the global transmission index

**Step 2:** Identification of an optimum region in the *parameter design space*.

Based on the analysis of the distributions presented in Figs. 4 and 5, an optimum region is identified with the constraints of $W_{GTOC} > 54°$ and $\Gamma_\varpi > 0.92$, and it is the shadowing area in Fig. 6.

**Step 3:** Selection of a candidate solution from the optimum region.

Here, as an example to present the design process, the manipulator with $r_1=0.4$, $r_2=1.8$ and $r_3=0.8$ is selected without any special reason from the optimum region. Values of its corresponding indices are $W_{GTOC} = 55.1250°$ and $\Gamma_\varpi = 0.9225$, respectively.

**Step 4:** Verification of the candidate.

Since this is only an example, supposing that the results can meet the application requirements and no modification should be made. If not, one may pick up another candidate from the optimum region. Of note is that, in this paper, the optimized results of geometric parameters are non-dimensional, since the orientational capability of the manipulator is only dependent on the ratio of these parameters. So, multiplying the non-dimensional parameters by a coefficient will not affect the GTOC and GTI. How much the coefficient will be depends on the application conditions. Once the coefficient is determined, the corresponding dimensional parameters can be derived.

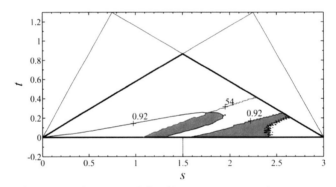

**Fig. 6.** An optimum area defined by $W_{GTOC} > 54°$ and $\Gamma_\varpi > 0.92$

## 4     Performance Comparison between Redundant and Non-redundant Manipulators

In this part, the GTOC and distribution of LMTI will be used to illustrate the difference of an actuation-redundancy manipulator from its non-redundant one. The LMTI distribution of the redundant 4-P̲SS-PU PKM with $r_1=0.4$, $r_2=1.8$ and $r_3=0.8$ can be generated as shown in Fig. 7.

Here, for the purpose of comparison, the 3-P̲SS-PU PKM with the same parameters is analyzed. The CAD model and kinematic scheme are presented in Fig. 8 and the LTI distribution is shown in Fig. 9.

From the LMTI distribution maps shown in Figs. 7 and 9, it can be concluded that the usable workspace (see Ref. [13] for the definition) is dramatically enlarged and the motion/force transmissibility and orientation capability are greatly improved by the introduction of actuation redundancy.

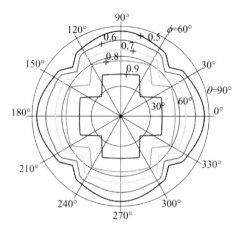

**Fig. 7.** LMTI distribution of the redundant 4-P̱SS-PU PKM with $r_1$=0.4, $r_2$=1.8 and $r_3$=0.8

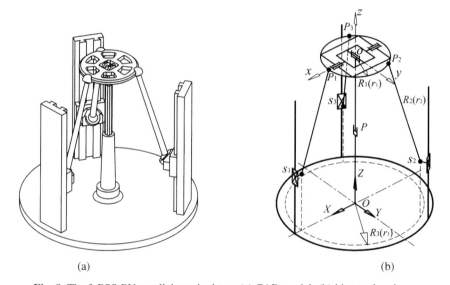

(a)                                                    (b)

**Fig. 8.** The 3-P̱SS-PU parallel manipulator: (a) CAD model; (b) kinematic scheme

## 5    Conclusions

This paper addresses the optimum kinematic design of the 4-P̱SS-PU parallel kinematic manipulator (PKM) with actuation redundancy. To this end, the *local minimized transmission index* (LMTI) is defined as the motion/force transmissibility evaluation criterion for PKMs with actuation redundancy. Based on this index, the *good-transmission orientational capability* (GTOC) and *global transmission index* (GTI) are introduced, and the corresponding atlases are presented. Consequently, the optimum kinematic design is carried out and the optimized parameters are given. To illustrate the improvement of motion/force transmissibility and orientation capability by the introduction of actuation redundancy, the transmission performance of 3-$\underline{P}$SS-PU PKM with the same parameters is analyzed, and the statement is confirmed by comparison. The LMTI proposed in this paper can be applied to the optimum kinematic design of other parallel manipulators with actuation redundancy.

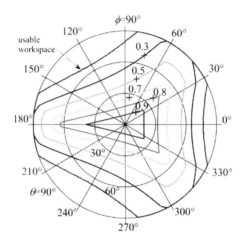

**Fig. 9.** LMTI distribution of the 3-$\underline{P}$SS-PU PKM with $r_1$=0.4, $r_2$=1.8 and $r_3$=0.8

**Acknowledgment.** This work was supported in part by the National Natural Science Foundation of China (Grant No. 51075222), and the Fund of State Key Laboratory of Tribology (Grant No. SKLT10C02 ).

# References

1. Cha, S.-H., Lasky, T.A., Velinsky, S.A.: Determination of the kinematically redundant active prismatic joint variable ranges of a planar parallel mechanism for singularity-free trajectories. Mechanism and Machine Theory 44, 1032–1044 (2009)
2. Dasgupta, B., Mruthyunjaya, T.S.: Force redundancy in parallel manipulators: theoretical and practical issues. Mech. Mach. Theory 33(6), 727–742 (1998)
3. Alberich-Carraminana, M., Garolera, M., Thomas, F., Torras, C.: Partially flagged parallel manipulators: singularity charting and avoidance. IEEE Transactions on Robotics 25(4), 771–784 (2009)
4. Mohamed, M.G., Gosselin, C.M.: Design and analysis of kinematically redundant parallel manipulators with configurable platforms. IEEE Transactions on Robotics 21(3), 277–287 (2005)
5. Lee, H.L., et al.: Optimal design of a five-bar finger with redundant actuation. In: Proc. IEEE Conf. Robotics and Automation, Leuven, Belgium, pp. 2068–2074 (1998)
6. O'Brien, J.F., Wen, J.T.: Redundant actuation for improving kinematic manipulability. In: Proceedings of the 1999 IEEE international Conference on Robotics & Automation, Detroit, Michigan (1999)
7. Abedinnasab, M.H., Vossoughi, G.R.: Analysis of a 6-DOF redundantly actuated 4-legged parallel mechanism. Nonlinear Dyn. 58, 611–622 (2009)

8. Kim, J., Park, F.C., Ryu, S.J., et al.: Design and analysis of a redundantly actuated parallel mechanism for rapid machining. IEEE Transactions on Robotics and Automation 17(4), 423–434 (2001)
9. Takeda, Y., Funabashi, H., Sasaki, Y.: Motion transmissibility of In-Parallel Actuated manipulators. JSME International Journal, Series C 38, 749–755 (1995)
10. Chen, C., Angeles, J.: Generalized transmission index and transmission quality for spatial linkages. Mechanism and Machine Theory 42, 1225–1237 (2007)
11. Wang, J.S., Liu, X.J., Wu, C.: Optimal design of a new spatial 3-DOF parallel robot with respect to a frame-free index. Sci. China Ser. E- Tech. Sci. 52, 986–999 (2009)
12. Wang, J.S., Wu, C., Liu, X.-J.: Performance evaluation of parallel manipulators: Motin/force transmissibility and its index. Mechanism and Machine Theory 45, 1462–1476 (2010)
13. Liu, X.J.: Optimal kinematic design of a three translational DoFs parallel manipulator. Robotica 24, 239–250 (2006)
14. Cha, S.-H., Lasky, T.A., Velinsky, S.A.: Kinematically-redundant variations of the 3-RRR mechanism and local optimization-based singularity avoidance. Mechanics based Design of Structures and Machines 35, 15–38 (2007)
15. Nokleby, S.B., Fisher, R., Podhorodeski, R.P., Firmani, F.: Force capabilities of redundantly-actuated parallel manipulators. Mechanism and Machine Theory 40, 578–599 (2005)
16. Tao, D.C.: Applied linkage synthesis, pp. 7–12. Addison-Wesley, Reading (1964)

# Integrated Structure and Control Design for a Flexible Planar Manipulator

Yunjiang Lou⋆, Yongsheng Zhang, Ruining Huang, and Zexiang Li⋆⋆

School of Mechanical Engineering and Automation
Shenzhen Graduate School, Harbin Institute of Technology
Shenzhen University Town, Xili, Shenzhen, China
`louyj@hitsz.edu.cn`

**Abstract.** Modern industries impose increasingly stringent performance requirements on equipments with very high acceleration and high precision. The integrated design method was proposed as a preferable technique to the traditional one. In this paper, a general framework of the integrated design for a parallel flexible planar linkage is presented. The dynamic model for a multi-link planar linkage with closed chains is derived by the finite element method. The proportional-derivative control strategy is applied in the closed-loop control system. The control parameters and structural parameters are optimized simultaneously by solving the integrated design problem. The differential evolution algorithm, a fast global optimization technique, is used to solve the optimal design problem. Simulation shows the integrated design method gives an over 20% improvement in settling time.

**Keywords:** Integrated design, multibody dynamics, flexible linkage, five-bar mechanism.

## 1   Introduction

Conventional mechanical design involves a sequence of designs performed separately within the structural and control disciplines. The controller design is conducted after a mechanical structure is designed and manufactured. This separated two-step approach has shown its success in various applications. Modern industries, however, impose even demanding requirements on the equipments. For example, the gold wire ball bonder, a crucial automatic equipment for IC (integrated circuit) packaging process, reaches a cycle time of 50 milliseconds with an accuracy of 2 microns for typical gold wires of a length of 2.54 mm [1]. The performance requirements of packaging equipments for the next generation

⋆ This research was supported by NSFC with Grant No. 51075085 and by the National High-Tech Research and Development Program of China (863 Plan, No. 2011AA04A103).
⋆⋆ Prof. Zexiang Li is with the Dept. ECE, the Hong Kong University of Science and Technology, and is also with the Dongguan HUST Manufacturing Engineering Research Institute.

S. Jeschke, H. Liu, and D. Schilberg (Eds.): ICIRA 2011, Part I, LNAI 7101, pp. 260–269, 2011.

IC will be even more stringent. The conventional design process may have difficulty to achieve the increasingly stringent precision requirement and increasingly
high productivity. By observing the coupled effects of structure and control parameters in performance, Maghami et al. [2] first proposed the integrated control
and structure design method. It features a simultaneous optimization of both the
structure and the control design, which can be an effective alternative to improve
the design.

In [2], the authors proposed the integrated design for a flexible spacecraft.
Later, it was generalized to design of a high-performance feed drive system [3],
a compliant two-axes mechanism [4], and a four-bar manipulator [5], etc. In this
paper, we try to apply the integrated design for a much more complicated machine, a flexible planar five-bar linkage.

It is necessary to model the manipulator as a *flexible-link* robotic system so
that the required operational accuracy can be achieved. The robotics systems
with flexible links are continuous dynamic systems characterized by an infinite
number of degrees of freedom and are governed by nonlinear coupled, ordinary
and partial differential equations. Fundamentally there are two methods used
to discretize and truncate the dynamic equations into finite dimensional model,
namely, the assumed modes method (AMM) [6] and the finite element method
(FEM). The AMM is difficult to model a manipulator with irregular shapes,
while the FEM is able to approximate an irregular manipulator in any precision
provided sufficient discretization [7]. For a manipulator link with various shapes
of cross section, the FEM is more suitable than the AMM for the dynamic modeling.

The paper is organized as follows. In section 2, a finite element model of the
linkage system is derived. The closed-chain condition is applied to derive the system dynamics via the Lagrange multiplier method. In section 3, A proportional-
derivative (PD) control strategy is applied to the closed-loop system and the
structural design problem is formulated as an optimization problem. In section
4, a computer simulation shows the result of the integrated design of the five-bar
linkage system. Finally, conclusion is drawn in section 5.

## 2    Dynamic Modeling of a Flexible Five-Bar Linkage

A five-bar linkage is the simplest 2-degree-of-freedom (DOF) parallel mechanism
and is widely used in robot manipulators [8], force reflecting interface [9]. In this
research, a 5R five-bar linkage is used for planar pick-and-place operations, as
shown in Fig. 1. Here, "R" means a revolute joint. The joints of A and E are
active and actuated by motors, while the other 3 joints are passive without
actuation. The end-effector is mounted in C. A coordinate frame is attached to
the midpoint of AE.

### 2.1    Kinetic and Potential Energy of a Five-Bar Linkage

In order to use the Lagrangian formulation to derive the dynamic model, the
first task is to find the kinetic and potential energy of the system. In the FEM,

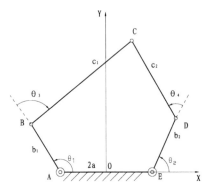

**Fig. 1.** 5R five-bar linkage

a link often is discretized into a finite number of beam elements. To give a clear description of deformation, we need to establish two coordinate frames: the inertia coordinate frame $OXY$ as shown in Fig. 1 and body coordinate frame $oxy$ in Fig. 2. Fig. 3 presents the way to set up other body coordinate frames and links deformation undergoing high velocity motion. The notations are defined in the table 1.

Based on the Bernoulli-Euler beam theory, the link AB is discretized into $n$ beam elements. Let us consider element $j$ between node $j$ and $j+1$. The position vector $p_1$ of any point $P_1$ on the element $j$ can be described as follows.

$$p_1 = \begin{bmatrix} \cos\theta_1 & -\sin\theta_1 \\ \sin\theta_1 & \cos\theta_1 \end{bmatrix} \begin{bmatrix} L_{1j-1} + x_{1j} \\ y_{1j} \end{bmatrix} \tag{1}$$

where $(x_{1j}, y_{1j})$ are the coordinate of $P_1$ with respect to the body frame $o_{1j}x_{1j}y_{1j}$. Note that the assumption of small flexural deformation has been applied in obtaining the coordinate $(L_{1j-1} + x_{1j})$. Therefore, the kinetic energy of the $j$-th element is the following integral.

$$T_{1j} = \frac{1}{2} \int_0^{l_{1j}} \rho A_{1j} \left( \frac{dp_1^T}{dt} \frac{dp}{dt} \right) dx_{1j} \tag{2}$$

Based on FEM theory, the displacement $y_{1j}$ can be approximated using the lateral displacement and slope of the node $i$ and $i+1$ as follows.

$$y_{1j} = [N_{1j}]^T U_{1j} \tag{3}$$

where $U_{1j} = \begin{bmatrix} \theta_1 & u_{1j} & v_{1j} & u_{1j+1} & v_{1j+1} \end{bmatrix}^T$ and $[N_{1j}]$ is the shape function matrix.

By some manipulation, the kinetic energy of the $j$-th element in (2) can thus be expressed as the following form.

$$T_{1j} = \frac{1}{2} \dot{U}_{1j}^T M_{1j} \dot{U}_{1j}^T \tag{4}$$

**Table 1.** Nomenclature

| Notations | Meaning |
|---|---|
| $i$ | the serial number of links $(i = 1, 2, 3, 4)$ |
| $j$ | the serial number of beam elements for each link$(j = 1, 2, n_i)$ |
| $OXY$ | the inertia coordinate frame |
| $o_{ij}x_{ij}y_{ij}$ | the body coordinate frame for element $j$ of link $i$ |
| $L_{ij-1}$ | sum of length of $j-1$ elements of link $i$ |
| $l_{ij}$ | length of element $j$ of link $i$ |
| $\theta_1, \theta_2$ | actuated angles of link AB and DE |
| $\theta_3$ | angle between link AB and BC |
| $\theta_4$ | angle between ED and CD |
| $(u_{ij}, v_{ij})$ | flexural displacement and slope of node $j$ of link $i$ |
| $(u_{ie}, v_{ie})$ | flexural displacement and slope at the end of link $i$ |
| $\tau_1, \tau_2$ | torque for $\theta_1$ and $\theta_2$ |
| $A_{ij}$ | section area of element $j$ of link $i$ |
| $\rho$ | material density |

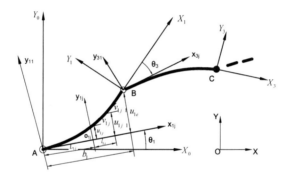

**Fig. 2.** Deformation of link AB, BC undergoing high velocity motion

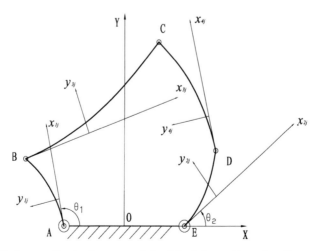

**Fig. 3.** Body coordinate frames and flexible deformation of entire mechanism

where $M_{1j}$ is the element mass matrix, and

$$M_{1j} = \rho A_i \int_0^{l_{1j}} \left( \frac{\partial p_1^T}{\partial U_{1j}} \frac{\partial p_1^T}{\partial U_{1j}} \right) dx_{1j} \tag{5}$$

Therefore, the kinetic energy of link 1 is

$$T_1 = \sum_{j=1}^{n_1} T_{1j} \tag{6}$$

Similarly, the link $i$ with $n_j$ beam elements has corresponding form.
Therefore, the total kinetic energy of five-bar linkage is

$$T = \sum_{j=1}^{n_1} T_{1j} + \sum_{j=1}^{n_2} T_{2j} + \sum_{j=1}^{n_3} T_{3j} + \sum_{j=1}^{n_4} T_{4j} + \sum_{j=1}^{5} T_{hj} + T_p \tag{7}$$

where, $T_{hi}$ is the kinetic energy of joints and $T_p$ the kinetic energy of the payload.

As a planar linage, the gravitational effect can be ignored. The potential energy of the linkage is the elastic potential energy depending only on flexural deformation. And it is independent of rigid body rotation $\theta$. Firstly, potential energy of element $j$ of link $i$ is

$$V_{ij} = \frac{1}{2} U_{ij}^T K_{1j} U_{ij}$$

where $K_{ij} = \begin{bmatrix} 0 & 0 \\ 0 & K_{ij22} \end{bmatrix}$, and $K_{ij22}$ is the element stiffness matrix for Bernoulli-Euler beam, which can be found in any elementary FEM textbook. Thus the potential energy of link i is

$$V_i = \sum_{j=1}^{n_1} V_{ij}$$

Therefore, the total potential of the linkage is

$$V = \sum_{j=1}^{n_1} V_{1j} + \sum_{j=1}^{n_2} V_{2j} + \sum_{j=1}^{n_3} V_{3j} + \sum_{j=1}^{n_4} V_{4j} \tag{8}$$

## 2.2   Boundary and Constraint Conditions

The head end of each link is clamped by the joint. So the boundary conditions can be determined

$$u_{11} = 0, \ v_{11} = 0, \ u_{21} = 0, \ v_{21} = 0, \ u_{31} = 0, v_{31} = 0, \ u_{41} = 0, \ v_{41} = 0.$$

By using the boundary conditions, the vector of generalized coordinate variables are obtained as

$$q = \begin{bmatrix} \theta_1 & \theta_2 & \theta_3 & \theta_4 & q_{1f}^T & q_{2f}^T & q_{3f}^T & q_{4f}^T \end{bmatrix}^T$$

where,

$$q_{if} = \begin{bmatrix} u_{i2} & v_{i2} & \cdots & u_{in_1-1} & v_{in_1-1} & u_{ie} & v_{ie} \end{bmatrix}^T, \ (i = 1, 2, 3, 4)$$

By using the generalized coordinate vector, the kinetic energy and potential energy in (7) and (8) can be summarized as

$$T = \frac{1}{2} \dot{q}^T M \dot{q} \tag{9}$$

$$V = \frac{1}{2} q^T K q \tag{10}$$

where $M$ and $K$ are respectively the total mass matrix and the stiffness matrix, obtained from those individual mass matrix and stiffness matrix.

From Fig. 1, we can see there is a closed loop in the mechanism. The loop is enclosed by two limbs ABC and EDC, which intersection at point C. In the inertia coordinate frame, the closure loop equation can be written as

$$\phi(q) = \begin{bmatrix} \phi_1(q) \\ \phi_2(q) \end{bmatrix} = 0. \tag{11}$$

## 2.3   Dynamic Equation Using Lagrangian Formulation

To deal with constraint condition, Lagrange multiplier $\lambda$ is introduced. By the Lagrangian formulation, the Lagrangian is $L = T - V - \phi^T(q)\lambda$. The dynamic equation is thus obtained as

$$\frac{d}{dt} \frac{\partial L}{\partial \dot{q}_k} - \frac{\partial L}{\partial q_k} = \tau_k, \ k = 1, 2, \cdots, N, \tag{12}$$

where $\tau_k$ is the generalized torque corresponding to the $k$-th generalized coordinate variable. By mathematic manipulation, the dynamic equation becomes

$$\begin{cases} M(q)\ddot{q} + C(q, \dot{q}) + Kq + \phi_q^T(q)\lambda = b\tau \\ \phi(q) = 0 \end{cases} \tag{13}$$

where $\phi_q$ is the Jacobian matrix of constraint condition (11).

The equation set (13) is a typical differential-algebraic equations (DAEs) problem. By differentiating (11) twice, constraint equations originally in terms of displacements are transformed to equations of velocities and accelerations.

Then (13) can be rewritten as

$$\begin{bmatrix} I & 0 & 0 \\ 0 & M(q) & \phi_q^T \\ 0 & \phi_q & 0 \end{bmatrix} \begin{bmatrix} \dot{q} \\ \ddot{q} \\ \lambda \end{bmatrix} = \begin{bmatrix} \dot{q} \\ b\tau - Kq - C(q, \dot{q}) \\ -\dot{\phi}_q(q, \dot{q})\dot{q} \end{bmatrix} \tag{14}$$

Then DAEs has become ODEs. By numerical integration such as Runge-Kutta method, we can solve (14).

# 3    Integrated Design Problem Formulation

## 3.1    Controller, Performance Indices and Design Variables

The PD controller is a simple but effective strategy for point-to-point motions. In practical control systems, the beam flexure is usually not able to be measured on line. The only quantity we can measure real time is the joint angle $\theta$. By difference technique, the velocity $\dot{\theta}$ can be further obtained. The input torque $\tau$ can be determined by the PD controller as follows.

$$\tau = K_p e + K_d \dot{e}, \tag{15}$$

where $e = \theta - \theta_d$, $\dot{e} = \dot{\theta} - \dot{\theta}_d$, and $\theta_d$ and $\dot{\theta}_d$ are the desired joint position and the desired joint angular velocity, respectively. Combined (14) and (15), a closed-loop control system is obtained containing both structural parameters and control parameters $K_p$, $K_d$. Therefore, it enables the determination of structural parameters and control parameters in an unified framework.

In this settings, the demanding requirements of high speed/acceleration and high accuracy for automatic equipments can be translated into requirements on transient and steady-state performance of a control system, which characterize a system in a direct way.

- *Settling time.* Settling time $t_s$ is a critical performance index reflecting rapidness of the system response. It gives a measure on how long it will take for the system response to enter a pre-specified accuracy. The shorter is the settling time, the faster is the response.
- *Overshooting.* In practical equipment, the overshooting $\sigma$ of the manipulator end-tip should be limited to a certain value. However, in order to achieve rapid response, it is inevitable to have an overshooting.
- *Steady-state error.* The performance index of steady-state error $e_{ss}$ is used to characterized accuracy of the system.

In integrated design, both structural and control parameters are optimized simultaneously. In the dynamic model, $A_{ij}$, $l_{ij}$ are structural parameters under determination. Therefore, the indeterminant structural parameters are $A_{ij}, l_{ij}$. Taking $\mathcal{A} = [A_{11}, A_{12}, \cdots A_{1n_1}, A_{21}, \cdots, A_{ij}, \cdots]^T$, $\mathcal{L} = [l_{11}, l_{12}, \cdots, l_{1n_1}, \cdots, l_{ij}, \cdots]^T$ as the vector of cross-section areas and length parameters, the set of design variables $\mathcal{P}$ are the collection of both control parameters and structural parameters as follows.

$$\mathcal{P} = [K_p^T, K_d^T, \mathcal{A}^T, \mathcal{L}^T]^T$$

## 3.2    Problem Formulation

In most industrial processes, productivity of qualified products is the crucial target. Hence, the consuming time for each product unit should be minimized. In our case, the settling time $t_s$ should be minimized to improve productivity. The overshooting should be limited to a certain threshold, and the steady-state error should be constrained to a pre-specified accuracy. Further, actuator torque $\tau$ is limited since actuator saturation exists for each actuator. Those constraints are imposed to guarantee product quality. By the analysis, the optimal (integrated) design problem is formulated as follows.

*Problem 1.* **Integrated design problem**

Find a set of optimal design parameters $\mathcal{P}$ to

$$
\begin{aligned}
&\min_{\mathcal{P}} \quad t_s \\
&\text{subject to } \sigma \leq \sigma_{\max}; \\
&\qquad\qquad e_{ss} \leq e_0; \\
&\qquad\qquad \tau_i \leq \tau_{\max}, \quad i = 1, 2;
\end{aligned}
$$

where $\sigma_{\max}$ is the largest overshooting that the system can tolerate, $e_0$ is the pre-specified steady-state error bound, and $\tau_{\max}$ is the given actuator torque limit.

# 4    Simulation and Discussion

In simulation implementation, the following settings are chosen and determined.

- The beam AB and DE are discretized into 2 elements and for beam BC and beam DC, $j = 3$. The cross section of each element is taken as rectangular shape, for ease of manufacturing. Let $w_{ij}$ be the width and $h_{ij}$ the height of the rectangle, respectively. In implementation, $h_{ij}$, $i = 1, 2$; $j = 1, \cdots, 3$ are fixed to a constant value $h_0$ to simplify the computation. Moreover, to obtain good isotropic capability, the mechanism is designed symmetrically. The beam 1 is identical to the beam 2, and the beam 3 is identical to the beam 4. Therefore, $\mathcal{A} = [w_{11}, w_{12}, w_{21}, w_{22}, w_{23}]^T$.
- By workspace requirement, the link lengths of the symmetric five-bar linkage are given as AB = DE = 0.23 $m$, BC = CD = 0.53 $m$. Further, the length of each beam element is equally divided in each link, i.e., $l_{1j} = 0.23/2 = 0.115$ $m$, $j = 1, 2$; and $l_{2j} = 0.53/3 \approx 0.1767$ $m$, $j = 1, \cdots, 3$.
- In evaluation of the performance indices, step response of point C is used. The settling time is calculated as the time it takes to enter 5% of the desired position.
- The overshooting bound is chosen as $\sigma_{max} = 15\%$, and the fixed beam height is given as $h_0 = 0.02$ $m$.
- The actuator saturation limit is taken as $\tau_{max} = 20$.

Hence, the integrated design problem is realized as follows.

*Problem 2.* **Integrated design problem of the flexible five-bar linkage**

Find a set of parameters $\mathcal{P} = [K_{p1}, K_{p2}, K_{d1}, K_{d2}, w_{11}, w_{12}, w_{21}, w_{22}, w_{23}]$ to

$$\min_{\mathcal{P}} \quad t_s$$
$$\text{subject to} \quad \sigma \le \sigma_{max};$$
$$e_{ss} \le e_0;$$
$$\tau_i \le \tau_{max} = 20, \quad i = 1, 2;$$
$$K_{p1}, K_{p2} \in (0, 400];$$
$$K_{d1}, K_{d2} \in (0, 20].$$

By investigating the integrated design problem 2, it is a nonconvex nonlinear optimization problem. The objective function $t_s$ and the constraints generically do not have analytic closed expression. Furthermore, the optimization problem is generally multi-modal, i.e., there exists multiple local optima in feasible region. A global optimization technique, the differential evolution (DE) algorithm is used to solve the integrated design problem.

**Table 2.** The Initial/Optimum Design and the Corresponding Initial/Optimum Performance

| | $w_{11}(m)$ | $w_{12}(m)$ | $w_{21}(m)$ | $w_{22}(m)$ | $w_{23}(m)$ | $K_{p1}$ | $K_{p2}$ | $K_{d1}$ | $K_{d2}$ | $t_s(s)$ |
|---|---|---|---|---|---|---|---|---|---|---|
| Initial | 0.02 | 0.02 | 0.02 | 0.02 | 0.02 | 150 | 150 | 5 | 5 | 0.153 |
| Optimum | 0.034 | 0.017 | 0.024 | 0.02 | 0.008 | 127 | 161 | 4.57 | 5.84 | 0.120 |

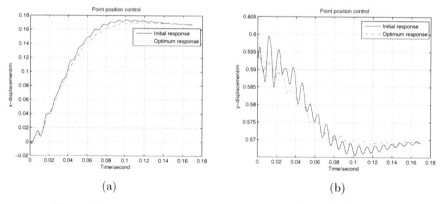

(a)                                        (b)

**Fig. 4.** The step responses: (a) in X-direction; (b) in Y-direction

There are applications that the manipulator is expected to move from one point to another point routinely. For this task, the end-effector is controlled to move from the home position $(0, 0.5927)$ to the desired position $(0.1668, 0.5697)$. By the close-loop model ,we can thus compute the dynamic response in $x$, $y$ directions, and determine settling time, overshooting, steady-state error accordingly. Starting from the initial design in Table 2, the DE algorithm reaches the optimum parameters,as shown in Table 2. Fig. 4 shows the dynamic response in $x$, $y$ directions of the initial and the optimum system. The optimum system gives improved performance on the critical index, settling time. The settling time of the initial system is 0.153 second while that of the optimum system is 0.120 second. This shows an improvement of over 20% compared with the initial design.

## 5    Conclusion

In the paper, the integrated design method is introduced to design a flexible five-bar parallel manipulator. The finite element method (FEM) is applied to derive system dynamic model. A PD control strategy is used in the closed-loop system. Typical control system performance indices, settling time, overshooting, and steady-state error, are considered as the design objective and major design constraints. The integrated design problem is then formulated as a nonlinear, multimodal optimization problem and the DE algorithm is used to locate the global optimum. The simulation shows that the integrated design method provides an obvious performance improvement for the five-bar linkage system.

## References

1. IConn,High Performance Wire Bonder,
   http://www.kns.com/UPLOADFILES/DGALLERY/ICONNSEPT%2009.PDF
   (access time: April 30, 2011)
2. Maghami, P., Joshi, S., Lim, K.: Integrated controls-structures designs: a practical design tool for modern spacecraft. In: Proceedings of the American Control Conference, pp. 1465–1473 (1991)
3. Chung, S.-C., Kim, M.-S.: A systematic approach to design highperformance feed drive systems. International Journal of Machine Tools & Manufacture 45(12-13), 1421–1435 (2005)
4. Rieber, J.M., Taylor, D.G.: Integrated control system and mechanical design of a compliant two-axes mechanism. Mechatronics 14, 1069–1087 (2004)
5. Wu, F.X., Zhang, W.J., Li, Q., Ouyang, P.R.: Integrated design and pd control of high-speed closed-loop mechanisms. Transactions of ASME, Journal of Dynamic Systems, Measurement, and Control 124, 522–528 (2002)
6. De Luca, A., Siciliano, B.: Closed-form dynamic model of planar multilink lightweight robots. IEEE Transactions on Systems, Man, and Cybernetics 21(4), 826–839 (1991)
7. Theodore, R.J., Ghosal, A.: Comparison of the assumed modes and finite element models for flexible multi-link manipulators. The International Journal of Robotics Research 14(2), 91–111 (1995)
8. Nenchev, D.N., Uchiyama, M.: A five-bar parallel manipulator with singularity-perturbed design. Mechanism and Machine Theory 33(5), 453–462 (1998)
9. Salcudeam, S.E., Stocco, L.: Isotropy and actuator optimization in haptic interface design. In: Proceedings of the IEEE International Conference on Robotics & Automation, San Francisco, pp. 763–769 (2000)

# Effects of Clearance on Dynamics
# of Parallel Indexing Cam Mechanism

Zongyu Chang[1], Lixin Xu[2], Yuhu Yang[3], Zhongqiang Zheng[1], and Tongqing Pan[1]

[1] Engineering College, Ocean University of China, Qingdao, 266100
[2] Mechanical Engineering College, Tianjin University of Technology and Education,
Tianjin, 300072
[3] Mechanical Engineering College, Tianjin University, Tianjin, 300072

**Abstract.** Indexing cam mechanisms are widely used in some kinds of light-industry machineries. They have great effects on dynamic performance of the machines. Some faults like clearance can not only worsen dynamic properties but also damage key components in the machines. This paper studies the dynamics of indexing cam mechanism with clearance fault between roller and cam. By using unilateral contact model clearance between roller and cam is modeled based on their physical characteristics. Then, dynamic model is developed of parallel indexing cam system with output shaft and rotary table. Numerical integration method is used to solve the differential equations, and the responses of parallel indexing cam mechanism considering clearance are obtained and analyzed. According to the result, reasons for impulse vibration on turret are mesh impacts when number of meshing roller changes in parallel indexing cam mechanism with clearance. Effects on response of turret and rotary table are investigated with increasement of clearance .This work will be helpful for fault diagnosis of indexing cam system.

**Keywords:** Indexing Cam Mechanism, Unilateral contact model, Clearance, Dynamics Analysis.

## 1 Introduction

Due to the requirements of high loading capacity, low noise, low vibration and high reliability, indexing cam mechanisms are widely used in automated machines, like food, medicine, beverage packaging machines and so on. As the "heart" of automated machine, quality of indexing cam mechanism has key effects on properties of whole machineries. Some fault factors like clearance, surface defects can not only cause serious vibration and noise, but also deteriorate the dynamic characteristic of indexing cam mechanism and result in failure of whole system. In the field of dynamics of indexing cam mechanism with clearance, lots of research work has been done. Jones [1] discussed that clearance affects the response and properties of in intermittent mechanism like Geneva mechanism. Xiao [2] summarized the research trends of dynamics of cam mechanism and pointed out that contact between roller and cam surface is one of the most important problems in study of dynamics of indexing cam mechanism and multibody flexible dynamic theory is an effective tool for modelling

S. Jeschke, H. Liu, and D. Schilberg (Eds.): ICIRA 2011, Part I, LNAI 7101, pp. 270–280, 2011.
© Springer-Verlag Berlin Heidelberg 2011

indexing cam mechanism. Koster [3], Shen and Yang [4], He[5] and Chang[6] developed dynamic model of roller cam mechanism and simulate the response. Chang [6] attempted explaining mechanism of effects of clearance on dynamic mechanism by dynamic analysis, and found that effects of clearance on response of turret are more serious than on rotary table. However until now dynamics model on indexing cam mechanism with clearance is based on motion rule of cam. This model can't affect the exact meshing situation between roller and cam.

In this paper, dynamics analysis of indexing cam mechanism is studied according to contact model between roller and indexing cam. Firstly profile of indexing cam is generated by applying Exponential Product Formula. Then by applying unilateral contact method clearance model and dynamic model of parallel indexing cam with clearance are developed. Numerical integration is applied to obtain the responses. Through the numerical results we analyze effects of clearance on dynamics response and the reasons for impact vibration on turret. It provides basis for obtaining the fault characteristic of indexing cam and implementing dynamic model-based fault diagnosis.

# 2    Modelling Indexing Cam Mechanism

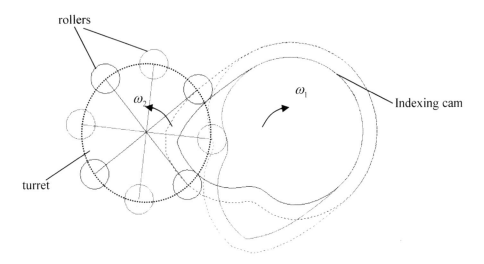

**Fig. 1.** Scheme of parallel indexing cam mechanism

## 2.1    Profile of Parallel Indexing Cam Based on Exponential Product Formula

The basic structure of parallel indexing cam mechanism is shown in Fig. 1. Profile of parallel indexing cam can be generated by the method of Exponential Product Formula. The general frame is built in Fig. 2, in which origin of frame is located in center of turret, axis $z$ is the rotation direction of turret and axis $x$ is defined as line from center of turret to cam center. In order to describe the motion of parallel indexing cam, skew is defined by rotation vector and coordinate of any point in rotation axis. The skew parameters are shown as table 1.

**Table 1.** Main Parameter of Product of exponential Formula for parallel indexing cam mechanism

| description | axis of turret | | axis of cam | | axis of  roller | |
|---|---|---|---|---|---|---|
| | Axis vector $\omega_1$ | A point coordinate in this axis $q_1$ | Axis vector $\omega_2$ | A point coordinate in this axis $q_2$ | Axis vector $\omega_r$ | A point coordinate in this axis $q_r$ |
| Value | $(0\ 0\ 1)^T$ | $(0\ 0\ 0)^T$ | $(0\ 0\ 1)^T$ | $(a\ 0\ 0)^T$ | $(0\ 0\ 1)^T$ | $(r\ 0\ 0)^T$ |

where $a$ is the center distance between cam axis and turret axis; $r$ is the radius of roller in turret.

Suppose $A_f(0)$ is a point in the center line of a roller, and its coordinate is

$$A_f(0) = (r_1\quad 0\quad 0)^T$$

According to exponential product formula and screw theory initial cam theoretical profile $A_c(\theta_1,\theta_2)$ can be obtained by following equation

$$e^{\hat{\xi}_1(\theta_{10}+\theta_1)}A_f(0) = e^{\hat{\xi}_2\theta_2}A_c(\theta_1,\theta_2) \tag{1}$$

Where $\theta_1$ is rotation angle of turret, $\theta_2$ is rotation angular of cam, $\xi_1$, $\xi_2$ are skew value of turret and cam shaft.

$$\xi_1 = \begin{bmatrix} -\omega_1 \times q_1 \\ \omega_1 \end{bmatrix} = (0\quad 0\quad 0\quad 0\quad 0\quad 1)^T ; \tag{2}$$

$$\xi_2 = \begin{bmatrix} -\omega_2 \times q_2 \\ \omega_2 \end{bmatrix} = (0\quad 0\quad -a\quad 0\quad 0\quad 1)^T . \tag{3)}$$

Where $\omega_1$, $\omega_2$ are angular velocity of turret and cam; $q_1$, $q_2$ are coordinates of points on cam axis and turret axis.

$$q_1 = (0\quad 0\quad 0)^T ; \quad q_2 = (a\quad 0\quad 0)^T$$

According to meshing relationship between turret center and cam profile, the theoretic profile of indexing cam $A_f(\theta_1,\theta_2)$ is

$$A_c(\theta_1,\theta_2) = (e^{\hat{\xi}_2\theta_2})^{-1}e^{\hat{\xi}_1\theta_1}A_f(0)$$

$$= \begin{bmatrix} \cos\theta_1\cos\theta_2 & -\sin\theta_1\cos\theta_2 & -\sin\theta_2 & -a\cos\theta_2 + a \\ \sin\theta_1 & \cos\theta_1 & 0 & 0 \\ \cos\theta_1\sin\theta_2 & \sin\theta_1\sin\theta_2 & \cos\theta_2 & -a\sin\theta_2 \\ 0 & 0 & 0 & 1 \end{bmatrix} A_f(0) \tag{4}$$

Then the geometry model can be derived as Fig. 3.

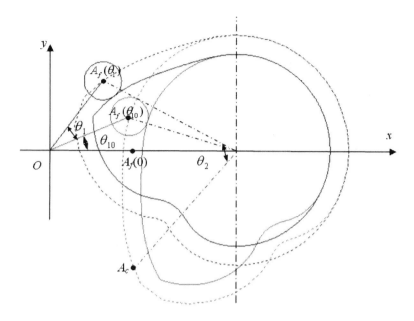

**Fig. 2.** Structure of kinematic analysis of parallel indexing cam mechanism

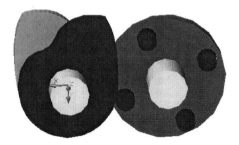

**Fig. 3.** Geometry of Parallel Indexing Cam Mechanism

## 2.2    Unilateral Contact Model and Clearance Model

In one automated machinery indexing cam system is combined by motor, indexing cam, roller and turret and rotary table as Fig. 4. Contact between cam and rollers of turret is the key factor affecting the system performance and is dealt by Unilateral contact model.

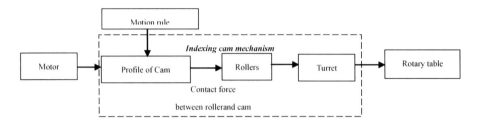

**Fig. 4.** Structure of indexing cam System

Unilateral contact model denotes a mechanical constraint which prevents penetration between two bodies. For parallel indexing cam mechanism, clearance between rollers and cam profile can be divided into three situations: Fig. 5 (a) presents that roller penetrated into cam profile, contact force is defined by complaint distance and curvature radius, roller radio, material property, oil film thick between roller and cam; (b) presents roller contract with roller justly. In his case, no compliant exist between the two ones and so no force generate. (c) Means that roller is separating with cam profile. No contact and no force exist. So we can obtain the unilateral contact model.

$$F_c = \begin{cases} f(\Delta, \rho_1, \rho_2, K_c, K_o) & \Delta > 0 \\ 0 & \Delta \le 0 \end{cases} \tag{5}$$

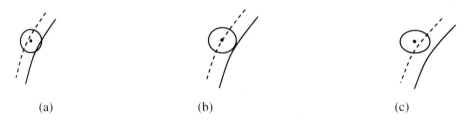

(a)                              (b)                              (c)

**Fig. 5.** Relative Positions between Cam Profile and Roller

Contact force can be calculated by stiffness and displacement based on Hertz law if compliance between two bodies exists. The relationship between contact normal force and contact displacement is shown as follows.

$$P = k\delta^{\frac{3}{2}} \tag{6}$$

Where 
$$k = \sqrt{\frac{16RE^2}{9}}$$

$$\frac{1}{R} = \frac{1}{R_1} + \frac{1}{R_2}, \quad \frac{1}{E} = \frac{(1-\mu_1^2)}{E_1} + \frac{(1-\mu_2)^2}{E_2}$$

$\mu_1$, $\mu_2$ are the Poisson's ratio of two cam and rollers; $E_1$, $E_2$ are Young's Modulus of two bodies, $R_1$, $R_2$ are curvature radius of contacting surface of two bodies.

More generally, normal contact force between cam and roller can be written as

$$P = k\delta^{\mathrm{e}} \tag{7}$$

Where stiffness value $k$ and force exponential value $e$ can be determined by material characteristics and geometry dimensions [13].

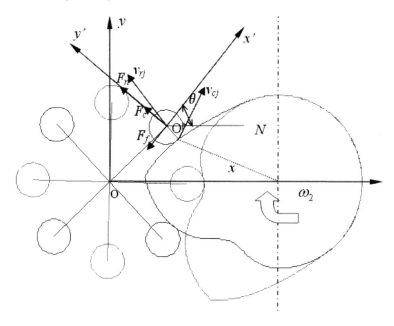

**Fig. 6.** Unilateral Contact Model in Parallel Indexing Cam Mechanism

Normal contact force $\vec{F}_{21n}$, damping force $\vec{F}_{21c}$ and friction force $\vec{F}_{21f}$ should be considered between cam1 and turret 2 during contact process. So the total contact force is

$$\vec{F}_{21} = \vec{F}_{21n} + \vec{F}_{21c} + \vec{F}_{21f} = P\vec{y}' + c\dot{\Delta}\vec{y}' - \mu P\vec{x}' \tag{8}$$

Where $c$ is the damping ratio, and $\mu$ is the friction coefficient.

According to kane equation, the differential equation of turret can be written as

$$I\ddot{\phi} + \sum_{i=1}^{6}(F_{ci}l_{ci} + F_{di}l_{di} + F_{fi}l_{fi}) = 0 \tag{9}$$

Where     $I$ is inertia of turret,

$\phi$ is angular displacement of turret,

$i$ presents the $i$th roller,

$F_{ci}$ is contact force of roller $i$,

$F_{di}$ is damping force of roller $i$,

$F_{fi}$ is friction force of roller $i$.

Integrate with other dof equation we can obtained whole system dynamics equation (6).

## 3    Simulation of Parallel Indexing Cam Mechanism with Clearance

### 3.1    Dynamics Response

According to clearance model, motion equations of parallel indexing cam mechanism are developed with clearance between roller and cam. The motion rule of cam is modified sine motion, speed of input cam shaft is 600r/min. The magnitude of clearance is supposed 0.01mm. By using numerical integration, the response of angular velocities and angular acceleration on turret and rotary table are shown in Fig. 7 and Fig. 8 individually.

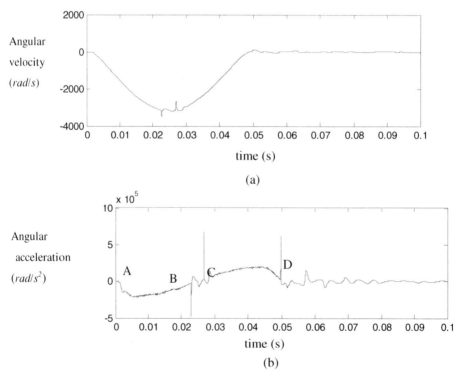

**Fig. 7.** Angular velocity and acceleration response on turret

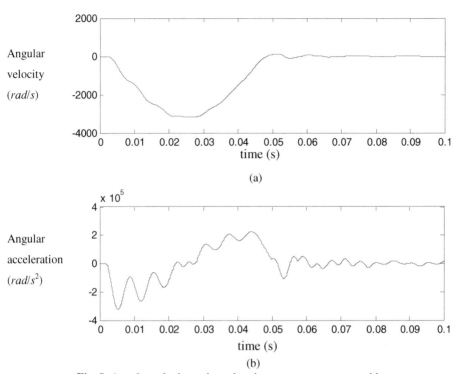

(a)

(b)

**Fig. 8.** Angular velocity and acceleration response on rotary table

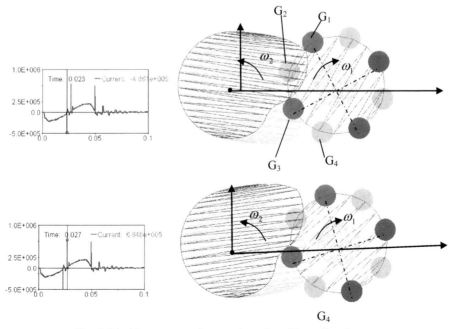

**Fig. 9.** Meshing process when number of meshing roller changes

From the results impulse occurs in the position B, C and D. Then we discuss the reason for the impulse vibration on turret. Fig. 9 showed position of indexing cam and turret when impulse vibrations occur. In fig 9(a) one roller exit meshing while two other rollers are meshing with two cams. In fig 10(b) roller enter meshing and three rollers are meshing with cams.

From the results clearance and contact play an important role in process of meshing. When meshing enter meshing or exit meshing the impulse impact exist in system. This is to say, the reason for impact vibration is that change of number of meshing rollers is changing. Table 2 presents that position of rollers and change of number of meshing rollers.

**Table 2.** Meshing relationship between rollers and cam

|  | Angle of roller G1(°) | Angle of roller G2(°) | Angle of roller G3(°) | Angle of roller G4(°) | Change of Roller No. in Meshing |
|---|---|---|---|---|---|
| Before B | 22.54 | -22.46 | -67.46 | -112.46 | |
| B | 61.18 | 16.18 | -28.82 | -73.82 | G1, G2, G3→G2, G3 |
| C | 73.41 | 28.41 | -16.59 | -61.59 | G2, G3 →G2, G3, G4 |
| D | 112.5 | 67.5 | 22.5 | -22.5 | G2, G3, G4→G3, G4 |

## 3.2    Effects of Change of Clearance on Responses of Turret and Rotary Table

Changing the magnitude of clearance between roller and indexing cam, effects of clearance on response of indexing cam mechanism are obtained. Fig 10 illustrates that the change of maximum acceleration response on turret and rotary table.

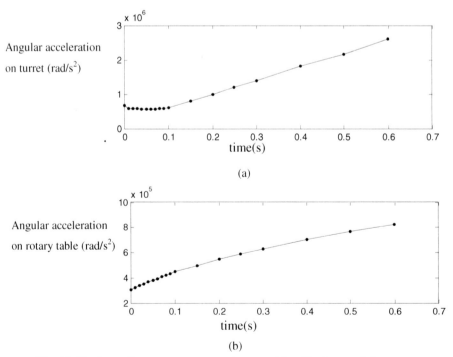

(a)

(b)

**Fig. 10.** Maximum Response on turret and rotary table with change of clearance

From Fig. 10(a) Maximum response of angular acceleration on turret keep nearly constant when clearance is 0—0.06mm; and when clearance is larger than 0.06mm, maximum response increases with clearance. Especially when clearance is larger than 0.2mm, the increasement of response is very obvious. And in rotary table, the angular acceleration is increasing generally with clearance as Fig. 10(b). These results suggest that in some case suitable clearance should be set in design and manufacture of parallel indexing cam mechanism.

# 4    Conclusion

In this paper dynamic model of parallel indexing cam mechanism with clearance fault is developed based on unilateral contact model. Numerical technique is used to solve the motion equations. According to the results clearance has a significant effect on response of output components. Comparing with rotary table, response of turret is more serious than on rotary table from clearance. In addition, when clearance is small (from 0mm to 0.001 mm) effects of clearance on turret is very small and the response increase very little with the increasement of clearance. Through the simulation of dynamics simulation of parallel indexing cam mechanism, we found the reason for impulse impact comes from changing of number of meshing.

**Acknowledgements.** This research was funded by the National Science Research Council of China, (No. 50605060). The author is also grateful for the help and discussion of Changmi Xu and Yi Cao.

# References

1. Jones, J.R.: Cams and Cam Mechanisms. Mechanical Engineering Publication Ltd. (1978)
2. Xiao, Z., Xiong, D.: Problems in the Frontier of Dynamics Analysis of Cam Mechanisms. Mechanical Science and Technology (4), 59–64 (1994)
3. Koster, M.P.: Vibration of Cam Mechanism. McMillan, London (1974)
4. Shen, Y., Yang, Y.: Dynamic Analysis of Indexing Cam Mechanism with Clearances. Mechanical Science and Technology 20(5), 714–715 (2001)
5. He, W., Hu, Y.: Nonlinear Dynamic Characteristics of Roller Gear Cam Mechanism. Chinese Journal of Mechanical Engineering 36(11), 33–38 (2000)
6. Chang, Z., Zhang, C., Yang, Y.: Dynamic Modeling of Roller Gear Cam Mechanism Using Multibody Method. Chinese Journal of Mechanical Engineering 37(3), 34–37 (2001)
7. Chang, Z., Zhang, C., et al.: A Study on Dynamics of Roller Gear Cam Mechanism Considering Clearances. Mechanism and Machine Theory 36(1), 143–152 (2001)
8. Pfeiffer, F.: Unilateral problems of dynamics. Archive of Applied Mechanics 69, 503–527 (1999)
9. Bottasso, C.L., Trainelli, L.: Implementation of Effective Procedures for Unilateral Contact Modeling in Multibody Dynamics. Mechanics Research Communications 28(3), 233–246 (2001)
10. Hippmann, G.: An Algorithm for Compliant Contact Between Complexly Shaped Bodies. Multibody System Dynamics 12, 345–362 (2004)

11. Yang, Y., Zhang, C.: Study on Profile Modification of Roller Gear Cam Mechanism. Journal of Tianjin University 28(4), 497–502 (1995)
12. Chang, Z., Xu, C.: A General Framework for Geometry Design of Indexing Cam Mechanism. Mechanism and Machine Theory 44(1), 2079–2084 (2009)
13. Fan, C., Xiong, G., Zhou, M.: Application and Improvement of Virtual Prototype Software MSC. ADAMS. Machine Industrial Press (2006)

# Design and Compliance Experiment Study
# of the Forging Simulator

Pu Zhang, Zhenqiang Yao, Zhengchun Du, Hao Wang, and Haidong Yu

The State Key Lab of Mechanical System and Vibration,
Shanghai Jiao Tong University, Shanghai 200240
{zhe,zqyao,zcdu,wanghao}@sjtu.edu.cn

**Abstract.** Force capability and compliance capability is the core performance of heavy forging manipulator, therefore the testing and calibration of heavy forging manipulator's these capabilities is very important. This paper presents a new forging simulator for the testing and calibration of heavy forging manipulator. The simulator has a good force capability and can reproduce working environment of forging manipulator by simulating force and movement. In this paper, firstly, a 2-DOF parallel planar mechanism is designed as the forging simulator based on the FEM simulation and kinematics analysis, and the optimal work space of the mechanism is obtained based on the dexterity, force capability and stiffness performance index. Secondly, the whole forging simulator platform is introduced, which includes the forging manipulator, the heavy force/moment sensor and the forging simulator. Finally, the compliance experiment of the simulator is done, the results show that the whole forging simulator platform is an effective approach for the testing and calibration of the heavy forging manipulator.

**Keywords:** Forging manipulator, Parallel mechanism, Force capability, Compliance.

## 1    Introduction

Force capability and compliance capability is the core performance of heavy forging manipulator, especially the passive compliance capability in clamp's axial is critical for protecting the forging manipulator's body[1], the bad compliance capability of forging manipulator will lead to serious accidents, such as the capsizing of forging manipulator, the fracture of manipulator clamp, the nonconformity of forging blank and so on, therefore the testing and calibration of heavy forging manipulator's force capacity and compliance capability is very important. Figure 1 shows the working environment of forging manipulator, and Figure 2 shows the fracture of manipulator clamp as a result of unsuitable compliance capability.

Heavy forging manipulator mainly depends on import at present in our country, correlative research has just begun, and the relevant content of testing and calibration for forging manipulator has not reported in the world. There are many cases about testing and calibration for the other equipments, such as: Zengxiang Fu [2] calibrated

S. Jeschke, H. Liu, and D. Schilberg (Eds.): ICIRA 2011, Part I, LNAI 7101, pp. 281–290, 2011.

the heavy press's force capability by forging specimens and found the best force capability through the specimens' stress-strain relationship; Yonggang Lin [3] built a pitch-controlled wind turbine system to test the electro-hydraulic actuator's performance; Hehua Zhu [4] used the soil box to simulate a variety of soil conditions, accordingly tested the shield's ground adaptability; Tongli Chang [5] built a HIL ground experiment simulator for testing the on-orbit docking mechanism. Literature [2] only calibrated the heavy press's force capability, but literatures [3-5] reproduced the working environment by experimental methods to testing a variety of performances of the equipments, therefore they enlighten us a new approach for the testing and calibration of the heavy forging manipulator.

**Fig. 1.** The working environment of forging manipulator

**Fig. 2.** The fracture of forging manipulator clamp

The rest of this paper is organized as follows: In Section 2, a 2-DOF parallel planar mechanism will be designed as the forging simulator based on the FEM simulation and kinematics analysis, and the optimal work space of the mechanism will be obtained based on the dexterity, force capability and stiffness performance index. In Section 3, the whole forging simulator platform will be introduced. In Section 4, the compliance experiment of the forging simulator will be introduced. Section 5 states the conclusions.

## 2    Design of the Forging Simulator

Analysis of forging compliance process is the basis of designing forging simulator. Wurong Wang and Kai Zhao et al [6] present the forging manipulator's kinematics and dynamics simulation in the rounding process of a long shaft. The results shows that the forging manipulator's clamp endures the deformation resistance in active compliance and passive compliance directions, force capability and compliance capability of forging manipulator in passive compliance direction is especially important.

Parallel mechanisms have been used more and more extensive because of characteristics of high rigidity, strong capacity, high precision and compact structure, therefore combined with analysis of forging compliance process we design a kind of parallel mechanism as the forging simulator to reproduce working environment by simulating force and movement of the forging blank.

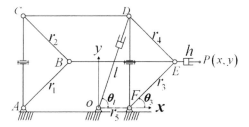

**Fig. 3.** 2-DOF parallel mechanism

As shown in figure 3, the 2-DOF parallel mechanism combines sarrut parallel mechanism with parallelogram mechanism. The fixed platform of parallel mechanism is AF, the movable platform is BP, and the end effector is the point P. The driving cylinder OD and EP make the platform BP move with 2-DOF by changing the length $l$、$h$ of cylinders.

## 2.1    Kinematic Analysis

The coordinate system is fixed to the platform AF, as shown in figure 3, $\overline{AB} = r_1$, $\overline{BC} = r_2$, $\overline{DE} = r_3$, $\overline{EF} = r_4$, $\overline{OF} = r_5$, $\overline{OD} = l$, $\overline{EP} = h$, $r_1 = r_2 = r_3 = r_4$, $\angle FOD = \theta_1$, $\angle XFE = \theta_3$, $\theta_1$、$\theta_3 \in (0 , \pi/2)$, $P = \{x, y\}^T$, the kinematics equation is:

$$\begin{cases} x = r_5 + \dfrac{\sqrt{4r_3^2 + r_5^2 - l^2(t)}}{2} + h(t) \\ y = \dfrac{\sqrt{l^2(t) - r_5^2}}{2} \end{cases} \tag{1}$$

The velocity Jacobian matrix is obtained as equation (2) from derivation of equation (1):

$$J = \begin{cases} 1 & -\varphi(\theta_1)\tan\theta_3 \\ 0 & \varphi(\theta_1) \end{cases} \tag{2}$$

In the equation (2), $\varphi(\theta_1) = \dfrac{1}{2\sin\theta_1} = \dfrac{\sqrt{4y^2 + r_5^2}}{4y}$, $\tan\theta_3 = \dfrac{y}{\sqrt{r_3^2 - y^2}}$.

Considering the ideal plane, force Jacobian matrix is:

$$G = \left(J^{-1}\right)^T = \begin{Bmatrix} 1 & 0 \\ \tan\theta_3 & 2\sin\theta_1 \end{Bmatrix} \tag{3}$$

## 2.2    Performance Analysis

The forging simulator is used to reproduce working environment by simulating force and movement of the forging blank, so it must has good performances including dexterity, force capability and stiffness performance, and an optimal work space of the mechanism should be obtained based on the performance analysis.

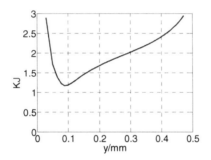

**Fig. 4.** Curve of the Jacobian's condition number

### 2.2.1    Dexterity Analysis

The condition number of Jacobian matrix is dexterity performance index of parallel mechanism [7], [8], [9], the condition number of this mechanism is:

$$\kappa_J = \|J\| \cdot \|J^{-1}\| \tag{4}$$

In the equation (4), $\|\bullet\|$ is arbitrary norm of matrix, usually taking Euclidean norm, $\|J\| = \sqrt{\lambda_{\max}(J^T J)}$, $1 \leq K_J < \infty$, if $K_J$ is smaller, dexterity and control accuracy will be better.

From equation (2), (4), we can know that the condition number of Jacobian matrix is decided by variable $y$. Figure 4 shows the curve of the Jacobian's condition number, minimum condition number is 1.17 when $y = 0.09\,$mm and condition number is between 1 and 2.5 when $y = 0.05 - 0.42$mm, where is the optimal condition number area.

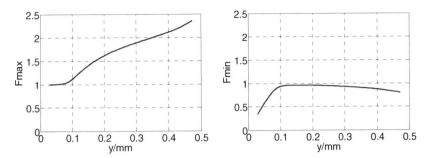

**Fig. 5.** Curve of the force capability index

### 2.2.2    Force Capability Analysis

Force capacity extremes are used to evaluate the force capacity of parallel mechanism in the work space, this parallel mechanism's maximum and minimum force capacity indexes [10] are:

$$F_{max} = \sqrt{\lambda_{F_{max}}\left(G^T G\right)} = \sigma_{F_{max}}(G) \tag{5}$$

$$F_{min} = \sqrt{\lambda_{F_{min}}\left(G^T G\right)} = \sigma_{F_{min}}(G) \tag{6}$$

In the equation (5), (6), $G$ is the force Jacobian matrix, $\lambda_{F_{max}}$, $\lambda_{F_{min}}$ are the Maximum and minimum eigenvalues of matrix $G^T G$, if $F_{max}$, $F_{min}$ are bigger, force capacity of the parallel mechanism will be better.

From equation (3), (5), (6), we can know that the force capacity index is decided by variable $y$. Figure 5 shows the curve of the force capacity index, parallel mechanism has a good force capacity performance when $0.1 < y < 0.4$ mm, force capacity performance will be better if variable $y$ is bigger in this area.

### 2.2.3    Stiffness Analysis

The end deformation extremes are used to evaluate the stiffness performance of parallel mechanism in the work space, this parallel mechanism's maximum and minimum stiffness performance indexes [10] are:

$$D_{max} = \sqrt{\lambda_{D_{max}}\left(C^T C\right)} = \sigma_{D_{max}}(C) \tag{7}$$

$$D_{min} = \sqrt{\lambda_{D_{min}}\left(C^T C\right)} = \sigma_{D_{min}}(C) \tag{8}$$

In the equation (7), (8), $C$ is the flexibility matrix, $C = JJ^T$, $\lambda_{D_{max}}$, $\lambda_{D_{min}}$ are the maximum and minimum eigenvalues of matrix $C^T C$, if $D_{max}$, $D_{min}$ are smaller, stiffness performance of the parallel mechanism will be better.

From equation (2), (7), (8), we can know that the stiffness performance index is decided by variable $y$. Figure 6 shows the curve of the stiffness performance index, parallel mechanism has a good stiffness performance when $0.1 < y < 0.4$ mm, stiffness performance will be better if variable $y$ is bigger in this area.

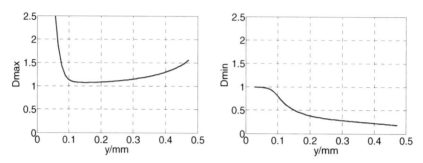

**Fig. 6.** Curve of the stiffness performance index

## 2.3    Optimal Work Space

Based on the dexterity, force capability and stiffness performance index analysis, we can get the optimal work space: $0.1 \leq y \leq 0.4$ mm.

# 3    Building of Forging Simulator Platform

The Figure 8 shows the whole forging simulator platform, which includes the forging manipulator, the six-axis force/moment sensor and the forging simulator.

The forging manipulator's specification is 150KN/300KNm, and the six-axis force/moment sensor's specification is 200KN/400KNm. As shown in Figure 7, the above 2-DOF parallel mechanism is designed as the forging manipulator. The forging simulator combines sarrut parallel mechanism with parallelogram mechanism, therefore it has a good force capability and can reproduce working environment of forging manipulator by simulating force and movement in two directions. In particular, as shown in Figure 7, a redundantly actuated mechanism is applied in forging simulator as the horizontal drive, which has advancements in force distribution and motion stability. The forging simulator drove by electric cylinders includes control system, power system, and mechanical system. The overall size of the forging simulator is 3.0m × 1.5m × 1.0m, and the maximum vertical velocity is 0.1m/s, the maximum vertical displacement is 0.25m, the maximum vertical force is 50KN; the maximum horizontal velocity is 0.12m/s, the maximum horizontal displacement is 0.25m, the maximum force is 76 KN.

The idea of reproduce working environment by the forging simulator platform is: first of all we can get the blank's deformation rule in the forging process by CAE software (ABAQUS, DEFORM, etc.), and then the control system changes the blank's deformation rule into every cylinder's force, displacement control signals, so cylinders can drive the mechanical system with 2 DOF to simulate force and movement of the forging blank, finally force and motion is transmitted to the forging manipulator for testing and calibration.

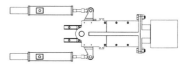

Fig. 7. The forging simulator

Fig. 8. The forging simulator platform

## 4    Compliance Experiment Study of the Forging Simulator

The Figure 8 shows the scene of compliance experiment of the forging simulator platform. Two experiments are done to test and calibrate the forging manipulator, which are: 1) the calibration of the overflow valve's value; 2) the reproducing of forging process.

### 4.1    Calibration of the Overflow Valve's Value

The Calibration of the overflow valve's value is the basis of compliance performance test. The Figure 9 shows the calibration experiment's result, we can know that there is error between the actual value and the theoretical value under 6.5MPa, and the actual value of the overflow value is smaller than the theoretical value; there is less error between the two above 6.5MPa.

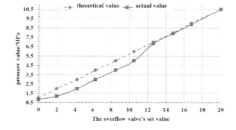

Fig. 9. The calibration of the overflow valve's value

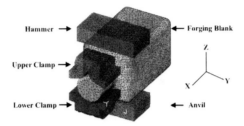

**Fig. 10.** The model of drawing process for quadrangle forging blank

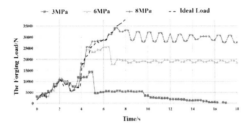

**Fig. 11.** The load of the clamp in horizontal direction

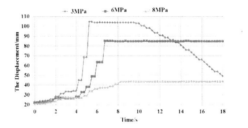

**Fig. 12.** The displacement of the clamp in horizontal direction

## 4.2    Reproducing of Forging Process

The drawing process for a quadrangle forging blank in steelworks is taken as an example in the experiment. As the Figure 10, the quadrangle blank weighs about 3 $\times 10^3$Kg, in the process, the hammer presses downward by 20 mm. We can test the forging manipulator's force capability and compliance capability in different overflow valve values (3MPa, 6MPa and 8MPa) by simulating force and movement in horizontal direction.

The Figure 11, 12 shows the load and displacement of the clamp in the experiment. We can know that the forging manipulator avoids the appearance of the peak force in three conditions (3MPa, 6MPa, and 8MPa) by overflowing, and when the valve value is between 0 to 4MPa the clamp's displacement has been very long at overflowing time and will be longer after overflowing because of the oil compressibility. Low stiffness of forging manipulator in horizontal direction will impact the forging blank's quality, so we suggest that the valve value should be set to 4 ~ 8MPa, which can protect the body of forging manipulator and guaranteed the quality of forging blank.

### 4.3    Conclusion of Experiments

The experiments calibrated the horizontal compliance system of the forging manipulator and tested the force capability and compliance capability in forging process. The experiment results show that it's necessary to test and calibrate the heavy forging manipulator and considering the forging safety and quality the valve value should be set to 4 ~ 8MPa .

## 5    Conclusion

In this paper, a parallel mechanism with a good force capability performance is designed as the forging simulator based on the forging process analysis, to reproduce working environment by simulating force and movement of the forging blank, and the optimal work space of the mechanism is obtained based on the dexterity, force capability and stiffness performance index. Then the whole forging simulator platform is built, which includes the forging manipulator, the heavy force/moment sensor and the forging simulator. Finally, the compliance experiment of the simulator is done, the results show that the whole forging simulator platform is an effective approach for the testing and calibration of the heavy forging manipulator.

**Acknowledgements.** The research is supported by National Basic Research Program of China (973 Program) under research grant No.2006CB705400.

## References

1. Wang, H., Zhao, K., Chen, G.: Energy Distribution Index for robot manipulators and its application to buffering capability evaluation. Science in China Series E: Technological Sciences 54(2), 457–470 (2011)
2. Fu, Z., Wang, H., Su, S.: The importance and key techniques for load/energy calibration of forging equipment with large capacity. Mechanical Science and Technology (6), 890–891 (2001)
3. Lin, Y., Xu, L., Li, W., et al.: Semi-physical simulation test-bed for electro-hydraulic proportional pitch-controlled wind turbine system. China Mechanical Engineering (8), 667–670 (2005)
4. Zhu, H., Xu, Q., Liao, S., et al.: Experimental study on working parameters of EPB shield machine. Chinese Journal of Geotechnical Engineering (5), 553–557 (2006)
5. Chang, T., Cong, D., Ye, Z., et al.: Simulation on HIL ground experiment simulator for on-orbit docking. Acta Aeronautica et Astronautica Sinica (4), 975–979 (2007)
6. Wang, W., Zhao, K., Lin, Z.: Evaluating interactions between the heavy forging process and the assisting manipulator combining FEM simulation and kinematics analysis. The International Journal of Advanced Manufacturing Technology 48(5), 481–491 (2010)
7. Salisbury, J.K., Craig, J.: Articulated hands: Kinematic and force control issues. International Journal of Robotics Research 1(1), 4–12 (1982)

8. Gosselin, C.M., Angeles, J.: A global performance index for the kinematic optimization of robotic manipulators. Transaction of the ASME, Journal of Mechanical Design 113, 220–226 (1991)
9. Xiong, Y., Ding, H., Liu, E.: Robotics. China Machine Press, Beijing (1993)
10. Liu, X.: The relationships between the performance criteria and link lengths of the parallel manipulators and their design theory. Yanshan University, Qinhuangdao (1999)

# Design of Compliant Bistable Mechanism
# for Rear Trunk Lid of Cars

Shouyin Zhang and Guimin Chen*

School of Mechatronics, Xidian University
Xi'an 710071, China
zhangshouyin2005@163.com, guimin.chen@gmail.com

**Abstract.** In traditional rear trunk lid designs, extra devices (e.g., hydraulic actuators and spring mechanisms) are employed to compensate the lid weight and reduce the efforts for both opening and closing it. Such devices often consist of a number of parts, thus leading to high costs for manufacture, assembly and maintenance. In this paper, we designed a compliant bistable mechanism to keep the lid's two states and compensate the lid weight, which leads to a system that requires only a small input force to switch between the two states. In the design, the pseudo-rigid-body model (PRBM) was employed to model the compliant mechanism, a particle swarm optimizer was used to optimize the PRBM parameters, and promising results were presented and discussed. The use of complaint mechanism can lead to reduction of the costs for manufacture, assembly and maintenance.

**Keywords:** trunk lid, compliant bistable mechanism, particle swarm optimizer.

## 1    Introduction

The rear trunk of a car is its main storage compartment. The rear trunk lid is the movable cover that shelters the things placed in the trunk. It is always required for the lid to steadily stay at two different positions, i.e., the open and closed states. Due to the weight of the lid, extra devices are often employed to reduce the efforts for both opening and closing it thus improving its use comfortableness. Such devices, e.g., hydraulic actuators and spring mechanisms, consist of a number of parts [1-2], thus leading to high costs for manufacture, assembly and maintenance.

In recent years, the research of compliant mechanisms has attracted a lot of attention in both academia and industry. A compliant mechanism, which utilizes the deflection of flexible segments rather than from articulated joints to achieve its mobility, provides many advantages over its rigid-body counterparts such as increased precision and reliability, ease to be miniaturized, and reduced part count (thus decreases the costs for manufacture, assembly and maintenance) [3]. A compliant mechanism also offers an economical way to achieve bistability [3] because the

---

* Corresponding author.

S. Jeschke, H. Liu, and D. Schilberg (Eds.): ICIRA 2011, Part I, LNAI 7101, pp. 291–299, 2011.

flexible segments store potential energy as they deflect. There has been a large amount of work done on different types of bistable compliant mechanisms [4-10].

Considering the trunk lid is required to steadily stay at two different positions, a bistable compliant mechanism could satisfy this requirement well. Furthermore, the bistable characteristics of the design must also compensate the weight of the lid to improve its use comfortableness.

In this paper, we designed a compliant bistable mechanism to keep the lid's two states and compensate the lid weight, which leads to a system that requires only a small input force to switch between the two states. In the design, the pseudo-rigid-body model (PRBM) [3] was employed to model the compliant mechanism and a particle swarm optimizer (PSO) [11] was used to optimize the PRBM parameters. The rest of the paper is organized as follows: Section 2 defines the design problem and presents the PRBM of a compliant four-bar mechanism; Section 3 optimizes the compliant mechanism; Section 4 discusses the results and concludes the main contribution and limitation of the work.

## 2    Problem Definition

To design a bistable compliant mechanism for rear trunk lid, its requirement should be well stated. First, the trunk lid could stably stay in the position when it is open or closed. Second, the trunk lid should have adequate range of motion, making it convenient to use. In this work, we assume the range of the trunk lid's motion is 75°. Third, for pursuing comfortableness, one can open or close the lid with a small force.

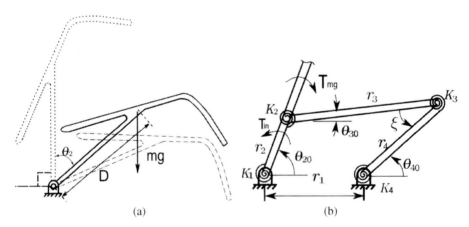

(a)                                    (b)

**Fig. 1.** (a) Model of trunk lid: opened position (dotted line); closed position (dot-dash); (b) PRBM of complaint four-bar mechanism

Fig. 1(a) shows a traditional trunk lid that rotates around a pivot, with the dotted line corresponding to the opened position and the dot-dash line to the closed position. And the weight (mg) of the lid is simplified at its center of mass with a distance of $D$ to the pivot. Here, we adopt a compliant four-bar mechanism to assist opening and closing the lid, which contains a link corresponding to the lid. So that in the process of lid closing ($\theta_2$ increases from zero to a certain angle), part of the positive work done by gravity will be stored in the compliant segments of the mechanism, thus only a small input load is required to compensate the residual positive work.

The PRBM of the complaint four-bar mechanism is shown in Fig. 1(b). Link $r_1$ is the ground or fixed link while link $r_2$ corresponds to the trunk lid. The moment ($T_{mg}$) is generated by the lid weight and exerts on link $r_2$. In Fig. 1(b), $r_i$ denotes the length of the links, $K_i$ the stiffness of torsional spring, $\theta_i$ the angle of the links to the horizontal axis, $T_{in}$ the moment required to actuate the lid. In the next section, for given $r_i$, $K_i$ and $\theta_{i0}$, we will deduce the relationship between $\theta_2$ and $T_{bar}$, where $T_{bar}$ is $T_{in}$ neglecting the lid weight.

## 3     Methods

In this section, based on the PRBM, we will deduce the expression of $T_{bar}$ with respect to $\theta_2$. Then by adding $T_{bar}$ to $T_{mg}$, we can get the resultant moment. Due to its simplicity in implementation and high computational efficiency in performing difficult optimization tasks, we use a PSO [11] to optimize the parameters of PRBM.

### 3.1     Moment

In the PRBM, the moment needed to drive a complaint four-bar mechanism is:

$$T_{bar} = K_1\psi_1 + K_2\psi_2\left(1 - \frac{d\theta_3}{d\theta_2}\right) + K_3\psi_3\left(\frac{d\theta_4}{d\theta_2} - \frac{d\theta_3}{d\theta_2}\right) + K_4\psi_4\frac{d\theta_3}{d\theta_2} \tag{1}$$

where $\psi_i$ is the change of angle $\theta_i$ as $\theta_2$ increases:

$$\psi_1 = \theta_2 - \theta_{20}$$
$$\psi_2 = \theta_2 - \theta_{20} - \left(\theta_3 - \theta_{30}\right)$$
$$\psi_3 = \theta_4 - \theta_{40} - \left(\theta_3 - \theta_{30}\right)$$
$$\psi_4 = \theta_4 - \theta_{40}$$

and kinematic coefficients [3] are:

$$\frac{d\theta_3}{d\theta_2} = \frac{r_2\sin\left(\theta_4 - \theta_2\right)}{r_3\sin\left(\theta_3 - \theta_4\right)}, \frac{d\theta_4}{d\theta_2} = \frac{r_2\sin\left(\theta_3 - \theta_2\right)}{r_4\sin\left(\theta_3 - \theta_4\right)}$$

We can see that $T_{bar} = 0$ when $\theta_2 = 0$. Thus, we consider $\theta_2 = 0$ as the opened position (corresponding to the dotted line in Fig. 1(a)). But since we have fixed the gravity of trunk lid on $r_2$, that the value of $T_{mg}$ under the condition of $\theta_2$ in Fig. 1(b) is not zero means this position is not stable. In this case, we rotate the PRBM together with the horizontal axis, to the position that $r_2$ is at the same position of trunk lid's open position in Fig. 1(a). At this position, $T_{mg}$ equals zero and corresponds to a stable equilibrium position. In this paper, we consider that the mass of the lid $m=10$ Kg, and the distance $D=0.6$ m. Then the moment exerted by the lib weight is:

$$T_{mg} = mgD \sin \theta_2 \tag{2}$$

To enhance the load capacity and improve the performance, two identical bistable mechanisms will be employed and symmetrically mounted on both sides of the lid to support the lid weight, thus each bistable mechanism will compensate half of the lid weight. The moment at the pivot can be expressed as:

$$T_{in} = T_{bar} - T_{mg} / 2 \tag{3}$$

This will be used to optimize the parameters of PRBM in the next subsection.

## 3.2     Optimization

PSO a population-based and stochastic optimization technique inspired by sociological behavior of bird flocking and fish schooling, which was first developed by Kennedy and Eberhart [12] in 1995. In PSO, the population is called the swarm, the individuals are called the particles, and each particle represents a potential solution for the problem being solved. Each particle "flies" through the solution space according to the previous experiences of its own and the particles within its neighborhood in search of better solution. PSO had been successfully applied to a wide variety of optimization tasks including artificial neural network training, job-shop scheduling, multi-objective optimization problems, etc.

Considering the assembly of the mechanism to the lid, we employ a partially compliant configuration which has two traditional rigid pivots, i.e., $K_1=0$ and $K_2=0$. The length of the fixed link ($r_1$) is set to 0.35 m. Then, the parameters to be optimized are: $[r_2, r_3, r_4, \theta_{20}, K_3, K_4]$. The constraints of the optimization include: (a) Because $r_2$ is fixed to the trunk lid, the motion range of $\theta_2$ must be no less than 75°; (b) The maximum stress in the compliant segments must be less than the yield strength of the material; (c) The values of $K_i$ are also limited due to the implementation difficulty.

To facilitate the optimization, we formulated an ideal bistable behavior of $T_{in}$ (denoted as $T_{target}$) with respect to $\theta_2$ as:

$$T_{target} = \frac{40\theta_2^3 + 85\theta_2^2 + 40\theta_2}{\theta_2^2 + 0.42\theta_2 + 1.2} \tag{4}$$

The curve for $T_{target}$ is plotted in Fig. 2. Then the fitness function of the optimization can be written as:

$$\text{min} \qquad T_{error} = T_{target} - T_{in}$$

$$\text{s.t} \qquad 0 \le r_i \le 0.5m_i \ (\ i = 2,3,4\ )$$
$$0 \le \theta_i \le 110°, (i = 3,4) \qquad\qquad (5)$$
$$75° \le \theta_2 \le 110°$$
$$0 \le K_i \le 20N \cdot m / rad, (i = 1,2,3,4)$$

In the optimization, the swarm size was set to 40 and the maximum iteration is 10000. Each particle is a 6-dimensional vector representing the PRBM of a candidate compliant four-bar mechanism design.

## 4    Results and Discussion

The optimized results of the parameters are given in Table 1. Using the results in Table 1, $T_{in}$ is plotted in Fig. 2. The corresponding PRBM is also presented in Fig. 3(a). From Fig. 2, we can see that $T_{in}$ approximates $T_{target}$ well before the unstable equilibrium position (the second position where $T_{target}=0$). Although $T_{in}$ is not equal to zero when $\theta_2 > 75°$, the sign of $T_{in}$ is negative and the trunk lid can be stopped by the lower part of the trunk to maintain the position. In summary, the design is acceptable for the trunk lid. The maximum value of $T_{in}$ is about 5 Nm, which represents a comfortable moment for users to open and close the lid.

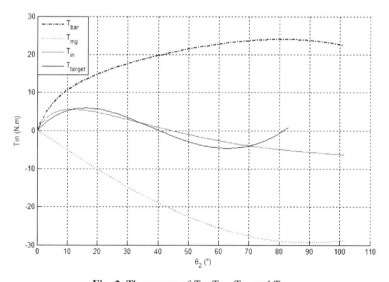

**Fig. 2.** The curves of $T_{in}$, $T_{mg}$, $T_{bar}$ and $T_{target}$

**Table 1.** Optimized parameters

| $r_2$(m) | $r_3$(m) | $r_4$ (m) | $\theta_{20}(°)$ | $K_3$ (Nm/rad) | $K_4$ (Nm/rad) |
|----------|----------|-----------|------------------|----------------|----------------|
| 0.37 | 0.4 | 0.39 | 12 | 0.38 | 16.5 |

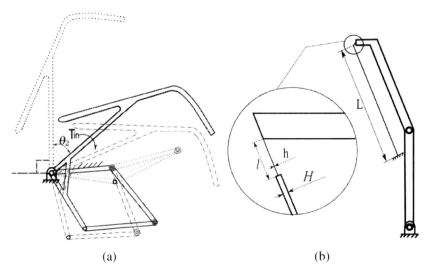

(a)                                        (b)

**Fig. 3.** (a) The PRBM of the optimized compliant four-bar mechanism and the trunk lid; (b) The implementation of the PRBM (ocantilevered segments and small-length flexural pivots)

Finally, a rigid-body replacement method [13] was used to finalize the bistable compliant mechanism from the PRBM. There are two flexural pivots in the PRBM. Because for $K_3$ is much smaller than $K_4$, we adopt a cantilevered segment for $K_4$ (with $b$, $H$ and $L$ are the out-of-plane thickness, the in-plane thickness and the length, respectively), and a small-length flexural pivot for $K_3$ (with $b$, $h$ and $l$ are the out-of-plane thickness, the in-plane thickness and the length, respectively). We set the out-of-plain thickness $b$ for both compliant segments to 0.03 m, so they can be fabricated from a single layer of material [14]. Titanium was selected due to its high ratio of yield stress to elastic modulus ($\sigma_y/E$). In the following, the dimensions of the two segments are determined using their stiffness listed in Table 1.

$$K_3 = \frac{EI}{l} = \frac{Ebh^3}{12l} \tag{6}$$

$$K_4 = \gamma K_\theta \frac{EI}{L} = \frac{\gamma K_\theta Ebh^3}{12L} \tag{7}$$

where $l$=0.02 m, $\gamma$ = 0.85, $K_\theta$= 2.85, $L = r_4/\gamma$ = 0.459 m. The in-plain thicknesses are:

$$h = 0.3 \times 10^{-3} \, \text{m}, \quad H = 2.3 \times 10^{-3} \, \text{m}$$

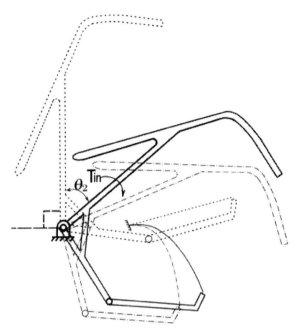

**Fig. 4.** The resultant design both at its open position (dotted line) and closed position (dot-dash)

It is also necessary to evaluate the stress level of the compliant segments. For given maximum rotation angle of the lid ($r_2$ in the PRBM), the maximum rotation angles of $\psi_3$ (corresponding to $K_3$) and $\psi_4$ (corresponding to $K_4$) are 66° and 90°, respectively. For the cantilevered segment, bending dominates its load, thus we have

$$\sigma_{max} = \frac{M_{max} H / 2}{I} = \frac{K_4 \psi_4 H}{2I} = 979.9 \ \text{MPa} \tag{8}$$

For the small-length pivot, both tension stress and bending stress are considered:

$$\sigma_{bend} = \frac{M_{max} h/2}{I} = \frac{K_4 \psi_4 h}{2I} = 972.7 \ \text{MPa} \tag{9}$$

$$\sigma_{pull} = \frac{F}{A} = \frac{(K_4 \psi_4 / r_4) \div \sin(\xi)}{bh} = 7.6 \ \text{MPa} \tag{10}$$

where angle $\xi$ is marked in Fig. 1(b). The maximum stress in total is:

$$\sigma_{max} = \sigma_{bend} + \sigma_{pull} = 927.7 + 7.6 = 935.3 \ \text{MPa} \tag{11}$$

In summary, the maximum stress in the compliant segments is less than the yield stress of Titanium ($\sigma_y$ = 1170 MPa), thus the design can meet the requirements of the lid design.

# 5    Conclusion

In this paper, we designed a compliant bistable mechanism to keep the lid's two states and compensate the lid weight, which leads to a system that requires only a very small force to switch between the two states. In the design, the pseudo-rigid-body model (PRBM) was employed to model the compliant mechanism, a particle swarm optimizer was used to optimize the PRBM parameters, and promising results were presented and discussed. The use of complaint mechanism can lead to reduction of the costs for manufacture, assembly and maintenance.

Nevertheless, this design could be improved in our future work by further reducing the lengths of the links and decreasing the stress level in the compliant segments. Also, trying other types of bistable compliant mechanisms for the design is also of our interests.

**Acknowledgment.** The authors gratefully acknowledge the financial support from the National Natural Science Foundation of China under Grant No. 50805110, the Scientific Research Foundation for the Returned Overseas Chinese Scholars under Grant No. JY0600100401, and the Fundamental Research Funds for the Central Universities under No. JY10000904010.

# References

1. Dowling, P.J.: Latch Device for Use with a Vehicle Trunk Lid. United States Patent, 5632515 (1997)
2. Queveau, G., Queveau, P., Guillez, J.-M.: Trunk Lid for Convertible Vehicle with Folding Roof, Adapted to Open from the Rear toward the Front and from the Front toward the Rear. United States Patent, 6092335 (2000)
3. Howell, L.L.: Compliant Mechanisms. Wiley, New York (2001)
4. Jensen, B.D., Howell, L.L.: Identification of compliant pseudo-rigid-body mechanism configurations resulting in bistable behavior. Trans. ASME, J. Mechan. Design 125, 701–708 (2003)
5. Su, H., McCarthy, J.M.: Synthesis of bistable compliant four-bar mechanisms using polynomial homotopy. Trans. ASME, J. Mechan. Design 129, 1094–1098 (2007)
6. Pucheta, M.A., Cardona, A.: Design of bistable compliant mechanisms using precision-position and rigid-body replacement methods. Mech. Mach. Theory 45(2), 304–326 (2010)
7. Qiu, J., Lang, J.H., Slocum, A.H.: A curved-beam bistable mechanism. J. Microelectromech. Syst. 13, 137–146 (2004)
8. Masters, N.D., Howell, L.L.: A self-retracting fully compliant bistable micromechanism. J. Microelectromech. Syst. 12, 273–280 (2003)
9. Wilcox, D.L., Howell, L.L.: Fully compliant tensural bistable micromechanisms (FTBM). J. Microelectromech. Syst. 14(6), 1223–1235 (2005)
10. Hwang, I., Shim, Y., Lee, J.: Modeling and experimental characterization of the chevron-type bi-stable microactuator. J. Micromech. Microeng. 13(6), 948–954 (2003)

11. Chen, G., Xiong, B., Huang, X.: Finding the optimal characteristic parameters for 3R pseudo-rigid-body model using an improved particle swarm optimizer. Precis. Eng. 3 (2011)
12. Kennedy, J., Eberhart, R.: Particle swarm optimization. In: Proceeding of IEEE International Conference on Neural Networks, pp. 1942-1948 (1995)
13. Pucheta, M.A., Cardona, A.: Design of bistable compliant mechanisms using precision–position and rigid-body replacement methods. Mechanism and Machine Theory 45(2), 304–326 (2010)
14. Jacobsen, J.O., Chen, G., Howell, L.L., Magleby, S.P.: Lamina emergent torsion (LET) joint. Mechanism and Machine Theory 44(11), 2098–2109 (2009)

# DynaMOC: A Dynamic Overlapping Coalition-Based Multiagent System for Coordination of Mobile Ad Hoc Devices

Vitor A. Santos, Giovanni C. Barroso, Mario F. Aguilar,
Antonio de B. Serra, and Jose M. Soares

Depto. de Eng. de Teleinformatica, Universidade Federal do Ceara
Campus do Pici - Bloco 725 - CEP 60455-970 Fortaleza, Brazil
`vitor@ufc.br, gcb@fisica.ufc.br,`
`{mario.fiallos,prof.serra,marques.soares}@gmail.com`

**Abstract.** In this work, we focus on problems modeled as a set of tasks to be scheduled and accomplished by mobile autonomous devices that communicate via a mobile ad hoc network. In such situations, the communication cost, computational efforts and environment uncertainty are key challenges.

It is intuitive to consider that keeping information about tasks globally known by devices can provide better schedules. However, there are some contexts - such as those where tasks require startup based on location - where information restricted to coalitions of devices can still produce satisfactory scheduling. The existing heuristics, however, do not consider this approach.

In this paper, we propose a multiagent system that coordinates the dynamic formation of overlapping coalitions and the scheduling of tasks within them. Heuristics for calculating the size of coalitions, as well as for scheduling tasks are proposed based on a Markov decision process. The system is applied to solve the problem of area coverage in a simulated environment and the results show that good schedules are obtained with lower cost of communication and computation compared with the solution based on globally known information.

**Keywords:** multiagent systems, coalitions, task scheduling.

## 1 Introduction

We consider the problem of coordinating teams of mobile devices that communicate via a mobile ad hoc network engaged in scheduling inter-dependent tasks geographically dispersed in an uncertain environment. Area coverage [1] and load transportation [2] are examples of those problems. Area coverage is a well-known problem in robotics with extensive research for the single robot coverage. In its distributed version, the whole area is splited in disjoint subareas so that covering each subarea is a task to be accomplished by a robot in a robot team. In the load transportation scenario, we may partition the load on a disjoint set and the path

S. Jeschke, H. Liu, and D. Schilberg (Eds.): ICIRA 2011, Part I, LNAI 7101, pp. 300–311, 2011.

on disjoint subpaths as well. In those situations, mobile devices react both to its environment and to messages received from neighboring in order to share tasks and domain data. As environments are frequently uncertain, tasks are allowed to be dinamically updated. Moreover, outcomes of tasks are frequently dependent on location of devices, because of the necessity of a startup travel. We say that those tasks have a setup cost.

Distributed control of mobile autonomous devices that cooperate to schedule and accomplish shared dynamic tasks is a notably challenging problem. First, scheduling of distributed tasks is a NP-complete problem. Second, the communication due to the sharing of tasks and domain data may compromise scalability. Clearly, both difficulties are sensitive to the number of devices and amount of tasks.

There are several heuristics to reduce the scheduling search space based on hierarchical task networks [3] or separate setup [4,5]. However, those schedulers either do not consider mobile teams or communication costs. Existing work that consider coalitions are primarily concerned with complete information sharing and situations where tasks require different skills [6,7].

We propose a multiagent system (MAS) [8] called DynaMOC. In this MAS, each agent is a dynamic driven data application which receive and evaluate data from physical system in real time. The system applies a mechanism for the reduction of computational and communication efforts based on overlapping coalitions of agents. Each agent is able to organize coalitions and to calculate their own schedules of tasks from the knowledge obtained within that coalitions.

We validate our system through the area coverage problem in a simulated environment. We show that dynamically formed coalitions can significantly reduce communication cost and produce good schedules.

In the remainder of this paper we formalize the problem to be solved (Section 2), the related work (Section 3), the proposed system (Section 4) and the case study (Section 5), which validates the system. Conclusion follow in Section 6.

## 2  Problem Definition

This work is related to the problem of coordinating autonomous units to perform shared tasks. A mobile device is an entity with mobility, computacional processing, arbitrary participation time and hops-based communication through a mobile ad hoc network. A mobile team is defined as the set $\Gamma = \{\gamma_1, \gamma_2, \ldots, \gamma_n\}$, $n \geq 1$, of mobile devices. Devices may be equiped with sensors and actuators to interact with the environment. Each device is associated with an agent.

Activities have capabilities of division and are dynamically assigned to different devices throughout its accomplishment. Moreover, aspects of performance of activities, such as cost and duration, may depend on the current state of the devices.

The domain of interest consider that tasks to be performed are geographically dispersed in the environment, denoted by $E$. The pair $(\Gamma, E)$ forms the *physical system*. Formally, the problem we aim to solve is denoted by the tuple:

$$\langle (\Gamma, E), A, S, F_s, R \rangle$$

where:

$(\Gamma, E)$ is the physical system formed by mobile team $\Gamma$ and the environment $E$.

$A = \{A_1, A_2, \ldots\}$ is the dynamic set of activities to be accomplished individually by agents.

$S = \{s_1, s_2, \ldots\}$ is the set of possible states to be undertaken by agents during the accomplishment of activities.

$F_s : \Gamma \times A \rightarrow S$ is the function that associates each agent (considering its current state) performing an activity to a state.

$R : A \times \Gamma \times S \rightarrow \mathbb{R}$ is the function that associates each activity performed by an agent in a given state to an outcome.

We want to find a schedule $\Xi : A \rightarrow \Gamma$ which produce the best overall outcome, according to the expression 1.

$$\sum_{A_i \in A} R(A_i, \Xi(A_i), F_s(\Xi(A_i), A_i)) \tag{1}$$

## 3    Related Work

Coalitions in multiagent systems are mainly concerned with the evaluation of optimal coalitions [8]. An optimal coalition structure partitions the team into subgroups without intersection and tasks are assigned to those subgroups. Early work related to overlapping coalitions in multiagent systems have been only recently developed. Some of these algorithms consider the formation of coalitions for joint accomplishment of tasks in the event that such tasks require different skills [9,6,7,10]. Our work, however, considers the formation of overlapping coalitions for reducing globally distributed information.

Lin e Hu [6] propose an algorithm to build overlapping coalitions to accomplish tasks. The algorithm, however, is based on complete information, unlike the problem domain considered here. Kraus et al. [10] consider the possibility of incomplete information. Their work, however, suggests protocols for the formation of coalitions based on sharing reward between agents and does not address activities scheduling.

Other heuristics reduce the scheduling search space when tasks require a separate setup [4]. However, those schedulers do not consider mobile teams and communication costs. Barbulescu et al. [5] propose a coordination mechanism to schedule tasks with setup requirements accomplished by mobile agent teams. However, they do not address communication issues. Another approach to reduce scheduling search space and communication cost is directed to the formation of coalitions. Existing work, however, are primarily concerned with complete information sharing and situations where tasks require different skills [6,7].

# 4    Description of DynaMOC

DynaMOC is composed by three main modules, according to the architecture illustrated in Figure 1. DynaMOC data structure keeps information about agent states and the subjective view of tasks. Decision Support Module is responsible by scheduling and coalition formation. The coordination of those functionalities and updating of data structure on each agent is carried out by the Coordination Module.

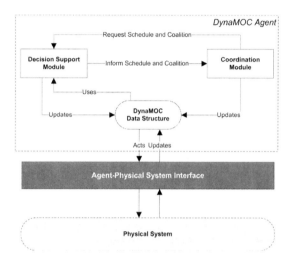

**Fig. 1.** Architecture of each DynaMOC agent

## 4.1    DynaMOC Data Structure

DynaMOC data structure has some similarities with C_TAEMS [11]. There are three main elements in it: agents organized as coalitions, activities and schedules.

- Activities: Activities represent small goals to be accomplished in order to complete large tasks. An agent $\gamma_i$ performs, therefore, a sequence $\{A_{i,1}, A_{i,2}, \ldots\}$ of activities. The activities of other agents and its own activites form the *Subjective View* of an agent. This is the part of the whole problem known by the agent. Each activity is performed as a sequence of actions. Numbers of a set $T_i$ of *logical times* are assigned to the actions of each agent $\gamma_i$.
  The outcome of an activity represents the value of performance metrics such as cost, quality and length [3].
- Schedules: A schedule is a structure that contains a sequence of activities to be carried out by an agent.
- Agents and Coalitions: An agent contains a list of attributes which describes domain-dependent features. Agents have the ability to form coalitions. Coalitions in a set $\Gamma$ are subsets of it. Coalitions are formed on the initiative of the agents. Each agent in a coalition is a *Former*, when it initiates coalition, or a *Visitor*, when it is invited by a former agent to participate in its coalition.

## 4.2   Decision Support Module

This module provides mechanisms for coalition formation and scheduling calculation.

**Coalition Formation.** A former agent $\gamma_i$ is capable of forming coalitions based on its *k-neighborhood*. The k-neighborhood of an agent $\gamma_i$ on logical time $t$ is denoted by $Cv(i, k, t)$ and is a set formed by the $k$ $\gamma_i$'s closest agents.

DynaMOC provides the following two mechanisms for defining the sizes of coalitions: static and dynamic. In the static approach, the size of coalitions is defined before the begining of missions. In the dynamic approach, the first coalition formed by each agent must involve all other agents. The next coalition are reduced in size according to the number of agents necessary to calculate the prior schedule. In other words, $\gamma_i$ consider the further agent which contributes with an activity in the prior schedule. This approach is described by the Algorithm 1.

---

**Algorithm 1.** Dynamic coalitions update

---

1: **procedure** UPDATECOALITIONASFORMER$(i, \Gamma)$
2:     **if** $C_i = \{\gamma_i\}$ **then**
3:         $C_i \leftarrow Cv(i, |\Gamma|, T(\xi_i))$
4:     **else**
5:         Identify the number $k$ of agents which contributed with the previous scheduled activities.
6:         $C_i \leftarrow Cv(i, k + 1, T(\xi_i))$
7:     **end if**
8: **end procedure**

---

**Scheduler.** The schedule of activities is based on their expected outcomes. The uncertainty of the physical system tends to dificult the calculation of those values. Usually, Markov Decision Processes (MDP) [12] are appropriate tools for decision support on scenarios with uncertainty. In a MDP, agent states are estimated, after actions, from a discrete probability distribution and outcomes are calculated by a function. In our work, outcomes are calculated through performance metrics. Thus, we propose the following MDP to model the behavior of agents within a coalition $C$ and the scheduling of activities:

$$\langle S_C, A_C, P_C, R_C, \pi_C \rangle \tag{2}$$

where:

$S_C = \bigcup_{\gamma_i \in C} S_i$ is the set of agent states in coalition $C$. We denote by $\xi_i$ the current state of $\gamma_i \in C$.

$A_C = \bigcup_{\gamma_i \in C} A_i$ are activities that can be carried out by the agents in a coalition $C$.

$P_C = \bigcup_{\gamma_i \in C} P_i$ where $P_i = \{Pr(e_{i,y}^{t+T(A')}|e_{i,x}^t, A')|x, y \in S_i, A' \in A_i\}$ is the probability of $\gamma_i$ to be in state $y$ on time $t + T(A') \in T_i$ after accomplishing $A'$ on state $x$ on time $t \in T_i$.

$R_C = \bigcup_{\gamma_i \in C} R_i$ where $R_i : S_i \times A_i \to \mathbb{R}$ is the expected outcome after the accomplishment of an activity by the agent $\gamma_i$ in a state $S_i$, ie $R_i(s', A') = R(\gamma_i, s', A')$.

$\pi_C = \bigcup_{\gamma_i \in C} \pi_i$ onde cada $\pi_i = e_{i,x}^0$ is the initial state of $\gamma_i$.

In order to improve the estimatives of outcomes we apply a learning mechanism based on *Q-learning* algorithm [13]. In this, the value $R_i(t, A')$ is updated through the real outcome $(V_i(t, A'))$ and the estimated outcome $(R_i(t, A'))$ to accomplish activity $A'$ on time $t$. There is a weighting $l_t$, which is the *learning factor* considered for both values. Furthermore, there is a exponetial moving average $w_t$, which considers the most recent activities. The learning mechanism is shown in the expression 3.

$$R_i(S_i(A_{i,j-1}), A_{i,j}) \leftarrow w_t(l_t(V_i(S_i(A_{i,j-1}), A_{i,j})) + R_i(S_i(A_{i,j-1}), A_{i,j})(1 - l_t)) +$$
$$(1 - w_t)(\sum_{\gamma_k \in C} \sum_{t < j_k} R_k(S_k(A_{k,t-1}), A_{k,t})),$$
$$(3)$$

where $A_{k,j_k}$ is the last most recent activity accomplished by $\gamma_k$.

An optimal solution to a MDP involving a large number of activities is a computationally intractable problem [14]. Thus, we propose a heuristic called k-Greedy Alternated Scheduling (Algorithm 2), which is partially based on Pick Minimum Weighted Processing Time(PMWP) heuristic [15]. In our algorithm, the best activities for each agent are alternately chosen. Its argument $k$ refers to the number of activities to be scheduled in the set $A$.

---

**Algorithm 2.** k-Greedy Alternated Scheduling

```
 1: function KGAS(i, C, A, k)
 2:     tempC ← C  cont ← 0
 3:     while A ≠ ∅ e cont ≤ k do
 4:         cont ← cont + 1
 5:         Find A' ∈ A and γ_j ∈ C corresponding to min_{A'∈A,γ_j∈C} R_j(T(A_j), A').
 6:         A_j ← A_j + A'
 7:         tempC ← tempC − γ_j
 8:         A ← A − A'
 9:         if tempC = ∅ then
10:             tempC ← C
11:         end if
12:     end while
13:     return A_i
14: end function
```

The algorithm's main loop is repeated alternately assigning activities to agents of $C$ until $k$ activities are assigned to $\gamma_i$ or there is no more activities of $A$ to be assigned. Each activity is chosen for an agent based on the best outcome considering the activities chosen so far, which is calculated by the MDP's function $R_j$.

### 4.3  Coordination Module

The coordination of the system is achieved from the concurrent execution of processes on each agent. This is modeled by a Petri Net [16], illustrated in Figure 2. After started, an agent has no activities scheduled. The first step is to update its own coalition through a protocol of coalition formation. The next step of the coordination process is to upgrade the subjective view of the agent. In our system, these structures are shared within coalitions. Subjective views are formed within an agent from two update processes: local and remote. The update of local activities refers to (i) removal of activities already carried out and (ii) definition new activities within the DynaMOC data structure, due to division of existing activities. After the local update, the update is performed remotely. Remote update of activities is the first phase of scheduling protocol and from which an agent knows the local activities of his peers within his coalition. If the subjective view has no activities to be performed, the agent is terminated. Otherwise, scheduling is calculated and distributed to the coalition.

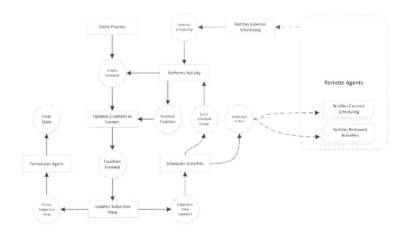

**Fig. 2.** A Petri Net for general coodination process

The main communication features within this module are related to coordination of sending messages within coalitions, and in a higher level, with the protocols that meet the needs of coalition formation and scheduling. We propose the structure shown in Table 1 for defining messages and its performatives. The structure is based on the FIPA ACL language [17].

**Table 1.** Message parameters

| Parameter | Description |
|---|---|
| Id | Message Identification. |
| Source | Agent that send the message. |
| Protocol | Type of communication protocol. |
| Performative | Performative which describes the message: request, inform, refuse, confirm, proposal, accept-proposal and refuse-proposal. |
| Content | Message content. |

# 5   Case Study

A case study was carried out in order to validate and evaluate the proposed multiagent system. We implemented the system and applied it to solve a problem that was simulated through a discrete event system. This section describes the problem, the simulated physical system, the application of the multiagent system in the problem and the performance tests.

## 5.1   Area Coverage and the Application of the System

Area coverage is one of the most important problems in robotics with many applicatons such as urban cleaning, areas recognition and rescue operations. The problem consists of finding a path that include all the coordinates within a given area.

One strategy for solving the problem is based on spiral paths, where the agents use obstacles, walls and areas already covered to build the circular paths. In this case study, we applied a spiral path algorithm known as BSA (Backtracking Spiral Algorithm) [18] as the method to define tasks and activities. In the BSA, the robot starts a spiral path until he reach a point surrounded by points already covered or obstacles. Then, he returns to a point known as *backtracking point* (BP). A BP is a candidate point to be the beginning of another spiral. Each activity in BSA algorithm is defined as a region to be covered. Initially, therefore, each agent has only one activity within its main task, which corresponds to the coverage of its initial assigned region. However, new areas may arise over time with new BP.

In order to evaluate the efficiency of the proposed dynamic coalition algorithm, we compare a *BSA with kGAS schedule and dynamic coalitions version* to other two versions: BSA with kGAS schedule and static coalitions version, in which the coalitions are formed statically as grand coalitions, and BSA-CM version (BSA - Cooperative Multirobot) [19], which is the distributed version of BSA. In BSA-CM, each robot consider the BP of all other robots, chosing the nearest one.

In our case study, the environment is modeled as a two-dimensional grid. A point in the grid is a minimum unit of the environment and is uniquely identified by its coordinates. Two environments with the same dimensions (80x80) and with different distribution of obstacles were employed. In the first, obstacles of arbitrary shapes were randomly distributed. In the second, obstacles in the form of horizontal walls were distributed in a standardized way. Horizontal walls with reduced vertical space between them provide the a greater number of backtracking points due to formation of different regions from which new spirals are formed.

In the tests, the agents have equal and constant speeds. In this case, time and distance can be considered equivalent concepts. Our charts, for example, show the amount of time as the minimum units of travel.

## 5.2   Performance Tests

Tests involving the solutions for the are coverage problem were performed based on *set tests*, denoted by $TS_{k,j,E,V}$, where:

- $k$ enumerates the tests sets.
- $j \in \{2, 4, 6, 8, 12, 16\}$ is the amount of agents.
- $E \in \{\text{ram}, \text{hor}\}$ identifies the type of environment: random obstacles and horizontal obstacles. horizontais.
- $V \in \{\text{BSA} - \text{CM}, \text{kS}, \text{kD}\}$ identifies the scheduling and coalition algorithms: BSA-CM, kGAS Greedy with static grand coalitions and EkGA with dynamic coalitions.

Each execution of a test set is called a *mission*. Eight missions were performed for each combination of $j$, $E$ and $V$. They differ about initial positions of the agents which were arbitraryly chosen [1]. The final results for each test set were calculated as an arithmetic average of each mission. These results were organized into charts according to the mission times and the amount of sent messages, as follows.

**Mission Times.** The time of a mission is the maximum amount of actions accomplished by a agent. The absolute mission times of all versions decrease as the number of agents is increased. These values, however, become meaningful when compared with a lower bound time. A lower bound time is calculated as the shortest time possible for a mission. This value is given by the open area (without obstacles) divided by the number of agents of the mission. For the case study, the environments considered have about $6,000$ area units of open area. This value is not the result of the optimal scheduling solution, since solving the MDP (expression 2) is unfeasible, given the number of activities. It is, however, an even more optimistic, since it disregards the setup time of activities.

Relations between absolute mission times and lower bound times are calculated by expression 4, for each amount of agents $j$, where $T_{\text{low}}(j)$ denotes the lower bound time.

$$\frac{\frac{\sum_{1 \le k \le 8} T_f(CT_{k,j,E,V})}{8}}{T_{\text{low}}(j)} \tag{4}$$

---

[1] More precisely, the environment to be covered is equally divided into virtual subareas according to the number of agents. Each device is positioned arbitrarily within its virtual subarea.

The mission times are shown in the charts of Figure 3 as percentage of the mission times of the lower bound time, according to the expression 4.

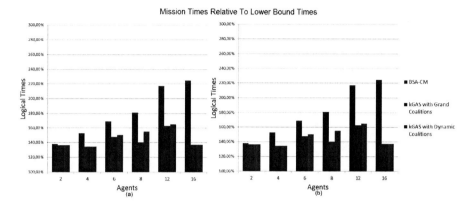

**Fig. 3.** Mission times relative to lower bound time in the simulated environment with: (a) arbitrarily randomly distributed obstacles. (b) horizontal obstacles.

**Sent Messages.** The amount of sent messagens is influenced by the necessary number of hops on mobile ad hoc networks communication. We refer, therefore, to the number of sent messages as the number of messages sendings. Figure 4 shows the sent messages charts.

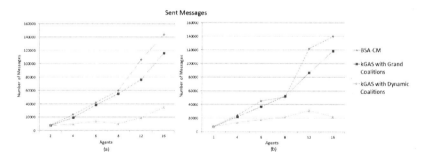

**Fig. 4.** Amount of sent messages in the simulated environment with: (a) arbitrarily randomly distributed obstacles. (b) horizontal obstacles.

## 6   Conclusions

In this paper we proposed a multiagent systems that aims to establish a cooperative behavior in situations where autonomous devices must work together to carry out shared activities. The system deal with several challenges. Scheduling of activities and the physical system uncertainty require efficient algorithms for decision-making so that processing capacity does not become a limitation. In the cases considered here, where the devices are interconnected by a mobile ad hoc network, and communication is based on hops, sending messages also becomes a factor to be controlled. Thus, we proposed a mechanism for the reduction of computational efforts and communication based on overlapping coalitions of agents. Each agent is able to organize coalitions and to calculate their own schedules of activities from the knowledge obtained within that coalitions.

The case study showed that the coalition formation mechanism proposed was able to reduce the search space for the building of schedules and the amount of sent messages. Reducing the search space did not substantially affect the ability to build good schedules. This is strongly due to the fact that the activities are sensitive to the locations of the devices.

As a future work, we will evaluate the system from the impact of communication failures due to the existence of obstacles and interference. A probabilistic model for signal loss will be used. Furthermore, the transmission range of each device can vary with the presence of obstacles. We will also investigate the system behavior on the problem of area coverage through the application of some conditions not yet considered, such as devices with different speeds and autonomies.

# References

1. Choset, H.: Coverage for robotics a survey of recent results. Annals of Mathematics and Artificial Intelligence 31, 113–126 (2001)
2. Murata, T., Nakamura, T.: Multi-Agent Cooperation Using Genetic Network Programming with Automatically Defined Groups. In: Deb, K., et al. (eds.) GECCO 2004. LNCS, vol. 3103, pp. 712–714. Springer, Heidelberg (2004)
3. Decker, K.S.: Taems a framework for environment centered analysis and design of coordination mechanisms. In: Foundations of Distributed Artificial Intelligence, Ch.16, pp. 429–448. John Wiley and Sons, Inc. (1996)
4. Allahverdi, A., Ng, C.T., Cheng, T.C.E., Kovalyov, M.Y.: A survey of scheduling problems with setup times or costs. European Journal of Operational Research 187(3) (2008)
5. Barbulescu, L., Rubinstein, Z.B., Smith, S.F., Zimmerman, T.L.: Distributed coordination of mobile agent teams: the advantage of planning ahead. In: Proceedings of the 9th International Conference on Autonomous Agents and Multiagent Systems, AAMAS 2010, vol. 1, pp. 1331–1338. International Foundation for Autonomous Agents and Multiagent Systems, Richland (2010)
6. Lin, C.-F., Hu, S.-L.: Multi-task overlapping coalition parallel formation algorithm. In: Proceedings of the 6th International Joint Conference on Autonomous Agents and Multiagent Systems, AAMAS 2007, pp. 211:1–211:3. ACM, New York (2007)
7. Cheng, K., Dasgupta, P.: Coalition game-based distributed coverage of unknown environments by robot swarms. In: Proceedings of the 7th International Joint Conference on Autonomous Agents and Multiagent Systems, AAMAS 2008, vol. 3, pp. 1191–1194. International Foundation for Autonomous Agents and Multiagent Systems, Richland (2008)
8. Wooldridge, M.: An Introduction to Multiagent Systems. John Wiley & Sons, Inc., New York (2009)

9. Shehory, O., Kraus, S.: Methods for task allocation via agent coalition formation. Artif. Intell. 101, 165–200 (1998)

10. Kraus, S., Shehory, O., Taase, G.: The advantages of compromising in coalition formation with incomplete information. In: Proceedings of the Third International Joint Conference on Autonomous Agents and Multiagent Systems, AAMAS 2004, vol. 2, pp. 588–595. IEEE Computer Society, Washington, DC, USA (2004)

11. Boddy, M., Horling, B., Phelps, J., Goldman, R., Vincent, R., Long, A., Kohout, R.: C_taems language specification v. 2.04 (April 2007)

12. Bellman, R.: A markovian decision process. Journal of Mathematics and Mechanics, 6 (1957)

13. Kaelbling, L.P., Littman, M.L., Moore, A.W.: Reinforcement Learning: A Survey. Journal of Artificial Intelligence Research 4, 237–285 (1996)

14. Papadimitriou, C., Tsitsiklis, J.N.: The complexity of markov decision processes. Math. Oper. Res. 12, 441–450 (1987)

15. Arnaout, J.-P., Rabadi, G., Mun, J.H.: A dynamic heuristic for the stochastic unrelated parallel machine scheduling problem. International Journal of Operations Research 3, 136–143 (2008)

16. Jensen, K., Kristensen, L.M.: Coloured Petri Nets. Springer, Heidelberg (2009)

17. Fipa acl message structure specification, version g (2002), http://www.fipa.org/specs/fipa00061/

18. Gonzalez, E., Alvarez, O., Diaz, Y., Parra, C., Bustacara, C.: Bsa: A complete coverage algorithm. In: Proceedings of the 2005 IEEE International Conference on Robotics and Automation, ICRA 2005, pp. 2040–2044 (April 2005)

19. Gonzalez, E., Gerlein, E.: Bsa-cm: A multi-robot coverage algorithm. In: Proceedings of the 2009 IEEE/WIC/ACM International Joint Conference on Web Intelligence and Intelligent Agent Technology, WI-IAT 2009, vol. 02, pp. 383–386. IEEE Computer Society, Washington, DC, USA (2009)

# Design of a High Performance Quad-Rotor Robot Based on a Layered Real-Time System Architecture

Jonas Witt[1], Björn Annighöfer[2], Ole Falkenberg[1], and Uwe Weltin[1]

[1] Hamburg University of Technology, Institute for Reliability Engineering,
Eißendorfer Str. 40, 21073 Hamburg , Germany
[2] Hamburg University of Technology, Institute of Aircraft Systems Engineering,
Nesspriel 5, 21129 Hamburg, Germany
{jonas.witt,bjoern.annighoefer,ole.falkenberg,weltin}@tu-harburg.de

**Abstract.** This work presents the results of an effort to create a high performance quad-rotor MAV named iQCopter for research in the field of swarm robotics and vision-based autonomous operation. During the design, navigational and computational capabilities have been of major priority. A distinctive feature of the iQCopter is its layered system architecture using a comparably powerful, hard real-time capable x86-computer even in the innermost control loop for maximum transparency and ease of use while a simple fixed-point microcontroller provides a low-level sensor interface and a fallback solution for safety reasons. Finally, a successful system identification and subsequent design of an aggressive $H_\infty$ controller are presented as benchmark cases to demonstrate the performance of the design.

**Keywords:** micro unmanned aerial vehicle (MAV), system design, architecture, robust control, system identification, quad-rotor.

## 1 Introduction

Micro unmanned aerial vehicles (MAVs) as a research platform have received strong attention in recent years. Whether for swarm experiments in a closed environment with external tracking [11,8] or as fully autonomous agents with on board intelligence [2,6,7,10], many different testbeds have been proposed. The quad-rotor setup with its simple construction, vertical take off and landing (VTOL) capability and quick response due to its unstable dynamics make it a frequently selected choice for UAV systems.

Our interest is in fully autonomous outdoor and indoor operation with single and swarming MAVs performing object transportation tasks and search-and-rescue operations in disaster areas. This poses demanding requirements on the capabilities of the testbed. High computational performance is required to be able to incorporate vision based simultaneous localization and mapping (SLAM) and obstacle avoidance algorithms while a solid inertial navigation system and

S. Jeschke, H. Liu, and D. Schilberg (Eds.): ICIRA 2011, Part I, LNAI 7101, pp. 312–323, 2011.
© Springer-Verlag Berlin Heidelberg 2011

**Fig. 1.** The iQCopter quadrotor MAV. The highest point is the IMU to achieve the largest possible separation between the actuator currents and the magnetometers. The iQCopter measures 72cm from rotor tip to rotor tip and weighs about 1250 grams including a 3300mAh 3-cell lithium polymer battery.

capable actuators are needed to realize aggressive control algorithms. The iQ-Copter (short for intelligent QuadroCopter) has been designed to provide a highly integrated easy to use research testbed that is able to meet these requirements [14].

## 1.1  Related Work

Several approaches to autonomous research grade quad-rotors and even more projects exist. This section describes a selection of successful projects to cover common choices that are made in the design phase.

Since quad-rotors enjoy great popularity not only in the research community, several open-source projects exist. In [6], an open-source project is used as a starting point to develop a fully autonomous quad-rotor equipped with a more accurate commercial IMU and a laser range finder executing SLAM on a wirelessly connected computer. An ARM based system is used for on board control and data streaming. The commercial IMU is limited to 120 Hz.

For the RANGE project of the MIT, a commercial MAV platform is used [2]. Also carrying a laser range finder, but a more powerful computer, it is able to execute SLAM on board of the MAV. In most commercial systems the inner loop is a black box for the researcher. This is convenient in some respect, but can be a struggle if one is interested in accessing signals at the innermost loop at high sampling rates for identification or controller development. This can even be infeasible.

The Stanford STARMAC [7] is based on a commercial IMU and a custom airframe. On board, two 16-bit microprocessors are used for control and communication. The utilized IMU is limited to 76 Hz.

The CSIRO X4-flyer [13] is a large custom built research quad-rotor with an IMU running at 50 Hz. A 16-bit microcontroller closes the inner loop and streams data via bluetooth.

For the Pixhawk project of the ETH Zürich, a new system was developed from the ground up including a custom IMU, airframe and integrated powerful x86 computer for on board stereo vision and pattern recognition [10]. The inner loop with state estimation and controllers runs on an ARM-based microcontroller. The x86 computer is only running soft real-time tasks.

The system in this paper is based on a commercial airframe [4] equipped with custom electronics. An 8-bit microcontroller acts as a low-level interface to all sensor components. The main architectural difference to the other systems is that loop closure is achieved through a powerful, hard real-time capable x86 computer (running Linux with real-time extensions), allowing to run all filter, control and also non-deterministic algorithms in parallel. A newly developed, script-driven real-time software framework routes signals to reusable and parameterizable modules. For research this setup has several benefits:

- All data flow is completely transparent, configurable and can be recorded at high rates
- The innermost loop can use extensive algorithms and run in double precision
- Modules can be developed for a known environment and be immediately deployed
- Familiar scientific software libraries can be used
- Stable fallback solutions on the 8-bit microcontroller provide safety against implementation errors during trials

The outstanding results of the linear system identification and controller experiments support the claim that a potent system has been designed.

### 1.2   Outline

This paper is laid out as follows. The system architecture is outlined in section 2 and proceeds with a description of the hardware components in section 3. Section 4 briefly describes the linear system identification with a grey box SIMO model and subsequent design of an aggressive $H_\infty$ controller to demonstrate the performance of the system. Finally a discussion of the results and an outlook on future projects is given in section 5.

## 2   MAV System Architecture

The driving aspects for the iQCopter were performance, size/weight, ease of use, safety/reliability and cost. Foremost a high computational and navigational performance have been identified as being crucial as a step towards fully autonomous operation. Accordingly, a potent x86 board computer and a high-fidelity MEMS IMU have been chosen as the foundation. To adhere to the goal of high navigational performance on the software side a high fidelity state estimator and controller algorithms preferably running with double precision and a sufficiently high sampling rate should be integrated.

Using a fixed-point microcontroller for this task, however, is problematic. Carrying out double precision floating point algorithms is usually highly inefficient or even impossible. Additionally, even if it is possible it introduces a burden for the researcher concerned with the development of complex algorithms to cross-compile for a proprietary platform, where familiar scientific libraries might not work and which offers low transparency during runtime and lacking debugging comfort.

An implementation on powerful computer hardware which runs an operating system is more convenient in that respect but problematic for safety and reliability reasons. Although erroneous code can also lockup the simplest microcontroller it does not suffer from determinism problems such as a computer running a regular operating system such as Linux or Windows. Another challenge arises with the ease of use of a computer. If it is easy to implement new functionality a researcher tends to do so and of course occasionally introduces conceptional mistakes or implementation errors. For safety critical functionality this is fatal for the whole system in the case of a MAV.

## 2.1 System Layers

To include the best aspects of a simple microcontroller and a powerful general purpose computer into the concept, the system architecture of the iQCopter consists of three hierarchic layers, each providing certain properties as shown in figure 2. The innermost layer is the "hardware layer" consisting of an 8-bit microcontroller which is connected to all critical sensors, actuators and a long range RF module. It is responsible for timing, the acquisition of sensor data and subsequent transfer to the computer board. This is illustrated in figure 3.

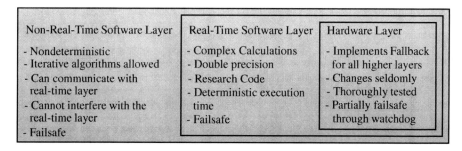

**Fig. 2.** The layered structure of our system design. Through the fallback mechanisms in the hardware layer, experimental code can be run in the software layer to accelerate research progress without sacrificing safety.

Safety, ease of use and performance are guaranteed by the combination of a solid fallback solution running on the fixed-point microcontroller in the hardware layer and the deterministic real-time software layer running more extensive algorithms on the computer. In case the main controller process on the computer is locked up or exited accidentally, the fallback solution automatically takes over within milliseconds. This way even software for the innermost control loop can easily and safely be researched while having the comfort of a familiar environment with advanced debugging and development tools.

Algorithms with nondeterministic execution time like many vision algorithms or iterative optimization are prohibited in the real-time layer, though. This is to be handled in the non-real-time layer. An important point is that a non-real-time task can never interfere with a real-time task even if it stresses the processor to 100%.

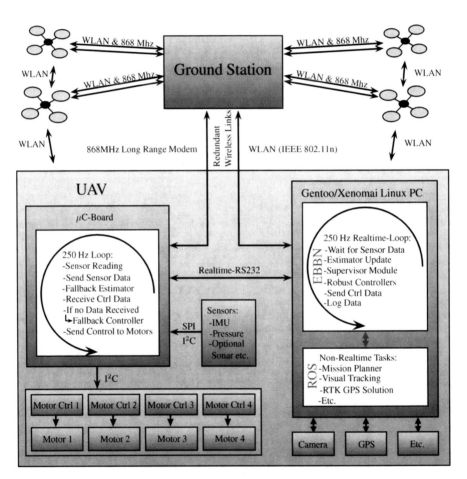

**Fig. 3.** The system architecture of an iQCopter communicating with multiple MAVs and a ground station. The two 250Hz loops are synchronized via the RS232-Link. If the board computer fails, the μC-Board is capable of both attitude estimation and control as a fallback solution.

## 2.2    Real-Time Software Framework

Having introduced the layered system architecture it was necessary to bring the endeavor to achieve high transparency and ease of use to the software level on the computer. This was realized by the development of a novel real-time capable framework named Executable Building Blocks Network (EBBN). It is a comprehensive suite of basic blocks such as math modules, hardware interfacing modules, control and state estimation modules etc. to form a runtime coalition for which the routing and parameterization is completely defined by configuration files.

# 3    Hardware Setup

## 3.1    Computer Board

The current iQCopter is equipped with a 1.6GHz Intel Atom embedded computer (consuming about 5W), with plans to upgrade to a laptop-level multicore computer board in the future. The board computer is easily replaceable in this system setup since no hardware specific code is executed on the computer. The ATMEL ATmega128 microcontroller functions as an abstraction layer between sensors and computer. The only hardware requirement for the computer is a RS232 serial port to form the real-time link to the microcontroller. The processing power of the Atom processor is sufficient to run all state estimation and control algorithms in double precision at 250Hz while running a pattern recognition algorithm with 400x300 pixels at about 5Hz in parallel.

The deployed operating system is a real-time enabled Gentoo Linux [5] since the control loop shall be closed via the board computer and thus requires deterministic timing. In order to make the Linux kernel real-time capable it is augmented with the Xenomai real-time framework [15]. During load tests the latencies where measured to never exceed $30\mu s$ which is well below the requirements considering $4ms$ period time.

## 3.2    Sensors

The most important sensors in a MAV are the inertial sensors like gyroscopes and accelerometers, since they provide the essential data for computation of the attitude. Commercially available complete inertial measurement units (IMU) including sensor data fusion were considered not appropriate for this project due to high price, weight and slow sampling rates (50-100Hz). The development of an IMU based on analog inertial sensors is challenging, though. Temperature sensitivity and high requirements for amplification and A/D-conversion complicate a high-performance solution. As a compromise an integrated intelligent sensor from Analog Devices' iSensor family has been chosen: the ADIS16405 IMU [1]. In a small package it houses high-accuracy temperature compensated MEMS accelerometers, gyroscopes and magnetometers for a reasonable price. Some specifications are given in table 1. Sensor readings are transferred via a

SPI interface. Data is internally acquired at 819.2Hz and filtered by a discrete low-pass configured to 17 taps improving gyroscope noise levels to $0.0045°/sec$ rms and changing their bandwidth to 32Hz.

**Table 1.** Quantities of the integrated Analog Devices ADIS16405 IMU. It also comprises a 3-axis magnetometer in the same package, weighing only 16 grams in total. Laid out as an intelligent sensor it provides temperature compensation and low pass filtering but not a complete state estimation solution.

| Gyroscopes | |
|---|---:|
| Typical Dynamic Range | $±350°/sec$ |
| Typical Sensitivity | $±0.05°/sec/LSB$ |
| Nonlinearity | 0.1% of FS |
| In-Run Bias Stability | $0.007°/sec$ |
| Angular Random Walk | $2°/\sqrt{hr}$ |
| Output Noise (unfiltered) | $0.9°/sec$ rms |
| Bandwidth | $330Hz$ |
| **Accelerometers** | |
| Typical Dynamic Range | $±18$ g |
| Typical Sensitivity | $±3.33$ mg/LSB |
| Nonlinearity | 0.1% of FS |
| In-Run Bias Stability | 0.2mg |
| Velocity Random Walk | $0.2m/sec/\sqrt{hr}$ |
| Output Noise (unfiltered) | $9mg$ rms |
| Bandwidth | $330Hz$ |
| Max. sampling rate | 819.2 Hz |
| Temperature Range | $−40°C$ to $85°C$ |

For sensor data fusion a simple yet efficient quaternion based Kalman filter has been implemented, running at 250 Hz. Although the sensor is high-end in the range of MEMS IMUs it is still important to estimate and compensate accelerometer and gyroscope biases during flight for satisfying performance. Additionally, a hard-iron calibration of the magnetometers has been done after the MAV assembly. The magnetometer biases are not estimated at flight time.

Position measurements are supplied either by a Real-Time Kinematic GPS (RTK-GPS) solution that is described in [12] or by visual measurements with a single camera or a stereo camera system. The RTK-GPS solution is based on a $\mu$-Blox LEA-6T chip passing raw data to the computer which iteratively determines the solution. At the time of writing both GPS-based and vision-based position control have successfully been tested in first flight tests.

### 3.3   Wireless Communication

The wireless communication capabilities comprise a 802.11n WLAN solution to provide a high performance mesh network structure between all MAVs and the ground station and a redundant long range 868Mhz link to provide a fallback solution.

### 3.4 Flight Frame and Actuators

For the flight frame and motor controllers the commercially available Conrad Quadrocopter 450 [4] toy quadrotor was chosen as the basis for the reason of easy and inexpensive availability of spare parts. The motor controllers are commanded via I$^2$C-bus in contrast to standard brushless controllers which only accept a rather inaccurate pulse width modulated signal as input. The motors are Robbe ROXXY 2827-34 brushless outrunner motors which drive 10"x4,5" airscrews providing a thrust up to 550 gram per motor with a 3-cell lithium polymer battery. The flight time is about 15 minutes with a 3300mAh battery and a total airborne weight of 1250 grams.

## 4 Performance Benchmark

In the following, two benchmark cases are briefly presented, which demonstrate the ability of the design to achieve remarkable performance with real flight experiments. All practical experiments strongly benefit from the highly modular, transparent and configurable EBBN framework, which has sped up development progress.

### 4.1 System Identification of the Roll and Pitch Axis

An important step for a research platform is the acquisition of an accurate system model for the purpose of model-based controller design and simulation. Unfortunately this is usually very difficult for quad-rotor MAVs since identification signals can not be fed into an uncontrolled and unsupervised flying vehicle. For a successful identification one ideally needs complete transparency down to the innermost control loops. This can be a problem with commercially available UAV platforms which only provide a blackbox solution for the stabilizing control loops or only slow sampling rates are provided externally. Even if the controller parameters are available it might pose problems to route the desired signals of a closed system to a data logger.

With EBBN and the presented system architecture, the innermost control loops with all signals are at the disposal of the researcher who can easily route all the desired signals to a data logger or the wireless communication system. It has been helpful to be able to quickly reparameterize or exchange stabilizing controllers during identification.

This paper can not comprehensively discuss the system identification for brevity (see [9] for a thorough review of closed-loop identification methods and [3] for modelling a quad-rotor). Instead the successful identification attempt for the roll and pitch axis is exemplarily described. For this, the indirect method is used where a stable closed-loop model is identified including the known controller $C(s)$. Afterwards the unstable open-loop model $G(s)$ can be extracted. Figure 4 shows the setup for a single axis. The identification signal $\gamma$ is a pseudo random binary sequence (PRBS) signal with a bandwidth of approximately 20Hz and a peak-to-peak amplitude of 0.15, which corresponds to 15% of the total valid

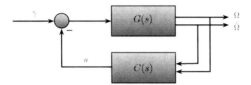

**Fig. 4.** The closed-loop SIMO identification setup for a single axis. The identification signal $\gamma$ is comprised of 20 periods of a PRBS-sequence to reduce noise influences.

motor control range. During the identification and validation experiments the iQCopter was fixed in all but the identification axis to be able to apply several unsupervised periods of the same PRBS-sequence without crashing the vehicle. The identification and validation data sets were acquired by averaging over all periods to reduce noise. Since 20 periods were averaged the signal-to-noise ratio improved by the factor 20. This was necessary since during initial experiments it was found that noise from vibration and process noise were significant.

Figure 5 shows the final identification result. The model is the result of an iterative identification, since the feedback controller $C(s)$ here is already an $H_\infty$-controller of 8th order which in turn was designed with a model that was acquired similarly, but with a hand-tuned PD-controller. The depicted single input multiple output (SIMO) model has been obtained by optimization of a grey box model with second order motor dynamics, an approximated delay of

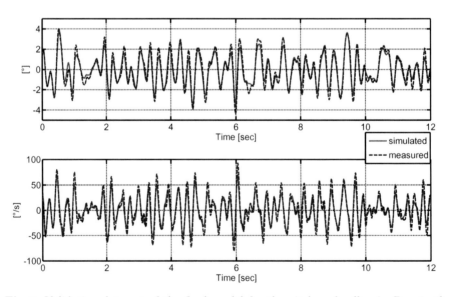

**Fig. 5.** Validation data set of the final model for the pitch and roll axis. Due to the unstable quad-rotor dynamics the simulation was run with the same stabilizing controller as during the experiment. From the plots of both outputs one can attest the model a very good approximation of the dynamics.

32ms and integral behavior for the angular rate and double integral behavior for the angle output:

$$G(s) = \begin{bmatrix} \frac{1}{s^2} \\ \frac{1}{s} \end{bmatrix} \frac{5.31(s+215.93)(s+131.56)}{(s+33.92)(s+13.14)} e^{-0.032s}$$

The acquired model resembles the system dynamics very well as will be proven with the design of an aggressive $H_\infty$ attitude controller for the pitch and roll axis in the next section.

## 4.2   An $H_\infty$ Controller Design for the Roll and Pitch Axis

Once a sufficient model has been acquired, model-based controller design techniques can be applied. Many UAVs rely on hand-tuned PID controllers due to

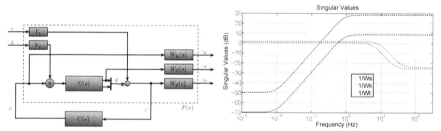

(a) The generalized plant (left) and the singular values of the shaping functions (right) that were used for the $H_\infty$ design

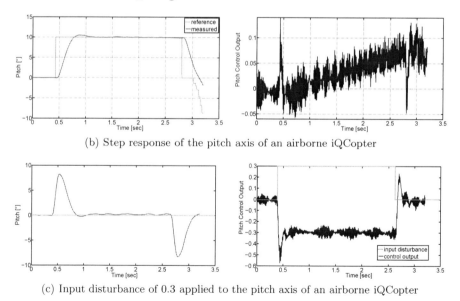

(b) Step response of the pitch axis of an airborne iQCopter

(c) Input disturbance of 0.3 applied to the pitch axis of an airborne iQCopter

**Fig. 6.** These plots prove the exceptional control performance of the iQCopter with its $H_\infty$ controller. The input disturbance of 30% of the total control range is a rather extreme example of the ability of the controller design.

the lack of a good system model. In [13], [3] and [7], linear model-based techniques are applied to quad-rotors. Due to model inaccuracies the results are not optimal, though.

The presented controller uses both, the angle and angular rate output, to achieve aggressive controller performance. This has been the driving idea behind the identification of a SIMO model. The generalized plant setup and shaping functions are shown in figure 6(a).

The performance of the resulting MISO $H_\infty$ controller for the pitch and roll axes is shown in figure 6(b) and 6(c) which depicts unfiltered plots from a free flight experiment. The improvement over the previously used hand-tuned PID controller has been found to be significant due to the high static gain that is achievable for both reference tracking and input disturbance rejection cases while keeping the overshoot as low as 6%. The rise time was optimized to about 300ms, accordingly the controller cycles about 75 periods meanwhile at 250Hz sampling rate. Although this might seem excessive we have observed that this yields superior results when compared to 50Hz sampling rate. This is probably due to the amplitude discretization that is necessary to generate the motor controller input. The oversampling effectively generates a higher resolution for actuator control. The designed controllers have quickly been incorporated into the UAV as state space models which are loaded from a Matlab generated file easing the transition from simulation to practical experiment.

## 5    Conclusion and Future Work

This paper has presented the iQCopter, a high-performance quad-rotor MAV with a layered system architecture to provide an easy to use testbed with high transparency down to the innermost control loops and mechanisms to ensure operational safety. With the successful model-based design of an aggressive controller it was shown that 1) the inertial measurement solution performs well, 2) the loop closure via a computer at 250Hz was successfully implemented and functions safely, 3) the linear model that was acquired represents the quad-rotor attitude dynamics well and 4) the physical setup with the chosen actuators and motor drivers is sufficient.

Future projects will focus on obstacle and collision avoidance with a swarm of iQCopters as well as localization and mapping with a stereo camera system for single agents. Additionally, dynamic mission planning for single and multiple cooperating MAVs will be addressed to allow operation in hazardous and changing environments.

## References

1. Analog Devices: ADIS 16405 (April 2011),
   http://www.analog.com/en/mems-sensors/inertial-sensors/
   adis16405/products/product.html
2. Bachrach, A., Winter, A.D., He, R., Hemann, G., Prentice, S., Roy, N.: RANGE-robust autonomous navigation in gps-denied environments. In: IEEE International Conference on Robotics and Automation (ICRA), pp. 1096–1097 (2010)

3. Bouabdallah, S., Noth, A., Siegwart, R.: PID vs LQ control techniques applied to an indoor micro quadrotor. In: IEEE/RSJ International Conference on Intelligent Robots and Systems (IROS), vol. 3, pp. 2451–2456 (2004)
4. Conrad Electronic: Quadrocopter 450 ARF (April 2011), http://www.conrad.de/ce/de/product/208000/QUADROCOPTER-450-ARF-35-MHz/
5. Gentoo: (April 2011), http://www.gentoo.org/
6. Grzonka, S., Grisetti, G., Burgard, W.: Towards a navigation system for autonomous indoor flying. In: IEEE International Conference on Robotics and Automation (ICRA), pp. 2878–2883 (2009)
7. Hoffmann, G., Rajnarayan, D.G., Waslander, S.L., Dostal, D., Jang, J., Tomlin, C.: The Stanford Testbed of Autonomous Rotorcraft for Multi Agent Control (STAR-MAC). In: The 23rd Digital Avionics Systems Conference. vol. 2 (2004)
8. How, J., Bethke, B., Frank, A., Dale, D., Vian, J.: Real-time indoor autonomous vehicle test environment. IEEE Control Systems Magazine 28(2), 51–64 (2008)
9. Ljung, L.: System identification: Theory for the user, 2nd edn. Prentice Hall information and system sciences series. Prentice Hall PTR, Upper Saddle River, NJ (1999)
10. Meier, L., Fraundorfer, F., Pollefeys, M.: The intelligent flying eye. SPIE Newsroom (2011)
11. Michael, N., Mellinger, D., Lindsey, Q., Kumar, V.: The GRASP Multiple Micro-UAV Testbed. IEEE Robotics & Automation Magazine 17(3), 56–65 (2010)
12. Pilz, U., Gropengießer, W., Walder, F., Witt, J., Werner, H.: Quadrocoter Trajectory Tracking Using RTK-GPS and Vision-Based Hovering. In: 4th International Conference on Robotics and Applications (2011)
13. Pounds, P., Mahony, R., Corke, P.: Modelling and Control of a Quad-Rotor Robot. In: Proceedings of the Australasian Conference on Robotics and Automation (2006)
14. Witt, J., Annighöfer, B., Falkenberg, O., Pilz, U., Weltin, U., Werner, H., Thielecke, F.: TUHH Quadrokopter Projekt (April 2011), http://www.tu-harburg.de/quadrokopter
15. Xenomai: (April 2011), http://www.xenomai.org/

# Simple Low Cost Autopilot System for UAVs

S. Veera Ragavan*, Velappa Ganapathy, and Chee Aiying

Monash University, Sunway Campus, Malaysia
{veera.ragavan}@monash.edu.my
University of Malaya, Kuala Lumpur, Malaysia
{velappa.ganapathy}@um.edu.my

**Abstract.** In this paper, we discuss the development of a Global Navigation and Path Planning System suitable for implementation on small, experimental, resource constrained, low cost, RC UAVs. The path planning algorithm generates short and feasible paths using waypoints and trajectories. Obstacle detection and avoidance which are important aspects of local path planning have also been incorporated. The developed path planning algorithm has a shorter computational time when compared with A* algorithm. The output from the path planning algorithm is fed to a GIS system and visually checked using $GoogleMaps^{TM}$ to ensure that UAV travels in the desired path. A telematics module and a JAUS Standard messaging interface for data exchange between the ground station and UAV has been developed and implemented to transmit and receive data from the UAV.

**Keywords:** Autonomous Path Planning, Navigation, UAVs, Waypoint based Navigation, JAUS based Messaging Interface, Mobile Object Database (MOD), Geographical information Systems (GIS).

## 1 Introduction

In the modern era, UAVs (Unmanned Aerial Vehicles) play an important role in search and rescue missions, target tracking, surveillance, scientific research and military reconnaissance. Hence, research in simple, low-cost autopilot system for UAVs would bring about greater benefits to the society. The development of autonomous autopilot systems for UAV has become important. UAVs that are employed in long range missions use Global Positioning System (GPS) modules not only to position themselves and be spatially aware, but also to send useful information for tracking, monitoring and recovery of lost machines through embedded communication modules and appropriate service interfaces provided to track them online. The UAV has to be autonomous and perform decision without human intervention. Suitable sensors and fusion techniques have been implemented [12]. A ground station monitors the status of UAV and also provides the user interfaces necessary to command the UAV and guides the UAV

---

* This work was supported in full by School of Engineering, Monash University Sunway Campus.

S. Jeschke, H. Liu, and D. Schilberg (Eds.): ICIRA 2011, Part I, LNAI 7101, pp. 324–334, 2011.

to reach its destination through a set of given waypoints from GIS systems such a Mobile Object Databases (MOD) and $GoogleMaps^{TM}$.

Multiple levels of suitable path planning algorithms must be applied in order to:(a) Select a feasible set of waypoints (from a MOD) connecting the start position and destination and (b) to generate a trajectory consistent with the vehicle kinematics between them. Local Path planning strategies also need to be developed so that UAV would be able to select the most optimal path to reach the next waypoint without colliding with obstacles. Common approaches that are used for Global Path Planning are A* algorithm, Dijikstra's algorithm and Genetic algorithm. In addition, trajectory generation or motion planning algorithms are required to determine the details of the path inbetween the waypoints. The approach used here is to divide the desired trajectory into smaller sections that can be approximated by polynomial equations of virtual arcs consistent with the UAV's kinematic constraints using virtual arc equation proposed in [1],[2].

The development of communication module interface is needed to ensure effective communication and handle coordination between the ground station and UAV. Important data such as the waypoints, UAVs location and UAVs flight status need to be monitored frequently by the ground station to determine the subsequent action taken. The current techniques used for communication are broadcast radio services, stand-alone two-way tactical data links (TDLs), overlay of GSM system and surrogate satellite services.

Existing tracking and navigation systems are concentrated on specific targets and do not inherit the flexibility to be diversified into a variety of applications. In this regard, this paper uses a generalized approach very similar in the mobile object tracking and navigation approaches using GPS data from a mobile device, a Mobile Object Database (MOD) and a GIS module implemented using Google Maps[3]. The path planning modules developed here are expected to be an extension to the development of a General Distributed framework that enables path planning and navigation based on waypoints for near real-time testing [4], [12].

The resultant path from the developed algorithm is Validated and checked using Geographical Information Systems (GIS). $GoogleMaps^{TM}$ APIs are used to develop customized User Interfaces (UIs) and using the overlay feature available, the path between any two given points is plotted. This paper also provides information on the elements required to construct an effective ground station for UAVs simple autopilot system. Tools used include $MATLAB^{TM}$ for path planning and $GoogleEarth^{TM}$ for visualization of the UAVs pre-planned flight path.

## 2 Problem Statement and Requirements

The Path planning problem investigated here can be described as : *Given a starting location A, destination location B and detailed description of environment in the form of a Map, Find the shortest path between the two specific locations. The path should be collision free, feasible and optimum.*

System Design Requirements:

- Develop a Friendly User Interface to simulate and plot the obtained flight path on a Local 3D Map using Matlab. Also plot the entire flight path using a visual 3D Plot and $GoogleMaps^{TM}$. .
- Implement a two way communication system based on a Standard Messaging Interface for data transfer between the ground station and UAV.

## 3   Path Planning System

A general flow of the system is shown in Fig.1.

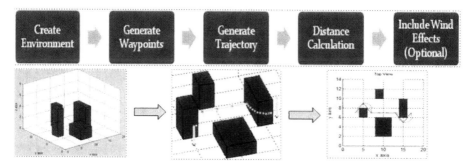

**Fig. 1.** General System Flow. (a) Creating a 3D Matlab Environment, (b) and (c) Generation of Waypoints and Trajectory, (d) Distance calculation and (e) Wind effect Viewer.

### 3.1   Environment Creation - MATLAB$^{TM}$ GUIs, GIS System Integration and Data Interaction

Firstly, a Virtual 3D Local environment Model which forms a part of Real world global environment and a subset of MOD is created using $MATLAB^{TM}$. The four primitives (Geometric building blocks of different dimensions) are used to represent the obstacles at the environment. The coordinates of blocks are in the form of an array of GeoFences that are declared as No-Fly Zones or obstacles. These Geo Fences can then be stored and retrieved from MODs. System Integration details of the GIS, MOD and Data Acquisition modules and their interactions is similar to [3]. The data sent is received over a TCP/IP connection and extracted components are stored in a Mobile Object Database developed using $MySQL^{TM}$. The Spatial extensions provided by $MySQL^{TM}$ are used in Mobile Object Database created.

### 3.2   Waypoints for Path Planning

A waypoint is a reference point in physical space used for purposes of navigation [4]. In this case, the waypoint coordinates would be in three dimensions, representing longitude, latitude and altitude. Using a set of Waypoints, the abstract routing paths of aircraft needed for UAV navigation is obtained.

The Waypoint Navigation has been used to gainfully augment if not replace traditional navigation systems. A Hybrid Waypoint Navigation System
attempted here offers a variety of added features and benefits. Conventional Autonomous Navigation Systems are either Deliberative or Reactive [4]. A hybrid
system provides a route from one waypoint to another or to multiple waypoints
depending on the destination and trip plan. The benefit is that, they not only
work for preplanning purposes, but they can also work as a Decision Support
System to direct the mobile robot back to its origin which is critical in UAV
recovery.

### 3.3   Proposed Path Planning Algorithm

The Path Planning Algorithm has been implemented in two levels: Way point
path planning and Trajectory generation.

A simple Waypoint based path planning algorithm was developed using
$MATLAB^{TM}$. After the environment is created, a set of the waypoints are
generated based on the given start point and destination. Once the start and
end points are selected by the user, a set of intermediate waypoint nodes denoting the shortest path is generated. Travelling along the hypotenuse of two points
results in the shortest distance. In this path planning algorithm, the object has
the flexibility to travel in eight directions instead of four as shown in Fig. 2(a).
Since the UAV can travel in eight possible directions , the shortest route to reach
destination would be to travel diagonally towards the end point instead of travelling in only four directions as shown in Fig. 2(b) and Fig. 2(c). Feasibility is
then checked using a rule base consisting mainly of $if - elseif - else$ conditions
to determine alternate route options that are available until the terminating
condition $(xstart == xfin)\&\&(ystart < yfin)$, is achieved. Nested $if - else$
conditions are used for obstacle detection and avoidance. If the pre-determined
waypoint is listed in the forbidden list (i.e. obstacles), then the Mobile Objecy
would manouvere around the obstacle and then return back to its original vertical route to reach the end point. Depending on the start and end conditions
one of the four different movement directions is selected.Additional conditions
were added to aid convergence and collision avoidance and tested for validity.
Trajectory defines the path and position of object through space over time.

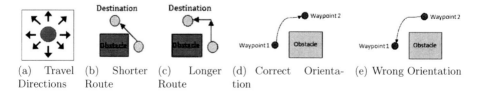

(a)   Travel    (b)   Shorter    (c)   Longer    (d)   Correct   Orienta-    (e) Wrong Orientation
Directions      Route            Route            tion

**Fig. 2.** Possible Orientations

The detailed path in between two waypoints can be obtained using trajectory generation. There are two types of equations generally applied to generate the trajectory: one is a linear equation as shown in Eq.1 and the other is the elliptic equation as shown by Eq.2 and Eq.3. Linear equation Eq.1 is used to generate straight line paths between two waypoints. The variable $x$ and variable $y$ represents the coordinates at any time $t$.Since the step size is set to 10, additional 10 points would be generated in between two waypoints to obtain a detailed path.

$$y = mx + b \tag{1}$$

$$X(t) = X_c + a\,cost\,cos\phi - b\,sint\,sin\phi \tag{2}$$

$$Y(t) = Y_c + a\,cost\,sin\phi - b\,sint\,cos\phi \tag{3}$$

In the ellipse equations Eqs. 2 - 3, the variable $a$ and $b$ are the major axis and minor axis respectively. $(X_c, Y_c)$ is the centre of the ellipse, and $\phi$ is the angle between the X-axis and the major axis of the ellipse. A $+ve\angle$ positive angle indicates a clockwise direction whereas a negative angle means that the ellipse is oriented in counter clockwise direction. The orientation of ellipse is important for trajectory generation since the waypoints generated could be in either direction. For e.g. in the 2(d), assuming object is travelling from Waypoint 1 to Waypoint 2, the orientation of ellipse must be in clockwise direction. A wrong orientation as shown in 2(e) results in the wrong trajectory. The ellipse equation is used to generate curvatures when the UAV manouvers to avoid obstacles. The step size is also set to 10 here so that 10 points are generated in between two waypoints.

Distance calculation is important to judge the performance of path planning algorithm. Algorithms that could produce shorter distances to reach destination are more preferable. More over shorter distances could mean lesser orientation changes in path. Two types of distance calculation methods are used: Euclidean distance and Vincenty Formula.

$$d = \sum \sqrt{(x_2 - x_1)^2 + (y_2 - y_1)^2 + (z_2 - z_1)^2} \tag{4}$$

The Euclidean distance calculation is the conventional approximate method used to calculate distance of two points as given by Eq. 4. The Vincenty Formula is a more accurate, iterative method to calculate distance between two latitude/longitude points on earth's surface based on an accurate ellipsoidal model of the earth. For accurate results WGS-84 an ellipsoidal model for earth is used with parameters : major semiaxes of ellipsoid, $a = 6378137m$, minor semiaxes of ellipsoid, $b = 6356752.3142m$ and flattening, $f = 1/298.257223563$ [5]. As calculations of angles are done in radians, the latitude and longitude in decimal is converted to radians using $rad = n.deg/180$ resulting in an accuracy of less than 0.5mm.

Finally, the wind effects obtained from [6] are added to the generated path. According to the Malaysian Meteorological Department, the average wind speed

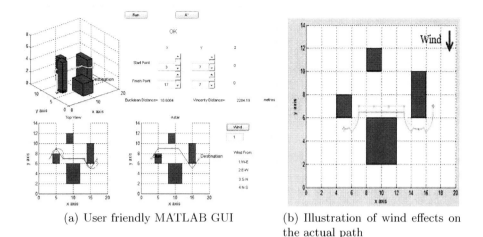

(a) User friendly MATLAB GUI

(b) Illustration of wind effects on the actual path

**Fig. 3.** Wind Effects

in Malaysia is approximately 3 km/h to 20 km/h. Wind directions considered are the four major directions : North, South, East and West. It can be seen from the simulation results shown in Fig. 3(b) the wind direction is from the North to South resulting in the actual path being displaced by a few units in the direction of wind. However, if the UAVs position is directly behind a tall building, then the actual path for that strech remains unaffected. The drift in path due to wind effect can be seen from the plots in Fig. 3(b) and Fig. 3(a).

## 3.4 Development of Joint Architecture for Unmanned Systems (JAUS) Based Intelligent Messaging Architecture(IMA)

There are no common standards available as yet to address the questions of measurability, comparability, interoperability, and resusability of architectural concepts and components in robotics [16]. Standards are crucial to enhance modularity, accelerate development, reduce cost, facilitate code reuse, provide a framework for technology insertion, and ultimately, to enable interoperability between systems developed by different vendors.While a large number of unmanned system products are being introduced to the market they are usually task dependent and non-interoperable.

JAUS (Joint Architecture for Unmanned Systems) is a DoD mandated SAE standard which is an ideal candidate for the messaging between elements of unmanned systems. JAUS provides the necessary definitions to develop architecture to support the following objectives [14],

– Support all classes of unmanned systems
– Rapid technology insertion
– Interoperable operator control unit

- Interchangeable/interoperable payloads
- Interoperable unmanned systems.

The development of a Standard Messaging Interface is important for data exchange between the ground station and UAV. After the path planning algorithm has generated a path towards the destination, the waypoints would be sent from the ground station to the Onboard Controller on the UAV. The Onboard controller sends location feed back to the ground station. Location Data transferred are latitude, longitude, altitude, roll, pitch, yaw, rates, velocity and Heading. To support message identification, routing and transfer, a modified version of a standard JAUS header was used. As the JAUS 16 byte header supports much more functionality than what is required, a reduced message header as shown in the table 1 was used in line with real time data transfer assumptions [13].

**Table 1.** Reduced JAUS Message Header And UAVs state Message

| No | Field | Bytes | No | Field | Bytes |
|----|-------|-------|----|-------|-------|
| No. | Field | Bytes | 1 | Latitude degrees (WGS 84) | 1 |
| 1 | Destination Node ID | 1 | 2 | Longitude degrees (WGS 84) | 1 |
| 2 | Source Component ID | 1 | 3 | Altitude | 1 |
| 3 | Data Control (bytes) | 2 | 4 | Roll , Pitch, Yaw | 1 |
| 4 | Sequence Number | 1 | 5 | Rate - Roll, Pitch, Yaw | 1 |
|  | Total Bytes | 5 |  | Total Bytes | 5 |

JAUS standard defines the format of messages that travel between unmanned systems. A Standard JAUS Message header has a length of 16 bytes consisting of twelve fields such as Message properties, Command Code, Destination ID's, Source ID's, data control and sequence numbers. Joint Architecture for Unmanned Systems (JAUS) consists of a number of hierarchical elements that work together to form a complete JAUS compliant unmanned system with components forming the lowest level of abstraction. Our motivation for using the JAUS arises from recent attempts to use JAUS messages for Smart Intelligent systems messaging for unmanned systems [13], [15].

### 3.5   A* Algorithm Implementation

The A* algorithm is widely used for path finding problems to achieve the path with the least cost. The A* algorithm follows the path of lowest cost, storing a priority queue for different path segments as it progresses. It abandons higher cost path segments as it progresses. The order of nodes visited in A* is determined using a distance plus cost function [7]. The process repeats until destination is reached. The A* uses heuristics to guide itself [8].

Before starting the A* algorithm, the cost map or search area must be defined. For this work, the map size is defined as 20 by 14 units and the number of obstacles as 8. The cost map is defined as follows; nodes where obstacles are placed are given value of -1; node representing the destination is given value of 0; nodes representing the object (UAV) are given a value of 1; nodes representing available space are given a value of 2. After obtaining the cost map, the search algorithm would proceed. The starting point is added to OPEN list. Then the successive nodes are searched by considering all the reachable points (value of cost map=0) adjacent to the starting point. The possible nodes are added to OPEN list. After the node on the OPEN list with lowest F-cost is selected, the node is removed from the OPEN list and then added to the CLOSED list. All the adjacent nodes are checked through. The nodes that are already on the CLOSED list or nodes which have obstacles are ignored. In certain cases, the adjacent node might be on the OPEN list. In this case, the new F, G and H-cost are computed. Then the new G-cost is compared to the G-cost of same node that is already located in the OPEN list. If the new G-cost is lower, the parent node is updated to the current node. For waypoints that are not on the OPEN list are added to the OPEN list and the parent node is defined. The steps above are repeated until the destination node is added to the CLOSED list, which implies that the shortest path has been found successfully. However, an empty OPEN list and the goal destination node reached would imply a failure in the search process. Once the destination node is successfully added to the CLOSED list, the A* would start at the destination node and backtrack moving from one node to its parent node. This path would lead to reaching the starting node again. The path generated would thus be the shortest path generated by A* algorithm.

## 3.6  Performance of the Developed Algorithm

The path planning algorithm that has been developed was compared with the A* algorithm. The factors chosen for comparison are the computational time and distance required for reaching the destination. Ten randomly selected starting points and destination points were chosen for testing and the results are shown in figure 4. In the table, the coloumns 'My' and 'A*' show performance of the developed path planning algorithm and a standard 'A*'algorithm. The computational time (in milliseconds) to run the program was obtained by using the 'cputime' command in MATLAB. The proposed path planning algorithm (My) is marginally better than those obtained with A* algorithm. A reduction in computational time is desirable since the results can be achieved in a shorter duration leading to increased response and energy efficiency of UAV. The reason for higher computational time required for A* algorithm is due to the frequent operations on the OPEN list and CLOSED list. On the other hand, the proposed path planning algorithm searches the shortest path through iterative conditional statements. It is shown that the distance travelled for both algorithms are similar. Hence, the path planning algorithm that has been developed here is comparable to A* and is proven to generate the shortest path.

| Start | Destination | cputime | | Distance (units) | |
|---|---|---|---|---|---|
| | | My | A* | My | A* |
| (7,3,0) | (17,9,0) | 50.3727 | 51.4179 | 15.31371 | 15.31371 |
| (1,7,0) | (17,9,0) | 46.3791 | 47.2215 | 18.48528 | 18.48528 |
| (5,11,0) | (15,3,0) | 29.6714 | 30.7322 | 13.31371 | 13.31371 |
| (17,11,0) | (7,1,0) | 45.5211 | 46.7223 | 16.48528 | 16.48528 |
| (17,3,0) | (7,11,0) | 47.7207 | 48.6567 | 13.31371 | 13.31371 |
| (15,5,0) | (3,7,0) | 50.1543 | 51.1995 | 14.48528 | 14.48528 |
| (9,1,0) | (11,11,0) | 18.0961 | 20.8885 | 12.48528 | 12.48528 |
| (7,11,0) | (17,7,0) | 44.0079 | 45.7551 | 13.31371 | 13.31371 |
| (15,11,0) | (3,7,0) | 53.4303 | 57.58 | 13.65685 | 13.65685 |
| (5,5,0) | (17,7,0) | 59.1244 | 60.3568 | 14.48528 | 14.48528 |
| | Average | 44.4478 | 46.05305 | | |

**Fig. 4.** Results of comparison of cputime and distance travelled

## 4    Testing and Simulation of Flight Path

### 4.1    Matlab Simulation

The MATLAB GUI was created to provide a user friendly interface to simulate the path in MATLAB environment. In the GUI shown in 3(a), users can specify the start Nodes and finish Nodes. Clicking on the 'Run' button, displays the path in 3D view and top views. The total Euclidean distance in units and distance travelled computed by Vincenty Formula in metres is also displayed. To compare the proposed path planning algorithm with A* algorithm, clicking on the 'A*' button on the top most row, generates the path by A* algorithm and superimposed on the graph. The path with wind effects is displayed by specifying the wind direction using the 'Wind' button. If the wind is obstructed by obstacle, the path directly behind the obstacle would not be displaced by the wind.

### 4.2    Google Earth Simulation

The Google Earth software displays satellite models of earth and is available as a free and open tool on the internet. In order to simulate the path in Google Earth, the xy-coordinates from MATLAB needs to be converted to longitude, latitude and altitude. The image overlay and polygon functions are used to create the environment in Google Earth. The latitude and longitude of four corners of the map are selected. Through interpolation method, the xy-coordinates from MATLAB can be converted into longitude and latitude respectively. A .*kml* file containing the longitude and latitude of entire path need is generated.

To plot the path from start point to destination on the map, in Google EarthTM polyline functions Commands are used. Execution of the m-file in MATLAB, generates a .kml file which can be used to vies the path in Google

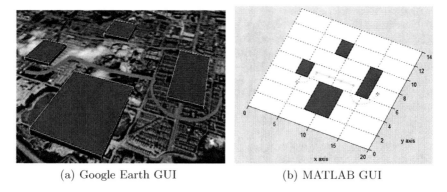

(a) Google Earth GUI                          (b) MATLAB GUI

**Fig. 5.** Illustration of MATLAB GUI

Earth. The limitation of Google Earth software is the restriction of zoom level to free users. Each zoom level contains information that could be appropriately displayed at that zoom level. The simulation of path in Google Earth in Fig. 5(a) matches the simulated path obtained using MATLAB Fig.5(b).

# 5   Limitations and Future Improvement

The path planning algorithm could be improved to include in dynamic environments. A D* algorithm implimentation capable of planning path in dynamic environments needs to be developed [10]. Failsafe systems capable of taking over when communication link is lost needs to be implemented.

# 6   Conclusion

The path planning algorithm that was developed provided marginally better results (w.r.t computational time) when compared to the A* algorithm. Both algorithms produce the shortest path and hence result in the same distance travelled from starting point to destination. Using the waypoint outputs from the proposed path planning algorithm, trajectory generation algorithm successfully generates the detail motion between two waypoints using polynomial equations. Effect of wind and deviation from the estimated path has been plotted.

A user friendly easy to use MATLAB GUI has been developed so that users are able to view the generated path and effects of wind in the path. The Google Earth interface provides a 3D view of flypath using waypoints.

A JAUS based IMA and the developed communication module were successfully interfaced to ensure effective data transmission from ground station to UAV. Using the MATLAB UDP interface object function and Telematics data interface, important waypoint data such as Longitude, Latitude and Altitude could be transferred almost instantaneously from ground station to UAV.

# References

1. McGee, T.G., Hedrick, J.K.: Path Planning and Control for Multiple Point Surveillance by an Unmanned Aircraft in Wind (2009)
2. Akthar, N., Whidborne, J.F., Cooke, A.K.: Real-time Trajectory Generation Technique for Dynamic Soaring UAVs, Department of Aerospace Sciences, Cranfield University
3. Alahakone, A.U., Ragavan, V.: Geospatial Information System for tracking and navigation of mobile objects. In: IEEE/ASME International Conference on Advanced Intelligent Mechatronics, AIM 2009, pp. 875–880 (2009)
4. Ibrahim, M.T.S., Ragavan, S.V., Ponnambalam, S.G.: Way point based deliberative path planner for navigation. In: IEEE/ASME International Conference on Advanced Intelligent Mechatronics, AIM 2009, pp. 881–886 (2009)
5. Vincenty Formula for Distance between Two Latitude/Longitude Points, http://www.movable-type.co.uk/scripts/latlong-vincenty.html (accessed: January 2010)
6. History: Weather Underground, http://www.wunderground.com/history/airport/WMKK/2010/6/1/DailyHistory.html?req_city=NA&req_state=NA&req_statename=NA (accessed: August 2011)
7. A*SearchAlgorithm, http://en.wikipedia.org/wiki/A*_search_algorithm (accessed: January 2010)
8. Amit's A*Pages, http://theory.stanford.edu/~amitp/GameProgramming/ (accessed: August 2011)
9. Miao, H.: Robot Path Planning in Dynamic Environments using a Simulated Annealing Based Approach (March 2009)
10. Stentz, A.: Optimal and Efficient Path Planning for Unknown and Dynamic Environments, Carnegie Mellon (1993)
11. M1206_User_guide, Wavecom Confidential (September 2003)
12. Ragavan, S.V., Ganapathy, V., Xian, E.C.M.: A reconfigurable FPGA framework for data fusion in UAV's. In: Proceedings of 2009 World Congress on Nature and Biologically Inspired Computing, NABIC 2009, Coimbatore, India, pp. 1626–1631 (2009)
13. Evans Iii, C.P.: Development Of A Geospatial Data Sharing Method For Unmanned Vehicles Based On The Joint Architecture For Unmanned Systems (JAUS), University of Florida (2005)
14. Yakin, Belet, F., Kutlu, F.: Developing JAUS Compliant Communication Infrastructures for C2 of Unmanned Systems through MDSD (2009)
15. Woo, H.J., Kim, M.H., Kim, J.H.: Development of multiple communication using JAUS message set for unmanned system. In: International Conference on Control, Automation and Systems 2007, Seoul, Korea, pp. 2374–2377 (2007)
16. Prassler, E., Nilson, K.: 1,001 robot architectures for 1,001 robots (Industrial Activities). In: Robotics & Automation Magazine, pp. 113–113. IEEE (2009)

# A Marsupial Relationship in Robotics: A Survey

Hamido Hourani[1], Philipp Wolters[1], Eckart Hauck[1], and Sabina Jeschke[2]

[1] Institute for Management Cybernetics (IfU),
[2] Institute of Information Management in Mechanical Engineering and
Center for Learning and Knowledge Management (IMA-ZLW),
RWTH Aachen University,
52068 Aachen, Germany
{hamido.hourani,philipp.wolters,eckart.hauck,
sabina.jeschke}@ima-zlw-ifu.rwth-aachen.de

**Abstract.** The diversity of tasks and work locations shows the need for heterogeneity among robot team members, where each group of robots is designed to fulfil specific tasks and to work efficiently in particular locations. To facilitate the missions of these specific task robots, logistic services have to be provided. A so called "marsupial relationship" – referring to the biological relationship between marsupial animals such as Kangaroos - can be one of these logistic services. This paper organizes and discusses the state of the art of this field. Besides, a precise definition of the marsupial relationship, which distinguishes it from other physical relationships in robotics, is presented. Moreover, a new organization and a detailed description of the marsupial members and their roles are given in this paper.

**Keywords:** Biological inspired robot, Marsupial robot, Physical cooperative, Multi-agent.

## 1 Introduction

In comparison to a single robot, a team of robots has several advantages such as robustness, faster accomplishment of tasks and higher quality of the result. Furthermore, some tasks can only be accomplished by a team of robots because of the character and the complexity of the tasks [1].

*Dudek*'s taxonomy for multi robots [2] classified teams of robots into three categories:

1. Identical composition COMP-IDENT (i.e. same software and hardware).
2. Homogeneous composition COMP-HOM (i.e. same hardware).
3. Heterogeneous composition COMP-HET (i.e. different software and hardware).

This paper focuses on heterogeneous robot teams.

Amongst the heterogeneous team members, each sub-group of robots is designed to efficiently carry out a specific group of tasks. The work domain of robots at the task site is limited, if the design of these robots complies with the characteristics of

S. Jeschke, H. Liu, and D. Schilberg (Eds.): ICIRA 2011, Part I, LNAI 7101, pp. 335–345, 2011.
© Springer-Verlag Berlin Heidelberg 2011

the task limits. This design restriction impacts their performance negatively when they are performing missions which are unrelated to their specific tasks. For instance, if the design of the robots is optimized for an underground environment but they would have to cross an open outdoor area to reach it.

Because time is a crucial factor in several applications, especially in rescue missions [3], a deployment service for the specific task robots (i.e. underground rescue robots) either near or inside their target location should be provided. This is achieved by providing a carrier robot for these robots. In this paper the carrier robot is called Container Robot while the carried robot team members, are called Passenger Robots. The Container is able to traverse difficult terrain, which the Passenger Robots cannot traverse easily without consuming their resources. Besides, the Container delivers them to their work locations faster and safer. Following this approach, the robots benefit from their heterogeneity by using the strengths of each team member and by overcoming their limitations [4].

This kind of physical relationship between robots is termed by *Murphy et al.* [5] as the marsupial-like relationship, analogue to the relationship between marsupial animals such as Kangaroos. Extended to the field of robotics, both the Container Robot and the Passenger Robots provide services to each other. For instance, while providing transportation to its Passenger Robots, the Container uses their sensors as extra mobile (non-attached) sensors [5].

A marsupial relationship in robotics comes into place in different fields of application which are underwater [6], underground [7], ground [8], aerial [9] and space [10].

Within this paper, the state of the art of different marsupial relationships in robotics will be presented and discussed. Moreover, a precise definition of the relationship and detailed descriptions of the marsupial members and their roles will be given. We believe that this paper will play a key role towards accelerating the research progress in this field.

The paper is structured as follows: Section 2 elaborates the characteristics of the marsupial relationship and defines it precisely. The roles of the marsupial members are discussed in section 3. Section 4 is devoted to the different applications of marsupial teams. In section 5, Summary and Open issues complete this paper.


## 2     The Marsupial Relationship and Its Definition

The marsupial relationship is a relatively new topic in robotics. Within this section, two research works are discussed to show the specific characteristics of the marsupial relationship and distinguish it from other physical relationships in robotics.

The first research work is the work of *Hirose et al.* [11]. They used a team of homogeneous robots where each member of the team carries out its tasks independently. In spite of this fact, they need to cooperate in some situations, such as crossing a cliff that a robot alone cannot cross. In order to do so, each robot carries one of its colleagues to build a connected chain. The carrying process is realized by equipping each robot with an arm and a knob. The arm is fixed on the front of the robot and the knob on its rear. Each robot holds the knob of its direct front robot to form that robot chain.

The second research work we discuss is the work of *Anderson et al.* [8]. They used a team of two heterogeneous robots; a small-sized robot (the Reduced Access Characterization Robot (RACS)) and a large-sized robot (the Mobile Automated Characterization Robot (MACS)). Both robots have the mission to explore an indoor environment. In addition to that, the MACS carries the RACS with it. Once the MACS reaches a tight door which it cannot pass, it deploys the RACS in front of the door, to let it explore inside of the room, and continues its work in another location. The MACS is equipped with a special container to place the RACS on it.

Between the works of *Hirose et al.* [11] and *Anderson et al.* [8] there are certain similarities but also differences. The similarities are:

1. Both of them considered physical relationships between robots.
2. Both of them used a robot to carry its colleague.
3. All team members share the same mission (i.e. exploration).
4. Robots depend physically on each other for a period of time (temporary dependency).

The differences are:

1. *Hirose et al.* [11] used a homogenous team while *Anderson et al.* [8] used a heterogeneous team.
2. The position of each robot within the physical relationship is not exchangeable in *Anderson*'s work while it is exchangeable in *Hirose*'s work. In other words, the MACS cannot exchange its position in the relationship with the RACS to being carried by the RACS, while the robots in [11] can exchange their positions within the physical chain.
3. Although the robots share the same mission in [8], they cannot exchange their work locations without a negative impact on their work performance. The MACS cannot enter the target work location of the RACS because of its size while the RACS needs a longer time to cover the MACS' work location. The robots in [11], on the other hand, can exchange their work locations without a negative impact on their performance.

These differences and similarities are the characteristics which distinguish the marsupial relationship from other physical relationships in robotics. On the one hand, the differences differentiate the marsupial relationship from other homogenous relationships. The heterogeneity of the team members is the key reason behind this decision. The similarities, on the other hand, form the marsupial relationship as a special case of the physical heterogeneous relationships. The carrying process is the main distinction between the marsupial relationship and other physical heterogeneous relationships. Furthermore, the dependency between Container and Passenger is temporary in the Marsupial relationship.

Several definitions tried to touch one of these characteristics to define the marsupial relationship. *Murphy et al.* [5] were the first research team who established this term. They used it to relate the robots' behaviour to the kangaroo lifestyle where a big robot ("mother robot") carries one or more small robots ("child robots"). It is worth mentioning that *Anderson et al.* [8] were the first research group who addressed the marsupial relationship, but did not term it.

*Ausmus et al.* [12] defined the marsupial robot as a group of mobile robots, a sub-group of which depends on other group members for transport, feeding, etc. This dependency can last either for a short period of time or for the entire mission. Despite the fact that *Ausmus'* definition narrows *Murphy's* definition, it does not consider the characteristics of the marsupial. *Ausmus et al.* [12] called the Container Robot the *Dispensing Agent* and the Passenger Robot the *Passenger Agent*. Another notation for Container and Passenger was presented by *Matusiak et al.* [13] who named them *Motherbot* and *Marsubot*.

*Leitner* [14] extended *Dudek's* taxonomy [2] by adding a special class for the marsupial relationship COMP-MAR. This class defines the physical relation of the marsupial. However, it does not refer to the characteristics and the roles of the marsupial members.

Since none of these definitions give a precise description of the marsupial relationship and its characteristics, we present a precise definition as follows:

*A marsupial relationship is a physical relationship between two or more heterogeneous mobile robots, which the robots establish to utilize their individual strengths and to overcome their individual weaknesses. This relationship is essentially used for the carrying process. The robots which are acting as carriers cannot exchange this role with their Passengers within the same application domain as well as they cannot exchange their target work locations with their Passengers without a negative impact on the performance of the involved robots. During this relationship, the dependency among the robots is temporary.*

By the same application domain constraint we mean that if robot *R1* is the Container for robot *R2* on the ground *G* (the marsupial application domain), *R2* cannot be the Container for *R1* on *G*. However, this constraint does not prevent *R2* from being the Container for *R1* on another application domain, like in the sky. Moreover, it does not prevent *R1* from being a Passenger of another robot *R3* on *G* (i.e. nested marsupial).

## 3    The Roles of the Marsupial Members

Two types of robots are needed to form a Marsupial relationship (i.e. Container Robot and Passenger Robot). The container roles are elaborated in section 3.1 and the passenger roles are elaborated in sections 3.2 and 3.3.

### 3.1    The Container Roles

*Murphy et al.* [5] mentioned four roles for the Container: Coach, Manager, Messenger, and Carrier. However, these roles do not cover the other possible roles of the Container Robot which are presented in the state of the art. Therefore, we add two more roles: the Processor and the Supporter. We elaborate each role and distinguish it from other Container roles. A Container Robot can play several roles during the execution of a task.

**The Carrier Role.** The Carrier Role is the fundamental role which forms the marsupial relationship. All Container Robots play this role. Within this role, a Container carries its Passenger Robots either inside of a closed box [6],[16], inside of an open box [15],[17], by using a gripper [18] or on its top [10], [15],[19]. The purpose of this role is to deliver the Passenger Robots faster to their deployment point, to save their energy, and to protect them during the carrying process. *Anderson et al.* [8] introduced a conceptual approach where the Container deploys the Passenger and a network hub to facilitate the communication to the Passenger. Once the Passenger finishes its task, it moves toward the network hub and waits for being collected by the Container.

**The Coach Role.** Generally, a Container Robot has two advantages which can be exploited after deploying its Passenger Robots at the target location.

1. The Container Robot can change its position to get another angle of view on the work location, since it can move freely after the deployment of its Passenger Robots.
2. The Container can be provided with various sensors to monitor the Passenger Robots and to work as an additional provider of information.

These advantages enable the Container Robot to act as a Coach by sending directive messages to its Passenger Robots. *Zhou et al.* [6] used a marsupial fish-like robot where the Container assists the Passenger with the Passenger's task.

**The Manager Role.** Acting as a Manager means that the Passenger Robots get their commands directly from the Container Robot. The Container sends a specific task to each Passenger.

The difference between the Coach Role and the Manager Role is the type of the message. As a Coach the Container broadcasts directive messages to its Passenger Robots and each Passenger interprets these messages based on its situation. As a Manager, in turn, the Container sends specific commands to each individual Passenger. Each Passenger has to execute its specific commands [12].

*Sukhatme et al.* [9] elaborated the Manager Role by using a marsupial aerial team of robots. The Container Robot is an unmanned aerial vehicle (UAV) which carries an unmanned ground vehicle (UGV). The Container Robot releases the Passenger and assigns a task to it. Once the task is accomplished, the Container Robot collects the Passenger.

**The Messenger Role.** Either the conditions at the target location (e.g. underground and underwater), the limited capabilities of the Passenger, or both make the communication between it and the external world difficult. To overcome this obstacle, a Container acts as a messenger between its Passenger Robots and the external world on the one hand, and between the Passenger Robots themselves on the other hand. This service can be used by a Passenger either through wired communication with the

Container (e.g. [5]) or through wireless communication (e.g. [6]). Generally a cable is used when the Passenger is already connected with the Container via a rope (e.g. [5]). Regarding the wireless communication, Zhao et al. [7] gave the marsupial team the ability to install a repeater between the Passenger and the Container. This repeater is needed either because of signal disruption or the weakness of the Passenger's capability. Anderson et al. [8] used the repeater as a landmark to help the Container with the collection of the Passenger, in addition to its hub functionality.

**The Processor Role.** Within this role, a Container Robot shares its computational capability with its Passenger Robots to overcome their weaker computational capabilities. This sharing happens on request from the Passenger. The Passenger Robot sends its input data to its Container. The Container, in turn, processes these data and returns them to the Passenger.

Initiating the communication session and determining the number of Passenger Robots which are involved in this communication session distinguish the Processor Role from the Coach Role and the Manager Role on the one hand and from the Messenger Role on the other hand. These differences are sketched in Figure 1.

1. In the Coach Role and the Manager Role, the Container Robot initiates the communication session to send messages to its Passenger Robots (The Manager Role section shows the difference between the Coach Role and the Manager Role). But, in the Processor Role the Passenger Robot initiates the communication session with its Container Robot.
2. In the Messenger Role, the Container passes the messages either among Passenger Robots or between Passenger Robots and the external world. However, the Container Robot, which plays the Processor role, exchanges messages just with one Passenger Robot and processes the requested data from its Passenger.

The Processor role is addressed by *Rybski et al.* [20] where four Passenger Robots depended partially on a Container Robot to process their sensor data.

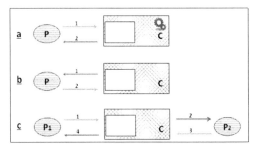

**Fig. 1.** A sketch of Marsupial members. *C* stands for Container Robot and *P* stands for Passenger Robot. The numbers above the arrows indicate the messages' sequences. (a) sketches a Processor role where the Passenger Robot initiates the communication. (b) sketches a Manager role where the Container Robot initiates the communication. (c) sketches the Messenger role where the Container Robot passes messages between two Passenger Robots; like in (a) the Container Robot exchanges messages with one Passenger Robot and processes the message.

**The Supporter Role.** This role includes the other logistic issues which require a physical interaction between a Container and its Passenger Robots on the one hand, and between the Container and the target environment on the other hand.

1. The physical logistic interaction between them includes for example recharging batteries [5]. This role is used when Passenger Robots are working for extended periods of time or the time which is required to accomplish their tasks is unknown. A Container provides its Passenger Robots with power either through a cable or through a docking station. *Murphy et al.* [5] used the cable approach to provide the Passenger with power. This approach limits the movement of the Passenger and the cable could be cut because of harsh terrain. *Matusiak et al.* [13] presented an approach to recharge the Passenger Robots' batteries through docking stations inside of the Container's body. Their Container Robot was able to feed three Passenger Robots at the same time. Feeding six Passenger Robots at the same time by one Container was presented by *Kottas et al.* [5]. Despite the fact that the docking approach gives Passenger Robots the freedom of movement, the Passenger Robots have to reserve part of their time for travelling back to their Container in order to recharge their batteries.
2. The physical logistic interaction between the Container and the target environment is for example removing obstacles which the Passenger faces (e.g. opening a closed door) and carrying the required equipment which is used by the Passenger to accomplish its task (e.g. first aid tools [7]). *Stroupe et al.* [10] presented a conceptual approach where a team of small space robots is carried by a large spider robot. Besides the Passenger Robots, the Container carries an orbital replacement unit (ORU). The mission of the marsupial team is to assemble and maintain an orbital unit in space. The Container Robot puts the ORU in its target place. After that, the Passenger Robots fix and connect this unit with the other units.

## 3.2   The Passenger Roles

The marsupial relationship exists in order to provide Passenger Robots with the required logistic services to accomplish their tasks smoothly. This means, the Passenger Robots are the service consumers. Therefore, most of the research works did not present roles or even contributions of Passenger Robots in the marsupial relationship. Instead, they assigned tasks to the Passenger after the deployment process. These can be surveillance [20], exploration [15], reconnaissance [18], communicating with trapped victims [16], and providing them with the required first aid tools [7], to name a few.

*Murphy et al.* [5] is the only exception of this trend. They presented a conceptual contribution of the Passenger Robots. In their work, the Container Robot, which plays a Manager Role, uses the sensors of its Passengers during the carrying process. For instance it uses them as extra mobile (non-attached) sensors while they are standing on its board.

### 3.3    Discussion

Some of the Passenger Robots' tasks could be seen as roles for these Passenger Robots. The project of SPAWAR Systems Centre (SSC) [19] is an example of these illusionary roles. In this project [19], they used Passenger Robots to expand the Container's force protection in military applications. Another example is presented by *Sukhatme et al.* [9]. They introduced a case study about an aerial Container Robot which uses its ground Passenger Robot to gain information about ground regions which the Container cannot cover from the sky.

These illusionary roles and others are reflections of the Container's roles, more precisely the Manager Role. A Container Robot, which has a Manager Role, sends specific tasks to each specific Passenger. The Passenger Robots, in turn, perform these tasks.

The confusion occurs when the Container Robot gains benefits from some of these tasks such as expanding its force protection [19].

To distinguish illusionary roles (e.g. [19]) from actual roles (e.g. [5]), we consider the carrying process as a distinction. If the Passenger Robot performs its task during the carrying process, it is an actual role. Otherwise, it is considered as an illusionary role.

Based on this rule, the Passenger Robots in [5] have an actual role because they perform the role during the carrying process, whereas the Passenger Robots in [9],[19] have illusionary roles because they perform their tasks after the deployment process.

## 4    Application of Marsupial Robots

Within this section, different applications of marsupial robots are discussed. The environment of the Container is used to organize this section in five categories: Space, Aerial, Ground, Underground, and Underwater marsupial.

### 4.1    Space

*Stroupe et al.* [10] presented a conceptual approach of a marsupial team in space. The Container Robot is a spider-like robot while the Passenger Robots are a team of Limbed Excursion Mechanical Utility Robots (LEMUR). The mission is to assemble and maintain an orbital unit in space. The Container Robot plays a Supporter Role and the Passenger Robots have construction and maintenance tasks. Both of them are working autonomously.

### 4.2    Aerial

*Sukhatme et al.* [9] presented a case study about an aerial marsupial robot team. The Container Robot plays a Manager Role and is an UAV, while the Passenger is an UGV. The mission of this marsupial team is to detect and track an intruder on the ground. If the Container cannot track the intruder from the sky, it deploys the

Passenger to follow the intruder on the ground. Once the intruder appears again, the Container collects the Passenger and starts tracking from the sky.

### 4.3 Ground

*Anderson et al.* [8] introduced the first marsupial team of robots. In their work, the Container Robot plays both, a Messenger Role and a Processor Role. The Container and the Passenger are UGVs. The mission of this marsupial team is to explore and map an indoor environment. *Murphy et al.* [5] addressed this mission by using a tethered marsupial team of robots where the Passenger is tied with the Container. Examples of other works that addressed the UGV Container with one or more UGV Passenger Robots are [4],[13],[15],[17],[20].

Using an UGV Container with an UAV Passenger was addressed by the project of SPAWAR [19]. In their research work, the marsupial team is used for military applications. The Container Robot plays a Messenger Role and a Supporter Role and the UAV Passenger expands the force protection of the Container. Besides the UAV Passenger, the Container has an UGV Passenger as well. Therefore, this work is the first work which applies heterogeneous Passenger robots on a real test bed.

Dealing with an underground Passenger was addressed by *Ferworn et al.* [18]. They used an UGV Container with an underground Passenger where the Container plays a Carrier Role. Once the Container reaches the target location, it drops the Passenger there. The mission of this team is urban search and rescue.

### 4.4 Underground

The underground marsupial team is addressed by *Zhao et al.* [7]. The Container Robot plays a Supporter Role and a Messenger Role and is connected to a remote control centre via a rope. The Passenger is kept inside of a closed box. The mission of this team is to search and rescue trapped victims inside of a collapsed coal mine. Besides, this team establishes a communication between the human rescue team and the trapped victims.

### 4.5 Underwater

*Zhou et al.* [6] presented a fish like marsupial robot team. The Container Robot plays a Coach Role and keeps the fish-like Passenger Robot inside of a specialized cabin. The mission of this team is to explore unreachable places such as underwater caves, sunken ships, and oil pipelines.

## 5 Summary and Open Issues

The marsupial relationship in robotics is a physical relationship among two or more heterogeneous robots. This relationship enables the heterogeneous robots to exploit their individual strengths and overcome their individual weaknesses. In addition, it provides several logistic services which expand the capabilities of the participating robots.

This physical relationship has a positive impact on Urban Search and Rescue (US&R) applications which need a fast and safe deployment of specific task robots either inside or near their target work location. Furthermore, the Container can be used as a mobile logistic station to provide a mobile service point which is near to its Passenger Robots' work location. Battery recharging is an example of logistic services the Container can provide.

This paper presents and discusses the state of the art of marsupial relationships. Besides, it specifies the characteristics of a marsupial relationship and uses these characteristics to come up with a new definition of this relationship. The marsupial relationship has been addressed by several research groups under different constraints and involving different roles. Moreover, the researchers applied it to different areas. We believe that this paper will play a key role towards accelerating the research progress in this field of robotics.

Some issues still need to be addressed such as:

**Efficient Rendezvous in Marsupial Relationships.** The process of collecting the Passenger Robots by the Container Robot has an important effect on the performance of the robot team. This can be seen when the Container plays a Supporter Role. If the Container is not able to attend the agreed rendezvous with one of its Passenger Robots, the Passenger Robot fails to continue its work either temporary or permanently (e.g. because its battery is discharged).

**Parasitistic Marsupial-Like Relationship.** This special case of marsupial relationship describes an ad hoc relationship between two heterogeneous robots. The formation of this relationship is carried out by the Passenger Robot and without prearrangement with the Container Robot. This means, a robot R1 utilizes the physical capability of another robot R2 to facilitate R1's work, without any negotiation with R2.

**Nested Marsupial Relationship.** The typical marsupial relationship is formed by a Container and one or more Passenger Robots. In the nested relationship, a Container Robot acts as a Passenger of another Container.

A suggested application for this marsupial robot is a rescue mission inside a burning nuclear plant. Due to harmful radiation, a safe distance should be maintained. At the same time, a quick deployment is required inside the plant. This scenario could be achieved by using a nested marsupial which consists of an UAV as an outer Container and an UGV as an inner Container. The inner Container, in turn, has a UGV Passenger Robot.

# References

1. Parker, L.: Multiple Mobile Robot Systems, Part E. Springer Handbook of robots. Springer, Heidelberg (2008)
2. Dudek, G., Jenkin, M., Millios, E., Wilkes, D.: A Taxonomy for Multi-Agent Robotics. Autonomous Robots 3(4) (December 1996)
3. Murphy, R., Todokoro, S., Nardi, D., Jacoff, A., Fiorini, P., Choset, H., Erkmen, A.: Search and rescue robotics, Part F. Springer Handbook of robots. Springer, Heidelberg (2008)

4. Kottas, A., Drenner, A., Papinkolopoulos, N.: Intelligent Power Management: Promoting Power-Consciousness in Teams of Mobile Robots. In: Proceeding of IEEE International Conference on Robotics and Automation, Japan (2009)
5. Murphy, R., Ausmus, M., Bugajska, M., Ellis, T., Johnson, T., Kelley, N., Kiefer, J., Pollock, L.: Marsupial-like Mobile Robot Societies. Autonomous Agent (1999)
6. Zhou, C., Cao, Z., Wang, S., Tan, M.: Marsupial Robotic Fish System. In: Proceeding of the 17th World Congress. The International Federation of Automatic Control (2008)
7. Zhao, J., Liu, G., Liu, Y., Zhu, Y.: Research on the Application of a Marsupial Robot for Coal Mine Rescue. In: Xiong, C.-H., Liu, H., Huang, Y., Xiong, Y.L. (eds.) ICIRA 2008. LNCS (LNAI), vol. 5315, pp. 1127–1136. Springer, Heidelberg (2008)
8. Anderson, M., McKay, M., Richardson, B.: Multirobot Automated Indoor Floor Characterization Team. In: Proceeding of the IEEE International Conference on Robotics and Automation, Minneapolis (1996)
9. Sukhatme, G., Montgomery, J., Vaughan, R.: Experiments with Cooperative Aerial-Ground Robots. Robot Teams: From Diversity to Polymorphism. AK Peters (2001)
10. Stroupe, A., Huntsberger, T., Kennedy, B., Aghazarian, H., Baumgartner, E., Ganino, A., Garrett, M., Okon, A., Robinson, M., Townsend, J.: Heterogeneous Robotic Systems for Assembly and Servicing. In: Proceeding of the 8th International Symposium on Artificial Intelligence, Robotics and Automation in Space – iSAIRAS, Munich, Germany (2005)
11. Hirose, S., Shirasu, T., Fukushima, F.: A proposal for cooperative robot "Gunryu" composed of autonomous Segments. In: Proceeding of International Conference on Intelligent Robots and Systems (1994)
12. Ausmus, M., Bugajska, M., Ellis, T., Johnson, T., Kelly, N., Kiefer, J., Pollock, L.: Marsupial-Like Mobile agent robot societies for urban search and rescue. Computer Science and Engineering, University of South Florida. Tampa, FL 33620-5399
13. Matusiak, M., Paanajärvi, J., Appelqvist, P., Elomaa, M., Vainio, M., Ylikorpi, T., Halme, A.: A Novel marsupial robot society: Towards Long-Term Autonomy. In: Distributed Autonomous Robotics System, Part VII, vol. 8, Springer, Heidelberg (2009)
14. Leitner, J.: Literature Review – Multi-robot Cooperation in Space applications. AS-0.3100 Seminar in Automation Technology (2009)
15. Kadioglu, E., Papinkolopoulos, N.: A method for transporting a team of miniature robots. In: Proceeding of the IEEE/RSJ Int. Conference on Intelligent Robots and Systems (2003)
16. Murphy, R.: Marsupial and shape-shifting robots for urban search and rescue. In: Proceeding of IEEE Intelligent Systems (2000)
17. Dellaert, F., Balch, T., Kaess, M., Ravichandran, R., Alegre, F., Berhault, M., McGuire, R., Merrill, E., Moshkina, L., Walker, D.: The Georgia Tech Yellow Jackets: A marsupial Team for Urban Search and rescue. AAAI Technical Report WS-02-18 (2002)
18. Ferworn, A., Hough, G., Manca, R.: Expedients for Marsupial Operations of USAR Robots. In: Proceeding of IEEE International Workshop on Safety, Security and Rescue Robotics (2006)
19. SPAWAR Systems Center: SSC San Diego's Marsupial Robotics, http://nosc.mil/robots/resources/marsupial/marsupial.html (Visited on the May 2, 2010)
20. Rybski, P., Stoeter, S., Erickson, M., Gini, M., Hougen, D., Papanikolopoulos, N.: A Team of Robotic Agent for Surveillance. In: Proceeding of the International Conference on Autonomous Agents (2000)

# Multi-objective Robot Coalition Formation
# for Non-additive Environments

Manoj Agarwal[1], Lovekesh Vig[2], and Naveen Kumar[1]

[1] Department of Computer Science, University of Delhi, Delhi-110007, India
[2] School of Information Technology, Jawaharlal Nehru University, New Delhi 110067, India

**Abstract.** Research towards the coalition formation problem in multi-robot systems has recently gained attention. The main objective of this research is to form the best teams of heterogeneous robots (coalitions) to cater to a given set of tasks. Due to the inherently NP-hard nature of the problem, it is being addressed employing a large number of techniques ranging from heuristics based solutions to evolutionary approaches. The problem becomes more complex when the resource-distribution needed to complete a task is non-additive in nature, i.e., it may not be sufficient to just add the resources to the individual robots forming the coalition to sum up to the resource requirement of the given task but also satisfy the minimum resource distribution on each individual member of the coalition. There may be multiple alternate coalitions for a task, each of which can complete the task but with different efficiency. Traditionally the coalition formation problem has been formulated as a single objective optimization problem wherein the objective is either to maximize the number of the tasks or to maximize the overall system efficiency. In this paper, the coalition formation problem has been modeled as a multi-objective optimization problem where both the number of tasks completed as well as the overall system efficiency are considered simultaneously. Two popular multi-objective approaches are implemented and the results demonstrate their superiority over single objective solutions.

## 1 Introduction

With advances in autonomous multi-robot systems, the complexity of the tasks involved has increased considerably. In many cases, the tasks are too complex to be performed by a single robot, i.e., tasks must be allocated to a team (coalition) of robots, often heterogeneous. This problem is referred to as the Single-Task Multiple-Robot (ST-MR) problem and is considerably harder than the Single-Task Single-Robot (ST-SR) problem[1]. A coalition represents assignment of robots to form a team for executing a common task and each such coalition (team) is responsible for execution of a single task. Thus, if all the tasks (say $N$) are to be completed, we need to form $N$ coalitions. The problem of choosing $N$ suitable coalitions from a set of $M$ robots ($M > N$) is a combinatorial problem and a brute force approach would be intractable. Tasks become even more complex in non-additive environments because in addition to satisfying the aggregate resource requirements of a task, a coalition must also satisfy the locational constraints on the individual sensory requirements[2]. The complexity of the system is increased further when a task can be completed by a number of alternate coalitions of robots

S. Jeschke, H. Liu, and D. Schilberg (Eds.): ICIRA 2011, Part I, LNAI 7101, pp. 346–355, 2011.

each having different resource distribution and task completion efficiency. Most robot coalition formation algorithms suffer from the limitation that they all attempt to maximize a single predefined objective function associated with task completion or resource utilization [3,4]. However, real life scenarios often require optimization of multiple objectives such as maximizing the number tasks completed and maximizing the efficiency of the system. As these objectives are often conflicting in nature optimizing all of them simultaneously is not possible. This paper addresses the coalition formation problem in the Single-Task Multiple Robot (ST-MR) category in the context of multiple conflicting objectives. A notion of coalition schemes is introduced here, where each scheme represents a mapping between the set of coalitions and the set of tasks. For each coalition scheme the following are evaluated:

– Number of tasks that the scheme is able to execute.
– Overall system efficiency of the coalition scheme.

As these objectives are in conflict, no single coalition scheme is likely to be optimal with respect to both the objectives and hence a multi-objective approach may yield superior schemes. In this paper, we apply variants of two popular evolutionary multi-objective optimization (EMO) algorithms namely Non-dominated Sorting Genetic Algorithm (NSGA-II) [5] and Strength Pareto Evolutionary Algorithm (SPEA-II) [6] to this problem.

Rest of the paper is organized as follows: section 2 briefly describes the related work, section 3 formally describes the coalition formation problem as a multi-objective optimization problem along with the proposed solution, section 4 outlines the implementations of the two multi-objective approaches, section 5 provides results of the simulations to demonstrate the usefulness of the proposed approach, and finally section 6 gives conclusions and scope of future work.

## 2   Related Work

In the context of task allocation, much work has focused on the ST-SR class of problems [1,7]. However, the single-task multi-robot (ST-MR) problem, better known as the coalition formation problem has recently begun to receive due attention [8,3].

Game theorists and economists have also studied the coalition formation problem with regard to market based selfish agents [9]. Distributed Artificial Intelligence (DAI) researchers have built upon the work in game theory and theoretical computer science to produce practical solutions to the multi-agent coalition formation problem [10,11]. However the portability of these solutions to the multi robot domain is not straightforward due to non-transferability of sensors amongst the robots [3,2].

Liu and Chen [12] provide a genetic approach for searching the coalition structure space to obtain the optimal coalition structure. Recently quantum-inspired approaches to coalition optimization have gained popularity. In particular Li et al. [13] propose a quantum evolutionary approach for coalition formation. Yu et al. [14] propose a quantum inspired ant colony optimization (QACO) method to improve the ability to search and optimize coalition structures.

Most of the work in the domain of multi-robot coalition formation [3,15,4] has addressed the problem of optimizing a single objective such as minimizing the task completion time or maximizing the system utility value. However, the objectives in real world scenarios are often conflicting in nature. Classical solutions to multi-objective optimization problem typically reformulate the problem as a single objective problem and subsequently employ one of the standard techniques to obtain a single optimal solution. However, when the objectives are conflicting, no single solution would serve as the optimal solution for all objectives simultaneously. Hence the end user should be provided with a set of trade-off solutions called the non-dominated[1] solutions or Pareto-optimal solutions [16]. This would enable the end user to choose a solution based on information external to mathematical formulation of the optimization problem. Evolutionary algorithms (EAs) have been the preferred choice for the search of Pareto-optimal solutions due to their capability to evaluate a population of solutions and generate a set of Pareto-optimal solutions [6,16,17,18].

An important facet of the coalition formation problem is that the resources of the individual members of a coalition are non-additive. It may not be enough for a coalition to have the necessary resource vector to complete a task, the resources must be appropriately distributed within the members of the coalition [2]. Recently Tang and Parker [19,15] developed the ASyMTRe system to autonomously synthesize coalitions whilst handling the locational constraints on the sensors. ASyMTRe was the first system that autonomously devised different potential coalitions for a particular task, by searching possible connections between motor schemas, communcation schemas, and perceptual schemas, both within and across robots. Taking a cue from this work, we have incorporated in our work multiple possible representations of a robotic task, where each representation corresponds to a potential coalition with an associated efficiency. While multi-objective approaches have been utilized for task allocation, they have been either applied to the single-task single robot problems [20] or to task allocation problems in scheduling environments [21]. To the best of our knowledge, multi-objective approaches have not been applied to the multi-robot coalition formation problem. This work aims to demonstrate the advantages of using multi-objective approaches to solve the coalition formation problem.

## 3    Problem Definition and Solution Strategy

The following entities describe the system:

1. The system has a set of $M$ robots $\{R_1, R_2, \ldots, R_M\}$, a set of $N$ tasks $\{T_1, T_2, \ldots, T_N\}$, and a set of $K$ types of resources $\{r_1, r_2 \ldots, r_K\}$.
2. Each robot $R_i$ has an associated resource distribution vector (say A) of size $K$, $\langle A_{i1}, A_{i2}, \ldots, A_{iK} \rangle$, where $A_{ij}$ represents the number of units of the $j^{th}$ resource type possessed by $R_i$.

---

[1] The domination between two solutions, $x^{(1)}$ & $x^{(2)}$ is defined in [16] as follows:
A solution $x^{(1)}$ is said to dominate another solution $x^{(2)}$, if both of the following are true:

1. $x^{(1)}$ is no worse than $x^{(2)}$ in all the objectives.
2. $x^{(1)}$ is strictly better than $x^{(2)}$ in at least one of the objectives.

3. As mentioned in section 1, a task may be completed by several coalitions, each having a unique resource requirement vector and corresponding efficiency. Thus, a task $T_i$ may be associated with multiple (say $p$) resource requirement vectors $\langle \rho_{i1}, \rho_{i2}, \ldots, \rho_{ip} \rangle$, corresponding to $p$ potential coalitions. $\rho_{ij}$ may be described by the triplet: $\langle m_j, e_j, \lambda \rangle$, where, $m_j$ and $e_j$ denote the number of robots and the corresponding efficiency of the $j^{th}$ resource requirement vector respectively, and $\lambda = \langle \lambda_1, \lambda_2, \ldots, \lambda_{m_j} \rangle$ denotes the resource requirement vector of the individual members of the coalition. Thus, the $j^{th}$ coalition would require $m_j$ robots and the resource requirement of any potential robot (say, $\lambda_l$) may be described by the vector $\langle \lambda_{l_1}, \lambda_{l_2}, \ldots, \lambda_{l_K} \rangle$, where $\lambda_{l_x}$ denotes the number of units of the $x^{th}$ resource type required by it. It may be noted that the resource requirement $\langle \lambda_{l_1}, \lambda_{l_2}, \ldots, \lambda_{l_K}, \rangle$ may be met by several robots in the system or in fact none at all. Thus the coalition $\rho_{ij}$ may be completely described by the vector
$$\rho_{ij} = \langle m_j, e_j, [\langle \lambda_{11}, \lambda_{12}, \ldots, \lambda_{1K} \rangle, \ldots, \langle \lambda_{m_j 1}, \lambda_{m_j 2}, \ldots, \lambda_{m_j K} \rangle] \rangle,$$

Based on the above specifications we list below the assumptions of the proposed system:

– Robots and tasks are randomly distributed in a plane.
– There is a central computing entity which has complete knowledge of the system and generates the desired coalition schemes.
– Number of tasks completed for any scheme can vary from 0 to $N$ and the efficiency of the scheme is defined as the average efficiency of all the tasks that could be completed using that scheme.
– Robots are allocated to task requirement ($\lambda_i$'s) using the best fit strategy.
– A task can only be completed by a coalition if the resource distribution of the coalition members satisfies at least one of the task coalition requirement vectors.

The proposed multi-objective robot coalition formation algorithms evaluate the following two conflicting objective functions for any coalition scheme:

– $f^1$: Number of tasks completed (to be maximized)
– $f^2$: Efficiency of the system (to be maximized)

To illustrate the above notions let us consider a system comprising of three robotic tasks namely box-pushing, transportation, and foraging as defined in [15] and having four robots. The four robots are described as follows: The vector $A_i$ describes the number of units of resources <laser, camera, communication, bumper, gripper, odometry>. For example, $A_2 = \langle 001101 \rangle$ indicates that robot $R_2$ possesses one unit of each of the resources: communication, bumper, and odometry. As mentioned earlier, each task has

**Table 1.** Robot Representations

| Robot | Representation | Location |
|-------|----------------|----------|
| $R_1$ | $< 111111 >$ | $< 14.2, 9.6 >$ |
| $R_2$ | $< 001101 >$ | $< 6.4, 15.4 >$ |
| $R_3$ | $< 111000 >$ | $< 4.6, 9.4 >$ |
| $R_4$ | $< 011011 >$ | $< 12.1, 14.2 >$ |

multiple possible representations with each representation containing members with sensory requirements similar to the resource requirement vector defined above. In addition, each representation also has task location. These are defined in Table 2. Accordingly Task 1 can be completed in three different ways as follows:

1. Three robots are required to complete the task with an efficiency of 0.9 amongst these one robot should have one unit of the third resource type (communication) only, another should have one unit each of the resource types communication and gripper, and yet another robot should possess one unit of laser, camera and communication.
2. A two-robot coalition can also complete the task but with an efficiency of 0.8 where one member should possess one unit of communication and odometry and the other member should have one unit of each communication, bumper, gripper and odometry.
3. Another two-robot coalition with an efficiency of 0.6 is also capable of executing the task, where one member needs one unit of communication and bumper and the other member requires one unit each communication, bumper, gripper and odometry.

**Table 2.** Task Representation

| Task | Representation | Location |
|------|----------------|----------|
| $Task_1$ | $< 3, 0.9, [(001000), (001010), (111000)] >$ | $< 2, 14 >$ |
| | $< 2, 0.8, [(001001), (001111)] >$ | |
| | $< 2, 0.6, [(001100), (001111)] >$ | |
| $Task_2$ | $< 1, 0.5, [(010010)] >$ | $< 9, 6 >$ |
| | $< 2, 0.2, [(000010), (010000)] >$ | |
| $Task_3$ | $< 2, 0.4, [(101000), (011000)] >$ | $< 14, 11 >$ |
| | $< 2, 0.1, [(001000), (111000)] >$ | |

The representation of an individual coalition scheme, $CS$ in the population is given by the bit vector $CS = \langle x_{11}, x_{12}, \ldots, x_{1M}; \ldots; x_{N1}, x_{N2}, \ldots, x_{NM} \rangle$, where $x_{ij} = 1(0)$ denotes the presence (absence) of the $j^{th}$ robot in the $i^{th}$ coalition. Starting with the first $M$ bits which denote the coalition for task $T_1$, each sequence of $M$ bits represents the coalition for one task. If $x_{ij} = 1$ for some $i$, then $x_{kj} = 0$, for $1 \leq k \leq N$ and $k \neq i$. A multi-objective algorithm starts (at $t = 0$) with a population, $P_t$ of size $n$ of randomly generated coalition schemes (also called chromosomes) and computes the values of the two objective functions (also called fitness values) for each of the chromosomes belonging to the initial population. A set of offspring chromosomes $Q_t$ is generated from $P_t$ by applying genetic operators and the best $n$ trade-off solutions from the combined population are propagated to the next generation $P_{t+1}$. This process of obtaining the next generation from the current generation by preserving the trade-off solutions from the parent and the offspring population is repeated a specified number of times or until the convergence criterion is satisfied, resulting in the generation of the best trade-off (non-dominated) solutions for the problem.

# 4    Multi-objective Approaches

In this paper we have evaluated the suitability of two popular elitist multi-objective evolutionary optimization algorithms, NSGA-II and SPEA-II to the problem of coalition formation. These algorithms differ in their method of evolving and maintaining the set of non-dominated solutions obtained over a number of generations. The two approaches are outlined below:

**SPEA-II**

1. Generate an initial population $P_0$ and create the empty archive (external set) $Q_0 = \phi$. Set $t = 0$.
2. Compute fitness values of individuals in $P_t$ and $Q_t$
3. Copy all non-dominated individuals in $P_t$ and $Q_t$ to $Q_{t+1}$. If size of $Q_{t+1}$ exceeds the specified archive size then reduce $Q_{t+1}$ by means of the truncation operator, otherwise fill $Q_{t+1}$ with dominated individuals in $P_t$ and $Q_t$.
4. If $t \geq T$ or another stopping criterion is satisfied then set A to the set of decision vectors represented by the non-dominated individuals in $Q_{t+1}$. Stop.
5. Perform binary tournament selection with replacement on $Q_{t+1}$ in order to fill the mating pool.
6. Apply recombination and mutation operators to the mating pool and set $Q_{t+1}$ to the resulting population. Increment generation counter ($t = t + 1$) and go to Step 2.

**NSGA-II**

1. The population $P_t$ at $t = 0$ is initialized with a random binary population of size N representing coalition schemes for all the tasks.
2. The population, $P_t$, is used to create an offspring population $Q_t$ (say), of size $N$ by using genetic operators selection and mutation.
3. $P_t$ and $Q_t$ are combined to get a population of size $2N$, denoted by $K_t$ (say), that is, $K_t = P_t \cup Q_t$
4. $K_t$ is subjected to non-dominated sorting process resulting in the formation of non-dominated fronts[2][16].
5. $N$ solutions are extracted from higher ranked fronts in $K_t$ to form the next generation population, $P_{t+1}$ as follows:
   (a) Initialize $P_{t+1} = \Phi$. Start with the first front $F_1$. If $| F_1 | \leq N$, do $P_{t+1} = P_{t+1} \cup F_1$.
   (b) Fill $P_{t+1}$ with the members of $F_2, F_3$, and so on until $| P_{t+1} | \leq N$. Since the total size of all fronts taken together is $2N$, not all fronts can be accommodated in $P_{t+1}$. Ignore all fronts that cannot be accommodated at all. For the last front (say, $F_l$) being considered for including solutions in $P_{t+1}$, if $F_l$ has more members than can be put in $P_{t+1}$, use a crowding distance[3] measure [5] to choose points which lead to maximum diversity.
6. Repeat steps 2 to 5 a specified number of times (generations).

---

[2] All solutions belonging to a given front, $F_i$, are considered to be of the same rank $i$, $F_1$ being the highest ranked front. Thus every solution in $K_t$ belongs to exactly one front.

[3] Crowding distance $d_i$ of a point $i$ is a measure of the sparsity in the objective space around $i$ [22].

## 5   Experiments

To demonstrate the efficacy of the multi-objective approaches, the two algorithms were run on the problem mentioned in section 3. The outputs generated by the multi-objective approaches were compared with the outputs generated by two single objective variants. The objectives considered for single objective optimization were $i)$ system efficiency and $ii)$ number of tasks completed. The results of applying the above approaches are shown in Table 3. Single objective optimization of the system efficiency yielded a coalition scheme that could complete only one task (Task 1) with a high efficiency of 0.9. Similarly, optimization of the number of tasks completed resulted in a coalition scheme with lower system efficiency of 0.3 but managed to complete two tasks (Task 2 and Task 3). Finally, both the multi-objective approaches generated a coalition scheme that also completed two tasks (Task 1 and Task 2) whilst maintaining a high efficiency of 0.7. Fig. 1(a) and Fig 1(b) show initial and final configurations respectively in a Player-stage simulation of the solutions produced by the multi-objective (MO) approaches. The robots utilized the wavefront path planner to navigate to their chosen tasks after the MO algorithm assigns them to specific tasks.

In order to carry out a more rigorous comparison between the above mentioned approaches, we conducted several rounds of numeric simulations. We considered three single objective functions: maximization of system efficiency(SO_Eff), maximization of the number of tasks completed (SO_Task) and maximization of a weighted function

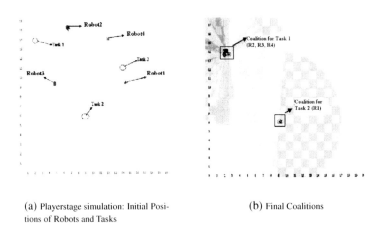

(a) Playerstage simulation: Initial Positions of Robots and Tasks

(b) Final Coalitions

**Fig. 1.** Robot Simulations using Player-Stage

**Table 3.** Toy Problem solutions

| Solution | Efficiency | Tasks Completed |
|---|---|---|
| Single-Objective(Efficiency) | 0.9 | 1 |
| Single-Objective(Tasks) | 0.3 | 2 |
| Multi-Objective | 0.7 | 2 |

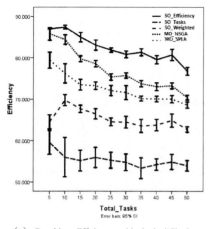 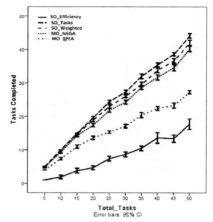

(a) Resulting Efficiency with both i)Single-Objective (SO) maximization of Completed Tasks and Efficiency and ii) Multi-Objective (MO) maximization of both objectives using NSGA-II (MO_NSGA) and SPEA-II (MO_SPEA)

(b) Resulting Task Completion with both i)Single-Objective (SO) maximization of CompleTasks and Efficiency and ii) Multi-Objective (MO) maximization of both objectives using NSGA-II (MO_NSGA) and SPEA-II (MO_SPEA)

**Fig. 2.** Simulations to contrast the solutions obtained with both Single-Objective (SO) and Multi-Objective (MO) approaches

of both efficiency and tasks completed (SO_Weighted). These were contrasted against the two multi-objective approaches outlined in Section 4, namely NSGA-II and SPEA-II. The number of tasks in the system were varied in the range 5-50 in steps of 5 while the number of robots were varied in the range 15-150 in steps of 15. Task requirement vectors and robot capability vectors were generated using normal distributions with parameters ($\mu = 2, \sigma^2 = 1$) and ($\mu = 3, \sigma^2 = 1$) respectively. The efficiency of the tasks followed normal distribution with parameters ($\mu = 50, \sigma^2 = 20$). The number of tasks completed, and the resulting efficiency were computed for all the three single objective approaches as well as the multi-objective approaches. For every pair (number of robots, number of tasks) ten simulations were executed for each of the approaches. Fig.2(a) shows comparison of the system efficiency achieved by all the five solution strategies. The multi-objective approaches generate coalition schemes with high efficiency comparable to SO_Eff and significantly higher than SO_Task and SO_Weighted. Similarly, Fig.2(b) shows comparison of the number of tasks completed by all the solution strategies. Again, the MO approaches generate coalition schemes with number of tasks completed comparable to SO_Task and SO_Weighted. It is evident the single objective solutions suffer from imbalance between the twin objectives while the multi-objective approach offers more balanced solutions from the non-dominated set. The weighted objective approach produces results similar to the multi-objective approaches in terms of number of tasks completed but performs much worse in terms of efficiency. It can be further observed that of the two multi-objective approaches NSGA-II outperform SPEA-II.

Comparison was also performed with a state of the art multi-robot coalition formation algorithm proposed by Manathara et al. [4]. The algorithm employed a particle swarm optimization (PSO) approach to generate coalition schemes for a multiple UAV search and prosecute mission. The problem was formulated as a single objective optimization problem to minimize the mission time. We reformulated the problem as a multi-objective problem with three conflicting objectives, namely maximizing the number of tasks completed, minimizing the time to complete all tasks, and minimizing the distance traveled by the robots. It was observed that the scheme generated by Manathara in 532 iterations of PSO was improved upon by NSGA-II in just ten iterations (see Table 4). Although the scheme $C_1$ takes the same amount of time (87 units) as Manathara's scheme, the distance traveled in case of $C_1$ is less than that of Manathara's scheme. It can also be seen from Table 4 that NSGA-II generated four non-dominated coalition schemes for the given problem.

**Table 4.** Final Fitness Matrix

| Coalition Scheme | Number of Completed Tasks | Time of Completion | Total Distance Travelled |
|---|---|---|---|
| $C_1$ | 3 | 87 | 1972 |
| $C_2$ | 1 | 20 | 200 |
| $C_3$ | 2 | 69 | 1286 |
| $C_4$ | 2 | 52 | 1325 |
| $C_{Manathara}$ | 3 | 87 | 2085 |

## 6    Conclusion and Future Work

In this paper, we have addressed the problem of mapping coalitions of robots to tasks having different requirements. This problem naturally falls in the realm of multi-objective optimization as real life scenarios have to deal with multiple conflicting goals such as maximization of the number of tasks completed, and maximization of the efficiency of the system. As a brute force method leads to exponential time requirement, we have used variants of the NSGA-II and SPEA-II. These algorithms lead to convergence to the Pareto-optimal set. In this paper, we have assumed that the placement of robots and tasks is static and that the algorithm running centrally determines the set of trade-off coalition schemes which can be used in conjunction with external information to choose the desired solution. The problem may be extended to a dynamic scenario and the possibility of a distributed mode of operation may be explored.

## References

1. Gerkey, B., Mataric, M.J.: A formal analysis and taxonomy of task allocation in multi-robot systems. International Journal of Robotics Research 23(9), 939–954 (2004)
2. Vig, L., Adams, J.A.: Issues in multi-robot coalition formation. In: Parker, L.E., Schultz, A., Schneider, F. (eds.) Multi-Robot Systems. From Swarms to Intelligent Automata, vol. III, Springer, Heidelberg (2005)
3. Vig, L., Adams, J.A.: Multi-robot coalition formation. IEEE Transactions on Robotics 22(4), 637–649 (2006)

4.  Manathara, J.G., et al.: Multiple UAV coalition for a search and prosecute mission. Journal of Intelligent and Robotic Systems, 1–34 (2010)
5.  Deb, K., Pratap, A., Agarwal, S., Meyarivan, T.: A fast and elitist multiobjective genetic algorithm: NSGA-II. IEEE Trans. Evol. Computation 6, 182–197 (2002)
6.  Zitzler, E., Laumanns, M., Thiele, L.: SPEA 2: Improving the strength pareto evolutionary algorithm. Technical Report 103, Computer engineering and Networks Laboratory (TIK), Swiss Federal Institute of Technology (ETH) Zurich (2001)
7.  Parker, L.E.: ALLIANCE: An architecture for fault tolerant multirobot cooperation. IEEE Transactions on Robotics and Automation 14(2), 220–240 (1998)
8.  Pedro, M.S., Mario, F.M.C.: CoMutaR: A framework for multi-robot coordination and task allocation. In: Proceedings of the IEEE/RSJ International conference on Intelligent Robots and Systems, St. Louis, USA (2009)
9.  Ray, D., Vohra, R.: A theory of endogenous coalition structures*. Games and Economic Behavior 26, 286–336 (1999)
10. Sandholm, T., Larson, K., Andersson, M., Shehory, O., Tohme, F.: Coalition structure generation with worst case guarantees. Artificial Intelligence 111(1-2), 209–238 (1999)
11. Shehory, O., Kraus, S.: Methods for task allocation via agent coalition formation. Artificial Intelligence 101(2), 165–200 (1998)
12. Liu, H.Y., Chen, J.F.: Multi-robot cooperation coalition formation based on genetic algorithm. In: Fifth International Conference on Machine Learning and Cybernetics, pp. 85–88. IEEE, Dalian (2006)
13. Li, Z., Xu, B., Yang, L., Chen, J., Li, K.: Quantum evolutionary algorithm for multi-robot coalition formation. In: Summit on Genetic and Evolutionary Computation, pp. 295–302. ACM/SIGEVO, Shanghai, China (2009)
14. Zhang, Y., Liu, S., Fu, S., Wu, D.: A quantum-inspired ant colony optimization for robot coalition formation. In: Control and Decision Conference, CCDC 2009, pp. 626–631. IEEE, Chinese (2009)
15. Parker, L.E., Tang, F.: Building multi-robot coalitions through automated task solution synthesis. Proceedings of IEEE 94, 1289–1305 (2006); Special Issue on Multi-Robot Systems
16. Deb, K.: Multi-Objective Optimization using Evolutionary Algorithms. John Wiley & Sons Inc., New York (2001)
17. Zitzler, E., Thiele, L.: Multiobjective evolutionary algorithms: A comparative case study and the strength Pareto approach. IEEE Transactions on Evolutionary Computation 3(4), 257–271 (1999)
18. Corne, D.W., Knowles, J.D., Oates, M.J.: The Pareto-envelope based selection algorithm for multiobjective optimization. In: Deb, K., Rudolph, G., Lutton, E., Merelo, J.J., Schoenauer, M., Schwefel, H.-P., Yao, X. (eds.) PPSN 2000. LNCS, vol. 1917, pp. 839–848. Springer, Heidelberg (2000)
19. Tang, F., Parker, L.E.: ASyMTRe: Automated synthesis of multi-robot task solutions through software reconfiguration. In: Proceedings of the IEEE International Conference on Robotics and Automation (ICRA), Barcelona, Spain (2005)
20. Shi, Z., Chen, Q., Li, S., Cai, H., Shen, X.: Cooperative task allocation for multiple mobile robots based on multi-objective optimization method. In: 2010 3rd IEEE International Conference on Computer Science and Information Technology (ICCSIT), vol. 1, pp. 484–489 (2010)
21. Yin, P.Y., Yu, S.S., Wang, P.P., Wang, Y.T.: Multi-objective task allocation in distributed computing systems by hybrid particle swarm optimization. Applied Mathematics and Computation 184(2), 407–420 (2007)
22. Deb, K.: A robust evolutionary framework for multi-objective optimization. In: GECCO 2008: Proceedings of the 10th Annual Conference on Genetic and Evolutionary Computation, pp. 633–640. ACM, New York (2008)

# Development of a Networked Multi-agent System Based on Real-Time Ethernet

Xiong Xu, Zhenhua Xiong, Jianhua Wu, and Xiangyang Zhu

State Key Laboratory of Mechanical System and Vibration,
School of Mechanical Engineering, Shanghai Jiao Tong University,
Shanghai 200240, P.R. China
{xiaoxu85,mexiong,wujh,mexyzhu}@sjtu.edu.cn

**Abstract.** This paper proposes a networked multi-agent system based on the real-time Ethernet. The developed system consists of a set of smart networked agents, which are connected by a ring topology through the real-time Ethernet. Each networked agent is designed to realize motion control tasks and real-time communication capabilities using digital signal processor and field-programmable gate array technologies. Furthermore, a real-time communication protocol is proposed to cope with the non-deterministic problem of Ethernet. Then, time delays caused by data processing and message transmission are analyzed. A platform is built to evaluate the capabilities of the developed networked multi-agent system. The experimental results demonstrate that the presented system achieves good performance in terms of real-time communication and servo-control performance.

**Keywords:** Networked multi-agent system, real-time Ethernet, real-time communication, smart agent, synchronous action.

## 1 Introduction

A major trend in modern industrial and commercial systems is to integrate computing, communication, and control into different levels of machine/factory operations and information processes [8]. Many types of manufacturing equipments, such as computer-numerically controlled machine tools, robots, printing machines, and semiconductor equipments, require control network "bus" architectures to transmit data in manufacturing systems. These network systems with common bus architectures are called networked multi-agent systems (NMASs) [9], where functional agents such as sensors, actuators and controllers are spatially distributed and interconnected by one communication network. Rather than traditional centralized point-to-point control systems, NMASs provide several advantages such as efficiency, flexibility and reliability. In addition, they reduce the problems of wiring connection and transmit-length limitation, and decrease installation, reconfiguration and maintenance time and costs.

Many different networked technologies, like control area network (CAN), Profibus, FIP, serial real-time communication specification (SERCOS), have

S. Jeschke, H. Liu, and D. Schilberg (Eds.): ICIRA 2011, Part I, LNAI 7101, pp. 356–365, 2011.

been presented in NMASs during the past decade [1,11]. But the bandwidth becomes the bottleneck of these field buses to provide high-speed communication for distributed control. Recently, many industrial automation components embed Ethernet as communication system because of its low price and high transmission speed [4,2]. With the development of NMASs, a large amount of control and feedback information is exchanged among the distributed nodes. And the important and challenging issues are how the control and feedback information is accurately and instantly transmitted, and how each individual sensor or actuator realizes the synchronous sampling or the synchronous action [5]. However, the Ethernet technology cannot be adopted directly in NMASs by the loss of deterministic communication and synchronized actions between field devices. It needs various modifications to support real-time communications at the factory floor. These proposals are referred as real-time Ethernet (RTE) [3], which is a fieldbus specification using Ethernet for the lower two layers of the open systems interconnection model (OSI model). Recently, the RTE becomes an emerging technology that attracts the research attention.

In this paper, we focus on the development of a networked multi-agent system based on the real-time Ethernet. The developed system consists of a set of smart networked agents, which are spatially distributed and connected one by one through the RTE. Each networked agent includes the following: an Ethernet PHY module, a digital signal processor (DSP) module, a field-programmable gate array (FPGA) module, and a digital-to-analog converter (DAC) module. Data processing to accomplish its own control tasks and communication capabilities are the key features of the designed networked agent. Furthermore, a real-time communication protocol is proposed to cope with the non-deterministic problem of Ethernet. Then, time delays caused by data processing and message transmission are analyzed. A platform is built to evaluate the real-time communication and servo-control performance of the developed networked multi-agent system.

The remainder of this paper is organized as follows. Section II is devoted to introduce the network architecture of the developed system. In Section III, we illustrate the hardware design of the networked agent, the real-time communication protocol and the real-time analysis of the RTE. A platform is built and experiments are conducted in Section IV. In the last section, a conclusion and future research perspectives are given.

## 2   Network Architecture

The main purpose of this work focuses on the development of the networked multi-agent system in the manufacturing field, especially for the computer numerical control (CNC) machines. The network of the system communicates physical signals such as position, velocity, and current by the means of network coding. The characteristics of this network including: messages are transmitted periodically and in real-time; data sizes are small, but the transmission frequency may be high. The network architecture of the system is shown in Fig. 1. A master-slave system architecture with a ring topology is used in the digital communication system.

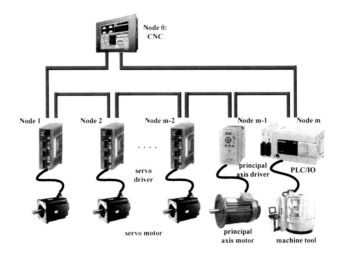

**Fig. 1.** Network architecture of a networked multi-agent system

The master node controls the entire digital communication. The master finishes the key functions of the CNC system, including interpolation, position control, NC code interpretation, tool compensation, motion control, etc. Servo and I/O are the field devices.

For example, the CNC master node is set as time-driven, whereas the sensor and actuator nodes are event-driven. And the sensor and actuator of the same axis (e.g., $X$ axis) are handled as one network node. At a fixed period $T_s$, the controller in the CNC master node computes a control signal and sends it over the network to the actuator node, where it is subsequently actuated. Then, the sensor samples the process and sends the measurement sample over the network to the master node.

## 3    Design and Development

Typical agents in the network include smart sensors, smart actuators and networked controllers [9]. Data processing to accomplish its own control tasks and communication capabilities are the key features of the designed networked agent. The following parts in this section illustrate the hardware design of the networked agent, the real-time communication protocol and the real-time analysis of the RTE.

### 3.1    Hardware Design

In order to realize concurrent and modular designs, we adopt both a DSP and a FPGA in the hardware structure of the networked agent. As shown in Fig. 2, the hardware structure of each networked agent includes the following: an Ethernet PHY module, a DSP module, an FPGA module, and a digital-to-analog

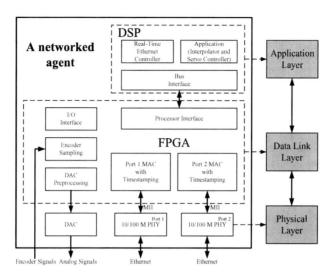

**Fig. 2.** Hardware structure of a networked agent

converter (DAC) module. The Ethernet PHY module adopts a commercial chip to implement the physical layer of the real-time communication, and provides media independent interface (MII) for the media access controller (MAC) in the FPGA module.

Next, we will describe the DSP module and the FPGA module in detail.

**DSP Module.** This module consists of three main blocks. The first one is the real-time Ethernet controller, which realizes the network configuration and the application layer of the communication. It is dedicated to real-time communication by adopting the master-slave approach in the master agent and event-driven mechanism of the slave agents, which will be discussed later. The seconde one is several application functions, such as a interpolator, a servo controller, and a sampling filter. The interpolator executes coordinated control functions, including velocity planning and real-time interpolation. It generates the reference positions for each axis. The proportional-integral-differential (PID) filter with velocity and acceleration feedforward compensation is used in the servo controller. However, not all application functions are included in a networked agent. It depends on the type of the networked agent. The interpolator and the servo controller are usually running on the master agent. The smart sensors have the sampling filter and the smart actuators need servo controller under the condition of the lumped servo/motor, as discussed in [12]. The third one is the bus interface with the FPGA module using the address mapping technology.

**FPGA Module.** The functional blocks of the FPGA provide the following characteristics and functions: encoder sampling, DAC preprocessing circuit, input/output (I/O) interface and media access controller (MAC) with timestamping. The encoder sampling consists of a quadruple-frequency circuit, a phase

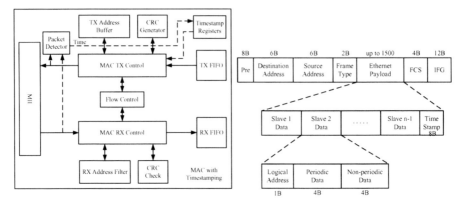

**Fig. 3.** "MAC with timestamping" block            **Fig. 4.** Frame format

discriminator and a position counter. The quadruple-frequency circuit is designed to improve the accuracy of orientation with four times the electrical drive signal. The phase discriminator is applied to judge the rotary direction of the motors. And the position counter is adopted to count the four times encoder signal according to the direction signal. The DAC preprocessing circuit achieves the pretreatment for the DAC module, which is developed to convert digital signals to analog signals and amplify the analog signals for servo drivers.

Ethernet ports of the networked agent are controlled by "MAC with Timestamping" blocks as shown in Fig. 3. Port 1 and Port 2 have the same functionalities. The timestamping approach is introduced in this work to realize the synchronous action. The key element of timestamping is the packet detector, which observes both the outbound and inbound paths of the MII interface. The packet detector is placed just before MII input and output stages. During the communication processes, the packet detector generates a signal when detecting the data packets. This signal latches the current value of the local clock into a dedicated register structure (RX timestamp or TX timestamp register). And the timestamp value is used to calculate the one-way delay during the network configuration phase. The media access controller (MAC) provides all features necessary to implement the Layer 2 protocol of the Ethernet standard (IEEE 802.3 specification). As shown in Fig. 3, the Ethernet MAC consists of several building blocks: TX module (including MAC TX Control, TX Address Buffer, 32-bit Cyclic Redundancy Check (CRC) Generator and TX FIFO); RX module (including MAC RX Control, RX Address Filter, 32-bit CRC Check and RX FIFO); MAC Control module; MII module. The TX and RX modules provide full transmit and receive functions. The CRC generator and the CRC check are designed for error detection. The MAC also handles preamble generation and removal. And the padding occurs automatically (when enabled) in compliance with the IEEE 802.3 standard. The MAC control module provides full duplex flow control, according to the IEEE 802.3u standard. The MII module provides the standard IEEE 802.3 media independent interface that defines the connection between the physical layer and the link layer.

## 3.2   Real-Time Communication Protocol

The real-time communication is implemented on the ring topology using the master-slave approach. Each slave agent is allocated a logic address during the network configuration phase. The master agent periodically sends the lumped frame, as shown in Fig. 4. Then the lumped frame is passed through all the slave agents, which process the frame by reading and writing pieces of information. Note that the slave agents adopt the event-driven mechanism to handle the lumped frame, for reducing the forwarding time of the packet inside the slave agents. Finally, the lumped frame comes back to the master agent. Through the entire communication process, the data collision in the network is avoided and the real-time capability can be guaranteed.

When the slave agent receives the lumped frame, the real-time Ethernet controller waits for a specific time slack, which equals to the time delay measured in the configuration phase. Then, the RTE controller immediately executes the encoder sampling or updates the command applied to the servo controller. Therefore, the networked agents can achieve the synchronous action.

## 3.3   Real-Time Analysis

First, let the RTE cycle time $T_{RTE}$ is the time necessary to execute a communication cycle on the distributed nodes. And the communication cycle time of the real-time Ethernet with the ring topology can be calculated from a timing diagram, as shown in Fig. 5.

Since we use the lumped frame technology, only one packet is required to handle all the RTE communication in a cycle. Hence, the cycle time $T_{RTE}$ can be obtained as follows:

$$T_{RTE} = N \times (T_{pre} + T_{tx} + T_{post}),  \tag{1}$$

where $T_{pre}$ is the preprocessing time for transmission at the source node; $T_{post}$ is the postprocessing time for reception at the destination node; $T_{tx}$ is the transmission time on network channel, including the total transmission delay of a frame and the propagation delay between any two connecting agents; $N$ is the number of networked agents. In this work, we assume that the sum of $T_{pre}$, $T_{tx}$ and $T_{post}$ between any two connecting agents are equal. This assumption

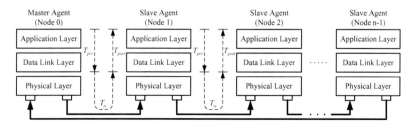

**Fig. 5.** Timing diagram of the real-time Ethernet with the ring topology

is consistent with the actual situation of the developed system. The detailed description of key components of the time delay can be found in [7].

In (1), the transmission time can be estimated using the following:

$$T_{tx} = DataSize \times 8/Bandwidth + T_{prop}, \tag{2}$$

where $DataSize$ is the data packet size in terms of bytes, including data payload and overhead; $Bandwidth$ is the data rate of the Ethernet bus; $T_{prop}$ is the propagation delay of the network. The propagation delay is the most deterministic parameter in a network system because it is proportional to the length of the cable between any two connecting agents. For example, for a 10-m cable, the propagation delay is about 50 $ns$ at the propagation speed of $2.0 \times 10^8 m/s$.

Here, we assume that the communication cycle is bounded by the sampling period $T_s$ of the master agent. Therefore, the number of networked agents can be calculated by

$$N = \left\lfloor \frac{T_s}{T_{pre} + T_{tx} + T_{post}} \right\rfloor, \tag{3}$$

where $\lfloor \cdot \rfloor$ means the floor function, and $\lfloor x \rfloor$ is the largest integer not greater than $x$.

## 4    Experimental Results

To evaluate the performance of the designed system, we have built an experimental platform based on real-time Ethernet communication. As shown in Fig. 6, three networked agents are set up in the developed platform. The main hardware of the networked agent consists of a 10/100-Mbps Ethernet PHY (Intel LXT973), a field programmable gate array (FPGA), a digital signal processor (DSP), a 16-b D/A chip, and a SRAM. Considering the future research, an Altera Cyclone II EP2C8Q208I8 FPGA was adopted, although the circuits of the networked agent only took up approximately 60% of the total FPGA logic elements.

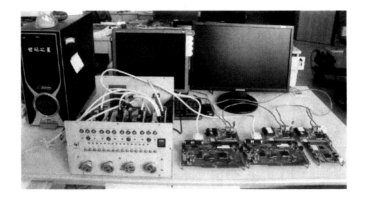

**Fig. 6.** Experimental set-up

## 4.1   Real-Time Performance

In this experiment, there was only two nodes, including a master agent and a slave agent. $N$ was selected as two. Standard cables up to $3m$ in length were used to connect two nodes, and the data rate of Ethernet was $100MHz$. The overhead of each packet was $12B$, with $8B$ preamble and $4B$ CRC. The experimental results, which were obtained from 1000 times with different data, are outlined in Table 1. The theoretical time $T_{tx}$ was calculated based on the Equation (2), where $DataSize$ equals to the data payload plus the overhead of each packet. Since the time delays inside the Ethernet PHY are not included in the theoretical time $T_{tx}$, the experimental results of $T_{tx}$ are a little larger than the theoretical ones.

**Table 1.** Experimental results of the real-time performance

| Data payload (Bytes) | $T_{RTE}$/us experiment | $T_{pre}$/us experiment | $T_{post}$/us experiment | $T_{tx}$/us experiment | $T_{tx}$/us theory |
|---|---|---|---|---|---|
| 20 | 31.25 | 4.153 | 8.402 | 3.07 | 2.575 |
| 64 | 66.93 | 11.487 | 15.235 | 6.743 | 6.095 |
| 100 | 109.43 | 17.487 | 27.826 | 9.402 | 8.975 |
| 200 | 195.53 | 34.155 | 46.095 | 17.515 | 16.975 |
| 500 | 485.75 | 84.157 | 117.216 | 41.502 | 40.975 |
| 1000 | 952.8 | 167.495 | 227.437 | 81.468 | 80.975 |

As a comparison to a fieldbus, we can consider the CAN-based system which is widely used in industrial automation. As mentioned in [10], the transaction time of the CAN system with $8B$ data payload (the maximum payload that CAN allows) is $10500us$ at the transmission speed of $1Mb/s$. And our presented system just consumes $31.25us$ with $20B$ data payload. With these results, we cannot make a direct comparison because the real-time Ethernet transmits more data (20 bytes versus 8 bytes) and the experimental conditions of them are different. However, it can be said that the designed system can achieve better real-time performance than the CAN as the real-time Ethernet has a faster transmission speed and transmits more data payload in one packet. And the CAN-based system often need multiple-packet transmission due to packet size constraints as adopted in [6].

## 4.2   Servo-Control Performance

To validate the servo-control performance of the proposed system, the experimental hardware consists of the following: three networked agents, two servo drivers (Panasonic Company), and two ac permanent-magnet synchronous motors (PMSMs) with pulse encoders. We selected one networked agent as the master. The other two agents, used as the smart sensor/actuator agents, controlled two motors respectively. The master agent performed two-axis trajectory interpolation and the position controls, and transmitted the actuation commands

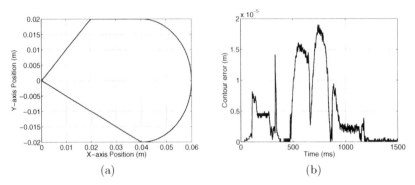

**Fig. 7.** Experimental results. (a) Desired trajectory; (b) Contour error.

to the slave agents every other $T_s$ through the real-time Ethernet. In the experiment, the sample period $T_s$ was $1ms$ and the data payload was $26B$.

As shown in Fig. 7(a), the desired trajectory with three linear segments and a semicircle, was chosen to verify the tracking performance of this developed prototype. The maximum velocity of the trajectory planning was set as $10m/min$. From the Fig. 7(b), we can obtain that the maximal value of contour error is $0.0190mm$. As discussed in [11], the experimental contour error of the SERCOS-based system is about $0.0448mm$. And the error using IEEE-1394 bus, introduced by Gu et al. [5], is $0.0187mm$. Hence, it can be said that the developed real-time Ethernet system can perform as well as SERCOS and IEEE-1394 do, in terms of servo-control performance. Otherwise, only the PID control law was used as the position-loop control. The contour error will be reduced when an advanced control law, such as cross-coupled control or synchronous tracking control, is adopted.

## 5    Conclusions and Future Work

In this paper, a networked multi-agent system based on the real-time Ethernet is designed. And a real-time communication protocol is proposed to cope with the non-deterministic problem of Ethernet. Also, time delays caused by data processing and message transmission are analyzed. A platform is built and experiments are conducted to demonstrate that the presented system achieves good performance in terms of real-time communication and servo-control performance. Our future efforts will focus on two areas. First, we will add message forwarding module of the RTE in the FPGA to reduce the cycle time of the designed system. Second, advanced control methodologies, such as synchronous tracking control, will be designed to achieve higher contour performance.

**Acknowledgments.** This research was supported in part by National Science and Technology Project 2009ZX02021-003, the Science & Technology Commission of Shanghai Municipality under Grant No. 11QH1401400 and Research Project of State Key Laboratory of Mechanical System and Vibration MSVMS201102.

# References

1. Cena, G., Demartini, C., Valenzano, A.: On the performances of two popular field-buses. In: Proceedings of IEEE International Workshop on Factory Communication Systems, pp. 177–186. IEEE (2002)
2. Ding, H., Zhang, B., Ding, Y., Tao, B.: On a novel low-cost web-based power sensor via the Internet. Sensors and Actuators A: Physical 136(1), 456–466 (2007)
3. Felser, M.: Real-time ethernet-industry prospective. Proceedings of the IEEE 93(6), 1118–1129 (2005)
4. Flammini, A., Ferrari, P., Sisinni, E., Marioli, D., Taroni, A.: Sensor interfaces: from field-bus to Ethernet and Internet. Sensors and Actuators A: Physical 101(1-2), 194–202 (2002)
5. Gu, G., Zhu, L., Xiong, Z., Ding, H.: Design of a distributed multi-axis motion control system using the IEEE-1394 bus. IEEE Transactions on Industrial Electronics 57(12), 4209–4218 (2010)
6. Lai, C.L., Hsu, P.L.: Design the Remote Control System With the Time-Delay Estimator and the Adaptive Smith Predictor. IEEE Transactions on Industrial Informatics 6(1), 73–80 (2010)
7. Lian, F.L., Moyne, J., Tilbury, D.: Network design consideration for distributed control systems. IEEE Transactions on Control Systems Technology 10(2), 297–307 (2002)
8. Lian, F.L., Moyne, J., Tilbury, D.: Modelling and optimal controller design of networked control systems with multiple delays. International Journal of Control 76(6), 591–606 (2003)
9. Lian, F., Yook, J., Tilbury, D., Moyne, J.: Network architecture and communication modules for guaranteeing acceptable control and communication performance for networked multi-agent systems. IEEE Transactions on Industrial Informatics 2(1), 12–24 (2006)
10. Sarker, M., Kim, C., Back, S., You, B.: An IEEE-1394 based real-time robot control system for efficient controlling of humanoids. In: 2006 IEEE/RSJ International Conference on Intelligent Robots and Systems, pp. 1416–1421. IEEE (2006)
11. Wei, G., Zongyu, C., Congxin, L.: Investigation on full distribution CNC system based on SERCOS bus. Journal of systems engineering and electronics 19(1), 52–57 (2008)
12. Yook, J., Tilbury, D., Soparkar, N.: A design methodology for distributed control systems to optimize performance in the presence of time delays. International Journal of Control 74(1), 58–76 (2001)

# A Conceptual Agent-Based Planning Algorithm for the Production of Carbon Fiber Reinforced Plastic Aircrafts by Using Mobile Production Units

Hamido Hourani[1], Philipp Wolters[1], Eckart Hauck[1],
Annika Raatz[2], and Sabina Jeschke[3]

[1] Institute for Management Cybernetics (IfU),
[3] Institute of Information Management in Mechanical Engineering (IMA) and
Center for Learning and Knowledge Management (ZLW),
RWTH Aachen University,
52068 Aachen, Germany
{hamido.hourani,philipp.wolters,eckart.hauck,
sabina.jeschke}@ima-zlw-ifu.rwth-aachen.de
www.ima-zlw-ifu.rwth-aachen.de
[2] Institute of Machine Tools and Production Technology,
TU Braunschweig University,
38106 Braunschweig, Germany
a.raatz@tu-bs.de
www.iwf.tu-bs.de

**Abstract.** In order to adapt to new modifications of a product, a new production line and competences should be developed. Enhancing this adaptability feature is the target of the presented conceptual approach. This target is achieved by constructing a product, which is fixed at its place, by heterogeneous mobile production units. In this paper, the product is an aircraft which is made of carbon fiber reinforced plastic. Having two types of agents (i.e. planning agents and representative agents), the conceptual approach supports flexibility and parallelism too. The planning agents depend on their general knowledge on the construction progress to provide an abstract plan. The representative agents, which represent the physical production units, depend on their local surrounding environment to draw a concrete plan from the provided abstract plan. Defining the roles of both types of agents are also within the scope of this paper.

**Keywords:** Assembly Automation, Composite Material Aircraft, Multi-Agent System, Planning.

## 1 Introduction

Due to the competition between different providers of a product, a rapid development process is needed to adapt to changing requirements. Therefore, the product life cycle is shortened [1]. Consequently, changes to the production lines are required and the competence of the development team (i.e. human operators) must be adapted to the new production lines.

S. Jeschke, H. Liu, and D. Schilberg (Eds.): ICIRA 2011, Part I, LNAI 7101, pp. 366–375, 2011.
© Springer-Verlag Berlin Heidelberg 2011

To avoid the cost of redesigning the production lines, a product can be constructed and assembled at the same place. However, this production approach reduces the throughput of the product, due to overlapping of the workspaces which each operator works on.

This paper introduces a conceptual approach to achieve the parallelism feature and the adaptation of changes at the same time. In this conceptual approach, a team of heterogeneous production units (i.e. robots) will be used to construct and assemble an aircraft. The fuselage of the aircraft is stationary while the production units are moving around and inside the fuselage to assemble the required pieces of the aircraft.

From this scenario we focus on the conceptual planning algorithm to construct an aircraft by a group of mobile heterogeneous production units. In addition to plan and schedule the activities of the production units, this planning algorithm supports the parallelism, adaptability and flexibility features. By parallelism feature we mean: The production units, which have different assigned tasks, are able to carry out their tasks in parallel even when their workspaces are overlapped. And by the adaptability feature we mean: Adding new customizations of an aircraft or changing its design is adapted by the production units. However, these changes are not applied to the currently running product. By the flexibility feature we mean: A centralized system supports each production unit with an abstract plan. Customizing this plan and generating a concrete plan by depending on the current situation of the workspace is achieved independently by each production unit. However, the abstract plan is used as a frame around the generated concrete plan.

This paper is organized as follows: The application scenario is elaborated in section 1.1. The related literature is presented in section 1.2. The requirements, which the planning algorithm must address, are presented in section 2. The architecture of the agent-based system is elaborated in the first part of this paper [2] but the main features are outlined in section 3.1. Section 3.2 is dedicated to the conceptual planning algorithm. The scientific contributions of this paper are presented in section 3.3 and section 3.4 gives an outlook for future work. The conclusion is presented in section 4.

## 1.1    Application Scenario

By depending on a new type of Carbon Fiber Reinforced Plastic (CFRP) technology, the fuselage of the aircraft will be designed as a geodetic lattice frame [3]. On this geodetic frame, small plates have to be fixed.

To achieve adaptability and parallelization in performing tasks, using small mobile production units is proposed to fix these plates and to assemble other pieces of the aircraft. However, the concurrency, the dependency among tasks and the overlapping of the workplaces are challenges which the group of mobile production units have to face.

In addition to the production units, several logistic units are involved. These units are responsible for providing the production units with the required tools and materials.

Apart from production and logistic units, several sensors are spread inside and outside the geodetic lattice frame. The task of these sensors is to update the central units about the progress of the tasks and the quality of each accomplished task. After each task, a quality step must be performed. In this system, if a task has not achieved the required quality, a recovery process is established.

Each production unit, logistic unit, and sensor is represented by an agent in a centralized system. This representation reduces the complexity of the system and enhances its scalability [4]. Each agent represents its corresponding external unit. In addition to these representative agents, planning agents are added to the system. These planning agents have the responsibility to schedule the tasks. The representative agents, in turn, have the responsibility to carry out these tasks.

The Market-Based Approach will be followed inside this system to allocate the tasks to the representative agents. In this approach, a task is announced by a specialized planning agent and the representative agents start bidding to seize it. Each representative agent specifies its price for the announced task.

This paper is based on the coordination between the institute of Information Management in Mechanical Engineering (RWTH Aachen) and the institute of Machine Tools and Production Technology (TU Braunschweig University). The scope of this paper is the conceptual planning algorithm. The Technological Requirements and Software Infrastructure of this planning algorithm are elaborated in [2].

## 1.2    Related Literature

Automated planning strategies are classified into two types: Off-line Planning and On-line Planning [5]. Off-line Planning takes place a priori and does not adapt to changes. On-line Planning, in turn, means adapting to changes and replanning based on them.

Since aircraft manufacturing techniques are precisely described and its assembly processes follow strict sequences [6], it fits under the Off-line Planning strategy. However, due to complexity of manufacturing an aircraft and the dependencies among the involved components, several defects are possible to appear during the manufacturing process [7]. Thus, correction steps are introduced to reduce the effect of these defects. In order to meet these corrections, a switching from an Off-line Planning to On-line Planning is required.

Multi agent systems can achieve considerable progress in the planning and control of complex commodity flows, compared to conventional flow concepts [8]. Furthermore, these agent systems have been introduced into the state of the art of industrial technology [4]. For the production, there are similar approaches which especially aim at flexibilisation of the material flow management, rapid start-up, or best possible reconfigurability [8],[9].

A planner has the responsibility to generate a plan which consists of a set of actions. Allocating resources to these actions and specifying the suitable time for executing them is the responsibility of a scheduler [5]. Designing a scheduling system for automated assembly in a non-deterministic environment was addressed by the institute of Information Management in Mechanical Engineering (RWTH Aachen) in a project within the scope of the Cluster of Excellence "Integrative Production Technology for High-Wage Countries". In this project, a scheduler for an automated assembly process was designed to adapt to random working piece conveyance, deduced solely from the current situation and a Computer Aided Design (CAD) description of the final product [11],[12].

The problem with task allocation is the process of assigning a set of tasks to a team of agents. Two main approaches address this problem [13]; the Behavior-Based Approach and the Market-Based Approach. In the Behavior-Based Approach each robot tries to estimate its colleagues' capabilities (i.e. sensors, power) and its state (i.e. busy, free). Based on that, each robot can determine which robot should do which task. Several algorithms belong to this category such as ALLIANCE [14] and Broadcast of Local Eligibility for Multi Target Observation [15]. In this approach there is no explicit communication among robots regarding task assignments. In addition, it depends on distributed coordination [13].

The Market-Based Approach, on the other hand, depends on explicit communication among robots regarding task assignments. It is based on the market theory and has been applied to a team of robots [10]. To determine which robot should do what, each robot has to attend an auction to get a task. To bid in this auction, a robot has to estimate its capabilities and availability in addition to the cost of doing this task. Then the robot sends the result to the auctioneer. The robot's capabilities, availability and cost together are called Robot Utility. Cost estimation depends on several factors such as the time which is needed to accomplish the task and the distance between the bidder robot and the task location [10].

In this proposed algorithm, the Market-Based Approach is used between the planning agents and the representative agents to announce and allocate the tasks. The Behaviour-Based Approach, on the other hand, is used among the representative agents to coordinate their activities when they are working at the same workspace.

## 2    Requirements

Several requirements must be addressed by the proposed planning algorithm in order to apply it to the production of the aircraft. This section presents the requirements which directly affect the planning algorithm, namely: task requirements and Agent requirements. Other requirements are discussed in [2].

Considering the tasks, most of the tasks of assembling aircrafts are known to the system in advance. But, these procedures must be represented in a language which can be interpreted by agents. Furthermore, dependencies among tasks and shared resources must be maintained. Performing two or more independent tasks at the same time issues the risk of collisions of physical units. This situation appears when the workspaces of these tasks overlap. Each task should have an associated documentation which shows the prerequisites to achieve it and the expected outcome as well as the expected quality. In case a task, which is accomplished by an agent, does not meet the required quality, a task recovery must be added to the list of tasks.

Apart from the requirements of tasks, agents on the other hands have their requirements. The dependencies among agents, material flows, and the selection of a suitable solution for integrating their activities must be considered by a planning algorithm. The skills of each agent play a role within the negotiation sessions (i.e. auction) to seize a task. If an individual agent does not meet the required skill to carry out the available task, an ad hoc group of agents will be formed. The gathered skills of this group should satisfy the available task. Since it is important to utilize all agents during the production process, each agent or group of agents has to participate in these negotiation sessions. This utilization approach assures that every agent is utilized. On the other hand, held tasks should be avoided. A held task is a task which is reserved by an agent, while this agent is busy with another task.

# 3    A Concept for Agent-Based Planning and Control of the Assembly of Carbon Fiber Reinforced Aircrafts

This section presents the conceptual architecture of the agent-based planning and control system. Inside this architecture, our conceptual planning algorithm works.

## 3.1    The Proposed Architecture

The core of this architecture is motivated by a market placed center concept. This core has interfaces with two main sides. The first being the task side and the second being the physical hardware side (e.g. the mobile production units). Figure 1 depicts this architecture.

To exemplify this architecture, let us suppose a new design of an aircraft is modelled using CAD. This model is the input of the system. The system interprets it by using certain transformation steps. This interpretation is decomposed into several simple tasks which can be accomplished by robots. These simple tasks are stored in the task database. Figure 2 depicts this decomposition.

The task database consist of two components: The first is the list of tasks and the second is the documentation of these tasks. In the documentation, the accomplished tasks and their associated quality management results are recorded. Once the task database is ready, the work inside the market place center starts.

The actors inside the market place center are agents. These agents are either planning agents or representative agents of physical entities. Tasks are allocated to the representative agents through the planning agents. The elaboration of this procedure is the scope of section 3.2.

Each representative agent has a direct communication channel with its corresponding physical entity. Using this channel, both of them update each other continuously about their activities. This tight communication allows agents to bid for tasks on behalf of their corresponding physical entity. Entities, on the other hand, perform these tasks and update their corresponding agents with their progress. These entities could be production units, feeders, logistic units or sensors.

On the right side of figure 1, a HMI component (Human Machine Interface) is placed, allowing a human to intervene in the system to solve some conflicted situations. For instance, a task does not meet the quality requirements and the recovery process cannot resolve this situation. In this case, a human operator is needed to resolve it. The detailed description of this architecture is presented in [2].

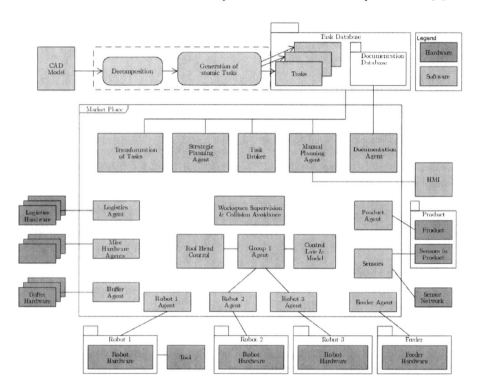

**Fig. 1.** The framework of the new concept for the production of CFRP aircrafts (c.f. [2])

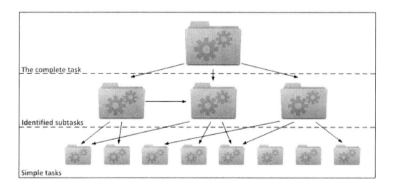

**Fig. 2.** Tasks decomposition

## 3.2    The Conceptual Planning Algorithm

The input of the market place is a set of simple tasks which are stored in the task database. Dependencies among these tasks are maintained and represented in a dependancy graph.

The planning agents are responsible for fetching the appropriate set of tasks from the task database. By the appropriate set we mean: The set of tasks which could be performed at the current status of the constructed aircraft. For instance, while the workspace at the end of the aircraft fuselage is crowded, the planning algorithm fetches a task which is performed on another workspace (e.g. on a wing). Once a task is fetched, the market based approach is carried out. In this approach, the task is announced to the representative agents.

Either a single representative agent or a group of agents bids its price to acquire the fetched task. The price depends on the agent's market unity. An agent market unity, among other things, consists of the agent's skills, its current distance from the task workplace, its status (e.g. busy, idle), and the number of its reserved tasks. If an agent wins the bidding, it is responsible for carrying out the task within the time and resources constraints, while maintaining the required quality of the task.

In addition to the planning and representative agents, the planning algorithm has a documentation agent. This special agent has the task to record the agents' performance and their allocated tasks. Besides, it has a direct communication channel to the documentation database to update it with the accomplished tasks.

**The Planning Agents.** The planning agents are depicted on the upper side of the market-place (figure 1). To exemplify these agents, we explain them by tracking a task which is passed through these agents. This task is to fix a plate in a specific place inside the aircraft fuselage.

The simple tasks are stored in the task database and they are the inputs of the market place center. Despite the fact that these tasks are simple, they need further analysis and transformation to describe how a task should be performed on a higher level. An agent transfers the task of fixing a plate into a set of instructions, such as through which entries of the fuselage can a representative agent use, to reach its target workspace. In this workspace, the representative agent has to fix the plate.

Due to its global knowledge about the progress of the construction and the crowded workspaces, the agent can control this scenario. The transformation step is done by the transformation agent (see figure 1, upper left corner of the market place).

Once a task is transferred by the transformation agent, the task broker agent begins the auction session for this task. The task transformation instructions are attached with the task. Thus, each representative agent can specify its suitable price. After a timer is expired, the broker agent announces the winner of the task.

Once the winner representative agent accomplishes the task by fixing the plate on the right place, a quality assurance process is issued. This process is needed to maintain the required quality of the accomplished task. For instance, if the plate is fixed and the gap between the plate and lattice is within the allowed range.

If the quality test shows that the task is accomplished successfully, the transformation agent fetches another task which depends on accomplishing the plate fixing task; for instance, to cover the fixed plate with another layer.

The previous mentioned workflow is termed as Off-line Planning because the simple tasks in the task database can be fetched in their usual sequence. This sequence is based on the dependencies among tasks. However, if the quality of an accomplished task does not meet the requirements, e.g. because the gap between the plate and the geodetic lattice exceeds the allowed range, an On-line Planning workflow takes place.

Besides cooperating with the transformation agent, the strategic planning agent takes the responsibility of solving this situation. Either it solves the situation by recovering the incomplete task or by ordering a task to remove the plate and re-scheduling it as a new task.

**The Representative Agents.** The representative agents are depicted on the lower side of the market-place in figure 1. Each agent of this set represents its corresponding external unit such as a production unit. The agent exchanges the data with a software application which runs inside the external unit.

Once a broker agent puts up a task for auction, the representative agents start publishing their utilities to participate in the auction. Agents can either participate in the auction individually or as a team of agents.

The winning agent or agent group defines the concrete plan for performing the task. For instance, in which way the production units can move the plate through the gap, which is specified by the transformation agent, without affecting other agents' work. This concrete plan includes the coordination with the other units such as logistic units or feeder units. And it includes the required coordination to avoid collisions with other production units on the same workspace.

The concrete plan, which each representative agent derives, depends on the local situation of each agent. Therefore, it is not part of the responsibility of the planning agents which work on a higher planning level.

This approach makes the complete system a hybrid system. The high level planning follows a centralized approach and is done by the planning agents. The concrete planning, on the other hand, follows a distributed approach and is performed by the representative agents.

## 3.3    The Scientific Contributions

The scientific contributions of this paper are the following:

**Adaptability and Flexibility.** These features are achieved in the production line by depending on mobile production units and a stationary aircraft fuselage. These production units can directly adapt to customization of the product, once the CAD model is provided to the system. To provide the system with flexibility, two levels of planning are supported; namely: High Level Planning and Low Level Planning. High level planning is based on a centralized system and the transformation agent has the responsibility to carry out this level of planning. The transformation agent depends on its global knowledge about the construction progress of the aircraft. Based on this knowledge, it produces an abstract plan for each task. Low level planning, in turn, is based on a distributed system and the representative agents have the responsibility to carry it out. The representative agents depend on their local situations to derive a concrete plan from the provided abstract plan.

**Parallelism and Workspace Overlapping.** Since the constructed product is stationary, overlapping of workspaces is highly probable. Consequently, independent tasks with overlapped workspaces cannot be performed in parallel. In this situation, the parallelism feature is achieved by depending on the two levels of planning. Based on its global knowledge, the transformation agent supports the representative agents with recommendations to facilitate the transportation of the required materials to the target workspace. The representative agents, in turn, depend on their local environment to notice the current activities of their neighbour colleagues. Thus, they can coordinate with them directly to synchronize their activities on the shared part of the workspace, when needed.

### 3.4    Outlook

The current conceptual system is designed as a centralized system. This concept will be extended to support a distributed system approach on a higher level. This feature will increase the scalability of the system; thus, the number of representative agents could be extended further. Yet, the representative agents should always deal with this distributed system as a single coherent system. This means a transparency layer must be considered in the future work. This layer has the important role to give all agents the same chance of winning an auction in real time, thus they are virtually attending the same auction session.

Participating in an auction as a group of agents requires awareness of the skills of the other agents. Furthermore, agents have to distribute the transformed task among them to carry it out. This topic and the cognitive skills of agents will be addressed in the future work.

## 4    Conclusion

Due to fast changes of requirements, the product life-time is short. Thus, a new product line and competences should be developed to adapt to these changes. This paper presents a new conceptual approach to address, among other things, this adaptation challenge. In addition to this adaptability feature, the flexibility and parallelism features are supported by this approach. These features are maintained by heterogeneous mobile production units while they are carrying out their tasks on a stationary fuselage of an aircraft. These units are represented inside a centralized system by so-called representative agents. These agents have the responsibility to acquire tasks. Defining these tasks and announcing them is carried out by another group of agents, the planning agents. Moreover, the planning agents have the responsibility to provide the representative agents with recommendations for carrying out their tasks. The planning agents have this responsibility because they have a global knowledge about the progress of the constructed aircraft. Each representative agent, in turn, draws its concrete plan independently, based on its local environment. These two levels of planning are important to achieve the flexibility and the parallelism features. In order to meet the required quality, each accomplished task is followed by a quality assurance step. If an accomplished task does not meet the required quality, the startegic planning agent initiates On-line Planning to recover the previous situation.

## References

1. Sallinen, M., Heikkila, T., Salmi, T., Kivikunnas, S., Pulkkinen, T.: A Concept for Isles of Automation: Ubiquitous Robot Cell for Flexible Manufacturing. In: International Conference on Control, Automation and Systems, Seoul Korea (2008)
2. Dietrich, F., Löchte, C., Jeschke, S., Raatz, A.: An Agent-Based Concept for Planning and Control of the Production of Carbon Fibre Reinforced Plastics Aircrafts with Mobile Production Units - Technological Requirements, Software Infrastructure and Architecture (to be published)
3. Vasiliev, V., Barynin, V., Rasin, A.: Anisogrid Lattice Structures - Survey of Development and Application. Composite Structures 54(2-3), 361–370 (2001)
4. Wurman, P., D'Andrea, R., Mountz, M.: Coordinating Hundreds of Cooperative, Autonomous Vehicles in Warehouse. AI Mag, Jg. 29(1), 9–19 (2007)
5. Nau, D.: Artificial Intelligence and Automation. In: Nof, S. (ed.) Springer Handbook of Automation, pp. 249–266. Springer, Heidelberg (2009)
6. Sarh, B., Buttrick, J., Munk, C., Bossi, R.: In: Nof, S. (ed.) Springer Handbook of Automation, pp. 894–909. Springer, Heidelberg (2009)
7. Jamshidi, J., Kayani, A., Iravani, P., Maropoulos, P., Summers, M.: Manufacturing and assembly Automation by Integrated Metrology Systems for Aircraft Wing Fabrication. Proceedings of the institution of Mechanical Engineers, Part B: Journal of Engineering Manufacture 224, 25–36 (2009)
8. Nejad, H., Sugimura, N., Iwamura, K., Tanimizu, Y.: Multi-agent Architecture for Dyanmic Incremental Process Planning in the Flexible Manufacturing System. J. Intell. Manuf., Jg. 21(4), 487–499 (2010)
9. Vrba, P., Radakovič, M., Obitko, M., Mařík, V.: Semantic Extension of Agent-Based Control: The Packing Cell Case Study. In: Mařík, V., Strasser, T., Zoitl, A. (eds.) HoloMAS 2009. LNCS (LNAI), vol. 5696, pp. 47–60. Springer, Heidelberg (2009)
10. Dias, B., Zlot, R., Kalra, N., Stentz, A.: Market-Based Multi-robot Coordination: A Survey and Analysis. IEEE 94(7) (2006)
11. Hauck, E., Ewert, D., Schilberg, D., Jeschke, S.: Design of a Knowledge Module Embedded in a Framework for a Cognitive System Using the Example of Assembly Tasks. In: 3rd Int. Conf. on Applied Human Factors and Ergonomics. CRC Press / Taylor & Francis, Ltd., Miami, USA (2010)
12. Hauck, E., Gramatke, A., Henning, K.: A Software Architecture for Cognitive Technical Systems for an Assembly Task in a Production Environment. In: Automation and Control, Theory and Practice, pp. 13–28. In-Teh (2009)
13. Parker, L.: Multiple Mobile Robot Systems. In: Siciliano, B., Khatib, O. (eds.) Springer Handbook of Robots, pp. 921–936. Springer, Heidelberg (2008)
14. Parker, L.: ALLIANCE -An Architecture for Fault Tolerant, Cooperative Control of Heterogeneous Mobile Robots. In: International Conference on Intelligent Robots and Systems (1994)
15. Werger, B., Mataric, M.: Broadcast of Local Eligibility for Multi-target Observation, pp. 347–356. Springer, Heidelberg (2000)

# Trajectory Tracking and Vibration Control of Two Planar Rigid Manipulators Moving a Flexible Object

Balasubramanian Esakki, Rama B. Bhat, and Chun-Yi Su

Department of Mechanical Engineering, VelTech Dr. RR and Dr. SR Technical University,
Chennai, Tamilnadu, India
Department of Mechanical and Industrial Engineering, Concordia University,
Montreal, Quebec, H3G 1M8, Canada
esak.bala@gmail.com, {rbhat,cysu}@encs.concordia.ca

**Abstract.** This paper deals with the robust design of a control system for two planar rigid manipulators required to move the flexible object in the prescribed trajectory while suppressing the vibration of the flexible object. Without approximating or discretizing the beam, the complete system of dynamic equations are derived by combining the manipulator and beam dynamics. The resulting equations have rigid as well as flexible parameters which are coupled together. By using singular perturbation technique, the two subsystems, namely, slow and fast subsystems, are identified. For slow subsystem, a regressor based sliding mode control scheme is developed to track the desired rigid body motion of the object. For fast subsystem, a corresponding feedback control algorithm has been developed to suppress the vibration of the object. Exponential stability results for the closed-loop system with the developed control laws for both slow and fast subsystems are presented. Simulation results demonstrate the versatility of the proposed composite control scheme.

**Keywords:** Robotic manipulator, singular perturbations, slow subsystem, fast subsystem, composite control, exponential stability, trajectory tracking.

## 1 Introduction

It is well known that robots have wide applications. However, in some situations single robot may not be able to grasp and move long slender flexible objects along a prescribed trajectory in a safe and efficient way and hence, two robots are used. The problem of two manipulators handling the flexible materials collaboratively is complex compared with handling the rigid parts. Especially the dynamics and control of flexible systems are more complex than that for the rigid systems. There are quite few studies on handling of flexible objects by two robots. Kosuge *et al.* [9] utilized the finite element model of the sheet metal and also implemented their control algorithm experimentally to reduce the vibration of the object. Sun and Liu [16] developed a new approach of modeling the beam and proposed a hybrid impedance controller which is used to stabilize the system while suppressing the vibrations and controlling internal forces. Al-Yahmali and Hsia [2] derived the sliding mode control algorithm for the case of two robot handling flexible object and the beam dynamics was derived using assumed mode method. Ali *et al.*

S. Jeschke, H. Liu, and D. Schilberg (Eds.): ICIRA 2011, Part I, LNAI 7101, pp. 376–387, 2011.
© Springer-Verlag Berlin Heidelberg 2011

[17] used two time scale controllers to track the desired trajectory for the rigid body motion, and also to suppress the vibration. In all the above studies on handling of flexible objects, namely sheet metal or beam, they are discretized using finite element model or approximated using assumed mode method. The truncation of the original model with infinite degree of freedom of a flexible beam to a finite dimensional model poses many issues mentioned in [5], importantly, measurement difficulties and also necessitates higher order controllers when more number of modes are considered. Considering these drawbacks, unlike in the earlier studies, in this study, the complete system of dynamic model is derived without using any approximated methods. The present study also develops a new robust control scheme for the two manipulators moving the flexible object and simultaneously suppressing the vibration.

## 2  Kinematics and Dynamics of Beam

The two manipulators rigidly grasping the Euler-Bernoulli beam shown in Fig. 1 can be considered to have simply supported end conditions, because the ends of the beam are allowed to rotate. Certainly, other end boundary conditions can be included for the derivation of the beam dynamics. However, the purpose of this paper is to illustrate the essential features of the controller designs avoiding confusion of the mathematical expressions.

### 2.1  Kinematics of Beam

The co-ordinate frames $X_1Y_1$ and $X_2Y_2$ shown in Fig. 1 are fixed frame and xy-frame is a moving coordinate frame which is attached to the beam. Consider a beam of length $L$ and mass $m = \rho L$, where $\rho$ is mass per unit length. $\{c_0\} = \{x_0, y_0, \theta\}^T$ are the mass center position and orientation of the beam with respect to $X_1Y_1$ frame. The Z and z directions are perpendicular to the plane. $F_{1x}, F_{1y}, F_{2x}, F_{2y}$ are the forces applied by the manipulators at the two ends of the beam. The transverse displacement $\eta(x,t)$ is measured with respect to xy-frame and deformation in the longitudinal direction is neglected. All kinematic relations are written with respect to $X_1Y_1$ frame.
Any point on the beam can be written as,

$$X = x_0 + x\cos\theta - \eta\sin\theta \tag{1}$$
$$Y = y_0 + x\sin\theta + \eta\cos\theta \tag{2}$$

where, $x$ is spatial co-ordinate ranging from $\frac{-L}{2}$ to $\frac{+L}{2}$. The beam has rigid body motion on which the flexible motion or vibration of beam is superimposed. Assuming that the slope due to transverse deflection is negligible compared to the orientation of the beam, slope at the two ends of the beam are neglected. The following relations are obtained from the Fig. 2.
The left end pose (position and orientation) of the beam is given by,

$$\{e_1\} = \{c_o\} - \{\tfrac{L}{2}\cos\theta \quad \tfrac{L}{2}\sin\theta \quad 0\}^T + \{-\eta\sin\theta \quad \eta\cos\theta \quad 0\}^T \tag{3}$$

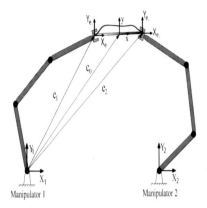

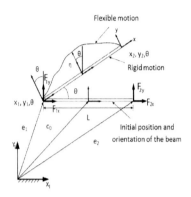

**Fig. 1.** Two planar manipulators grasping a flexible object

**Fig. 2.** Flexible beam with coordinate frames and forces

and the right end pose of the beam is given by,

$$\{e_2\} = \{c_o\} + \{\frac{L}{2}cos\theta \quad \frac{L}{2}sin\theta \quad 0\}^T + \{-\eta \sin \theta \quad \eta \cos \theta \quad 0\}^T \qquad (4)$$

Differentiating (3) and (4), these relations can be written in compact form with respect to the Cartesian coordinates as,

$$\{\dot{e}\} = [R]\{\dot{X}_{rf}\} \qquad (5)$$

where $\dot{X}_{rf} \triangleq \{\dot{x}_0 \; \dot{y}_0 \; \dot{\theta}\}^T$ denotes the velocity of the mass center of the object, $\{\dot{e}\} = \{\dot{e}_1 \; \dot{e}_2\}^T$ and $R = [1 \; 0 \; \frac{L}{2}sin\theta - \eta \cos \theta; 0 \; 1 \; -\frac{L}{2}cos\theta - \eta \sin \theta; 0 \; 0 \; 1; 1 \; 0 \; \frac{L}{2}sin\theta - \eta \cos \theta; 0 \; 1 \; \frac{L}{2}cos\theta - \eta \sin \theta; 0 \; 0 \; 1]^T$.

## 2.2 Dynamics of Beam

In order to determine the dynamic equations of motion of beam, the kinetic energy, potential energy due to elasticity of the beam and also due to gravitational force have to be obtained. By applying extended Hamilton's principle [6], the dynamic equation of motion of beam will be derived.

Differentiating (1) and (2) to obtain the velocities, kinetic energy of the beam is given as,

$$T = \frac{1}{2} \int_{-\frac{L}{2}}^{\frac{L}{2}} \rho [\dot{x}_0^2 + \dot{y}_0^2 + \dot{\theta}^2 \eta^2 + (x\dot{\theta} + \dot{\eta})^2 - 2\dot{\theta}\eta(\dot{x}_0 cos\theta + \dot{y}_0 sin\theta)$$

$$+ 2(\dot{\theta}x + \dot{\eta})(\dot{y}_0 cos\theta - \dot{x}_0 sin\theta)]dx \qquad (6)$$

Neglecting the shear deformation and considering the bending of the beam, potential energy due to elasticity and gravitational force can be combined together results in,

$$U = \frac{1}{2} \int_{-\frac{L}{2}}^{\frac{L}{2}} \left[ EI\eta''^2 \right] dx + mgy_0 \qquad (7)$$

Work done due to the external forces (Fig. 2) are formulated as,

$$W = F_{1x}(x_0 - \frac{L}{2}\cos\theta) + F_{1y}(y_0 - \frac{L}{2}\sin\theta) + F_{2x}(x_0 + \frac{L}{2}\cos\theta)$$

$$+ F_{2y}(y_0 + \frac{L}{2}\sin\theta) + (F_{2y}+F_{1y})\eta\cos\theta - (F_{1x}+F_{2x})\eta\sin\theta \tag{8}$$

By applying extended Hamilton's Principle,

$$\int_{t_1}^{t_2}(\delta T - \delta U + \delta W)dt = 0 \tag{9}$$

the beam dynamics with respect to Cartesian coordinates $X_{rf} = \{x_0, y_0, \theta\}^T$ can be written in a compact form as,

$$M_{rf}\ddot{X}_{rf} + C_{rf} + \eta_{rf} + G_{rf} = F_{rf}(-f) \tag{10}$$

where,

$$M_{rf} = \begin{bmatrix} m & 0 & -\rho\cos\theta\int_{-\frac{L}{2}}^{\frac{L}{2}}\eta dx \\ 0 & m & -\rho\sin\theta\int_{-\frac{L}{2}}^{\frac{L}{2}}\eta dx \\ -\rho\cos\theta\int_{-\frac{L}{2}}^{\frac{L}{2}}\eta dx & -\rho\sin\theta\int_{-\frac{L}{2}}^{\frac{L}{2}}\eta dx & \frac{mL^2}{12}+\rho\int_{-\frac{L}{2}}^{\frac{L}{2}}\eta^2 dx \end{bmatrix} ; \quad G_{rf} = \left\{ \begin{array}{c} 0 \\ mg \\ 0 \end{array} \right\} ;$$

$$C_{rf} = \left\{ \begin{array}{c} \dot{\theta}^2(\rho\sin\theta\int_{-\frac{L}{2}}^{\frac{L}{2}}\eta dx) \\ -\dot{\theta}^2(\rho\cos\theta\int_{-\frac{L}{2}}^{\frac{L}{2}}\eta dx) \\ 0 \end{array} \right\} ; \quad \eta_{rf} = \left\{ \begin{array}{c} -\rho\sin\theta\int_{-\frac{L}{2}}^{\frac{L}{2}}\ddot{\eta} dx - 2\rho\dot{\theta}\cos\theta\int_{-\frac{L}{2}}^{\frac{L}{2}}\dot{\eta} dx \\ \rho\cos\theta\int_{-\frac{L}{2}}^{\frac{L}{2}}\ddot{\eta} dx - 2\rho\dot{\theta}\sin\theta\int_{-\frac{L}{2}}^{\frac{L}{2}}\dot{\eta} dx \\ \rho\int_{-\frac{L}{2}}^{\frac{L}{2}}x\ddot{\eta} dx + 2\rho\dot{\theta}\int_{-\frac{L}{2}}^{\frac{L}{2}}\eta\dot{\eta} dx \end{array} \right\}$$

$$F_{rf} = \begin{bmatrix} 1 & 0 & 0 & 1 & 0 & 0 \\ 0 & 1 & 0 & 0 & 1 & 0 \\ \frac{L}{2}\sin\theta - \eta\cos\theta & -\frac{L}{2}\cos\theta - \eta\sin\theta & 0 & -\frac{L}{2}\sin\theta - \eta\cos\theta & \frac{L}{2}\cos\theta - \eta\sin\theta & 0 \end{bmatrix}$$

The flexible motion is nothing but transverse vibration of beam dynamics which can be given by,

$$-\sin\theta\ddot{x}_0 + \cos\theta\ddot{y}_0 + x\ddot{\theta} + \ddot{\eta} - \eta\dot{\theta}^2 + \frac{EI}{\rho}\eta^{iv} = F_{ff}(f) \tag{11}$$

where, $F_{ff} = [-\sin\theta \ \cos\theta \ 0 \ -\sin\theta \ \cos\theta \ 0]$ and $\{f\} = \{F_{1x}, F_{1y}, M_{O1}, F_{2x}, F_{2y}, M_{O2}\}^T$
Equation (10) has rigid as well as flexible parameters are coupled together and in (11) also has similar parameters are coupled.

## 3   Manipulator Dynamics and Combined Dynamics

### 3.1   Manipulators Dynamics

Using the general manipulator dynamic equation, the two manipulators equations in the assembled form in joint space can be written as,

$$M_r\ddot{q} + C_r\dot{q} + G_r = \tau + J^T f \tag{12}$$

where,

$$M_r = \begin{bmatrix} M_1 & 0 \\ 0 & M_2 \end{bmatrix}; \quad C_r = \begin{bmatrix} C_1 & 0 \\ 0 & C_2 \end{bmatrix}; \quad G_r = \begin{Bmatrix} G_1 \\ G_2 \end{Bmatrix}; \quad \tau = \begin{Bmatrix} \tau_1 \\ \tau_2 \end{Bmatrix}; \quad J = \begin{bmatrix} J_1 & 0 \\ 0 & J_2 \end{bmatrix};$$

where, $\{f\} = \{f_1 \ f_2\}^T$ and $\{q\} = \{q_1 \ q_2\}^T$.

### 3.2   Combined Dynamics

The manipulators dynamics (12) is represented in joint space and it should be converted into Cartesian space. Then the resulting equation will be combined with the beam dynamics yileds the combined dynamics in Cartesian space.

In general differential kinematic relations of manipulator relates the end-effector and joint velocity which is given by,

$$\{\dot{q}\} = [J^{-1}]\{\dot{e}\} \tag{13}$$

Differentiating (5) and substituting the result into the derivative of (13) gives,

$$\ddot{q} = J^{-1}\dot{R}\dot{X}_{rf} + J^{-1}R\ddot{X}_{rf} + \dot{J}^{-1}R\dot{X}_{rf} \tag{14}$$

For simplicity, the vectors represented in parentheses and matrices represented in the square brackets are omitted above and it is followed further.

Substituting (13) and (14) into (12), we obtain the manipulator dynamics in Cartesian space,

$$M_r J^{-1}R\ddot{X}_{rf} + (M_r\dot{J}^{-1}R + M_r J^{-1}\dot{R} + C_r J^{-1}R)\dot{X}_{rf} + G_r = \tau + J^T f \tag{15}$$

The dynamics of manipulators and beam are represented with respect to Cartesian coordinates are combined to formulate the kinematically closed loop system.

Due to the assumption of simply supported beam boundary conditions, the moments at the two ends are not considered. But in reality manipulators experience forces as well as moments at the two ends of the beam. Conisdering the moments in $F_{rf}$ and then $R^T$ becomes $F_{rf}$. Using (10) and premultiplying (15) by $R^T J^{-T}$ and also taking into account the transverse vibration of beam dynamics (11), the complete manipulators-beam system dynamics is represented as

$$M_{orf}\ddot{X}_{rf} + C_{orf}\dot{X}_{rf} + G_{orf} + \eta_{orf} = u_{orf} \tag{16}$$

$$-\sin\theta\ddot{x}_0 + \cos\theta\ddot{y}_0 + x\ddot{\theta} + \ddot{\eta} - \eta\dot{\theta}^2 + \frac{EI}{\rho}\eta^{iv} = F_{ff}(f) \tag{17}$$

where,

$$M_{orf} = R^T J^{-T} M_r J^{-1} R + M_{rf}; \quad C_{orf} = R^T J^{-T}(M_r\dot{J}^{-1}R + M_r J^{-1}\dot{R} + C_r J^{-1}R) + C_{rf}$$
$$G_{orf} = R^T J^{-T} G_r + G_{rf}; \quad \eta_{orf} = \eta_{rf}; \quad u_{orf} = R^T J^{-T}\tau$$

## 4  Singular Perturbation Model

The system dynamics derived without using any approximation methods given in (16) and (17) have rigid as well as flexible parameters that are coupled together. These flexible parameters have to be uncoupled by using singular perturbation technique. Using a perturbation parameter, say $\varepsilon^2$, order of the system dynamics can be changed and this small parameter depends upon the system variable. Keeping that in mind, the term $EI/\rho$ in (17), which has large magnitude compared to other coefficients [10], can be re-defined as $EI/\rho = a \cdot K$. where, $K$ is a dimensionless parameter which has large value for the different materials [8] and [10], its order is equal to $EI/\rho$ and also the variable "$a$" satisfies the equalities. The beam's rigid body motion with respect to the state variables $X_{rf} = \{x_0, y_0, \theta\}^T$ and also the transverse vibration $\eta$ with respect to the state variable occurs in different time scales. Then, one need to introduce a new variable $w(x,t)$ in the same order of the state variable by the following,

$$\eta(x,t) \triangleq \varepsilon^2 . w(x,t) \tag{18}$$

where $\varepsilon^2 = 1/K$ is the so-called perturbed parameter. Incorporating (18), the singularly perturbed model of the complete system of dynamic equation is obtained which is given by,

$$\tilde{M}_{orf}\ddot{X}_{rf} + \tilde{C}_{orf}\dot{X}_{rf} + \tilde{G}_{orf} + \eta_{orf} = \tilde{u}_{orf} \tag{19}$$

$$-\sin\theta\ddot{x}_0 + \cos\theta\ddot{y}_0 + x\ddot{\theta} + \varepsilon^2\ddot{w} - \varepsilon^2 w\dot{\theta}^2 + aw^{iv} = F_{ff}(f) \tag{20}$$

where,
$$\tilde{M}_{orf} = \tilde{R}^T J^{-T} M_r J^{-1}\tilde{R} + \tilde{M}_{rf}; \quad \tilde{C}_{orf} = \tilde{R}^T J^{-T}(M_r J^{-1}\tilde{R} + M_r J^{-1}\dot{\tilde{R}} + C_r J^{-1}\tilde{R}) + \tilde{C}_{rf}$$
$$\tilde{G}_{orf} = \tilde{R}^T J^{-T} G_r + \tilde{G}_{rf}; \quad \tilde{\eta}_{orf} = \tilde{\eta}_{rf}; \quad u_{orf} = \tilde{R}^T J^{-T}\tau$$
The components such as $\tilde{M}_{orf}$, $\tilde{C}_{orf}$, $\tilde{G}_{orf}$, $\tilde{\eta}_{orf}$ and $\tilde{R}$ are obtained by substituting $w$ instead of $\eta$. In the following sections, two subsystems, namely slow and fast, are obtained by following the typical steps of singular perturbation approach.

### 4.1  Slow Subsystem

When the perturbation parameter $\varepsilon$ approaches zero, the equivalent quasi-steady-state system [15] represents the slow subsystem. By setting $\varepsilon = 0$, in (19) and (20) yields the slow subsystem which is given in compact form as,

$$M_{or}\ddot{X}_{rf} + C_{or}\dot{X}_{rf} + G_{or} = u_{or} \tag{21}$$

where,
$$M_{or} = M_o + M_{rd} \text{ and } M_o = R_1^T J^{-T} M_r J^{-1} R_1; \quad C_{or} = R_1^T J^{-T}(M_r J^{-1} R_1 + M_r J^{-1}\dot{R}_1 + C_r J^{-1} R_1); \quad G_{or} = G_o + G_{rd} \text{ and } G_o = R_1^T J^{-T} G_r; \quad u_0 = R_1^T J^{-T}\tau \text{ and the beam dynamic equation parameter becomes,}$$

$$M_{rd} = \begin{bmatrix} m & 0 & 0 \\ 0 & m & 0 \\ 0 & 0 & \frac{mL^2}{12} \end{bmatrix}; \quad F_{rd} = \begin{bmatrix} 1 & 0 & 0 & 1 & 0 & 0 \\ 0 & 1 & 0 & 0 & 1 & 0 \\ \frac{L}{2}\sin\theta & -\frac{L}{2}\cos\theta & 1 & -\frac{L}{2}\sin\theta & \frac{L}{2}\cos\theta & 1 \end{bmatrix}; \quad G_{rd} = \left\{ \begin{array}{c} 0 \\ mg \\ 0 \end{array} \right\}$$

$R_1 = [1 \ 0 \ \frac{L}{2}sin\theta; 0 \ 1 \ -\frac{L}{2}cos\theta; 0 \ 0 \ 1; 1 \ 0 \ \frac{L}{2}sin\theta; 0 \ 1 \ \frac{L}{2}cos\theta; 0 \ 0 \ 1]^T$. and also the equation of motion for transverse vibration of the beam (20) becomes,

$$[-\sin\theta.\ddot{x}_0 + \cos\theta\ddot{y}_0 + x\ddot{\theta} + aw^{iv}]_s = F_{ff}(f_s) \qquad (22)$$

where $f_s$ corresponds to $f$ when $\varepsilon = 0$.

The slow subsystem given in (21) represents the rigid body motion without involving any flexible parameters. It will be used further to design a control algorithm to track a desired trajectory of the object.

## 4.2  Fast Subsystem

Equation (20) represents the perturbed flexible model obtained with perturbation parameter $\varepsilon$ which is very small and solely depends upon the $E, I$ and $\rho$.

In order to study the dynamic behavior of fast system, the so called boundary layer phenomenon [8] and [15] must be obtained. This can be identified by ensuring that the slow variables are kept constant in the fast time scale $v = \frac{t - t_0}{\varepsilon}$. From the typical steps of singular perturbation [8] one can define the fast variable $w_f = w - w_s$. Differentiating the fast time scale two times gives,

$$\ddot{w} = \ddot{w}_s + \frac{dv}{dt}\frac{d}{dv}\hat{w}_f = \ddot{w}_s + \frac{1}{\varepsilon^2}\hat{\ddot{w}}_f \qquad (23)$$

where $\hat{w}_f$ denotes differentiating fast variable with respect to fast time scale.

Using the fast varible, (20) can be rewritten as,

$$-\sin\theta.\ddot{x}_0 + \cos\theta\ddot{y}_0 + x\ddot{\theta} + \varepsilon^2\ddot{w} - \varepsilon^2(w_s + w_f)\dot{\theta}^2 + a(w_s^{iv} + w_f^{iv}) = F_{ff}(f) \qquad (24)$$

Using (22) and (23), (24) becomes,

$$F_{ff}(f_s) + \hat{\ddot{w}}_f + \varepsilon^2\ddot{w}_s - \varepsilon^2(w_s + w_f)\dot{\theta}^2 + aw_f^{iv} = F_{ff}(f) \qquad (25)$$

By defining $F_{ff}(f_f) = F_{ff}(f) - F_{ff}(f_s)$, the above equation can be rewritten as,

$$\hat{\ddot{w}}_f + \varepsilon^2\ddot{w}_s - \varepsilon^2(w_s + w_f)\dot{\theta}^2 + aw_f^{iv} = F_{ff}(f_f) \qquad (26)$$

However, in the boundary layer system, the slow variable $w_s$ is constant which implies $\ddot{w}_s = 0$ and also $\varepsilon = 0$ [15]. Then, the fast dynamics can be represented as,

$$\hat{\ddot{w}}_f + aw_f^{iv} = F_{ff}(f_f) \qquad (27)$$

Following [11] and [14], an operator A is defined as,

$$D(A) = \{w_f | w_f^{iv} \in H, w_f(0) = w_f''(0) = w_f(L) = w_f''(L) = 0\}$$
$$Aw_f = aw_f^{iv}, \quad \forall w_f \in D(A) \qquad (28)$$

where, $D(A)$ denotes the domain of the operator $A$ and $H$ denotes the Hilbert space. Using (28), the partial differential equation (27) can be rewritten as an abstract differential equation on $H$ as,

$$\hat{\ddot{w}}_f(v) + Aw_f(v) = F_{ff}(f_f) \qquad (29)$$
$$w_f(0) = w_{f0}, \quad \dot{w}_f(0) = w_{f1}$$

Equation (29) represents the fast subsystem which will be used for designing fast feedback control.

## 5   Composite Control

A composite control for the two manipulators and beam system is given by,

$$u = u_s(\dot{X}_{rf}, X_{rf}, t) + u_f(\hat{w}_f, w_f)$$

where $u_s$ is designed based on slow subsystem (21) and $u_f$ is designed to stabilize the fast subsystem (29).

### 5.1   Robust Controller Design for Slow Subsystem

The key issue is that with the unknown manipulators and beam parameters the design of $u_s(\dot{X}_{rf}, X_{rf}, t)$ can not be arbitrary. It has to guarantee the exponential tracking of the desired trajectories so that the Tikhnov's theorem can be satisfied, which will be clear in the later development. For that purpose, a sliding mode control approach will be adopted.

Define the tracking error as,

$$e_r = X_{rf} - X_{rfd} \tag{30}$$

where $X_{rfd}$ is the desired trajectory and the auxiliary trajectory can also be defined as,

$$\dot{X}_r = \dot{X}_{rfd} - \lambda e_r \tag{31}$$

where $\lambda$ is a positive definite matrix whose eigenvalues are strictly in the right half of the complex plane.

The sliding surface can be chosen as,

$$S = \dot{X}_{rf} - \dot{X}_r = \dot{e}_r + \lambda e_r \tag{32}$$

The sliding mode controller can be given as,

$$u_s = u_{or} = Y_{or}\psi - K_D S \tag{33}$$

where $K_D$ is a positive definite gain matrix, $Y_{or}(\ddot{X}_r, \dot{X}_r, \dot{q}, q)$ is the regressor matrix, $\alpha_{or}$ is the parameter vector and $\psi = [\psi_1 \dots \psi_m]^T$ are the switching functions which are given by,

$$\psi = -\Gamma \frac{Y_{or}^T S}{\|Y_{or}^T S\|} \tag{34}$$

where $\Gamma \geq \|\alpha_{or}\|$ and $\Gamma$ is upperbound of $\alpha_{or}$ which is assumed to be known.

### 5.2   Control Design for Fast Subsystem

The objective of the controller is to suppress the vibration of the flexible object by incorporating following feedback control law,

$$u_f = (f_f) = -\Pi F_{ff}^\dagger \hat{w}_f(v) \tag{35}$$

where $F_{ff}^{+}$ can be found using pseudo inverse. The operator $\Pi$ is well studied in [11] and [12]. Also, the velocity signal $\hat{w}_f(v)$ can be measured using velocity sensor. The presented control algorithm uses only velocity feedback which is irrespective of boundary conditions. This controller is simple to implement in real time and reduces the need of number of sensors.

Substitute (35) into (29) and also incorporating the operator $\Pi = kQA$ gives,

$$\hat{w}_f(v) + kQA\hat{w}_f(v) + Aw_f(v) = 0 \tag{36}$$
$$w_f(0) = w_{f0}, \quad \dot{w}_f(0) = w_{f1}$$

where $k$ is the positive gain and the term $QA\hat{w}_f(v)$ is the special damping term [12]. This damping has been studied by various researchers especially [3]-[4]. The two operators $Q$ and $A$ are related by $Q = A^{\beta}$ and $\beta$ varies between $[\frac{-1}{2},0]$. When $\beta = \frac{-1}{2}$, the damping term $QA\hat{w}_f(v)$ becomes $A^{\frac{1}{2}}\hat{w}_f(v)$. This corresponds to structural damping which can be also seen in [3].

### 5.3   Stability Analysis

Tikhnov's theorem [7] is used to justify the composite control strategy that uses slow control based on a slow subsystem together with fast feedback control to stabilize the fast subsystem. According to Tikhnov's theorem, both the subsystems has to be exponentially stable.

**Exponential Stability of Slow Subsystem:** Based on Tikhnov's theorem, slow subsystem has to be exponentially stable. The following derivation will illustrate the exponential stability of slow subsystem for all $t > 0$.

Differentiating the sliding surface (32), using (21) and (32) and also multiplying both sides by $M_{or}$ yields,

$$M_{or}\dot{S} = u_{or} - Y_{or}(\ddot{X}_r, \dot{X}_r, \dot{q}, q)\alpha_{or} - C_{or}S \tag{37}$$

where,

$$(M_{or}\ddot{X}_r + C_{or}\dot{X}_r + G_{or}) = Y_{or}(\ddot{X}_r, \dot{X}_r, \dot{q}, q)\alpha_{or}$$

Consider a Lyapunov function candidate as,

$$V_1(t,S) = \frac{1}{2}S^T M_{or}S \tag{38}$$

Differentiating (38), using (37) and also the property $\dot{M}_{or} - 2C_{or} = 0$ yields,

$$\dot{V}_1(t,S) = S^T[u_{or} - Y_{or}\alpha_{or}] \tag{39}$$

Substituting the control law given in (33) and (34) into (39) one can have,

$$\dot{V}_1(t,S) \leq -S^T K_D S \tag{40}$$

The solution of (40) with the help of $K_D = M_{0r}\kappa$ becomes,

$$V_1(t,S) \leq V_1(0,S(0))e^{-2\kappa t} \tag{41}$$

It is evident from the above equation that the sliding surface will converge exponentially to zero. Thus the sliding surface is related to the tracking error $e_r$ in (32) which also converges exponentially to zero which satisfies the Tikhnov's theorem.

**Exponential Stability of Fast Subsystem:** According to Tikhnov's theorem, the fast subsystem also has to be exponentially stable. The energy multiplier method used by [12] is followed to prove the exponential stability to satisfy the theorem given in [13], [theorem 4.1].
Let the energy function for (36) is in the following form,

$$E(v) = \frac{1}{2}\|Aw_f(v)\|^2 + \frac{1}{2}\|A^{\frac{1}{2}}\hat{w}_f(v)\|^2 \tag{42}$$

where $E(v)$ is weakly monotone decreasing function with respect to fast time scale $v$. The fast time scale derivative of $E(v)$ from the above equation will be,

$$\hat{E}(v) = -k\langle QA\hat{w}_f(v).A\hat{w}_f(v)\rangle \leq 0 \tag{43}$$

Let us choose $0 < \varepsilon < 1$ and the Lyapunov function candidate is given by,

$$V_2(v) = 2(1-\varepsilon)vE(v) + \langle \hat{w}_f(v).A\hat{w}_f(v)\rangle \tag{44}$$

There exists a constant $C_1$ such that, the following holds,

$$[2(1-\varepsilon)v - C_1]E(v) \leq V_2(v) \leq [2(1-\varepsilon)v + C_1]E(v) \tag{45}$$

The derivative of $V_2(v)$ with respect to fast time scale after some manipulation becomes,

$$\hat{V}_2(v) = [(2-\varepsilon)\|A^{-\frac{1}{2}}\|^2 + \frac{C_2^2 k}{2}\lambda_{max}(Q) - 2kv(1-\varepsilon)\lambda_{min}(Q)]\|A\hat{w}_f(v)\|^2$$
$$-(\varepsilon - \frac{k}{2C_2^2}\lambda_{max}(Q))\|Aw_f(v)\|^2 \tag{46}$$

where $\lambda_{max}(Q) = max_{w_f \in H}\langle Qw_f.w_f\rangle$ and $\lambda_{min}(Q) = min_{w_f \in H}\langle Qw_f.w_f\rangle$.
If $C_2$ can be chosen as large then $(\varepsilon - \frac{k}{2C_2^2}\lambda_{max}(Q)) > 0$,

$$\hat{V}_2(v) \leq 0 \qquad \forall v > v_2 \tag{47}$$

where $v_2$ can be, $(2-\varepsilon)\|A^{-\frac{1}{2}}\|^2 + \frac{C_2^2 k}{2}\lambda_{max}(Q) - 2kv_2(1-\varepsilon)\lambda_{min}(Q) = 0$.
The above result in (47) shows that derivative of Lyapunov function has decreasing nature for $v > v_2$ and it is also evident from (43) that the energy will also be dissipating for $v > 0$. Using these facts, for $v > T := max\{v_1, v_2\}$ and also from (45) $E(v)$ can be estimated as,

$$\int_T^\infty E(v)^2 dv \leq \int_T^\infty \frac{[2(1-\varepsilon)T + C_1]^2 E(0)^2}{2(1-\varepsilon)v - C_1} < \infty \tag{48}$$

which satisfies the theorem provided in [13] to guarantee the exponential stability.

## 6   Simulation Studies

In the simulation, two planar rigid manipulators each with three links are used to move the flexible beam along a desired trajectory specified by, $X_{rfd} = \{sin(t), cos(t), 0\}^T$ is taken into account. The manipulators and beam parameters are considered to be similar as given in [1]. The control parameters such as, $K_D = diag(424.2)$, $\lambda = diag(7.9)$, $\Gamma = 0.4$ and $k = 1$ are considered for the simulation. The value of $\Gamma$ was chosen based on the $L_\infty$ norm of the time independent parameters of the regressor in this case, vector $\alpha_{or}$. The regressor for the slow subsystem is very lengthy and due to space limitations not provided. The simulation was carried out in Matlab with a sampling time of 0.001 sec. Figs. 3 to 5 show the tracking of planar motion of center of the object along X and Y direction and also rotation about Z axis respectively. It can be observed that, the tracking of position and orientation is achieved within 1 sec, which shows the effectiveness of the controller.

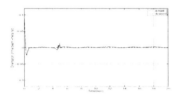

**Fig. 3.** X-Position tracking

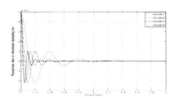

**Fig. 4.** Y-Position tracking

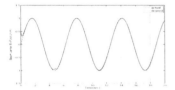

**Fig. 5.** Orientation of the beam

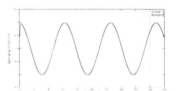

**Fig. 6.** Structural damping $\beta = -0.5$

In the case of fast subsystem, the initial disturbance of 5 mm with zero initial velocity is considered for the simulation. Although, the beam dynamic equation is not assumed with number of modes, simulation has to be performed with the assumption of modes. As the first few modes are dominant in yielding higher amplitude of vibration, first four modes are considered here. For the case of structural damping characteristics when $\beta = -0.5$, in Fig. 6 the amplitude of vibration initially yields oscillatory motion and completely suppressed around 1 second.

## 7   Conclusion

In this article, the problem of two planar rigid manipulators used to move a flexible object in the desired trajectory and suppressing the vibration of the flexible object is considered. Without using any approximated methods, the complete system of dynamic equations have been derived. The resulting equations are separated into slow and fast subsystems by using singular perturbation method. Furthermore, a regressor based sliding mode control algorithm is designed for the slow subsystem to control the rigid body motion of the object. Also, the special damping term is included in the feedback control law for fast subsystem to demonstrate the effect of damping in suppressing the vibration of the flexible beam. Tikhnov's theorem has also been justified by investigating the exponential stability of both slow and fast subsystems. The simulation results show that the proposed composite controller is an efficient choice for tracking the desired trajectory and suppressing the vibration of the flexible object.

# References

1. Ahmad, S., Zribi, M.: Predictive adaptive control of multiple robots in cooperative motion. Journal of Dynamics and Control 5, 139–161 (1995)
2. Al-Yahmali, A.S., Hsia, T.C.: Modeling and control of two manipulators handling a flexible object. Journal of the Franklin Institute 344, 349–361 (2007)
3. Burns, J.A., King, B.B.: A note on mathematical modeling of damped second order systems. Journal of Mathematical Systems, Estimation and Control 8, 1–12 (1998)
4. Chen, G., Russell, D.L.: A Mathematical model for linear elastic systems with structural damping. Quarterly Applied Mathematics 39, 433–454 (1981)
5. Ge, S.S., Lee, T.H., Zhu, G.: Improving regulation of a single-link-flexible manipulator with strain feedback. IEEE Transactions on Robotics and Automation 14, 179–185 (1998)
6. Greenwood, D.T.: Classical Dynamics. Dover publications, Prentice Hall (1997)
7. Khalil, H.K.: Nonlinear Systems, 3rd edn. Prentice Hall (2002)
8. Kokotovic, P.: Khalil. H. K., O'Reilly, J.: Singular Perturbation Methods in Control:Analysis and Design. SIAM (1999)
9. Kosuge, K., Yoshida, H., Fukuda, T., Sakai, M., Kanitani, K.: Manipulation of sheet metal by dual manipulators based on finite element model. In: Proceedings of IEEE Int. Conf. on Robotics and Automation, pp. 199–204 (1995)
10. Lotfazar, A., Eghtesad, M., Najafi, A.: Vibration control and trajectory tracking for general in-plane motion of Euler-Bernoulli beam via two-time scale and boundary control methods. ASME Journal of Vibrations and Acoustics 130, 051009-1 – 051009-10 (2008)
11. Luo, Z.H.: Direct strain feedback control of flexible robot arms:New theoretical and experimental results. IEEE Tranascations on Auomatic Control 38, 1610–1622 (1993)
12. Luo, Z.H., Guo, B.: Further theoretical results on direct strain feedback control of flexible robot arms. IEEE Tranascations on Auomatic Control 40, 747–751 (1995)
13. Pazy, A.: Semigroups of linear operators and applications to partial differential equations. Springer, Heidelberg (1983)
14. Sakawa, Y., Matsuno, F., Fukushima, S.: Modeling and feedback control of a flexible arm. Journal of Robotic Systems 2, 453–472 (1985)
15. Spong, M.W.: Adaptive control of flexible joint manipulators:Comments on two papers. Automatica 31, 585–590 (1995)
16. Sun, D., Liu, Y.H.: Position and force tracking of a two manipulator system manipulating a flexible beam. Journal of Robotic Systems 18, 197–212 (2001)
17. Tavasoli, A., Eghtesad, M., Jafarian, H.: Two-time scale control and observer design for trajectory tracking of two robot manipulators moving a flexible beam. Journal of Robotics and Autonomous Systems 57, 212–221 (2009)

# Concept and Design of the Modular Actuator System for the Humanoid Robot MYON

Torsten Siedel, Manfred Hild, and Mario Weidner

Neurorobotics Research Laboratory
Humboldt-Universität zu Berlin
Unter den Linden 6
10099 Berlin, Germany
{siedel,hild}@informatik.hu-berlin.de,
weidner@uv.hu-berlin.de

**Abstract.** When developing a humanoid robot, the choice of the system driving its joints is of crucial importance for the robot's robustness, technical reliability, ease of maintenance, as well as its degree of autonomy. Here, we present a novel, modular actuator system of the humanoid robot MYON. Both the concept of the actuator system and the composition of the individual modules which it consists of are described. In addition to the design of the robot's joints the way how the actuator components are integrated in the assembly of MYON is addressed. Finally, the characteristics of the different modes of actuating the joints by the actuator system are explained, and future prospects of its application considered.

**Keywords:** humanoid robot, modular actuators, compliant actuators, parallel actuation, serial elasticity.

## 1 Introduction

Humanoid robots nowadays are mainly being developed for research purposes. Here, their development is directed towards a multitude of research fields such as biped locomotion [1,2,3,4], interaction between man and machine [5,6,7], artificial intelligence [8], or for various servicing applications [7] where the robot is used as a tool.

For investigations in the area of motion control, like the locomotion of a humanoid robot, the design of the actuator system actuating the respective robot plays a crucial role. Different types of actuators are being applied here. The actuator systems most frequently used with humanoid robots are based on either electromechanical [1,3,7], pneumatic [4,9], or hydraulic principles [6], respectively. These principles differ from each other in many regards. Some important properties concern their power density, energetic efficiency, structural shape, controllability, as well as the kind of energy supply. The latter is among the decisive aspects concerning the robot's quality of autonomy. For instance, robots based on pneumatic or hydraulic actuators are often linked to a stationary external energy supply [4]. Thus, their autonomy is restricted compared to robots which carry along a source of energy by themselves.

S. Jeschke, H. Liu, and D. Schilberg (Eds.): ICIRA 2011, Part I, LNAI 7101, pp. 388–396, 2011.
© Springer-Verlag Berlin Heidelberg 2011

Furthermore, the compliance of the actuator system is an important attribute for the use with humanoid robots since this compliance may have a significant influence, e.g., on the energetic efficiency during walking movements, or on the shock tolerance of the robot's joints [4,10]. Last but not least, the ease of the robot's serviceability is an important quality criterion, not only for routine maintenance but also for, e.g., making adjustments.

The objective of the present work was to develop a actuator system in a modular style which allows for an individual adaptation to the different joints of a humanoid robot. The advantage of a modular construction is that even complex yet stable structures can be generated with only few different components if they provide versatile linkage possibilities. In the first section the concept of the actuator system is explained. Further, it is illustrated how the single components of the actuator system are realized and implemented into the robot. Concluding, the advantages generated by the actuator system are shown.

## 2   Concept of MYON's Actuator System

The humanoid robot MYON (see figure 1, right panel) has a height of 1.25 m and weighs 15 kg. It was developed in line with the project ALEAR (Artificial Language Evolution on Autonomous Robots) [11] for which, among others, it provides a library of motion.

A central concept having been realized with the development of MYON is its modularity [12]. This modularity is split into two types. First, the modularity of the individual body parts: Each of these (head, torso, arms, and legs) represent a module which are autonomous with regard to sensor system, computation power,

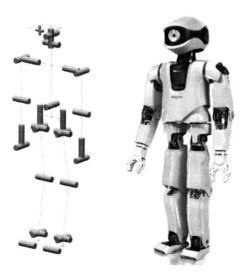

**Fig. 1.** Left panel, arrangement of MYON's individual joints. Right panel, the humanoid robot MYON.

actuating elements and energy supply and which can be connected by an flange system. Second, the modularity of its inner configuration. This type of modularity concerns technical components which MYON consists of. These components comprise local processor nodes (called *AccelBoard3D*) [12], sensors, battery modules, adaptors, as well as the actuator system. Each of these components is to be considered a module being integrated in the robot at different positions but having one and the same general assembly (except for minor changes when needed for an adaptation to individual structural conditions in the robot). To guarantee the mobility of MYON, its actuating system was developed according to the following concept: Modular configuration, compliance, one single type of actuator and maintenance. The advantages and the relevance of this concept are elucidated more closely in the following.

MYON consists of 26 active joints (see figure 1, left panel). They differ from each other in their performance characteristics concerning torque and angular velocity. Thus, the knee joint is actuated more strongly than that of the elbow. To allow for adapting the actuator system to the individual requirements of the different joints, it itself again consists of several *modules*. The actuator's performance characteristics can be adjusted by the choice of a certain combination of those modules.

This characteristic of *compliance* in particular provides protection against shock-kind torque impulses. Compliance in the joints, however, offers further advantageous properties, such as the possibility of an improved torque controllability, as well as an intermediary storage of kinetic energy [4].

The *modules* integrated in MYON are adjusted to each other concerning their capacity. This avoids a possible need of oversizing components, or of special additional elements between the components at their mechanical or electronic interfaces and facilitates their assembly [13]. For this reason, one and the same actuator type can be used for the actuation of the whole body of MYON, and the electronic interface of the *AccelBoard3D* needs to be configured for this actuator only. Furthermore, this allows for the use of a uniform type of the mechanical connection between actuator and joint in all positions of the robot.

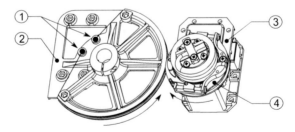

**Fig. 2.** Arrangement of the actuator components for actuating a joint. (1) shows, where the ends of the steel wire rope are mounted. (2) marks the pulley that is connected with the joint which shall be actuated. (3) represents the servomotor whose output shaft is mounted on the clutch (4). To transmit the torque between the clutch, both components are connected by the steel wire rope which is wired in a crosswise manner. Hence, the rotation of the pulleys is opposed, as shown by the arrows.

A humanoid robot usually is a complex device. To ascertain its safe operation a fail-proof construction is required which also takes care of an easy maintenance. In particular, the actuator components should therefore be positioned in a manner providing simple serviceability.

## 3   Realization and Implementation

The actuator system of MYON relies on three components: Actuator, coupler, and steel wire rope. A joint which consists of these three components is depicted in figure 2. The electromechanically operating actuator (see figure 2, part number 3) converts electrical into mechanical energy and is connected with a coupling (see figure 2, part number 4). This coupling in turn is connected by a steel wire rope with a pulley (see figure 2, part number 2). Depending on its layout, this steel wire rope connection represents a transmission between actuator and joint. The application and layout of the three components depends on the specification of the joint to be driven. In addition, joints which are not directly driven by a servomotor are equipped with an absolute angle sensor in order to detect the exact position of the joint independently from the actuator system [14]. The realization of the actuator components is explained in detail in the following.

### 3.1   Realization of the Components

As basic device of the MYON actuator system an electromechanically operating servomotor type RX-28 is used (see figure 3, panel A). It already contains the power electronics needed for its operation and can be serially connected with further servomotors of the same type. In addition, this servomotor possesses an absolute manner working angle sensor for measuring the position of the actuator's output shaft. Up to four of such servomotors can be connected with one *AccelBoard3D* which in turn serves as a nodal point for its control.

To generate a further transmission from the output side of the servomotor to the respective joint, a cable pull is applied. This consists of a pulley which is mounted on the servomotor, and another pulley placed on the respective joint.

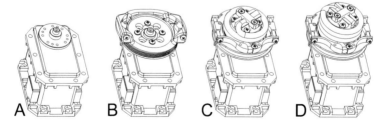

**Fig. 3.** Illustration of a single actuator in different configurations. (A) shows the RX-28 without any modifications. (B) shows the RX-28 combined with a rigid pulley, and (C) and (D) with a stiff (C) and less stiff (D) steel spring.

The pulley connected with the joint consists of ABS plastics and is manufactured by the Rapid prototyping. The transmission ratio is determined by the difference of either pulley's diameter. The pulleys themselves are connected with two steel wire ropes of 0.7 mm in diameter which withstand a traction of up to 400 N. Their ends are fastly bound to the pulleys (see figure 3, point 1). The cables are pre-stressed and therefore exert a drag force. To avoid that the axles on which the pulleys are mounted are being pulled together too strongly both cables between the pulleys run crosswise (see figure 2, 5). By this means the pulling forces are compensated during idleness of the actuator, thus reducing the load both on the bearings and the skeleton.

### 3.2   Implementation of the Components

The coupling module has been realized in three variants (cf. figure 3). Each of these variants comprises the mounting interfaces for the servomotor output and the attachment of both steel cables. Therefore the coupling also constitutes one of the two pulleys which enable an additional transmission. Coupler B (fig. 3) consists of ABS plastics and has been manufactured by the Rapid prototyping method. In contrast, couplings C and D are made of aluminum and equipped with torsion springs. They represent serial resilience and confer compliance to the actuator system at their installation positions. Both torsion springs exhibit a linear spring characteristic. The working spring rate $k$ of the coupler C is $k_1 = 163\,mNm/°$, and that of the coupler D is $k_2 = 100\,mNm/°$.

Fig. 4, on the left side shows a mounted coupler of type D, and on the right side its individual main components. To adjust the tension of the cables even after their mounting there are two cable clamp screws (1) as well as two cable clamp slides (2) located at the drive side ring (4) of the coupling at the latter of which the ends of the steel cables are attached. By turning the cable clamp screws, the cable tension is adjusted due to a simultaneous change in the position of the cable clamp slides. The drive side ring (4) is rotatable bedded on the drive shaft (5) by a ball bearing (3). The torsion spring (6) is, on its right end, connected

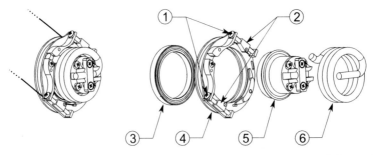

**Fig. 4.** Left panel, a mounted coupling of type D with implied ends of the steel cables; right panel, exploded view of a coupling of type D with numbered single components. (1) Cable clamp screws, (2) cable clamp slide, (3) ball bearing, (4) drive side ring, (5) drive shaft, (6) torsion spring.

with the drive shaft (5), and on its left end with the drive side ring (4). Due to this arrangement the drive side ring (4) and the drive shaft (5) can contort relative to each other depending on the torque impact.

The design of a actuator system for a particular joint directs itself according to the requirements given by this joint. To such requirements there belong the characteristics of maximum torque, maximum angular velocity, maximum angular deflection range, as well as the spatial situation around the joint. Furthermore, the weight of the actuator system is an important factor which is strongly influenced by the inclusion of additional servomotors and couplings. Joints which have to exert a strong torque can either be enforced by several servomotors, or/and another transmission ratio by means of the pulleys. In table 1 all actuator system variations with respect to the actuation of joints are listed.

As can be seen, the modules of the actuator system are integrated in MYON in different configurations. Simple joints such as that of the wrist are equipped with only one servomotor but no further actuator components. In contrast the ankle roll joint, as the strongest of all, is being actuated by four servomotors, and an additional transmission. As depicted in fig. 5, both the couplings and the pulleys are mounted on the exterior of the robot's skeleton which significantly facilitates their accessibility. Moreover, this assembly offers the possibility of exchanging servomotors without the need of dismantling surrounding structures.

The inclusion of several servomotors in a single joint actuation depends on the spatial conditions around the joint. As can be seen from figure 5, panels B,

**Table 1.** Listing of MYON's active joints. For every joint, the construction regarding the number of used servomotors, type of coupling, gear ratio and operating range is listed. Furthermore, it can be seen which joints are equipped with an additional angle sensor.

| MYON's joints actuation | | | | | | |
|---|---|---|---|---|---|---|
| Part | Joint | Number of Actuators | Type of Clutch | gear ratio | Operating Range | Angle Sensor |
| Head | Pitch | 1 | A with Spring | 1:1 | 78° | no |
| | Roll | 1 | A | 1:1 | 110° | no |
| | Yaw | 1 | A | 1:1 | 180° | no |
| Arm | Shoulder Roll | 1 | B | 1:2 | 144° | yes |
| | Elbow | 1 | B | 1:2 | 127° | yes |
| | Wrist | 1 | A | 1:1 | 290° | no |
| Torso | Shoulder Pitch | 2 | C | 1:1.65 | 235° | yes |
| | Waist Roll | 1 | C | 1:4 | 60° | yes |
| | Hip Yaw | 1 | B | 1:2.73 | 80° | yes |
| Leg | Hip Roll | 2 | D | 1:2.5 | 60° | yes |
| | Hip Pitch | 3 | D | 1:2.5 | 129° | yes |
| | Knee | 3 | D | 1:2.5 | 171° | yes |
| | Ankle Roll | 1 | C | 1:2.5 | 30° | yes |
| | Ankle Pitch | 4 | B | 1:2.5 | 129° | yes |

E, and F, in an ideal situation the servomotors and the connected couplings are located directly at the joint to be actuated. This minimizes structural loads by forces from the cable pull system. If the spatial situation does not allow for such an alignment, the servomotors can be, e.g., positioned consecutively, as shown in fig. 5, panels A, C and D. Due to this adaptability of the actuator system the available installation space can be optimally used.

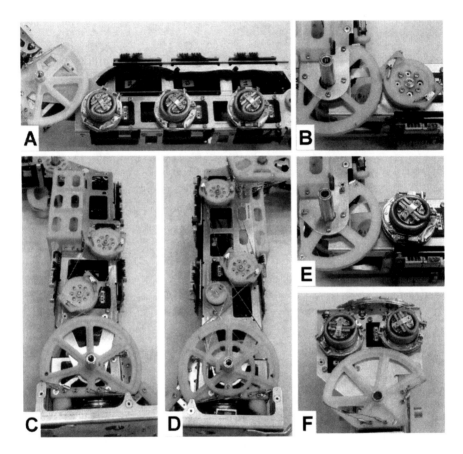

**Fig. 5.** Illustration of different joints of Myon. (A) Hip pitch, (B) elbow without compliance, (C) ankle pitch exterior, (D) ankle pitch interior, elbow with compliance, (F) hip roll.

## 4    Conclusion and Outlook

In this paper we have presented the composition of a novel, modular actuating system for movable robot parts and their integration into the apparatus' skeleton. We showed that by variation of only few but generally suitable actuator modules each joint of the humanoid robot Myon can be equipped. The application of serial resilience with heavily strained joints of the robot primarily provided shock resistance both of the joints and the actuator system. The arrangement of the actuator system components in an easily maintenance manner enables an uncomplicated exchange of the coupling components for, e.g., reasons of adjusting a joint's elasticity. For instance, the elbow joint as depicted in fig. 5, panel (B), and equipped with a rigid coupling variant B, can, as shown in fig. 5, panel (E), be modified with an elastic coupling C. More heavily strained joints of the robot are driven by up to four servomotors. In parallel with the number of actuators per joint, the amount of parameters available for steering purposes can be increased. This opens many new applications of Myon for research purposes. Among others, the possibility for antagonistic control of the joints connected with two or more actuators.

**Acknowledgements.** This work has been supported by the European research project ALEAR (FP7, ICT-214856). The authors would like to thank Mario Lühmann for his help with mechanical assemblies.

# References

1. Lohmeier, S., Buschmann, T., Ulbrich, H.: Humanoid Robot LOLA. In: Proceedings of the IEEE International Conference on Robotics and Automation, ICRA (2009)
2. Ogura, Y., Aikawa, H., Shimomura, K., Morishima, A., Lim, H., Takanishi, A.: Development of a new Humanoid Robot WABIAN-2. In: Proceedings of the IEEE International Conference on Robotics and Automation, ICRA (2006)
3. Pratt, J., Krupp, B.: Design of a Bipedal Walking Robot. In: Proceedings of the SPIE (2008)
4. Vanderborght, B.: Dynamic Stabilisation of the Biped Lucy Powered by Actuators with Controllable Stiffness. Springer, Heidelberg (2010)
5. Edsinger, A., Kemp, C.C.: Human-Robot Interaction for Cooperative Manipulation: Handing Objects to One Another. In: Proceedings of the 16th IEEE International Symposium on Robot and Human Interactive Communication, RO-MAN (2007)
6. Oztop, E., Franklin, D.W., Chaminade, T., Cheng, G.: Human-Humanoid Interaction: Is a Humanoid Robot Perceived as a Human? International Journal of Humanoid Robotics (2005)
7. Sakagami, Y., Watanabe, R., Aoyama, C., Matsunaga, S., Higaki, N., Fujimura, K.: The Intelligent ASIMO: System Overview and Integration. In: Proceedings of the IEEE/RSJ International Conference on Intelligent Robots and Systems, IROS (2002)
8. Tsagarakis, N.G., Metta, G., Sandini, G., Vernon, D., Beira, R., Becchi, F., Righetti, L., Santos-Victor, J., Ijspeert, A.J., Carrozza, M.C., et al.: iCub: The Design and Realization of an Open Humanoid Platform for Cognitive and Neuroscience Research. In: Advanced Robotics (2007)
9. Daerden, F., Lefeber, D.: Pneumatic Artificial Muscles: Actuators for Robotics and Automation. European Journal of Mechanical and Environmental Engineering (2002)

10. Raibert, M.H., Brown, H.B., Chepponis, M.: Experiments in Balance with a 3D One-legged Hopping Machine. The International Journal of Robotics Research (1984)
11. Website of the ALEAR-Project (Artificial Language Evolution on Autonomous Robots), http://www.alear.eu/
12. Hild, M., Siedel, T., Benckendorff, C., Kubisch, M., Thiele, C.: Myon: Concepts and Design of a Modular Humanoid Robot Which can be Reassembled During Runtime. In: Proceedings of the 14th International Conference on Climbing and Walking Robots, CLAWAR (2011)
13. Siedel, T.: Entwicklung eines Elektromechanischen Antriebssystems für Gehroboter in Anlehnung an Biologische Prinzipien. Master's thesis, Rheinische Fachhochschule Köln (2009)
14. Benckendorff, C.: Technische Realisierung Multimodaler Sensorik für Humanoide Roboter. Master's thesis, Humboldt-Universität zu Berlin (2010)

# Design of a Passive, Bidirectional Overrunning Clutch for Rotary Joints of Autonomous Robots

Manfred Hild, Torsten Siedel, and Tim Geppert

Neurorobotics Research Laboratory
Humboldt-Universität zu Berlin
Unter den Linden 6
10099 Berlin, Germany
{hild,siedel,geppert}@informatik.hu-berlin.de

**Abstract.** Joint design and load transmission are crucial factors when building autonomous robots. On the one hand, heavy torques are often needed which result in multi-stage gearboxes, on the other hand the latter exhibit massive friction which gets in the way of energy-efficient actuation systems. Furthermore, the immense impact forces of a tumbling robot can easily break its joints, gears, and motors. This holds especially true for tall humanoid robots. In this paper we present a novel clutch for rotary joints which is able to resolve the aforementioned dilemma.

**Keywords:** overrunning clutch, frictionless decoupling, energy-efficient actuation, compliant parallel actuation.

## 1   Introduction

Joint design and load transmission are crucial factors when building autonomous robots, especially humanoid robots. On the one hand, heavy torques are often needed, e. g. at the knee and ankle joints of a humanoid robot. As a consequence, this normally results in multi-stage gearboxes which exhibit massive friction. On the other hand, an equally important goal of robot design is energy-efficiency. Obviously, the friction of multi-stage gearboxes gets in the way of energy-efficient actuation systems. Furthermore, the immense impact forces of a tumbling robot can easily break its joints, gears, and motors. This holds especially true for tall humanoid robots.

In order to resolve the aforementioned dilemma, we present a novel overrunning clutch for rotary joints which is able to automatically connect the geared motor to the limb of an autonomous robot, e. g. an arm, whenever the motor applies torque – and to disconnect the limb during energy preserving phases of a motion. This way, a multi-stage gearbox can be used to deliver the necessary torque for the robot to lift its arm including heavy weights, but the robot is also able to let the arm swing freely, e. g. during walking.

Clutches which couple or decouple a drive shaft from a driven shaft are well-known and used in a wide field of applications. An exhaustive overview is, e. g., given in [8]. The unique and novel property of the overrunning clutch presented

S. Jeschke, H. Liu, and D. Schilberg (Eds.): ICIRA 2011, Part I, LNAI 7101, pp. 397–405, 2011.

in the paper at hand, is that the clutch works both passively and bidirectional, i.e., no additional active actuation is needed for coupling and decoupling, independent of the rotational direction. In the rest of the paper, we first reference existing clutch designs, then describe in detail the construction and operating modes of our clutch design, and finally present first experimental data which verifies the successful operation of the clutch.

## 2     Construction and Functional Principle

There exist various design principles for unidirectional overrunning clutches, namely the spring clutch, roller or ball clutch, sprag clutch, and ratchet and ball clutch – just to list the most common types [11]. More sophisticated designs make use of electro-rheological fluids [7, 9] or exhibit special non-linear dynamics [12, 13]. Clutches which are used for autonomous robots need to work bidirectional. Existing approaches control the coupling [4] and thus need additional actuation, e.g. an electromagnetic mechanism to engage the clutch [5]. In contrast, our clutch uses a special mechanism which works fully passively. Often, series elasticities are used [10] to combine several actuators at the same joint. Our clutch already exhibits a small amount of serial elasticity which may be used for multi-actuated joints. Using such techniques, one may eventually reach the power of pneumatic or hydraulic actuators without the need for compressors, which is always difficult to achieve on autonomous robots, although some robots of this kind do exist [1, 2].

**Fig. 1.** Picture of the bidirectional overrunning clutch

## 2.1   Overview

Overall, the bidirectional overrunning clutch (see Figure 1) is 22 mm long, has an outer diameter of 40 mm and weighs approximately 50 g. All parts consist of aluminium and ABS plastic. A traction principle is used to tranmit the torque from input and output. Furthermore, the clutch works in a passive manner, i.e., no additional actuation is needed to connect or disconnect the actuator from the driven shaft. The mechanism only depends on the relative position between the internal drive shaft, the driven hub, and the case inside which the actuator is mounted (see Figure 2).

## 2.2   Basic Components

The functional parts of the clutch are shown in Figure 2. Part 2 is the drive shaft of the clutch that is directly connected to the actuator (part 5). It transfers the actuator's torque to the interior of the clutch. Within the drive shaft, four clamping wedges (parts 4) are pivoted radially symmetrical. They are connected to the mechanical grounding (part 1). The internal structure of the clutch is enclosed by the driven hub (part 3). Depending on the current operational mode, the driven hub either rotates freely or transmits the actuator's torque to the hub. The inner cylindrical surface of the driven hub is rubber-coated in the area where the wedges operate. For actuation, a servo motor of the type Dynamixel RX-28 (Robotis, Inc.) is used (part 5).

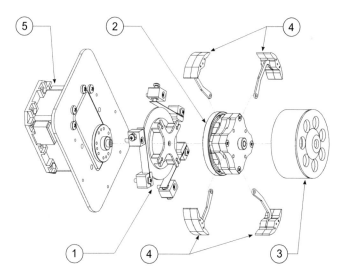

**Fig. 2.** Exploded view exposing the main components: mechanical grounding (1), drive shaft (2), driven hub (3), wedges (4), and actuator (5)

## 2.3 Description of the Internal Structure

We now detail the internal construction. Figure 3 illustrates step by step how the basic parts are mounted: the top side of the drive shaft (2), the driven hub (3), and one of the four wedges (4) are shown in section A. Drive shaft and driven hub rotate around the main axis $a$. The wedge is mounted to the drive shaft and rotates around axis $b$ until the wedge touches the outer surface of the drive shaft. As can be seen in Figure 3 B, all four wedges are mounted radially symmetrical to the drive shaft and rotate as explained before. All four wedges are covered by the bottom of the drive shaft (see Figure 3 C). Both parts of the drive shaft have the same thickness, therefore opposite wedges are mounted symmetrically to the middle of the drive shaft. This reduces backlash between parts 2, 3, and 4, leading to a reliable function of the overall clutch. Figure 3 D shows a synchronization (grounding) cross mounted to the bottom of the drive shaft. This synchronization cross rotates around the main axis $a$ and is connected to all wedges by small guidances. Each of these guidances consists of a 1 mm pin on the bottom of each wedge and a corresponding slot at one the four ends of the synchronization cross.

## 2.4 Mechanical Grounding

For reliable operation, a frictional engagement between the wedges and the gearbox housing is crucial. This traction is referred to as the mechanical grounding (see part 1 in Figure 2) and serves the following two purposes:

1. Creation of friction torque between wedges and gear housing to avoid random connections of the clutch.
2. Radially symmetrical alignment of the clamping wedges.

The friction torque $\tau$ can be fine-tuned using adjustment screws, as shown in Figure 4). A modified pretension of the flat springs results in an alteration of the contact force $F$. The friction torque of rigid bodies is $\tau = 3\mu r F$, wherein $\mu$ is the coefficient of friction and $r$ the radius of the friction washer. The coefficient of friction is an empirical property of the contacting materials, i. e., the type of metal of both the flat springs and the friction washer. With respect to the materials used in our clutch, we have $\mu = 0.19$. The friction torque is necessary for the stable operation of the clutch. However, it is small in comparison to the driven torque of the actuator. Energy waste due to traction is thus negligible.

## 2.5 Operational Modes and Coupling Sequences

In the following, we will explain the functional sequences of coupling in clockwise rotation and subsequent decoupling. The coupling sequence starts with the clutch in the neutral position as shown in the middle of Figure 5. In this position, the driven hub can freely rotate in both directions.

First, we assume that the drive shaft is directly driven clockwise by the actuator. Due to the mechanical grounding, the wedges do not rotate around the main axis, but instead stay in place. Relative to the drive shaft, they actually rotate counter-clockwise around axis $b$ (review Figure 3). As soon as the clamping wedges achieve a rotation of three degrees relative to the drive shaft, they start to touch the inner rubberized surface of the driven hub. Immediately after that, the clamping wedges also touch the outside of the drive shaft, whereby the clamping wedges are pushed further outwards against the inside of the driven hub (see Figure 5). As a result of the entrapment of the clamping wedges between drive shaft and drive hub, the actuator's torque is fully transmitted to the driven hub. If the actuator rotates further clockwise, then the synchronization cross also starts to rotate into the same direction.

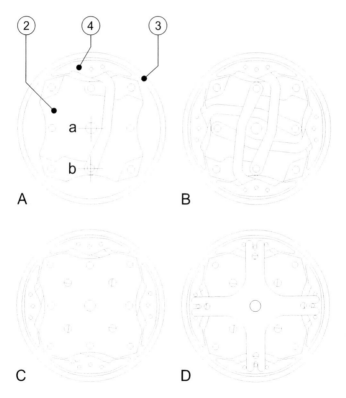

**Fig. 3.** Internal structure of the clutch. Drawing. A shows the basic components, incorporating the drive shaft (2), the driven hub (3) and a wedge (4), as well as the main axis $a$ of the clutch and the axis $b$ around which the wedge rotates. All clamping wedges are shown exposed in drawing. B and covered in drawing. C, respectively. Drawing. D displays the synchronization cross which synchronizes the four wedges and connects them to the actuator's chassis (grounding).

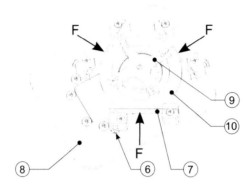

**Fig. 4.** Overview of the components which generate the friction forces as needed for the mechanical grounding: adjustment screw (6), flat spring (7), gearbox (8), synchronization cross (9), and friction washer (10)

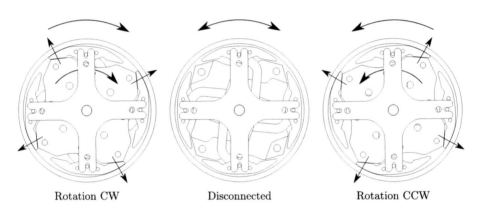

Rotation CW                    Disconnected                    Rotation CCW

**Fig. 5.** Operational modes of the clutch. Left: Frictional engagement between drive shaft and driven hub for clockwise rotation. Middle: Uncoupled (neutral) position of the clamping wedges. Consequently, the driven hub can rotate freely. Right: Friction between drive shaft and driven hub for counter-clockwise rotation.

In case of an externally acting torque which turns the driven hub into clockwise direction, the wedges will be released from their clamping positions, so the driven hub can overrun the internal movement. Traction will be released due to a *resetting movement* until the wedges reached their neutral position. The coupling sequence counter-clockwise is analogous to the clockwise one.

## 3   Experimental Validation

Using a straightforward adaption of the measurement apparatuses in [3] and [6], we experimentally verified the proper operation of the described clutch. The

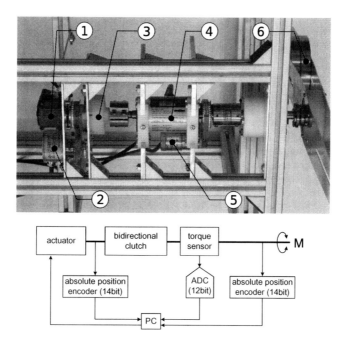

**Fig. 6.** Picture and schematic diagram of the measurement apparatus. The main components are as follows: Actuator RX-28 (1), angle sensor for the drive shaft (2), bidirectional overrunning clutch (3), torque sensor (4), angle sensor for the driven hub (5), pendulum (6).

setup is shown in Figure 6, along with the corresponding schematic diagram. A pendulum has been lifted and released, using either the clutch or instead a simple metal rod for torque transmission. The results can be seen in Figure 7. In the control condition with the simple metal rod, almost no torsion takes place. The actuator's torque is transmitted directly from the actuator to the pendulum. The expected linear relationship between torque and torsion can be observed.

Using the clutch, this changes significantly. After three degrees of rotational displacement the clutch starts to couple and transmits the actuator's torque up to a specific limit (approx. 1.2 Nm, depending on the rubber coating used). The clutch exhibits a certain amount of series elasticity which can be useful when designing multi-actuator driven joints for autonomous robots. After reversal of the rotational direction, first the torque decreases, then the clutch decouples (see arrows in Figure 7).

Besides the rather slow decoupling process, the clutch can also be decoupled within milliseconds but just switching the motor to free-run operation. As can be seen in Figure 8, the pendulum then immediately swings freely and (almost) frictionless after decoupling, since the gear's friction does not disturb the pendulum's motion.

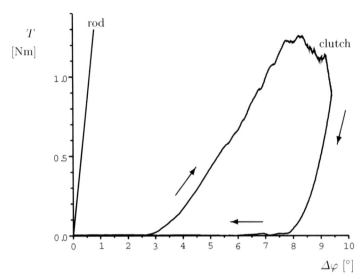

**Fig. 7.** Torque transmission over degrees of torsion. Compared to the linear direct coupling of a metal rod, the clutch begins to transmit torque after three degrees of angular displacement. There is an upper transmission limit of approx. 1.2 Nm where a stick-slip effect is observable. Sensitive fade-in of torque is eased by the clutch's serial elasticity, whereas decoupling happens more quickly. These properties can be utilized within the mechanical design of angular joints of autonomous robots.

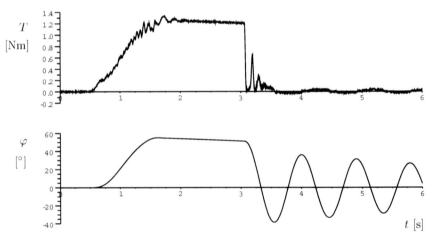

**Fig. 8.** Coupling and decoupling sequence of the clutch over time. After 0.5 s the actuator increases torque up to approx. 1.2 Nm at 1.5 s. A stick-slip effect can be observed for high torque values. During the 1 s steady-state phase there is no stick-slip effect, but the torque transmission ratio declines slightly due to the rubber coating. Decoupling can either be achieved by slowly decreasing the actuators torque into the opposite turning direction (not shown here, see Figure 7), or by abruptly switching the motor to free-run operation. As can be seen, the pendulum immediately starts to swing freely – the gear's friction is irrelevant.

# 4   Conclusion and Outlook

We have presented the design of a passive bidirectional overrunning clutch which can be used for the design of rotary joints of autonomous robots. Although further tests are needed, we could demonstrate that the clutch works as supposed. The clutch's series elasticity, bounded torque transmission, and frictionless mode are useful within the mechanical design of robots, since they ease the construction of multi-actuator driven joints and protect the gears and motors from external forces like impacts. Currently, different rubber coatings and morphological design variations are investigated. In parallel, the clutch is used within sensorimotor loops so that control paradigms can be evaluated and extended as to include the quick decoupling mechanism, e. g. in the case of an impending impact during a downfall.

# References

1. Buehler, M., Playter, R., Raibert, M.: Robots step outside. In: Int. Symp. Adaptive Motion of Animals and Machines (AMAM), Ilmenau, Germany, pp. 1–4 (2005)
2. Daerden, F., Lefeber, D.: Pneumatic artificial muscles: actuators for robotics and automation. European Journal of Mechanical and Environmental Engineering 47(1), 11–21 (2002)
3. Holgerson, M.: Apparatus for measurement of engagement characteristics of a wet clutch. Wear 213(1-2), 140–147 (1997)
4. Hurst, J.W., Chestnutt, J., Rizzi, A.: An actuator with mechanically adjustable series compliance. Technical Report CMU-RI-TR-04-24, Robotics Institute, Pittsburgh, PA (April 2004)
5. Klug, S., Möhl, B., von Stryk, O., Barth, O.: Design and application of a 3 dof bionic robot arm. In: Proc. of the 3rd Int. Symposium on Adaptive Motion in Animals and Machines, AMAM 2005 (2005)
6. Liu, K., Bamba, E.: Frictional dynamics of the overrunning clutch for pulse-continuously variable speed transmissions: rolling friction. Wear 217(2), 208–214 (1998)
7. Liu, K., Bamba, E.: Analytical model of sliding friction in an overrunning clutch. Tribology International 38(2), 187–194 (2005)
8. Orthwein, W.C.: Clutches and brakes: design and selection. CRC (2004)
9. Papadopoulos, C.A.: Brakes and clutches using ER fluids. Mechatronics 8(7), 719–726 (1998)
10. Pratt, J.E., Krupp, B.T.: Series elastic actuators for legged robots. In: Proceedings of SPIE–The International Society for Optical Engineering, vol. 5422, pp. 135–144 (2004)
11. Roach, G.M., Howell, L.L.: Evaluation and comparison of alternative compliant overrunning clutch designs. Journal of Mechanical Design 124, 485 (2002)
12. Welge-Luessen, T., Glocker, C.: Modelling and application of the self-locking phenomenon in the context of a non-discrete impact clutch. PAMM 5(1), 221–222 (2005)
13. Zhu, F., Parker, R.G.: Non-linear dynamics of a one-way clutch in belt-pulley systems. Journal of sound and vibration 279(1-2), 285–308 (2005)

# DeWaLoP-Monolithic Multi-module In-Pipe Robot System

Luis A. Mateos and Markus Vincze

Automation and Control Institute (ACIN)
Vienna University of Technology
Gusshausstrasse 27 - 29 / E376, A - 1040 Vienna, Austria
{mateos,vincze}@acin.tuwien.ac.at

**Abstract.** This paper describes the multi-module configuration of the Developing Water Loss Prevention – DeWaLoP – in-pipe robot system. The system objective is to redevelop the pipes of the over 100 years old fresh water supply systems of Vienna and Bratislava by crawling into water canals of about 1 meter in diameter and applying a restoration material to repair the pipes. In-pipe robots with multiple modules are commonly arranged as a chain, one module linked to the next one, with at least one driving module if the robot's working environment consist of straight pipelines and with two driving modules if the pipelines contains bifurcations, where one driving module is used to move the robot *in* and the other is used to move *out* of the pipeline. The DeWaLoP robot is required to work in pipelines with bifurcation; the in-pipe robot system consists of two modules, a mobile robot (driving module) and a maintenance unit. Nevertheless, its mechanical design has been modified from the classic "*chain-link-module*", enabling the robot to move *in* and *out* of the pipe with only one driving module as a monolithic robot.

**Keywords:** Robotics, Multi-module robot, Wheeled locomotion, In-pipe robot.

## 1 Introduction

Fresh water pipe-lines are prevalent, important, valuable, unnoticed and often in a damaged state. Water pipes carry fresh water into buildings from the municipal water systems; these types of pipes are frequently made of polyvinyl chloride (PVC/uPVC), ductile/cast iron, polyethylene, or copper. Water pipe systems are prone to damage due to aging, excessive traffic, geological change and earthquakes. Resulting from these damages, the pipe joints may not be completely hermetic and external materials (such as soil, polluted water, among others) may contaminate the fresh water system. Commonly, due to high cost of pipe replacement, pipe cleaning and repairing is preferred [1].

In-pipe robots, which have a long history of development in robotics, can be classified into several elementary forms according to movement patterns, as shown in figure 1, although most of them have been designed depending upon specific applications [2].

S. Jeschke, H. Liu, and D. Schilberg (Eds.): ICIRA 2011, Part I, LNAI 7101, pp. 406–415, 2011.
© Springer-Verlag Berlin Heidelberg 2011

**Fig. 1.** In-pipe robot classification. (a) Pig type. (b) Wheel type. (c) Caterpillar type. (d) Wall-press type. (e) Leg type. (f) Inchworm type. (g) Screw type.

In fact, the goals of the in-pipe robot have close relations with the working environment, because the principal requirement of the in-pipe robot is to be able to explore wherever it has to go within its working environment.

Existing robots generally travel along horizontal pipelines successfully, but only some of them can cope with complicated pipeline configurations, such as $Y$-shaped pipelines configuration. Furthermore, few of them can negotiate $L$-shaped pipelines (elbows) and/or $T$-shaped pipelines (also called branches). For successful navigation, however, in-pipe robots are strongly demanded to have the ability of negotiating elbows and branches, because urban water pipelines are configured with a number of special fittings, such as elbows, branches, and their combinations.

## 1.1    Common In-Pipe Robot Systems

In-pipe robots can be classified into several elementary forms according to the movement patterns. Wheel-driven-systems guarantee under regular circumstances within the straight pipes a very efficient movement [3]. Actual research and development is dedicated to the realization of flexible, multi segment platforms instead of monolithic robots to guarantee movement in pipes with turn-offs and curves. Further, to get more stability in moving within pipes, the wheels are distributed over the entire cross-section of the robot covering the entire diameter of the pipe.

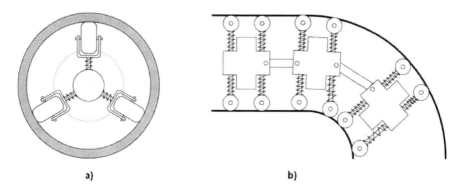

a)                                      b)

**Fig. 2.** a) Wheel-drive-system. b) Multi-segment in-pipe wheel-drive-system

The traction force is proportional to the friction coefficient and the pressing force between the wheel and the pipeline surface, and the friction coefficient depends on the material of the wheel and the surface condition of the pipelines. The disadvantage of this method is the lack of flexibility to adjust to pipe diameters bigger than ±10%.

In-pipe robots using a wheel-drive-system are commonly used for inspection, cut or superficially repair a pipe. Examples of this kind of robot can be found in [4 - 6].

## 1.2    DeWaLoP – Developing Water Loss Prevention Robot System

The DeWaLoP – Developing Water Loss Prevention – robot system objective is to redevelop the pipes of the over 100 years old fresh water supply systems of Vienna (3000 km length) and Bratislava (2800 km), by crawling into water canals of about one meter diameter and applying a restoration material to repair the pipes.

Attempts to redevelop these types of pipes included operators inside the one-meter pipe diameter, which creates a special situation that presents safety and health risk.

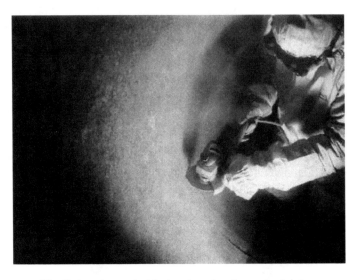

**Fig. 3.** An operator inside the pipe, cleaning a pipe joint

Currently, the applications of robots for the maintenance of the pipeline utilities are considered as one of the most attractive solutions available. The DeWaLoP robot is intended to be a low cost robot with high reliability and easiness in use, the robot system includes the conventional inspection of the pipe system, which is carried out using a cable-tethered robot with an onboard video system. An operator remotely controls the movement of the robot systems.

There are no commercial robots able to perform this specific redevelopment tasks. Nevertheless, there are several robots on the market; these robots have different objectives, as well as different working environments. Some of them may be used to cut, or superficially repair or scan pipes, either in gas or water pipes. In the same way, these robots can be remotely operated, or autonomous; powered with batteries or powered with cables from a control station. Robots available in the market are mainly designed for pipes with diameters between 300 to 800mm. There are no commercial robots working in pipes with 1000mm diameter or bigger.

The proposed DeWaLoP robot system is more complex than the typical commercial system; it is designed to perform several tasks (inspect, clean and redevelop) instead of a single one. The proposed solution consists of three main subsystems: a control station, a mobile robot (similar to a vehicle) and a maintenance system.

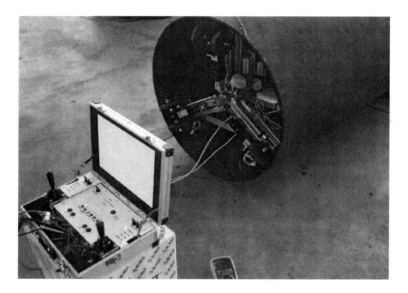

**Fig. 4.** Control station, mobile robot and maintenance system

- Control station

The control station is in charge of monitoring and controlling all the systems of the in-pipe robot. The main controller is composed of a couple of SBC (single board computers), one is in charge of monitoring and displaying the video images from the cameras on a LCD display, the second SBC is in charge of the robot system's remote control, which receives the information from the physical remote control (the joysticks, buttons and switches), in order to control the robot systems [7].

- Mobile robot

The mobile robot enables the in-pipe system modules to move inside the pipe, in the same way, carries the electronic and mechanical components of the system, such as power supplies, restoration material tank, motor drivers, among others. It uses a differential wheel drive which makes the robot able to promptly adjust its position to remain in the middle of the pipe while moving.

- Maintenance unit

Structure able to expand or compress with a Dynamical Independent Suspension System (DISS) [8]. By expanding its wheeled-legs, it creates a rigid structure inside the pipe, so the robot's cleaning and restoration tools work without any vibration or involuntary movement from the inertia of the tools and accurately restore the pipe; by compressing its wheeled-legs, the wheels become active so the maintenance structure is able to move along the pipe by the mobile robot. The structure consists of six wheeled legs, distributed in pairs of three, on each side, separated 120°, supporting the structure along the centre of the pipe. The maintenance system combines a wheel-drive-system with a wall-press-system, enabling the system to operate in pipe diameters varying from 800mm to 1000mm.

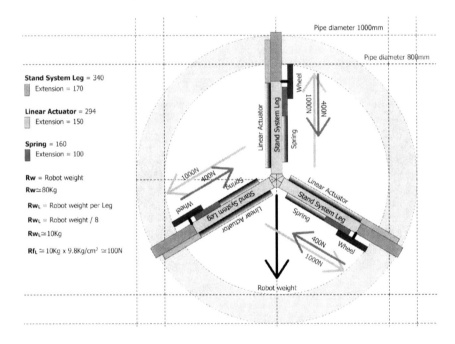

**Fig. 5.** DeWaLoP maintenance system, geometric and force diagram inside the 800mm and 1000mm pipe

## 2    In-Pipe Multi-module Robot System

The locomotion of a multi-module in-pipe robot in *"chain-link-module"* configuration is directly related to the pipeline configuration. For a straight pipeline without *Y* or *T* configuration, the multi-module robot can be moved *in* and *out* of the pipe with only one driving module. If the pipeline contains bifurcation of any type, then the multi-module system must contain two driving modules, one for moving *in* the pipe and one for moving *out*. In these pipelines, if the multi-module system only contains one driving module, it can move *in*, but it cannot be moved *out*. This is because the module of the robot when moving *out* is a passive module, not a driving module, and it is not possible to direct a passive module in a *chain-link* configuration.

The multi-module robot shown in figure 6 consist of two equal opposite parts, with a common component, the *support 2* module. These two parts contain a *camera*, *drive*, *battery*, *support* and *sensor* modules; the only difference between both parts is that are opposite, one is for moving the robot inside the pipe and the other is for moving the robot out the pipe.

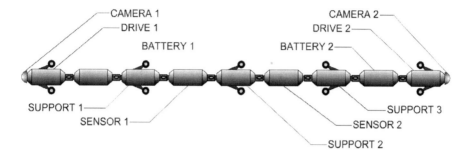

**Fig. 6.** In-pipe multi-module system with two *driving* modules

## 2.1    In-Pipe Robot Size

Pipeline configurations give geometric limitations and the size of a robot should be determined to satisfy the limitations. In an *L*-shaped pipelines (elbow), the robot can be modeled as a cylinder and relations can be derived between the diameter of the elbow, the curvature, and the size of the robot. The worst placement of the robot is when it is inclined with 45 degrees. If the size of the robot is not the proper for the pipe diameter, the robot may get stuck. Therefore, a relation between the pipe diameter and the length of the robot has been calculated, for a robot to be able to turn a $45°$ elbow pipe configuration [9]. This relation assures that any module will be able to move freely in the pipe, $D < L_r < 1.75D$, where $D$ is the diameter of the pipe and $L_r$ is the length of the robot or the length of each system module. In the same way the width $w$ of each module must satisfy $\{(R+D/2) \sin 45° - (R - D/2)\} < w < D$, where $R$ denotes the radius of curvature.

## 3    DeWaLoP Monolithic Multi-module Robot System

An important requirement for the DeWaLoP robot system is to be portable, to easily integrate into the pipeline. This is, to design the robot system in a simple way; with the less number of modules as possible. As previously mentioned, if the pipe line is not straight, if it contains bifurcation (*T* or *Y* pipeline configuration) and the robot system is multi-module, then it is needed to have two driving modules, one to move the robot *in* and one to move it *out*.

The DeWaLoP in-pipe robot consists of two modules, the mobile robot (driving module) and the maintenance unit (pipe-joint redevelopment module). If following the *chain-link* configuration, an extra driving module is required to enable the robot to move in pipelines with bifurcations. Nevertheless, to simplify the multi-module configuration for the DeWaLop robot, a re-design of the modules *link* is essential.

By analyzing the mechanical properties of the in-pipe modules (the mobile robot and the maintenance unit), it is possible to observe, that the link between these two modules is omni-directional, it can be move in $x$, $y$ and $z$ - *axis*. This means that the mobile robot can push or pull the maintenance module in any direction.

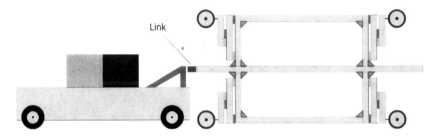

**Fig. 7.** Omni-directional link between the mobile robot (driving module) and the maintenance unit in *chain-link* configuration

The re-design consist in relocate the points of contacts of the modules with respect to the *link*. Instead of linking both modules with a single point of contact, the *link*, will become multi-contact, so the mobile robot push or pull the maintenance module in different points over its structure. This is done, by adjusting the structure and size of the mobile robot to fit under the maintenance system as shown in figure 8.

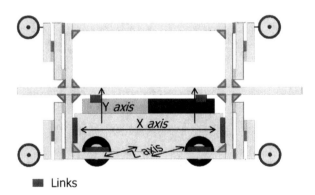

**Fig. 8.** 3D points of contact (*link*) between mobile robot and maintenance unit

The points of contact are arranged to enable the maintenance unit module movement over the 3D space without interfering between the axes. The structure of the maintenance module is triangular and the mobile robot is rectangular, making possible to arrange the maintenance unit over the mobile robot. Moreover, the mobile robot is the active module, which drives the entire robot system, while the maintenance system is the passive module.

On the mobile robot, extensions arms are added to each of its four corners, under the triangular structure of the maintenance module. These extensions enable movement to the maintenance module over the $x - axis$, when the mobile robot moves $x+$ or $x-$. In the same way it will enable movement of the maintenance unit over the $z- axis$, when the mobile robot moves $z+$ or $z-$. In the $y - axis$, it is only possible to be move in the positive $y+$, as shown in figure 9.

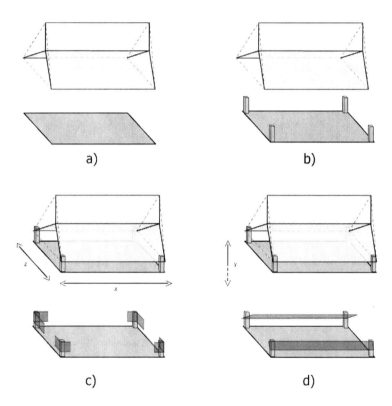

**Fig. 9.** 3D points of contact between the mobile robot and the maintenance unit. a) Mobile robot and maintenance unit. b) Mobile robot extensions. c) Points of contact in $x$ and $z$-axis. d) Points of contact in $y$-axis.

Thus, the final version of the system is a monolithic robot composed by two aggregated independent modules, one active and one passive. When the robot is moving in the pipeline, the mobile robot is the active module and the maintenance unit is the passive, and vice versa when redeveloping the pipe [7][8].

**Fig. 10.** DeWaLoP robot. a) Mobile robot. b) Maintenance system. c) Mobile robot extension arms as *x* and *z-axis* points of contact.

## 4    Conclusion

The proposed monolithic multi-module in-pipe robot system is simple and compact, in contrast to the in-pipe multi-module *chain-link* configuration, which requires the robot to have two driving modules, in order to navigate in pipelines with bifurcations, where one driving module is for moving *in* and the other one is for moving *out* of the pipe.

The proposed 3D contact-link enables the entire DeWaLoP robot, consisting of two independent modules, to be driven by a single driving module, simplifying the robot system.

**Acknowledgments.** This work is part-financed by Project DeWaLoP from the European Regional Development Fund, Cross-Border Cooperation Program Slovakia-Austria 2007-2013.

# References

1. Amir, A.F., Kawamura, Y.: Concept and Design of a Fully Autonomous Sewer Pipe Inspection Mobile Robot "KANTARO". In: IEEE International Conference on Robotics and Automation (2007)
2. Roh, S., Ryeol, H.: Differential-Drive In-Pipe Robot for Moving Inside Urban Gas Pipelines. IEEE Transactions on Robotics 21(1) (2005)
3. Ilg, W., Berns, K.: A Wheeled Multijoint Robot for Autonomous Sewer Inspection. In: Intelligent Robots and Systems, IROS 2007 (2007)
4. Hirose, S.: Biologically inspired Robots-Snake-Lake Locomoters and Manipulators. Oxford Science Publications (1993)
5. Shiao, Y., Chi, C.L., Nguyen, Q.: The Analysis of a Semi-Active Suspension System. In: SICE 2010, pp. 2077–2082 (2010)
6. Roth, H., Schilling, K., Futterknecht, S., Weigele, U., Reisch, M.: Inspection- and Repair Robots for Waste Water Pipes – A Challenge to Sensorics and Locomotion. In: Proceedings ISIE (1998)
7. Mateos, L.A., Sousa, M., Vincze, M.: DeWaLoP Robot – Remote Control for In-pipe Robot. In: ICAR 2011, pp. 518–523 (2011)
8. Mateos, L.A., Vincze, M.: DeWaLoP Robot – Dynamical Independent Suspension System. In: ICMET 2011 (2011)
9. Choi, H.R., Roh, S.: In-pipe Robot with Active Steering Capability for Moving Inside of Pipelines. In: Bioinspiration and Robotics: Walking and Climbing Robots, p. 544 (2007) ISBN 978-3-902613-15-8

# Design and Control of a Novel Visco-elastic Braking Mechanism Using HMA

Keith Gunura, Juanjo Bocanegra, and Fumiya Iida[*]

Institute of Robotics and Intelligent Systems,
Swiss Federal Institute of Technology,
LEO D, Leonhardstrasse 20,
CH-8092 Zurich, Switzerland
www.birl.ethz.ch

**Abstract.** Many forms of actuators have been developed with the capability of braking. Most of these braking mechanisms involve numerous mechanical components, that wear with time and lose precision, furthermore the mechanism are difficult to scale down in size while maintaining relatively large holding torques. In this paper, we propose the use of an off-the-shelf economic material, Hot-Melt-Adhesive (HMA), as a brake mechanism. HMA exhibits visco-elastic characteristics and has interesting properties as it can change phases from solid to plastic to liquid and vice versa. Its advantage is that it is reusable and durable. Experiments were performed to display the holding strength as well as the HMAs visco-elasticity in its solid state as a brake mechanism. The HMA requires no constant application of power when solid, and acts as a brake and visco-elastic damper depending on temperature. Results show that HMA can add compliance and high torque braking of joints.

**Keywords:** Hot Melt Adhesive Mechanism, Damper, Brake, High Torque Braking, Visco-elastic damping.

## 1 Introduction

Hot-Melt-Adhesives (HMAs), are polymer-based solvent-free thermal plastic materials that are applied in the molten state and are capable of producing moderate to high strength bonds upon cooling [1]. HMAs are capable of bonding with almost any material. Their bond is unaffected by water, humidity or moisture. HMAs are primarily used for processes such as packaging, labels, pressure sensitive applications and product assemblies. What puts HMAs apart from normal strong bond adhesives is that they can be reused even after cooling by simply reheating them to their operating temperature.

A lot of research has been carried out on HMAs thermal and adhesion properties based on their chemical compositions, *bond strength* and *visco-elasticity* [2], but there has been little exploration into its application in robotics apart from

---

[*] This work was supported by Swiss National Science Foundation, Grant No. PP00P2123387 / 1.

S. Jeschke, H. Liu, and D. Schilberg (Eds.): ICIRA 2011, Part I, LNAI 7101, pp. 416–425, 2011.

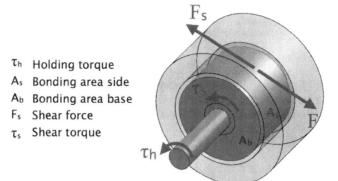

$\tau_h$  Holding torque
$A_s$  Bonding area side
$A_b$  Bonding area base
$F_s$  Shear force
$\tau_s$  Shear torque

**Fig. 1.** The HMA braking mechanism concept. The shaft is immersed in HMA inside a tightly sealed capsule. The HMA is heated through the capsule walls. The shear force $F_s$, which cancels out forward force $F$, is generated by the adhesion of HMA to the shaft and capsule and hence braking occurs.

bonding structural robotic components together [3]-[7]. A notable implementation of HMA to robotics has been the use of active grippers for hot melt joining of micro components [8]. The active gripper system comprises of a flat surface coated with HMA, and by heating or cooling the HMA, the gripper can release or attach a component. Furthermore there was exploration of a detachable actuator [9] which used HMA as a means of attaching itself to a wall. Though not explicitly used for robots the detachable actuator was modified for HMA application exploration in the field of climbing robots by [10]. Osswald *et al.* demonstrated the bonding strength and transition speed of HMA during continuous operation which inherently proved the controllability of HMA.

A concept has been proposed and developed that uses very cheap off-the-shelf HMA material to apply a braking force on a shaft as shown in Figure 1. By exploiting the thermal properties of HMA, illustrated in Figure 2, it is possible to produce three functionalities: 1) in liquid phase, the shaft is free to rotate, 2) as the HMA temperature decreases it transitions through low and high viscosity damping as the phase changes from liquid to solid, 3) in solid phase the HMA creates an adhesive bond between the shaft and the capsule, preventing the shaft from turning thus it acts as a brake.

The immediate advantages of using HMA as a brake is that the braking force does not require constant application of a clamping force from mechanical components or systems, ergo removing the need for sophisticated bulky components. Additionally it is generally difficult to achieve large holding torque without dissipating a large amount of energy. The HMA braking mechanism requires little to almost no energy for applying a large braking torque. There is no long term surface wear, brake fade or noise from rubbing friction surfaces as there is no such mechanical component involved. Compliance and damping is intrinsic to the HMA and does not require mechanical intervention. Further advantages are that HMA is very cheap and economical for the properties it displays. One can find HMA sticks in almost any hobby and craft outlet.

A typical scenario for the HMA mechanism as a brake would be for legged minefield robots or long legged robots that require a long operating time and patience in a static position. Applying the HMA brake (i.e turning off the heaters) requires no energy and removes any stress on the actuators. Furthermore if HMA brake is applied, all remaining power can be directed to other more important processes. As a dampener, the mechanism can be used in any slow moving system with, maybe, passive joints that require damped motion and braking such as in the field of soft robotics.

The main objective of this paper is to propose and demonstrate the functionality and application of using cheap off-the-shelf HMA in robotics. The for-mentioned mechanism, HMA braking mechanism, exploits the physical properties and characteristics of HMA materials to achieve relatively high static braking force and variable dynamic damping with no mechanical effort. The paper will demonstrate the holding torques achievable using the economical HMA mechanism, with further demonstration on an application platform. The first sections will briefly introduce HMA physical properties and brief on braking mechanism, following on with a description of the experiments, a discussion of the results and the conclusion.

# 2   Hot Melt Adhesive and Braking

An intrinsic property of HMA is that it can shift from solid to liquid phase by increasing temperature. During the phase changes its viscosity changes resulting in change of bonding strength. To further demonstrate the HMA capabilities, this section sheds some perspective on the HMA dynamics and force/torque models followed by the concept of the HMA mechanism.

## 2.1   HMA Thermodynamics

HMA exhibits unique properties that can be used for many tasks if carefully controlled. There is a growing interest on how to use HMA in industry for pick and place tasks because by controlling the temperature it is easy to shift between the HMA phases as shown in Figure 2. For the HMA used for this paper, transparent Pattex Hot Sticks with $\varnothing$11 mm and length 200 mm, the optimal operating temperature for liquid phase is typically around 120-200 $^o$C. The plastic phase can be described as that which accompanies the melting of a solid substance to liquid or *vice versa*. In this phase, the HMA bond is weak and viscous , and occurs typically between 50-90 $^o$C. In the solid phase of the HMA, the bond strength is strong and the temperature is typically below 50 $^o$C.

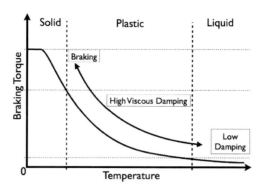

**Fig. 2.** The conceptual HMA torque profile. As temperature increases the torque drops from compliant high torque braking through high viscous damping to very low viscous damping of motion.

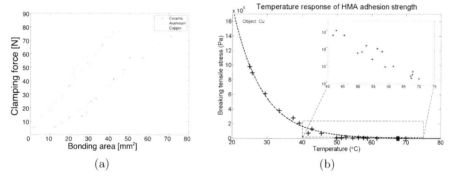

**Fig. 3.** a) Clamping force of HMA, on ceramic, aluminium and copper [10]. The clamping force is in essence the bonding strength of HMA, which is the force measured just before bond failure. Copper and aluminium show high bonding strengths. b) The temperature response of adhesion strength between HMA and copper. Breaking tensile stress decreases exponentially with temperature rise. Inset: a detailed logarithmic plot for a temperature window for copper.

## 2.2   HMA Bonding Strength

An important property of HMA is the strong bond it can make when adhered to an object. Figure 3a shows results collected from measuring the bonding strength of the HMA in relation to a flat bonding area for a climbing robot using the same type of HMA used in this paper. It can be seen that there is a strong linear relationship between the bonding strength and the bonding area for the various materials tested. Thus it can be inferred that, for the general case when surface is cylindrical, increasing the contact area of HMA to the surface by increasing radius can provide a large holding torque. Osswald *et al.* demonstrated

that the shear torque, $\tau_b$, of one circular surface area, $A_b$, shown in Figure 1 can
be calculated by equation 1.

$$\tau_b = \frac{2 \cdot \pi}{3} \cdot k \cdot r^3 \tag{1}$$

The paper extends this formula by calculating the the shear torque, $\tau_s$, due to
shaft surface area $A_s$, given that torque is proportional to surface area.

$$\tau_s = k \cdot 2 \cdot \pi \cdot h \cdot r^2 \tag{2}$$

then adding equation 1 and 2 will give the total torqe $\tau_b$ as

$$\tau_b = 2 \cdot k \cdot \pi \cdot r^2 \cdot \left(\frac{2}{3} \cdot r + h\right) \tag{3}$$

where $k$ is constant used for linear regression on Figure 3, $r$ is radius of cylinder
and $h$ is length of cylinder. Equation 3 is crude but it gives a good guide in the
demonstration of the HMA braking concept. Of course there are other methods
of increasing the surface area such as drilling holes on surface, making the surface
corrugated e.t.c. but these will not be necessary in the demonstration.

### 2.3   Standard Brake Design and Mechanism

Braking is essentially inhibiting motion and to accomplish this, a force equal
and opposite to the motive force is required. The most common braking force is
generated by friction, usually implementing rough disks that are pressed at high
forces against a moving surface. Mechanisms of applying compression or tension
force to the disks vary from hydraulic to electric and even physical strength such
as bicycle brakes for example. The drawback of such mechanisms is that they
require a lot of energy to apply a relatively large braking torque. In robotics
the common so far is electric (such as servo brakes) and magnetorheological
brakes for haptic devices [11]-[12]. These brakes still use the general mechanism of
braking which requires a friction disk, pad or gear and a mechanism for applying
compressive or tension force. The drawbacks, however, is that the surfaces wear
with time.

## 3   Experiment and Results

Figure 3a shows that the contact surface area is an important parameter for
generating a relatively large holding torque. To validate this torque-surface area
relationship for cylindrical surfaces, two shafts of different contact surface areas
(i.e. one shaft had double the radius of the other) were constructed and evaluated against each other. Note that Brake 1 will be the brake with half the
radius of Brake 2. Further investigations were performed to demonstrate the viability of controlling HMA temperature for continuous operation. The following
subsections describe the investigations in detail.

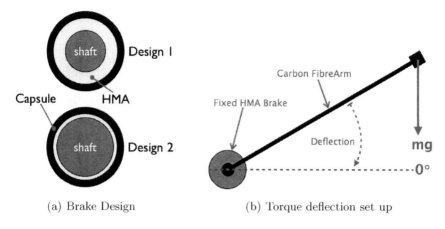

(a) Brake Design                    (b) Torque deflection set up

**Fig. 4.** Experiment set up

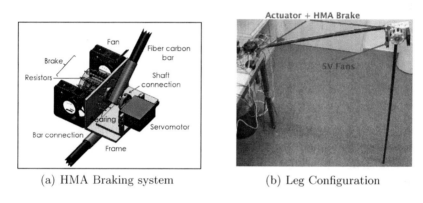

(a) HMA Braking system             (b) Leg Configuration

**Fig. 5.** Demonstration platform

## 3.1   Holding Torque and Deflection

A pivot and lever set up was used to measure the holding torque of the HMA brake designs as shown in Figure 4a. The lever was a 1 metre long arm connected to the shaft of the brake i.e. the pivot. The HMA within the brake was left to cool to a room temperature of about 23°C while fixing the arm at a specific angle position, 15° to the horizontal. This angle was selected as a threshold in which any deflection angle between 0 and 15° is acceptable, the horizontal being 0°. The term "deflection angle" defines the angle achieved by the deformation of HMA under a load on the arm. Deflection angle helps in characterising the elasticity and the rate of angle change due to the HMAs visco-elastic properties. The arm was very light in weight and was made from carbon fibre tube, with a ⌀15mm and 2mm thick capsule wall. A light arm did not add unnecessary load to the brake. To generate a torque on the shaft, weights were added to the tip of the arm. The angle deflection was recorded visually using a high definition

**Table 1.** Summary Evaluation of Heaters

| Device | Characteristics and Performance |
|---|---|
| Resistor | cheap and easy to implement, however they require a medium to create an adequate thermal contact with a metal surface. |
| Resistor wire | flexible and wounds around the capsule, consequently prone to damage and short circuit. |
| Hot glue gun heater | reaches a large enough operation temperature but required direct mains voltage, potentially dangerous if extreme care not practised. |
| Peltier | switches from hot to cold depending on the direction of the current but requires at least 5 minutes before switching polarity to prevent damage, easily damaged at high temperatures. |

camera placed directly in front of the shaft. The image was captured only if there was no further movement of the arm. The carbon fibre arm did not bend under the heavy loads that were applied at its tip.

## 3.2   Heating and Cooling

Heating and cooling is a means of controlling the HMA phase transitions. The faster it takes to heat or cool the faster it is to release or brake respectively. To apply heat to the HMA several devices were evaluated as shown in Table 1. Inevitably simple resistors were used. The surface to surface contact problem was overcome by coating the surfaces with a thermal paste similar to that used for heat-sinks and microprocessors.

A small precision temperature sensor was placed on the exterior surface of the aluminium capsule. The sensor was able to measure the heat dissipated through the capsule. The capsule dimensions were approximately 15mm thick, 50mm in diameter and 30mm in length. The resistors were placed in holes, drilled inside and along the interior of the capsule wall, and immersed in a thermal paste. A total of eighteen resistors were used in each HMA braking mechanism.

The HMA braking mechanism, attached to the knee servo, used $3\Omega$ resistors, two in series by nine in parallel generating a power of approx. 103 Watts. The resistors were arrange in parallel in order to have the same voltage current to flow through them resulting in large heat dissipation. The brake on the hip had the same configuration but with $1.5\Omega$ resistors generating a power of approx. 216 Watts. The resistor configuration was to demonstrate the effects of different resistor values on temperature control. See Figure 5 for more layout details.

The adverse effect of cooling was done by electric fans. It is important to state that the experiments are for proving the concept.

## 3.3   Results

The HMA mechanism discussed above is a first prototype of the novel braking mechanism. However the results, shown in Figure 6a, demonstrate that relatively

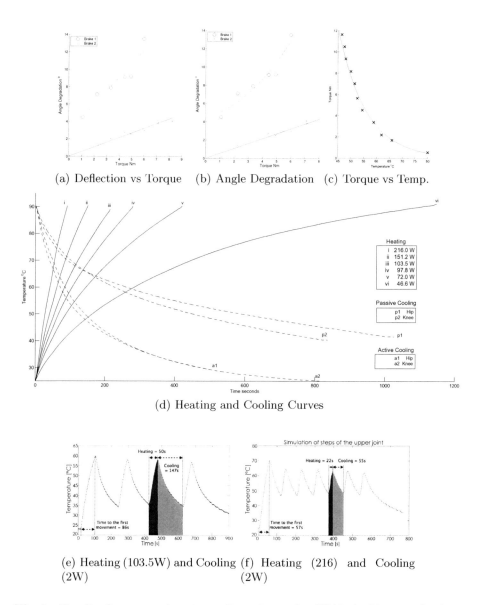

(a) Deflection vs Torque     (b) Angle Degradation     (c) Torque vs Temp.

(d) Heating and Cooling Curves

(e) Heating (103.5W) and Cooling (f) Heating (216) and Cooling
(2W)                                  (2W)

**Fig. 6.** Results from experiments performed on the HMA braking mechanism.
(a)Comparison of two brakes of different shaft radii. (b) Comparison of angle degradation due to HMA viscous properties of Brake 1 and 2. (c) General torque vs temperature
profile of HMA. (d) Solid lines represent heating curves of six different power outputs
and dashed line represents cooling. (e-f) Continuous heating and cooling profiles of
different heater power outputs.

large torques were generated, for the size of the mechanisms. The slopes define the rate of deflection per unit torque where by Brake 1 had an estimated slope of approximately 3.64°/Nm and Brake 2 1.04 °/Nm. The difference in slopes, for each brake profile, indicates that the separation distance of the shaft surface from the capsule inner wall affects the deformation of the HMA.

Unlike a spring, a visco-elastic material does not return completely to its initial undeformed state after deformation, this paper defines the difference between the first initial state and new initial state as degradation. Figure 6b shows a strong linear dependency, with $R^2 = 0.956$, on the angle degradation and the amount of torque applied on Brake 2 which could be interpreted as linear visco-elastic behaviour only because the deformations are small. Brake 1 exhibits a non-linear visco-elastic behaviour between the degradation and torque with $R^2 = 0.987$ for a power fit trendline. Evidently the degradation is larger. The results suggest that the HMA, in its solid phase, can behave as either a linear or non-linear visco-elastic material depending on the contact surface area.

The viscous property of the HMA allows it to degrade its torque exponentially as temperature increases as can be seen in Figure 6c. The implications of this dependency are quite phenomenal. It should be known that the viscosity of visco-elastic materials is strongly affected by temperature. Figure 6c, therefore, implies that it is possible to change between linear and non-linear visco-elastic behaviour by intelligently controlling the temperature.

The above discussion identifies that the control of the braking mechanism depends on the speed at which the HMA can be cooled and heated. The results shown in Figure 6d demonstrate that it is possible to achieve relatively fast heating in the range of 100-250 seconds to get from room temperature to 90°C and cooling between 160-450 seconds from 90°C to solid phase or room temperature respectively. The adverse drawback of fast heating being the large power consumption.

As displayed in Figure 6e and f, the change from heating to cooling is instantaneous. The low threshold temperature was enough to apply a large holding torque and the high threshold temperature was enough for smooth movement of the joints but with damping. The damping allowed for passive swinging downward of the loaded arm without large impact with the floor.

## 4   Conclusion and Future Work

The paper has introduced a new braking mechanism that adopts HMA material as a braking component and demonstrated the viability of using HMA through an application platform. The platform demonstrated that it is possible to brake a joint using HMA material and achieve relatively larger holding strength than most brakes of that scale in size. It is further demonstrated that the holding strength of the HMA material can be regulated by controlling the temperature. In addition to this advantage, the HMA brake has the simplicity in mechanism to be scaled down and still achieve relatively high torques. This is due the fact that there is no mechanical mechanisms to implement the braking or damping force like most conventional brakes. The mechanism can also be used as a damper for impact and motion as an extension of its primary application.

However, the response time is still not ideal compared with the other forms of brakes. Therefore, the application of this type of brake is limited to some tasks that do not need quick response of braking. The design optimisation of the HMA mechanism is an obvious path for further research and future work. The HMA brake has demonstrated its application and concept, and only with further investigation and work will the mechanism realise its full functionality.

**Acknowledgement.** The authors would like to thank Marc Osswald and Liyu Wang for their fruitful research into HMA properties that contribute to this project. This work was supported by Swiss National Science Foundation, Grant No. PP00P2123387 / 1.

# References

1. Pocius, A.: Physical properties of polymers. In: Chemistry and Materials Science, Springerlink, Part V, pp. 479–486 (2007)
2. Li, W., Bouzidi, L., Narine, S.S.: Current research and development status and prospect of Hot-Melt-Adhesives: A Review. Ind. Eng. Chem. Res. 47, 7524–7532 (2008)
3. Wright, P.K., Cutkosky, M.R.: Handbook of industrial robotics, pp. 91–111. John Wiley and Sons (1985)
4. Llievski, F., Mazzeo, A., Shepherd, R.F., Chen, X., Whitesides, G.M.: Soft robotics for chemists. Angewandte Chemie 50, 1890–1895 (2011)
5. Bark, C., Binnenbose, T., Vogele, G., Weisener, T., Widmann, M.: Gripping with low viscosity fluid. In: 11th International Workshop on Micro Electro Mechanical Systems, Heidelberg, Germany, January 25-29, pp. 301–305. IEEE Press (1998)
6. Gerberich, W.W., Cordill, M.J.: Physics of adhesion. Rep. Prog. Phys. 69, 2157–2203 (2006)
7. Park, Y.-J., Joo, H.-S., Kim, H.-J., Lee, Y.-K.: Adhesion and rheological properties of EVA-based Hot-Melt-Adhesives. Int. J. Adhesion Adhesives 26, 571–576 (2006)
8. Rathmann, S., Raatz, A., Hesselbach, J.: Active gripper for hot melt joining of micro components. In: Ratchev, S. (ed.) IPAS 2010. IFIP AICT, vol. 315, pp. 191–198. Springer, Heidelberg (2010)
9. Osakabe, Y., Kikuchi, K., Tomita, H., Saito, Y.: Detachable actuator using induction heating and thermalplastic adhesive. In: Int. Conf. on Elect. Machines and Sys. (ICEMS), Tokyo, pp. 1–6 (2009)
10. Osswald, M., Iida, F.: A Climbing robot based on Hot Melt Adhesion (HMA). In: IEEE/RSJ Int. Conference on Intelligent Robots and Systems (IROS 2011) (2011)
11. Conti, F., Khatib, O.: A New Approach for haptic interface design. The International Journal of Robotics Research 28(6), 834–848 (2009)
12. Goldfarth, M., Durfee, W., Korkowski, K., Harrold, B.: Evaluation of a controlled-brake orthosis for FES-Aided gait. IEEE Trans. Neural Syst. Rehab. Eng. 11(3), 241–248 (2003)

# Topological Design of Weakly-Coupled 3-Translation Parallel Robots Based on Hybrid-Chain Limbs

Huiping Shen[1], Tingli Yang[1], Lvzhong Ma[2], and Shaobin Tao[3]

[1] School of Mechanical Engineering, Changzhou University, 213016, P.R. China
[2] School of Mechanical Engineering, Jiangsu University, 212013, Zhengjiang, P.R. China
[3] DTL Mori Seiki, West Sacramento, CA, USA
Shp65@126.com

**Abstract.** This paper presented a novel and systematic design method for topological structure of weakly-coupled parallel robots with three pure translations by using hybrid chains. First, the general design steps for hybrid-chain limb (HCL) were presented, with which many practical hybrid-chain limbs containing three translations used for connecting the moving platform with the fixed platform of parallel robots were derived by using HCL. Then, based on these limb structures, eight promising weakly-coupled parallel structures three pure translations were originally synthesized. Meanwhile, many generic structures could be formulated by changing the type of driving joints, the relative position of driving joints and the local sub-structures of limbs. Finally, the eight novel parallel robots were classified based on structural stability and symmetry in topology, complexity of kinematics and dynamics, and the ability to be manufactured and assembled.

**Keywords:** Parallel robots, Topological structure design, Type synthesis.

## 1 Introduction

In recent decades, parallel robot mechanisms with less DOF have attracted many researchers because of their greater rigidity, high loading capability, precise position capability, smaller weight to load ratio. They are prospective in robots, machine building, simulation platform, and high precision micromanipulators. Most of the time, parallel robot mechanisms whose motion output have less DOF(2~5)have more practical applications. These are many more new structures and patents, especially for parallel mechanisms with three pure translations. Such translational three-DOF are ones with three limbs each with U-P-U joints, P-U-U joints, R-C-C joints[1].The Delat mechanism is one of the earliest and the most famous spatial translational three-DOFs robots, as it has been marketed and used industrially for pick and place applications[2]. Each of these limbs actually is a R-R-Pa-R(Revolute-Revolute-Parallelogram-Revolute) kinematic chain. Many variations of that Delta mechanism has been proposed and implemented, such as R-Pa-R-R kinematic chain, P-Pa-R-R kinematic chain[3]. However, these translational three-DOF parallel mechanisms are all coupled from input-output kinematics points of view[4-5].

S. Jeschke, H. Liu, and D. Schilberg (Eds.): ICIRA 2011, Part I, LNAI 7101, pp. 426–435, 2011.
© Springer-Verlag Berlin Heidelberg 2011

This paper presents a new systematic method for weakly-coupled parallel mechanisms with three pure translations by using hybrid-chain limb(HCL), which considers hybrid chain as "limps" connecting the moving platform with the base. The design rules and general design steps for hybrid-chain limb are presented. Furthermore, this paper enunciates in detail the synthesis process of the topological structures of 3-dof parallel mechanisms, the moving platform of which can generate three translations. Eight promising weakly-coupled parallel structures with three pure translations were originally synthesized. Meanwhile, the structure classification of these parallel structures is identified according to the four structures evaluation criteria suggested in the paper.

## 2  Basic Theory[6]

### 2.1    The Motion Output Matrix of a Parallel Robot

The motion output matrix $M_p$ of a parallel robot mechanism refers to the position and orientation of its output link, i.e. moving platform. In matrix form, it can be represented as

$$M_p = \begin{pmatrix} x(\theta_i) & y(\theta_i) & z(\theta_i) \\ \alpha(\theta_i) & \beta(\theta_i) & \gamma(\theta_i) \end{pmatrix}, \quad i = 1 \sim F \tag{1}$$

Where, F≤6, x $\theta(i), y(\theta_i), z(\theta_i)$ are the Cartesian coordinates of the moving coordinates system origin fixed with the moving platform and $\alpha(\theta_i), \beta(\theta_i), \gamma(\theta_i)$ are three Euler angles of the moving coordinate system with respect to the global coordinate system. $\theta_i$ is the $i^{th}$ input of the parallel robot; F is the degree of freedom of the parallel robot.

It is obvious that Equation(1) can also be used to describe a limb structure. The output motion matrix of a limb structure is written as $M_l$.

### 2.2    The Motion Output Equation of Parallel Robot

Furthermore, a parallel robot mechanism with $n_s$ limbs can be seen as one fixed platform and one moving platform connected with $n_s$ limbs. The moving platform moves within the constraints of all limbs. Thus, its motion output matrix $M_P$ is the intersection union of the motion output matrix of all limbs, i.e.,

$$M_p = \bigcap_{i=1}^{n_s} M_l \tag{2}$$

Where $M_l$ is the motion output matrix of the $i^{th}$ limb, which is determined by its structure type and configuration between the fixed platform and the moving platform. The equation shows that the motion output matrix $M_l$ of every limb should include all components of expected output matrix $M_p$ of parallel mechanisms,  that is $M_i \supseteq M_p$.

## 2.3    Degree of Freedom

A general equation for calculating the degree of freedom can be found in the paper.

$$F = \sum_{i=1}^{m} f_i - \min\left\{\sum_{j=1}^{v} \xi_j\right\} \qquad (3)$$

Where F is the DOF of the mechanism; $f_i$ is the DOF of the $i^{th}$ kinematic pair; $m$ is the number of kinematic joints; $v$ is the number of basic loops in the mechanism and $v=m-n+1$($n$ is the number of the links of the mechanism); $\xi_j$ is the number of independent equations of $j^{th}$ basic loop; There are different ways for selection of the $v$ loops, Operator $\min\{\cdot\}$ means that we choose the way whose $\Sigma\xi_j$ is the minimum. For most common loops, $\xi$ is 6. For over-constrained loops, $\xi$ should be determined according to whether it is a general over-constrained loop or a special over-constrained loop.

# 3    Design of Hybrid Chain Limb

## 3.1    Hybrid-Chain Limb

In general, there are two types of limb structures that connect the fixed and the moving platform of parallel mechanisms, i.e., simple chain and hybrid chain.

Simple chain means serial open kinematic chain composed of links and kinematic joints, which is corresponding to general over-constrained loops. For example, the outputs of a simple chain composed of three parallel-axle revolute joints are two independent translations and one rotation. On the contrary, the outputs of a simple chain with two parallel-axle revolute joints are only one independent translation and one rotation.

If the motion output of a chain with intermediate loops is the same with motion output of another simple chain without any loops(i.e. equivalent simple chain),then the chain is called hybrid chain. It is evident that when we design the hybrid chain we need to design a loop first and make its output link realize a part of motion outputs of the overall expected motion outputs .Then, one-open simple chain, which can generate the rest of motion output, can be appended to the output link of the loop. Thus, the motion output should be equal or greater than the overall motion outputs of the parallel mechanism.

For example, in Fig.1(a),prism joint $P_1$ can be replaced by a parallelogram with four revolute joints ,i.e. $R_1$-$R_2$-$R_3$-$R_4$,in Fig.1(b).Output link in the simple chain in Fig.1(a) and one in the hybrid chain in Fig.1(b) has the same output matrix , .i.e.

$$\begin{pmatrix} X & Y & \bullet \\ \alpha & \bullet & \bullet \end{pmatrix}$$

Both of them can generate two translations along x-axis and y-axis as well as one rotation around x-axis (See the coordinate system in Fig.2.here, "$\bullet$"means a constant).

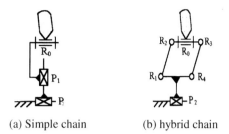

(a) Simple chain          (b) hybrid chain

**Fig. 1.** Two chains with the same output matrix

In this paper, Hybrid chain limb is being used as main limb structures connecting the moving platform and the fixed platform of parallel mechanisms, which not only will extends numbers of novel topological structures, but also benefits to topological structure optimizations and the coupling degree of synthesized mechanisms are as lower as zero or one. In another words, the direct kinematics solutions of these synthesized parallel mechanisms are much more easier.

## 3.2 Design Steps of HCL

According to the construction rules of HCL[7] ,the design steps are illustrated below with a HCL which can generate three translations and two rotations output as an example.

**Step 1.** Write the desired motion output matrix $M_l$ of the HCL being designed.
As an example, select a global coordinate system, if its motion output matrix $M_l$ be three translations x,y,and z and two rotations about x and z axes, which are $\alpha$ and $\gamma$, then, in matrix form, it is

$$M_l = \begin{pmatrix} x & y & z \\ \alpha & \bullet & \gamma \end{pmatrix} \tag{4}$$

**Step 2.** Seek the equivalent simple chain.
It is easy to be found that the corresponding equivalent simple chain can be $R//R//R \perp R//R$. Comparing it with $M_l$, the configuration of the simple chain in the global coordinate system can be drawn as in Fig.2, where the axis of revolute joint A,B and C, and joint D,E are respectively parallel with each other ,while axis of joint C is perpendicular to that of joint D.

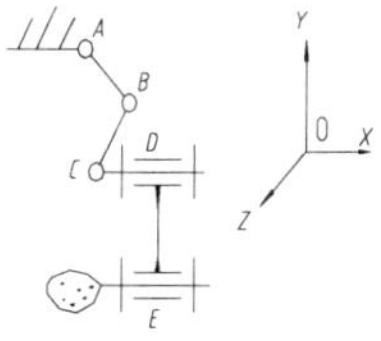

**Fig. 2.** Equivalent simple chain 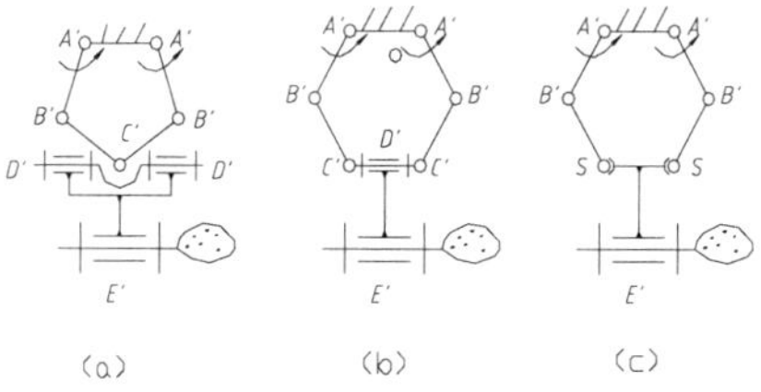          **Fig. 3.** Construction of the HCL$_s$

**Step 3.** Construction the part of the HCL.

Loops, such as a five bar or six bar planner loop mechanism is used to construct the loop of the HCL, can be introduced in the mechanism to generate some of the translation and rotation components of $M_l$, Here, the A-B-C part of the three parallel revolute joints, which can generate x,y translation along x, y-axis and $\gamma$ rotation around z-axis, of above equivalent simple chain can be partially replaced by one planar 5-bar mechanism as in Fig.3(a) or one planar 6-bar mechanism as in Figure3(b).To be precise, the middle revolute joint $C'$ in Fig.3(a)or the output link of $C'- C'$ in Fig.3(b)opposite to the fixed link $A'- A'$ is respectively output joint or link.

**Step 4.** Constuct the open-chain part of HCL

According to $M_l$ in Equation (4),an open-chain, D-E part, with two parallel revolute joints can be appended to the output joint $C'$ or output link $C'- C'$ to make up the another one translation and one rotation in $M_l$. Up to now, the construction of a HCL is done.

**Step 5.** Generate the generic structures of  HCL

As known, the two revolute joints $C'$ in Fig.3(b)can be replaced by using a spherical joint S in Fig.3(c) because the DOF around $C'- C'$ axis can be replaced by the local rotation DOF around the connecting line between two spherical joints. In this way, more generic structures can be derived.

In brief, Step 1 is the design goal of a HCL. Step 2 is the construction basis of HCL. Step 3 to step 4 construct the loop and open-chain part of HCL respectively. Step 5 can be used to find more generic type structures of HCL.

By following above steps, three types of basic HCL found are $C_{II}$ (2),$C_{II}$ (3), $C_{II}$ (4) as in Table 1 which satisfy the requirements of $M_l$ in Equation (4).

Similarly, four basic HCL types which can output three translations and one rotation found are $B_l(2), B_l(3), B_l(4), B_{III(2)}$ as in Table 1;The basic HCL for three translations and three rotations are $D(2),D(3),D(4)$ as in Table 1.

## 4   The Design Procedures for 3-Translation Parallel Mechanisms

The design procedures for 3-translation Parallel mechanism may be described as follows.

**Step 1.** Write the design motion output matrix $M_p$ of the parallel mechanism being designed.

$$M_P = \begin{bmatrix} x & y & z \\ \bullet & \bullet & \bullet \end{bmatrix} \tag{5}$$

**Step 2.** Designing the limb structure

According to Equation (2), the motion output of every limb should include all components of the expected motion output matrix $M_p$, i.e., $M_{li} \supseteq M_p$ .Most of practical hybrid-chain limb that satisfy the requirement have been listed in Table 1.

**Table 1.** Hybrid -chain limbs which can generate three translations

| Type | Motion output matrix of HCL | Equivalent SC | Hybrid -chain Limb (HCL) | | |
|------|------|------|------|------|------|
| | | 1 | 2 | 3 | 4 |
| A | $M_P = \begin{bmatrix} x & y & z \\ \bullet & \bullet & \bullet \end{bmatrix}$ | | | | |
| $B_I$ | | | | | |
| $B_{II}$ | $M_P = \begin{bmatrix} x & y & z \\ \alpha & \bullet & \bullet \end{bmatrix}$ | | | | |
| $B_{III}$ | | | | | |
| $C_I$ | $M_P = \begin{bmatrix} x & y & z \\ \alpha & \bullet & \gamma \end{bmatrix}$ | | | | |
| $C_{II}$ | | | | | |
| D | $M_P = \begin{bmatrix} x & y & z \\ \alpha & \beta & \gamma \end{bmatrix}$ | | | | |

**Step 3.** Enumerate feasible assembling plans of limb structures.

For this design, there are eight practical assembling plans which can generate three translations, as in Table 2 .i.e., $3 - B_I$ (2) , $B_{III}$ (2) $- B_{II}$ (1) , $B_I$ (2) $- C_I$ (2) , $B_I$ (2) $- C_I$ (3) , $B_I$ (2) $- B_I$ (2) $- C_I$ (1) , $B_I$ (2) $- C_I$ (1) $- C_I$ (1) , $B_{II}$ (1) $- C_I$ (2) and $B_{II}$ (1) $- C_I$ (3)

Where, $B_I(2) - C_I(2)$ means the moving platform and fixed platform are connected by one $B_I(2)$ type HCL and $C_I(2)$ type HCL, the same notation is taken in the text.

**Table 2.** Eight novel three-translation parallel mechanisms

| | No.1 | No.2 |
|---|---|---|
| Assembly plan | 3−BI（2） | BIII（2）−BII（1） |
| Configuration chart | | |
| BKC 及 κ | One BKC, κ =1 | One BKC, κ =1 |
| | No.3 | No.4 |
| Assembly plan | BI（2）−CI（2） | BI（2）−CI（3） |
| Configuration chart | | |
| BKC 及 κ | BKC1, κ 1=0；BKC2, κ 2=0； | 一个 BKC, κ =1； |
| | No.5 | No.6 |
| Assembly plan | BI（2）−BI（2）−CI（1） | BI（2）−CI（1）−CI（1） |
| Configuration chart | | |
| BKC 及 κ | One BKC, κ =1 | One BKC, κ =1 |
| | No.7 | No.8 |
| Assembly plan | BII（1）−CI（2） | BII（1）−CI（3） |
| Configuration chart | | |
| BKC 及 κ | BKC1, κ 1=0；BKC2, κ 2=0 | 一个 BKC, κ =1 |

**Step 4.** Determine the $\xi_j$ of independent displacement equations of basic loops

It is possible that a parallel mechanism with three pure translations can be constructed by using every assembling plan above. Therefore, the number ($\xi_j$) of independent equations of basic loops composed of all limbs should be determined. Because DOF, $f_i$, of every joint of each limb and the total DOF of the parallel mechanism being designed are known, $min \sum \xi_j$ can be calculated according to Equation(3). Then, the number $\xi_j (j = 1,2,...)$ of independent displacement equation can be assigned to each basic loops.

For example, for the assembly plan $B_I(2) - C_I(1) - C_I(1)$ in step 3, the DOF of $B_I(2)$ type hybrid chain is seven and the DOF of $C_I(2)$ type hybrid chain is five. Thus, $min \sum \xi_j = (7+5+5) - 3 = 14$ .Furthermore, the assembly plan contains 15 links, therefore, the number of the basic loop, $v=m-n+1=(7+5+5)-15+1=3$.There is a planar loop in $B_I(2)$ hybrid chain and the number of the independent equation $\xi_1 = 3$, therefore the rest two basic loops can be distributed as $\xi_2 = 5, \xi_3 = 6$.

**Step 5.** Determine if the structure type of basic loops exist.

According to $\xi_j$ value of the independent equation distribution plan of step 4, these basic loops with all $\xi_j$ can be determined if they exist.

For example, for the assembly plan $B_I(2) - C_I(1) - C_I(1)$ ,the planar loop structure with $\xi_1 = 3$ can exist within $B_I(2)$ type hybrid chain. While limb $B_I(2) - C_I(1)$, as well as limb $C_I(1) - C_I(1)$ can constitute two basic loops with $\xi_2 = 6, \xi_3 = 5$ respectively. Therefore, this assembly plan can build the required parallel mechanism.

**Step 6.** Determine the configurations of all limbs between the fixed and the moving platform.

According to the assembly plan of limbs in step 3, $\xi_j$ distribution plan in step 4,corresponding loop structures in Step 5,the configuration of all limbs between the fixed and the moving platform can be determined according to Equation(2).

For example, for the assembly plan $B_I(2) - C_I(1) - C_I(1)$ ($\xi_1 = 3, \xi_2 = 6, \xi_3 = 5$), if its configuration of three limbs is arranged as the No.6 configuration in Table 2, according to Equation (2) the motion output matrix of the moving platform can be expressed as follows:

$$\begin{bmatrix} x & y & z \\ \bullet & \beta & \bullet \end{bmatrix}_{B2} \cap \begin{bmatrix} x & y & z \\ \alpha & \bullet & \gamma \end{bmatrix}_{C1} \cap \begin{bmatrix} x & y & z \\ \alpha & \bullet & \gamma \end{bmatrix}_{C1} = \begin{bmatrix} x & y & z \\ \bullet & \bullet & \bullet \end{bmatrix}_{P}$$

For other seven assembly plans in this paper, the special configurations of corresponding limb branches between the fixed platform and moving platform can be determined as in Table 2.Thus, we obtain originally eight novel parallel mechanisms driven by three prism joints located at the fixed platform, whose platform can pose three pure translations.

**Step 7.** Determine the driving joints.

According the existence rule[9],the three prism joints located at the fixed platform of eight novel parallel mechanism can be used as driving joints.

**Step 8.** Derive the generic parallel mechanisms

Another eight generic mechanisms can be derived by replacing prism driving joints in Table 2 with revolute joints. More generic types can also be formulated by replacing hybrid-chain limb $C_l(2)$ with $C_l(3)$ ,$C_l(4)$ etc. In this way, the solution space of types synthesis can be expanded greatly.

# 5   Topological Structure Classification

The eight novel three-translation parallel mechanisms were invented in this paper and have been granted China patents. These parallel mechanisms use the hybrid-chain limb as the limb structure, hence most of them have lower coupling degree $k$ between basic loops, which is only zero or one, their direct kinematic solution is easy to be obtained. While those 3-translation parallel mechanism which use equivalent simple chain as limbs, their coupling degree is much more greater, which results that their direct kinematic solution is more difficult.

Basic classifications are needed in order to find potential industrial applications for the eight promising parallel mechanisms. Therefore, the authors formulated four classification criteria:

(1)  Structural stability and symmetry in topology

There are only two connection points for moving platform of the second, third, fourth, seventh, and eighth parallel structures. So, they all have worse stability and can be used mainly for motion output; while there are three connection points for the moving platform of the first, fifth, and sixth parallel structures. Their moving platform can be used in heavy load or motion output. For these three types, two limbs of three are the same. Therefore, they are partly symmetric.

(2)  Complexity of kinematics and dynamics

The kinematics and dynamics complexity of the third and seventh structure is the lowest because the coupling degree of their two BKC are zero. Their kinematics and dynamics can be solved directly; while the coupling degree of the first, second, fourth, fifth, sixth and eighth structures are one and their kinematics and dynamics can be solved only if one dimensional kinematics or dynamics equation is solved.

(3)  The ability to manufacture and assemble.

The eight parallel structures are easy to manufacture with given precision. In terms of manufacturing quantity, generally, the more the sum of links and joints, the more works are needed to manufacture and assemble. Thus, the least works are needed for the seventh and the eighth structures and the following is the second, third, sixth, fifth, fourth and the first parallel structure.

Above three criteria will help understand the properties of the eight novel 3-translation parallel mechanisms.

# 6   Conclusions

The construction rules and general design steps for hybrid chain were presented in this paper. Further, an effective and systematic design method for weakly-coupled parallel mechanism with three pure translations which use hybrid chains as the connecting limbs was further forwarded. This method is general enough to the synthesis of other parallel mechanisms which have different $DOF_s$ and different motion outputs.

The eight weakly-coupled parallel mechanisms with three translations presented here were not previous literatures. They have been classified according to structural stability and symmetry in topology, complexity of kinematics and dynamics, and the ability to manufacture and assemble. Furthermore, more generic structure types were easily derived by exchanging prism with revolute joints, changing the position of driving joints, changing the local sub-structure of limbs and changing the assemble plans of limbs.

The parallel mechanisms used hybrid chains as limbs are weakly coupled and their direct kinematic solutions are easy to obtain. The works in the paper will provide scientific foundations for the development and application of these novel parallel mechanisms with less complexity.

**Acknowledgment.** Authors would like to appreciate the support by the National Natural Science Foundation of China (No. 51075045,50875261), Jiangsu Province Key S & T Support Projects(No.BE2010074,No.BE2010061) and Changzhou City S& T Project(No.CE20100050).

# References

1. Gosselin, C., Angeles, J.: The optimum kinematic design of a spherical three-degree-freedom parallel manipulator. ASME J. of Mechanical Design III, 202–207 (1989)
2. Clavel, R.: Delta, A fast robot with parallel geometry. In: 18th Int. Symp. on Indus. Robots, pp. 91–100 (1988)
3. Tsai, L.W., Sameer, J.: Kinematics and Optimization of a Spatial 3-UPU Parallel Manipulator. ASME J. of Mechanical and Design. 122, 439–446 (2000)
4. Kong, X.W., Gossline, C., Clement, M.: Type Synthesis of Parallel mechanism. Springer, Heidelberg (2007)
5. Gogu, G.: Structural Synthesis of Parallel Robots, Part 1: Methodology. Springer, Heidelberg (2008)
6. Yang, T.L., Jin, Q., Lu, Y.F., et al.: Structures Synthesis and Classification of 3-dof Translational Parallel Robotic Mechanisms based on the units of Single-opened-Chain. Chinese J. of Mechanical Engineering 38(8) (2002)
7. Shen, H.P., Yang, T.L., Ma, L.Z.: Synthesis and Structure Analysis of Kinematic Structures of 6-dof Parallel Robotic Mechanisms. Mechanisms and Machine Theory 40, 1164–1180 (2005)

# Working Space and Motion Analysis on a Novel Planar Parallel Manipulator with Three Driving Sliders

Huiping Shen[1], Wei Wang[1], Changyu Xue[2], Jiaming Deng[1], and Zhenghua Ma[1]

[1] Research Institute of Robotics, Changzhou University, Changzhou, 213016, P.R. China
[2] Brockport, NY 14420, USA
Shp65@126.com

**Abstract.** The change of position and orientation of workpieces is often required in CNC machining, workpiece conveying and product testing. A novel practical planar parallel mechanism with three sliders driven on two parallel guide rails is presented. The direct and inverse kinematic solutions are deduced. The workspace analysis on the end-effector is conducted under given position and orientation. The simulation of motion characteristics of three sliders is completed when it is in given orientation. The virtual prototype is demonstrated. This paper is useful to real-time control and industrial application of this 3-DOF parallel manipulator.

**Keywords:** Parallel mechanism, Kinematics, Workspace.

## 1 Introduction

During processing of a large workpiece, its position and orientation may vary from time to time, which is realized by controlling the movement of work platform. Because the motion of cutting tool is limited, different position and orientation of workpiece become indispensable in order to enhance the ability of numerical machine and improve its production efficiency and manufacturing precision. The change of position and orientation is also required in workpiece conveying and product testing. During the conveying process, the posture of object to be delivered may be changed manually or with the use of manipulators. On the one hand, the use of hard labor cannot guarantee the operation accuracy and consistency; on the other hand, the use of manipulators will increase the complexity and cost of production line. If the convey device itself can change the posture of object during the delivery process, it will improve the efficiency and meet the production requirement better. The error detection of large format photovoltaic products, such as solar cell module and LED panel, requires lighting and must be carried out from different positions and perspectives. The detection automation will be realized if the detection equipment can change its position and orientation.

Compared with the series counterparts, Parallel Kinematic Mechanism (PKM) have been widely applied in many research fields due to the high stiffness, structural

S. Jeschke, H. Liu, and D. Schilberg (Eds.): ICIRA 2011, Part I, LNAI 7101, pp. 436–444, 2011.
© Springer-Verlag Berlin Heidelberg 2011

stability, high load capacity, small exercise load and high micro precision. In recent years, 3-DOF PKM have been paid increasing attention to in both the academics and industry. Arakelian studied the dynamic model of one symmetrical 3-DOF planar PKM 3-RRR and the balance of force and torque on the rack [1]. Gao proposed the relationship between the workspace shape and structural dimensions of one symmetrical 3-DOF planar PKM 3-RRR [2]. Kucuku compared and analyzed seven 3-DOF planar PKM with the use of Genetic Algorithm [3]. Han presented a nonsymmetrical planar parallel mechanism with three guide rails 3-PRR and analyzed its singularity and workspace [4]. Qian presented a planar PKM with one guide rail 2-PRR+RPR and applied it onto virtual axis machine tools [5]. Based on a nonsymmetrical planar non-redundant parallel mechanism 3-PRR, Yang analyzed the actuator singularity of three redundant parallel mechanisms [6].

Different from the non-redundant parallel mechanism 3-PRR [6,7], the 3-DOF planar parallel manipulator presented in this paper includes three sliders moving reciprocatively along two parallel rails [8]. Its work platform can change  position and orientation to achieve high precision location of the workpiece. This mechanism has large workspace and can be widely applied onto numerical machines.

## 2   Innovative Design and Kinematic Model

### 2.1   Innovative Design

As listed in Fig. 1, the 3-DOF planar parallel manipulator consists of three sliders A, B and C, three connecting rods 1, 2 and 3, and work platform 4. The work platform is connected to the rod 3 by revolute hinge D on one end and connected to rods 1 and 2 with multiple hinge E on the other end. The rods 1, 2 and 3 are also connected with revolute hinges to sliders A and B on one guide rail K' and connected to slider C on another guide rail K, which is parallel to rail K'. This structure is simple and easy of manufacture. It has high positioning accuracy as well.

### 2.2   Direct Kinematics

In Fig. 1, the Cartesian coordinate system XOY is established. A, B, C, D and E are five hinges in the mechanism; $S_i$ ($i$=1, 2, 3) represents x-displacement of three sliders A, B and C on the rails, respectively; P($x_P$, $y_P$) is the central position of work platform 4, whose length is $L$; $\theta$ represents the angle between the work platform and the positive x-axis; $L_i$ ($i$=1, 2, 3) are length of connecting rods 1, 2 and 3, respectively; $\theta_i$ ($i$=1, 2, 3) represents the angle between each connecting rod and the positive x-axis; H is the distance between the two parallel rails.

Direct kinematics is used to solve the posture of work platform ($x_P$, $y_P$, $\theta$) when $S_1$, $S_2$ and $S_3$ are known.

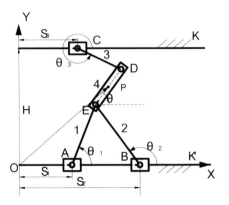

**Fig. 1.** 3-DOF planar parallel manipulator

By the vector method, kinematics vector equation is written as:

$$\begin{cases} \overrightarrow{H} + \overrightarrow{S_3} + \overrightarrow{L_3} = \overrightarrow{S_1} + \overrightarrow{L_1} + \overrightarrow{L} \\ \overrightarrow{S_1} + \overrightarrow{L_1} = \overrightarrow{S_2} + \overrightarrow{L_2} \end{cases} \tag{1}$$

Its x-axis and y-axis projections are:

$$\begin{cases} S_3 + L_3 \cos\theta_3 = S_1 + L_1 \cos\theta_1 + L\cos\theta & (2-1) \\ S_1 + L_1 \cos\theta_1 = S_2 + L_2 \cos\theta_2 & (2-2) \end{cases}$$

$$\begin{cases} H + L_3 \sin\theta_3 = L_1 \sin\theta_1 + L\sin\theta & (3-1) \\ L_1 \sin\theta_1 = L_2 \sin\theta_2 & (3-2) \end{cases}$$

To eliminate $\theta_2$ from both equations (2-2) and (2-3) and simplify, $\theta_1$ will be derived:

$$\theta_1 = \arccos\left(\frac{L_2^2 - L_1^2 - (S_1 - S_2)^2}{2L_1(S_1 - S_2)}\right) \tag{4}$$

To eliminate $\theta_1$ from both equations (2-2) and (2-3) and simplify, $\theta_2$ will be derived:

$$\theta_2 = \arccos\left(\frac{L_1^2 - L_2^2 - (S_1 - S_2)^2}{2L_2(S_2 - S_1)}\right) \tag{5}$$

To eliminate $\theta$ from both equations (2-1) and (3-1) and simplify, $\theta_3$ will be derived:
$$A\sin\theta_3 + B\cos\theta_3 + C = 0$$

i.e., $\theta_3 = 2\arctan(\dfrac{A \pm \sqrt{A^2 + B^2 - C^2}}{B - C})$ (6)

where:

$$A = 2L_3(H - L_1 \sin\theta_1), \quad B = 2L_3(S_3 - S_1 - L_1 \cos\theta_1)$$
$$C = L_1^2 + L_3^2 - L^2 + S_1^2 + S_3^2 + H^2 - 2S_1S_3$$
$$+ 2L_1(S_1 - S_3)\cos\theta_1 - 2HL_1 \sin\theta_1$$

$\theta$ can be derived directly from equation (3-1):

$$\theta = \arcsin\left(\frac{H + L_3 \sin\theta_3 - L_1 \sin\theta_1}{L}\right) \tag{7}$$

and

$$\overrightarrow{OP} = \overrightarrow{S_1} + \overrightarrow{L_1} + \frac{1}{2}\overrightarrow{L} \tag{8}$$

Thus, the posture of the work platform can be written as:

$$\left\{ \begin{array}{ll} x_p = S_1 + L_1 \cos\theta_1 + \dfrac{L}{2}\cos\theta = f(S_1, S_2, S_3) & (9-1) \\[2mm] y_p = L_1 \sin\theta_1 + \dfrac{L}{2}\sin\theta = f(S_1, S_2, S_3) & (9-2) \\[2mm] \theta = \arcsin\left(\dfrac{H + L_3 \sin\theta_3 - L_1 \sin\theta_1}{L}\right) = f(S_1, S_2, S_3) & (9-3) \end{array} \right.$$

From the above solutions, the position $(x_P, y_P)$ and orientation $\theta$ of work platform are related with displacement of sliders A, B and C, thus this is a non-decoupling control mechanism.

## 2.3    Inverse Kinematics

Inverse kinematics is used to solve the displacements of $S_1$, $S_2$ and $S_3$ when the posture of work platform $(x_P, y_P, \theta)$ is known.

By equation (9-2),(3-2) and (3-1), we get

$$\theta_1 = \arcsin\frac{y_p - \dfrac{L}{2}\sin\theta}{L_1} \tag{10}$$

$$\theta_2 = \pi - \arcsin\frac{y_p - \dfrac{L}{2}\sin\theta}{L_2} \tag{11}$$

$$\theta_3 = \pi - \arcsin\frac{y_p + \dfrac{L}{2}\sin\theta - H}{L_3} \tag{12}$$

By equation (9-1), (2-2) and (2-1), we get

$$\left\{ \begin{array}{l} S_1 = x_p - L_1 \cos\theta_1 - \dfrac{L}{2}\cos\theta = f(x_p, y_p, \theta) \\[2mm] S_2 = S_1 + L_1 \cos\theta_1 - L_2 \cos\theta_2 = f(x_p, y_p, \theta) \\[2mm] S_3 = S_1 + L_1 \cos\theta_1 - L_3 \cos\theta_3 + L\cos\theta = f(x_p, y_p, \theta) \end{array} \right. \tag{13}$$

Inverse velocity equation can be obtained by inverse kinematics using the first time derivative as follows.

$$
\begin{cases}
\dot{S}_1 = \dot{x}_p + (L_1^2 - (y_p - \dfrac{L}{2}\sin\theta)^2)^{-\frac{1}{2}}(y_p\ \dot{y}_p - \dfrac{L}{2}\dot{y}_p\sin\theta) \\[2mm]
\dot{S}_2 = \dot{S}_1 - (L_1^2 - (y_p - \dfrac{L}{2}\sin\theta)^2)^{-\frac{1}{2}}(y_p\ \dot{y}_p - \dfrac{L}{2}\dot{y}_p\sin\theta) \\[2mm]
\quad -(L_2^2 - (y_p - \dfrac{L}{2}\sin\theta)^2)^{-\frac{1}{2}}(y_p\ \dot{y}_p - \dfrac{L}{2}\dot{y}_p\sin\theta) \\[2mm]
\dot{S}_3 = \dot{S}_1 - (L_1^2 - (y_p - \dfrac{L}{2}\sin\theta)^2)^{-\frac{1}{2}}(y_p\ \dot{y}_p - \dfrac{L}{2}\dot{y}_p\sin\theta) \\[2mm]
\quad -(L_3^2 - (y_p + \dfrac{L}{2}\sin\theta - H)^2)^{-\frac{1}{2}}(y_p\ \dot{y}_p + \dfrac{L}{2}\dot{y}_p\sin\theta - H\ \dot{y}_p)
\end{cases}
\tag{14}
$$

## 3    Workspace Analysis

### 3.1    Maximal Range of Swing Angle under Given Position

(1) In Fig. 2, when the connecting rods 1 and 2 are collinear, point E is on the guide rail. If the slider C moves reciprocatively, the work platform 4 will have different postures. The angle between the connecting rod and the positive x-axis reaches its maximum (as shown in Fig. 2(b)) and its minimum (as shown in Fig. 2(e)), respectively; the maximal swing angle of the work platform 4 is:

$$
\Delta\theta = \theta - \theta' = \pi - 2\arcsin\frac{H - L_3}{L}
\tag{15}
$$

It demonstrates that the increase of $L$ and $L_3$ and the decrease of $H$ will increase the swing angle of the work platform 4.

(2) In Fig. 3, $L_1 < L_2$, neither $L_1$ nor $L_2$ is collinear with the horizontal guide rail, the shorter one of connecting rods 1 and 2 is perpendicular to the guide rail. When the slider C moves reciprocatively, the work platform 4 will have different postures. The angle between the connecting rod and the positive x-axis reaches its maximum (as shown in Fig. 3(b)) and its minimum (as shown in Fig. 3(f)), respectively. The following case $L_1 + L_2 > H$ is studied and its maximal swing angle of the work platform 4 is:

$$
\Delta\theta = \theta - \theta' = \pi + 2\arcsin\frac{L_1 + L_3 - H}{L}
\tag{16}
$$

It demonstrates that the increase of $L_1$ and $L_3$ and the decrease of $H$ and $L$ will increase the swing angle of the work platform 4.

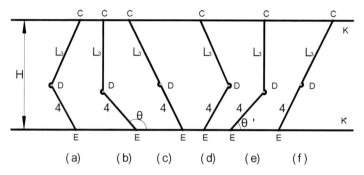

**Fig. 2.**    Postures of work platform ($L_1$ and $L_2$ are collinear)

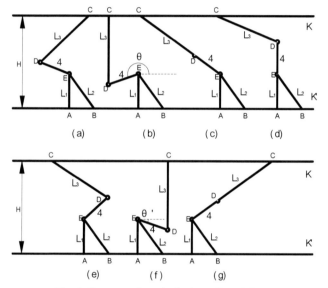

**Fig. 3.** Postures of work platform ($L_1 < L_2$)

In the experiment, $L_1 = L_2 = 500$ (unit: mm, same hereafter), the length of work platform $L = 500$, the distance between guide rails $H = 1000$. As $L_3$ increases from 500 to 1000, the maximal swing angle of work platform 4 is demonstrated in Fig. 4.

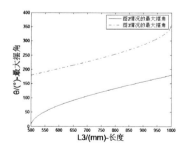

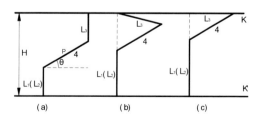

**Fig. 4.** Maximal swing angle of platform        **Fig. 5.** Limit positions of connecting rods

## 3.2    Maximal Range of Position (X, Y) under Given Orientation

To simplify the process, only one case is discussed ($L_1 = L_2 = L_3 = L$). The angle between the work platform and the positive x-axis $\theta$ is fixed. $L_k$ is the length of guild rails. Point $P(x_P, y_P)$ is the central position of work platform 4.

In Fig. 5(a), $L_0$ reaches its minimum, $L_{min} = \dfrac{H - L\sin\theta}{2}$, the movement of point P is linear and parallel to the guide rails. In Fig. 5(b), $L_0$ reaches its critical value, $L_{mid} = \dfrac{L^2 + H^2 - 2HL\sin\theta}{2(H - L\sin\theta)}$, $L_3$ reaches the left limit position of the guide rail. In Fig. 5(a), $L_0$ reaches its maximum, $L_{max} = H - L\sin\theta$, the movement of point P is linear and parallel to the guide rails.

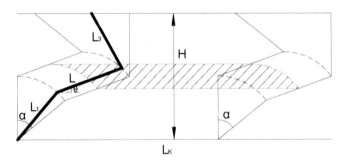

**Fig. 6.** Workspace of point P ($L_{min} < L_0 < L_{mid}$)

In Fig. 6, when $L_{min} < L_0 < L_{mid}$, the workspace of point P is:

$$S_1 = (L_0 - L_0\cos\alpha)(L_K - L_0\sin\alpha - L\cos\theta)$$

Where $\alpha = \arccos(\dfrac{H - L\sin\theta - L_0}{L_0})$

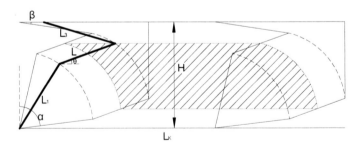

**Fig. 7.** Workspace of point P ($L_{mid} < L_0 < L_{max}$)

In Fig. 7, when $L_{mid} < L_0 < L_{max}$, the workspace of point P is:

$$S_2 = (L_0 - L_0\sin\beta)(L_K - L\cos\theta + L_0\sin\alpha)$$

Where $\alpha = \arccos(\dfrac{H - L\sin\theta - L_0}{L_0})$, $\beta$ is the angle between $L_3$ and the guild rail when the slider C reaches its left limit position.

By comparing Fig. 6 against Fig. 7, the following conclusion may be drawn: when $L_{mid} < L_0 < L_{max}$, the workspace of point P is larger.

## 4    Application and Experimental Prototype

Of various technological trajectories in industry, lines and circles are the most commonly used curves. Fig. 8 shows a trajectory composed of these basic curves, in which the specific coordinates are listed. In order to allow point P (Fig. 1) to move along the above-mentioned trajectory under same velocity, the corresponding displacement characteristics of three sliders must be met, which is shown in Fig.(9).

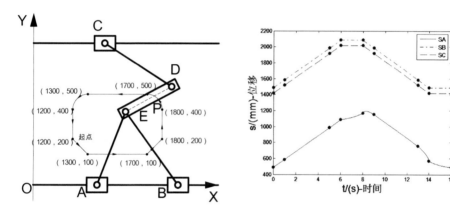

**Fig. 8.** Motion trajectory             **Fig. 9.** Displacement of three sliders

Figure 10 is the virtual experimental prototype of 3-DOF planar parallel manipulator. The physical prototype is under research and development.

**Fig. 10.** Virtual experimental prototype

## 5 Conclusions

A novel practical planar parallel mechanism with three sliders driven on two parallel guide rails is presented in this paper. Its work platform can change position and orientation to achieve high precision location of workpieces. The structure is simple and the manufacturing cost is low. It is easy to realize real-time control.

The direct and inverse kinematic solutions are deduced. The workspace analysis on the end-effector is conducted. Under the given orientation, the end-effector moves along the composite trajectory.The MATLAB simulation of displacement characteristics of three sliders is completed. The virtual experimental prototype is demonstrated. It lays the foundation for the precise control and industrial application of the 3-DOF planar parallel manipulator.

By allowing the end-effector to move in Z-direction or to rotate around A or B-axis, four, five- or six-axis manipulator would be composed. The industrial application of this 3-DOF parallel manipulator is promising and can be widely used in CNC machining, workpiece conveying and product testing.

**Acknowledgment.** Authors would like to appreciate the support by the National Natural Science Foundation of China (No. 51075045, 50875261) and Jiangsu Province Key Scientific & Technological Support and Self-innovation Projects(No.BE2010074, No.BE2010061) and Changzhou City S & T Project(No.CE20100050).

## References

1. Arakelian, V.H., Smith, M.R.: Design of Planar 3-DOF 3-RRR Reactionless Parallel Manipulators. Mechatronics 18(10), 601–606 (2008)
2. Gao, F., Liu, X.J., Chen, X.: The Relationships between the Shapes of the Workspaces and the Link Lengths of 3-DOF Symmetrical Planar Parallel Manipulators. Mechanism and Machine Theory 36(2), 205–220 (2001)
3. Kucuk, S.: A Dexterity Comparison for 3-DOF Planar Parallel Manipulators with Two Kinematic Chains Using Genetic Algorithms. Mechatronics 19(6), 868–877 (2009)
4. Han, X.Z., Huang, Y.M., Chen, C., Ma, B.L., Xu, H.W.: Kinematics Analysis of a New 3-DOF Planar Parallel Mechanism. Journal of Xi'an University of Technology 25(1), 23–27 (2009)
5. Qian, Y.M., Cao, Q.L.: Analysis of Planar Parallel Connected Mechanism With 3 – Freedom. Machine Design and Manufacturing Engineering 30(6), 29–33 (2001)
6. Yang, J.X., Yu, Y.Q.: Actuator Singularity Analysis of Planar 3-DOF Redundant Parallel Mechanisms. China Mechanical Engineering 17(6), 629–632 (2006)
7. Liu, S.Z., Yu, Y.Q., Si, G.N., Yang, J.X., Su, L.Y.: Kinematic and Dynamic Analysis of a Three-degree-of-freedom Parallel Manipulator. Journal of Mechanical Engineering 45(8), 11–17 (2009)
8. Shen, H.P., L, J., Wang, W., Ma, Z.H., Deng, J.M.: Three-slider Planar Type Numerical Control Operation Platform. China Patent Application CN 201010256966.3 (2010)

# Optimal Kinematic Design of a 2-DoF Translational Parallel Manipulator with High Speed and High Precision

Gang Zhang, PinKuan Liu, and Han Ding

State Key Laboratory of Mechanical System and Vibration, School of Mechanical Engineering,
Shanghai Jiaotong University, Shanghai 200240, China
{zgrobot,pkliu,hding}@sjtu.edu.cn

**Abstract.** This paper addresses the performance analysis and kinematic optimization of a 2-DoF translational parallel manipulator (TPM) with high speed and high precision. By combining the advantages of parallel manipulator and direct drive linear (DDL) motors, a new type of 2-DoF translational parallel manipulator is presented and explicit expressions of inverse and direct kinematic equations are derived. Based on the kinematic performance analysis of the 2-DoF TPM, a global and comprehensive performance index (GCPI), which is based on dexterity, stiffness, workspace and singularity avoidance, is proposed. The optimization results according to different performance indices are discussed. The proposed 2-DoF TPM is particularly suitable for applications requiring high-speed and high-precision motions.

**Keywords:** Translational parallel manipulator, direct drive, optimal kinematic design, global and comprehensive performance index (GCPI).

## 1    Introduction

The need for high-speed and high-precision positioning devices has been increasing in many fields of technology, particularly in high-speed machining [1], semiconductor manufacturing industries [2] and surgical robotic applications [3]. Compared with serial manipulators, parallel manipulators [4] are potential solutions to high-speed and high-precision applications due to their outstanding advantages, such as stiffness, dynamic characteristics, position accuracy, and load-to-weight ratio. However, parallel manipulators suffer from some drawbacks including small workspace, presentation of singular configuration and complicated dynamic model.

The first translational parallel manipulator (TPM), *i.e.* Delta, was proposed by Clavel [5], which used spatial parallelograms to realize translational motions in 3-D space. Since then, many TPMs with 3-DoF [6] and 2-DoF [7-8] have been introduced and intensively studied. Generally, the desired lower-mobility translational parallel manipulators should be symmetrical with identical limbs to meet the requirement of kinematic isotropy.

Conventionally, the positioning control of TPMs has been conducted with rotational motors with extra transmission mechanisms such as ball screws. These transmission mechanisms may introduce backlash and friction, which represents a

S. Jeschke, H. Liu, and D. Schilberg (Eds.): ICIRA 2011, Part I, LNAI 7101, pp. 445–454, 2011.

major drawback for high-speed applications. On the other hand, mechanisms with direct drive motors [9-10] seem very promising in motion speed, accuracy and reliability promotion, because the backlash is completely removed and friction is significantly reduced. These features may result in better control performances, higher positioning accuracy and much wider bandwidth for control response.

Optimal kinematic design is important in the development of parallel manipulators [11-12]. Workspace [13-14], manipulability [15-16], dexterity [17], isotropy [18-19], stiffness [20] and singularity [21] have been utilized to the kinematic optimization and performance evaluation of robotic manipulators. Merlet [22] pointed out the inconsistencies and concluded that these indices should not be satisfactory for parallel manipulators involving both translational and rotational motions.

By combining the advantages of parallel mechanism and direct drive, a new translational parallel manipulator is proposed. Firstly, the geometric description of the 2-DOF translational parallel manipulator is given in Section 2. Then, the position and velocity analysis of the TPM is performed and the explicit expressions of inverse and direct kinematics are derived in Section 3. Afterwards, kinematic performance indices of the TPM, including dexterity, stiffness, singularity and isotropy, are studied in Section 4. Moreover, based on the above kinematic performance indices, a global and comprehensive performance index (GCPI) is proposed as the objective function in Section 5. The optimization results are discussed with respect to different optimization criteria and important conclusions are drawn in Section 6.

## 2     Geometry of the TPM

The 2-DoF translational parallel manipulator is shown in Fig.1. It is composed of a moving platform, a fixed base, two sliders and two kinematic chains. The two sliders are parallel configured and horizontally mounted on the fixed base. The moving platform is connected to the sliders by two identical kinematic chains, each containing a parallelogram linkage. The parallelogram linkage can keep the moving platform parallel to the base, thus the output motion of moving platform is a planar 2-DoF rigid

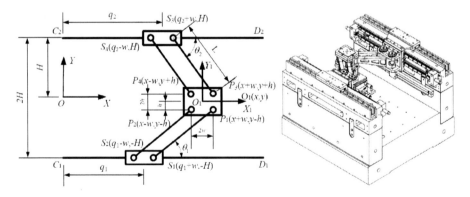

(a)    Schematics of the 2-DoF over-constrained TPM,          (b) CAD model of the TPM

**Fig. 1.** The Schematics and CAD model of the 2-DoF over-constrained TPM

translations of the moving platform with respect to the fixed base. As a result, the proposed TPM is denoted as 2-$\underline{P}$(Pa), where $\underline{P}$ is the actuated prismatic joint and Pa stands for the planar parallelogram. The proposed TPM is over-constrained to enable the static and dynamic symmetry and improve the stiffness in the direction normal to the plane of motion of the mechanism. In order to improve the dynamic performance and precision of the TPM, each slider is directly driven by a permanent magnet synchronous servo motor. Each direct drive linear (DDL) motor is equipped with an optical linear scale of sub-micrometer resolution for displacement measurement. By integrating the advantages of direct drive and parallel mechanisms, the over-constrained TPM can meet the requirements of applications requiring high-speed and high-precision motions.

# 3    Kinematic Analysis

## 3.1    Position Analysis

As illustrated in Fig.1(a), a reference coordinate system $o-XY$ is fixed on the fixed base and a body coordinate system $O_1-X_1Y_1$ is rigidly attached to the moving platform. The distance of the two sliders is 2H, the dimensions of the moving platform is $2w \times 2h$ and the length of links is L. $q = [q_1, q_2]^T$ is the joint space coordinates vector, where $q_1$ and $q_2$ are the actuated input displacements of two linear motors. $X = [x, y]^T$ is the vector of the operational space coordinates, where $(x, y)$ is the coordinates of the origin $O_1$ with respect to the reference coordinate system $O-XY$. $\theta = [\theta_1, \theta_2]^T$ is the vector of passive joint angles.

From Fig.1(a), the inverse kinematics of the TPM is analyzed via solving the constraint equations

$$|S_i P_i| = L, \quad i = 1,\dots,4. \tag{1}$$

Thus, the inverse kinematics of the TPM can be solved as

$$q_1 = x \pm \sqrt{L^2 - (y - h + H)^2} \tag{2}$$

$$q_2 = x \pm \sqrt{L^2 - (y + h - H)^2} \tag{3}$$

It can be seen that there are four solutions for the inverse kinematic problem. Corresponding to Fig.1(a), the signs "$\pm$" in Eqs. (2) and (3) are both "$-$".

The explicit expressions of direct kinematics analysis problem of the 2-DoF TPM are derived from Eqs. (2) and (3)

$$y = ax + b \tag{4}$$

$$x = \frac{-d \pm \sqrt{d^2 - 4ce}}{2c} \tag{5}$$

where $a = \dfrac{q_1 - q_2}{2(H - h)}$, $b = \dfrac{q_2^2 - q_1^2}{4(H - h)}$, $c = a^2 + 1$, $d = 2a(b - h + H) - 2q_1$, $e = q_1^2 + (b - h + H)^2 - L^2$

## 3.2    Velocity Analysis and Jacobian Matrix

By differentiating Eq.(1) with respect to time, one can obtain the velocities equations

$$J_x \dot{X} = J_q \dot{q},$$
(6)

where  $J_x$ — direct Jacobian matrix,

$J_q$ — inverse Jacobian matrix,

$\dot{X} = [\dot{x} \quad \dot{y}]^T$ — vector of the operational space velocities,

$\dot{q} = [\dot{q}_1 \quad \dot{q}_2]^T$ — vector of the joint space velocities.

If matrix  $J_q$  is non-singular, the inverse kinematics can be written

$$\dot{q} = J\dot{X}$$
(7)

where

$$J = J_q^{-1} J_x = \begin{bmatrix} 1 & \tan\theta_1 \\ 1 & \tan\theta_2 \end{bmatrix},$$
(8)

is the Jacobian matrix of the 2-DoF TPM.

# 4     Kinematic Performance Analysis

Optimal kinematic design is one of the most important issues in the development of parallel manipulators and the evaluation of the kinematic performances is important in the process of manipulators design and applications.

## 4.1    Dexterity

The dexterity of a manipulator is considered as the ability to perform small displacements of its end-effector at a specified pose of its workspace. It is defined on the basis of the condition number of the Jacobian matrix

$$1 \le \kappa_J = \frac{\sigma_{max}}{\sigma_{min}} \le \infty$$
(9)

where  $\sigma_{max}$ , $\sigma_{min}$  represent the maximum and minimum singular values of the Jacobian matrix and $1,\infty$ correspond to the isotropic and singular configuration respectively. The reciprocal of the condition number is often used for it is better behaved than  $\kappa_J$  over the whole workspace. In fact, it is bounded as

$$0 \le \frac{1}{\kappa_J} \le 1,$$
(10)

The condition number is related to a given configuration and thus is called local conditioning index (LCI) of parallel manipulators. For the investigated TPM in this paper, closed-form solution to the condition number can be obtained as

$$\kappa_J = \frac{\sigma_{max}}{\sigma_{min}} = \left( \frac{2 + J_{12}^2 + J_{22}^2 + \sqrt{(2 + J_{12}^2 + J_{22}^2)^2 - 4(J_{12} - J_{22})^2}}{2 + J_{12}^2 + J_{22}^2 - \sqrt{(2 + J_{12}^2 + J_{22}^2)^2 - 4(J_{12} - J_{22})^2}} \right)^{\frac{1}{2}},$$
(11)

where  $J_{12} = \cos\theta_1$  and  $J_{22} = \cos\theta_2$ .

The distribution of the LCI for the investigated TPM is shown in Fig.2, from which we can see that LCI is symmetric with respect to the $X$ axis.

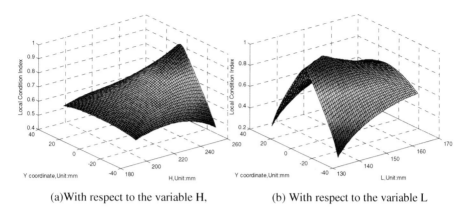

(a)With respect to the variable H,          (b) With respect to the variable L

**Fig. 2.** Distribution of local conditioning index over the workspace

To obtain a performance measure of the global behavior of the manipulator condition number, global conditioning index (GCI) [23] should be used to assess the distribution of condition index over the whole workspace. Similar to GCI proposed by Huang and Gosselin [7], a global performance measure is adopted.

$$1 \leq \eta_1 = \frac{\int_w \kappa_J \, dw_t}{\int_w dw_t} \leq \infty ,$$  (12)

where $w_t$ is the task workspace of the robot manipulator.

Since GCI itself could not give a full-scaled description of the overall global kinematic performance. Another conditioning index [7], denoted by $\eta_2$, is adopted.

$$1 \leq \eta_2 = \frac{\max(\kappa_J)}{\min(\kappa_J)} \leq \infty ,$$  (13)

where $\max(\kappa_J)$ and $\min(\kappa_J)$ represent the maximum and minimum value of $\kappa_J$ in the task workspace of the 2-DoF TPM.

## 4.2   Isotropy

According to the definition given by Ref.[17], a general parallel manipulator is called isotropic if it can attain at least one configuration in which the conditions below are simultaneously met

$$J_x^T J_x = \begin{bmatrix} \alpha^2 \mathbf{I}_3 & \mathbf{0}_3 \\ \mathbf{0}_3 & \alpha^2 \mathbf{I}_3 \end{bmatrix}, J_q^T J_q = \begin{bmatrix} \beta^2 \mathbf{I}_3 & \mathbf{0}_n \\ \mathbf{0}_n^T & \beta^2 \mathbf{I}_3 \end{bmatrix} ,$$  (14)

where $\mathbf{0}_3$ and $\mathbf{I}_3$ are $3 \times 3$ zero and identity matrices respectively, while $\mathbf{0}_n$ is the $n \times (m - n)$ zero matrix and $\alpha$ and $\beta$ are real-valued constants.

From Eq.(14), The conditions of kinematic isotropy of the 2-DoF TPM can be expressed as following

$$\theta_1 = \theta_2 = \frac{\pi}{4}, H - h = \frac{\sqrt{2}}{2} L \cdot \qquad (15)$$

### 4.3    Stiffness

The stiffness matrix of parallel manipulator is given [20] by the following expression:

$$S = kJ^T J , \qquad (16)$$

where $k$ is a scalar representing the stiffness of each actuator. In order to measure of the uniformity of the stiffness among the direction defined by parallel manipulator's generalized coordinates, local stiffness index (LSI) is proposed, which is defined as the condition number of the stiffness matrix

$$\kappa_s = \frac{\lambda_{max}}{\lambda_{min}} , \qquad (17)$$

where $\lambda_{max}$ and $\lambda_{min}$ represent the maximum and minimum singular values of the stiffness matrix $S$ . The distribution of the LSI for the 2-DoF TPM is shown in Fig.3, from which we can see that LSI is also symmetric with respect to the $X$ axis.

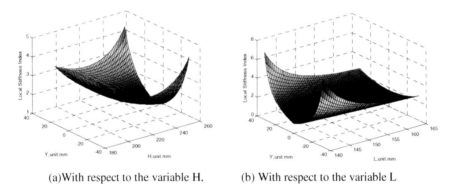

(a)With respect to the variable H,        (b) With respect to the variable L

**Fig. 3.** Distribution of local stiffness index over the task workspace of the 2-DoF TPM

The global stiffness index (GSI) of parallel manipulator is defined as the condition number of stiffness matrix integrated over the prescribed task workspace and divided by the volume of the task workspace, which can be written as

$$1 \leq \eta_3 = \frac{\int_w \kappa_s dw_t}{\int_w dw_t} \leq \infty \cdot \qquad (18)$$

Similar to the conditioning index proposed by Ref. [7], another stiffness index, denoted by $\eta_4$, can be defined to describe the deviation between the maximum and minimum value of $\kappa_s$ over the prescribed task workspace of parallel manipulator

$$1 \leq \eta_4 = \frac{\max(\kappa_s)}{\min(\kappa_s)} \leq \infty , \qquad (19)$$

where $\max(\kappa_s)$ and $\min(\kappa_s)$ represent the maximum and minimum value of $\kappa_s$ .

## 4.4     Singularity Avoidance

To avoid singularity and get better force transmission behaviors, the passive joint angles $\theta = [\theta_1, \theta_2]^T$ should be kept within a given range. Therefore, according to the given range of passive joint angles, the maximum workspace along the $Y$-axis can be defined. Thus, a measure of the workspace index $(WI)$ can be defined

$$1 \leq WI = \frac{y_{max}}{y_w} \leq \infty \tag{20}$$

As illustrated in Fig.4, $y_{max}$ and $y_w$ represent the reachable workspace and the prescribed task workspace along the $Y$-axis.

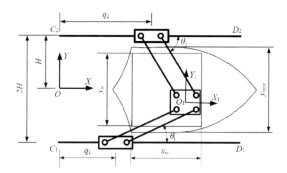

**Fig. 4.** Reachable workspace and prescribed task workspace of the 2-DoF TPM

# 5     Optimal Kinematic Design

According to the requirements of electrical packaging [2], the proposed 2-DoF TPM is designed to have a task workspace of $x_w \times y_w = 70mm \times 70mm$ in $o - xy$ plane and an acceleration exceeding 10 g ($1g = 9.81m/s^2$) with a resolution of micron level. In this section, the optimal kinematic design of the 2-DoF TPM is studied.

## 5.1     Objective Function

Based on the previous discussion, different global and comprehensive kinematic performance indices can be defined as an objective function to be minimized.

1. Global and comprehensive conditioning index (GCCI)

$$\eta_C = \sqrt{(w_1 \eta_1)^2 + (w_2 \eta_2)^2}, (w_i \neq 0, i = 1, 2). \tag{21}$$

This index has been used in Ref. [7] as a performance criterion for the dimensional synthesis of a novel 2-DoF translational parallel robot for pick-and-place operations.

2. Global and comprehensive stiffness index (GCSI)

$$\eta_S = \sqrt{(w_3 \eta_3)^2 + (w_4 \eta_4)^2}, (w_i \neq 0, i = 3, 4). \tag{22}$$

3. Global and comprehensive performance index (GCPI)

$$\eta = \sqrt{(w_1\eta_1)^2 + (w_2\eta_2)^2 + (w_3\eta_3)^2 + (w_4\eta_4)^2} , (w_i \neq 0, i = 1, \cdots, 4) , \qquad (23)$$

where $w_i (i = 1, \cdots, 4)$ are the weights associated to the different performance criteria.

From Eq.(8), it can be seen that the vector of design variables is $[x_1, x_2]^T = [H - h, L]^T$, since the element of the Jacobian matrix is only related to $H - h$.

## 5.2 Constraints

The prescribed task workspace of the TPM should be kept away from singularity. This can be done by the constraints of the passive joint angles within the range of $[15°, 75°]$ to avoid singularity and ensure acceptable force transmission behavior.

Another constraint to be considered is the workspace index For the investigated TPM, the workspace index can be set as

$$1 \leq WI \leq 1.5 . \qquad (24)$$

Thus, the optimization problem can be formulated as follows.

To find a set of optimal design parameters $[x_1, x_2]^T \in \mathbb{R}^2$ such that

$$\min \quad \eta$$

Subject to:         $15° \leq \theta_i (X, q) \leq 75°$   $i = 1, 2$

$1 \leq WI \leq 1.5$

$x_i \in [x_{i,min}, x_{i,max}]$   $i = 1, 2$

$\forall (x, y) \in (x_w, y_w)$

## 5.3 Optimization Results and Discussion

For the computer implementation, the kinematic optimization problem of the 2-DoF TPM is solved by the sequential quadratic programming (SQP) algorithm available in the MATLAB optimization toolbox and $\eta_i$ is calculated by

$$\eta_1 = \frac{1}{N}\sum_{i=1}^{N}\kappa_{J,i}, \quad \eta_2 = \frac{\max(\kappa_{J,i})}{\min(\kappa_{J,i})}, \quad \eta_3 = \frac{1}{N}\sum_{i=1}^{N}\kappa_{S,i}, \quad \eta_4 = \frac{\max(\kappa_{S,i})}{\min(\kappa_{S,i})} \qquad (25)$$

where $\kappa_{J,n}$ and $\kappa_{S,n}$ are the values of the condition number of Jacobian and stiffness matrix evaluated at node $i$ of equally meshed task workspace in the $Y$ axis.

The optimization design starts from the initial values of isotropic configuration. The results in terms of different criteria and the time used to calculate the optimization results are listed in Table 1 and shown in Fig.5.

Table 1. Original values of design variables and optimized results of the 2-DoF TPM

| Index | Weight values | Original values | Optimized results | Time (s) |
|---|---|---|---|---|
| GCCI | $w_1 = w_2 = 1$ | $x_1 = 100, x_2 = 141$ | $x_1 = 96.6704, x_2 = 170.6612$ | 28.1404 |
| GCSI | $w_3 = w_4 = 1$ | $x_1 = 110, x_2 = 156$ | $x_1 = 95.2255, x_2 = 165.0789$ | 30.1472 |
| GCPI | $w_i = 1, (i = 1, \ldots, 4)$ | $x_1 = 120, x_2 = 170$ | $x_1 = 95.4763, x_2 = 166.0476$ | 41.8932 |

It is shown From Table.1 and Fig.5 that the optimization scheme is robust since different initial values converge to the same optimization result. Although the condition of isotropy can provide an isotropic configuration in the workspace, it does not guarantee the optimal performance over the whole workspace, thus, the global and comprehensive performance indices should be used in the optimal kinematic design of parallel manipulators.

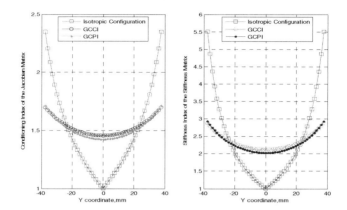

Performance indices of the (a) Jacobian matrix and (b) Stiffness matrix

**Fig. 5.** Initial values and the optimization results of the 2-DoF TPM

## 6    Conclusions

In this study, we investigated the optimal kinematic design of a 2-DoF translational parallel manipulator. The following conclusions can be drawn:

1. By combining the advantages of parallel mechanism and direct drive, a novel translational parallel manipulator is proposed in this paper, which can meet the requirements of applications requiring high-speed and high-precision motions.

2. A global and comprehensive kinematic performance index (GCPI) in terms of both dexterity and stiffness indices is proposed in this paper. This index can also be extended to the optimal kinematic design of other parallel manipulators when the performance indices of dexterity and stiffness have priority.

3. Based on the optimization results, the proposed TPM has been employed to the development of a prototype (Fig.1), which is being constructed in the Advanced Electronic Manufacturing Center of Shanghai Jiaotong University.

**Acknowledgement.** This work is supported in part by the Important National Science & Technology Specific Projects under Grant No. 2009ZX02006-002 and the Science & Technology Commission of Shanghai Municipality under Grant No. 09JC1408300.

## References

1. Heisel, U., Gringel, M.: Machine tool design requirements for high-speed machining. CIRP Annals - Manufacturing Technology 45(1), 389–392 (1996)
2. Ding, H., Xiong, Z.: Motion stages for electronic packaging design and control. IEEE Robotics and Automation Magazine 13(4), 51–61 (2006)

454 G. Zhang, P.K. Liu, and H. Ding

3. Taylor, R.H., Stoianovici, D.: Medical Robotics in Computer-Integrated Surgery. IEEE Transactions on Robotics and Automation 19(5), 765–781 (2003)
4. Tsai, L.W.: Robot analysis: The mechanics of serial and parallel manipulators. In: Robot Analysis: The Mechanics of Serial and Parallel Manipulators (1999)
5. Clavel, R.: Delta, a fast robot with parallel geometry. In: 18th International Symposium on Industrial Robots, pp. 91–100 (1988)
6. Tsai, L.W., Joshi, S.: Kinematics and optimization of a spatial 3-UPU parallel manipulator. Journal of Mechanical Design, Transactions of the ASME 122(4), 439–446 (2000)
7. Huang, T., et al.: Conceptual design and dimensional synthesis of a novel 2-DOF translational parallel robot for pick-and-place operations. Journal of Mechanical Design, Transactions of the ASME 126(3), 449–455 (2004)
8. Liu, X.J., Wang, Q.I.M., Wang, J.: Kinematics, dynamics and dimensional synthesis of a novel 2-DoF translational manipulator. Journal of Intelligent and Robotic Systems: Theory and Applications 41(4), 205–224 (2005)
9. Asada, H., Youcef-Toumi, K.: Direct Drive Robots: Theory and Practice (1987)
10. Pritschow, G.: A comparison of linear and conventional electromechanical dives. CIRP Annals - Manufacturing Technology 47(2), 541–548 (1998)
11. Liu, X.J.: Optimal kinematic design of a three translational DoFs parallel manipulator. Robotica 24(2), 239–250 (2006)
12. Stock, M., Miller, K.: Optimal kinematic design of spatial parallel manipulators: Application to linear delta robot. Journal of Mechanical Design, Transactions of the ASME 125(2), 292–301 (2003)
13. Merlet, J.E.: Designing a parallel manipulator for a specific workspace. International Journal of Robotics Research 16(4), 545–556 (1997)
14. Gosselin, C.M., Guillot, M.: Synthesis of manipulators with prescribed workspace. Journal of Mechanical Design 113(4), 451–455 (1991)
15. Yoshikawa, T.: Manipulability of Robotic Mechanisms. International Journal of Robotics Research 4(2), 3–9 (1985)
16. Yoshikawa, T.: Dynamic Manipulability of Robot Manipulators. Journal of Robotic Systems 2(1), 113–124 (1985)
17. Gosselin, C.M.: The optimum design of robotic manipulators using dexterity indices. Robotics and Autonomous Systems 9(4), 213–226 (1992)
18. Alici, G., Shirinzadeh, B.: Optimum synthesis of planar parallel manipulators based on kinematic isotropy and force balancing. Robotica 22(1), 97–108 (2004)
19. Zanganeh, K.E., Angeles, J.: Kinematic isotropy and the optimum design of parallel manipulators. International Journal of Robotics Research 16(2), 185–197 (1997)
20. Gosselin, C.: Stiffness mapping for parallel manipulators. IEEE Transactions on Robotics and Automation 6(3), 377–382 (1990)
21. Gosselin, C., Angeles, J.: Singularity analysis of closed-loop kinematic chains. IEEE Transactions on Robotics and Automation 6(3), 281–290 (1990)
22. Merlet, J.P.: Jacobian, manipulability, condition number, and accuracy of parallel robots. Journal of Mechanical Design, Transactions of the ASME 128(1), 199–206 (2006)
23. Gosselin, C., Angeles, J.: Global performance index for the kinematic optimization of robotic manipulators. Journal of Mechanisms, Transmissions, and Automation in Design 113(3), 220–226 (1991)

# Modeling and Control of Cable Driven Parallel Manipulators with Elastic Cables: Singular Perturbation Theory

Alaleh Vafaei[1], Mohammad A. Khosravi[2], and Hamid D. Taghirad[2]

[1] Electrical and Computer Engineering Department,
[2] Advanced Robotics and Automated Systems (ARAS),
Faculty of Electrical and Computer Engineering, University of Tehran,
K.N. Toosi University of Technology

**Abstract.** This paper presents a new approach to the modeling and control of cable driven parallel manipulators and particularly KNTU CDRPM. First, dynamical model of the cable driven parallel manipulator is derived considering the elasticity of the cables, and then this model is rewritten in the standard form of singular perturbation theory. This theory used here as an effective tool for modeling the cable driven manipulators. Next, the integrated controller, applied for control of the rigid model of KNTU CDRPM in previous researches, is improved and a composite controller is designed for the elastic model of the robot. Asymptotic stability analysis of the proposed rigid controller is studied in detail. Finally, a simulation study performed on the KNTU CDRPM verifies the closed-loop performance compared to the rigid model controller.

## 1 Introduction

Cable driven parallel robots are a special kind of parallel robots in which rigid links are replaced by cables. This has produced some advantages for cable driven ones that has attracted the attention of researches [1,2,3]. High acceleration due to the reduced mobile mass, larger workspace, transportability and ease of assembly/disassembly, economical structure and maintenance are among these advantages. The most important limitation of cable driven robots is that, the cables suffer from unidirectional constraints that can only be pulled and not pushed. In this class of robots, the cables must be in tension in the whole workspace. Cables are sagged under compression forces, and therefore, to enable tension forces in the cables throughout the whole workspace, the mechanism must be designed over-constrained [4]. KNTU CDRPM is an over-constrained parallel manipulator that uses a novel design to achieve high stiffness, accurate positioning for high-speed maneuvers [5]. Controller must ensure that the cables are always in positive tension by using an appropriate redundancy resolution scheme, [5].

The major challenge in the controller design of these robots is deformation of the cables under tension. Elongation is one kind of these deformations that causes position and orientation errors. Moreover, the flexibility of the cables may

S. Jeschke, H. Liu, and D. Schilberg (Eds.): ICIRA 2011, Part I, LNAI 7101, pp. 455–464, 2011.

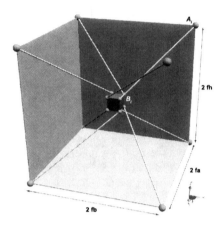

**Fig. 1.** The KNTU CDRPM, a perspective view

lead the system to vibration, and cause the whole system to be uncontrollable [6]. Although cable behavior has been the subject of researches in civil engineering but different use of them in parallel robots requires new studies. Cables in parallel robots are much lighter than one used in civil engineering and usually we have large changes in cable length and the tension exerted to them. Reported studies on the effect of cable flexibility on modeling, optimal design and control of such manipulators are very limited and usually neglected.

It should be noticed that a complete dynamic model of cable robots is very complicated. Furthermore, such complicated models are useless for controller design strategies, although they can accurately describe dynamic intrinsic characteristics of cables. Thus, in practice it is proposed to include only the dominant effects in the dynamics analysis. For this reason in many robotics applications, cables mass have been neglected and cable has been considered as a rigid element [7,8]. With those assumptions the dynamics of cable driven robot is reduced to the end-effector dynamics, that will lead to some inaccuracies in tracking error and especially the stability of the manipulator. In this paper a more precise model of the cable driven robot considering cable flexibility is derived and being used in the controller design and stability analysis. Using natural frequencies of system, Diao and Ma have shown in [9] that in fully constrained cable driven robots the vibration of cable manipulator due to the transversal vibration of cables can be ignored in comparison to that of cable axial flexibility. By this means, this model can describe the dominant dynamic characteristics of cable and can be used in the dynamic model of cable robot. Based on this observation, in this paper axial spring is used to model cable dynamics.

In this paper, considering axial flexibility in cables, a new dynamical model for cable driven robots is presented. This model is formulated in the standard form of *singular perturbation theory*. The most contribution of this theory in solving the control problems of the systems is in the modeling part [10]. By using the obtained model, the control of the system is studied. Next, the stability of the system is analyzed through Lyapunov second method and it is proven that the closed–loop system with the proposed control algorithm is stable. Finally the performance of the proposed algorithm is examined through simulation.

## 2   Singular Perturbation Standard Model

The singular perturbation model of a dynamical system is a state space model where the derivatives of some of the states are multiplied by a small positive scalar $\varepsilon$, that is [11]

$$\dot{x} = f(x, z, \varepsilon, t) \ \ x \in R^n \tag{1}$$

$$\varepsilon \dot{z} = g(x, z, \varepsilon, t) \ \ z \in R^m \tag{2}$$

It is assumed that $f$, $g$ have continuous derivatives along $(t, x, z, \varepsilon) \in [0, t_1] \times D_1 \times D_2 \times [0, \varepsilon_0]$, on their domains $D_1 \subset R^n$ and $D_2 \subset R^m$. Putting $\varepsilon = 0$, the dimension of the standard model reduces from $m + n$ to $n$, since the differential equation (2) changes to

$$g(x, z, \varepsilon, t) = 0 \tag{3}$$

The model (1) and (2) is an standard model, if and only if, the equation (3), has $k \geq 1$ distinct real solutions:

$$z = h_i(t, x) \ \forall [t, x] \in [0, t_1], i = 1, 2, 3, \dots \tag{4}$$

This assumption ensures that the reduced model with appropriate order of $n$ is related to the roots of equation (3). For achieving the $i$-th reduced order model, substitute (4) in (1) and assume $\varepsilon = 0$, then:

$$\dot{x} = f(t, x, h(t, x), 0) \tag{5}$$

This approximation is a wise simplification of the dynamic system in which the high frequency dynamics is neglected, which is sometimes called a quasi-steady model. Since the velocity of variable $z$ i.e. $\dot{z} = g/\varepsilon$ can be a large number while $\varepsilon$ is small and $g \neq 0$, therefore, variable $z$ converges rapidly to the roots of equation $g = 0$, the quasi-steady form of (2). The equation (5) is often called slow model.

## 3   Dynamics

Due to redundancy characteristic of KNTU CDRPM and other over–constrained cable driven parallel manipulators, the sagging of the cables is neglected. A simple model that can hold elastic characteristic of the cable and also can be used in controller design procedure, is to model the cable as a spring. This simple model can be well included in singular perturbation theory in order to derive a dynamic model for KNTU CDRPM considering elasticity of the cables. In what follows, we will first describe the dynamics of rigid robot briefly and then dynamic equations of the elastic system are derived using rigid ones. In the next step the dynamics equations are formulated in the standard form of singular perturbation theory.

## 3.1  Dynamics with Ideal Cables

The rigid model of parallel robots can be formulated into the general form of [12]:

$$M(x)\ddot{x} + C(x, \dot{x})\dot{x} + G(x) = J^T \tau \tag{6}$$

in which, $x$ is the vector of generalized coordinates showing the position and orientation of the end-effector, $M(x)$ is a $6 \times 6$ matrix called mass matrix, $C(x, \dot{x})$ is a $6 \times 6$ matrix representing the *Coriolis* and *centrifugal* forces, $G(x)$ is a $6 \times 1$ vector of gravitational forces, $J$ $n \times 6$ denotes the Jacobian matrix, $\tau$ $n \times 1$ is the cable tension vector. $n$ is equal to the number of cables and for KNTU CDRPM it is equal to 8. The actuator dynamics can be represented as

$$M_m \ddot{L} + D\dot{L} + \tau = u \tag{7}$$

in which, $L$ is the $n \times 1$ cable length vector, $M_m$ is a diagonal $n \times n$ inertia matrix of actuators, $D$ a diagonal $n \times n$ matrix including viscous friction coefficients for actuators (pulleys), $\tau$ $n \times 1$ cable tension vector, $u : n \times 1$ actuator input vector. Use equations (6) and (7) to derive

$$M_{eq}(x)\ddot{x} + C_{eq}(x, \dot{x})\dot{x} + G_{eq}(x) = J^T u \tag{8}$$

in which,

$$\begin{aligned}
M_{eq}(x) &= M(x) + J^T M_m J \\
C_{eq}(x, \dot{x}) &= C(x, \dot{x}) + J^T M_m \dot{J} + J^T D J \\
G_{eq}(x) &= G(x)
\end{aligned} \tag{9}$$

## 3.2  Dynamics with Real Cables

In parallel manipulators with elastic cables, actuator position is not directly related to end-effector position, and therefore, both the actuator and the end-effector positions must be taken into state vector. In other words both the cable length in the unloaded state and the cable length under tension are taken as state vector. For modeling a parallel manipulator with $n$ cables, we assume $\hat{L}_{1i} : i = 1, 2, ..., n$ indicate the length of $i$-th cable under tension and $\hat{L}_{2i} : i = 1, 2, ..., n$ indicate the $i$-th cable without tension. In the case of rigid system, we have: $\hat{L}_{1i} = \hat{L}_{2i} (\forall i)$. In vector representation

$$L = (\hat{L}_{11}, ..., \hat{L}_{1n}, \hat{L}_{21}, ..., \hat{L}_{2n})^T = (L_1^T | L_2^T) \tag{10}$$

The kinetic energy of the system is

$$T = \frac{1}{2}\dot{x}^T M(x)\dot{x}^T + \frac{1}{2}\dot{L}_2^T M_m \dot{L}_2 \tag{11}$$

The sum of total potential energy of the system is

$$P = P_1 + P_2(L_1 - L_2) \tag{12}$$

In which $P_1$ is the potential energy of the rigid robot and the second term, the potential energy of the $i$-th cable which its elasticity is approximated with a linear spring, is as follows

$$P_2 = \frac{1}{2}(L_1 - L_2)^T K (L_1 - L_2) \tag{13}$$

and $K$ is the matrix of the stiffness coefficients of cables. Now the Lagrangian of the system is derived by $L = T - P$, as

$$L = \frac{1}{2}\dot{x}^T M(x)\dot{x} + \frac{1}{2}\dot{L}_2^T M_m \dot{L}_2 - P_1 - \frac{1}{2}(L_1 - L_2)^T K(L_1 - L_2) \tag{14}$$

The total dynamic equations of the system is derived simply by applying the Lagrange equations

$$\begin{cases} M(x)\ddot{x} + C(x,\dot{x})\dot{x} + G(x) = J^T K(L_2 - L_1) \\ M_m \ddot{L}_2 + K(L_2 - L_1) + D\dot{L}_2 = u \end{cases} \tag{15}$$

in which, the relation between $x$ and $L_1$ is obtained by $\dot{L}_1 = J\dot{x}$. Furthermore, in eq. (15), $K$ is the $n \times n$ diagonal stiffness matrix of the cables, $M(x)$ the $6 \times 6$ inertia matrix, $C(x,\dot{x})$ a $6 \times 6$ matrix with *Coriolis* and *centrifugal* terms, $G(x)$ the $6 \times 1$ vector of gravitational forces, $J$ the $n \times 6$ Jacobian matrix, $M_m$ the diagonal $n \times n$ inertia matrix of actuators(pulleys), $D$ the diagonal $n \times n$ matrix including viscous friction coefficients for actuators, and $n = 8$ for KNTU CDRPM.

## 3.3    Singular Perturbation Model

The spring stiffness matrix $K$ which connects two equations in (15) enables us to formulate these equations in singular perturbation form. /without loss of generality, assume that all of the cables stiffness are equal. Then write the elastic forces in the cables in the form $z = k(L_1 - L_2)$, $K = kI$. Since the singular perturbation theory is defined usually for small terms, define $\varepsilon = 1/k$, therefore $\varepsilon \to 0$ as $k \to \infty$. Multiplying two sides of the first line of equation (15) by $M^{-1}$ and consider $z = k(L_1 - L_2)$, we have

$$\begin{cases} \ddot{x} = -M^{-1}(x)J^T z - M^{-1}(x)(C(x,\dot{x})\dot{x} + G(x)) \\ -\varepsilon\ddot{z} = M_m^{-1}z - M_m^{-1}D\dot{L}_2 + M_m^{-1}u - \ddot{L}_1 \end{cases} \tag{16}$$

Considering the following equations,

$$\begin{aligned} \dot{L}_2 &= \dot{L}_1 - \varepsilon\dot{z} \\ \dot{L}_1 &= J\dot{x} \\ \ddot{L}_1 &= J\ddot{x} + \dot{J}\dot{x} \end{aligned} \tag{17}$$

We can summarize equation (16), which is in the standard form of singular perturbation theory in the form

$$\begin{cases} \ddot{x} = a_1(x,\dot{x}) + A_1(x)z \\ \varepsilon\ddot{z} = a_2(x,\dot{x},\varepsilon\dot{z}) + A_2(x)z + B_2 u \end{cases} \tag{18}$$

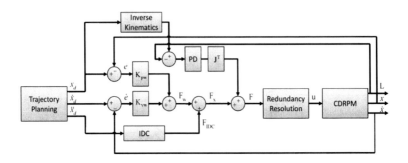

**Fig. 2.** The cascade control scheme

In which

$$A_1 = -M^{-1}(x)J^T$$
$$a_1 = -M^{-1}(x)(C(x,\dot{x})\dot{x} + G(x))$$
$$a_2 = -\varepsilon M_m^{-1}D\dot{z} + M_m^{-1}DJ\dot{x} - JM^{-1}(x)(C(x,\dot{x}) + G(x)) + \dot{J}\dot{x}$$
$$A_2 = -(J(x)M^{-1}(x)J^T(x) + M_m^{-1}),$$
$$B_2 = -M_m^{-1}$$

Note that the rigid model is the marginal mode of the elastic model of eq. (6), when the stiffness of the cables tends to infinity or $\varepsilon \to 0$.

## 4   Control

### 4.1   Control Law for the Rigid Model

The controller applied to the rigid model is a combination of two control loops with an inverse-dynamic controller. The first control loop is a PD controller in joint-space and the second one in work space (Fig. 2). It is shown that this controller can improve the performance of the control system up to 80% compared to conventional single loop controllers [5]. The structure of this controller is illustrated in Fig. 2 and the control law is defined as:

$$F = F_j + F_x$$
$$F_j = J^T(K_{pj}(L_d - L) + K_{vj}(\dot{L}_d - \dot{L}))$$
$$F_x = K_{pw}(x_d - x) + K_{vw}(\dot{x}_d - \dot{x}) + M_{eq}\ddot{x}_d + G_{eq} + C_{eq}\dot{x}_d \qquad (19)$$
$$u = P + P_n = (J^T)^\dagger F + (I - J^{T\dagger}J^T)k_e$$

in which, $(\cdot)^\dagger$ denotes the pseudo inverse and $(\cdot)_d$ denote the desired values. $P$ and $P_n$ are defined as

$$F = J^T P$$
$$0 = J^T P_n$$

and $k_e$ is an $n$ dimensional vector which is optimized through redundancy resolution scheme, [5]. $K_{pj}, K_{vj}, K_{pw}$ and $K_{vw}$ are diagonal positive definite matrices.

**Stability Analysis of the Closed-loop System.** First, let us derive the error dynamics to prove the stability of the closed-loop system using the controller in equation (19). According to the robot dynamic equations (8) and control law we can write

$$
\begin{aligned}
M_{eq}\ddot{x} + C_{eq}\dot{x} + G_{eq} &= K_{pw}(x_d - x) + K_{vw}(\dot{x}_d - \dot{x}) + M_{eq}\ddot{x}_d + \\
&\quad G_{eq} + C_{eq}\dot{x}_d + J^T(K_{pj}(L_d - L) + K_{vj}(\dot{L}_d - \dot{L}))
\end{aligned}
\tag{20}
$$

Or,

$$
M_{eq}\ddot{e} + (K_{vw} + J^T K_{vj} J)\dot{e} + K_{pw}e + J^T K_{pj}e_L + C_{eq}\dot{e} = 0
\tag{21}
$$

in which, $e_L = L_d - L$ and $e = x_d - x$. Now, introduce a Lyapunov candidate to prove the stability of the system under control.

$$
V = \frac{1}{2}\dot{e}^T M_{eq}\dot{e} + \frac{1}{2}e^T K_{pw}e + \frac{1}{2}e_L^T K_{pj}e_L
\tag{22}
$$

in which, $M_{eq}$, $K_{pw}$ and $K_{pj}$ matrices are positive definite, therefore V is positive definite. The derivative of Lyapunov function is:

$$
\dot{V} = \dot{e}^T M_{eq}\ddot{e} + \frac{1}{2}\dot{e}^T \dot{M}_{eq}\dot{e} + e^T K_{pw}\dot{e} + e_L^T K_{pj}\dot{e}_L
\tag{23}
$$

Substitute the term $M_{eq}\ddot{e}$ from the dynamic equations of the system.

$$
\begin{aligned}
\dot{V} &= \dot{e}^T(-(K_{vw} + J^T K_{vj} J)\dot{e} - K_{pw}e - J^T K_{pj}e_L - C_{eq}\dot{e}) \\
&\quad + \tfrac{1}{2}\dot{e}^T \dot{M}_{eq}\dot{e} + e^T K_{pw}\dot{e} + e_L^T K_{pj}\dot{e}_L
\end{aligned}
\tag{24}
$$

Hence,

$$
\begin{aligned}
\dot{V} &= -\dot{e}^T(K_{vw} + J^T K_{vj} J)\dot{e} + \frac{1}{2}\dot{e}^T(\dot{M}_{eq} - 2C_{eq})\dot{e} \\
&= -\dot{e}^T(K_{vw} + J^T K_{vj} J + 2J^T DJ)\dot{e} \leq 0
\end{aligned}
\tag{25}
$$

note that $J^T K_{vj} J$ is a positive semi-definite (PSD) matrix, because $K_{vj}$ is PD and

$$
y^T(J^T K_{vj} J)y = y^T(J^T K_{vj}^{1/2} K_{vj}^{1/2} J)y = z^T z \geq 0.
\tag{26}
$$

Therefore, $K_{vw} + J^T K_{vj} J + 2J^T DJ$ which is sum of two PSD matrices and a PD matrix, is a PD matrix. Then we can conclude $\dot{V} \leq 0$. Therefore, we know that the motion of the robot will converge to the largest invariant set that satisfies $\dot{V} = 0$. In this case, $\dot{V} = 0$ results in $\dot{e} = 0$. Therefore, from equation (21) the largest invariant set is

$$
K_{pw}e + J^T K_{pj}e_L = 0
\tag{27}
$$

It is shown in Appendix that $J.e$ has the same sign of $e_L$, hence, we can write $e_L = \alpha Je$, $\alpha > 0$ and then we can rewrite equation (27) in this form:

$$
(K_{pw} + \alpha J^T K_{pj} J).e = 0, \ \alpha > 0
\tag{28}
$$

According to the above equation and positive definiteness of $(K_{pw} + \alpha J^T K_{pj} J)$ it is concluded that $e = 0$. Therefore, as time tends to infinity we have $x = x_d$ and this means the end-effector position converges to the desired trajectory.

**Table 1.** Geometric and Inertial Parameters of the KNTU CDRPM

| Description | Quantity |
|---|---|
| $K$: Spring stiffness matrix | $100I_{8\times8}$ |
| $M_m$: Inertia matrix of actuators | $0.006I_{8\times8}$ |
| $D$: Viscous friction coefficients for actuators | $0.244I_{8\times8}$ |
| The parameters of controllers: | |
| $\tilde{K}_p = 13500,\ \tilde{K}_v = 700$ | |
| $K_{pj} = 10^5 I_{8\times8},\ K_{dj} = 10^4 I_{8\times8}$ | |
| $K_{pw} = 10^7 \mathrm{diag}(80, 50, 1000, 77.5, 14, 19.5)$ | |
| $K_{dw} = 10^7 \mathrm{diag}(24, 9, 600, 16.5, 1.14, 5.7)$ | |

## 4.2   Control Law for the Elastic Model

Control of the systems with real cables can be done using a composite control scheme that is a well-known technique in the control of singularly perturbed systems [10]. In this framework the control effort $u_{tot}$ consists of two main parts, i.e. $u$ the control effort for slow subsystem, the model in eq. (8), and $u_f$ the control effort for fast subsystem. Here we use a control law that is combination of rigid model control and a PD controller for the fast dynamics

$$u_t = u + \tilde{K}_p(L_1 - L_2) + \tilde{K}_v(\dot{L}_1 - \dot{L}_2) \tag{29}$$

As a practical point of view, it must be said that $L_1$ can be measured by an encoder and $L_2$ by a *string pot*. In next section, it is shown through simulation that this controller can stabilize the closed-loop system with real cables and reach to a desired tracking error. Stability analysis of the system with this composite controller will be discussed in later researches.

## 4.3   Simulation Study

In this section, the performance of the proposed controller is demonstrated through simulating the KNTU CDRPM. The dynamic equations of the CDRPM

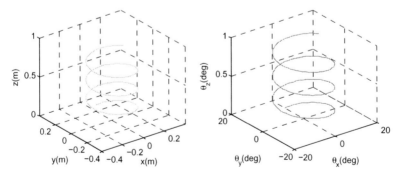

**Fig. 3.** Desired path in the workspace

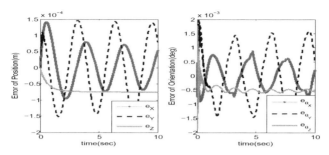

**Fig. 4.** The tracking error of the controller for elastic model

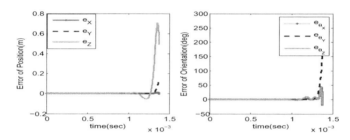

**Fig. 5.** The tracking error of the rigid model controller on the elastic model

considering the elasticity of the cables are shown in eq. (15).These equations in the standard form of singular perturbation theory are shown in eq. (18). Table 1 shows robot and controller specifications, other parameters are the same as what is given in [5]. The desired path of the manipulator in 3D is cylindrical and is shown in Fig. 3. The tracking performance of the CDRPM using the proposed controller is shown in Fig. 4. As seen in this figure, the proposed control topology is capable of reducing the tracking errors less than 0.15 millimeters in position and less than $2 \times 10^{-3}$ degrees in orientation. The tracking error of a single controller for the rigid model i.e.$u$ in eq. (19) is shown in Fig. 5 for comparison. It is obvious that this controller cannot stabilize the cable driven manipulator.

## 5   Conclusions

A dynamical model for cable driven manipulators considering the flexibility of the cables is proposed using cable model as a linear axial spring. The model is formulated in standard form of singular perturbation theory. A composite control is employed for control of cable driven manipulators, which is composition of the controller for the rigid model and a PD controller for controlling the fast dynamics. It is shown that the rigid control law can stabilize the system with ideal and inflexible cables asymptotically. The efficiency of the proposed controller is verified through simulations on KNTU CDRPM.

# A    Appendix

Here, we will show that $\boldsymbol{J}\boldsymbol{e}_x = \boldsymbol{J}(\boldsymbol{x}_d - \boldsymbol{x})$ has the same sign of $\boldsymbol{e}_l = (\boldsymbol{\ell}_d - \boldsymbol{\ell})$, the proof will be done *by reduction to the absurd* ( or *contradiction*). Therefore, assume that they have different sign:

$$l_d - l = \alpha \boldsymbol{J}(x_d - x)\,, \alpha < 0 \tag{30}$$

Therefore, $\exists M \gg \frac{1}{\varepsilon} \Rightarrow \frac{\Delta l}{M} = \frac{\alpha}{M}J\Delta x$.
$\frac{\Delta l}{M} = dl$ and we know that $dl \simeq \boldsymbol{J}dx$, so from equation (30) we have:

$$\boldsymbol{J}dx = dl \simeq \frac{\alpha}{M}\boldsymbol{J}\Delta x \tag{31}$$

$$dx \simeq \frac{\alpha}{M}\Delta x \tag{32}$$

Which is a wrong expression when $\alpha < 0$. Thus by contradiction, we can conclude that $\alpha > 0$, i.e. $\boldsymbol{J}(x_d-x)$ and $(l_d-l)$ have the same sign.

□

# References

1. Albus, J., Bostelman, R., Dagalakis, N.: The nist robocrane. J. of Robotic Systems 10, 709–724 (1993)
2. Kawamura, S., Kino, H., Won, C.: High-speed manipulation by using parallel wire-driven robots. Robotica, 13–21 (2000)
3. Merlet, J.-P., Daney, D.: A new design for wire driven parallel robot. In: 2nd Int. Congress, Design and Modeling of mechanical systems, Monastir (March 2007)
4. Pham, C., Yeo, S., Yang, G., Kurbanhusen, M., Chen, I.: Force-closure workspace analysis of cable-driven parallel mechanisms. Mechanism and Machine Theory 41, 53–69 (2006)
5. Vafaei, A., Aref, M.M., Taghirad, H.D.: Integrated controller for an over-constrained cable driven parallel manipulator: Kntu cdrpm. In: IEEE Int. Conf. on Robotics and Automation (ICRA), pp. 650–655 (May 2010)
6. Khosravi, M.A., Taghirad, H.D.: Dynamics analysis and control of cable driven robots considering elasticity in cables. Presented at CCToMM 2011 Symposium (2011)
7. Gorman, J., Jablokow, K., Cannon, D.: The cable array robot: Theory and experiment. In: IEEE International Conference on Robotics and Automation (2001)
8. Alp, A.B., Agrawal, S.K.: Cable suspended robots: feedback controllers with positive inputs. In: American Control Conference, pp. 815–820 (2002)
9. Diao, X., Ma, O.: Vibration analysis of cable-driven parallel manipulators. Multibody Syst. Dyn. 21, 347–360 (2009)
10. O'Reilly, J., Kokotovic, P.V., Khalil, H.: Singular Perturbation Methods In Control: Analysis and Design. Academic Press (1986)
11. Khalil, H.K.: Nonlinear Systems, 3rd edn. Prentice-Hall (2002)
12. Aref, M.M., Gholami, P., Taghirad, H.D.: Dynamic analysis of the KNTU CDRPM: a cable driven redundant manipulator. In: IEEE/ASME International Conference on Mechtronic and Embedded Systems and Applications (MESA), pp. 528–533 (2008)

# CAD-2-SIM – Kinematic Modeling of Mechanisms Based on the Sheth-Uicker Convention

Bertold Bongardt

Robotics Innovation Center DFKI, Bremen, Germany

**Abstract.** This paper describes methods of kinematic modeling and of forward kinematics computation that are implemented in a new *kinematic modeling* software – named `CAD-2-SIM` – that transfers models of mechanisms from *computer-aided design* software to *simulation*. In particular, the software is based on a convention developed by Sheth and Uicker in 1971 that we call the *two-frame convention*, since it requires the definition of *two* specifically placed and named frames per joint. This convention simplifies the *kinematic specification* of an arbitrary mechanism and enables computing its *forward kinematics*. The presented notation uses an indexing scheme based on *graph theory*.

**Keywords:** Kinematic Modeling, Parallel Mechanisms, Graph Theory, Computer-Aided Design, Open Source Software.

## 1 Introduction

*Design* on the one hand, and *testing*, *simulation*, and *control* on the other hand, are two complementary aspects in the process of engineering new *mechanisms*, e.g., robots. Nowadays, the design process – also called *kinematic synthesis* – is supported by (mainly proprietary) *computer-aided design* (CAD) tools, while control and *kinematic-dynamic analysis* is supported by a multitude of *simulation software*, e.g., `Openrave` [4]. However, the process of *transferring* a *kinematic model* from one software to another often is a time-consuming task. The novel, open-source program `CAD-2-SIM` is a tool to simplify this transfer by creating an automated interface between the two sides of software. Thus, it can significantly increase the overall development speed for new mechanisms.

Fig. 1 shows the general processing of `CAD-2-SIM`: the software needs two kinds of *input*: first, a CAD model of the mechanism is needed. This model is enriched with a set of frames. Secondly, a `Python` class which provides further information about that mechanism needs to be provided. The *output* of `CAD-2-SIM` is three-fold: first, a *specification* of the mechanism for `Openrave` is composed in XML format, second, an automatic computation of the *forward kinematics* (FK) is conducted, and third, a documentation in LaTeX format can optionally be created. This paper focuses on the description of the FK-computation (Sec. 4) and the generation of the XML specification (Sec. 5).

S. Jeschke, H. Liu, and D. Schilberg (Eds.): ICIRA 2011, Part I, LNAI 7101, pp. 465–477, 2011.

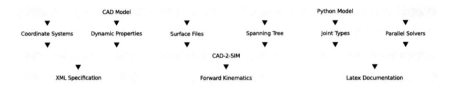

**Fig. 1.** Schematic sketch of the program CAD-2-SIM: The transfer of kinematic models from CAD to simulation software, the computation of forward kinematics, and some LaTeX documentation are provided by the central Python program

One of the most important features of CAD-2-SIM is the placement of the frames in CAD software. They are all placed at the *anchor points*[1] of the joints (Sec. 3.3) which results in a very intuitive handling for the designer. In contrast, when using DH conventions [3], certain geometric constraints must be obeyed (Sec. 3.1), that are stemming from the *link geometry*. Also, the two-frame convention provides a precise separation between *time-variant* and *time-invariant* displacements of a mechanism. From that follows, for example, that the displacment of a simple joint can be expressed as a pure screw displacement. Due to the automatic computation for tree-like structures (Sec. 4.1), it is possible to define an arbitrary number of end-effectors: this is a convenient opportunity to define certain frames of interest. Finally, any *parallel substructure* can be included in the CAD-2-SIM-framework by implementing a solver in a Python class and embedding this into the computation via a plugin mechanism. The presented modeling is consistent in the sense that *parallel substructures* simply act as *complex joints* (Sec. 4.2).

The structure of this paper is as follows: In Sec. 2, an introduction to basic necessary entities is provided. Subsequently, in Sec. 3, we introduce three different conventions for specification of mechanisms. In particular, the Sheth-Uicker convention is presented. This convention builds the basis for the method of computing the forward kinematic in CAD-2-SIM, which is explained in Sec. 4. In Sec. 5, the generation of a mechanism specification for use with Openrave is briefly described. Finally, we present some outlook in Sec. 6.

## 2   Preliminaries

### 2.1   Terminology

In this section, a few standard terms are presented which are needed for this paper. A *link* is a rigid body of a mechanism. A link $L$ may connect more than two joints. A *joint* $J$ is a kinematic element that connects exactly *two* links in a defined manner and with a defined number of degrees of freedom. A *frame* $F$ is the short name for a *local coordinate system*. Its pose is defined by *position* and *orientation* and may change over time. The *origin* $O$ is a short name for the (time-invariant) *global coordinate system*, or in other terms, the *basis* of the

---

[1] The *anchor point* of a joint is the intersection of the joint axis with the *plane of touch*.

vector space. In the entire paper, we work with the standard basis of $\mathbb{R}^3$ and the standard basis of $GL(4)$.

## 2.2  Transformations and Displacements

The group of *proper rigid body transformations* in three-dimensional Euclidean space is denoted by

$$SE(3) = SO(3) \ltimes \mathbb{R}^3, \tag{1}$$

the Special Euclidean Group, according to [17, Sec. 2.5]. In this paper, we work with the *homogeneous representation* $GL(4)$. For this matrix, we use the symbol $S$. The matrix $S$ consists of a rotation matrix $R$ and a translation vector $t$.

$$S = \begin{pmatrix} R & t \\ 0 & 1 \end{pmatrix} \tag{2}$$

In general, an element of $SE(3)$ represents a (finite frame) *displacement*. We use this term as a short term for a *proper rigid body transformation*. Since several algebraic structures are suitable to express finite displacements [7,13,15,17], in the remainder of this paper, we work with functions instead of matrices and denote any displacements by $D$. However, for any displacement, a representation as a homogeneous matrix $S$ is available and suitable.

*Poses.* A *pose* is a special displacement. It describes a displacement relative to the origin. To indicate this, for a pose we use the notation $P$ instead of $D$.

*Simple Joint Displacements.* According to [9], joints can be categorized into three classes of *lower-pair*, *higher-pair*, and *wrapping* joints. In this paper, we constrain the discussion to lower-pair joints that only have *one* degree of freedom, namely any rotative, prismatic or screw joint. The displacement of such a joint can be expressed via a *finite screw* (see, e.g., [2]), and we call it a *simple joint*. A nonsimple joint, we call a *complex joint*. In [18] it was demonstrated how modeling of other lower pairs can easily be integrated into the two-frame convention.

If $S$ represents a pure translation, the rotation matrix $R$ equals the identity element of $SO(3)$, the identity matrix $I_3$. If $u$ denotes the unit vector of the *direction* of a pure translation, and $q$ the *magnitude* of the movement, the translation vector $t$ is computed as

$$t = t(q) = q \cdot u \,. \tag{3}$$

If $S$ represents a pure rotation, the translation vector $t$ equals the identity element of $\mathbb{R}^3$, the zero vector $0_3$. If $u$ denotes the unit vector of the *axis* of a pure rotation, $\hat{u}$ the corresponding skew-symmetric matrix[2], and $q$ the *magnitude* (i.e., angle) of the rotation. The rotation matrix $R$ is computed as

$$R = R(q) = \exp(q \cdot \hat{u}) \,. \tag{4}$$

The expression $\exp(q \cdot \hat{u})$ can be computed by the well-known *Rodrigues formula*[3]

$$\exp(q \cdot \hat{u}) = I + \sin q \cdot \hat{u} + (1 - \cos q) \cdot \hat{u}^2 \,. \tag{5}$$

---

[2] Notation is chosen to be consistent with [12].
[3] See [12, Sec. 2.2.] for a derivation.

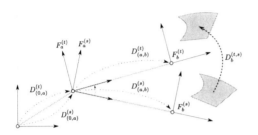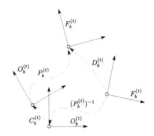

**Fig. 2.** Displacement examples: spatial displacements (e.g., $D^{(t)}_{a,b}$) are marked by dotted arrows. The dashed arrow ($D^{(t,s)}_b$) indicates a temporal displacement.

**Fig. 3.** Example of similar displacements. $D^{(t)}_b$ is similar to $C^{(t)}_b$ with respect to $P^{(t)}_b$.

### 2.2.1 Spatial Displacement

Let $t$ be a fixed and arbitrary timestep, let $F_a$ and $F_b$ be two frames in the same global coordinate system. Let $P^{(t)}_a$ and $P^{(t)}_b$ describe the poses of these frames at timestep $t$. Then, the *spatial displacement* between the two frames from $F_a$ to $F_b$ is expressed via

$$D^{(t)}_{(a,b)} : F^{(t)}_a \underset{P}{\mapsto} F^{(t)}_b \qquad\qquad D^{(t)}_{(a,b)} = (P^{(t)}_a)^{-1} \circ P^{(t)}_b \qquad (6)$$

The spatial displacement $D^{(t)}_{(a,b)}$ describes a *passive interpretation* of a transformation. This is indicated by the usage of the symbol $\underset{P}{\mapsto}$. This notation is chosen so that it matches the notation in classic robotics textbooks (e.g., [16]). The FK *map* of a kinematic chain is computed as $D_{(0,n)} = D_{(0,1)} \circ D_{(1,2)} \circ \cdots \circ D_{(n-1,n)}$ , where the interpretation works from right-to-left because of the *passive interpretation*.

### 2.2.2 Similar Displacements

During the forward kinematics computation, the following *similarity relation* is needed (see, e.g., [1, Sec. 2.6]):

$$D^{(t)}_b = (P^{(t)}_b)^{-1} \circ C^{(t)} \circ P^{(t)}_b . \qquad (7)$$

The displacement $D^{(t)}_b$ is *similar* to the displacement $C^{(t)}$ with respect to the similarity transform $D^{(s)}_b$. See Fig. 3 for a simplified sketch.

### 2.3 Mechanisms and Graph Theory

A graph is a pair $G = (V, E)$ of sets such that $E \subseteq V \times V$: The elements of the set $V$ are called *vertices*, the elements of the set $E$ are called *edges* (e.g., [5]). The combinatorics of a graph are defined by means of an incidence or adjacency structure. A characterization by McPhee reads 'Linear graph theory is that branch of mathematics that studies the description and manipulation of system topologies' [11]. Specifically, in application to kinematics, graph theory provides the tools to distinguish between *kinematic chains, trees,* and *graphs.* Our modeling (Sec. 3.3) is similar to the one presented in [10] in terms of working with a *frame graph*. However, while the authors of [10] perform *dynamics* computations, we focus only on *kinematics* computations.

*Spanning Trees.* A *spanning tree* $T = (V, E')$ of a graph $G = (V, E)$ is a subgraph of $G$ that connects all vertices by exactly one path. In a spanning tree, the *parent vertex* of a vertex $v$ is denoted as $\lambda(v)$.[4] We call a *vertex indexing* that fulfills the relation $\text{ind}(v) > \text{ind}(\lambda(v)) \; \forall \; v \in V$ a *T-compatible* indexing.

### 2.3.1  Link Graph

Before the frames are introduced, a few notation requirements have to be fulfilled. The first one is the *link enumeration*. If the CAD model contains $n$ different links, all these links are enumerated with a simple index $i \in \{1, \dots, n\}$, thus the set of all links can be denoted by $\mathcal{L} = \{L_1, \dots, L_n\}$. The second requirement is the usage of *joint tuple-indices*: Whenever two links $L_i$ and $L_j$ are connected via a joint, then this joint is denoted as $J_{ij}$, where the tuple index $(i, j)$ is element of $\{1, \dots, n\} \times \{1, \dots, n\}$.[5] Thus, the set of all joints can be denoted by $\mathcal{J} = \{J_{ij} \mid L_i \text{ and } L_j \text{ adjacent }\}$. The notation is chosen so that the definition of the *link graph* $G_\mathcal{L} = (V_\mathcal{L}, E_\mathcal{L})$ is easily achieved: The *vertex set* $V_\mathcal{L}$ is created by the set of *links* and the *edge set* $E_\mathcal{L}$ is created by the set of *joints*, $V_\mathcal{L} = \mathcal{L}$ and $E_\mathcal{L} = \mathcal{J}$. To enable an automated FK computation, a *spanning tree* of the *link graph* has to be defined. The spanning tree we denote as $T_\mathcal{L} = (V_\mathcal{L}, E'_\mathcal{L})$. For simplicity, we assume that the *link enumeration* has been conducted in $T_\mathcal{L}$-compatible manner (see above). Let $L_j$ be an arbitrary link of the spanning tree, then we call $L_i = \lambda(L_j)$ the *predecessor link* of $L_j$. The link that does not have a predecessor (it is $L_1$) is the *root* of the tree.

*Configuration Vector.* Let $D_{(ij)}$ denote the degree of freedom of joint $J_{(ij)}$. The set $Q_\mathcal{J}$ contains all single degrees of freedom $q_{(i,j)_k}$ of all joints, like

$$Q_\mathcal{J} = \left\{ q_{(i,j)_k} \mid J_{(ij)} \in \mathcal{J}, \; k \in \{1, 2 \dots, D_{(ij)}\} \right\}. \tag{8}$$

The configuration vector $q = (q_1, q_2, \dots, q_N)$ is obtained from the set $Q_\mathcal{J}$ by first sorting it *lexicographically* and then casting it into an ordered vector. In case of the triple indices used, the lexicographic comparator $<_{\text{lex}}$ is defined as

$$(i, j)_k <_{\text{lex}} (l, m)_n \quad :\Leftrightarrow \quad (i < l) \lor (i = l \land j < m) \lor (i = l \land j = m \land k < n).$$

We use an underline notation $\underline{D}$, to indicate the independence of some displacement $D$ from the configuration vector $q = q(t)$, and thus its time-invariance. In cases of $q(t)$-dependence, we use an overline notation $\overline{D}$ to emphasize this.

## 3  Kinematic Notation Conventions

### 3.1  The Convention by Denavit and Hartenberg

In most classic robotics textbooks (e.g., [16]), kinematics is introduced by means of a kinematic chain and by means of the Denavit-Hartenberg (DH) convention.

---

[4] – According to [6, Sec. 4.1.1, 4.1.4]. –

[5] To work with a unique notation, all joints should be defined so that the index tuple $(i, j)$ is lexicographically sorted (thus $i < j$).

The convention specifies a certain displacement for a link-joint couple $i$ in a mechanism by defining four parameters: the link length $a_i$, link offset $d_i$, the link twist angle $\alpha_i$, and the joint angle $\theta_i$. Due to the fact that the placement of the frames is dependent on the *geometry* of the links, modeling becomes unintuitive. For example, in case of skew joint axes, frames may be placed in *open space* instead of *on* the links. Further, the zero-pose cannot be arbitrarily chosen.

### 3.2 The Convention by Gupta

In 1981, Gupta introduced the *zero reference position method* [8] as a new convention for dealing with kinematics. The computation of the *current pose* $P^{(t)}$ of a mechanism is not based on joint-to-joint computations, but on the displacement of the mechanism against its *zero reference pose* $P^{(1)}$. Gupta shows how to analyze a complex joint "as a separate entity and then 'add on' this solution to the rest of the manipulator solution". The basic concept that enables this is the similarity transformation (Sec. 2.2.2). The FK computation in CAD-2-SIM (Sec. 4) also works with help of the *zero reference pose* $P^{(1)}$. Displacements of joints and parallel substructures are modularly 'added' to the overall kinematics computation.

### 3.3 Sheth and Uicker's Two-Frame Convention

*The Frame Naming and Placing Routine.* For two arbitrary links $L_i$ and $L_j$ that are connected by a joint $J_{ij}$, *two frames* are introduced. The naming as well as the poses of the two frames follow certain conventions so that the CAD-2-SIM program can reconstruct the entire combinatoric and geometric structure of the mechanism. The two frames are both associated with joint $J_{ij}$. One is named $F_{(ij)_i}$ and attached to link $L_i$, the other is named $F_{(ij)_j}$ and attached to link $L_j$.

- For any joint $J_{ij}$ that connects a link $L_i$ and a link $L_j$, define *two* frames that are named as $F_{(ij)_i}$ and $F_{(jk)_j}$. Place these two frames so that:
    1. The *origins* of the frames are identical to the anchor point of joint $J_{ij}$.
    2. The *z-axes* of the frames are identical to the axis of joint $J_{ij}$.
    3. The *x-axes* of the frames are chosen conveniently, e.g., according with the local geometry of the link they are attached to (see example in Fig. 4).
    4. The *y-axes* of the frames are chosen according to the right-hand rule.

The set of the defined frames we denote with $\mathcal{F}$. Since for each joint-link pair there is exactly *one frame* defined in the CAD software, the set $\mathcal{F}$ contains $|\mathcal{F}| = |\mathcal{L}| \cdot |\mathcal{J}|$ frames in total.

*Comparison.* In comparison with simple DH-chain modeling, the two-frame convention 'adds' an additional frame per joint. By adding this redundancy, one gains generality[6] and symmetry[7] of the description. As a first advantage, the x-axes of the frames can be chosen according to the geometry of that single

---

[6] – *Any* mechanism can be modeled –
[7] – Each link *looks the same* from perspectives of any adjacent link –

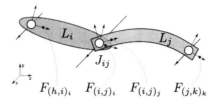

**Fig. 4.** Modeling a joint $J_{(ij)}$ connecting link $L_i$ and $L_j$ with two frames $F_{(ij)_i}$ and $F_{(ij)_j}$ according to the two-frame convention: frame $F_{(ij)_i}$ is attached and aligned to link $L_i$, and frame $F_{(ij)_j}$ to link $L_j$

link the frame is attached to. This significantly simplifies the situation for the designer. As a second advantage, the redundancy defined by *two* joint frames in the CAD-software can be used for verifying the consistency of joint axes. [8]

### 3.3.1 Frame Graph

Having introduced all frames, next to the link graph (Sec. 2.3.1) a second graph, namely the *frame graph* $G_{\mathcal{F}} = (V_{\mathcal{F}}, E_{\mathcal{F}})$, can be observed: The vertex set $V_{\mathcal{F}}$ of $G_{\mathcal{F}}$ is created by set of the frames $\mathcal{F}$. The edge set $E_{\mathcal{F}}$ is created by all frame displacements, link, and joint displacements (see Sec. 3.3.2). Note that the combinatorics of the frame graph are entirely determined by the combinatorics of the link graph $G_{\mathcal{L}}$. Also, the spanning tree $T_{\mathcal{F}} = (V_{\mathcal{F}}, E'_{\mathcal{F}})$ can be deduced from the spanning tree $T_{\mathcal{L}} = (V_{\mathcal{L}}, E'_{\mathcal{L}})$.

*Kinematic Specification.* Roughly, a mechanism $\mathcal{M}$ can then be specified in its zero pose via the triple
$$\mathcal{M} = (\mathcal{L}, \mathcal{J}, \mathcal{F}) . \tag{9}$$
Here, it is assumed that the joints also contain information about their type. Compare also [19] for a similar approach. To compute the kinematics for a given configuration vector $q$, the spanning tree together with solvers for parallel substructures needs to be provided. Fig. 5 displays a mechanism that is neither a kinematic chain (since it contains branches, links $L_2, L_4, L_7$, and two end-effectors, links $L_8, L_{13}$) nor a kinematic tree (since it contains a loop, gray joints), with a $T_{\mathcal{L}}$-compatible link enumeration and tuple-indexed joint set. Fig. 6 shows its link graph, and Fig. 7 shows parts of its frame graph.

### 3.3.2 Displacements

For any mechanism modeled with the two-frame convention, the frame displacements can be partitioned into two kinds of displacements. Let $F_b$ be an arbitrary frame of a spanning tree of a mechanism and let $F_a = \lambda(F_b)$ be the predecessor of $F_b$. Then, one can distinguish two cases: either $F_a$ and $F_b$ are attached to the same link (rigid body), or $F_a$ and $F_b$ are part of the same joint. We

---

[8] However, it was mentionend in [18] that for computation purposes, one frame of each tuple of joint frames can be canceled.

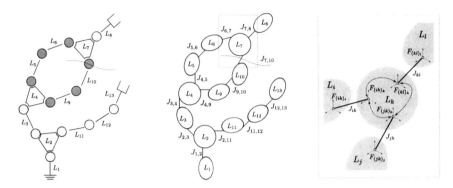

**Fig. 5.** Sketch of the physical appearance of a mechanism. Combinatorially, a joint hypergraph $H_{\mathcal{J}} = (\mathcal{J}, \mathcal{L})$ is shown.

**Fig. 6.** Depiction of *link graph* $G_{\mathcal{L}}$ that is constructed by taking the line graph of $H_{\mathcal{J}}$ (Fig. 5) $L(H_{\mathcal{J}}) = G_{\mathcal{L}}$

**Fig. 7.** Detailed view of Fig. 6 with generalized indices showing parts of the *frame graph* $G_{\mathcal{F}} = (V_{\mathcal{F}}, E_{\mathcal{F}})$

call the former a *link displacement*, the latter a *joint displacement*. In the next two paragraphs, these two displacements are introduced.

*Link Displacements.* As mentioned earlier, for each joint adjacent to a link $L_j$ there is a frame attached to the link $L_j$. Let $J_{(ij)}$ and $J_{(jk)}$ be two example joints at $L_j$, having frames $F_{(ij)_j}$ and $F_{(jk)_j}$. The displacement between these frames is denoted as $D^{(t)}_{(ij)_j,(jk)_j}$ for timestep $t$ and computed via Eq. 6. A simpler notation which omits redundant information can be achieved by defining the triple $(ijk) := (ij)_j, (jk)_j$. The link displacement can therefore be written as $D_{(ijk)} := D_{(ij)_j,(jk)_j}$. Since the two frames are attached to the same rigid body, their relative displacement is *time-invariant* ($D^{(t)}_{(ijk)} = D^{(1)}_{(ijk)}, t > 0$). We note this invariance by using the underline notation (Sec. 2.3.1) and omitting the superscript $\underline{D}_{(ijk)} := D^{(t)}_{(ijk)}$:

$$\underline{D}_{(ijk)} : F_{(ij)_j} \underset{p}{\mapsto} F_{(jk)_j} \qquad\qquad \underline{D}_{(ijk)} = (P^{(1)}_{(ij)_j})^{-1} \circ P^{(1)}_{(jk)_j} \qquad (10)$$

In contrast to displacements for the DH-convention, the displacement $\underline{D}_{(ijk)}$ can be *arbitrary* due to the arbitrary geometry of a link $L_j$.

*Joint Displacements.* Let $J_{(ij)}$ be an arbitrary joint that connects two links $L_i$ and $L_j$. Then, according to the two-frame convention, there is one frame $F_{(ij)_i}$ attached to link $L_i$ and another frame $F_{(ij)_j}$ attached to link $L_j$. The displacement between these two frames $D^{(t)}_{(ij)_i,(ij)_j}$ at timestep $t$ is computed in *two steps*. The *first* step is to compute the initial joint displacement $D^{(1)}_{(ij)_i,(ij)_j}$. Since the initial joint displacements are needed as offsets in all timesteps, we define $\underline{D}_{(ij)} := D^{(1)}_{(ij)_i,(ij)_j}$, omitting redundant subsubscripts. According to Eq. 6 this is defined as

$$\underline{D}_{(ij)} : F^{(1)}_{(ij)_i} \underset{p}{\mapsto} F^{(1)}_{(ij)_j} \qquad\qquad \underline{D}_{(ij)} = (D^{(1)}_{(ij)_i})^{-1} \circ P^{(1)}_{(ij)_j} . \qquad (11)$$

The *second* step is to compute the current joint displacement $D_{(ij)}^{(t)}$ at any timestep $t > 1$ composed from the previous $\underline{D}_{(ij)}$ and the $q(t)$-dependent joint displacement $\overline{D}_{(ij)_j}^{(t)}$. The latter is the similar displacement (Eq. 7) to $\overline{J}_{(ij)_j}^{(t)}$ with respect to $\underline{P}_{(ij)_j}^{(t)}$:

$$\overline{D}_{(ij)_j}^{(t)} : \underline{F}_{(ij)_j}^{(t)} \underset{\text{p}}{\mapsto} F_{(ij)_j}^{(t)} \qquad\qquad \overline{D}_{(ij)_j}^{(t)} = (\underline{D}_{(ij)_j}^{(t)})^{-1} \circ \overline{J}_{(ij)_j}^{(t)} \circ \underline{D}_{(ij)_j}^{(t)} . \qquad (12)$$

The current joint displacement $D_{(ij)}^{(t)}$ is composed from the constant joint offset and current displacement, like

$$D_{(ij)}^{(t)} : F_{(ij)_i}^{(t)} \underset{\text{p}}{\mapsto} F_{(ij)_j}^{(t)} \qquad\qquad D_{(ij)}^{(t)} = \underline{D}_{(ij)} \circ \overline{D}_{(ij)_j} . \qquad (13)$$

Due to the two-frame placing convention, the $z$-axes of the two frames always coincide. In case of simple joints, the time-invariant $\underline{D}_{(ij)}$ as well as the time-variant $\overline{J}_{(ij)}$ are screw displacements.

At this point, all entities (links, joints, configuration vector, frames, displacements) that are necessary to compute the forward kinematics have been introduced in a unified manner. This adresses the ambiguities of notation which where pointed out in [14].

## 4    Computation of Forward Kinematics

In the given context, a forward kinematics (FK) computation means the determination of the poses of *all* frames $F \in \mathcal{F}$, where the pose of each frame $F^{(t)}$ is a function of the mechanism $\mathcal{M}$ and the configuration vector $q^{(t)} = (q_1^{(t)}, q_2^{(t)}, \ldots, q_N^{(t)})$, such that $F^{(t)} = f(\mathcal{M}, q^{(t)}) \forall F \in \mathcal{F}$. The 'trick' to enable CAD-2-SIM to compute the FK automatically for any tree-like mechanism is to define frames in the CAD program according to the two-frame convention that is presented in the previous section. These frames provide a description of the mechanism at timestep $t = 1$ in its zero reference configuration. $F^{(1)} = f(\mathcal{M}, q^{(1)} = 0) \forall F \in \mathcal{F}$.

*Complexity.* While computation of forward kinematics for chain- and tree-like mechanisms is polynomial, the computation for kinematic loops is as complex as the inverse kinematics problem of the chains that build the loops. Within these complexity classes, the runtime of kinematic algorithms is influenced by the algebraic structures that represent the displacements. Notation conventions like Denavit-Hartenberg or Sheth-Uicker's two-frame convention deliver a set of parameters that only *specify* the displacements, but do not fix the algebraic structure, so that the question of runtime is not considered in this paper.

*Examples.* In the following, we describe the principal computations that are implemented in CAD-2-SIM. Due to space limitations, this paper does not contain computations of an example mechanism. However, several examples are available together with the source code of the software.

*Requirements.* For FK computation, two inputs are required by CAD-2-SIM: First, the mechanism needs to be aligned to an arbitrarily chosen, suitable zero pose in the CAD software and needs to be equipped with the set of frames $\mathcal{F}$ as described in Sec. 3.3. Second, a Python class according to Fig. 1 has to be implemented that provides the following information: First, for all joints in $\mathcal{J}$ the *joint type* is saved. Second, the *spanning tree* is provided here. Third, for each frame $F_b$ in the mechanism the *dependency* is saved: Either the pose of the frame can be determined via the pose of the parent frame $\lambda(b)$ in the spanning tree, or the frame is part of a parallel substructure. In the latter case, the Python class must also provide dedicated *solver* routines for those substructures. The *computation for trees* and the *computation for parallel substructures* are described in the following two subsections.

*Initial and Regular Traversals.* For both cases – tree-like and parallel structure computation – we distinguish between *two* kinds of traversals of the mechanism: the initialization phase is identified with timestep $t = 1$ and described in Par. 4.1.1 and 4.2. Here, all frame poses of the mechanism are computed for the zero reference configuration $q^{(1)} = \mathbf{0}$. The actual computation of poses for a configuration vector $q^{(t)} \neq \mathbf{0}$ is executed in a *regular traversal* of the algorithm. This is identified with a timestep $t > 1$ and described in Par. 4.1.2 and 4.2.1.

## 4.1   Automated FK-Computation for Frames in the Spanning Tree
### 4.1.1   Initial Traversal
The mechanism is traversed once completely in the initial iteration at timestep $t = 1$. In this traversal, the *initial link displacements* $\underline{D}_{(ijk)}$ (Eq. 10) and the *initial joints displacements* $\underline{D}_{(ij)}$ (Eq. 11) are computed. They are stored for each frame-tuple of the spanning tree. In addition, CAD-2-SIM performs validations of preconditions in the initial traversal: it is verified whether the *naming* and the *placing* of the frames are correct, according to Sec. 3.3.

### 4.1.2   Regular Traversals
The mechanism is traversed once completely in each regular iteration at some timestep $t > 1$.

*Regular Link Displacements.* The displacement of the frame at the end of the link $D^{(t)}_{(jk)_j}$ is computed as the composition of the current $q$-dependent $D^{(t)}_{(ij)_j}$ of the parent frame $F_{(ij)_j}$ and the time-invariant link displacement $\underline{D}_{(ijk)}$:

$$D^{(t)}_{(jk)_j} = D^{(t)}_{(ij)_j} \circ \underline{D}_{(ijk)} . \tag{14}$$

*Regular Joint Displacements.* The displacement of the frame at the end of the joint $D^{(t)}_{(ij)_j}$ is computed in two steps. First, the current relative joint displacement $D^{(t)}_{(ij)}$ is computed as in Eq. 13. The *second* step is analogous to the computation in Eq. 14 for the *regular link displacement*. To determine $D^{(t)}_{(ij)_j}$, the joint displacement $D^{(t)}_{(ij)}$ is composed with the displacement $D^{(t)}_{(ij)_i}$ of the parent frame:

$$D^{(t)}_{(ij)_j} = D^{(t)}_{(ij)_i} \circ D^{(t)}_{(ij)} . \tag{15}$$

The computation defined by the above equation traverses the entire tree, from the root of the tree (base link) to the leaves of the tree (end-effectors).

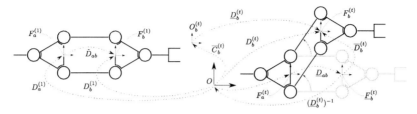

**Fig. 8.** An example mechanism with a parallel substructure. Shown are the zero pose at timestep $t = 1$ and a second pose at another timestep $t > 1$, together with the related displacements, so that the chain $D_b^{(t)} = D_a^{(t)} \circ \underline{D}_{(a,b)} \circ (\underline{D}_b^{(t)})^{-1} \circ \overline{C}_b^{(t)} \circ D_b^{(t)}$ expressed in Eq. 19 is visible.

## 4.2  Embedding FK-Computations for Parallel Substructures

Let $F_a$ be the predecessor in the spanning tree of the parallel substructure that can be computed automatically (since it only has one predecessor) and $F_b$ the 'last' frame of the parallel substructure[9]. We note that $F_a$ and $F_b$ can be arbitrarily chosen 'on' the predecessor and the successor links, so typically they are chosen suitable to the *substructure geometry*[10]. The embedding of the parallel substructure into the overall FK computation works in an analogous manner as the embedding of *regular joint displacements* (Sec. 4.1.2). The displacement of a parallel substructure is therefore a relaxation of a constraint joint displacement to any rigid body transformation. In this interpretation, the parallel substructure simply acts as a *complex joint*. Since the CAD model defines a feasible (zero) configuration for timestep $t = 1$, an initial solution for the FK of the parallel substructure is available. This solution can help to select a unique configuration from the 'symmetric' solution set for the parallel problem.

*Initial Parallel Traversal.*  The computation of initial, time-invariant displacement $\underline{D}_{(a,b)}$ works in accordance with Eq. 11, so that

$$\underline{D}_{(a,b)} = D_{(a,b)}^{(1)} = (P_a^{(1)})^{-1} \circ (P_b^{(1)}) . \tag{16}$$

### 4.2.1  Regular Parallel Traversals
In the *first* step (analogous to Eq. 13), the current displacement $D_{(a,b)}^{(t)}$ of a parallel mechanism is computed via its initial displacement $\underline{D}_{(a,b)}$ and via the temporal change $\overline{D}_b^{(t)}$ of its last element $F_b$:

$$D_{(a,b)}^{(t)} = \underline{D}_{(a,b)} \circ \overline{D}_b^{(t)} . \tag{17}$$

In the *second* step (analogous to Eq. 15), the relative displacement is combined with the current pose $D_a^{(t)}$ of the predecessor $F_a$ to compute the current displacement $D_b^{(t)}$ of the last element $F_b$

$$D_b^{(t)} = D_a^{(t)} \circ D_{(a,b)}^{(t)} . \tag{18}$$

---

[9] That again may act as a unique predecessor for another frame.

[10] See example in Fig. 8 where the frames $F_a$ and $F_b$ are placed on the 'base lines'.

This functions maps $F_{(0)}$ to $F_b^{(t)}$ in the passive interpretation. The functions in the equations above define the following chain:

$$F_{(0)} \xrightarrow[p]{D_d^{(t)}} F_a^{(t)} \xrightarrow[p]{D_{(a,b)}} \underline{F}_b^{(t)} \xrightarrow[p]{(D_b^{(t)})^{-1}} O_b^{(t)} \xrightarrow[p]{\bar{C}_b^{(t)}} O_b^{(t)} \xrightarrow[p]{D_b^{(t)}} F_b^{(t)} . \tag{19}$$

Fig. 8 provides an example for the situation: the pose of $F_b$ at timestep $t$ is determined by displacement $D_b^{(t)}$.

### 4.3 Remarks

The displacements that occur in the computation of FK fall into two classes: *link displacements* can be arbitrary but are time-invariant, whereas *joint displacements* are time-variant but come in the form of screw displacements in the case of simple joints. The latter constraint is relaxed for complex joints and for parallel substructures. The algorithm in CAD-2-SIM combines these two classes of displacements in the FK computation: a sequential computation 'along the tree' is performed for link displacements, whereas a computation relative to the zero configuration is conducted for joint displacements and parallel substructures.

## 5   Generation of the Mechanism Specification

The specification of a mechanism for Openrave in XML format[11] mainly consists of the following information. In one part of the file, all rigid *bodies* are listed together with their initial *pose*, their *mass properties* and their *graphical representation*. In another part of the file, all *joints* are listed together with the link connections, their joint type, and their initial pose in terms of *axis* and *anchor point*.

To generate this information, CAD-2-SIM has to perform only one traversal of the entire mechanism. The main steps can be described as: checking the *consistency* of *namings* of the given input files (kinematic frames, dynamic properties, and shape files), checking the consistency of the kinematic frames (*namings* and *placings*), and optionally unifying *physical units*. Finally, some file work is executed and the XML file is generated by Python's dedicated libraries.

## 6   Conclusion and Outlook

This paper announces a novel open source software CAD-2-SIM for transferring *models of mechanisms* from CAD to simulation software and describes how it computes forward kinematics based on the Sheth-Uicker *two-frame convention*. To derive a uniform description, an indexing based on graph theory is introduced. Since the convention provides a rigorous split between constant and variable displacements, it is demonstrated that the convention can also easily integrate parallel substructures into the kinematics computation. The presented computation can be regarded as a blend of classical computation "along the chain" for

---

[11] See http://openrave.programmingvision.com/wiki/index.php/Format:XML

link displacements and computation via the displacement against Gupta's *zero reference pose* for joint displacements.

In future, CAD-2-SIM will be extended to support an automated *code generation* for fast languages like C++. Further, an automated treatment of standard parallel structures can be provided. As a next step, we will document the connections between the Sheth-Uicker's two-frame convention we have used and the minimal Denavit-Hartenberg convention.

**Acknowledgement.** The research presented in this article was funded by the German Ministry of Education and Research (BMBF) within the projects *VI-Bot* (Grant Number 01-IW-07003) and *CAPIO* (Grant Number 01-IW-10001).

# References

1. Angeles, J.: Fundamentals of Robotic Mechanical Systems: Theory, Methods, and Algorithms, 3rd edn. Springer-Verlag New York, Inc., Secaucus (2007)
2. Davidson, J.K., Hunt, K.H., Pennock, G.R.: Robots and Screw Theory: Applications of Kinematics and Statics to Robotics. In: ASME, vol. 126 (2004)
3. Denavit, J., Hartenberg, R.S.: A kinematic notation for lower-pair mechanisms based on matrices. Trans. of the ASME. Journal of Applied Mechanics 22, 215–221 (1955)
4. Diankov, R.: Automated Construction of Robotic Manipulation Programs. PhD thesis, Carnegie Mellon University, Robotics Institute (2010)
5. Diestel, R.: Graph Theory. Springer, Heidelberg (2005)
6. Featherstone, R.: Rigid Body Dynamics Algorithms. Springer, Heidelberg (2008)
7. Funda, J., Paul, R.P.: A computational analysis of screw transformations in robotics. IEEE Transactions on Robotics and Automation 6, 348–356 (1990)
8. Gupta, K.C.: Kinematic analysis of manipulators using the zero reference position description. Int. J. Rob. Res. 5, 5–13 (1986)
9. Hartenberg, R.S., Denavit, J.: Kinematic Synthesis of Linkages (1964)
10. Lai, H.-J., Haug, E.J., Kim, S.-S., Bae, D.-S.: A decoupled flexible-relative co-ordinate recursive approach for flexible multibody dynamics. International Journal for Numerical Methods in Engineering 32(8), 1669–1689 (1991)
11. McPhee, J.: On the use of linear graph theory in multibody system dynamics. Nonlinear Dynamics 9(1), 73–90 (1996)
12. Murray, R.M., Shankar Sastry, S., Li, Z.: A Mathematical Introduction to Robotic Manipulation. CRC Press, Boca Raton (1994)
13. Perez, A., McCarthy, J.M.: Dual quaternion synthesis of constrained robotic systems. Journal of Mechanical Design 126, 425–435 (2004)
14. Roth, B.: Overview on advanced robotics: Manipulation. In: Proceedings ICAR, pp. 569–580 (1985)
15. Sahu, S., Biswal, B.B., Subudhi, B.: A novel method for representing robot kinematics using quaternion theory. In: IEEE Sponsored Conference on Computational Intelligence, Control And Computer Vision In Robotics & Automation (2008)
16. Sciavicco, L., Siciliano, B.: Modelling and Control of Robot Manipulators, 2nd edn. Kluwer Academic Publishers (1999)
17. Selig, J.M.: Geometric Fundamentals of Robotics, 2nd edn. Springer, Berlin (2005)
18. Sheth, P.N., Uicker, J.J.: A generalized symbolic notation for mechanisms. Journal of Engineering for Industry, Series B 93(70), 102–112 (1971)
19. Thomas, U., Maciuszek, I., Wahl, F.M.: A Unified Notation for Serial, Parallel, and Hybrid Kinematic Structures. In: ICRA, pp. 2868–2873 (2002)

# Non-rigid Object Trajectory Generation
# for Autonomous Robot Handling

Honghai Liu[1] and Hua Lin[2]

[1] Intelligent Systems & Biomedical Robotics Group, School of Creative Technologies,
University of Portsmouth, UK
[2] School of Mechanical Materials and Manufacturing Engineering,
University of Nottingham, UK

**Abstract.** It is evident that there is no feasible solution to non-rigid object manipulation using robots. This paper proposed a two-stage strategy for planning of garment handling systems, i.e., generating trajectory of non-rigid objects and robot manipulation planning. The paper is focused on the former of presenting a generic approach to trajectory generation. A graph representation is first adapted based on garment folding creases, representing the trajectory position and a clothes handling sequence of each clothes partition, then configuration transformations are employed to form the continuous folding process. Finally the handling sequence is calculated based on the analysis of the adjacency matrix of the graph description of the garment. The proposed approach is evaluated on generating trajectory for the handling procedure of a female shirt in this paper.

## 1 Introduction

Automatic handling systems that can be reprogrammed to perform a different task in relation to rigid objects are readily available [1]. However, the use of robotics for automatic handling of textile materials brings serious difficulties for automation as their shape, position, orientation and other physical and mechanical properties can vary in unpredictable ways; depending on the dynamics of the material and the environmental conditions [2]. Moreover, the unique characteristics of floppy material and the complex interaction between the material properties and handling devices can make automated processes become inefficient if the processes are unable to adjust systematically to the changes of properties of the materials to be handled [3]. Therefore, intelligent control of handling textile material is indispensable if the handling system is to be effective. Intelligent control relies on a knowledge base and a suitable reasoning procedure for arriving at a control decision, which will in turn initiate a corresponding control action [4]. Intelligent control of handling limp materials involves multidisplinary knowledge and requires extensive study. There are several active research areas for the automated manipulation of a highly flexible and complex material such as cloth: Sensing techniques [5], Handling mechanism performance [6], Material properties relevant for automated handling [7], Modelling and prediction of the

S. Jeschke, H. Liu, and D. Schilberg (Eds.): ICIRA 2011, Part I, LNAI 7101, pp. 478–485, 2011.

interaction between material properties [8] and handling devices and Intelligent planning strategy.

It is evident intelligent planning strategies for textile material handling are scarce in the literature. Our interest is to develop an intelligent planning strategy for garment handling systems. Though not much literature exists in garment manipulation, similar concepts can be found in the sequence problems of handling other material such as carton folding, sheet metal bending and even protein folding. A Computer-Aided Process Planning (CAPP) [9] was used based on a tolerance tree to generate bending sequences. Gupta and Guo [10] proposed an automated robotic system for planning and executing bending on sheet metal blanks. There is also a need to generate a sound and straightforward algorithm based on the intricate geometry properties of a carton to generate a trajectory in carton packaging. Liu and Dai [11,4] proposed a generic approach to carton-folding applications. One of the main characteristics of garment handling is symmetry, which could lead to simplification of the design of handling mechanisms. The aims of this study are to investigate and understand the handling characteristics of a garment, to derive a generic handling sequence in order to reduce the design complexity of an intelligent gripper.

Two major issues of the handling problem of textile materials are handling mechanisms, e.g., robotic grippers, and planning strategies, e.g., handling sequences [12,13,14]. It is too difficult to solve the two issues at the same time so that we make an assumption to separate them. The assumption is that a handled part of materials retains a virtual plane during materials operation. This assumption meets both development requirements of handling mechanisms and planning strategies. Handling systems have to keep the handled material, e.g., clothes partitions, in a virtual plane as the systems can avoid their shape and posture vary in such predictable ways as dynamics of the materials, and the output of previous handling. It also is one of the design requirements for handling mechanisms, e.g., an intelligent gripper.

The paper is organised as follows; Section 2 derives a generic representation of a clothes based on the standards of clothes industries so that a variety of clothes can be mathematically described. Section 3 presents the analysis of clothes handling operation. Finally conclusions are presented.

## 2    Generic Representation of Clothes

The development of a generic garment model has been inspired by a garment lifecycle, which can be described as a closed loop: textile manufacturing, garment design, garment manufacturing, marketing, customers and recycle or reuse. Due to the fact that the garment handling concerned herein is an internal link between clothes manufacturing and marketing, It is a natural starting point to build a generic garment models based on the standards of clothes design and manufacturing industries. Fig. 1 provides the example of a female shirt in both flat and folded situations.

In accordance with the assumption of a virtual plane of each partition of a garment, which is decomposed by its folding creases. A virtual plane is further

**Fig. 1.** A unfolded and folded female shirt

simplified as a position of the plane and its relation to its base garment partition
in three dimension. The aim of a garment-handling gripper design has to meet
the fact that the gripper must keep each partition of a garment within a virtual
plane as much as it can, its handling positions can be fixed by those which are
relevant to the 3D trajectories, which are generated from a garment planning
strategy. In other words, the garment handling task can be viewed as that of
articulated objects, each of which is a rigid plane. Hence the handling motion can
be described as the combination of position trajectories and their operational
sequence.

Each partition, modelled as a virtual plane, of a garment is mathematically
denoted by a linear vector and its relation to its base, which is randomly defined
from all partitions. The center partition is usually selected as a base partition
since it is fixed during handling procedure. It indicates that only a linear vector
$pq$ of the $s$th partition $\mathbf{G}^s$ needs to be defined, because the geometric center of
its base defaults to the origin of the Cartesian coordinates. The linear vector $pq$
is described at its $j$th time instant as,

$$
\begin{aligned}
\mathbf{G}_j^s &= {}^s\mathbf{H}_{i,j}(\mathbf{p}_i - \mathbf{q}_i) \\
&= {}^s\mathbf{h}_{i,j}^p \mathbf{P}_j - {}^s\mathbf{h}_{i,j}^q \mathbf{q}_j \\
&= T_{i,k}^p\left(u_x, u_y, u_z\right) \cdot R_k^p\left(\phi, \theta, \psi\right) \cdot T_{k,j}^p\left(v_x, v_y, v_z\right) \mathbf{p}_j - \\
&\quad T_{i,k}^q\left(u_x, u_y, u_z\right) \cdot R_k^q\left(\phi, \theta, \psi\right) \cdot T_{k,j}^q\left(v_x, v_y, v_z\right) \mathbf{q}_j
\end{aligned}
\tag{1}
$$

where

$$
T_{i,j}^p\left(v_x, v_y, v_z\right) =
\begin{bmatrix}
1 & 0 & 0 & v_x \\
0 & 1 & 0 & v_y \\
0 & 0 & 1 & v_z \\
0 & 0 & 0 & 1
\end{bmatrix}
$$

and $R_k(\phi, \theta, \psi) = \mathbf{R}_x(\phi) \cdot \mathbf{R}_y(\theta) \cdot \mathbf{R}_z(\psi)$, and $\mathbf{p}_i$, $\mathbf{q}_i$ are positions in the $i$th folding
procedure. $T$, $R$ stand for a translation transformation and orientation. $v_x, v_y, v_z$
represent a linear displacement from virtual panel $j$ to joint $k$ , and $u_x, u_y, u_z$
represent a linear displacement from joint $k$ to virtual panel $i$. The mapping of
the linear vector $pq$ from $i$th trajectory position to $j$th is represented as,

$$^{s}\mathbf{H}_{i,j} : p_i q_i \rightarrow p_j q_j$$

With the relationship between the linear vector and its base, the above mapping is also that of the virtual plane $s$ from $i$th trajectory position to $j$th. Concerning all partitions of a garment, a concise description of the garment handling configurations' mapping can be derived as,

$$[\mathbf{G}_{goal}]_{n \times 1} = [\mathbf{H}]_{n \times n} \cdot [\mathbf{G}_{ini}]_{n \times 1} \tag{2}$$

and

$$\mathbf{H}_{n \times n} : [\mathbf{G}_{ini}]_{n \times 1} \rightarrow [\mathbf{G}_{goal}]_{n \times 1}$$

Where $[G_{ini}]_{n \times 1}$ denotes the initial configuration of a garment, $[G_{goal}]_{n \times 1}$ denotes the final configuration. Though Equation 2 represents the mapping of the folding procedure from an initial configuration of a garment to its final configuration, it mixes folding positions of garment partitions and sequences together so that it cannot provide feasible trajectories for intelligent grippers or garment handling systems due to existence of motion collisions. The method of Liu and Dai [11] in carton-folding applications has been adapted to solve this problem. They extracted a folding sequence from the simplified graph model of a carton, then combined with carton-folding trajectory positions to generate the carton-folding trajectories. It inspires one to decompose equation 2 into a composite description of garment folding trajectory positions and their handling sequences. In order to solve the problem, equation 2 has been rearranged as another description, which comprises of separated trajectory positions of garment partitions and their sequences. Consequently the trajectory positions can be supervised by their sequence to be fed into the effectors of garment handling systems such as intelligent grippers. Due to the fact that the number of partitions of a garment is limited, a final configuration of $[\mathbf{G}_{goal}]$ can be represented and calculated by $Diag\,[H \cdot G] \cdot [\mathbf{I}]$ in a matrix, and the folding sequence can be achieved heuristically by the adjacency matrix of a graph $[\mathbf{A}] \cdot [\mathbf{I}]$ [11], Equation 2 is rewritten as,

$$[\mathbf{G}_{goal}]_{n \times 1} = \left( Diag\,[\mathbf{H} \cdot \mathbf{G}]_{n \times n} + [\mathbf{A}]_{n \times n} \right) \cdot [\mathbf{I}]_{n \times 1} \tag{3}$$

Where $Diag\,[\mathbf{H} \cdot \mathbf{G}]$ is a diagonal matrix whose description is replaced by Equation 1, $[\mathbf{I}]$ is a $n \times n$ unit matrix, $\mathbf{A}$ is an adjacency matrix of the graph of a garment.

For instance, the graph version of the shirt in Fig. 1 is given in Fig. 2, where the graph partitions are outlined by its folding crease. The partitions are labelled by numbers, partitions labelled with $i$ and $i^*$ means that they are geometrically symmetric, and partition labelled as 1 is its base partition since it does not have motion during such a handling process. The mathematical description of the initial configuration of the shirt is given in Equation 4,

$$[G] = \begin{bmatrix} IG_{10} & 1 & 0 & 0 & 1 & 1 & 0 & 0 \\ 1 & H_{2,1}G_{20} & 1 & 1 & 0 & 0 & 0 & 0 \\ 0 & 1 & H_{3,2}G_{30} & 0 & 0 & 0 & 0 & 0 \\ 0 & 1 & 0 & H_{4,(2,5)}G_{40} & 1 & 0 & 0 & 0 \\ 1 & 0 & 0 & 1 & H_{5,1}G_{50} & 0 & 0 & 1 \\ 1 & 0 & 0 & 0 & 0 & H_{2*,1}G_{2*0} & 1 & 1 \\ 0 & 1 & 0 & 0 & 0 & 0 & H_{3*,2*}G_{3*0} & 0 \\ 0 & 0 & 0 & 0 & 1 & 1 & 0 & H_{4*,(2*,5)}G_{4*0} \end{bmatrix}$$

(4)

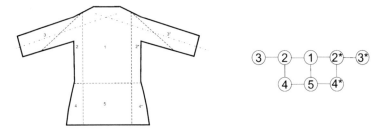

**Fig. 2.** Graph version of the example in Fig. 1

Equation 4 combines the garment handling sequence of the partitions and their corresponding trajectory positions. Its diagonal entries are configuration positions and changes of garment partition, For example, entry $G(5,5) = H_{5,1}G_{50}$ denotes the trajectory position of partition 4 in Fig. 2 at the initial configuration. The states of the other partitions in the column and row of a diagonal entry determine the position of the corresponding partitions in handling sequence of a garment. Hence the value of a garment partition is calculated using equation 1 while its folding state changes are determined by a heuristic algorithm to work out the garment handling sequence based on its graph representation.

## 3   Garment Handling Sequence

The analysis of a garment handling sequence is performed to, firstly, produce a graph model of the garment based on its folding creases and its adjacency matrix, second it is to generate its folding sequence based on heuristic rules and finally it is to produce folding trajectories of the garment by merging its folding sequence and trajectory positions together. A heuristic algorithm is presented for the calculation of a garment folding sequence. The sequence is calculated based on the combination of graph theory, particular to adjacency matrix analysis and empirical rules from clothes designers and clothes manufacturers. With the adaptation of Liu and Dai's approach to carton-folding applications, heuristic rules for generation of a garment folding sequence are as,

1. Identify if there are close loops in a garment graph, if yes, removing them from the graph because a partition positioned as a close loop usually is passively handled,
2. Detect if there are symmetric garment partitions, if yes merging the folding actions of symmetric partitions together because empirical indicates that symmetric partitions always are handled by similar actions,
3. The longer branch of the graph, the later the partition positioned are handled.

The folded female shirt in graph description is shown in Fig. 3f.

$$[G] = \begin{bmatrix} IG_{10} & 1 & 0 & 1 \\ 1 & H_{2,1}G_{20} & 1 & 0 \\ 0 & 1 & H_{3,2}H_{2,1}G_{30} & 0 \\ 1 & 0 & 0 & H_{5,1}G_{50} \end{bmatrix} \tag{5}$$

Consider the example in Fig. 1 again and merging the above-mentioned results leads to the simulation result in Fig. 4, in which the trajectory in solid lines gives the active folding process actuated by a clothes handling system such as a intelligent robotic arm with a gripper. The trajectory in dashed lines gives the passive folding process actuated by adjacent clothes partitions. Symbols ○ represent initial configurations of the geometric centres of the clothes partitions, symbols ◇ represent the folding process of these clothes partitions, symbols * represent the folded positions of these clothes panels. The handling trajectory in the simulation represents the configuration transformation between the initial configuration, process configurations and folded configuration. For example, the trajectory of clothes partition 3 is given from the start position $(-51.82, 6.8, 0)$cm to the processing position $(24.72, 6.8, 0)$cm, then the final position $(-3.17, -18.2, 0)$cm.

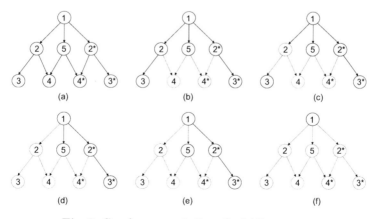

**Fig. 3.** Graph representation of a folding process

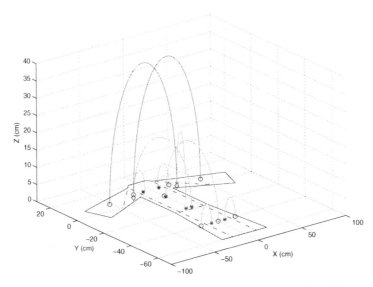

**Fig. 4.** The handling trajectory sequence of the example in Fig. 1

## 4    Concluding Remarks

A heuristic algorithm has been proposed for the folding procedures of intelligent garment handling systems in this paper. First, a generic model is constructed for general clothes based on standards of clothes designers and the clothes manufacturing industry. Then, the handling procedure has been described as trajectory positions and the handling sequence of garment partitions. Finally three heuristic rules were defined to help generate a feasible handling procedure based on graph theory. This work assumes each garment partition as a virtual plane, which is described by a linear vector and its relation to its base. It indicates that a robotic mechanism with a gripper having the capability to hold a garment partition approximately in a virtual plane during handling processes, can combine the proposed handling strategies together to develop an intelligent garment handling systems. This work has addressed a novel path to the development of intelligent flexible material handling systems, a full version can be found at [15]. Future work aims at integrate the proposed approach with existing computational models in order to achieve a feasible approach which practically handles computational cost and modelling precision for real-time packaging systems.

## References

1. Taylor, P.M., Taylor, G.E.: Progress towards automated garment manufacture. In: Taylor, P.M. (ed.) Sensory Robotics for the Handling of Limp Materials. Springer, Berlin (1990)
2. Paraschidis, H., Fahantidis, N., Petridis, V., Doulgeri, Z., Petrou, L., Hasapis, G.: A robotic system for handling textile and non rigid flat materials

3. Nicholls, H.R. (ed.): Advanced tactile sensing for robotics (series in robotics and automated systems) (1995)
4. Liu, H., Dai, J.S.: An approach to carton-folding trajectory planning using dual robotic fingers. Robotics and Autonomous Systems 42, 47–63 (2003)
5. Paraschidis, K., Fahantidis, N., Petridis, V., Doulgeri, Z., Petrou, L., Hasapis, G.: A robotic system for handling textile and non rigid flat materials. Computer in Industry 26, 303–313 (1995)
6. Kolluru, R., Valavanis, S., Smith, K.P., Tsourveloudis, N.: An overview of the university of louisiana robotic gripper system project. Transaction of the Institute of Measurement and Control 24(1), 65–84 (2002)
7. Taylor, P.M., Pollet, D.M.: Low-force dynamic lateral compression of fabrics. Textile research Journal 72(10), 845–853 (2002)
8. Lin, H., Taylor, P.M., Bull, S.J.: A mathematical model for grasping analysis of flexible materials. Modelling and Simulation in Materials Science and Engineering 13, 1–17 (2005) (to appear)
9. De Vin, L.J., De Vries, J., Streppel, A.H., Klasssen, E.J.W., Kals, H.J.J.: The Generation of Bending Sequences in A CAPP System for Sheet-Metal Components. Journal of Materials Processing Technology 41, 331–339 (1995)
10. Gupta, K.K., Guo, Z.: Motion planning for many degrees of freedom: sequential search with backtracking. IEEE Trans. Robotics and Automation 11(6), 897–906 (1995)
11. Liu, H., Dai, J.S.: Carton manipulation planning using configuration transformation. Proc. Instn Mech.Engrs, Part C: J. of Mech. Eng. Sci. 216(5), 543–555 (2002)
12. Dai, J.S., Taylor, P.M., Liu, H., Lin, H.: Garment handling and corresponding devices - technology in roboitc ironing. In: Proc. the 11th World Congress in Mechanism and Machine Science, Tianjin, China (2003)
13. Taylor, P.M., Dai, J.S., Lin, H., Liu, H.: Technologies for automated ironing. In: International Textile Design and Engineering Conference, Heriot-Watt University, Galashields (2003)
14. Lee, M.: Tactile sensing: new directions, new challenges. International Journal of Robotics Research 19(7), 636–643 (2000)
15. Liu, H., Lin, H.: Sequence trajectory generation for garment handling systems. Journal of Applied Mathematical Modelling 32(6), 1017–1026-80 (2008)

# Robotized Sewing of Fabrics
# Based on a Force Neural Network Controller

Panagiotis N. Koustoumpardis and Nikos A. Aspragathos

Mechanical Engineering and Aeronautics Department,
University of Patras Rio Patras, 26504, Greece
{koust,asprag}@mech.upatras.gr

**Abstract.** The robotized sewing of a wide range of fabrics is presented. A conventional industrial sewing machine in cooperation with a scara robot manipulator is used for producing straight line seams in single pieces of rectangular fabrics. A force controller based on neural networks is implemented in order to control the robot end-effector motion so as to ensure that a desired tensional force is applied to the fabric throughout the process of the sewing. The force controller scheme is designed and closes the loop outside the standard robot control law. All the necessary algorithms are implemented and executed inside the robot's controller board. The 12-specimens of fabrics, which have been used for the robotized sewing experiment, represent a broad range of fabric types and compositions. The seams produced by the robot are compared with seams that are produced by a human operator under the same sewing machine conditions. The results reveal that the seams produced by the robot are comparable with that produced by the human operator and in few cases better.

**Keywords:** Neural networks, force control, robotized sewing, handling fabrics.

## 1    Introduction

Robotized handling of fabrics raises new and challenging difficulties that require robotic manipulation techniques beyond the current ones. Such handling techniques could be based on computational intelligence methods. The very low fabric's resistance, their large deformations and the materials' non-linearity are the main reasons for the handling difficulties. In the robotized sewing problem, where a sewing machine is involved in the chain robot-fabric-environment, the fabric should be kept taut and simultaneously should be fed in the sewing machine.

A few schemes for force control for robotic feeding a sewing machine were proposed in the relevant literature. A PID force control has been used in [1], where the fabric was fixed from one edge and pulled by a robot from the opposite edge. Another approach was presented in [2], where the sewing feed mechanism has been replaced by an especially designed manipulator. This fixed manipulator has been attached after modifications to the sewing machine. Their system was tested under high sewing speeds, while straight line and circular seams for joining multiple fabrics have been realized. A model-reference adaptive system has been proposed in [3] and is

S. Jeschke, H. Liu, and D. Schilberg (Eds.): ICIRA 2011, Part I, LNAI 7101, pp. 486–495, 2011.

compared with a PI controller. Fung et.al. [3], used a pair of two-link mechanisms that exerts a prescribed tension to fabrics to facilitate inspection processes.

In our previous work [4, 5] the efficiency of neural networks force control for the handling of a fabric during the sewing process has been studied. Recently, the control of the tensional force has been based on a fuzzy model reference adaptive controller [6] with promising preliminarily results.

In this paper the integration of our previous work is presented towards fully automated sewing process without any prior knowledge of the fabric type and sewing machine settings. An extensive experimental investigation of the seams derived by the developed robotized sewing system as well as its capabilities is presented. A wide range of knitted and woven fabrics with varying compositions are sewed by the system and by a human operator and the results are compared and explained.

This paper is organized as follows. The complexity of the sewing problem and the difficulties appeared in its automation are discussed in the next section. The topology of the neural network and the architecture of the force controller are presented in section 3. The experimental results with the seams produced by the robot and the human operator as well as the conclusion are presented in the lasts two sections.

## 2     The Robotized Sewing Problem and Its Difficulties

The experimental stage for the robotic sewing tests is shown in Fig 1. A rectangular specimen of fabric is gripped by a robot manipulator holding the right edge while the opposite (left) edge of the fabric is moving with unknown velocity by the feed dog mechanism of the sewing machine. During the sewing process the fabric should be kept taut so as to prevent the buckling and ensure high quality of stitches. The desired tensional forces for each fabric depend on the fabric type and properties [4]. The sewing process is separated into two phases. In the first one (Step A initial phase), shown in Fig 1, the robot approaches the fabric from the top (↓①) until the gripper fingers touch the table with a force greater than a predefined one (4 N). Then the downward movement stopped and the fingers close and pinch the fabric. The gripper is moving up (↑②) for 5mm so as to avoid the contact of the robot with the table during the sewing. Afterwards, the controller is activated and the robot is moving to the right (→③) in order to apply the desired tensional force to the fabric. This initial step is identical with the work presented in [5]. In the second phase (Step B sewing phase), shown in Fig. 2, the sewing machine is started performing a seam while the neural network controller moves the robot towards the needle and ensures that the desired tensional force is applied to the fabric.

The aim of the presented approach is to develop a flexible controller that could be able to perform the above described process and handle a wide range of fabric types without any previous knowledge concerning the properties or the model of each fabric, since the modeling of the fabric's behavior is a very difficult and complicated problem. A simplified mechanical model [7], which describes the tensional part of the viscoelastic behavior of the fabric, is shown in Fig. 3a.

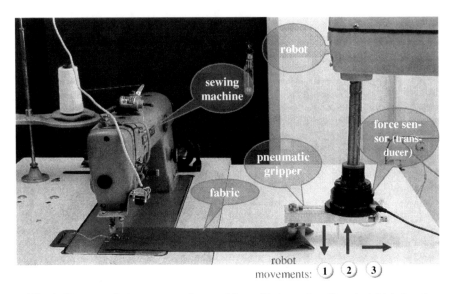

**Fig. 1.** The controlled system: sewing machine – fabric – robot (Step A: initial phase)

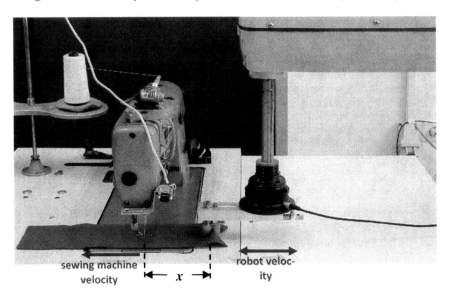

**Fig. 2.** The controller system: sewing machine – fabric – robot (Step B: sewing phase)

The fabric properties: spring with stiffness coefficient $k(x)$, damper with damping coefficient $b(x)$ and the friction force $f(x)$ between the fabric and the table, are nonlinear parameters and functions of the length $(x)$ between the gripper and the sewing needle, which is reduced during the sewing process. These properties are depending on the fabrics types as well as on the fabrics dimensions. For example, a very extensible fabric has quite different properties from a fabric with a very low extensibility (which approaches the rigid body behavior). Besides that, even for the case of the same fabric, during the sewing process the length of the fabric is reduced and consequently the fabric stiffness is increased. Moreover, this model is valid only in the case of tension because the fabric cannot support compressive forces in contradiction with the simple mechanical model shown in Fig. 3a. Therefore, it is considered that the model of the fabric is unknown and so a neural network controller is designed where the model of the fabric is not necessary.

Our previous work towards the automation of the sewing of fabrics is integrated as follows. The force/strain curves of the 12 fabrics that are used in the experiments are presented in Fig. 3b, where the fabric 12 is a very extensible fabric and fabric 1 is a fabric with a very low extensibility. The data for these curves have been obtained by robotized fabrics tensile tests [8]. From each of these curves the extensibility of each fabric is estimated using a trained neural network. The desired constant tensional force for each fabric needed for the sewing process is determined by a fuzzy decision mechanism [4] using as an input the extensibility obtained by the neural network appeared in [8]. These tensional forces are shown in the third column in Table 1.

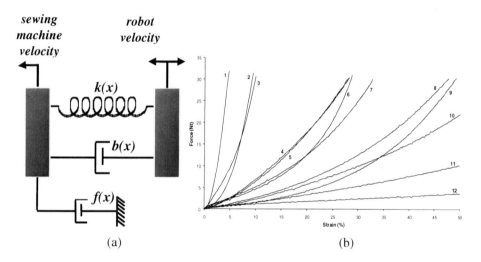

(a)                                    (b)

**Fig. 3.** Mechanical model of fabric tension (a) and fabrics' force/strain curves

The aim of the proposed controller is to apply the desired constant tensional force to the fabric in the beginning and during the sewing process, independently of the sewing machine velocity, which is unknown. This is achieved by determining the robot end-effector's incremental displacements along the sewing line direction. This neural network controller is characterized by on-line and endless learning as well as it has the capability of memorizing prior behaviors of sewed fabrics as explained in [5]. The neural network controller is presented in the next section and illustrated in Fig. 4. The force sensor mounted on the wrist of the robot manipulator is used to measure the force applied to the fabric, which is the only feedback signal in the control loop, in order to derive the appropriate incremental displacement. The proposed neural network controller and by extension the whole system is tested in a number of fabric specimens and the evaluation of its efficiency is based on the seams quality.

It should be declared that the orientation of the fabric and the rotation of the fabric around the needle in order to stitch in curved lines are not examined in this study. For the convenience of the presented experiments it is assumed that the fabric is already placed on the feed dog mechanism [9] and aligned with the sewing line [10].

Apart from the problem of the handling itself, there are a lot of other sewing machine's parameters that affecting the seam quality. These are the pressing force, the rotational frequency of the main shaft, the different sewing modes, the stitch length, the tension of the thread etc. All these parameters have been initially set and are kept constant in all experiments that are presented in this paper. Therefore, they have the same influence in the seam quality in both cases of the robotized or manual feeding of the fabric.

## 3      The Experimental Setup and the Neural Network Control Scheme

The Adept Cobra s800 robotic manipulator is used for the sewing process. A simple ad hoc pneumatic pinch gripper is mounted on the robot, as shown in Fig 1. The force is measured using the F/T system (Gamma 65/5) from ATI Industrial Automation, which is mounted on the wrist of the robot. All the necessary algorithms, i.e., the FNN force controller, the communication with the force sensor controller etc. are implemented and executed inside the robot's controller board (SmartController CX), as shown in Fig. 4, in order to meet the increased demands for high cycle rates in the force control loop.

The neural network control scheme, presented by the authors of this paper in [5], is used for sewing the fabric specimens. This control scheme, which is illustrated in the flowchart with the rounded rectangular callout ① in Fig. 4, formulates the feedback error between the applied tensional force and the desired one. This force error is used by the back-propagation algorithm in order to adapt the network's weights. In addition, the applied tensional force is fed to the input of the network. Eventually, the output of the controller is the robot's incremental displacement.

For the experiments presented in the next section, a conventional industrial sewing machine is used, where the sewing speed is set to 20% of the maximum one.

## 4      Discussion of Sewing Results

The 12-specimens of fabrics are covering a wide range concerning their extensibility, from a very extensible fabric (specimen 12) to a fabric with a very low extensibility (specimen 1), in other words a fabric approaching the behavior of a "rigid body". Moreover, the selected specimens are knitted and woven fabrics with varying composition as shown in Table 1. The length of the produced seams is initially set to be 15 cm, while the initial length of the part of the fabric that is between the robot end effector and the sewing machine is set to 18 cm. The robot end effector is stopped at 3 cm before the sewing machine's feed dog mechanism due to the mechanical limits and to avoid collision of the devices.

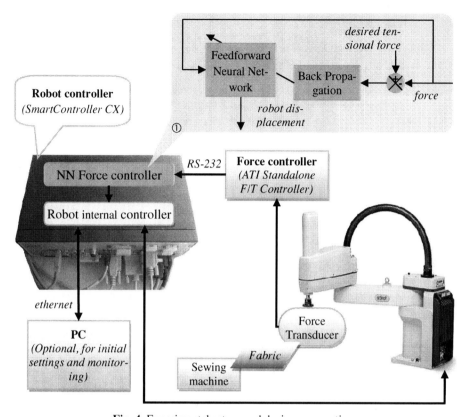

**Fig. 4.** Experimental setups and devices connections

In the last two columns of Table 1, the seams produced by the robot as well as the seams produced by the human operator are illustrated. The high resolution files of these pictures can be found in [11]. As a general conclusion, the seams produced by the robot are comparable with that produced by the human operator and in few cases better, as shown in specimens 1 and 6. Moreover, the advantage of the robot to follow a straight line, in contrast to a human operator, is obvious in the most of the specimens.

Puckering occurred in both cases of: robot or human operator. The wrinkles or wrinkled parts, originated in tightly stitched fabrics, and appear largely in specimens 1 and 12. These specimens can be considered as the boundaries of the trained force controller and as it is known a neural controller that works close to its boundaries exhibits a reduced performance. Especially, the specimen 1 presents more and higher wrinkles in the case of the human operator. This can be explained given that the human cannot keep the tensional force constant and a very low variation in the applied force could activate the puckering more easily in a fabric with a very low extensibility. On the other hand, these wrinkles can be reduced in acceptable levels

**Table 1.** Fabric specimens and seams produced by the robot and the human operator

| No. | Construction<br>*Composition* | Desired force (N) | Seams produced by the robot | Seams produced by the human operator |
|-----|-------------------------------|-------------------|-----------------------------|---------------------------------------|
| 1 | **Woven**<br>*viscose 65%*<br>*polyester 35%* | 0.1 | | |
| 2 | **Woven**<br>*synthetic*<br>*wool 50%-*<br>*50%* | 0.3 | | |
| 3 | **Woven**<br>*cotton 100%* | 0.3 | | |
| 4 | **Knitted**<br>*polyester 60%*<br>*cotton 40%* | 0.5 | | |
| 5 | **Knitted**<br>*acrylic*<br>*cotton* | 0.5 | | |
| 6 | **Woven**<br>*cotton 92%*<br>*elastane 8%* | 0.5 | | |
| 7 | **Knitted**<br>*acrylic 100%* | 0.5 | | |
| 8 | **Knitted**<br>*cotton 100%* | 0.7 | | |
| 9 | **Knitted**<br>*cotton 49%*<br>*acrylic 49%*<br>*lycra 2%* | 0.6 | | |

**Table 2.** (*continued*)

| | | | | |
|---|---|---|---|---|
| 10 | **Knitted** *polyester 60% cotton 40%* | 0.7 | | |
| 11 | **Knitted** *nylon 100%* | 0.7 | | |
| 12 | **Knitted** *cotton 94% elastane 6%* | 0.9 | | |

when the fabric is stretched before and after the seam. In most cases a human expert follows this handling approach to facilitate the quality of the seam, i.e. stretches the fabric while putting the one hand before the sewing needle and the other one after the sewing needle. In the presented experiments the human operator is restricted to sew the fabrics using only one hand, before the sewing needle, so as to be comparable with the robotic handling approach. The use of a second robotic manipulator or the use of a second gripper in order to imitate the actual human handling approach is under consideration.

Indicatively and due to pages limits, the applied tensional force and the appropriate desired force for the cases of specimens 1 and 12 is presented in Fig. 5. Each case is separated in two steps. The Step A is the initial phase where the desired tensional force should be applied to the fabric in order to start the sewing. The Step B is the sewing phase where the sewing machine is started and the robot follows while trying to apply the desired tensional force.

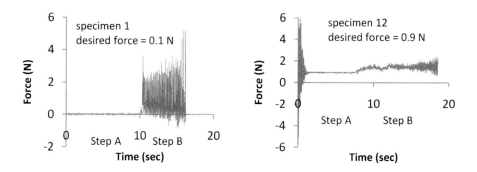

**Fig. 5.** Applied forces during the Step A initial phase and Step B sewing phase of specimens 1 and 12

From both cases, it is obvious that as the robot approaches the sewing machine, i.e. as the remaining length of the fabric to be taut (to be sewed) decreases, the fabric becomes more 'stiffer' and therefore the force oscillations increased. A comparison between these and the respective ones when a human operator sews the same fabrics, would be very useful. Therefore, a fabric tension measurement system that could be able to measure the applied tension when a human operator sews a fabric is under consideration and will be presented in a future work.

It should be mentioned that the fabric specimens have not been ironed after its sewing. A careful ironing of the specimens, which is a common procedure when a cloth is sewed, can improve the appearance of the fabrics and by extension could improve the quality of the seams. On the other hand, a system or an objective technique to "measure" the quality of the seams would be necessary in such automatic systems. A lot of automatic quality control of seams have been already researched and presented in the international literature [12].

## 5    Conclusion

The robotized sewing of fabrics using a conventional industrial sewing machine is presented. Our previous work towards the sewing automation is integrated into one system and a variety of fabric types are sewed without using any prior knowledge of the fabric properties or the sewing machine settings. The robot controller is based on neural networks and has on-line learning and memorizing capabilities. The produced by the robot seams of the 12 fabric specimens are comparable with that produced by the human operator and in few cases better. The known and complex problem of puckering that appeared in a sewed fabric is occurred in some of the experiments presented here. The investigation of the controller boundaries under greater sewing speeds will be the next step in this work. The feedback of the results (assessment of seams quality) so as to adapt the controller performance will be also investigated.

## References

1. Patton, R., Swern, F., Tricamo, S., Veen, A.: Automated Cloth Handling Using Adaptive Force Feedback. Journal of Dynamic Systems, Measur. and Control 114, 731–733 (1992)
2. Winck, R.C., Dickerson, S., Book, W.J., Huggins, J.D.: A novel approach to fabric control for automated sewing. In: IEEE/ASME International Conference on Advanced Intelligent Mechatronics, AIM, pp. 53–58 (2009)
3. Fung, E.H.K., Yuen, C.W.M., Hau, L.C., Wong, W.K., Chan, L.K.: A robot system for the control of fabric tension for inspection. In: Proceedings of ASME International Mechanical Engineering Congress and Exposition, pp. 813–819 (2008)
4. Koustoumpardis, P., Aspragathos, N.: Fuzzy Logic Decision Mechanism Combined with a Neuro-Controller for Fabric Tension in Robotized Sewing Process. Journal of Intelligent and Robotics Systems 36(1), 65–88 (2003)
5. Koustoumpardis, P., Aspragathos, N.: Neural network force control for robotized handling of fabrics. In: International Conference on Control, Automation and Systems, ICCAS 2007, October 17-20, pp. 566–571. COEX, Seoul (2007)

6. Triantafyllou, D., Koustoumpardis, P., Aspragathos, N.: Model Reference Fuzzy Learning Force Control for Robotized Sewing. In: 19th Mediterranean Conference on Control and Automation, Corfu, Greece, June 20-23, pp. 1460–1465 (2011)
7. Gershon, D.: Strategies for Robotic Handling of Flexible Sheet Material. Mechatronics 3(5), 611–623 (1993)
8. Koustoumpardis, P., Fourkiotis, J., Aspragathos, N.: Intelligent evaluation of fabrics' extensibility from robotized tensile test. International Journal of Clothing Science and Technology 19(2), 80–98 (2007)
9. Zoumponos, G.T., Aspragathos, N.A.: Fuzzy logic path planning for the robotic placement of fabrics on a work table. Robotics and Computer-Integrated Manufacturing 24(2), 174–186 (2008)
10. Zacharia, P., Aspragathos, N., Mariolis, I., Dermatas, E.: A robotic system based on fuzzy visual servoing for handling flexible sheets lying on a table. Industrial Robot 36(5), 489–496 (2009)
11. Robotics Group, `http://robotics.mech.upatras.gr/portal`
12. Mariolis, I.G., Dermatas, E.S.: Automated assessment of textile seam quality based on surface roughness estimation. Journal of the Textile Institute 101(7), 653–659 (2010)

# Dynamic Insertion of Bendable Flat Cables with Variation Based on Shape Returning Points

Yuuki Kataoka and Shinichi Hirai

Department of Robotics, Ritsumeikan University,
Kusatsu, Shiga 525-8577, Japan

**Abstract.** This paper focuses on the insertion of flat cables with variance. Manipulation of flat cables must cope with the variance of their deformed shapes. Here we will propose a method to guide the cable end to its desired location using static images of the cable. First, we will introduce the insertion of flat cables. Second, we will describe the concept of a shape returning point, where dynamically deformed shape coincides with static shape of a cable. Based on this concept, we will construct the procedure to determine the trajectory of a robot manipulating cables. We will show experimental results to demonstrate how the proposed procedure works.

## 1 Introduction

Cable insertion is one of basic and common operations in manufacturing in electric and automotive industries. This operation depends on human work up to now though automatic cable insertion is desired for the past decades. The barrier against the automatic insertion of bendable cables is the variance of their deformed shapes. Individual cables exhibit different deformation, even though their natural shapes are identical. This suggests that motion of an assembly robot must be changed according to individual cables.

Manipulation of deformable objects has been studies in the past decade [1,2,3,4]. Along this literature, insertion of flexible wires has been extensively studies [5,6,7,8]. These studies are based on object models, implying that behavior of objects to be inserted follows the predetermined models. Models for wires and cables have been studied as well [9,10,11]. Unfortunately, objects often exhibit behavior deviated from the models due to the variance among objects. Variance among objects is out of focus in the previous studies, suggesting that the model-based methods have difficulty in performing cable insertion despite of the variance. One approach to change the motion of an assembly robot is *visual servoing*, where visual images are fedback to the robot synchronously to the robot motion. This approach can cope with any deformation that may happen in actual operation. Unfortunately, capturing successive images, transmitting them to an image processor, and image processing synchronous to robot motion control require special hardwares, which results in high cost and low applicability. Thus, alternative approach is needed.

S. Jeschke, H. Liu, and D. Schilberg (Eds.): ICIRA 2011, Part I, LNAI 7101, pp. 496–508, 2011.

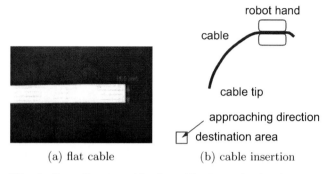

(a) flat cable                    (b) cable insertion

**Fig. 1.** Operation to guide the cable tip to destination area

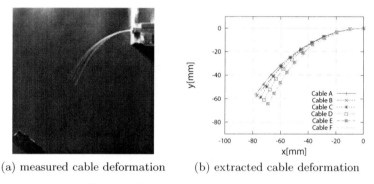

(a) measured cable deformation        (b) extracted cable deformation

**Fig. 2.** Different deformation of cables

This paper focuses on the insertion of flat cables with variance. We will propose a method to guide the cable end to its desired location using static images of the cable. Namely, our approach need not obtain successive images dynamically.

## 2   Insertion of Bendable Flat Cables

Figure 1 illustrates the operation to be tackled in this paper. Figure 1-(a) shows an example of a flat cable. We focus on two-dimensional flexural deformation of a cable. An assembly robot, which works in the vertical plane, grips a bendable flat cable at one point on the cable, as shown in Figure 1-(b). The gripping point is apart from the tip so that the cable can be inserted into the hole. Operation is to guide the tip of a bendable flat cable to the predetermined destination area, which represents a hole in which the cable is inserted, and along with the predetermined approaching direction, which characterizes the direction of the hole.

One difficulty in flat cable insertion comes from the variation of cable deformation. Figure 2 demonstrates variation in static deformation of cables. We used flat cables of 0.1 mm in thickness, 16.0 mm in width, and 7.4 g/m in line density. A robot, Denso Wave VP–6242G, grasps a flat cable at the point 100 mm apart from its tip. We used RC7M–VPG5, a robot controller, and PAC, a robot

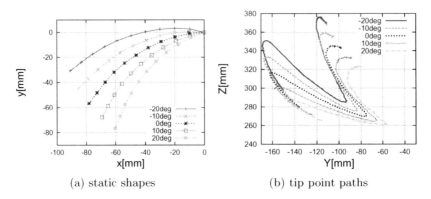

(a) static shapes                    (b) tip point paths

**Fig. 3.** Different deformation according to gripping posture

programming language, to control the robot motion. Figure 2-(a) shows a super-imposed image that shows the deformation of six cables. As shown in the figure, the static shapes of six deformed cables differ from one another, despite of their same geometry. The difference at the tip reached to 13.1 mm at its maximum. It is often the case that the size of the hole is smaller than this difference, imply-ing that teaching-and-playback approach does not work well in such operation. We applied a sequence of image processing algorithms to extract the deformed shape of a cable. We divided the total length of a cable into 10 regions, implying that the extracted shape consists of 11 points. Figure 2-(b) shows the extracted shapes of deformed cables given in the superimposed image.

Another difficulty in flat cable insertion comes from the deformation during operation. Figure 3 demonstrates the dependency of cable shapes to gripping posture. We used one flat cable to measure deformed shapes at different grip-ping postures. Gripping posture is given by the orientation angle of the gripper attached to the assembly robot, as we focus on operation in vertical plane. As shown in Figure 3-(a), static shapes depend on the orientation angles. Let us move the robot end by 50 mm downward in 0.4 s and 50 mm leftward in 0.4 s. A camera, Photonfocus MV2–D1280–640 with a lens, MYUTRON FV5026W–F, captures successive images of a deforming cable at 400 frames per second. The captured images are sent to a PC through AproLink microenableIV. Image pro-cessing are performed on the PC to extract the shape of a deformed cable. Due to the dynamic deformation of a flat cable, the cable tip moves differently from the robot end motion, as shown in Figure 3-(b). In addition, we find that cable tip motion depends on the orientation angle.

Figure 4 demonstrates dynamic deformation of a cable. The gripping angle was $0°$. The robot end moved along the same trajectory as that in Figure 3. Figure 4-(a) shows the path of the cable tip and Figures 4-(b) through (f) show deformed shapes, compared with the static shape of the cable. Deformed shapes are basically different from the static shape but deformed shape in Figure 4-(e) is similar to the static shape. This suggests that a flat cable may exhibit a deformed shape similar to its static shape during operation.

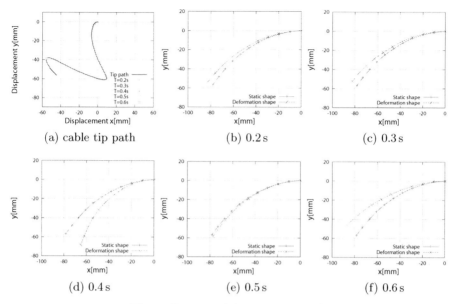

**Fig. 4.** Dynamic deformation of cable

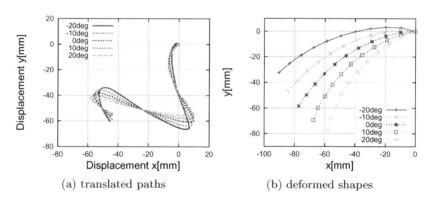

**Fig. 5.** Intersection of translated cable tip paths

Consequently, we have to cope with the variance of cable deformation as well as dynamic deformation of cables to successfully perform the insertion of bendable flat cables. Observation of dynamic deformation suggests the deformed shape of a flat cable may return to its static shape during operation.

## 3   Shape Returning Points

As mentioned in the previous section, the deformed shape of a flat cable may return to its static shape during operation. Let us investigate this phenomena

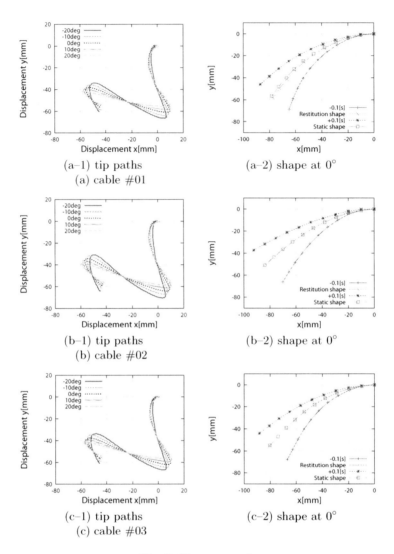

**Fig. 6.** Shape returning

experimentally. Recall that Figure 3-(b) shows cable tip paths according to different orientation angles. Since static shapes differ from one another as shown in Figure 3-(a), the starting points of paths (top right points of individual paths) are different from one another. Translating each path so that its starting point coincides with the origin of the coordinate system, we obtain Figure 5-(a). As shown in the figure, all paths intersect at one point: $(x, y) = (-23.3, -51.3)$ mm. Deformed shapes at this intersecting point are shown in Figure 5-(b). Comparing this figure and Figure 3-(a), we find that each deformed shape at the intersecting point is similar to its corresponding static shape. This intersecting point is thus referred to as *shape returning point*. Note that shape returning points at different orientation angles coincide to one another, suggesting that we can guide the cable tip point to the destination once the corresponding static shape is measured, since the deformed shape at the point coincides to the static shape.

Let us verify shape returning phenomena with different cables. We used three different cables, #01, #02, and #03. Figure 6-(a–1) shows tip point paths of cable #01 at different orientation angles. As shown in the figure, paths intersect at one point. We confirmed that all deformed shapes are closed to one another at the intersecting point. Figure 6-(a–2) shows one deformed shape (orientation angle is 0 degree) and the statically deformed shape of the cable. As shown in the figure, the deformed shape almost coincides to the static shape. The figure includes two deformed shapes 0.1 s before and after the time corresponding to the intersecting point. The two deformed shapes are far from the static shape, implying that shape returning is sensitive to time. Figures 6-(b) and (c) show the results for cables #02 and #03. We find that shape returning concept is valid for different cables.

## 4   Guidance of Cable Tip

**Procedure to Determine Robot end Trajectory.** Based on the concept of shape returning point, we will determine the trajectory of the robot end point and the orientation angle at the end point. Recall that the shape returning point is independent of the orientation angle, suggesting that we can determine the trajectory of the robot end point and the orientation angle at the end point independently. Let $x_r$ be the position of the end point of a robot and $\theta_r$ denote the orientation angle at the robot end point. Let $x_e$ be the tip position of a cable and $\theta_e$ denote the tangential direction along with the cable at its tip. Let $x_e^*$ be the center of the destination area and $\theta_e^*$ denote the approaching direction. We should determine $x_r$ and $\theta_r$ so that $x_e$ and $\theta_e$ be guided to their desired values $x_e^*$ and $\theta_e^*$.

Assume that the robot is in its home location, where its end point position and orientation are given by $x_{rs}$ and $\theta_{rs}$, as illustrated in Figure 7-(a). Let $x_{es}$ and $\theta_{es}$ be cable tip position and orientation corresponding to robot home location. Note that the tangential direction $\theta_e$ along with the cable changes according to the orientation angle $\theta_r$ at the robot end. This suggests that we can guide angle $\theta_e$ from its initial value $\theta_{es}$ to its desired value $\theta_e^*$ by controlling $\theta_r$. Let $\theta_{ro}$ be the orientation angle where $\theta_e$ coincide to its desired value $\theta_e^*$, as shown in Figure 7-(b). Since orientation angle $\theta_r$ changes from its initial value $\theta_{rs}$ to $\theta_{ro}$, cable shape may change. Let $x_{eo}$ be the position of the cable tip at the changed shape. Now, assume that the robot end moves along a predetermined trajectory $d(t)$ from $x_{rs}$. Let $x_{SRP}$ be the position of the shape returning point along this trajectory, as shown in Figure 7-(c). Then, let us translate the starting position $x_{rs}$ by $d_r = x_e^* - x_{SRP}$ so that the shape returning point coincides to the desired

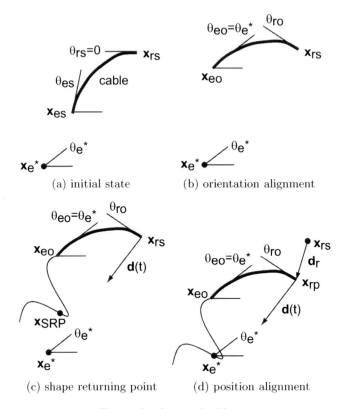

**Fig. 7.** Guidance of cable tip

position $x_e^*$, as shown in Figure 7-(d). Consequently, the starting position and orientation of robot end point are given by

$$x_{rp} = x_{rs} + d_r,$$
$$\theta_{rp} = \theta_{ro}.$$

Recall that the tangential direction at the shape returning point coincides to that at the starting point: $\theta_{ro} = \theta_e^*$. As a result, the cable tip position and orientation are guided to their desired values: $x_e^*$ and $\theta_e^*$.

For the above procedure, we have to determine $\theta_{ro}$ and $d_r$ for each cable to be inserted. The following sections describe how to determine them.

**Orientation Alignment.** In the procedure mentioned in the previous section, we need to determine robot end orientation angle $\theta_{ro}$ that makes the tangential direction of a flat cable coincide to the approaching direction. Assume that we can measure static shapes of a cable to be inserted at a finite number of different orientation angles in advance. Let $\theta_e^i$ be the tangential direction of a cable corresponding to the $i$-th robot end orientation angle $\theta_r^i$. We apply linear

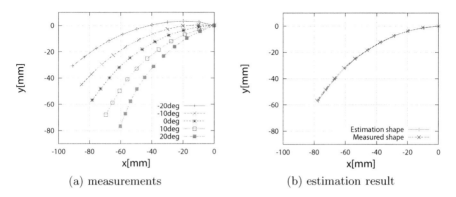

(a) measurements    (b) estimation result

**Fig. 8.** Interpolation of static shape

interpolation in calculating angle $\theta_{ro}$. We first minimize the absolute difference between $\theta_e^i$ and $\theta_{es}$. Namely, we determine $k$ satisfying:

$$E_k = \| \theta_e^k - \theta_{es} \| = \min_i \| \theta_e^i - \theta_{es} \| .$$

Then, we determine $\theta_e^l$ that is adjacent to $\theta_e^k$ and $\theta_{es}$ is between the two. Let us calculate $E_l = \| \theta_e^l - \theta_{es} \|$. Orientation angle $\theta_{ro}$ is then determined by the following linear interpolation:

$$\theta_{ro} = \frac{E_l \theta_e^k + E_k \theta_e^l}{E_k + E_l}.$$

This interpolation can apply not only at the cable tip but also at any point along the cable. Since cable shape can be specified by all angles at points along the cable, we can interpolate the static shape at any value of $\theta_r$. Figure 8 shows one example of shape interpolation. Figure 8-(a) describes a set of static shapes corresponding to different orientation angles. Let us interpolate the static shape at $\theta_r = 0$ from two static shapes at $-10°$ and $10°$. Figure 8-(b) shows the interpolated and the measured shapes, which are similar to each other.

**Estimating Shape Returning Point.** In the procedure mentioned in the previous section, we need to estimate the position of the shape returning point for each cable to be inserted. Measuring dynamic deformation of a cable enables us to directly determine the position of the shape returning point, but this approach is time consuming and should be avoided. Thus, we will approximate a static shape of the cable to be inserted from a finite number of static shapes of sample cables so that we can estimate the position of the shape returning point of a cable to be inserted.

Recall that we have the static shape $S_0^{cur}$ of a cable to be inserted at $\theta_r = 0$ in the orientation alignment process. We collect many static shapes corresponding to different cables. Let $S_0^i$ be the shape of the $i$-th cable sample at $\theta_r = 0$. Let us apply linear approximation. First, we determine $k$ satisfying:

$$D_k = dist(S_0^k, S_0^{cur}) = \min_i \ dist(S_0^i, S_0^{cur}),$$

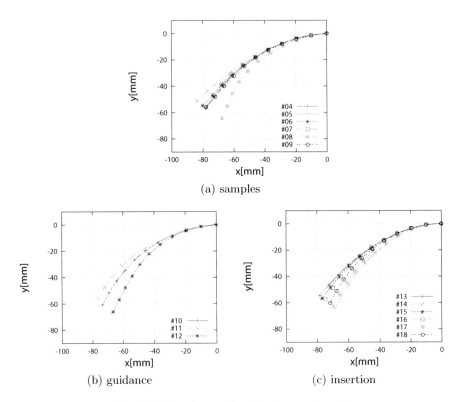

(a) samples

(b) guidance

(c) insertion

**Fig. 9.** Static shapes of cables in experiments

where *dist* denote the difference between two shapes. Second, we determine $l$ satisfying:

$$D_l = dist(S_0^l, S_0^{cur}) = \min_{i \neq k} \; dist(S_0^i, S_0^{cur}).$$

Namely, $S_0^k$ and $S_0^l$ are the best and second best approximation of shape $S_0^{cur}$. Let $\boldsymbol{x}_{\mathrm{SRP}}^k$ and $\boldsymbol{x}_{\mathrm{SRP}}^l$ be the positions of the shape returning point of the $i$-th and $k$-th cable samples. We will estimate the position of the shape returning point of the cable to be inserted by

$$\boldsymbol{x}_{\mathrm{SRP}} = \frac{D_l \boldsymbol{x}_{\mathrm{SRP}}^k + D_k \boldsymbol{x}_{\mathrm{SRP}}^l}{D_k + D_l}.$$

Once we can estimate the position of the shape returning point, we can calculate the translation of robot end point by $\boldsymbol{d}_r = \boldsymbol{x}_e^* - \boldsymbol{x}_{\mathrm{SRP}}$.

## 5    Experiments on Cable Guidance and Insertion

**Cables Used in Experiments.** This section describes experimental results on flat cable guidance and insertion. First, we built static shape sets for six

**Table 1.** Error in cable guidance experiment

| (a-1) $P_1$ and 55° | | | (a-2) $P_1$ and 65° | | | (a-3) $P_1$ and 75° | | |
|---|---|---|---|---|---|---|---|---|
| $x$ [mm] | $y$ [mm] | $\theta_e$ [°] | $x$ [mm] | $y$ [mm] | $\theta_e$ [°] | $x$ [mm] | $y$ [mm] | $\theta_e$ [°] |
| −0.09 | −1.08 | 1.26 | 0.16 | −0.58 | 0.42 | −0.09 | −0.33 | 0.91 |
| −0.37 | 0.93 | 3.17 | −1.62 | 1.18 | 3.46 | 1.38 | 0.18 | 3.55 |
| 0.46 | −1.15 | −0.81 | −2.04 | 0.10 | 3.50 | −0.91 | 0.10 | −2.04 |

| (b-1) $P_2$ and 55° | | | (b-2) $P_2$ and 65° | | | (b-3) $P_2$ and 75° | | |
|---|---|---|---|---|---|---|---|---|
| $x$ [mm] | $y$ [mm] | $\theta_e$ [°] | $x$ [mm] | $y$ [mm] | $\theta_e$ [°] | $x$ [mm] | $y$ [mm] | $\theta_e$ [°] |
| −0.34 | −0.83 | 1.16 | 0.66 | −0.58 | −1.45 | 0.91 | −0.08 | 1.91 |
| 1.13 | −0.07 | 2.88 | 0.88 | −0.07 | 2.36 | 1.16 | 0.18 | 3.18 |
| 0.21 | −0.65 | 0.69 | 0.96 | −0.40 | 4.24 | −0.16 | 0.10 | −0.36 |

| (c-1) $P_3$ and 55° | | | (c-2) $P_3$ and 65° | | | (c-3) $P_3$ and 75° | | |
|---|---|---|---|---|---|---|---|---|
| $x$ [mm] | $y$ [mm] | $\theta_e$ [°] | $x$ [mm] | $y$ [mm] | $\theta_e$ [°] | $x$ [mm] | $y$ [mm] | $\theta_e$ [°] |
| 0.66 | −1.08 | 0.74 | 0.19 | −0.33 | 0.36 | 0.91 | −0.08 | 0.54 |
| 1.38 | −0.32 | 2.99 | 1.88 | −0.32 | 1.93 | 1.88 | −0.07 | 3.65 |
| 0.21 | −0.65 | 0.12 | 0.46 | −0.40 | 3.62 | 1.46 | −0.15 | 3.90 |

cables: #04 through #09. Shapes corresponding to $\theta_r = 0$ of these cables are shown in Figure 9-(a). We used three cables #10 through #12 for guidance test. Shapes corresponding to $\theta_r = 0$ of these cables are shown in Figure 9-(b). Note that shapes of cables #10 through #12 are different from those of cables #04 through #09. The maximum difference of the tip position among cables #10 through #12 reaches to 13.99 mm. We used six cables #13 through #18 for insertion test. Shapes corresponding to $\theta_r = 0$ of these cables are shown in Figure 9-(c). Note that shapes of cables #13 through #18 are different from those of cables #04 through #09. The maximum difference of the tip position among cables #13 through #18 reaches to 13.97 mm.

**Experiment on Cable Guidance.** We used three cables: #10 through #12. A cable should be guided to its desired position $P_1 = (-140, 310)$ mm, $P_2 = (-140, 300)$ mm, or $P_3 = (-130, 310)$ mm. Desired angle is set to 55°, 65°, or 75°. Namely, we have nine desired locations. Table 1 summarizes the experimental result. This figure shows the positional error along $x$- and $y$-axes and orientation error. The absolute positional error is less than 2.1 mm and the absolute orientation error is less than 4°.

**Experiment on Cable Insertion.** We have performed cable insertion experiment to demonstrate our method. A cable should be inserted into a slit of 5 mm in height and 25 mm in width. As mentioned in the previous section, the absolute positional error was less than 2.1 mm in cable guidance experiment. This error is less than the slit height 5 mm, suggesting that our method is applicable to actual cable insertion. We used six cables: #13 through #18. Note that the variation of cable end position, 13.97 mm, exceeds the slit height, 5 mm. The position of

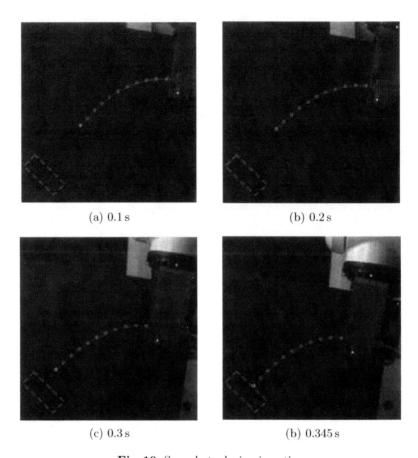

(a) 0.1 s                    (b) 0.2 s

(c) 0.3 s                    (b) 0.345 s

**Fig. 10.** Snapshots during insertion

the slit is $(-140, 300)$ mm. The orientation of the slit is set to $45°$, $55°$, or $65°$. We applied the following three trajectories:

$T_1$ : move 70 mm in 0.6 s with $55°$ from the horizon downward,

$T_2$ : move 70 mm in 0.6 s with $45°$ from the horizon downward,

$T_3$ : move 70 mm in 0.6 s with $35°$ from the horizon downward.

Thus, we conduced 54 trials for insertion and found that all trials were successfully performed. Figure 10 shows an example of snapshots during cable insertion. This figure shows the insertion of cable #13 along trajectory $T_1$ into a slit with angle $45°$. The cable was successfully inserted into the slot in 0.35 s. Figure 11 shows a sequence of corresponding deformed shapes. As shown in the figure, the deformed shape of a cable turns into its static shape at the moment of insertion.

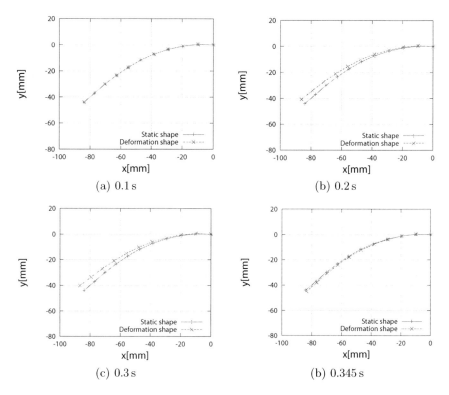

**Fig. 11.** Deformed shapes during insertion

## 6    Concluding Remarks

We have proposed a method to guide bendable cables based on their shape returning points. This method does not require to take successive images of a deforming cable during its insertion. Instead, our method requires a several images of the statically deformed cable. We demonstrated that the variance of the cable tip position can be reduced to one sixth. The proposed method can be applied to any assembly robot with a camera to measure static shapes of cables. Future issues are 1) reduction of images of statically deformed cable, 2) investigating shape returning phenomena, and 3) three-dimensional insertion of a flat cable with twist deformation.

**Acknowledgement.** This research was supported in part by Canon Inc.

## References

1. Taylor, P.M., et al.: Sensory Robotics for the Handling of Limp Materials. Springer, Heidelberg (1990)
2. Hopcroft, J.E., Kearney, J.K., Krafft, D.B.: A Case Study of Flexible Object Manipulation. Int. Journal of Robotics Research 10(1), 41–50 (1991)

3. Henrich, D., Wörn, H. (eds.): Robot Manipulation of Deformable Objects. Advanced Manufacturing Series. Springer, Heidelberg (2000)
4. Shibata, M., Ota, T., Hirai, S.: Wiping Motion for Deformable Object Handling. In: Proc. IEEE Int. Conf. on Robotics and Automation, Kobe, May 12-17, pp. 134–139 (2009)
5. Zheng, Y.F., Pei, R., Chen, C.: Strategies for Automatic Assembly of Deformable Objects. In: Proc. IEEE Int. Conf. on Robotics and Automation, pp. 2598–2603 (1991)
6. Chen, M.Z., Zheng, Y.F.: Vibration-Free Handling of Deformable Beams by Robot End-Effectors. Journal of Robotic Systems 12(5), 331–347 (1995)
7. Nakagaki, H., Kitagaki, K., Ogasawara, T., Tsukune, H.: Study of Deformation and Insertion Tasks of a Flexible Wire. In: Proc. IEEE Int. Conf. Robotics and Automation, pp. 2397–2402 (1997)
8. Yue, S., Henrich, D.: Manipulating Deformable Linear Objects: Sensor-Based Fast Manipulation during Vibration. In: Proc. IEEE Int. Conf. Robotics and Automation, pp. 2467–2472 (2002)
9. Pai, D.K.: STRANDS: Interactive Simulation of Thin Solids using Cosserat Models. Computer Graphics Forum 21(3), 347–352 (2002)
10. Wakamatsu, H., Hirai, S.: Static Modeling of Linear Object Deformation Based on Differential Geometry. Int. J. of Robotics Research 23(3), 293–311 (2004)
11. Wakamatsu, H., Arai, E., Hirai, S.: Fishbone Model for Belt Object Deformation. In: Burgard, W., Brock, O., Stachniss, C. (eds.) Robotics: Science and Systems III, pp. 89–96. The MIT Press (2007)

# A Vision System for the Unfolding of Highly Non-rigid Objects on a Table by One Manipulator

Dimitra Triantafyllou and Nikos A. Aspragathos

University of Patras, Dept. of Mechanical Engineering & Aeronautics, Robotics Group, Greece
{dtriant,asprag}@mech.upatras.gr

**Abstract.** In this paper, a systematic approach is presented in order to detect and classify the characteristic features of a folded piece of fabric to be unfolded by a robot. The manipulations can be made by only one manipulator on a working table and with machine vision feedback. The main goal of this method is to detect, evaluate and classify the regions of interest (ROIs) which, in the particular case, are the corners of the fabric lying on the table.

**Keywords:** unfolding of fabrics, detection of critical features, vision system.

## 1   Introduction

Last decades, the increase of life expectancy and the drop of birth rate, has led to a society which is rapidly aging. Additionally, the number of single-person households is rising and the need to exempt from tedious house works is getting bigger. As a result, robotics' researchers are expected to provide solutions which will facilitate everyday life for everyone and, especially, for older people and caregivers.

Home service robots face a lot of tasks concerning the handling of non rigid objects such as cloths. The robotic research literature shows that the robotic handling of non-rigid objects, such as fabrics, is a very complicated problem since it is very difficult to model and predict the behavior of the fabric. The non-linearity, the large deformations and the very low bending resistance of the fabrics increase the complexity and difficulty of the robotic handling. In addition, fabrics, unlike solid objects, cannot be represented by a geometric model, thus there is no stable posture for grasping.

A quite challenging house work concerning handling of fabrics is the folding and, in order to do that, unfolding of clothes. Actually, to start the task of folding a piece of cloth, it has to be fully extended, without wrinkles, either in the air or on a working table. This procedure is essential in order to recognize the shape of the clothes and identify it, if it is not a priori known, and subsequently, to fold them.

Usually, the efforts to fold a cloth using one robotic arm consider the shape of the cloth known and already extended and grabbed from an area of the cloth suitable for folding [1], [2]. In contrast, most of researchers that used two robotic arms aim at first to accomplish a successful unfolding and then proceed to the folding. The main goal was to find the proper grasping points which usually are two of its corners [3], [6] or two not neighbor points at the cloth's outline [4] ,[5]. The manipulations were made

S. Jeschke, H. Liu, and D. Schilberg (Eds.): ICIRA 2011, Part I, LNAI 7101, pp. 509–519, 2011.

mainly in the air and the corners were detected with the help of machine vision. Mai-tin-Shepard et al [3], implemented a vision algorithm that takes into account the sharpness of curvature of the cloth in order to find two neighbor corners and to man-age the unfolding and folding of towels. Osawa [4], proposed a recurrent procedure, where a corner of the cloth was detected and grasped and then the lowest point of the hanging cloth was grasped by the other manipulator and expanded in order to recog-nize its shape and proceed to folding. Hamajima [5] used the relationships that exist between the shadows that appear on clothes and the approximate outline of clothes in hung-up state in order to detect their hemlines. Salleh [6] presented an inchworm gripper for tracing the edge of a piece of clothing. This gripper assists the two robotic manipulators to get into the state of holding a piece of cloth by two neighbor corners.

This paper presents part of an ongoing research work toward the unfolding of clothes on a working table by one manipulator using vision sensing. In this paper, an approach is presented for the classification of the critical features of a folded piece of fabric for the unfolding manipulation. In addition, a technique is presented for the detection and identification of the critical features. Experimental results are presented and discussed for the demonstration of the efficiency of this technique.

## 2     Basic Observations /Characteristics

The first step of the introduced approach is the systematic study of one human hand movements trying to unfold a fabric. So, some basic observations are made concern-ing: a) the fabric's behavior, b) the movements of the human hand and their effects on the cloth's possible configurations, c) the characteristic features of the folded cloth's shape that the human specified to proceed the unfolding.

In subsection 2.1, the unfolding procedure studied during the experiments and some manipulations and their correlation with the fabric's behavior and possible con-figurations are briefly presented, while, in subsection 2.2, the fabric's features of in-terest are described and classified.

### 2.1     A Brief Description of the Unfolding Procedure

The number of possible deformations that a piece of fabric can have is infinite. So, in a random position, it is usually difficult to detect the regions of interest of the piece of clothing under consideration (Fig 1.a).

After experimentation the following manipulations have proven to be very helpful for the initial part of the unfolding task. It is observed that when a piece of fabric, at random configuration, is grabbed from a random point, lifted in the air, shaken in order to remove its wrinkles and thrown with a flick of the wrist onto a table, then the corner the most distant from the point where the fabric is grabbed is one of the cor-ners that the fabric has when it is fully extended/unfolded (Fig 1.b). If this procedure is repeated once again but this time the fabric is grabbed from the corner founded from the previous manipulation, then a second not neighbor corner of the fabric is determined (Fig 1.c).

(a)                              (b)                              (c)

**Fig. 1.** The first part of the unfolding algorithm: a) the fabric at random configuration, b) the fabric after the first throw and the detection of the first fabric's corner A, c) the fabric after its second throw and the detection of the second corner B

After these manipulations, the fabric has obtained a configuration that will facilitate the detection of the features that are used for the unfolding. These features are corners, either corners of the cloth when it is fully extended or corners formed by folds of the fabric, and their corresponding unfolding axis (see subsection 2.2).

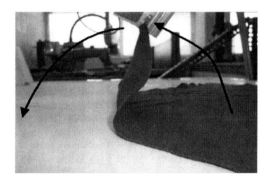

**Fig. 2.** The unfolding movement

After the detection and classification of the corners, a basic unfolding manipulation was observed during the experiments. The corner of a folded area is grabbed and a semicircular path is followed (Fig 2). The axis around which the movement is made is the corresponding unfolding axis of this corner.

The procedure described is iterated until the fabric gets in a fully extended-unfolded configuration.

## 2.2     The Cloth's Regions of Interest

As it was mentioned in the previous paragraph, in order to detect the characteristic features of a piece of fabric, it has to be in a configuration that will make at least some of them visible. So, at this part, the fabric is considered thrown appropriately on the working table (Fig 1.c).

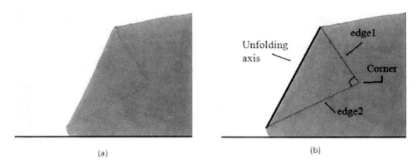

**Fig. 3.** (a) A fold, (b) the corner and the unfolding axis of the fold

The regions of interest in the task of unfolding are the corners of the fabric and, whenever they exist, their corresponding unfolding axes (Fig 3). The critical features are specific corners and edges of folded or unfolded shape which can be found either inside or in the contour of the fabric. A corner of the fabric is the point where two of its edges, with different directions meet. The edges either belong to the perimeter of the cloth when it is unfolded, or occur from folds. A corner's corresponding axis, is the edge opposite from the corner, which together with the two edges of the corner form a triangle. The axis should end at the points of intersection with the other two edges.

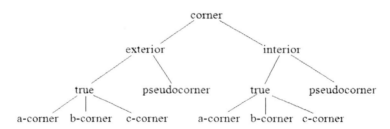

**Fig. 4.** The corner's classification tree

As a result, a corner can either belong to the corners of the unfolded shape or occur from folds, either be located at the contour of the lying fabric or in its interior. In addition, pseudocorners that occur from overlapping parts of the fabric have to be recognized as well. Three criteria are used for the classification of the corners in the corner's tree shown in Fig 4.

The first criterion used is the location of the corner in the current shape of the folded fabric (Fig 5). The corners are classified in two categories: a) exterior corners, which are located on the contour of the fabric, b) interior corners, which are located in the interior area of the fabric. The distinction is easily made, since the exterior corner is formed by two edges of the contour and for the interior one, both edges do not belong to the contour. Corners with one edge on the contour and the other in its interior are not taken into account.

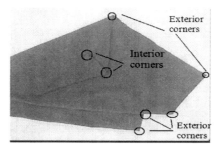

**Fig. 5.** Detection of interior and exterior corners

A second criterion for the classification of the corners is whether they occur from two overlapping parts of the fabric (Fig 6). According to this distinction the corners are classified in pseudocorners and true corners. When a pseudoconrner is an exterior corner it can be easily recognized since it's a corner looking outwards the fabric. Corners inside other corners, with one common edge can be also considered as pseudocorners. Another kind of pseudocorner is detected when one of its edges does not end at the point of their intersection.

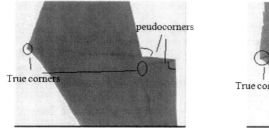 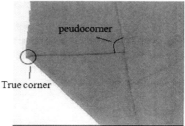

**Fig. 6.** Detection of true corners and pseudocorners

The third criterion classifies the true corners in three categories (Fig 7.a): a) the corners that occur from the folding of the fabric and the folded part is above the rest of the fabric and visible to an observer (a-corners) , b) the corners that occur from the folding of the fabric and the folded part is below the rest of the fabric and is not visible to an observer (b-corners), c) the corners that do not occur from folding, which are the corners of the unfolded shape of the fabric when it is fully extended (c-corners). The a-corners can be detected from the existence of an edge in the interior of their angle. In the b and c corners such a edge is not visible.

A case often met is when several folds, one at the top of the other, occur (Fig 7.b). The detection of the formed corners is made from the exterior a-corners to the interior corners, thus from the bottom to the top of folds. Firstly, an exterior a-corner is detected and the edge starting from its interior leads to another corner. The second corner is evaluated and classified and, if it is an a-corner, the same procedure is iterated until a b or c corner is found. The corresponding unfolding axis for the last found corner is detected in order to start the unfolding procedure from the top layer to the bottom.

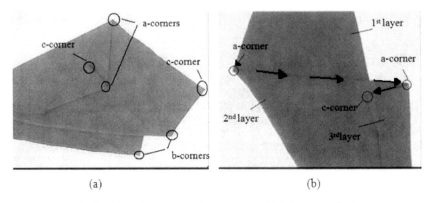

(a)                                    (b)

**Fig. 7.** a) The three types of true corners, b) Subsequent folds

As it is analyzed in the next section, apart from the corners, the detection of their corresponding "unfolding axis", if it exists, is also necessary (Fig 8). This axis is an edge located opposite to the corner, which together with the two edges of the corner form a triangle. The axis' line ends at the points of intersection with the other two edges, otherwise it is not an unfolding axis.

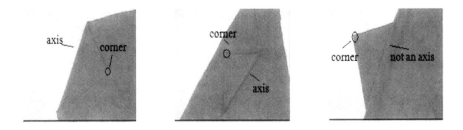

**Fig. 8.** Corners and their axes

## 3    The Vision System

In this paper, already known techniques and methods of machine vision are implemented to detect and recognize the proposed features of the fabric's configuration.

The true exterior corners of the fabric, when it is thrown on the working table, are detected by a curvature based corner detector that detects both fine and coarse features [7]. The contour is extracted with the help of a Canny detector, then the absolute value of curvature of each point on a contour at a low scale is computed and local maxima of absolute curvature are regarded as initial corner candidates. An adaptive curvature threshold is used to remove round corners from the initial list and false corners due to quantization noise and trivial details are eliminated by evaluating the angles of corner candidates in a dynamic region of support (Fig 9).

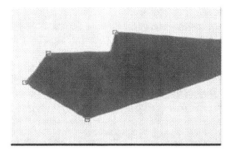

**Fig. 9.** Detection of the corners of the contour of the fabric

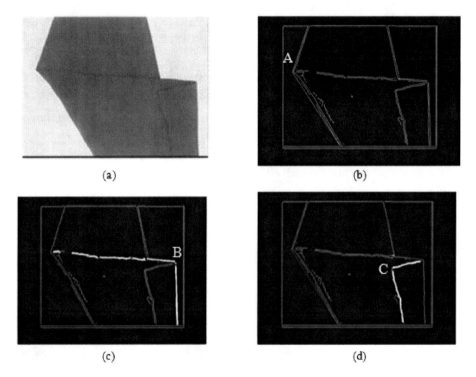

(a)

(b)

(c)

(d)

**Fig. 10.** Detection of subsequent folds: a) the folded fabric, b) the fabric after the implementation of Canny detector/ corner A is detected, c) the detection of: the A's corner interior edge, the edge of different direction and the a-corner B, d) the detection of B's interior double edge, the edge of different direction and a new b or c-corner C

As it is already mentioned, corners can be divided in a, b and c-corners . In order to find the corresponding category of each corner, the double line created by the contour of the folded fabric and its shadow is detected using the Canny edge detector (Fig 10.b). If a double edge exists, the corner corresponds to an a-corner. Otherwise, the fabric's corner must be lifted slightly so that the side that was facing the working table is revealed. If a double edge is detected then the corner corresponds to a b-corner. In different occasion the corner is a c-corner, thus one of the corners of the unfolded fabric when it is fully extended.

As it was mentioned before, when a double edge starts from a corner, a fold exists. Following this edge, other corners that may have occurred from several folds one on the top of the other, can be detected. Actually, corners like these are detected to the point where the double edge following the initial direction ends and another one, with different direction starts (Fig 10.c, 10.d).

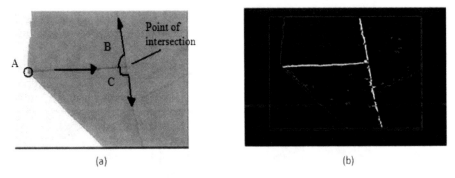

(a)                                             (b)

**Fig. 11.** Detection of a pseudocorner created from overlapping: a) the edge starting from the a-corner A intersects with an edge extending to two opposite directions, b) the vision algorithm detects the intersecting edges and classifies corners B and C as pseudocorners

This procedure might lead to pseudocorners, which occur when one part of the fabric is overlapped by another one. To avoid this situation, whenever a change of direction is observed the algorithm checks whether the new detected double edge starts from the point of intersection with the previous edge or the edge is extended to the opposite direction as well (Fig 11). In the second case, the detected corner can be characterized as a pseudocorner.

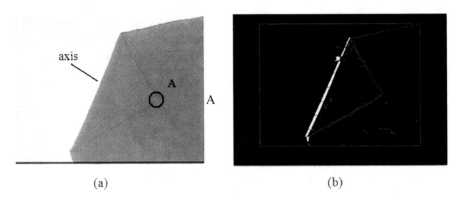

(a)                                             (b)

**Fig. 12.** Detection of the unfolding axis: a) corner A and its unfolding axis, b) the vision algorithm detects the unfolding axis

Finally, in order to find the axis around which an unfolding movement will be made, the algorithm searches once again for a double edge opposite to the corner under examination (Fig 12). This axis and the two edges of the corresponding corner form a triangle.

## 4    Experimental Results

The experiments were conducted with one orthogonal piece of fabric 45x40 cm, under relatively steady lighting conditions. The camera's locations varied in order to take pictures of the whole surface of the fabric and also to zoom in regions of interest so as to facilitate the detection of their characteristic features.

As the figures of section 3 show, in most cases the vision algorithm managed to detect and classify successfully the regions of interest. However, wrinkles, different lighting conditions and the incapability to avoid gaps at the detected edges may cause problems or even lead to failure.

**Fig. 13.** The noise caused by wrinkles of the fabric

Figure 13 shows the noise that occurs from wrinkles. This noise has computational cost since the white pixels have to be checked if they belong to an edge or not.

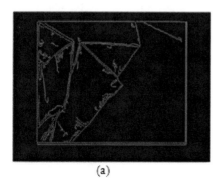
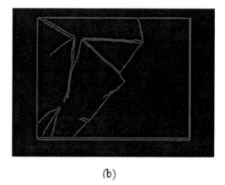

(a)                                           (b)

**Fig. 14.** Different threshold for Canny detectors: a) low threshold, b) high threshold

Different lighting conditions that may occur during the day or even various differences of intensities along the edges of the same picture may cause either the existence of extra white pixels or the lack of them. As a result, either extra unwanted edges (Fig 14.a), or gaps along the desired edges (Fig 14.b), may occur. To overcome this problem a sufficient, for the most cases, threshold for the Canny detector was found after experimentation, but still small changes at lighting conditions may cause noise. In addition, there is a gap tolerance of some pixels for the edge detection (Fig 10.b). In cases where two edges are close to each other this tolerance may lead to the detection of corners and edges that do not exist (Fig 15).

Finally, the use of stereoscopic vision is expected to solve a lot of the problems presented and improve the vision algorithms.

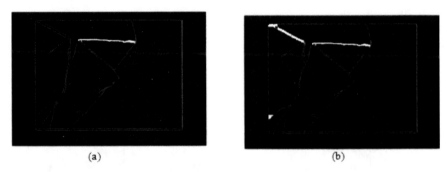

(a)                                    (b)

**Fig. 15.** Different gap tolerances for the gap detection: a) the edge detection with small gap tolerance, b) the edge detection with big gap tolerance

# 5    Conclusion

In this paper, an effort is made to classify and detect the critical features for the task of unfolding a piece of fabric of unknown dimensions and shape. This effort is a part of an ongoing research work on the unfolding of clothes on a working table by one manipulator with machine vision feedback.

The presented approach manages to detect and classify the critical features of any piece of fabric of polygonal shape. For future work, the approach should be generalized so as to include circular fabrics or fabrics with circular corners. In addition, further investigation is necessary in order to improve the vision algorithms. Finally, future work will include the implementation of the manipulations by a robotic manipulator.

# References

1. Paul, F.W.: Acquisition, placement, and folding of fabric materials. International Journal of Clothing Science and Technology 16, 227–237 (2004)
2. Zoumponos, G., Aspragathos, N.: Vision Aided Neuro-Fuzzy Control for the Folding of Fabric Sheets. In: International Conference on Control, Automation and Systems (2007)

3. Maitin-Shepard, J., Cusumano-Tower, M., Lei, J., Abbeel, P.: Cloth Grasp Point Detection based on Multiple-View Geometric Cues with Application to Robotic Towel Folding. In: IEEE International Conference on Robotics and Automation (2010)
4. Osawa, F., Seki, H., Kamiya, Y.: Unfolding of massive laundry and classification types by dual manipulator. Journal of Advanced Computational Intelligence and Intelligent Informatics 11(5) (2007)
5. Hamajima, K., Kakikura, M.: Planninig Strategy for task of unfolding clothes. Robotics and Autonomous Systems 32, 145–152 (2000)
6. Salleh, K., Seki, H., Kamiya, Y., Hiziku, M.: Inchworm Robot Grippers in Clothes Manipulation –Optimizing the Tracing Algorithm. In: International Conference on Intelligent and Advanced Systems (2007)
7. He, X.C., Yung, N.H.C.: Corner detector based on global and local curvature properties. Optical Engineering 47(5), 057008-1–057008-12 (2008)

# Optimizing Motion of Robotic Manipulators in Interaction with Human Operators

Hao Ding[1,3], Kurniawan Wijaya[1], Gunther Reißig[2], and Olaf Stursberg[1,*]

[1] Institute of Control and System Theory,
Dept. Elect. Eng. and Comput. Sci., University of Kassel, Germany
{hao.ding,stursberg}@uni-kassel.de
[2] Chair of Control Eng. (LRT-15), Dept. Aerospace Eng.,
University of the Federal Armed Forces Munich, Germany
http://www.reiszig.de/gunther/
[3] Group of Robotics and Manufacturing,
ABB Corporate Research, Ladenburg, Germany

**Abstract.** Recently, the problem of how to manipulate industrial robots that interact with human operators attracts a lot of attention in robotics research. This interest stems from the insight that the integration of human operators into robot based manufacturing systems may increase productivity by combining the abilities of machines with those of humans. In such a Human-Robot-Interaction (HRI) setting, the challenge is to manipulate the robots both safely and efficiently. This paper proposes an online motion planning approach for robotic manipulators with HRI based on model predictive control (MPC) with embedded mixed-integer programming. Safety-relevant regions, which are potentially occupied by the human operators, are generated online using camera data and a knowledge-base of typical human motion patterns. These regions serve as constraints of the optimization problem solved online to generate control trajectories for the robot. As described in the last part of the paper, the proposed method is realized for a HRI scenario.

**Keywords:** Human-robot-interaction, robot motion planning, safety-aware control, behavior estimation, predictive control.

## 1 Introduction

The traditional spatial separation of industrial robots and human operators in production sites of the manufacturing industries is often chosen to ensure safety for the human. However, in times of pushing productivity to the limit, it is increasingly often noted that this separation is not beneficial for the efficiency of some production processes [10,21], in particular when production steps that have to be carried out by humans and those that can be accomplished by robots are

---

* This work is partially supported by the project EsIMiP funded by the Bavarian Research Foundation (AZ-852-08).

S. Jeschke, H. Liu, and D. Schilberg (Eds.): ICIRA 2011, Part I, LNAI 7101, pp. 520–531, 2011.
© Springer-Verlag Berlin Heidelberg 2011

interleaved. Such situations may appear, for example, if high-speed assembly procedures are carried out by robots and if a human operator randomly picks assembled workpieces to perform quality checks, or if high-precision assembly (carried out by a robot) and manufacturing steps requiring human flexibility alternate. If robots and humans operate in the same area simultaneously to increase the productivity, it of course remains a crucial goal to guarantee safe operation. For both, efficiency and safety, it is important to consider the human behavior – not only the current observable motion of a human in the work space, but also the likely one over a future time horizon for which a robot trajectory is planned. This results in human-robot-interaction (HRI) or human-robot-collaboration (HRC), in which models of human behavior for prediction play an important role for computing safe and efficient robot trajectories.

The above-mentioned requirements for motion planning lead to non-convex optimization problems which are hard to be solved efficiently. Thus, several approaches that are based on solving approximations to the original problem have been proposed: [16] discusses a potential field method, but optimality of motion is not considered and the inclusion of robot kinematics and dynamics is difficult. Cell decomposition methods in the configuration space take advantage of the fact that the configuration of the manipulator reduces to a single point [18]. To account for the difficulty of proper and efficient obstacle representation in the configuration space, sampling-based approaches like rapidly-exploring random trees (RRTs, [17]) and probabilistic roadmaps (PRMs, [15]) have been proposed, as well as kinodynamic planning [11], RRT* [14], elastic roadmaps [25] as variants. The idea is to plan the path in the configuration space, but to check for collisions in the workspace by using forward kinematics. Note that velocity limits of joints are of the prescribed relative to the obstacle movement in HRI, which can be easily dealt with in the workspace. Along this line, the approaches [2,7] were proposed and further developed for increasing the efficiency of computation in [4,5]. For considering the safety aspect, a method for the efficient estimation of safety-relevant regions (i.e. regions that are occupied by a human with considerable probability) was described in [6]. These regions, which are derived from probabilistic models of the human behavior, can be embedded into the optimization-based computation of robot controls as optimization constraints.

This paper proposes a method for online computation of optimized paths of the robotic manipulator while identifying dynamic obstacles, like a human operator, from measured data and considering typical (and thus likely) motion patterns of the operator. For enabling online-optimization in a real-time setting, the computation is accelerated by using the moving horizon scheme known from model predictive control (MPC) rather than optimizing at once over the complete time span required to reach a goal position of the end-effector. At each control interval, a finite horizon open-loop optimal control problem is solved to yield a (sub-)optimal control sequence, and the first control input of the sequence is applied to the real plant. The procedure is repeated at any sampling time; for more details, see [3,20]. While previous own work on the generation of safety-relevant regions was restricted to the motion of a human hand, this paper does also consider the motion of a human elbow.

The paper is organized as follows: In Section 2, the problem of optimal motion planning for robotic manipulators interacting with humans is defined first. The following subsections describe the generation of safety-relevant regions and the motion planning by mixed-integer programming. The application of the proposed method to a realistic HRI scenario is contained in Sec. 3, followed by the conclusions.

## 2  Optimization-Based Robotic Manipulation for HRI

One of the fundamental problems in the field of motion planning is to safely and efficiently drive the end effector of a robotic manipulator to a specified goal position. Here, *safety* refers to the requirement that the robotic manipulator must have no collision with surrounding obstacles including human operators. At the same time, *efficiency* requires that the motion of the manipulator should minimize a specified objective function such as transition time, energy consumption, or distance to the goal. Additionally, the motion of the manipulator should be *feasible*, i.e., be consistent with kinematic and dynamic constraints. Moreover, a motion planning method may be required to be adaptive and to be applicable online, especially in the presence of time-varying obstacles like humans. In order to be able to treat this complex motion planning problem, we first give it a mathematically precise meaning. To this end, the following notation is used:

- *Workspace*: the Euclidean space $Z = \mathbb{R}^3$.
- *Configuration space*: $C = \mathbb{R}^n$; points $[q_1, q_2, \ldots, q_n]^T \in C$ represent joint angles of the robotic manipulator with $n$ degrees of freedom.
- *State space*: $X = \mathbb{R}^{2n}$; points $x(t) = [q(t), \dot{q}(t)]^T \in X$ represent the state of the robotic manipulator.
- $z(q_j) \in Z$ denotes the position of joint $q_j$ including the position of the end effector in the workspace with $j \in \{1, \ldots, n+1\}$. For the sake of notational simplicity, $z_j$ is used as a shortcut for $z(q_j)$.
- *Observation space*: $\mathbb{O} = Z \times Z$; $O(t) = [z^1(t), z^2(t), z^3(t), \dot{z}^1(t), \dot{z}^2(t), \dot{z}^3(t)]^T \in \mathbb{O}$ represents data measured or derived; specifically, one observation consists of position and velocity in the workspace.

The complex task of motion planning in HRI scenarios can then be formulated as an abstract optimization problem as follows:

$$\min_{u(\cdot)} \sum_{\tau=0}^{g} J_\tau(x(\tau), u(\tau)) \tag{1a}$$

$$s.t.\quad x(t+1) = f(x(t), u(t)), t \in \{0, 1, \ldots, g-1\} \tag{1b}$$

$$x(0) = x_0, \ z_{n+1}(g) \in G \tag{1c}$$

$$x(t) \in M, \quad u(t) \in U \tag{1d}$$

$$\Omega(x(t)) \cap F(t) = \emptyset, \quad t \in \{0, 1, \ldots, g\}. \tag{1e}$$

Here, the dynamics of the robot is modeled by the discrete-time control system (1b), and the input $u$ represents a sequence of controls such as torques. This discrete-time control system is derived from the differential equations modeling the robot's motion (e.g. [13]), where the discrete time instances $0, 1, \ldots, g$ correspond to the sampling instances $0, \Delta t, \ldots, g \cdot \Delta t$ in continuous time. The model may consist of robot kinematics, actuator and transmission dynamics, inertial parameters, friction estimation, load dynamics, etc. The constraint (1c) forces the robot to start at the initial state $x(0)$ (position, velocity) and also requires that its end effector reaches the target set $G \subseteq \mathbb{R}^n$ at the terminal time $g$. (1d) represents control and state constraints, where the latter may be used to avoid e.g. infeasible configurations of the robot. Safety of the robot's motion is guaranteed by (1e), where $F(t) \subseteq Z$ denotes the set of points possibly occupied at time $t$ by (possibly time-varying) obstacles, and $\Omega(x(t)) \subseteq Z$ is the set of points occupied at time $t$ by the robot. We would like to emphasize that safety and feasibility may also be guaranteed everywhere in between the sampling instances by appropriately tighten the constraints (1d) and (1e) [8], [19, Section 5.3.4]. Finally, $J_\tau$ denotes a cost function representing a performance measure whose sum is to be minimized.

Two questions immediately arise, namely, how to determine the *safety-relevant region* $F(t)$, especially in HRI scenarios, and how to solve the optimization problem (1), which is in general non-convex. The following sections address these.

## 2.1   Determination of Safety-Relevant Regions

In order to model and predict human motion and to determine the safety-relevant regions $F(t)$, we use a combination of Hidden Markov Models (HMMs) and reachability analysis.

In a training phase, HMMs are constructed using experimental data. These models then yield a conditional probability density function $P(O(t + r) = O_n | O(t))$ which gives the probability of reaching the point $O_n$ at future time $t + r$, $r \in \{1, \ldots, H\}$ with prediction horizon $H$, under the condition that the current observation is $O(t)$ [1,12,23]. The safety-relevant region $F(t + r)$ is then determined numerically under the constraint

$$\delta \leq \int_{F(t+r)} P(O(t + r) = O_n | O(t)) \, dO_n, \qquad (2)$$

which means that the probability of the event that $O(t+r) \in F(t+r)$ is not less than $\delta$ [6]. Here, the probability threshold $\delta$ is a parameter of the method with $0 < \delta < 1$. Moreover, the safety-relevant regions so determined are not unique, which represents another degree of freedom of the method.

In contrast to HMMs, reachability analysis depends on prior knowledge of constraints of human motion such as velocity and acceleration bounds. The method we propose is based on the following reachability result, in which a function $\gamma$ represents one component of the position vector $z \in \mathbb{R}^3$. For the sake of simplicity of presentation, the position is shifted in time to the interval $[0, T]$ for definition of $\gamma$.

**Lemma 1.** *Let $T > 0$ and assume $\gamma\colon [0,T] \to \mathbb{R}$ is twice differentiable and fulfills the following conditions:*

(i) $\gamma(0) \in [\gamma_-, \gamma_+]$ *for some bounds $\gamma_- \leq \gamma_+$; (measurement error)*
(ii) $\dot{\gamma}(0) \in [\dot{\gamma}_-, \dot{\gamma}_+]$ *for some bounds $\dot{\gamma}_- \leq \dot{\gamma}_+$; (measurement error)*
(iii) $\forall_{t \in [0,T]}\ \dot{\gamma}(t) \in [v_-, v_+]$ *for some $v_-$, $v_+$ with $v_- \leq \dot{\gamma}_- \leq \dot{\gamma}_+ \leq v_+$, where $v_-$ and $v_+$ represent bounds on the speed of the human motion;*
(iv) $\forall_{t \in [0,T]}\ \ddot{\gamma}(t) \in [a_-, a_+]$ *for some $a_-$, $a_+$ with $a_- \leq a_+$ where $a_-$ and $a_+$ represent bounds on the acceleration of the human motion.*

*Then $\gamma(t) \leq \gamma(t)_u$ for all $t \in [0,T]$, where*

$$\gamma(t)_u = \gamma_+ + \begin{cases} t \cdot \dot{\gamma}_+ + t^2 \cdot \frac{a_+}{2}, & \text{if } a_+ = 0 \text{ or } t \leq t_1, \\ t_1 \cdot \dot{\gamma}_+ + t_1^2 \cdot \frac{a_+}{2} + v_+ \cdot (t - t_1), & \text{otherwise,} \end{cases} \tag{3}$$

*and $t_1 = \frac{v_+ - \dot{\gamma}_+}{a_+}$. In addition, $\gamma(t) \geq \gamma(t)_l$ for all $t \in [0,T]$, where $\gamma(t)_l$ is obtained from $\gamma(t)_u$ by substituting $'+'$ with $'-'$.*

This result allows to determine an over-approximation $\psi(t+r)$ of the reachable set at time $t+r$ in the future,

$$\psi(t+r) := [\bar{\gamma}(r)_l, \bar{\gamma}(r)_u], \tag{4}$$

where the interval is a subset of $\mathbb{R}^3$ and the vector-valued bound $\bar{\gamma}_u$ is the vector of the bounds (3) obtained for the three components of the position $z \in \mathbb{R}^3$, and analogously for the lower bound $\bar{\gamma}_l$.

HMMs are based on *motion patterns*, which are, roughly speaking, typical motions observed in the training phase. In the case that an atypical motion is observed during the prediction phase, the HMM is updated accordingly online [23]. However, the HMM can only be updated once a motion pattern is completed, from the initial position to the target, which usually leads to inaccurate predictions during newly observed motion pattern, see Fig. 1.

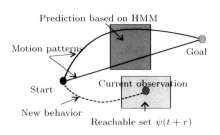

**Fig. 1.** Schematic example

On the other hand, while reachability analysis usually leads to predictions that are less accurate than those obtained from HMMs, reachable sets depend on dynamic constraints only, and hence, the quality of their predictions does not deteriorate when an unknown motion pattern occurs.

In a work currently under review, we have therefore proposed to combine HMMs with reachability analysis in order to arrive at uniformly more accurate predictions than could be achieved from either method alone. The idea is to take advantage of the fact that *any* region $F(t+r)$ that fulfills (2) is a valid safety-relevant region. So, roughly speaking, we may first try to satisfy (2) for some $F(t+r)$ contained in the reachable set, and enlarge $F(t+r)$ beyond the latter only if this is necessary to fulfill (2). Hence, if the prediction that could be obtained from the HMM alone is of a high quality, the safety-relevant region should be a subset of $\psi(t+r)$ and the difference to the original method (based solely on the HMM) is negligible. However, if an unexpected motion pattern occurs, then the prediction that could be obtained from the HMM alone is of a low quality. The probability density will be rather small on the reachable set, hence the reachable set will be a subset of the computed safety-relevant region. The latter then contains the future observation with certainty.

We finally remark that for the purpose of reducing the complexity of solving the optimal control problem in (1a), the safety-relevant region $F(t+r)$ may also be over-approximated by sets that have a simpler structure, e.g. [22].

## 2.2 Solution of the Motion Planning Problem

Due to the complexity and non-convexity of the cost function (1a), of the dynamics (1b), and of the safety constraint (1e), the solution of the optimization problem (1) represents a challenge even if the safety-relevant region $F(t)$ is known for all times $t$ in advance. We here present a method to approximately solve the following special case of (1):

$$\min_{z(\cdot)} \ \|z_{n+1}(g) - \hat{z}\|_\infty, \tag{5a}$$

$$\text{s.t.} \quad V_j^- \Delta t \le z_j(t+1) - z_j(t) \le V_j^+ \Delta t, t \in \{0, 1, \ldots, g-1\}, j \in \{1, \ldots, n+1\}, \tag{5b}$$

$$x(0) = x_0, \tag{5c}$$

$$\|z_{j+1}(t) - z_j(t)\|_2 = r_{j,j+1}^2, t \in \{0, 1, \ldots, g\}, j \in \{1, \ldots, n\}, \tag{5d}$$

$$\Omega(x(t)) \cap F(t) = \emptyset, t \in \{0, 1, \ldots, g\}. \tag{5e}$$

Here, we assume that $\hat{z}$ is an interior point of the target region $G$, e.g. its center, that $\Omega(x(t))$ is a union of straight line segments joining the joint positions $z_j(t)$ and $z_{j+1}(t)$. For all times $t$, the safety-relevant region $F(t)$ is (the interior of) a polyhedron:

$$F(t) = \{z \in Z \mid A(t)z < b(t)\}, \tag{6}$$

where $A(t) \in \mathbb{R}^{N \times 3}$ is a matrix with rows $A_k(t)$, $k \in \{1, \ldots, N\}$, $N$ the number of hyperplanes for representing the polyhedron, and $b(t) = (b_1(t), \ldots, b_N(t))^T$. The joint velocities in the workspace are bounded to $[V_j^-, V_j^+]$.

The cost (5a), which aims at coming as close as possible to the target region $G$, has been introduced since we will later solve (5) within an MPC scheme, where $g$ is usually too small to actually reach $G$ in the first part of the iteration. Nevertheless, if $G$ can be reached within the given time horizon and if $G$ is a cuboid, then the formulation (5a) guarantees that $G$ is actually reached.

The bounds on the joint velocities in (5b) represent the dynamics of the robot. This simplification is justified because the joint positions of industrial robots are usually controlled by built-in lower-level controllers. Depending on the capability of the latter, bounds on velocities can be chosen to guarantee that the robot can successfully track the optimized trajectories. In the constraint (5d), the constants $r_{j,j+1}$ represent the lengths of the links of the robot.

We aim at approximately solving (5) as a Mixed-Integer Linear Program (MILP), which requires a formulation as a linear program in both continuous and binary decision variables. We first observe that the dynamic constraint (5b) is linear, and that the cost (5a) may be equivalently represented using a linear cost function, $\min \xi$, and additional linear constraints, $-\xi \leq z_{n+1}^i(g) - \hat{z}^i \leq \xi$ for all $i \in \{1, 2, 3\}$.

While a direct treatment of (5d) would lead to a quadratically constrained problem [2], this constraint may be approximated arbitrarily closely by a combination of linear constraints and binary decision variables, as shown in [7].

The constraint (5e) may also be represented as a linear program in both continuous and binary decision variables [2,7]. First observe that the statement $z \notin F(t)$ is equivalent to the set of constraints

$$A(t)z \geq b(t) + (v - 1) \cdot M, \tag{7}$$

$$\sum_{k=1}^{N} v_k = 1, \tag{8}$$

where $v = (v_1, \ldots, v_N)^{\mathrm{T}}$ is a vector of binary variables $v_k \in \{0, 1\}$ and $1 = 1^{N \times 1}$ is a vector of ones. $M$ is a sufficiently large constant[1]. The constraint (7) formulates that the $k$th scalar inequality in $A(t)z \geq b(t)$ is enforced if and only if $v_k = 1$, and the constraint (8) ensures that the latter equality holds for exactly one $k$. Consequently, the constraints (7)-(8) avoid, roughly speaking, collision of the point $z$ with the safety-relevant region $F(t)$ given by (6). In order to avoid collision of the line segment $\|z_j, z_{j+1}\|$ joining $z_j$ and $z_{j+1}$, we choose a finite number of particles $p_{sj} \in [\![z_j, z_{j+1}]\!]$,

$$p_{sj} = \lambda_s \cdot z_j + (1 - \lambda_s) \cdot z_{j+1}, \tag{9}$$

where $\lambda_s \in [0, 1]$, $s \in \{1, \ldots, S\}$, and avoid the collision of each particle $p_{sj}$ with $F(t)$ by introducing constraints (7)-(8) with $p_{sj}$ at the place of $z$. By increasing the number $S$ of particles in each link $j$, we approximate the line segment $\|z_j, z_{j+1}\|$ arbitrarily closely. Moreover, we could even treat more general link geometries than just straight line segments and still provably avoid collision between links and the safety-relevant region $F(t)$ by appropriately enlarging $F(t)$ by some safety margin [8,19]. One drawback with ordinary particle based methods is that they usually lead to a huge number of binary variables, and hence, to unacceptable computational time for the planning. However, we proposed

---

[1] Hence the name 'big-M method' [24]. The way of choosing the value of $M$ can be found in [24, p. 205].

geometric results, which can drastically reduce the number of binary decision variables in the aforementioned MILPs, for 2D and 3D motion planning problems in [4] and [5], respectively.

The crucial point here is that $v$ does not anymore depend on the particle index $s$. This greatly reduces the number of binary decision variables, and leads to a speedup of about 200 in typical scenarios.

## 3  Application Results

### 3.1  A Human-Robot-Interaction Scenario

We have realized the proposed methods in the following HRI scenario, shown in Fig. 2. A human operator moves his hand from its start position $S_H$ to the goal position $G_H$ and backwards, while an industrial robot moves its end-effector from its start $S_R$ to its goal $G_R$. For simplification, only the motion of the end-effector $z_{ee}(t)$ in the robot coordinate $z^1 z^2 z^3$, which has the nearest distance to the human operator, is considered in this scenario. A lower-level built-in controller of the robot is used to track the reference trajectory for the positions of each joint, where the trajectory represents the sequence of points over time obtained in the motion planning step. A red and a yellow marker is attached to the human's hand and elbow, respectively, which is detected by a stereo camera system. In order to efficiently compute safety-relevant sets $F(t)$, we need to avoid working with an infinite number of points in the observation space as proposed in [6]. Therefore, the workspace of the human operator is divided into 252 cells in the camera coordinate $z'^1 z'^2 z'^3$, which are translated copies of the cuboid $[0, 12.27] \times [0, 12.75] \times [0, 13.5] cm^3$ that are arranged in a $12 \times 7 \times 3$-grid. For better illustration, the 3D workspace is represented as a combination of three planes (shown in Fig. 3), which correspond to cross-sections parallel to the $z'^1 - z'^2$-plane.

 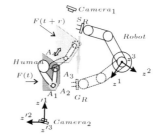

**Fig. 2.** A scenario for an industrial robot interacting with a human arm. The top view of the scenario is shown in the right figure, where the safety-relevant region $F(t)$ is over-approximated by 4 faces with normal vectors $A_1$ to $A_4$.

### 3.2  Generation of the Safety-Relevant Regions Using Probabilities

The motion of the hand and the elbow with different motion patterns are identified as two HMMs. The safety-relevant region $F(t+r)$ with $r = \{1, \ldots, H\}$

that is possibly occupied by the human arm is generated according to (2) with the prediction horizon[2] $H = 8$ and a given probability threshold $\delta = 0.9996$. In Fig. 3, the gray areas mark the region for the hand, the orange areas for the elbow, and red for the overlap. $F(t + r)$ is over-approximated by 4 supporting half-spaces with outside pointing normal vectors $A_1$, $A_2$, $A_3$, and $A_4$. Thus, the end-effector position $z_{ee}$ outside $F(t + r)$ is guaranteed by the given constraints (7) and (8) with $N = 4$ hyperplanes. For simplification, the normal vectors are fixed, while the positions of the half-spaces are time-varying: $b_k(t+r) = max\{A_k \cdot ver(t+r)\}$, $\forall ver(t+r) \in F(t+r)$, where $ver(t+r)$ denotes the vertices of the cells that are inside of $F(t + r)$.

Dynamic limits such as bounds for the velocity and acceleration of human motion, and particularly, of the motion of the hand, are well known, e.g. [9]. Here, we use the parameters $v_\pm = \pm 15cm/s$ and $a_\pm = \pm 15cm/s^2$, In addition, we use the bounds $\gamma_\pm = z'(t) \pm 5cm$ and $\dot{\gamma}_\pm = \dot{z}'(t) \pm 8cm/s$ needed in the application of Lemma 1, while $z'(t)$ and $\dot{z}'(t)$ are the actual measurements.

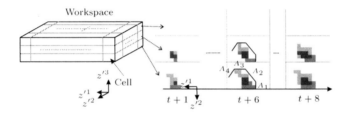

**Fig. 3.** Generation of the safety-relevant regions over the prediction horizon

### 3.3   Optimized Trajectories of the Robot Using MPC

An optimized position sequence to drive the robot from a specified start to a goal state is computed by solving a model-based optimization problem over a prediction horizon, while taking into account time-varying dynamic constraints (obstacle avoidance). The technique used here is *model predictive control* (MPC) with embedded mixed-integer programming. The following optimization problem is solved for any $t$ until the goal is reached.

$$\min_{z_{ee}(t+1),\ldots,z_{ee}(t+H)} \sum_{r=1}^{H} \|z_{ee}(t + r) - \hat{z}\|_\infty, \tag{10a}$$

$$s.t. \quad (5b),\ (5c),\ (7),\ and\ (8), \tag{10b}$$

where the velocity limits in the directions $z^1$, $z^2$, and $z^3$ are $[-10, 10]cm/s$, $[-6, 6]cm/s$, and $[-4, 4]cm/s$, respectively.

---

[2] In order to realize the real-time computability, the prediction horizon for generating $F(t + r)$ needs to be carefully chosen. $H = 8$ is chosen here as a good compromise between computational effort and prediction quality.

With respect to the prediction of the safety-relevant regions, the optimized position sequences of the robot end-effector based on the current measurement $z_{ee}(t)$ (denoted by the green square) are shown in Fig. 4. With the prediction horizon $H = 8$, the sequence of end-effector positions $z_{ee}(t + 1), \ldots, z_{ee}(t + 8)$ is optimized using the regions $F(t + 1), \cdots, F(t + 8)$. The sequence is marked by red circles, while the optimized sequence with no obstacle consideration is marked by the blue stars. The positions of the 3rd and 4th faces are the same for $F(t + 1)$ and $F(t + 3)$, as well as for $F(t + 6)$ and $F(t + 8)$.

The proposed method for generation of $F(t + r)$, $r \in \{1, \ldots, 8\}$ is implemented in C++ on an $i5$-CPU PC with 2.67 GHz clock rate. $F(t + r)$ can be computed online with the camera frequency at 10 frames per second. The optimizer is implemented in C++ using Concert Technology libraries in CPLEX Studio Academic Research 12.2, and run on 4 threads of another $i5$-CPU PC with 2.67 GHz clock rate. Data are transmitted via UDP between the two PCs. We define the sampling time in the optimization as $\Delta t = 0.1sec$. With the

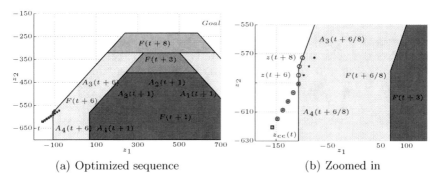

(a) Optimized sequence          (b) Zoomed in

**Fig. 4.** Optimized sequence of the robot end-effector based on the current measurement $z_{ee}(t = 0)$ (denoted by the green square), $z_{ee}(t + 1), \ldots, z_{ee}(t + 8)$ (red circles) with consideration of the safety-relevant regions $F(t + r)$ and (blue stars) with no obstacle consideration (view from top)

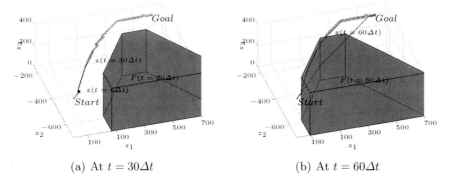

(a) At $t = 30\Delta t$          (b) At $t = 60\Delta t$

**Fig. 5.** Optimized trajectories in 3D from the start to the goal

provided $F(t + r)$, the optimized sequence at each time interval can be computed within $0.01sec$ and the first desired position $z_{ee}(t + 1)$ is applied to the robot in end iteration of the MPC cycle.

The optimized trajectories in 3D for $t = 30\Delta t$ and $t = 60\Delta t$ are shown in Fig. 5. The optimized trajectory with collision avoidance is denoted by the circles. The past positions are marked in black, the current in green, and the future in red. The red areas represent the safety-relevant regions $F(t = 30\Delta t)$ and $F(t = 60\Delta t)$, respectively. The optimized trajectory without any obstacle is denoted by blue stars, shown in Fig. 5(b).

## 4    Conclusions and Current Work

For optimization-based online motion planning of robotic manipulators, a predictive control scheme with embedded mixed-integer programming interacting with dynamic obstacles modeling human operators has been proposed. The human arm behavior is modeled and predicted by combination of two HMMs for hand and elbow, respectively, and reachability analysis. Based on the proposed method, the safety-relevant regions, which serve as constraints in the optimization, can be generated online with multiple patterns. The control scheme for online motion generation has been successfully demonstrated by the realization for an HRI scenario. The optimized trajectory of the robot end-effector with identification of the human arm can be computed in $0.01sec$ with prediction horizon $H = 8$. Additionally, the approach is being applied to and examined for different scenarios. The performance of the proposed methods compared to other approaches is to be further investigated.

## References

1. Bennewitz, M., Burgard, W., Cielniak, G., Thrun, S.: Learning motion patterns of people for compliant robot motion. Int. J. of Robot. Research 24(1), 31–48 (2005)
2. Blackmore, L., Williams, B.C.: Optimal manipulator path planning with obstacles using disjunctive programming. In: American Control Conf., pp. 3200–3202 (2006)
3. Camacho, E.F., Bordons, C.: Model Predictive Control. Springer, Heidelberg (2004)
4. Ding, H., Reißig, G., Groß, D., Stursberg, O.: Mixed-integer programming for optimal path planning of robotic manipulators. In: IEEE Conf. on Autom. Sci. and Eng. (accepted 2011)
5. Ding, H., Reißig, G., Stursberg, O.: Increasing efficiency of optimization-based path planning for robotic manipulators. In: IEEE Conf. on Decision and Control and European Control Conf. (accepted 2011)
6. Ding, H., Reißig, G., Wijaya, K., Bortot, D., Bengler, K., Stursberg, O.: Human arm motion modeling and long-term prediction for safe and efficient human-robot-interaction. In: IEEE Int. Conf. Robot. and Autom., pp. 5875–5880 (2011)
7. Ding, H., Zhou, M., Stursberg, O.: Optimal path planning in the workspace for articulated robots using mixed integer programming. In: IEEE/RSJ Int. Conf. on Intell. Robots and Syst., pp. 5770–5775 (2009)
8. Fainekos, G., Girard, A., Kress-Gazit, H., Pappas, G.: Temporal logic motion planning for dynamic robots. Automatica 45(2), 343–352 (2009)

9. Flash, T., Hogan, N.: The coordination of arm movements: an experimentally confirmed mathematical model. J. of Neuroscience 5(7), 1688–1703 (1985)
10. Haddadin, S., Schaeffer, A., Hirzinger, G.: Requirements for safe robots: measurements, analysis and new insights. Int. J. of Robot. Research 28, 1507–1527 (2008)
11. Hsu, D., Kindel, R., Latombe, J.C., Rock, S.: Randomized kinodynamic motion planning with moving obstacles. Int. J. of Robot. Research 21(3), 233–255 (2002)
12. Hu, W., Xiao, X., Fu, Z., Xie, D., Tan, T., Maybank, S.: A system for learning statistical motion patterns. IEEE Trans. Pattern Anal. Mach. Intell. 28(9), 1450–1464 (2006)
13. Johanssona, R., Robertssona, A., Nilsson, K., Verhaegenc, M.: State-space system identification of robot manipulator dynamics. Mechatronics 10, 403–418 (2000)
14. Karaman, S., Frazzoli, E.: Sampling-based algorithms for optimal motion planning. Int. J. of Robot. Research 30(7), 846–894 (2011)
15. Kavraki, L., Svestka, P., Latombe, J., Overmars, M.: Probabilistic roadmaps for path planning in high-dimensional configuration space. IEEE Trans. on Robot. and Autom. 12(4), 566–580 (1996)
16. Khatib, O.: Real-time obstacle avoidance for manipulators and mobile robots. Int. J. of Robot. Research 5(1), 90–98 (1986)
17. Kuffner, J., LaValle, S.: RRT-connect: An efficient approach to single-query path planning. In: Proc. IEEE Int. Conf. on Robot. and Autom., pp. 995–1001 (2000)
18. Latombe, J.: Robot Motion Planning. Kluwer (1991)
19. LaValle, S.: Planning Algorithms. Cambridge University Press (2006)
20. Mayne, D., Rawlings, J., Rao, C., Scokaert, P.: Constrained model predictive control: stability and optimality. Automatica 36, 789–814 (2000)
21. Santis, A., Siciliano, B., Luca, A., Bicchi, A.: An atlas of physical human-robot interaction. Mechanism and Machine Theory 43, 253–270 (2008)
22. Stursberg, O., Krogh, B.H.: Efficient Representation and Computation of Reachable Sets for Hybrid Systems. In: Maler, O., Pnueli, A. (eds.) HSCC 2003. LNCS, vol. 2623, pp. 482–497. Springer, Heidelberg (2003)
23. Vasquez, D., Fraichard, T., Laugier, C.: Growing hidden markov models: An incremental tool for learning and predicting human and vehicle motion. Int. J. of Robot. Research 28(11-12), 1486–1506 (2009)
24. Williams, H.P.: Model building in mathematical programming, 2nd edn. Wiley (1985)
25. Yang, Y., Brock, O.: Elastic roadmaps - motion generation for autonomous mobile manipulation. Autonomous Robots 28, 113–130 (2010)

# Haptic Display of Rigid Body Contact Using Generalized Penetration Depth

Jun Wu[1,2], Dangxiao Wang[1], and Yuru Zhang[1]

[1] State Key Lab of Virtual Reality Technology and Systems,
Beihang University, Beijing, 100191, China
[2] Computer Graphics & Visualization Group,
Technische Universität München, 85748, Germany
wujun@me.buaa.edu.cn, {hapticwang,yuru}@buaa.edu.cn

**Abstract.** Rigid body contact with multiple regions is common in virtual environments. The traditional penalty based haptic display treats translational penetration depth at each contact region independently, and hence causes the undesired effect of visual interpenetration since it does not guarantee all geometrical constraints simultaneously. It may also introduce force discontinuity due to the singularity of penetration depth. To overcome these artifacts, we present a method based on the concept of generalized penetration depth (GPD), which considers both translation and rotation to separate two overlapping objects. The method could be viewed as an extension of the classic god-object method from Euclidean space to configuration space in which GPD is defined. We demonstrate the method for 3-DoF rigid bodies using pre-computed contact space. For 6-DoF rigid bodies where pre-computation is not feasible, we propose an efficient method to approximate the local contact space based on continuous collision detection and quadratic programming.

**Keywords:** Haptic display, Rigid body contact, Generalized penetration depth.

## 1 Introduction

When an object (referred as the tool) undergoing both translational and rotational motion contacts other objects (referred as obstacles), reactive wrench (i.e., force and torque) naturally arises in response to the contact event. This is common in many real world manipulations, e.g., a dental handpiece contacts teeth and the surrounding gum, a mechanical part contacts other parts in assembly [10]. In the virtual world, however, the tool manipulated by an operator may penetrate into obstacles. This penetration is inevitable since the reactive wrench is calculated after the contact occurs. Unfortunately this intersection is not visually negligible, especially if the operator pushes against the obstacle, which is often the case in some medical treatments. The visual display of interpenetration will confuse the operator's interpretation of the virtual world. Furthermore, the interpenetration of virtual objects will decrease the operator's perceived stiffness

S. Jeschke, H. Liu, and D. Schilberg (Eds.): ICIRA 2011, Part I, LNAI 7101, pp. 532–541, 2011.

of the virtual object [17]. Therefore, the computation of a non-penetration configuration of the tool for visual display is a problem associated with the reactive wrench computation.

In this paper, we present a haptic display method based on generalized penetration depth (GPD), which is defined as a minimum combination of translational and rotational motion to separate two overlapping objects. In this formulation, we first compute a *reasonable* configuration of the tool, and then use it to calculate the reactive wrench. Meanwhile, this non-penetration configuration serves for visual display. The proposed GPD based method can be interpreted as a direct extension of the classic god-object method [21] from Euclidean space to configuration space, i.e., from the position of the god-object to the position and posture of the god-object. Since the method is formulated in the configuration space, it handles situations with both a single contact area and multiple simultaneous contact areas in a uniform way.

The paper is organized as follows. We review related works on rigid body simulation and generalized penetration depth computation in Section 2. Then we give an overview of the proposed method in Section 3. In Section 4, a 3-DoF rigid body in a planar scenario is constructed to valid the proposed method. In Section 5, we introduce a practical method to handle 6-DoF rigid bodies. Finally, we conclude with future research directions in Section 6.

## 2   Related Work

Haptic display of single point-object interaction is almost mature; some methods are widely recognized, e.g., the god-object method [21] and its variation [16]. The benefits of this approach are non-penetration visual display and orthogonal feedback force. It also overcomes the force discontinuity problem introduced in penalty based method (vector based method termed in [21]).

For object-object interaction, McNeely et al. [10] proposed a penalty based 6-DoF display method using volumetric representation. 6-DoF haptic display using other representations (e.g., [1, 3, 12, 15]) is also investigated. In these works, visual interpenetration is inevitable especially when the operator pushes hard. The interpenetration depth is roughly proportional to the stiffness of the penalty spring. While stiffer spring coefficient decreases the depth, it introduces stiffer numerical equations and increases the possibility of instability of the simulation. In simulation based haptic display an intermediate configuration, governed by penalty force and virtual coupling force, is used for visual display. Then a big penalty spring coefficient (beyond the limitation of haptic device) could be applied to reduce the interpenetration. However, virtual coupling would lead to other kinds of undesired effects such as artificial friction [14]. Moreover, special consideration still should be paid to local penetration depth estimation; sophisticated algorithms for contact clustering (e.g., [7, 15]) are needed in penalty based methods. Berkelman et al. [2] proposed a constraint based method also using a virtual coupling.

Recently, Kolesnikov and Zefran [8] proposed a method for wrench computation based on generalized penetration depth. They provide an analytic solution for an object interacting with a plane (only one contact area). We extend this approach to more general cases where multiple contacts are naturally considered in the formulation. Ortega et al. [14] also extend the classic god-object method to object-object interaction. Their method makes an assumption that the god-object moves in a quasi static way, and optimizes on the acceleration using Gauss' principle. In this paper, a formulation using GPD is given. We directly optimize on the configuration other than on the acceleration. This makes the interpretation much simpler (see the 3-DoF example in Section 4).

Penetration depth (PD) is a distance measure to quantify the extent of intersection between two overlapping models. The classic version is the translational penetration depth, which is a minimum amount of translational distance by which to separate two overlapping models. Zhang et al. [19] extended the notion to generalized PD, which takes into account both translation and rotation. A challenging issue is the high computation complexity for the computation of generalized PD. For a low DoF rigid body, contact space could be pre-computed. However for a high DoF rigid body, pre-computing is not feasible. Zhang et al. [19] proposed a convexity-based algorithm to compute the lower and upper bounds on GPD. Some constraint optimization approaches have also been proposed (e.g., [18] [11]). These approaches are generally not fast enough for haptic rendering. An iterative approach for translational PD computation is investigated in [5].

## 3    Haptic Display Using GPD

The extended god-object method is formulated in configuration space (shortened as C-space), which is the set of all possible configurations of the manipulated tool. As shown in Fig. 1, first, we compute a configuration, $c_g$, at which the god-object barely touches the obstacle without penetration. Similar to that in classic god-object method, $c_g$ should be a local closest configuration to the configuration of the haptic interface object, $c_h$, according to a distance metric $\sigma$.

$$\sigma(c_g, c_h) = \min\left(\{\sigma(c, c_h) \,|\, c \in \mathcal{C}_{contact}\}\right) \tag{1}$$

$\mathcal{C}_{contact}$ denotes contact space, which is defined as the set of configurations at which the object barely touches the obstacle without penetration. We denote $\mathcal{F}$ as free space, the set of configurations at which the object does not intersect with an obstacle, and $\mathcal{O}$ as the obstacle space which is the complement of $\mathcal{F} \cup \mathcal{C}_{contact}$ in C-space.

The distance, $\sigma(c_g, c_h)$, is a minimum combination of translation and rotation to separate the tool from the obstacle, and is termed as the generalized penetration depth. Several distance metrics have been proposed, here we choose one which can be efficiently evaluated.

$$\sigma(c, c_h) = (c - c_h)^T M (c - c_h) \tag{2}$$

where $M$ is the mass matrix, its specific formulation in different cases will be introduced later. The unit of the metric is $kgm^2$.

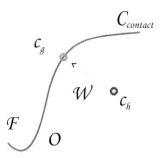

**Fig. 1.** For a penetration configuration $c_h$, a nearest non-penetration configuration $c_g$ is computed for feedback wrench computation and visual display

Once the configuration of the god-object is determined, feedback wrench can be calculated accordingly.

$$W = kM(c_g - c_h) \tag{3}$$

where the vector $k$ is penalty constants for force and torque.

The benefits of this method are straightforward. Since the resulting configuration lies in the contact space, it maintains only contact, without penetration. The object-object interaction in Euclidean space is formulated to point-object interaction in configuration space, thus avoids the sophisticated penetration handling in Euclidean space. By locally tracking the nearest configuration in the contact space, force discontinuity and pop-through are avoided.

## 4 Pre-computed C-Space for Planar 3-DoF Rigid Body

For a low DoF rigid body, such as a rigid body in a planar scenario, its contact space could be constructed in a preprocess step. Then the problem of finding a closest configuration can be efficiently solved using proximity query packages designed for Euclidean space.

### 4.1 Implementation

In this planar scenario, a rigid body translates along $x$ and $y$ axis and also rotates around $z$ axis, as shown in Fig. 2a. The rigid body's configuration is represented by $(x, y, \theta)$. The mass matrix $M$ in distance metric Eq. 2 is a $3*3$ diagonal matrix with $(m, m, I_z)$ as the diagonal, where $I_z$ is the moment of inertial around $z$ axis. Therefore, the distance of two configurations is equal to the Euclidean distance in 3D Euclidean space with axis $(x, y, z = \sqrt{\frac{m}{I_z}}\theta)$.

To build the contact space, we first uniformly sample the configuration space (resolution is chosen as $120^3$) and classify each configuration as intersection or non-intersection with the obstacle in Euclidean space. Then the contact space is

constructed using marching cubes algorithm to extract boundary between free
space and obstacle space. In each cross section of the constructed contact space,
the contour is the Minkowski sum of the obstacle with the given posture of the
tool. The time for the preprocess is about several minutes. During real-time
interaction, as it is transformed to a single point interacts with a 3D surface,
conventionally approaches (e.g., [4, 16]) could be employed.

## 4.2   Results

A series of pictures captured during a typical interaction is shown on the left of
Fig. 2, while the right reports the reactive wrench during this process. The red
rectangle is a tool controlled to contact a black concave obstacle, while the green
one is the computed god-object representation of the tool for visual display. In this
interaction, the tool first rotates around $z$ axis, then translates along $-x$ direction
to (b), translates along $-y$ direction to (d), finally along $x$ direction to (f).

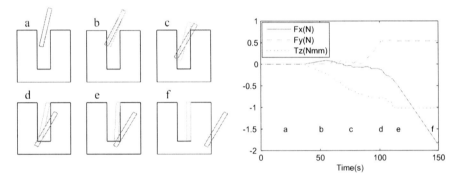

**Fig. 2.** Left: Snapshots of a typical planar interaction. The red rectangle is a tool
controlled to contact a black concave obstacle, while the green one is the computed
god-object representation of the tool for visual display. Right: Force curve during this
interaction.

It can be seen in the free space (a), the god-object is equal to the actual tool,
no force will be exerted. When there is only one contact (b), the god-object
tends to rotate to avoid penetration. When the penetration depth is big, both
significant rotation and translation is needed (f). During the whole process, the
god-object maintains only contact with the obstacle without penetration, even
when there are multiple contact areas as in (c) and (d). Since the configuration
of god-object is locally tracked, it avoids pop-through as (f) shows. Otherwise,
the god-object in (f) should be on the right of the actual tool.

## 5   Local Construction of C-Space for Spacial 6-DoF Rigid Body

A challenge for this approach is that when the degree of freedom is high, such
as 6-DoF, it is not feasible to compute its contact space. Rather than build its

exact whole contact space, we introduce a method to approximate its contact space locally around an initial contact configuration.

## 5.1   Algorithm

For a penetration configuration of the haptic tool, we need to compute a locally closest configuration in the contact space according to a distance metric. The configuration is represented by the tool's position and orientation, i.e., $(x, y, z, \theta_x, \theta_y, \theta_z)$. Suppose in the previous time step the configuration of the haptic tool, $c_{hap}^{-1}$, is in the free space. The idea is to find an initial guess of the closest configuration in contact space, and then use optimization technic to compute a closer configuration than the initial one. The algorithm is given in Algorithm 1.

---

**Algorithm 1.** God-object Computation using Local Approximation of C-space

---

1:  $CCD(c_{hap}^{-1}, c_{hap}) -> c_{ini}$
2:  **if** collision **then**
3:     Query contact points $I_k$, $k = 1, ..., m$
4:     Update contact Jacobian $J_{m*6}$
5:     Compute $c_{tgt}$ using quadratic programming
6:     $CCD(c_{ini}, c_{tgt}) -> c_{col}$
7:     **if** collision **then**
8:        $c_{god} = c_{col}$
9:     **else**
10:        $CCD(c_{tgt}, c_{hap}) -> c_{god}$
11:    **end if**
12: **else**
13:    $c_{god} = c_{hap}$
14: **end if**

---

The initial guess of the closest configuration is computed using continuous collision detection (CCD) [20]. The CCD algorithm evaluates whether a interpolated motion between an initial and a final configuration collides with the obstacle. If so, it reports the time of first contact and the configuration at that moment.

If collision occurs (i.e., $c_{hap} \in \mathcal{O}$) during the first CCD, the local refinement is needed. The purpose of local refinement is to track a local closest configuration while the tool slides on the obstacle. The local refinement is based on the given initial guess, and the information of contact points in Euclidean space. Given a configuration in the contact space, its normal is characterized by its Jacobian as follows. Let $P_k$ and $n_k$ denote the position and normal of the $k^{th}$ contact point in Euclidean space. The constraints of non-penetration motion is

$$a^T n_k + \alpha^T (OP_k * n_k) \geq 0 \tag{4}$$

where $OP_k$ is the vector from the origin of the dynamic coordinate to the contact point, $a$ and $\alpha$ are translation and rotational components of the configuration

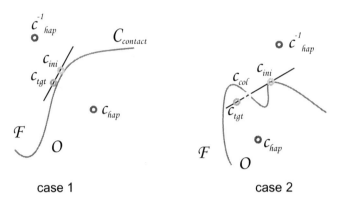

**case 1**                          **case 2**

**Fig. 3.** Local tracking of the closest configuration in the contact space

displacement $\Delta c = c - c_{ini}$. These $m$ non-penetration constraints can be concatenated to form a single constraint on the generalized coordinate of the god-object: $J\Delta c \geq 0$, where $J$ is the $m * 6$ Jacobian.

Equation 4 serves as the non-penetration condition. Then the closest configuration is formulated as an optimization problem defined by the distance metric Eq. 2.

$$\begin{cases} \min : (c - c_h)^T M (c - c_h) \\ s.t. \quad J (c - c_{ini}) \geq 0 \end{cases} \tag{5}$$

here, the mass matrix $M$ is a $6 * 6$ diagonal matrix with $(m, m, m, I_x, I_y, I_z)$ as the diagonal, $I_i$ is the moment of inertial around axis $i$. This quadratic program can be efficiently solved using an active set method [13]. In most cases, the non-singular contact points will be less than 12 (each contact point constrains half a DoF), the quadratic program is not a large system.

In the formulation of Jacobian, we make a linearization assumption, thus the computed target configuration is not necessarily in the contact space; it may be in the free space (Fig. 3 case 1) or in the obstacle space (Fig. 3 case 2). To solve this problem we employ CCD again to find a first intersect configuration between the motion from initial to target. Note that although repeating the optimization step would refine the result iteratively, it would need much more computing power thus is not adopted here.

## 5.2   Results and Discussion

We first evaluate the quality of feedback wrench using some basic geometry models. Figure 4 shows manipulating a tetrahedron to slide on a static L shape model. Both models are represented by triangles. Several snapshots of the tool during the sliding (and rotating) process are merged together to show the sequence, from a to g on the left side of Fig. 4. The red tetrahedron is the actual configuration of the tool, while the green one is the computed god-object configuration.

These solid models are rendered in a semi-transparent manner to illustrate the penetration. The corresponding force and torque curves are shown on the right side. Generally, the tool moves along $x$ axis from left to right, then along the $y$ axis up. At (b) the first contact happens between an edge of the L model and an edge of the tetrahedron. As it moves further, this edge-edge contact evolves to vertex-face contact at (c). At this transition, the force in $x$ direction disappear, i.e., the feedback force is only in y direction. Torque also changes as show in the lower right of Fig. 4. At (d) the tool is rotated and pushed down, an increase of feedback force and torque can be observed. At (e), there are two contact pairs, producing a force in both $x$ and $z$ direction. During the whole process, force in $z$ direction is always zero since the frictionless contact plane is parallel to $z$ axis.

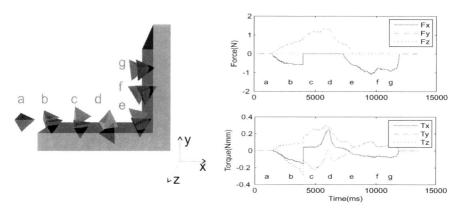

**Fig. 4.** A red tetrahedron slides (and rotates) on the surface of an L shape model

Some other models are also tested. Figure 5 left shows a tetrahedron sliding on a bunny (1 174 triangles), and right shows a cylinder (216 triangles) against a torus (576 triangles). In all these scenes, we perceive no visual interpenetration between the god-object and the obstacle. The computation is finished within $1 \sim 2$ ms which satisfies haptic display.

**Fig. 5.** Left: A tetrahedron slides on a bunny. Right: A cylinder model contacts a torus.

While the above result on simple models is promising, there is a practical problem when extending the method to more complex triangle models. To address this, CCD packages with more accurate and robust result are needed. Meanwhile, due to the time-consuming CCD algorithm we used, the haptic display update rate for complex models may be below $1kHz$. Multi-rate approaches (e.g., [14]) may alleviate this. These will be investigated in the near future.

## 6    Conclusions

We have presented an extension of the classic god-object method for point-object interaction to haptic display of general rigid body contact. This framework provides haptic display with non-interpenetrating visual effect, thus to improve the fidelity of virtual simulators. Meanwhile, it avoids contact area clustering and treatments on the singularity of penetration depth in traditional penalty based methods. The effectiveness of this framework is validated by a fast implementation of planar 3-DoF rigid body interaction using pre-computed contact space. Furthermore, the framework is demonstrated on spacial 6-DoF simple geometries, using a local C-space construction method.

There remains several directions on the basis of this framework. First, to extend the general method to more complex geometry models, the algorithm for 6-DoF rigid body will greatly benefit from better CCD algorithm, from both computational efficiency aspect and robustness of the contact information. Second, incorporating friction in this approach will produce more realistic haptic sensation. Third, user evaluation of different haptic display methods may lead to some unknown aspects of human haptic perception. Finally, it would be interesting to extend the approach to articulated rigid bodies, such as finger based grasping for rehabilitation.

**Acknowledgments.** The authors would like to thank Dr. Xinyu Zhang for his help on continuous collision detection, and Xiaowei Dai on quadratic programming. This work is supported by the National Natural Science Foundation of China (No. 60605027), and by the research project of State Key Lab of Virtual Reality Technology and Systems of China.

## References

1. Barbič, J., James, D.L.: Six-dof haptic rendering of contact between geometrically complex reduced deformable models. IEEE Transactions on Haptics 1(1), 39–52 (2008)
2. Berkelman, P.J., Hollis, R.L., Baraff, D.: Interaction with a real time dynamic environment simulation using a magnetic levitation haptic interface device. In: IEEE ICRA 1999, vol. 4, pp. 3261–3266 (1999)
3. Gregory, A., Mascarenhas, A., Ehmann, S., Lin, M., Manocha, D.: Six degree-of-freedom haptic display of polygonal models. In: IEEE VIS 2000, pp. 139–146 (2000)
4. Ho, C.H., Basdogan, C., Srinivasan, M.A.: Efficient point-based rendering techniques for haptic display of virtual objects. Presence: Teleoper. Virtual Environ. 8(5), 477–491 (1999)

5. Je, C., Tang, M., Lee, Y., Lee, M., Kim, Y.J.: Polydepth: Real-time penetration depth computation using iterative contact-space projection, Ewha Technical Report CSE-TR-2010-02 (2010)
6. Kazerounian, K., Rastegar, J.: Object norms: A class of coordinate and metric independent norms for displacement. In: ASME Design Technical Conference, pp. 271–275 (1992)
7. Kim, Y.J., Otaduy, M.A., Lin, M.C., Manocha, D.: Six-degree-of-freedom haptic rendering using incremental and localized computations. Presence: Teleoper. Virtual Environ. 12(3), 277–295 (2003)
8. Kolesnikov, M., Zefran, M.: Generalized penetration depth for penalty-based six-degree-of-freedom haptic rendering. Robotica 26(4), 513–524 (2008)
9. Lin, Q., Burdick, J.W.: Objective and frame-invariant kinematic metric functions for rigid bodies. The International Journal of Robotics Research 19(6), 612–625 (2000)
10. McNeely, W.A., Puterbaugh, K.D., Troy, J.J.: Six degree-of-freedom haptic rendering using voxel sampling. In: SIGGRAPH 1999, pp. 401–408 (1999)
11. Nawratil, G., Pottmann, H., Ravani, B.: Generalized penetration depth computation based on kinematical geometry. Computer Aided Geometric Design 26(4), 425–443 (2009)
12. Nelson, D.D., Johnson, D.E., Cohen, E.: Haptic rendering of surface-to-surface sculpted model interaction. In: ACM SIGGRAPH 2005 Courses, p. 97 (2005)
13. Nocedal, J., Wright, S.: Numerical optimization. Springer, Heidelberg (2006)
14. Ortega, M., Redon, S., Coquillart, S.: A six degree-of-freedom god-object method for haptic display of rigid bodies with surface properties. IEEE Transactions on Visualization and Computer Graphics 13(3), 458–469 (2007)
15. Otaduy, M.A., Lin, M.C.: A modular haptic rendering algorithm for stable and transparent 6-dof manipulation. IEEE Transactions on Robotics 22(4), 751–762 (2006)
16. Ruspini, D., Khatib, O.: Collision/contact models for the dynamic simulation of compex environmnets. In: IEEE/RSJ IROS 1997 (1997)
17. Srinivasan, M.A., Beauregard, G.L., Brock, D.L.: The impact of visual information on the haptic perception of stiffness in virtual environments. In: ASME Winter Annual Meeting (1996)
18. Zhang, L., Kim, Y.J., Manocha, D.: A fast and practical algorithm for generalized penetration depth computation. In: Robotics: Science and Systems Conference, RSS 2007 (2007)
19. Zhang, L., Kim, Y.J., Varadhan, G., Manocha, D.: Generalized penetration depth computation. Computer Aided Design 39(8), 625–638 (2007)
20. Zhang, X., Lee, M., Kim, Y.J.: Interactive continuous collision detection for nonconvex polyhedra. Vis. Comput. 22(9), 749–760 (2006)
21. Zilles, C.B., Salisbury, J.K.: A constraint-based god-object method for haptic display. In: IEEE/RSJ IROS 1995, vol. 3, pp. 146–151 (1995)

# Assistive Robots in Eldercare and Daily Living: Automation of Individual Services for Senior Citizens

Alexander Mertens[1], Ulrich Reiser[2], Benedikt Brenken[3], Mathias Lüdtke[2], Martin Hägele[2], Alexander Verl[2], Christopher Brandl[1], and Christopher Schlick[1]

[1] Institute of Industrial Engineering and Ergonomics of RWTH Aachen University, Germany
{a.mertens,c.brandl,c.schlick}@iaw.rwth-aachen.de
[2] Fraunhofer Institute for Manufacturing Engineering and Automation, Germany
{ulrich.reiser,mathias.luedtke,martin.haegele,
alexander.verl}@ipa.fraunhofer.de
[3] Research Institute for Operations Management (FIR) at RWTH Aachen, Germany
benedikt.brenken@fir.rwth-aachen.de

**Abstract.** This paper presents the latest results with regard to the design of service robots and interfaces for human-robot interaction in recent empirical research projects. Focus is on establishing services for health care, nursing homes, rehabilitation and homely aftercare in respect of the demands coinciding with demographic change.

Within several user studies and clinical trials relevant application scenarios, arrangement of working spaces and the stature layout of robots were elicited and their influence on intuitive understanding and technical acceptance investigated. Additionally the implementation of information input with help of swabbing movements on touch screens for people suffering from hand tremor was accomplished, considering the specific requirements and computer literacy of the prospective users.

**Keywords:** AAL, Eldercare, Human-Robot Interaction, Robot, Service.

## 1    Introduction

Demographic changes cause large-scale changes in the population´s age structure. Particularly serious is the steady increase of elderly people, as this poses a challenge for medical care. While in 2008 five percent of the German population was 80 years or older, it is expected that by 2060 every seventh person (14 % of the population) will belong to this group [1].

It can be observed that with advanced age an increase of health problems arises, both, in terms of number of patients and the complexity of health impairment [2]. It is therefore necessary to develop innovative concepts and products regarding the areas aging in your own home, rehabilitation and homely aftercare in order to stay abreast of the changes in the population´s age structure.

The main aim is to increase the quality of life of the elderly and sick. Staying independent is the crucial requirement for aging in your own home. According to a survey by the TNS Emnid, seniors do prefer to live alone and only be supported by

S. Jeschke, H. Liu, and D. Schilberg (Eds.): ICIRA 2011, Part I, LNAI 7101, pp. 542–552, 2011.
© Springer-Verlag Berlin Heidelberg 2011

their partner or family in cases of emergency. Family members should be supported in taking care of their relatives, because caring of family members should not turn into a wearisome duty. It should rather be held as easy as possible by integrating intensified and purpose-optimized robot-based technologies in daily life scenarios.

Another focus is on home care subsequent to surgery which includes extensive rehabilitation activities. Hospital stays are very expensive where home care could cut costs significantly [3]. Besides that most patients want to leave hospital as quickly as possible to return to their usual environment and continue their daily life in order to maintain a fixed structure in their lifestyle.

In 2009 350.000 heart surgeries have been performed in Germany. By integrating technology appropriately (such as telemedical monitoring and home help), it becomes possible to support patients in their own environment once they have left hospital. An integrated and interdisciplinary approach is necessary to design and test scenarios and strategies for the use of technology in prospective, personal services. One of the key issues during testing will be: How users can be introduced to and qualified for the usage of the applications. Studies have shown the enormous potential for increased use of technology in home care services and medical care (see Fig. 1).

Service robots, systems which partially or fully perform services autonomously, are an important step into the right direction and will be particularly focused on in the following.

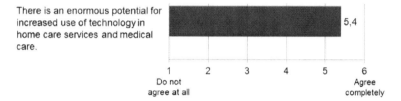

**Fig. 1.** Forecast on technologies in personal services [4]

## 2    Related Work and Lessons Learned in Developing Service Robots

### 2.1    Care-O-bot 3

Care-O-bot 3 was created as a product vision of a future household assistant that is able to ease the everyday life of people in their homes. Typical tasks for the robot include for example cleaning the table, clearing the dish washer or bringing objects like a cold drink from the fridge or the keys lying on the floor. Before the robot was constructed, these task descriptions along with results from user studies [5] were considered to create the overall design concept of the robot.

The key features of this concept include the explicitly non-anthropomorphic design and the 'two-sides' human robot interaction concept. A humanoid shape should be avoided, as according to the user studies [5] the appearance of a device elicits always corresponding expectations of its capabilities. Therefore the appearance of the robot should fit to its actual capabilities. The second major design feature, the 'two-sides' concept (see Fig. 2, left), defines the way the robot interacts with its environment and the way it interacts with humans.

544     A. Mertens et al.

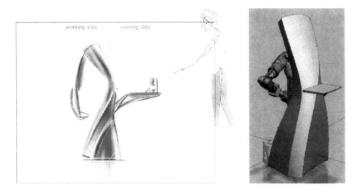

**Fig. 2.** Left: The 'two-sides' human-robot interaction concept. *Right:* First technical rendering.

The working space of the robot was therefore separated into a representative side, which is turned to the user to give instructions to the robot. A special component in this respect is the tray, which serves as input terminal and provides for natural and safe handing over of objects. In contrast, the working side encompasses the manipulator of the robot that interacts with the environment. Through this separation into the two sides, the intrinsic safety of the robot is increased as much as possible while at the same time the human robot interaction is as comfortable as possible. In addition to the two-sides concept, human-robot interaction is supported furthermore by a flexible hull, which enables the robot to provide feedback to the user through simple gestures like bowing. Having defined this design concept, corresponding hardware components were chosen with which both the functional capabilities and the design concept could be implemented. In [6] an overview of the hardware and software components of Care-O-bot 3 is given. Special attention was paid to the design of the user interface. Derived from different application scenarios, different designs were created (see Fig. 3).

**Fig. 3.** Developed user interfaces for Care-O-bot 3 for the implementation on different input devices like tablet pc, smart phones or the touch screen integrated into the tray of the robot [7]

A simple user interface for a serving drink scenario was finally implemented on the touch screen integrated into the tray of the robot [7]. In the following sections, further application scenarios related to assistance of elderly people both at home and in eldercare facilities are described in more detail.

## 2.2    Examples for Service Robot Application Scenarios

Although Care-O-bot 3 was designed as a general household assistant not restricted to elderly people, the most dominant and also most pressing application scenarios in research projects are focused on the eldercare sector. In the following, two scenarios from European research projects SRS (Multi-Role Shadow Robot for Independent Living) [8] and Wimi-Care (Supporting the Knowledge Transfer for a Participative Design of the Care Work Sector through Microelectronics) [9] are presented along with first results of real live testings.

**Home Assistant Scenario.** The goal of the European research project SRS [8] is to allow elderly persons to live longer in their own homes instead of moving into an eldercare facility. Care-O-bot 3 is used in the project context in a partly tele-operated, semi-autonomous mode to assist elderly persons at fulfilling household tasks. The key feature of the concept lies in the close cooperation of the patients, their relatives and the technology providers. The interaction between the different groups was hereby accomplished throughout all project phases. Relatives or private caregivers are actively integrated into the services provided by the robot. The participation can e.g. consist of controlling the robot remotely to initiate certain tasks, to communicate with the patients via robot or to help the robot through tele-operation in case it cannot solve its task completely autonomously. This potentially results in a higher reliability of the robot's services and a closer integration of the different user groups. The project started in 2010 with a survey to identify appropriate scenarios for a tele-operated home assistant among the following three user groups:

- elderly persons as local users and beneficiary
- private caregivers, e.g. relatives of the elderly person as remote operators
- employees of 24-hour teleassistance centers as professional remote operators

From the results of the survey the following fetch-and-carry scenario was chosen: The robot is requested by the local user to bring an object to a certain location, e.g. glass of water (see Fig. 4, lower left), or in particular difficult to reach objects like a book from the shelf (see Fig. 4, upper right). The robot then navigates to the location where the object resides, detects it by using its sensors, grasps the object and drives back to the location of the local user where it delivers the object. In case of problems, it can contact the remote operator for help. This help may e.g. consist of instructing the robot to find objects by taking a look at the picture of the scenario presented by the robots camera. In addition, preparing food was envisaged as a slight variation of the fetch-and-carry scenario (see Fig. 4, upper left). Giving support in emergency situations was determined to be a second group of relevant applications, e.g. helping a fallen person to stand up or starting a video call to the tele-operator (see Fig. 4, lower right). The remote operator can then use the robot to observe the elderly person and decide whether to set up an emergency call. The scenarios are planned to be evaluated within the SRS project in facilities for assisted living.

**Fig. 4.** Envisaged SRS Scenarios (from top left to bottom right): preparing food, retrieving difficult to reach objects, serve drinks or assist in emergency situations

**Scenarios to Support Service Personal in Eldercare Facilities.** The German research project WiMi-Care [7] aims in contrast to the SRS project at helping service personal in eldercare facilities in their daily work, taking over routine tasks such as transporting goods and journalizing their work to leave them more time for work in direct contact with the inhabitants.

Two scenarios for Care-O-bot 3 were identified through a requirement analysis conducted in an eldercare facility, the scenario "beverage supply" (Fig. 5, left) and an entertainment scenario (Fig. 5, right).

The main goal of the beverage supply scenario consists of offering water to the patients. As they tend to drink to little of their own accord, it is usually very time-consuming for nursing staff offer drinks on a regular basis while registering the drinking statistics of the single inhabitants. In addition, journalizing the amount of consumed potation is usually error-prone as they often have to do several tasks at once and have to react to sudden alarms. In detail, the scenario consists of the following steps:

- Care-O-bot 3 draws a cup of water from water dispenser.
- Care-O-bot 3 identifies the inhabitants sitting at the tables and chooses a person which according to the potation supply journal has not drunk enough water and offers the drink.
- The robot motivates the elderly people to drink, for example by addressing the people individually via speech output.
- If the drink is taken, Care-O-bot 3 thanks the inhabitant and moves back to the kitchen area.

It is also necessary that the Care-O-bot3 performs its application safe and reliable, especially in sitting areas or on a crowded corridor. In the entertainment scenario, Care-O-bot 3 offers individual functions and activities to entertain or also train the patients, e.g. by playing games or music. The activity can hereby be started via touch screen or a smartphone. The evaluation of real live testings of the potation supply scenario is given in the next section.

**Fig. 5.** Left, middle: potation supply scenario, right: entertainment scenario

## 2.3    Evaluation of Care-O-bot 3 in an Eldercare Facility

The first evaluation of the potation supply scenario in May 2010 took place in a eldercare facility in Stuttgart [10] and focused on the feasibility and overall acceptance of the scenario. Furthermore the need for required enhancements and adaptions of Care-O-bot 3 was identified during the project in order to ensure a reliable performance of the robot in the second and final practical evaluation which will take place in June 2011.

The task was conducted according to the scenario description before. The following single steps are illustrated in Fig. 6: The robot first drives to the kitchen in the eldercare facility, draws water from a water dispenser, transports the cup on a long corridor frequented by inhabitants and staff members and offers the drink to people sitting at a table.

From the functional point of view, the scenario was found to be feasible with respect to the autonomous retrieval of drinks. Water was successfully offered and handed over to inhabitants more than 20 times in a regular supply service [10].The acceptance of Care-O-bot 3 was very high, also mainly due to an elaborate preparation of the test phase including several information evenings during which nursing staff and inhabitants got the chance to understand the idea of a robot supporting the staff without replacing them and that the interaction with the machine must not be feared.

In many cases the elderly people did not drink the water, but just placed it in front of them. A reason for this might be that the inhabitants during testing were already offered beverages by the nursing staff. The inhabitants also were aware that the robot was tested and might have taken the drink to support the work of the scientists which of cause also was a distraction from their daily routine. Generally the expectations towards the robot seemed to match its abilities, which is surely due to the functional design of Care-O-bot 3.

**Fig. 6.** Course of the potation supply scenario: Drawing water from a water cooler (upper left), transporting it to a sitting area (upper right) and offering it to the inhabitants (bottom)

Nevertheless, some inhabitants tended to treat the robot like a life form and for example thanked Care-O-bot 3 and even tried to caress it when it brought them a drink.

# 3     Evaluation of Target-Group Specific Human-Robot Interfaces

Target group specific interfaces for human-robot interaction are crucial for an efficient and self-reliant access to the provided services and for communicating individual needs. Many currently available telemedical systems e.g. are not adequate for people suffering from kinetic tremor, ametropia or who do not have adequate computer literacy. This inability abates efficiency, effectiveness and satisfaction of the user and even causes social isolation due to the hindered maintaining and establishing of contacts. For this target group of people depending on assistance and support new concepts of interaction have been developed and evaluated. Creating a sufficient interaction for these people is the key to several identified barriers occurring with current demographic change and related problems with technical acceptance. Optimizing the user interface can help to integrate service robots in daily life scenarios of the people in need and retain the trust in these assistive technologies.

## 3.1     Information Input for People Suffering from Kinetic Tremor

To allow an appropriate interaction between people suffering from kinetic tremor in the upper extremities and IT-based robot systems, the information input has to be focused as prevalent user interfaces do not respect the specific limitations and occurring deviations [11].

**Solution Concept and Hypotheses.** Theoretically the problem occurring with a kinetic tremor, namely the inaccurate input, may be counteracted by simply increasing the space available on the input area (paper, touch screen, etc…). This would compensate the expected deviation caused by the tremor. However, this method has limitations when it comes to stronger tremor deviations and limitation of input space on human-robot interfaces. This leads to either the limitation of options concurrently displayed or the reduction of button size on the screen, in order to maintain the amount of choices offered [12]. This will almost certainly increase the error ratio because of distinct tremor symptoms and resulting deviation.

In order to enable correct and independent input for the previously described target group a touch screen is used as user interface. The principle behind the enlargement is Fitt's Law. The width of the target, measured along the axis of motion on the screen, is not restricted through the screen dimensions, characterized in that the user can perform a continuous input movement beyond the borders. The electronic tracking of the input appears only on the touch screen but inhibits tremor symptoms because no deceleration is necessary. For the whole contact phase data which helps to retrace the movement, as direction, orientation, velocity and starting point, is collected. It is hypothesized that this very close approximation of the user movement helps to allocate the desired input from the user much more reliably than the ordinary point input method.

Furthermore it is expected that precision is also increased through a raised friction on the screen surface and through this generated dumping effect, physically reducing tremor deviation.

**Participants and Procedure.** 20 clinically diagnosed tremor patients were recruited from the Department of Neurology at the University Hospital of Aachen University (age: min=53, q1=66, med=76, mean=74.5, q3=78, max=84). The participants had not used touch screens before this study. All participants used the index finger of their dominant hand in the experiment.

Testing the generated swabbing input method faces the test person with the following setup: A standard multi touch notebook is placed in front of the user via a holding frame which enables an angular positioning (20° from desk surface) to suit the test person's needs relative to the desk height. The probands chair is adjusted so that the table height is approximately similar to the elbow height while the arm points towards the ground. On the screen the test person is presented with highlighted items which he or she has to select in order to perform the task. The test person is asked to perform an "input" and will receive a visual feedback whether the input was correctly performed or not. The interaction area is a square of 800 x 800 pixels (164 mm each side), and the participants have to rest the test finger on a crosshairs after each input which is located at the same side of the used hand.

The items are arranged circular (tapping & swabbing) or in grid layout (tapping) on the screen. The trials are accomplished with rising resolution starting with 9 items, 16 items, and finally 25 items. Each condition is repeated for 10 trials resulting in a total of 90 trials. The user starts by resting the finger on the crosshairs before either tapping or moving the finger to the center of the screen to swab. For introduction and to minimize the influence of learning effects the probands got a short hands-on demonstration for each of the three different layouts with a maximum of ten inputs per layout. Subsequently an accelerometer and gyroscope were attached to the input finger to measure oscillation for different interaction techniques.

To guarantee comparability of the results a high consistency during each test was conducted. A standardized test protocol helped to achieve this. To prevent learning effects, we counterbalanced the order of patterns with even-size Latin Square.

**Results.** In the following results, we used two-way, repeated measures ANOVA models with significance level of $\alpha=0.05$; data is normally distributed. We found no interaction between layout and resolution ($F(2.13)=0.814$, n.s.), and no significant difference between different layouts in tapping ($F(1.47)=2.978$, n.s.). Then, a comparison between methods in radial layout shows significant effect of methods ($F(1.54) = 5.106$, p<0.05). As seen in Fig. 7, the error rates of swabbing in 16- and 25-buttons resolutions are lower than tapping. Post-hoc analysis with pairwise t-test with Bonferroni correction supports the effect in both resolutions (16: p=0.0043, 25: p=0.032).

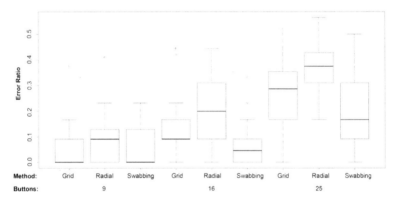

**Fig. 7.** Box plots of error ratio by resolutions and methods

The acceleration data is Fast-Fourier transformed into frequency domains. This enables an analysis of tremor frequencies during rest and interaction with the touch screen. The frequency domain of data shown in Fig. 8 is transformed into spectrum plots in Fig. 9.

**Fig. 8.** An excerpt of acceleration data from each stage of interaction

Each plot represents frequency in an axis of a stage of interaction. The investigated patterns show that measured effects are strongly dependent on the tremor type (resting and action (intention/posture/contraction) tremor), especially regarding the axes of movement on which the tremor agitation appears. The sliding movement shows the best effect for those patients suffering from an intention and resting tremor, as here deviations among the main axes of movement are reduced, while for persons with contraction tremor sliding worsens the symptoms. The results further show, that people encumbered with medium and strong tremors, who use wiping movements as interaction, show a significantly reduced error rate of input compared to those who use touching standard button environments. It is also shown that patients suffering from a minor tremor agitation experience no noteworthy improvement during their interaction.

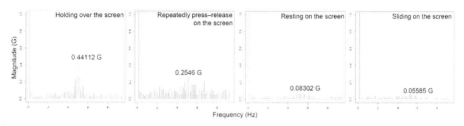

**Fig. 9.** Spectrum plots of finger oscillation frequencies and magnitude in axis orthogonal to the ground. The number indicates the value of the highest peak.

## 4    Conclusion

The importance of robot-based assistance for present and future medical care with regard to demographic change is undisputed. However, due to a lack of specifications for elderly users, today's systems do not adequately recognize requirements of senior users. The feedback about the probands' experiences during the experiment shows that success and sustainability of novel technology is strongly dependant on overcoming individual user barriers and the integration of medical technology in the environment without stigmatizing.

So far, the users' perspectives and preferences have not been systematically integrated in the product development process which makes it difficult to establish assistance technologies in this market segment. Utilization not only increases the quality of life of elderly people but it also is strategically important for many companies entering the "senior market".

The scenarios carried out in these studies represents fundamental research in order to adequately design age-adapted robot-based systems, which take into account the requirements and living conditions of the ordinary "best-ager", not least generating a positive stand towards technology.

**Acknowledgment.** This research is funded by the German Federal Ministry of Education and Research BMBF (01FG10004) and the body responsible for the project is DLR.

# References

1. Bundesamt, S.: Bevölkerung Deutschlands bis 2060 - Ergebnisse der 12. koordinierten Bevölkerungsvorausberechnung, Wiesbaden (2009)
2. Saß, A.-C.: Somatische und psychische Gesundheit. In: Bohm, K. (ed.) Gesundheit und Krankheit im Alter, p. 31. Robert Koch Institut, Berlin (2009)
3. Mahomed, N.: Inpatient compared with home-based rehabilitation following primary unilateral total hip or knee replacement: a randomized controlled trial. PubMed, Toronto (2008)
4. FIR at RWTH Aachen University: Technologieintegration bei Dienstleistungen. Aachen (in print, 2011)
5. Parlitz, C., Hägele, M., Klein, P., Seifert, J., Dautenhahn, K.: Care-O-bot 3 — Rationale for human-robot interaction design. In: International Federation of Robotics u.a.: ISR 2008: 39th International Symposium on Robotics, Seoul, Korea, pp. 275–280 (2008)
6. Reiser, U., Connette, C., Fischer, J., Kubacki, J., Bubeck, A., Weisshardt, F., Jacobs, T., Parlitz, C., Hägele, M., Verl, A.: Care-O-bot® 3 – Creating a product vision for service robot applications by integrating design and technology. In: The 2009 IEEE/RSJ International Conference on Intelligent Robots and Systems (IROS), pp. 1992–1997 (2009)
7. Reiser, U., Parlitz, C., Klein, P.: Care-O-bot® 3 – Vision of a robot butler. In: Beyond Gray Droids: Domestic Robot Design for the 21st Century: Workshop, HCI 2009, Cambridge, UK, September 1 (2009)
8. Multi-Role Shadow Robot for Independent Living (SRS), funded in the 7th European framework with Grant agreement no.: 247772, Duration: (February 2010 - January 2013), http://www.srs-project.eu
9. Supporting the Knowledge Transfer for a Participative Design of the Care Work Sector through Microelectronics (WiMi-Care), funded by the German Federal Ministry of Research and Technology (BMBF, support code: 01FC08024-27), Duration: (November 2008 - October 2011), http://www.wimi-care.de
10. Jacobs, T., Graf, B.: Working Brief 23: Pilotanwendungen: Ergebnisse für die Weiterentwicklung des Care-O-bot® 3 hinsichtlich benötigter Fähigkeiten und Akzeptanz (2010), http://www.wimi-care.de/outputs.html#Briefs
11. Plumb, M., Bain, P.: Essential Tremor: The Facts. Oxford University Press (2006)
12. Jones, L.A., Sarter, N.B.: Tactile Displays: Guidance for Their Design and Application. Human Factors: The Journal of the Human Factors and Ergonomics Society 50, 90–111 (2008)

# Key Factors for Freshmen Education Using MATLAB and LEGO Mindstorms

Alexander Behrens, Linus Atorf, Dorian Schneider, and Til Aach

Institute of Imaging & Computer Vision, RWTH Aachen University,
52056 Aachen, Germany
{alexander.behrens,til.aach}@lfb.rwth-aachen.de

**Abstract.** Undergraduate engineering courses with strong focus on theoretical concepts often have an adverse effect on student motivation due to a lack of illustrative applications to real–world problems. To identify and overcome this problem we point out educational key factors to design practical laboratories for first semester students using MATLAB and LEGO Mindstorms robots. By means of evaluation results of the freshmen course "MATLAB meets LEGO Mindstorms" and follow–up projects using the same teaching concept, we show that freshman students can develop creative applications and solutions, even if only first fundamentals have been taught. Using the RWTH – Mindstorms NXT Toolbox for development, beginners foster their programming and engineering skills in a fast and intuitive way. Providing successive tasks and ensuring enough room for creativity, a surprising variety of sophisticated projects is reported by student teams in final presentations and competitions, thus boosting their motivation and interest in future engineering tasks.

**Keywords:** Educational robotics, Freshmen, Practical Course, MATLAB, LEGO Mindstorms, RWTH – Mindstorms NXT Toolbox.

## 1 Introduction

The integration of new practical introduction courses and hands–on projects for freshman students is more and more becoming a hallmark of today's engineering curricula. Thus, traditional undergraduate courses in electrical engineering, which deal with mathematical basics and principles of electrical engineering from a strictly theoretical point of view, are gradually restructured [13]. The concept of teaching broad theoretical foundations first, and to establish complex and intensive practical courses only in advanced semesters loses relevance, since the students' motivation often drops due to difficulties relating theoretical concepts to practical engineering tasks. In contrast, several education projects [7, 11, 14] show that especially first semester laboratories can increase the students' course achievements, as well as boost their motivation in engineering. Based on this hands–on concept, a new first semester introduction course into practical engineering, termed "MATLAB meets LEGO Mindstorms"[1] has been developed [3]

---

[1] http://www.lfb.rwth-aachen.de/mindstorms

S. Jeschke, H. Liu, and D. Schilberg (Eds.): ICIRA 2011, Part I, LNAI 7101, pp. 553–562, 2011.
© Springer-Verlag Berlin Heidelberg 2011

and established in the Bachelor of Science curriculum of Electrical Engineering and Information Technology of RWTH Aachen University, Germany, in 2007. In this project three learning targets, viz. mathematical methods, MATLAB® programming, and practical engineering, are addressed after only a two–months series of lectures. In an eight–day, full–time mandatory block–course about 400 freshman students are required to transfer mathematical basics to algorithms in MATLAB in order to control LEGO® Mindstorms® NXT robots. Based on the open–source RWTH – Mindstorms NXT Toolbox for MATLAB [15], a surprisingly wide variety of creative inventions are developed and presented by first semester students each year. In this paper we point out the major aspects of this teaching concept, address the deliberate choice of using MATLAB and LEGO Mindstorms robots, and discuss its applications to freshman students based on four years of experience. Furthermore, we give a review how this approach was transferred and adopted to follow–up projects at other universities and colleges.

## 2   Educational Project Environment

### 2.1   Programming Software

MATLAB is a powerful programming and simulation tool, which provides an intuitive way to map matrices and vector algebra from mathematical expressions, discussed in lectures and educational text books, to program algorithms. It allows an easy and fast implementation of programming basics and supports extensive debugging methods, especially for beginners. Beyond its detailed documentation and adaptive syntax verification, its functionality enables the user to abstract and solve complex mathematical problems and engineering tasks using high and low–level descriptions. Its intuitive access and flexibility allow to use it for teaching core computing and signal processing concepts to freshman students. Thus, MATLAB demos are often applied in education to address and solve real–world problems from a practical point of view [6], like digital signal processing (DSP) [9,10], applied automatic controls [12], computer programming [1], as well as to graphical user interface (GUI) design. Furthermore, MATLAB programming skills become more and more important for engineers, since MATLAB is widely used in industry for algorithm and simulation development.

### 2.2   Educational Robotics

The usage of LEGO Mindstorms robots for practical courses is widely spread [2,16], since the LEGO bricks are modular and robust which makes it possible to realize and re–build robots in a fast and straightforward way. Furthermore, many students are often already familiar with LEGO, which quickly leads to a high level of creativity. The Mindstorms NXT hardware kit provides a programmable NXT brick with a 32–bit ARM processor, and a USB and Bluetooth communication interface. Also, analog and digital sensors, like e.g. touch, sound, light, color, ultrasonic distance sensors, servo motors, and different plastic LEGO bricks are included. Several more specific ones, such as RFID, acceleration, compass, and infrared sensors are available from third party vendors.

## 2.3    MATLAB–Mindstorms NXT Interface

Different tools have been developed to control Mindstorms NXT robots via MATLAB. A free MATLAB–Simulink® implementation [5] using robot simulation models with advanced control engineering is available for professional users. Here, the robot's behavior can be previewed in a virtual environment. For real–time execution the program code is embedded into the NXT, which impedes the opportunity to debug code step–wise and interactively.

The RWTH – Mindstorms NXT Toolbox[2] [4] supports a direct control interface using a Bluetooth or USB connection via MATLAB. It provides four different command layers with low and high–level functionality. Based on the LEGO communication protocol, data packages are transmitted and directly accessible. Furthermore, an object–oriented and user–friendly interface is established, and advanced motor control programs with high precision control can be optionally activated. With support for many sensors and a detailed documentation embedded into the MATLAB help browser, the toolbox provides an intuitive interface for beginners as well as advanced programmers. As an open–source software, the toolbox is also supported and recommended by MathWorks [8].

## 3    Hands–on Project "MATLAB Meets LEGO Mindstorms"

A first hands–on project, called "MATLAB meets LEGO Mindstorms" was established for Bachelor students at RWTH Aachen University, Germany, using MATLAB, LEGO Mindstorms NXT robots, and the RWTH – Mindstorms NXT Toolbox. The content of this laboratory reflects three key objectives: Mathematical methods, MATLAB programming, and practical engineering. Mathematical fundamentals and a first MATLAB introduction are taught in an affiliated lecture "Mathematical Methods of Electrical Engineering" (MMET), which covers discrete–time signals, digital signal processing, and system theory, all in a manner suitable to freshman students. Based on the basic knowledge of the first two months series of lectures, the students develop and program NXT robots in teams using MATLAB. Within eight days, the students are required to solve six mandatory basic exercises, which address NXT motors and sensors on the first five project days. During the last three days the students are free to develop their own robot applications, and finally give a presentation. Furthermore, they can enter the MATLAB Team Award competition for the most creative and inventive robotic construction. Since the project is intentionally conducted as a full–time block–course, all students (about 400) are distributed among 23 institutes of the Electrical Engineering Department, where they are guided by a total of 80 supervisors. Besides participating in the MMET lecture and the MATLAB introduction course, the students have to pass a mandatory online self–assessment test for preparatory work. For evaluation, voluntary surveys are carried out each term. Summarized evaluation results of the last four years are illustrated in Fig. 1. The results show, that the teaching concept achieves the

---

[2] http://www.mindstorms.rwth-aachen.de

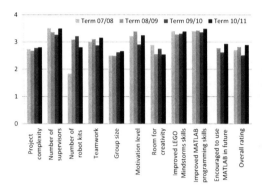

**Fig. 1.** Project evaluation results based on anonymous student surveys (4: excellent, 3: good, 2: average, 1: below average, 0: inadequate) (left). Individual student project: Autonomous forklift robot detects and transports objects along different paths (right)

desired learning targets, boosts the students' motivation, and improves the peer–learning process. The overall rating of the project is very high and considerable improvements of the students' MATLAB skills are confirmed. The motivation level, teamwork, and the opportunity to be creative are highly rated, while the project complexity is considered adequate to good. Compared to other laboratories, where students conduct only predefined experiments and verify their results in protocols and tests based on a weekly time schedule, our learning concept is favored by the students. Based on quantitative results published by the Faculty (see Table 1), also the overall evaluation scores are rated higher.

**Table 1.** Overall evaluation scores of different laboratories of the B. Sc. ET/IT curriculum. The school grades (1: very good – 5: inadequate) are published for the semester terms 2007–2011 by the Faculty of Electrical Engineering and Information Technology.

|  | Semester | 07/08 | 08/09 | 09/10 | 10/11 |
|---|---|---|---|---|---|
| MATLAB meets LEGO Mindstorms | 1st | — | 1.87 | — | 2.06 |
| Electrical Engineering Laboratory 1 | 2nd | 2.53 | 2.56 | 2.51 | 2.37 |
| Computer Engineering Laboratory 1 | 3rd | 3.44 | 3.22 | 2.93 | 2.44 |

## 4   Educational Key Factors

Based on these results and four years of experience we identify the major educational aspects of this project, which lead to meet the learning targets, and increase the students' motivation and interest in engineering.

***Development Environment:*** For a high–quality output and motivation boost of freshmen projects the provided software and hardware components have to be adjusted to the need of first semester students. MATLAB provides several advantages compared to other programming software, since the students are able to transfer mathematical expressions directly into programming code. Also, the program execution within the debug mode proved to be a valuable feature. The students can monitor program variables and intermediate outputs. In a step–wise and interactive manner errors are quickly identified. Furthermore, the different MATLAB file types, like scripts, functions and figures, as well as the detailed syntax highlighting and interactive documentation assist also the supervisors in verification and understanding of the developed programs. Finally, MATLAB is a script based language that needs no compiling or linking of the program code. This way, any overhead for code compilations is avoided such as library version inconsistencies.

Constructing robots with modular LEGO bricks provides an opportunity to design robots very fast and give new construction ideas a quick try. This constructive component is strongly appreciated by the students. Furthermore, mobile NXT robots controlled by a wireless Bluetooth connection are favored, since they can explore new and unknown environments. Although the number of bricks and their plastic design may lead to limited and less than perfectly precise robot constructions, working with limited resources trains engineering.

For robot control, RWTH – Mindstorms NXT Toolbox functions provide a suitable interface for programming beginners. Processing each control command at a time makes the communication between NXT and PC more transparent, and facilitates debugging compared to software solutions embedded in the NXT. Although bandwidths of the USB and Bluetooth data channel are limited and can lead to time lags during robot control – which impede wireless applications with hard real–time requirements – the MATLAB interface nevertheless turns out to be very flexible and extendable. Additional toolbox functionalities and hardware devices like web cameras and external controllers, as well as graphical user interfaces can easily be integrated into the applications. One example is given by an individual student project, shown in Fig. 2. A haptic scanner samples a glass using a test prod and displays the reconstructed 3D points in a MATLAB plot. The scanning process is started by pushing control buttons on a graphical user interface.

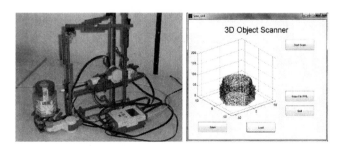

**Fig. 2.** 3D haptic scanner sampling a honey glass (left), and its 3D point reconstruction shown in a MATLAB GUI (right)

***Project Timing and Duration:*** The introduction of practical courses right at the beginning of a course of study is important to make students understand how theoretical concepts are related to solutions for real–world problems. The project evaluations show that the course goals are fulfilled and motivation levels are high, even if freshman students have only been taught mathematical fundamentals for two months. Thus, already short insights into mathematical and engineering principles enable the students to develop new and individual projects.

The full–time block–course concept with a duration of several days provides enough time and room for creativity. Compared to projects on a weekly basis, the students are given more time to focus and concentrate on the specific project tasks, without being "distracted" by other lectures. Solutions are then found faster and more inventive application ideas come up.

***Exercise Design and Scope for Creativity:*** The project exercises should be designed to exhibit a successively increasing level of complexity. First, basic exercises address programming fundamentals and hardware specifics, like e.g. motor control and sensor characteristics. More complex tasks like timer control, search and detection algorithms are applied in subsequent exercises. Based on the acquired knowledge and experiences, the students are then able to develop and realize their own more complex robot applications, as illustrated in Fig. 3. Providing additional predefined construction tasks as backup proved valuable to assist and inspire less creative students.

**Fig. 3.** Students teams constructing their own creative robot applications

Although it is well–known that educational robotics alone already boosts the motivation level, providing the students sufficient room to design, develop, and program their own and individual robots is also of high importance. Only making advanced and flexible robots available for programming without any option to extend, redesign, or rebuild the robot may often lead to short motivation effects. Thus, only lessons in which the students "feel like engineers" will be remain in the students' minds.

***Supervision and Assistance:*** Since the project is limited in time, a sufficient preparation, like reading the experiment documentations and getting familiar with the programming software is essential for a smooth exercise execution during the project. Instead of reviewing the students' knowledge by oral or written preliminary tests, we developed a mandatory online self–assessment test. The students are asked to solve basic mathematical and programming problems using MATLAB and a primer tutorial, and answer questions about the experimental setup. Very few students fail to pass the test in time. They are invited to an additional pre–seminar to be trained individually.

During the project a sufficiently high ratio between supervisors and students is essential. Especially in the beginning, when the students are confronted with completely new challenges, instructions and assistance from tutors accelerate the work progress. Furthermore, individual robotic projects should be discussed and coordinated with the supervisors before execution, to prevent too complex and time–consuming project tasks. Thus, from our experience a ratio between supervisors and students of 1:5 ensures a good performance in practice.

***Teamwork and Peer–Learning:*** Because program codes can be written by only one student at a time using one computer, student teams are formed as groups of two. Each team is equipped with a LEGO Mindstorms NXT set to work on the mandatory basic exercises. In the second project phase, in which students are free to develop their own robot application, teams of four students are formed. Having two computers and two robot kits, more complex tasks and constructions can be distributed among the team and realized in parallel. Furthermore, working in teams increases the peer–learning process, and may lead to different points of view and fruitful debates.

***Presentation and Competition:*** At the end of the project the students are requested to demonstrate and present their individual robotic applications and MATLAB implementations in a 15 minute slide presentation. Since the presentation is scheduled on the last project day, the students thus also train to finalize their programs and robots on time. Furthermore, each student project is demonstrated to the other students and supervisors (cf. Fig. 4). To make the projects visible to third parties, robot descriptions and videos can be uploaded and archived on the project web page. Beyond the presentations, the students are welcome to participate in a MATLAB Team Award competition. MathWorks awards a prize for the best student team, based on the robot design, innovation, construction, and implementation.

**Fig. 4.** Student presentations

## 5    Follow-Up Projects

"MATLAB meets LEGO Mindstorms" has inspired several other educational institutions to develop new freshman projects. In the following, we highlight few third party projects that employ MATLAB, LEGO Mindstorms NXT, and the RWTH–Mindstorms NXT Toolbox for teaching purposes.

### 5.1    University of Cambridge, UK

The project *Week 1 Exercise: Engineering LEGO* at University of Cambridge, UK, is intended for over 300 freshmen of the Department of Engineering to design and build LEGO systems that demonstrate aspects of engineering science. This introductory course takes place during the first week of study, and thus before any lecture has started. Established as a block–course, it provides the very first contact between students and university. The syllabus consists of a six day laboratory, with a weekend as optional work time in between.

The course structure is also scheduled into three parts. First of all, an introduction into MATLAB and the basic functions of the NXT Toolbox is given. The second phase is scheduled for three days and allows the students to design individual robots. In this process simple "toy robots", such as e.g. remotely controlled cars, are not accepted as project idea. Instead, constructions which verify the laws of physics by measuring physical constants or material properties, for example, are expected. Students are encouraged to use search engines, LEGO communities, and video portals to brainstorm for ideas and get a grasp of what kind of projects are realizable. The last two days are used for presentation, deconstruction and clean–up.

A high level of supervision is provided during the project. Once a group has proposed a suitable robot design, a supervisor needs to approve the idea. Thus, the students do not run the risk of not completing the project in time and failing the design requirements. If no own proposal can be elaborated, the teams can choose from five ready–made models. These well–described machines, such as e.g. a replica of a steam engine, leave room for further modifications and extensions. The students are then free to work on their own.

With a strong focus on teamwork the students, formed into groups of three, are encouraged to specialize and assign specific tasks to each other. Especially in the first exercise, one student should begin building a barcode scanner which is later used, while the others continue to familiarize themselves with MATLAB and the toolbox. This concept is also motivated by the fact that learning programming is only effective if at most two students share one PC.

During presentations the student teams demonstrate their project in less than ten minutes. Teams are graded based on the quality of their presentation, design aspects, formalities such as punctuality, and regular course attendance. Furthermore, prizes are awarded for the best and most ingenious systems, and prize winners are invited to present their constructions to the complete audience.

In conclusion, this course applies a very similar teaching concept to "MATLAB meets LEGO Mindstorms", but also shows interesting new aspects of using

LEGO Mindstorms and the RWTH–Mindstorms NXT Toolbox for education. The strong focus on teamwork and the contest–like atmosphere are well suited for a freshman week at university. The laboratory boosts motivation and fosters enthusiasm by encouraging the students to propose their own project ideas. It is noteworthy that a potential lack of previous MATLAB skills poses no problem for successful robot applications. The intense first day's preparation course establishes a foundation of skills, sufficient for simple algorithms and analyses.

### 5.2   Other Projects

Other practical courses and theses using MATLAB, LEGO Mindstorms, and the RWTH – Mindstorms NXT toolbox have been designed for different and more specific educational projects. For instance, Clemson University, USA, introduced a *Freshman Engineering Robotics Project* for their College of Engineering and Science students. The syllabus consists of six introductory lessons aiming to convey the handling of the NXT, and a final project task. The students can take the Mindstorms kits home for self–contained work, and are encouraged to report their progress, based on a weekly course schedule. The final project, predetermined by a given topic like a walking biped or segway robot, is finally submitted and presented in a video presentation. In a practical course at New Jersey's Science & Technology University, about 60 biomedical engineering students are encouraged to build Mindstorms robots to solve robotic surgery tasks. An introduction course to control systems to characterize PID–controllers is given at the School of Information technology and Engineering, University of Ottawa, Canada. Further projects are listed in more detail on the web page [15].

## 6   Conclusions

Based on evaluation results over four years of the freshmen course "MATLAB meets LEGO Mindstorms" we described our teaching concept and discussed the major educational key factors for first semester students using MATLAB and LEGO Mindstorms NXT robots. The combinations of these two development environments is proved successful for freshmen education, resulting in high motivation levels and advanced programming skills. A course structure with basic exercises in the beginning and subsequent more complex tasks towards the end, giving the students teams enough room to be creative and build their own and individual robot application, leads to self–contained activities and high performances. Shown also by other follow–up projects, freshmen are eager to work in practical courses, even if they have been only briefly taught basic fundamentals beforehand. The introduction of a block–course induces the students to focus strongly on the project tasks. By encouraging the students to describe their own robot applications in oral presentations as well as on the Internet, and establishing an award competition, many teams regularly exceed the expectations of the supervisors. Compared to other more traditional laboratories in the same curriculum the overall evaluation scores of this learning concept are rated higher.

Finally, other follow–up projects show how the educational key factors can be applied and successfully adopted to other robotic courses in freshmen education using MATLAB, LEGO Mindstorms robots and the RWTH–Mindstorms NXT Toolbox.

# References

1. Azemi, A., Pauley, L.: Teaching the Introductory Computer Programming Course for Engineers Using Matlab. In: Frontiers in Education (FIE), pp. T3B 1–23 (2008)
2. Azlan, N., Zainudin, F., Yusuf, H., Toha, S., Yusoff, S., Osman, N.: Fuzzy Logic Controlled Miniature LEGO Robot for Undergraduate Training System. In: IEEE Conf. on Industrial Electronics and Applications (ICIEA), pp. 2184–2188 (2007)
3. Behrens, A., Atorf, L., Schwann, R., Neumann, B., Schnitzler, R., Ballé, J., Herold, T., Telle, A., Noll, T.G., Hameyer, K., Aach, T.: MATLAB Meets LEGO Mindstorms - A Freshman Introduction Course into Practical Engineering. IEEE Transactions on Education 53(2), 306–317 (2010)
4. Behrens, A., Atorf, L., Aach, T.: Teaching Practical Engineering for Freshman Students using the RWTH - Mindstorms NXT Toolbox for MATLAB. In: Matlab - Modelling, Programming and Simulations, SCIYO, ch. 3, pp. 41–65 (2010)
5. Chikamasa, T.: Embedded Coder Robot NXT Demo (2006), http://www.mathworks.com/matlabcentral/fileexchange/ (accessed on April 14, 2011)
6. Devens, P.: MATLAB & Freshman Engineering. Proc. American Society for Engineering Education, ASEE (1999)
7. Goodmann, P.E.: Teaching ECET Students to Be Self-Directed Learners with First-Year Projects and Amateur Radio. Journal of Engineering Technology (2007)
8. MathWorks: Matlab support for lego mindstorms nxt (2010), http://www.mathworks.com/academia/ (accessed on April 14, 2011)
9. McClellan, J., Schafer, R., Yoder, M.: Experiences in Teaching DSP First in the ECE Curriculum. In: Frontiers in Education (FIE), vol. 2, pp. 891–895 (1997)
10. McClellan, J., Rosenthal, J.: Animating Theoretical Concepts for Signal Processing Courses. Proc. American Society for Engineering Education, ASEE (2002)
11. Michaud, F.: Engineering Education and the Design of Intelligent Mobile Robots for Real Use. Int. Journal of Intell. Autom. and Soft Computing 13(1), 19–28 (2007)
12. Narayanan, G.: Select MATLAB commands used in Teaching Applied Automatic Controls. In: Proc. American Society for Engineering Education, ASEE (2005)
13. Pop-Iliev, R., Nokleby, S.B.: Concurrent Approach to Teaching Concurrent Design Engineering. In: Proc. Int. Conf. Design Education, Innovation, and Practice (2005)
14. Roselli, R.J., Brophy, S.P.: Effectiveness of Challenge-Based Instruction in Biomechanics. Journal of Engineering Education 93(4), 311–324 (2006)
15. RWTH Aachen University, Aachen, Germany: RWTH - Mindstorms NXT Toolbox for MATLAB (2008), http://www.mindstorms.rwth-aachen.de
16. Vallim, M., Farines, J.M., Cury, J.: Practicing Engineering in a Freshman Introductory Course. IEEE Transactions on Education 49(1), 74–79 (2006)

# Adaptive Dynamic Path Following Control of an Unicycle-Like Mobile Robot

Victor H. Andaluz[1], Flavio Roberti[1], Juan Marcos Toibero[1],
Ricardo Carelli[1], and Bernardo Wagner[2]

[1] Instituto de Automática, Universidad Nacional de San Juan,
Av. San Martín Oeste 1109, J5400ARL, Argentina
{vandaluz,froberti,rcarelli}@inaut.unsj.edu.ar
[2] Leibniz Universität Hannover, Institute for Systems Engineering,
Real Time Systems Group, D-30167 Hannover, Germany
wagner@rts.uni-hannover.de

**Abstract.** This work presents a new adaptive dynamic control to solve the path following problem for the unicycle-like mobile robot. First, it is proposed a dynamic modeling of a unicycle-like mobile robot where it is considered that its mass center is not located at the center the wheels' axle. Then, the design of the control algorithm is presented. This controller design is based on two cascaded subsystems: a kinematic controller with command saturation, and an adaptive dynamic controller that compensates the dynamics of the robot. Stability and robustness are proved by using Lyapunov's method. Experimental results show a good performance of the proposed controller as proved by the theoretical design.

**Keywords:** Dynamic model, path following, compensation dynamic.

## 1 Introduction

Mobile Robotics is an active research area where researchers from all over the world find new technologies to improve mobile robots intelligence and areas of application. Among different mobile platforms, unicycle-like mobile robots are frequently used to perform different tasks due to their good mobility and simple configuration. This robot structure has been used in various applications like surveillance, floor cleaning, and industrial load transportation using autonomous guided vehicles [1],[2].

Fundamental problems of motion control of autonomous mobile robots can be roughly classified in three groups [3]: 1) *point stabilization*: the goal is to stabilize the vehicle at a given target point, with a desired orientation; 2) *trajectory tracking*: the vehicle is required to track a time parameterized reference, and 3) *path following*: the vehicle is required to converge to a path and follow it, without any time specifications. This work is focused to resolve the last control problem.

The path following problem has been well studied and many solutions have been proposed and applied in a wide range of applications. Let $\mathcal{P}_d(s) \in \Re^2$ -be a desired

S. Jeschke, H. Liu, and D. Schilberg (Eds.): ICIRA 2011, Part I, LNAI 7101, pp. 563–574, 2011.

geometric path parameterized by the curvilinear abscissa $s \in \Re$. In the literature it is common to find different control algorithms for path following where $s(t)$ is considered as an additional control input. In [3],[4],[5],[6],[7], the rate of progression ($\dot{s}$) of a virtual vehicle has been controlled explicitly. Another method for path following of mobile robots is the image-based control. The main objective of this method is to detect and follow the desired path through vision sensors [5],[8].

In order to reduce performance degradation, on-line parameter adaptation is relevant in applications where the mobile robot dynamic parameters may vary, such as load transportation. It is also useful when the knowledge of the dynamic parameters is limited. As an example, the trajectory tracking task can be severely affected by the change imposed to the robot dynamics when it is carrying an object, as shown in [9]. Hence, some path following control architectures already proposed in the literature have considered the dynamics of the mobile robots [3],[5],[6].

In such context, this paper proposes a new method to solve the path following problem for a unicycle-like mobile robot. Additionally, it is proposed a dynamic model of the uniclycle-like mobile robot which, differently to previous works [10],[11], has reference velocities as input signals to the robot, as it is common in commercial robots. Also, it presents an adequate structure for control law designing. It is important to remark that this dynamic model was developed considering lateral deviations of the center of mass produced by load transport or by the location and/or motion of the tool. For example, the location, motion and manipulation of a robotic arm mounted on the mobile robot can produce that the center of mass of the mobile robot will not be located at the center of the robots' axle. The proposed control scheme is divided into two subsystems, each one being a controller itself: 1) the first one is a kinematic controller with saturation of velocity commands, which is based on the mobile robot's kinematics. The path following problem is addressed in this subsystem. It is worth noting that the proposed controller does not consider $s(t)$ as an additional control input as it is frequent in literature. 2) An adaptive dynamic compensation controller updates the estimated parameters, which are directly related to physical parameters of the mobile robot. In addition, both stability and robustness properties to parametric uncertainties in the dynamic model are proven through Lyapunov's method. To validate the proposed control algorithm, experimental results are included and discussed.

The paper is organized as follows: Section 2 shows the complete dynamic modeling of the unicycle-like mobile robot, while Section 3 describes the path following formulation problem and it also presents the controllers design. Furthermore, the analysis of the system's stability is developed. Next, experimental results are presented and discussed in Section 4, and finally the conclusions are given in Section 5.

## 2    Dynamic Modeling

In this section the dynamic modeling of a unicycle-like mobile robot is developed considering lateral deviations of the center of mass produced by load transportation or by the location and/or motion of the tool. The unicycle-like mobile robot presents the advantages of high mobility, high traction with pneumatic tires, and a simple wheel configuration. It has two driven wheels which are controlled independently by two D.C. motors and a castor wheel to maintain balance.

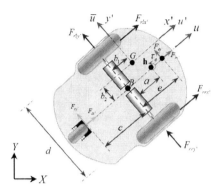

**Fig. 1.** Unicycle-like mobile robot with lateral deviations of its center of mass

Fig.1 illustrates the unicycle-like mobile robot considered in this paper. The position of the mobile robot is given by point G, representing the center of mass; $\mathbf{h} = [x \ \ y]^T$ represents the point that is required to track a path in $\mathcal{R}$; $\psi$ is the orientation of the mobile robot. On the other hand, $u'$ and $\bar{u}$ are the longitudinal and lateral velocities of the center of mass; $\omega$ is the angular velocity; $d$, $b_1$, $b_2$, $a$ and $c$ are distances; $F_{rrx'}$ and $F_{rry'}$ are the longitudinal and lateral tire forces of the right wheel; $F_{rlx'}$ and $F_{rly'}$ are the longitudinal and lateral tire forces of the left wheel; $F_{cx'}$ and $F_{cy'}$ are the longitudinal and lateral force exerted on $C$ by the castor wheel; $F_{ex'}$ and $F_{ey'}$ are the longitudinal and lateral force exerted on $E$ by the tool; and $\tau_e$ is the moment exerted by the tool.

The force and moment equations for the mobile robot are:

$$\sum F_{x'} = m(\dot{u}' - \bar{u}\omega) = F_{rlx'} + F_{rrx'} + F_{ex'} + F_{cx'} \tag{1}$$

$$\sum F_{y'} = m(\dot{\bar{u}} - u'\omega) = F_{rly'} + F_{rry'} + F_{ey'} + F_{cy'} \tag{2}$$

$$\sum M_z = I_z\dot{\omega} = \tfrac{d}{2}(F_{rrx'} - F_{rlx'}) + b_2(F_{rrx'} + F_{rlx'}) - b_1(F_{rly'} + F_{rry'})$$
$$+ b_2 F_{cx'} + (c - b_1)F_{cy'} + b_2 F_{ex'} + (e - b_1)F_{ey'} \tag{3}$$

where $m$ is the robot mass; and $I_z$ is the robot moment of inertia about the vertical axis located in $G$. The kinematics of point $\mathbf{h}$ is defined as:

$$\dot{x} = u\cos\psi - \bar{u}\sin\psi - (a - b_1)\omega\sin\psi; \quad \dot{y} = u\sin\psi + \bar{u}\cos\psi + (a - b_1)\omega\cos\psi \tag{4}$$

$$u = u'b_2\omega \tag{5}$$

According to Zhang [10], velocities $u$, $\omega$ and $\bar{u}$, including the slip speeds, are:

$$u = \tfrac{1}{2}\left[r\left(\omega_r + \omega_l\right) + \left(u_r^s + u_l^s\right)\right]; \qquad \omega = \tfrac{1}{d}\left[r\left(\omega_r - \omega_l\right) + \left(u_r^s - u_l^s\right)\right] \tag{6}$$

$$\bar{u} = b_1\omega + \bar{u}^s \tag{7}$$

where $r$ is the right and left wheel radius; $\omega_r$ and $\omega_l$ are the angular velocities of the right and left wheels; $u_r^s$ and $u_l^s$ are the longitudinal slip speeds of the right and left wheel, $\bar{u}^s$ is the lateral slip speed of the wheels.

The motor models attained by neglecting the voltage on the inductances are:

$$\tau_r = \frac{k_a\left(v_r - k_b\omega_r\right)}{R_a}; \qquad \tau_l = \frac{k_a\left(v_l - k_b\omega_l\right)}{R_a} \tag{8}$$

where $v_r$ and $v_l$ are the input voltages applied to the right and left motors; $k_b$ is equal to the voltage constant multiplied by the gear ratio; $R_a$ is the electric resistance constant; $\tau_r$ and $\tau_l$ are the right and left motor torques multiplied by the gear ratio; and $k_a$ is the torque constant multiplied by the gear ratio. The dynamic equations of the motor-wheels are:

$$I_e\dot{\omega}_r + B_e\omega_r = \tau_r - F_{rrx}R_t; \qquad I_e\dot{\omega}_l + B_e\omega_l = \tau_l - F_{rlx}R_t \tag{9}$$

where $I_e$ and $B_e$ are the moment of inertia and the viscous friction coefficient of the combined motor rotor, gearbox, and wheel, and $R_t$ is the nominal radius of the tire.

In general, most market-available robots have low level PID velocity controllers to track input reference velocities and do not allow the motor voltage to be driven directly. Therefore, it is useful to express the mobile robot model in a suitable way by considering rotational and translational reference velocities as input signals. For this purpose, the velocity controllers are included into the model. To simplify the model, a PD velocity controller has been considered which is described by the following equations:

$$\begin{bmatrix} v_u \\ v_\omega \end{bmatrix} = \begin{bmatrix} k_{PT}\left(u_{ref} - u_{me}\right) + k_{DT}\left(\dot{u}_{ref} - \dot{u}_{me}\right) \\ k_{PR}\left(\omega_{ref} - \omega_{me}\right) + k_{RT}\left(\dot{\omega}_{ref} - \dot{\omega}_{me}\right) \end{bmatrix} \tag{10}$$

where

$$u_{me} = \tfrac{r}{2}\left(\omega_r + \omega_l\right); \qquad \omega_{me} = \tfrac{r}{d}\left(\omega_r - \omega_l\right) \tag{11}$$

$$v_u = \tfrac{v_r + v_l}{2}; \qquad v_u = \tfrac{v_r - v_l}{2} \tag{12}$$

Variables $\dot{u}_{ref}$ and $\dot{\omega}_{ref}$ are neglected in (10) in order to simplify the model. From (1 – 12) the following dynamic model of the mobile robot is obtained:

$$\dot{\mathbf{h}}(t) = \mathbf{J}(\psi)\mathbf{v}(t)$$
$$\omega = \dot{\psi}$$
(13)

$$\mathbf{M}\dot{\mathbf{v}} + \mathbf{C}(\mathbf{v})\mathbf{v} = \mathbf{v}_{\text{ref}}$$
(14)

where: $\mathbf{J} = \begin{bmatrix} \cos\psi & -a\sin\psi \\ \sin\psi & a\cos\psi \end{bmatrix}$; $\mathbf{M} = \begin{bmatrix} \chi_1 & -\chi_7 \\ -\chi_8 & \chi_2 \end{bmatrix}$; $\mathbf{C} = \begin{bmatrix} \chi_4 & -\chi_3\omega \\ \chi_5\omega & \chi_6 \end{bmatrix}$; $\mathbf{v} = \begin{bmatrix} u \\ \omega \end{bmatrix}$;

$\mathbf{v}_{\text{ref}} = \begin{bmatrix} u_{\text{ref}} \\ \omega_{\text{ref}} \end{bmatrix}$; $\Omega_h = \begin{bmatrix} \delta_x \\ \delta_y \end{bmatrix}$; and $\Omega_v = \begin{bmatrix} \delta_u \\ \delta_w \end{bmatrix}$. Hence, the full mathematical model of the

unicycle-like mobile robot is represented by: (13) the kinematic model and (14) the dynamic model, taking the reference velocities of the robot as input signals.

## 3      Formulation Problem and Controllers Design

This section presents the formulation of the path following problem for mobile robots. In addition, it shows the proposed methodology to solve the path following problem for the unicycle-like mobile robot.

### 3.1      Formulation Problem

The solution of the path following problem for mobile robots derived in [3] admits an intuitive explanation. A path following controller should aim to reduce to zero both: i) the distance from the vehicle to a point on the path, and ii) the angle between the vehicle velocity vector and the tangent to the path at this point.

As represented in Fig. 2, the path to be followed is denoted as $\mathcal{P}$. The actual desired location $\mathbf{P}_d = [P_{xd} \quad P_{yd}]^T$ is defined as the closest point on $\mathcal{P}$ to the mobile robot, with a desired orientation $\psi_d$. In Fig. 2, $\rho$ represents the distance between the robot position $\mathbf{h}$ and $\mathbf{P}_d$, and $\tilde{\psi}$ is the error orientation between $\psi_d$ and $\psi$.

Given a path $\mathcal{P}$ in the operational space of the mobile robot and the desired velocity module $\upsilon$ for the robot, the path following problem for the mobile robot consists in finding a feedback control law $\mathbf{v}_{\text{ref}}(t) = (s, \upsilon, \rho, \tilde{\psi})$, such that

$$\lim_{t\to\infty} \rho(t) = 0 \qquad \text{and} \qquad \lim_{t\to\infty} \tilde{\psi}(t) = 0.$$

The error vector of position and orientation between the robot and the point $\mathbf{P}_d$ can be represented as, $\tilde{\mathbf{h}} = \mathbf{P}_d - \mathbf{h}$ and $\tilde{\psi} = \psi_d - \psi$. Therefore, if $\lim_{t\to\infty}\tilde{\mathbf{h}}(t) = \mathbf{0}$ then $\lim_{t\to\infty} \rho(t) = 0$ and $\lim_{t\to\infty}\tilde{\psi}(t) = 0$, as it will be explained in the following sections.

Hence, the desired position and desired velocity of the mobile robot on the path $\mathcal{P}$, are defined as $\mathbf{h}_d(s,h) = \mathbf{P}_d(s,h)$ and $\mathbf{v}_{hd}(s,h) = \upsilon_p(s,h)$. Where $\upsilon_p$ is the desired velocity of the robot at location $\mathbf{P}_d$. Note that the component of $\upsilon_p$ has to be tangent to the trajectory due to kinematics compatibility.

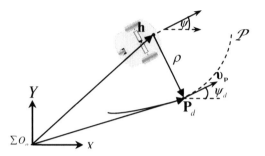

**Fig. 2.** Path following problem for a mobile robot

## 3.2    Controllers Design

The proposed control scheme to solve the path following problem is shown in Fig. 3, the design of the controller is based mainly on two cascaded subsystems.

1) *Kinematic Controller* with saturation of velocity commands, where the control errors $\rho(t)$ and $\tilde{\psi}(t)$ may be calculated at every measurement time and used to drive the mobile robot in a direction which decreases the errors. Therefore, the control aim is to ensure that $\lim_{t\to\infty}\rho(t)=0$ and $\lim_{t\to\infty}\tilde{\psi}(t)=0$.

2) *Adaptive Dynamic Compensation Controller*, which main objective is to compensate the dynamics of the mobile robot, thus reducing the velocity tracking error. This controller receives as inputs the desired velocities $\mathbf{v}_c = [u_c \quad \omega_c]^T$ calculated by the kinematic controller, and generates velocity references $\mathbf{v}_{ref}(t)$ to the mobile robot. The velocity control error is defined as $\tilde{\mathbf{v}} = \mathbf{v}_c - \mathbf{v}$. Hence, the control aim is to ensure that $\lim_{t\to\infty}\tilde{\mathbf{v}}(t) = \mathbf{0}$.

### 3.2.1    Kinematic Controller

The problem of control is to find the control vector of maneuverability $\left(\mathbf{v}_c(t) \mid t \in [t_0, t_f]\right)$ to achieve the desired operational motion. Thus, the proposed kinematic controller is based on the kinematic model of the unicycle-like mobile robot (13), *i.e.*, $\dot{\mathbf{h}} = f(\mathbf{h})\mathbf{v}$. Hence the following control law is proposed,

$$\mathbf{v}_c = \mathbf{J}^{-1}\left(\upsilon_\mathbf{p} + \mathbf{L}\tanh\left(\mathbf{L}^{-1}\mathbf{K}\,\tilde{\mathbf{h}}\right)\right) \tag{15}$$

where $\tilde{\mathbf{h}} = [\tilde{h}_x \quad \tilde{h}_y]^T$ represents the position error of the robot defined as $\tilde{h}_x = P_{xd} - x$ and $\tilde{h}_y = P_{yd} - y$; $\upsilon_\mathbf{p} = [\upsilon\cos\psi_d \quad \upsilon\sin\psi_d]^T$ is the desired velocity vector on the path; $\mathbf{L}$ and $\mathbf{K}$ are definite positive diagonal matrices that weigh the control error. In order to include an analytical saturation of velocities in the mobile robot, the **tanh(.)** function, which limits the error $\tilde{\mathbf{h}}$, is proposed. The expression $\tanh(\mathbf{L}^{-1}\mathbf{K}\,\tilde{\mathbf{h}})$ denote a component by component operation. Now, the behaviour of the control position error of the robot is analyzed assuming -by now- perfect velocity tracking *i.e.*, $\mathbf{v} \equiv \mathbf{v}_c$. By substituting (15) in (13), it is obtained,

$$\left( \mathbf{v}_{hd} - \dot{\mathbf{h}} \right) + \mathbf{L} \tanh \left( \mathbf{L}^{-1} \mathbf{K} \, \tilde{\mathbf{h}} \right) = \mathbf{0} \tag{16}$$

Now defining $\Upsilon$ as the difference signal between $\dot{\mathbf{h}}_d$ and $\mathbf{v}_{hd}$, *i.e.*, $\Upsilon = \dot{\mathbf{h}}_d - \mathbf{v}_{hd}$ and remembering that $\dot{\tilde{\mathbf{h}}} = \dot{\mathbf{h}}_d - \dot{\mathbf{h}}$, (16) can be written as

$$\dot{\tilde{\mathbf{h}}} + \mathbf{L} \tanh \left( \mathbf{L}^{-1} \mathbf{K} \, \tilde{\mathbf{h}} \right) = \Upsilon \tag{17}$$

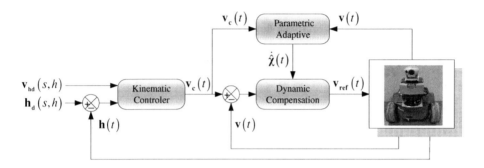

**Fig. 3.** Adaptive dynamic controller: block diagram

*Remark 1.* $\mathbf{v}_{hd}$ is collinear to $\dot{\mathbf{h}}_d$, then $\Upsilon$ is also a collinear vector to $\mathbf{v}_{hd}$ and $\dot{\mathbf{h}}_d$.

For the stability analysis the following Lyapunov candidate function is considered

$$V \left( \tilde{\mathbf{h}} \right) = \tfrac{1}{2} \tilde{\mathbf{h}}^T \tilde{\mathbf{h}} \; > 0 \tag{18}$$

Its time derivative on the trajectories of the system is, $\dot{V} \left( \tilde{\mathbf{h}} \right) = \tilde{\mathbf{h}}^T \Upsilon - \tilde{\mathbf{h}}^T \mathbf{L} \tanh \left( \mathbf{L}^{-1} \mathbf{K} \, \tilde{\mathbf{h}} \right)$. Then, a sufficient condition for $\dot{V} \left( \tilde{\mathbf{h}} \right)$ to be negative definite is,

$$\left| \tilde{\mathbf{h}}^T \mathbf{L} \tanh \left( \mathbf{L}^{-1} \mathbf{K} \, \tilde{\mathbf{h}} \right) \right| > \left| \tilde{\mathbf{h}}^T \Upsilon \right| \tag{19}$$

*Remark 2.* For large values of $\tilde{\mathbf{h}}$, it can be considered that: $\mathbf{L} \tanh \left( \mathbf{L}^{-1} \mathbf{K} \, \tilde{\mathbf{h}} \right) \approx \mathbf{L}$. $\dot{V}$ will be negative definite only if $\| \mathbf{L} \| > \| \Upsilon \|$; establishing a design condition which makes path following errors $\tilde{\mathbf{h}}$ to decrease.

*Remark 3.* As aforementioned, the desired path velocity can be written as $\mathbf{v}_{hd} = \dot{\mathbf{h}}_d - \Upsilon$. So, for small values of $\tilde{\mathbf{h}}$, $\mathbf{L} \tanh \left( \mathbf{L}^{-1} \mathbf{K} \, \tilde{\mathbf{h}} \right) \approx \mathbf{K} \tilde{\mathbf{h}}$. Thus, the closed loop equation of the system can now be written as $\dot{\tilde{\mathbf{h}}} + \mathbf{K} \, \tilde{\mathbf{h}} = \Upsilon$. Applying Laplace representation, one gets

$$\dot{\tilde{\mathbf{h}}}(s) = \frac{1}{s\mathbf{I} + \mathbf{K}} \Upsilon(s).$$

Hence, the direction of the vector of control errors $\tilde{\mathbf{h}}(s)$ tends to the direction of the error velocity vector $\Upsilon(s)$. Therefore, since for finite values $\tilde{\mathbf{h}}(s)$ this location error is normal to $\mathbf{v}_{hd}$ -criterion of minimum distance between the robot and the path- and thus to $\Upsilon$ (see *Remark 1*), then $\tilde{\mathbf{h}}$ has to be zero. It can now be concluded that $\rho(t) \to 0$ and, due to the non-holonomic constrain of the robot, $\tilde{\psi}(t) \to 0$ for $t \to \infty$ asymptotically.

### 3.2.2    Adaptive Dynamic Compensation Controller

The objective of the adaptive dynamic compensation controller is to compensate the dynamics of the mobile robot, thus reducing the velocity tracking error. This subsystem receives the desired velocities $\mathbf{v}_c = [u_c \quad \omega_c]^T$ and generates velocity references $\mathbf{v}_{ref} = [u_{ref} \quad \omega_{ref}]^T$ to be sent to the mobile robot.

Now, relaxing the perfect velocity tracking assumption of Subsection 3.1, then $\mathbf{v} \ne \mathbf{v}_c$ and the velocity error is defined as, $\tilde{\mathbf{v}} = \mathbf{v}_c - \mathbf{v}$. This velocity error motivates to design of an adaptive dynamic compensation controller with a robust parameter updating law. The dynamic compensation control law for the mobile robot is,

$$\mathbf{v}_{ref} = \eta\hat{\chi} = \eta\chi + \eta\tilde{\chi} = \mathbf{M}\sigma + \mathbf{C}\mathbf{v} + \eta\tilde{\chi} \tag{20}$$

where $\eta(\mathbf{v},\sigma) \in \mathfrak{R}^{2\times8}$, $\chi = [\chi_1 \quad \chi_2 \quad \cdots \quad \chi_8]^T$ and $\hat{\chi} = [\hat{\chi}_1 \quad \hat{\chi}_2 \quad \cdots \quad \hat{\chi}_8]^T$ are respectively the unknown vector, real parameters vector and estimated parameters vector of the robot, whereas $\tilde{\chi} = \hat{\chi} - \chi$ is the vector of parameter errors and $\sigma = \dot{\mathbf{v}}_c + \mathbf{L}_v \tanh(\mathbf{L}_v^{-1}\mathbf{K}_v\tilde{\mathbf{v}})$. A Lyapunov candidate function is proposed as

$$V(\tilde{\mathbf{v}},\tilde{\chi}) = \tfrac{1}{2}\tilde{\mathbf{v}}^T\mathbf{M}\tilde{\mathbf{v}} + \tfrac{1}{2}\tilde{\chi}^T\gamma\tilde{\chi}$$

where $\gamma \in \mathfrak{R}^{8\times8}$ is a positive definite diagonal matrix and $\mathbf{M} \in \mathfrak{R}^{2\times2}$ is a positive definite matrix defined in (14). The time derivative of the Lyapunov candidate function is,

$$\dot{V}(\tilde{\mathbf{v}},\tilde{\chi}) = -\tilde{\mathbf{v}}^T\mathbf{M}\mathbf{L}_v \tanh(\mathbf{L}_v^{-1}\mathbf{K}_v\tilde{\mathbf{v}}) - \tilde{\mathbf{v}}^T\eta\tilde{\chi} + \tilde{\chi}^T\gamma\dot{\tilde{\chi}} + \tfrac{1}{2}\tilde{\mathbf{v}}^T\dot{\mathbf{M}}\tilde{\mathbf{v}}. \tag{21}$$

The robust updating law

$$\dot{\hat{\chi}} = \gamma^{-1}\mathbf{L}^T\tilde{\mathbf{v}} - \gamma^{-1}\Gamma\hat{\chi} \tag{22}$$

is adopted to update the parameter estimated, where $\Gamma \in \mathfrak{R}^{8\times8}$ is a diagonal positive gain matrix. Let us consider that the dynamic parameters can vary, *i.e.*, $\chi = \chi(t)$ and $\dot{\tilde{\chi}} = \dot{\hat{\chi}} - \dot{\chi}$. Now, substituting (22) in (21), the following expression it is obtained,

$$\dot{V}\left(\tilde{\mathbf{v}}, \tilde{\chi}\right) = -\tilde{\mathbf{v}}^{\mathsf{T}} \mathbf{M} \mathbf{L}_{v} \, \tanh\left(\mathbf{L}_{v}^{-1} \mathbf{K}_{v} \, \tilde{\mathbf{v}}\right) - \tilde{\chi}^{\mathsf{T}} \mathbf{\Gamma} \tilde{\chi} - \tilde{\chi}^{\mathsf{T}} \mathbf{\Gamma} \chi$$
$$- \tilde{\chi}^{\mathsf{T}} \gamma \dot{\chi} + \tfrac{1}{2} \tilde{\mathbf{v}}^{\mathsf{T}} \dot{\mathbf{M}} \tilde{\mathbf{v}} \tag{23}$$

In [12], it has been shown the stability of the adaptive dynamic compensation controller for a mobile manipulator, where it was proved that velocity error and parameter errors are ultimately bounded. Hence, we can conclude that $\tilde{\mathbf{v}}(t)$ and $\tilde{\chi}(t)$ are ultimately bounded.

### 3.2.3    Stability Analysis Considering $\tilde{\mathbf{h}}_i(t)$ and $\tilde{\mathbf{v}}_i(t)$

The behaviour of the tracking error of the mobile robot is now analyzed relaxing the assumption of perfect velocity tracking.

$$\dot{\tilde{\mathbf{h}}} + \mathbf{L} \tanh\left(\mathbf{L}^{-1} \mathbf{K} \, \tilde{\mathbf{h}}\right) = \mathbf{J} \tilde{\mathbf{v}} + \Upsilon . \tag{24}$$

The Lyapunov candidate (18) is proposed, and its time derivative is $\dot{V}\left(\tilde{\mathbf{h}}\right) = \tilde{\mathbf{h}}^{\mathsf{T}} \left(\mathbf{J}\tilde{\mathbf{v}} + \Upsilon\right) - \tilde{\mathbf{h}}^{\mathsf{T}} \mathbf{L} \tanh\left(\mathbf{L}^{-1} \mathbf{K} \, \tilde{\mathbf{h}}\right)$. A sufficient condition for $\dot{V}\left(\tilde{\mathbf{h}}\right)$ to be negative definite is

$$\left| \tilde{\mathbf{h}}^{\mathsf{T}} \mathbf{L} \tanh\left(\mathbf{L}^{-1} \mathbf{K} \, \tilde{\mathbf{h}}\right) \right| > \left| \tilde{\mathbf{h}}^{\mathsf{T}} \left(\mathbf{J}\tilde{\mathbf{v}} + \Upsilon\right) \right| . \tag{25}$$

For large values of $\tilde{\mathbf{h}}$, it can be considered that: $\mathbf{L}\tanh\left(\mathbf{L}^{-1}\mathbf{K}\,\tilde{\mathbf{h}}\right) \approx \mathbf{L}$. Therefore, $\dot{V}\left(\tilde{\mathbf{h}}\right)$ will be negative definite only if $\|\mathbf{L}\| > \|\mathbf{J}\tilde{\mathbf{v}} + \Upsilon\|$, thus making the velocity errors $\tilde{\mathbf{h}}$ to decrease.

Now, for small values of $\tilde{\mathbf{h}}$, it can be expressed that: $\mathbf{L}\tanh\left(\mathbf{L}^{-1}\mathbf{K}\,\tilde{\mathbf{h}}\right) \approx \mathbf{K}\tilde{\mathbf{h}}$, and (25) can be written as, $\|\tilde{\mathbf{h}}\| > \|\mathbf{J}\tilde{\mathbf{v}} + \Upsilon\| / \lambda_{\min}\left(\mathbf{K}\right)$, thus implying that the error $\tilde{\mathbf{h}}$ is ultimately bounded as,

$$\left\|\tilde{\mathbf{h}}\right\| \leq \|\mathbf{J}\tilde{\mathbf{v}} + \Upsilon\| / \lambda_{\min}\left(\mathbf{K}\right) \tag{26}$$

For the case of perfect velocity tracking $\mathbf{v} \equiv \mathbf{v}_c$, i.e., $\tilde{\mathbf{v}} \equiv \mathbf{0}$ and consequently from (26), and by recalling from Section 3.2.1, it is concluded that $\rho(t) \to 0$ and $\tilde{\psi}(t) \to 0$, thus accomplishing the control objective for the path following problem. On the other hand, by considering the adaptive dynamic compensation controller with robust updating law (22), which include the $\sigma$-modification term, it was proved that $\tilde{\mathbf{v}}(t)$ is ultimately bounded. Then, the conclusion is that the control error will also be ultimately bounded by (26).

## 4     Experimental Results

In order to show the validity of the dynamic model and the performance of the proposed controller, several experiments were executed. Some of the results are presented in this section. First, the identification and validation of the proposed dynamic model is shown. The experimental test was implemented on a Pioneer 3-AT robot, which admits linear and angular velocities as input reference signals. The identification of the mobile robot was performed by using least squares estimation [13] applied to a filtered regression model [14]. The identified parameters of the Pioneer 3-AT mobile robot are:

$$\chi_1 = 0.1972 \qquad \chi_2 = 0.2315 \qquad \chi_3 = -0.0008 \qquad \chi_4 = 1.0013$$

$$\chi_5 = -0.0056 \qquad \chi_6 = 0.9778 \qquad \chi_7 = -0.0006 \qquad \chi_8 = -0.1661$$

Fig. 4 shows the validation the proposed dynamic model, where it can be seen the good performance of the obtained dynamic model.

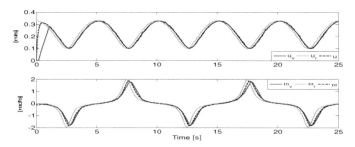

**Fig. 4.** Validation of the proposed dynamic model. Subscript $v$ represents the proposed dynamic model signals while the subscript $r$ refers to the reference signals.

Next experiment corresponds to the control system shown in Fig. 3. It was implemented on a Pioneer 3-AT robot, using the control laws in (15) and (20), with the updating law given in (22). It is worth noting that the distance $a$ in Fig. 1 is nonzero. Note that for the path following problem, the desired velocity of the mobile robot will depend on the task, the control error, the angular velocity, etc. For this experiment, it is consider that the reference velocity module depends on the control errors. Then, reference velocity in this experiment is expressed as $|\mathbf{v}_{hd}| = v_p / (1 + k\rho)$, where $k$ is a positive constant that weigh the control error module. Also, the desired location is defined as the closest point on the path to the mobile robot.

Figures 5-6 show the results of the experiment. Fig. 5.a shows the stroboscopic movement on the $X$-$Y$-$Z$ space. It can be seen that the proposed controller works correctly. Figure 5.b shows that $\rho(t)$ remains close to zero. Figure 6.a illustrates the control actions for the mobile robot, while the Fig. 6.b shows the evolution of the adaptive parameters, where it can be seen that all the parameters converge to fixed values.

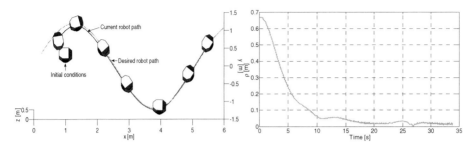

**Fig. 5.** (a) Motion of the mobile robot based on the experimental data. (b) Distance between the robot and the closest point on the path

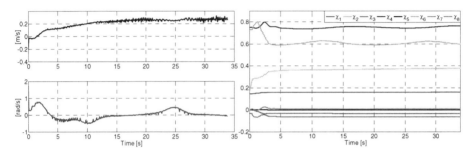

**Fig. 6.** (a) Velocity commands to the mobile robot Pioneer. (b) Adaptive parameters evolution.

## 5    Conclusions

In this work, it is proposed an adaptive dynamic controller for solving the path following problem of an unicycle-like mobile robot. In addition it is proposed a dynamic model for the unicycle-like mobile robot, which has reference velocities as control signals to the robot. Also, in the modeling it was considered a lateral deviation of the center of mass produced by load transportation or by the location and/or motion the tool. It has been proposed an adaptive controller which updates the mobile robot dynamics on-line. The design of the whole controller was based on two cascaded subsystems: a kinematic controller which complies with the task objective (path following), and an adaptive controller that compensates the dynamics of the mobile manipulator. Both the kinematic controller and the adaptive controller have been designed to prevent command saturation. Robot commands were defined in terms of reference velocities. Finally, the stability and robustness are proved by considering the Lyapunov's method, and the performance of the proposed controller is shown through real experiments.

## References

1. Patel, S., Sanyal, R., Sobh, T.: RISCBOT: A WWW-Enabled Mobile Surveillance and Identification Robot. Journal of Intelligent Robotic Systems 45(1), 15–30 (2006)
2. Prassler, E., Ritter, A., Schaeffer, C., Fiorini, P.: A Short History of Cleaning Robots. Autonomous Robots 9(3), 211–226 (2000)

3. Soeanto, D., Lapierre, L., Pascoal, A.: Adaptive non-singular path-following, control of dynamic wheeled robots. In: Proceedings of 42nd IEEE/CDC, Hawaii, USA, December 9-12, pp. 1765–1770 (2003)
4. Egerstedt, M., Hu, X., Stotsky, A.: Control of Mobile Platforms Using a Virtual Vehicle Approach. IEEE Transactions 46(11) (November 2001)
5. Xu, Y., Zhang, C., Bao, W., Tong, L.: Dynamic Sliding Mode Controller Based on Particle Swarm Optimization for Mobile Robot's Path Following. In: International Forum on Information Technology and Applications, pp. 257–260 (2009)
6. Ghommam, J., Saad, M., Mnif, F.: Formation path following control of unicycle-type mobile robots. In: IEEE Int. Conf on Robotics and Automation Pasadena, CA, USA, May 19-23 (2008)
7. Wangmanaopituk, S., Voos, H., Kongprawechnon, W.: Collaborative Nonlinear Model-Predictive Collision Avoidance and Path Following of Mobile Robots. In: ICROS-SICE International Joint Conference 2009, Japan, pp. 3205–3210 ( August 2009)
8. Cherubini, A., Chaumette, F., Oriolo, G.: A position-based visual servoing scheme for following paths with nonholonomic mobile robots. In: IEEE/RSJ International Conference on Intelligent Robots and Systems Acropolis Convention Center Nice, France, September 22-26 (2008)
9. Martins, F.N., Celeste, W., Carelli, R., Sarcinelli-Filho, M., Bastos-Filho, T.: An Adaptive Dynamic Controller for Autonomous Mobile Robot Trajectory Tracking. Control Engineering Practice 16, 1354–1363 (2008)
10. Zhang, Y., Hong, D., Chung, J.H., Velinsky, S.A.: Dynamic Model Based Robust Tracking Control of a Differentially Steered Wheeled Mobile Robot. In: Proceedings of the American Control Conference, Philadelphia, Pennsylvania, pp. 850–855 (1998)
11. De La Cruz, C., Carelli, R.: Dynamic model based formation control and obstacle avoidance of multi-robot systems. Robotica 26, 345–356 (2008)
12. Andaluz, V., Roberti, F., Carelli, R.: Robust Control with Redundancy Resolution and Dynamic Compensation for Mobile Manipulators. In: IEEE-ICIT International Conference on Industrial Technology, pp. 1449–1454 (2010)
13. Aström, K.J., Wittenmark, B.: Adaptive Control. Addison-Wesley (1995)
14. Reyes, F., Kelly, R.: On parameter identification of robot manipulator. In: IEEE International Conference on Robotics and Automation, pp. 1910–1915 (1997)

# A Study on Localization of the Mobile Robot Using Inertial Sensors and Wheel Revolutions

Bong-Su Cho, Woosung Moon, Woo-Jin Seo, and Kwang-Ryul Baek

Deptartment of Electronics Engineering,
Pusan National University,
Busan, Korea
{mscho97,crenmoon,krbaek}@pusan.ac.kr
seowoojin@gmail.com

**Abstract.** INS (Inertial Navigation System) is composed of inertial sensors such as accelerometers and gyroscopes and navigation computer. INS can estimate attitude and position by itself with no outside help and has acceptable stability in the short time, but poor stability in the long time. If a navigation system uses only INS, position and attitude errors are accumulated. The most basic and simple localization method is using encoders attached to robot's wheels. However, measuring errors occur due to the slip between of wheel and ground. In this paper, we discuss about position estimation of the mobile robot in indoor environment. In order to achieve the optimal solution, the error model of encoder system and the Kalman filter will be designed. The system described in this paper shows better accurate position information.

**Keywords:** Localization, INS, Mobile robot, Encoder, Odometry, IMU, Kalman filter.

## 1 Introduction

A mobile robot is automatic machine that navigates in a given environment and recognizes its surroundings using many sensors. A research of the mobile robot has been being developed rapidly in a various field. A localization of the mobile robot for an autonomous movement is important technique and, currently, is the field that a various research is necessary. The dead reckoning evaluates the position of the object using velocity and direction that are measured by encoders or inertial sensors [1][2].

In the dead reckoning, it uses IMU (Inertial Measurement Unit) or a control variable such as the encoders and it is not dependent on external signals. This method will be able to estimate the position easier than other methods. IMU can provide the position and attitude of the mobile robot at a high rate. If initial information of the mobile robot is known, then the position and attitude can be evaluated by the accelerations and the angular rates. However, low frequency noises and sensor biases are amplified due to this integrative nature. So IMU has accumulation position and attitude errors. Therefore, IMU may need other supporting signals [1][3].

S. Jeschke, H. Liu, and D. Schilberg (Eds.): ICIRA 2011, Part I, LNAI 7101, pp. 575–583, 2011.

When the mobile robot moves indoors, the position and attitude of the mobile robot is measured by encoders attached to the robot's wheels. However, measuring errors occur due to the slip between the wheels and ground. Although these errors are relatively small, they are accumulated in a long term [2].

In this paper, we discuss about the position and attitude of the mobile robot in indoor environment. The standalone encoders system or INS is not suitable for dead-reckoning for a long period of time. We combine encoders system and INS to reduce accumulation errors in the dead-reckoning. Although each INS and encoders system has accumulation errors, tightly-coupled system will reduce the errors to acceptable level. In order to achieve the optimal tightly-coupled system, the Kalman filter will be designed [4][5].

# 2      Localization

The purpose of proposal system that combines INS and encoders system is to estimate the attitude and position of the mobile with small errors, using information of two systems with different features. This chapter derives the fundamental equation of navigation system and describes proposal navigation algorithm.

## 2.1      Localization Using Inertial Sensors

IMU is an assembly of the inertial sensors which include tri-axial accelerometers, tri-axial gyroscopes and at least dual axial magnetic sensors. Tri-axial accelerometers measure the three dimension acceleration with respect to a body frame. These measured accelerations are used to evaluate the attitude and position of the mobile robot. When the mobile robot is stationary, tri-axial accelerometers can provide very accurate attitude information. Three orthogonal gyroscopes provide rotation rates about three axes. The integrations of tri-axial gyroscopes can provide the attitude when the object is not only stationary but also moving [6].

### 2.1.1      Initial Alignment Algorithm

Initial alignment is to initially calculate the attitude of the body frame from the outputs of IMU on the navigation frame and to calibrate biases of the inertial sensors. The acceleration on the body frame is measured at a complete standstill in the following manner

$$\mathbf{f}^b = \begin{vmatrix} f_x \\ f_y \\ f_z \end{vmatrix} = \mathbf{C}_n^b \mathbf{f}^n = \mathbf{C}_n^b \begin{vmatrix} 0 \\ 0 \\ -g^n \end{vmatrix} = \begin{vmatrix} g^n \sin \theta \\ -g^n \cos \theta \sin \phi \\ -g^n \cos \theta \cos \phi \end{vmatrix} \tag{1}$$

where $\mathbf{f}^b$, $\mathbf{f}^n$ are acceleration on the body and navigation frame and $g^n$ is acceleration of gravity.

In Eq. 1, the roll angle and pitch angle become

$$\phi = \tan^{-1}\left(\frac{-g^n \cos\theta \sin\phi}{-g^n \cos\theta \cos\phi}\right) = \tan^{-1}\left(\frac{f_y}{f_z}\right) \tag{2}$$

$$\theta = \tan^{-1}\left(\frac{g^n \sin\theta}{g^n \cos\theta}\right) = \tan^{-1}\left(\frac{f_x}{\sqrt{f_y^2 + f_z^2}}\right) \tag{3}$$

The calculation of yaw angle uses earth rotation angular velocity at a complete standstill. However, it is difficult to measure the earth rotation angular velocity because it demands gyroscopes with very high resolutions to measure very small angular acceleration value. The magnetic sensor measures the magnitude of earth's magnetic field. Therefore, the compass sensor consisted of two magnetic sensors will be able to measure the yaw angle

$$\alpha = \tan^{-1}\left(\frac{H_{ey}}{H_{ex}}\right) \tag{4}$$

$$\lambda = \varphi - \alpha, \quad \varphi = \lambda + \alpha \tag{5}$$

Where $\alpha$ is a magnetic north angle and $\lambda$ is a declination angle.

### 2.1.2   Positioning
On the Newton's law of motion, the velocity of the mobile robot is evaluated by single integration of the acceleration. Also the position is evaluated by single integration of the velocity. After the measured acceleration transform body frame into navigation frame, applying the acceleration of gravity, the equations of the velocity and position become as follows.

$$\mathbf{v}_{k+1}^n = \mathbf{v}_k^n + \left(C_b^n \mathbf{f}_k^b + g^n\right)\Delta t \tag{6}$$

$$\mathbf{P}_{k+1}^n = \mathbf{P}_k^n + \mathbf{v}_k^n \Delta t + \frac{1}{2}\left(C_b^n \mathbf{f}_k^b + g^n\right)\Delta t^2 \tag{7}$$

Here, $\mathbf{v}_k^n = \left|v_{N_k} \quad v_{E_k} \quad v_{D_k}\right|^T$ and $\mathbf{P}_k^n = \left|P_{N_k} \quad P_{E_k} \quad P_{D_k}\right|^T$ denote the velocity and position vector on navigation frame at time k.

### 2.2   Localization Using Rotor Encoders

Rotor encoder is the equipment that converts the position of rotor into a digital signal. The velocity, position and heading angle of the mobile robot are calculated with a position change quantity of rotor. Fig.1 shows the movement prediction of the mobile robot by each wheel's rotary angle.

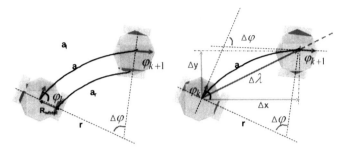

**Fig. 1.** The movement prediction by each rotary angle

The mobile robot's moving distance can be expressed in terms of its wheel's radius, and each wheel's rotary angle [2].

$$a_k = \frac{a_{k,l} + a_{k,r}}{2} \quad \text{with} \quad a_{k,l} = R_{wheel}\eta_{k,l}, \quad a_{k,r} = R_{wheel}\eta_{k,r} \tag{8}$$

The mobile robot's change quantity in the heading direction is calculated with the width of the robot and the distance travelled by each wheel.

$$\Delta\varphi_k = \frac{a_{k,l} - a_{k,r}}{d_{width}} \tag{9}$$

In this case, the robot's rotation radius is as follows.

$$r_k = \frac{a_k}{\Delta\varphi_k} \tag{10}$$

According to the law of cosine, the mobile robot's change in position is expressed as follows

$$\lambda_k^2 = r_k^2 + r_k^2 - 2r_k^2 \cos\Delta\varphi_k = 2(1 - \cos\Delta\varphi_k)r_k^2 \tag{11}$$

If the robot moves straight, the change-quantity in the heading direction becomes zero. In such case, the rotation radius will become arbitrarily large, and the term in parenthesis in Eq. 30 will become zero. Eq. 30 is expanded using Taylor series, which is shown below.

$$\lambda_k^2 = 2a_k^2 \left( \frac{1}{2!} - \frac{\Delta\varphi_k^2}{4!} + \frac{\Delta\varphi_k^4}{6!} - \frac{\Delta\varphi_k^6}{8!} + \cdots \right) \tag{12}$$

The following is the mobile robot's change quantity in position transformed into Navigation frame.

$$\Delta P_{N_k} = \lambda_k \cos\left(\varphi_{k-1} + \frac{\Delta\varphi_k}{2}\right), \quad \Delta P_{E_k} = \lambda_k \sin\left(\varphi_{k-1} + \frac{\Delta\varphi_k}{2}\right) \tag{13}$$

Finally, the mobile robot's the velocity, position and heading direction define as follows.

$$v_{N_k} = \frac{\Delta P_{N_k}}{\Delta t}, \quad v_{E_k} = \frac{\Delta P_{E_k}}{\Delta t} \tag{14}$$

$$P_{N_{k+1}} = P_{N_k} + \Delta P_{N_k}, \quad P_{E_{k+1}} = P_{E_k} + \Delta P_{E_k} \tag{15}$$

$$\varphi_{k+1} = \varphi_k + \Delta \varphi_k \tag{16}$$

# 3    The Kalman Filter

A dead reckoning is a common method to predict position of the mobile robot by inertial sensors or control variables such as the encoder. The position estimation using this dead reckoning has acceptable accuracy over short times, however it has unbounded errors in the long times.

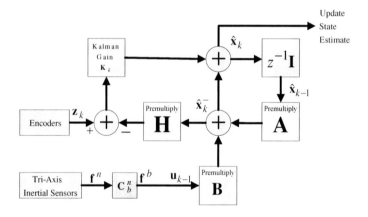

**Fig. 2.** The block of the Kalman filter for the dead reckoning

In this paper, we use the inertial sensors and the encoders attached to the robot's wheels for dead reckoning. The integration of measured tri-axial accelerations will increase the unbounded errors for velocity and position of the mobile robot. In encoders system, the unbounded errors occur due to the measuring error of the encoders, the mechanical defect of the mobile robots in the design, the slip between of the wheels and ground, etc. An accurate dead reckoning of a mobile robot using the inertial sensors or the encoders is difficult to achieve due to the unbounded error in each system. Although each inertial sensors and encoders have unbounded velocity and position error, tightly-coupled system will reduce the error to acceptable level. The Kalman filter is known to be the most ideal filter to estimate state variable in dynamic system [4][5].

In dead reckoning, the linear stochastic difference equations for the Kalman filter are given below.

$$\mathbf{x}_{k_{dr}} = \mathbf{A}_{dr}\,\mathbf{x}_{k-1_{dr}} + \mathbf{B}_{dr}\,\mathbf{u}_{k-1_{dr}} + \mathbf{w}_{k-1_{dr}} \tag{17}$$

$$\mathbf{z}_{k_{dr}} = \mathbf{H}_{dr}\,\mathbf{x}_{k_{dr}} + \mathbf{v}_{k_{dr}} \tag{18}$$

Here, $\mathbf{x}_{k_{dr}}$ is state variable and define $\mathbf{x}_{k_{dr}} = \begin{vmatrix} v_{N_k} & v_{E_k} & P_{N_k} & P_{E_k} & \varphi_k \end{vmatrix}^T$ into velocity, position and heading angle of the mobile robot.

The estimated and predicted state variables are a linear combination. And the correlations of between the position and the velocity are measurement period. The system matrix is same as following matrix.

$$\mathbf{A}_{dr} = \begin{vmatrix} 1 & 0 & 0 & 0 & 0 \\ 0 & 1 & 0 & 0 & 0 \\ \Delta t & 0 & 1 & 0 & 0 \\ 0 & \Delta t & 0 & 1 & 0 \\ 0 & 0 & 0 & 0 & 1 \end{vmatrix} \tag{19}$$

The system input variables are outputs of accelerometers and outputs of attitude algorithm. The correlations of each input are zero. And the input variable and state variable are related to the only measurement period.

$$\mathbf{u}_{dr} = \begin{vmatrix} a_{N_k} & a_{E_k} & \varphi_k \end{vmatrix}^T \tag{20}$$

$$\mathbf{B}_{dr} = \begin{vmatrix} \Delta t & 0 & 0 \\ 0 & \Delta t & 0 \\ \dfrac{1}{2}\Delta t^2 & 0 & 0 \\ 0 & \dfrac{1}{2}\Delta t^2 & 0 \\ 0 & 0 & \Delta t \end{vmatrix} \tag{21}$$

The measurement variable and state variable are linear combination. And the correlations of measurement variable are zero. The measurement matrix becomes a unit matrix.

$$\mathbf{H}_{dr} = \mathbf{I}_{5\times5} \tag{22}$$

$$\mathbf{z}_{k_{dr}} = \mathbf{H}_{dr}\,\mathbf{x}_{k_{dr}} \tag{23}$$

The process noise covariance is the error covariance that is measured with the inertial sensors. The white noises of the velocity and position are related to the acceleration white noise and the measurement period. And the heading angle noise covariance is same as the covariance of yaw-angle-noise that is output white noise of the attitude algorithm.

$$\mathbf{Q}_{dr} = \begin{vmatrix} Q_{v_N} & 0 & Q_{v_N,P_N} & 0 & 0 \\ 0 & Q_{v_E} & 0 & Q_{v_E,P_E} & 0 \\ Q_{P_N,v_N} & 0 & Q_{P_N} & 0 & 0 \\ 0 & Q_{P_E,v_E} & 0 & Q_{P_E} & 0 \\ 0 & 0 & 0 & 0 & Q_\varphi \end{vmatrix} \tag{24}$$

Where $Q_{v_x}$, $Q_{P_x}$ and $Q_{v_x,P_x}$ are the white noise covariance of accelerometer and define $Q_{v_x} = Q_{a_x}\Delta t^2$, $Q_{P_x} = Q_{a_x}\left(\dfrac{1}{2}\times\Delta t^2\right)^2$ and $Q_{v_x,P_x} = Q_{v_x}\dfrac{1}{2}\Delta t^3$.

The measurement noise covariance is the error covariance that is measured with encoders. In this case, we assume that the correlations of measurement variable are zero. Then, the measurement noise covariance is same as following.

$$\mathbf{R}_{dr} = \begin{vmatrix} R_{v_N} & 0 & 0 & 0 & 0 \\ 0 & R_{v_E} & 0 & 0 & 0 \\ 0 & 0 & R_{P_E} & 0 & 0 \\ 0 & 0 & 0 & R_{P_E} & 0 \\ 0 & 0 & 0 & 0 & R_\varphi \end{vmatrix} \tag{25}$$

where $R_{v_N}$, $R_{v_E}$, $R_{P_N}$, $R_{P_N}$, $R_\varphi$ are the measured white noises covariance from the encoders, respectively.

## 4    The Experiment Results

The mobile robot is operated using two DC motors. Each motor are equipped with two channel encoder which measures rotating velocity and rotating direction of wheels. Sensor module used for INS is ADIS16354 inertia sensor from the Analog Devices Inc. This module is made up of tri-axial gyroscope and tri-axial accelerometer. Compass sensor is HMC6352 from the Honeywell. TMS320F28335 DSP from the Texas Instrument Inc. was used to calculate the navigation solution and to control the mobile robot. To estimate the position, the mobile robot moves as drawing circles in the interest space. Fig 3 shows the estimated velocity and position from proposal algorithm. The estimated velocity and position are observed as a sinusoid because the mobile robot is a circular motion. Although the result has not been provided in this paper, the positioning using only inertial sensor has shown unbounded position error due to double integration. Also, the odometry method estimates a smaller circular position than true position because the calculated yaw angle changes faster than the true yaw angle. In the experiment results, the proposal algorithm provides reliable position with acceptable level compared to the method that only used odometry or inertial sensors.

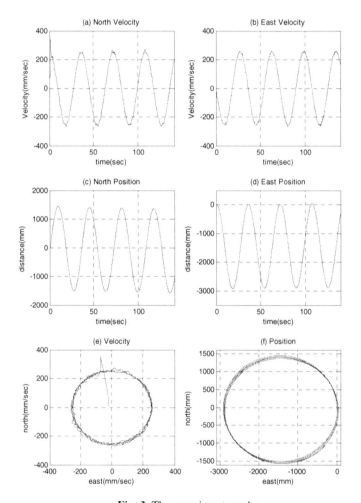

**Fig. 3.** The experiment results

## 5    Conclusions

IMU offers quick and accurate response in the short time, however the errors of position estimation are amplified due to the integrative nature. The position estimation using encoders attached to wheels have negative bias due to the slips between wheels and ground, and unbounded position error due to the integrative nature of the rotating speed. In this paper, we have discussed position estimation of mobile robot in indoor environment. The velocity and position are sampled in 50ms interval. The Kalman filter is applied to reduce the accumulated errors. The proposed method also compensates for the yaw angle errors that generate position errors in odometry therefore it has smaller position errors. If system modeling algorithm and the two systems' combination algorithm are further developed, more accurate position estimation is able to be accomplished.

**Acknowledgements.** This research was financially supported by the Ministry of Education, Science Technology (MEST) and Korea Industrial Technology Foundation (KOTEF) through the Human Resource Training Project for Regional Innovation.

# References

1. Titterton, D.H., Weston, J.L.: Strapdown inertial navigation technology. The Institute of Electrical Engineers (2004)
2. Moon, W., Cho, B.S., Jang, J.W., Baek, K.R.: A Multi-Robot Positioning System using a Multi-Code Ultrasonic Sensor Network and a Kalman Filter. International Journal of Control, Automation and Systems 8(6), 1349–1355 (2010)
3. Vaganay, J., Aldon, M.J., Fournier, A.: Mobile Robot Attitude Estimation by Fusion of Inertial Data. In: 1993 IEEE International Conference on Robotics and Automation, pp. 277–282 (1993)
4. Honghui, Q., Moore, J.: Direct Kalman Filtering Approach for GPS/INS Integration. IEEE Trans. on Aerospace and Electronic Systems 38(2), 687–693 (2002)
5. Welch, G., Bishop, G.: An Introduction to the Kalman Filter, July 24. UNC-Chapel Hill, TR 95-041 (2006)
6. Savage, P.G.: Strapdown Inertial Navigation Integration Algorithm Design Part 1: Attitude Algorithm. Journal of Guidance, Control, and Dynamics 21(1), 19–28 (1998)

# Robust and Accurate Genetic Scan Matching Algorithm for Robotic Navigation

Kristijan Lenac[1], Enzo Mumolo[2], and Massimiliano Nolich[2,3]

[1] Faculty of Engineering, University of Rijeka, Croatia
klenac@riteh.hr
[2] DI3, University of Trieste, Italy
mumolo@units.it
[3] IFACE s.r.l., Trieste, Italy
mnolich@units.it

**Abstract.** In this paper we propose a scan matching algorithm for robotic navigation based on the combination of ICP and genetic optimization. Since the genetic algorithm is robust but not very accurate, and ICP is accurate but not very robust, it is natural to use the two algorithms in a cascade fashion: first we run a genetic optimization to find an approximate but robust matching solution and then we run ICP to increase accuracy. The proposed genetic algorithm is very fast due to a lookup table formulation and very robust against large errors in both distance and angle during scan data acquisition. It is worth mentioning that large scan errors arise very commonly in mobile robotics due, for instance, to wheel slippage. We show experimentally that the proposed algorithm successfully copes with large localization errors.

**Keywords:** scan matching, genetic optimization, ICP, robotics.

## 1  Introduction

The matching and analysis of geometric shapes is an important problem that arises in various application areas, in particular computer vision, pattern recognition and robotics. In a typical scenario we have two objects and we want to find the optimal transformation (translation and rotation), which matches one object on the other one as accurately as possible. Objects are typically represented by finite sets of points in two or three dimensions. An important area of matching of geometric shapes is scan matching applied to robot self-localization. A fundamental requirement of mobile robots is, in fact, the need to ascertain their pose (position and orientation) while navigating or exploring an environment. Using a range device, such as a laser, ultrasonic or infrared device, the obstacles in front of the device are measured in terms of distance and angle. A set of such measurements can be performed which, from the point of view of the robot, forms a scan of the environment. Depending on the used device, the scans are characterized by an according data density. Scan matching techniques are methods to compare scans taken at different locations which estimate the relative displacement between scans.

S. Jeschke, H. Liu, and D. Schilberg (Eds.): ICIRA 2011, Part I, LNAI 7101, pp. 584–593, 2011.

Generally speaking, scan matching can be classified into local and global. Local scan matching is when an Initial Position Estimate (IPE) is available from which to start the search. It is generally used for robot position tracking where some other localization methods like odometry provide an IPE. The provided IPE has typically a small localization error and local scan matching is used to further reduce this error. On the other hand, with global scan matching we are able to generate and evaluate a position hypotheses independently from initial estimates, thus providing the capacity to correct position errors of arbitrary scale. The literature on scan matching is very large. Here we outline some important methods proposed so far. If an approximate alignment of two scans prior to performing the matching is available, the scan matching can be performed as a feature to feature, point to feature or point to point correspondences. The first (used for example in [1]) and the second cases (used in [2]) are limited to structured environments. In [1], geometric features like line segments, corners or range extrema are extracted from the actual and reference scans and matched between them while [2] considered Gaussian distributions with mean and variances computed from the point falling into cells of the grid. The last type of approaches are variations of the Iterative Closest Point algorithm (ICP) proposed by Besl and McKay [3]. Basically, ICP has three basic steps: first, pair each point of the first set to the second one using a corresponding criterion; second, compute the rotation and translation transformations which minimize the mean square error between the paired points and finally apply the transformation to the first set. The optimum matching is obtained by iterating the three basic steps. However, ICP has several drawbacks. First, its proper convergence is not guaranteed, as the problem is characterized by local minima. Second, ICP requires a good pre–alignment of the views to converge to the best global solution. Lu and Milios [4] were the first to apply this approach for localization of mobile robots. They use ICP to compute translations and propose techniques for corresponding points selection. Pfister et al. [5] developed a method which extends the approach of [4] considering also the uncertainty of the estimated motion in order to integrate the scan matching-based motion with odometry information. Most of the versions of the ICP algorithm use the Euclidian distance to estimate the correspondences between scans. However, this distance does not take into account that small rotations of the sensor mean large displacements as the distance is increased. To overcome this limitation several approaches have been proposed. Lu-Milios in [4] proposed to compute two sets of correspondents, one by the Euclidean distance and the other by the angular distance (to capture the sensor rotation). The Metric-based Iterative Closest Point algorithm described in [6] establishes a new distance concept which captures the sensor displacement and rotation at the same time.

The main contributions of this paper are related to the introduction of a hybrid algorithm for robot localization, called h-GLASM, which obtains a robust and fast convergence to the correct position, and to solve global scan matching using the same algorithm. Differently from other hybrid approaches [7], in fact, the proposed genetic scan matching extends the search area of the position of the robot, allowing the subsequent ICP based approach to converge rapidly and accurately.

The structure of this paper is the following. Section 2 addresses the problem of scan matching in general, and briefly describes some solutions proposed in the past which are important to this work. Section 3 summarize a recently proposed genetic algorithm, called GLASM, and Section 4 describes h-GLASM, the proposed hybrid algorithm based on GLASM and ICP. In Section 5 some localization results obtained with h-GLASM are reported and discussed. Final remarks and conclusion are discussed in Section 6.

## 2   Previous Solutions to the Scan Matching Problem

### 2.1   ICP Based Scan Matching

Scan matching can be described in an intuitive way by considering one point of a reference scan and one of the new scan under the assumption that they sample the same point in the environment but from different positions. Consider a point $P_1(x_1, y_1)$ in the $(x_1, y)$ coordinate system and a point $P_2(x_2, y_2)$ in the $(x_2, y_2)$ coordinate system. The two coordinate systems differ by a rotation $\varphi$ and a translation, represented by a bias vector $\bar{b} = (b_x, b_y)$. A reference scan is made by a sequence of points $P_1$ and the new scan by a sequence of points $P_2$ acquired after a rotation and translation movement of the robot. Using a rotation/translation operator, the point $P_1$ is seen in the $(x_2, y_2)$ reference frame as follows:

$$\begin{cases} x_1 \cos(\varphi) - y_1 \sin(\varphi) + b_x \\ x_1 \sin(\varphi) + y_1 \cos(\varphi) + b_y \end{cases}$$

If the point $P_1(x_1, y_1)$ in the first scan corresponds to the point $P_2(x_2, y_2)$ in the second scan, we define the following errors:

$$\begin{cases} e_x(1, 2) = x_2 - x_1 \cos(\varphi) - y_1 \sin(\varphi) + b_x \\ e_y(1, 2) = y_2 - x_1 \sin(\varphi) + y_1 \cos(\varphi) + b_y \end{cases}$$

The scan matching problem consists in estimating the robot movement by finding the two factors $\bar{b}$ and $\varphi$ that make the two scans overlap as much as possible. This can be performed iteratively as follows. The first operation of each iterations is to pair each points of the two sequences (correspondence problem). This pairing is performed by finding the couple of points such that $P_i$ corresponds to $P_j$ if the value $\sum_{j=1}^{N} \{e_x(i, j)^2 + e_y(i, j)^2\}$ is minimized given the actual value of $\bar{b}$ and $\varphi$, where $N$ is the number of points in the scans. This defines a correspondence index function $I$ such that $i = I(j)$. The second operation of the iterations is to refine the two factors $\bar{b}$ and $\varphi$ by solving $(\varphi, b) = argmin_{(\varphi, b)}(\sum_{j=1}^{N} \{e_x(I(j), j)^2 + e_y(I(j), j)^2\}$. The iteration proceeds until convergence. The final operation is to apply the transformation to the new scan. In this way the two scans are aligned and the map of the environment is built.

## 2.2   Metric Based ICP

In the conventional ICP algorithm correspondences between two scans are chosen based on the closest-point rule, normally using the Euclidean distance. However, as pointed out by many authors [4,5], this distance does not take into account that the points in the new scan, which are far from the sensor, could be far from their correspondences in the previous scan due to a rotation. To overcome this limitation, the mbICP [6] proposes a distance based on the translation and rotation simultaneously. Introducing this new distance into the ICP framework, translational and rotational movements are taken into account at once while looking for the correspondences as well as during the minimization process. In other words, given a certain displacement vector $\mathbf{q} = (x, y, \theta)$ where $\theta = [-\pi, +\pi]$, a norm function can be defined as $|q| = \sqrt{x^2 + y^2 + L^2\theta^2}$, where $L$ is a positive real number which renders the factor $L^2\theta^2$ homogeneous to a length. This distance is used in the ICP framework becoming the basis of mbICP. The inputs are the reference scan $Sref$ with points $ri, (i = 1..n)$, the new scan $Snew$ with points $nj, (j = 1..m)$ and the initial relative displacement estimation $q$. The procedure is iteratively executed until convergence.

## 2.3   Genetic Based Scan Matching

Genetic Algorithm (GA) applied to Scan Matching aims at finding the $(x, y)$ translation and the rotation $\varphi$ that obtains the best alignment between two different scans. Its advantage is that GA, due to its stochastic nature, is able to avoid local minima. Each parameter of the scan position $(x, y, \varphi)$ is coded in the chromosome as a string of bits as follows: nbitx for coding $x$, nbity for $y$ and nbitrot for $\varphi$. The problem space is discretized in a finite solution space with a resolution that depends on the extension of the search area and on the number of bits in each gene. The search area limits can be set based on the problem at hand. In the case of pose tracking where odometry measurements are available they are usually set on the basis of odometry error model.

Typically the most relevant characteristic of a genetic scan matching is the definition of the fitness function. The fitness function used by Yamany et al. [8] is a mean squared error cost function. Robertson and Fisher [9] used the mean squared error objective function and perform optimization in the six-parameter space. In [10,7] the fitness is defined as $\sum_{k=1}^{N} e_j(k)/N$ where $N$ is the number of points and $e_j$ is the difference between the point in the reference and new scans.

## 2.4   GLASM Genetic Algorithm

According to [11], classical genetic algorithm can be improved by computing the fitness function using a lookup table which divides the plane of scan readings in a grid. As soon as the reference scan is available, a look-up table is created as depicted in Fig. 1. Each cell represents a portion of the 2D plane of scan readings. In the case of pose tracking the lookup table is centered in the reference scan position. The overall dimensions of the lookup table are such to cover all possible

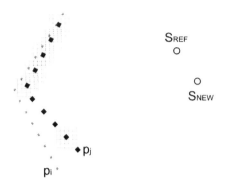

**Fig. 1.** Corresponding points of two different scans in different reference frames

sensor readings of the two scans. For position estimation with an a-priori given map the lookup table should at least cover the map. Each cell in the table is initialized with 0. Cells close to a reference scan point are marked with values inversely proportional to the distance from the reference scan point to award points closer to ref point according to some function. In the proposed genetic algorithm the simple binary function is used to mark the cells close to a reference scan point with 1 leaving others with 0.

The fitness is computed as follows: for each point of the new scan a direct lookup is made in the lookup table to establish if the cell corresponding to the point has 1. The number of points of a new scan having a corresponding point in a reference scan is then taken as a fitness value for this chromosome, i.e. for the new scan evaluated in the position coded in a chromosome. This in fact is directly proportional to the overlapping of two scans, i.e. the degree of matching between the two. In other words: $f_{S_{NEW},S_{REF}} = \sum_{i=1}^{N} \rho(i)$, where $S_{NEW}$ and $S_{REF}$ are the two scans to be matched, N is the number of points in $S_{NEW}$, and the value of $\rho$ is as follows:

$$\rho(i) = \begin{cases} 1 & \text{if a point of } S_{NEW} \text{ lies in the square around a point in } S_{REF} \\ 0 & \text{otherwise} \end{cases}$$

The positional information is coded in the genes using the Gray code. The inverse Gray code value of the bit string is taken to obtain the position from the gene. In this way the variations in the bit string caused by the mutation or crossover operators translate in the proportional variations in the position they represent. Using a simple binary code a change in one bit may cause a significant variation in the position. Experiments showed that for the scan matching application, simple binary code leads to a reduced efficiency of the genetic algorithm. The genetic algorithm starts with a population of Popsize chromosomes randomly selected with uniform distribution in the search space. Each individual represents a single position of the new scan. The goal of the scan matching is to estimate the position of the new scan relative to a reference scan or a given map which is best fitted according to a fitness value.

## 2.5  Hybrid Solution

Many authors [12,7] point out that the combination of ICP and optimization methods would increase the robustness of scan matching. In [7] Martinez et al. propose a hybrid GA-ICP method for mobile robot localization and motion estimation. Their approach consists of two steps: first a GA search of the robot movement parameters is performed around the odometric estimation, and then the ICP technique is applied to refine the transformation. The genetic optimization, based on a polar correspondence of the scans, aims at estimating an initial point for ICP that can improve its convergence ratio.

# 3  The Proposed Hybrid Scan Matching Algorithm

The genetic scan matching based on lookup table is suited for both local and global scan matching. In the proposed h-GLASM algorithm the search space is increased to cope with large odometric errors, that can be caused by particular problems like wheel slippage on carpet, holes, etc or by the fact that the odometry correction is performed at really low rate. The initial position estimate is roughly estimated by the genetic lookup based algorithm using just a few generations. Then a correspondence matching using mbICP [6] is performed, as the problem is reduced to the classical case where ICP works properly and is fast. As the genetic typically produces good initial estimates, ICP typically converges really fast. As a result, the hybrid approach can be computed in a time that is comparable to the computational time of mbICP alone. h-GLASM is suited for both local and global scan matching. Local scan matching can be performed as reported in Fig. 2. In this case, the new scan $snew$, evaluated starting from the odometric estimation of robot movements, is fed as input to GLASM, together with the previous scan, $sref$. The output of GLASM $x'$, $y'$, $\theta'$ is then used as starting point of the mbICP algorithm that compares $sref$ and $snew$. h-GLASM can also be used for global scan matching, as reported in Fig. 3. In this case, the search space is initially wide and known. The initial position estimate for the new scan is not available so the search space is centered in the reference scan position. GLASM estimates poses of the robot that correspond to best matching between snew and sref, and these poses are then refined using mbICP.

LOCAL

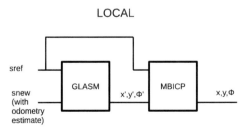

**Fig. 2.** Block diagram of h-GLASM used for local scan matching

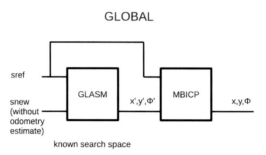

**Fig. 3.** Block diagram of h-GLASM used for global scan matching

# 4   Experimental Results

The experimental results described in this section have been obtained implementing the described algorithms in a Player-Stage simulator. We used the two classical environments reported in Fig. 4, called Cave and Autolab. The scans are obtained with a simulated laser device where the range measurements are multiplied with a random variable taken from a gaussian distribution with mean equal to 1 and variance equal to 0.05. According to [6], the localization performances are described in terms of True Positives (the method converges to the correct solution) and False Positives (the method converges to a wrong solution). If the algorithm does not converge after a maximum number of iterations, and the solution is wrong, a True Negatives counter is incremented. Finally, in the False Negatives case, the algorithm does not converge, even if the solution is correct.

Table 1 and Table 2 summarize the results. The measurements reported in these tables are obtained as follows: as the robot moves, consecutive scans of the environment are taken. For each pair of consecutive scans the first scan is the reference scan while the second is the new scan. The position of the new scan is given by the odometry motion estimation. In the simulation perfect odometry is used to which a known random value is added to represent localization errors. Large localization errors may in practice be due for example to wheel slippage. The genetic search is performed in a genetic search space centered in this modified position which represents the coordinates where the robot thinks to be in. The $(x, y, \varphi)$ errors are random variables from $(0, 0, 0)$ and $(x_{max}, y_{max}, \varphi_{max})$. Although a huge number of experiments have been performed, eight experiments are reported in this paper, where the actual values $(x_{max}, y_{max}, \varphi_{max})$ are $(0.15m, 0.15m, 8.6^o)$ (these values are the same of Experiment 3 of [6]), $(0.2m, 0.2m, 17.3^o)$, $(0.2m, 0.2m, 34.3^o)$, $(0.2m, 0.2m, 45.0^o)$ (these values are the same of Experiment 6 of [6]). Two additional results with respect to [6] are obtained with random errors up to $(0.5m, 0.5m, 100.0^o)$ and $(2m, 2m, 360.0^o)$. Given that the False Negatives are always equal to zero they have been omitted from the Tables for convenience. Then, for the two environments, the True Positives are always very high for the proposed algorithm while

**Table 1.** Localization errors in the AUTOLAB environment

| Experiments | Errors | mbICP | h-GLASM |
|---|---|---|---|
| Experiment 3 | True Positive | 98,85 | 100,0 |
| random error up to 0.15m, 0.15m, 8.6$^o$ | True Negative | 1,15 | 0,0 |
| | False Positive | 0,0 | 0,0 |
| Experiment 4 | True Positive | 84,71 | 98,82 |
| random error up to 0.20m, 0.20m, 17.3$^o$ | True Negative | 10,59 | 1,18 |
| | False Positive | 4,71 | 0,0 |
| Experiment 5 | True Positive | 50,0 | 98,91 |
| random error up to 0.20m, 0.20m, 34.3$^o$ | True Negative | 27,17 | 0,0 |
| | False Positive | 22,83 | 1,09 |
| Experiment 6 | True Positive | 42,86 | 97,80 |
| random error up to 0.20m, 0.20m, 45.0$^o$ | True Negative | 42,86 | 1,10 |
| | False Positive | 14,29 | 1,10 |
| Experiment 7 | True Positive | 11,63 | 95,35 |
| random error up to 0.50m, 0.50m, 100.0$^o$ | True Negative | 82,56 | 2,33 |
| | False Positive | 5,81 | 2,33 |
| Experiment 8 | True Positive | 2,30 | 97,70 |
| random error up to 2.00m, 2.00m, 360.0$^o$ | True Negative | 96,55 | 2,30 |
| | False Positive | 1,15 | 0,0 |

**Table 2.** Localization errors in the CAVE environment

| Experiments | Errors | mbICP | h-GLASM |
|---|---|---|---|
| Experiment 3 | True Positive | 96,43 | 97,62 |
| random error up to 0.15m, 0.15m, 8.6$^o$ | True Negative | 1,19 | 1,19 |
| | False Positive | 2,38 | 1,19 |
| Experiment 4 | True Positive | 73,42 | 94,94 |
| random error up to 0.20m, 0.20m, 17.3$^o$ | True Negative | 11,39 | 2,53 |
| | False Positive | 15,19 | 2,53 |
| Experiment 5 | True Positive | 43,68 | 98,85 |
| random error up to 0.20m, 0.20m, 34.3$^o$ | True Negative | 32,18 | 1,15 |
| | False Positive | 24,14 | 0,00 |
| Experiment 6 | True Positive | 46,91 | 98,77 |
| random error up to 0.20m, 0.20m, 45.0$^o$ | True Negative | 32,10 | 1,23 |
| | False Positive | 20,99 | 0,00 |
| Experiment 7 | True Positive | 12,36 | 98,88 |
| random error up to 0.50m, 0.50m, 100.0$^o$ | True Negative | 76,40 | 1,12 |
| | False Positive | 11,24 | 0,00 |
| Experiment 8 | True Positive | 2,47 | 96,30 |
| random error up to 2.00m, 2.00m, 360.0$^o$ | True Negative | 97,53 | 1,23 |
| | False Positive | 0,00 | 2,47 |

for the MbICP method proposed in [6] decrease as the errors increase. At the same time, the True Negatives, i.e. the cases where the MbICP does not even converge, remain at about the same value in both the environments.

It is worth noting that the last two experiments are related to very large rotation and translation errors and represent global localization conditions. With these large errors, the proposed hybrid solution works remarkable well, giving a rate of True positives of about 96-97%, while the mbICP algorithm gives only around 2%.

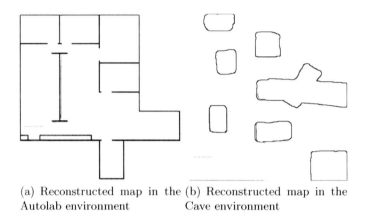

(a) Reconstructed map in the Autolab environment

(b) Reconstructed map in the Cave environment

**Fig. 4.** Map building using scan matching in the test environments

In Fig. 4(a) and Fig. 4(b) we report finally the reconstructed maps (overlap of scans, depicted in red) of the considered environments using the proposed algorithm, considering a systematic odometric error affecting at each step the rotation angle ($\frac{\pi}{4}$) in ten moves of 0.5 m. The trajectory of the robot, moving from left to right, is represented by the black dots in Fig. 4(a) and in Fig. 4(b).

## 5   Final Remarks and Conclusions

In this paper we have described and discussed a hybrid optimization algorithm for aligning two partially overlapped scans, i.e. for solving the scan matching problem for robot localization. The algorithm is based on genetic optimization and ICP. The fitness function gives the genetic algorithm several important properties, namely does not require to compute any point to point or feature to feature correspondence. The genetic part of the algorithm is performed by evaluating the fitness directly by matching points which, after the projection on the same coordinate frame, fall in the search window around the previous scan. The ICP part is performed using the metric based ICP algorithm described in [6]; in fact the genetic algorithm in some cases has some remaining rotation error which must be recovered in the ICP phase. The described approach does not require to solve the point correspondence problem and is very fast because based on a look up table computation. As a matter of fact, it has a linear computational complexity $O(N)$, whereas GCP and ICP corresponding phases have a quadratic cost of $O(N^2)$. The experiments have shown that the limitations to the overall accuracy posed by the finite solution space (set by a number of bits used to code a position in the genes and by the extension of the search space) and quantization of the fitness function as defined with a lookup table, are small if an appropriate size of the marked area is chosen for the problem at hand.

# References

1. Lingemann, K., Surmann, H., Nuchter, A., Hertzberg, J.: Indoor and outdoor localization for fast mobile robots. In: Proceedings of the 2004 IEEE/RSJ Int. Conference on Intelligent Robots and Systems, IROS (2004)
2. Biber, P.: The normal distributions transform: A new approach to laser scan matching. In: Proceedings of the 2003 IEEE/RSJ Int. Conference on Intelligent Robots and Systems, IROS (2003)
3. Besl, P.J., McKay, N.D.: A method for registration of 3d shapes. IEEE Trans. PAMI, 239–256 (1992)
4. Lu, F., Milios, E.: Robot pose estimation in unknown environments by matching 2d range scans. J. of Intelligent and Robotic Systems 18, 249–275 (1997)
5. Pfister, S., Kriechbaum, K., Roumeliotis, S., Burdick, J.: Weighted range sensor matching algorithms for mobile robot displacement estimation. In: Proceedings of the 2002 IEEE Int. Conference on Robotics and Automation (ICRA), pp. 1667–1674 (2002)
6. Minguez, J., Montesano, L., Lamiraux, F.: Metric-based iterative closest point scan matching for sensor displacement estimation. IEEE Transactions on Robotics 22(5), 1047–1054 (2006)
7. Martinez, Gozales, Morales, Mandow, Garcia-cerezo: Mobile robot motion estimation by 2d scan matching with genetic and iterative closest point algorithms. Journal of Field Robotics 23(1), 21–34 (2006)
8. Yamany, S., Ahmed, M., Farag, A.: A new genetic based technique for matching 3d curves and surfaces. Pattern Recognition 32, 1817–1820 (1999)
9. Robertson, C., Fisher, R.B.: Parallel evolutionary registration of range data. Comput. Vis. Image Underst. 87, 39–50 (2002)
10. Martinez, J.: Mobile robot self-localization by matching successive laser scans via genetic algorithms. In: 5th IFAC International Symposium on Intelligent Components and Instruments for Control Applications, pp. 1–6 (2003)
11. Lenac, K., Mumolo, E., Nolich, M.: Fast Genetic Scan Matching Using Corresponding Point Measurements in Mobile Robotics. In: Giacobini, M. (ed.) EvoWorkshops 2007. LNCS, vol. 4448, pp. 375–382. Springer, Heidelberg (2007)
12. Luck, J., Little, C., Hoff, W.: Registration of range data using a hybrid simulated annealing and iterative closest point algorithm. In: Proceedings of IEEE International Conference on Robotics and Automation, ICRA 2000, vol. 4, pp. 3739–3744 (2000)

# Beacon Scheduling Algorithm for Localization of a Mobile Robot

Jaehyun Park, Sunghee Choi, and Jangmyung Lee[*]

Dept. of Electrical Engineering, Pusan National University, South Korea
{jae-hyun,dhmgbds,jmlee}@pusan.ac.kr

**Abstract.** This paper proposes the localization scheme using ultrasonic beacons in a multi-block workspace. Indoor localization schemes using ultrasonic sensors have been widely studied due to their cheap price and high accuracy. However, ultrasonic sensors are susceptible to environmental noises from their propagation characteristics. On account of their decay phenomena when they are transmitted over a long distance, ultrasonic sensors are not suitable for application in large indoor environments. To overcome these shortages of ultrasonic sensors while emphasizing their advantages, a multi-block approach has been proposed by dividing the indoor space into several blocks with multiple beacons in each block. This approach, however, is hard to divide into several blocks when beacons are not installed in a certain pattern, and in case of having newly installed beacons, all blocks placement is reconstructed. Therefore, this paper proposes a real time localization scheme to estimate the position of mobile robot without effecting beacons placement. Beacon scheduling algorithm has been developed to select the optimal beacons according to robot position and beacon arrangement for the mobile robot navigation. The performance of the proposed localization system is verified through simulations and real experiments.

**Keywords:** Mobile robot, Localization, Ultrasonic, Beacon, Beacon Scheduling.

## 1    Introduction

With the development of robot technology such as microprocessor, sensors and computer, the practical use of mobile robots is widely increased. Real examples are cleaning robots and tour guide robots in the indoor environments such as museum and exhibition hall. And at outdoor environments, patrol and exploration of the mobile robot to be used for various purposes have been developed. For service applications in various environments, position recognition, environments perception using sensors, obstacle avoidance and path planning for autonomous navigation is vitally necessary. Especially, the precise localization of the mobile robot is one of the most important issues in the robotics field.

Localization schemes of mobile robots are classified into two categories that is relative and absolute position estimation. Relative position estimation is dead

---

[*] Corresponding author.

S. Jeschke, H. Liu, and D. Schilberg (Eds.): ICIRA 2011, Part I, LNAI 7101, pp. 594–603, 2011.
© Springer-Verlag Berlin Heidelberg 2011

reckoning method using odometry, gyro and accelerometer sensors [1], [2]. This method is easy and cheap to implement. However, with increasing driving distance, the accumulative error becomes larger, thus making precise localization difficult [3]. The absolute position estimation obtained using GPS, laser, infrared, vision, RFID, and ultrasonic sensors may resolve the problems of the relative position estimation [4-9]. However, it has problems due to the uncertainty of sensor information and the difficulty of installing the sensor.

This paper used ultrasonic sensors for indoor localization of mobile robot. The ultrasonic sensors have been widely used since they are cheap, easy to be controlled and have high accuracy. However, ultrasonic sensors are susceptible to environmental noises from their propagation characteristics. On account of their decay phenomena when they are transmitted over a long distance [10], ultrasonic sensors are not suitable for application in large indoor environments. To overcome these shortages of ultrasonic sensors while emphasizing their advantages, a new approach has been proposed by dividing the indoor space into several blocks with multiple beacons in each block [11]. As a representative scheme, the block ID recognition scheme has been developed by Ninety System to widen the operating area of the mobile robot [12]. However, in using this system, the user needs to specify all the coordinates of the active beacons and the block ID manually, which may lead to a high cost for the initial setting up of the working environment [18], [19]. Also, in case of unstructured placement of beacons or having newly installed beacons, dividing blocks to specify placement is difficulty and the placements of all blocks are reconstructed. The localization is not possible when the mobile robot moves out of the workspace, which is defined by the user a priori.

In this paper, a localization scheme in unstructured beacon placement has been proposed. The mobile robot is able to estimate own position using multi-block scheduling without effecting beacons placement. This paper is organized as follows. In section II, the indoor localization system, iGS, is introduced in detail, and a beacon scheduling algorithm in the multi-block environment is described in section III. In section IV, the effectiveness and usefulness of the multi-block scheduling algorithm has been verified by experiments. Finally, section V concludes this research work and mentions possible future related work.

# 2    Multi-block Localization Using iGS

## 2.1    Introduction to iGS(indoor GPS System)

The indoor localization system, developed by Ninety System and the Intelligent Robot Laboratory of PNU, has been utilized as a platform for mobile robot navigation. Its localization accuracy is ±5 cm and the localization period is 200 msec. The basic operating space is defined as 5 m (width) x 5 m (depth) x 2.5 m (height).

Figure 1 illustrates the navigational environment of the mobile robot in the iGS space. There are at least three active beacon sensors in the room and one localizer on the mobile robot. The localizer calls a specific beacon to send ultrasonic signals which are received by the localizer to measure the distance to the beacon. When such distance data from three known locations are available, the unknown location of the mobile robot can be estimated by the trilateration method [13], [14]. The localizer uses an RFID signal to select a specific beacon, which sends out ultrasonic signals to stably provide the distance data to the localizer. The distance from the localizer to the beacon can be easily obtained by the multiplication of the speed of the ultrasonic signal and the time of flight, even though the environment temperature changes the speed of the ultrasonic signal in a known pattern.

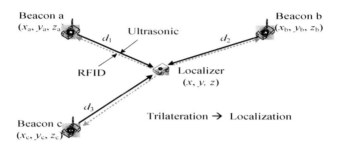

**Fig. 1.** Beacons in the iGS space

## 2.2     Distance Measurement and Calculation of the Absolute Location

The distance can be calculated by the multiplication of the speed of the ultrasonic signal and the measured TOF [15].

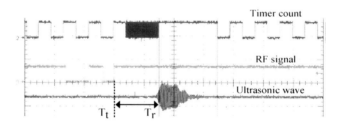

**Fig. 2.** TOF diagram

Figure 2 shows an illustration of the starting time for the counter, $T_t$, and the arrival time of the ultrasonic signal at the localizer, $T_r$, where the counter starts when the RF signal is transmitted and stops when the ultrasonic signal is detected by the localizer with a certain threshold value.

$$TOF = T_r - T_t \tag{1}$$

The distance between the localizer and an active beacon, d, can be obtained as the multiplication of $v$ and the *TOF*.

$$d = v \cdot TOF \tag{2}$$

where the speed of the ultrasonic signal, $v$, is a function of the environmental temperature and is represented as

$$v \cong 331.5 \sqrt{\frac{T}{237}} \ [m/s] \tag{3}$$

where $T$ represents the absolute temperature [16].

When the absolute positions of the beacons are pre-specified as $(x_a, y_a, z_a)$, $(x_b, y_b, z_b)$, and $(x_c, y_c, z_c)$, and the distances between the localizer and beacons are obtained as d1, d2 and d3, the absolute position of the mobile robot, $P(x, y, z)$, can be represented by the following equations.

$$\begin{bmatrix} (x-x_a)^2 + (y-y_a)^2 + (z-z_a)^2 \\ (x-x_b)^2 + (y-y_b)^2 + (z-z_b)^2 \\ (x-x_c)^2 + (y-y_c)^2 + (z-z_c)^2 \end{bmatrix} = \begin{bmatrix} d_a^2 \\ d_b^2 \\ d_c^2 \end{bmatrix} \tag{4}$$

From these equations, the absolute position of the mobile robot, $P(x, y, z)$, can be computed as

$$P = A^{-1}B$$

$$\text{where} \quad A = 2 \begin{bmatrix} x_b - x_a & y_b - y_a & z_b - z_a \\ x_c - x_b & y_c - y_b & z_c - z_b \\ x_a - x_c & y_a - y_c & z_a - z_c \end{bmatrix}, \ P = \begin{bmatrix} x \\ y \\ z \end{bmatrix}, \tag{5}$$

$$\text{and} \ B = \begin{bmatrix} d_a^2 - d_b^2 - x_a^2 + x_b^2 - y_a^2 + y_b^2 - z_a^2 + z_b^2 \\ d_b^2 - d_c^2 - x_b^2 + x_c^2 - y_b^2 + y_c^2 - z_b^2 + z_c^2 \\ d_c^2 - d_a^2 - x_c^2 + x_a^2 - y_c^2 + y_a^2 - z_c^2 + z_a^2 \end{bmatrix}.$$

## 2.3   Multi-block Localization System

The localization of the mobile robot becomes extremely complex and difficult within a multi-block workspace, which has multiple beacons installed. A new multi-block localization system, based on the iGS, is proposed in this paper for the most precise localization of the mobile robot. Figure 3 shows the structure of the multi-block localization. Multi-block scheduling algorithm is implemented to select optimal beacons set. The RFID transmitter in the localizer sends trigger signals to activate the selected beacons. When the active beacon receives its own ID, it sends an ultrasonic signal back to the localizer on the mobile robot. The distance from the beacon to the mobile robot can be calculated by multiplying the TOF and travel speed of the ultrasonic signal. A sleep mode is also adopted for the active beacons, to save power while they are not in active use.

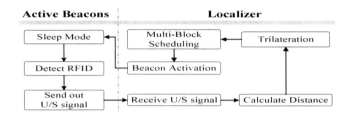

**Fig. 3.** The structure of the multi-block localization

# 3    Beacon Scheduling

Since the strength of ultrasonic signals decay by the inverse square of the distance from the source [17], one set of the iGS can only covers an area of about 5 m x 5 m (assuming that there are no obstacles in the room). When it is necessary to localize mobile robots globally, the overcoming of obstacles, as well as decay problems, needs to be also addressed. In these cases, the sensor space can be divided into multiple blocks to provide a solution for the global localization.

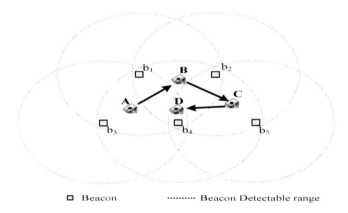

**Fig. 4.** The example of beacon scheduling

Since the performance of the trilateration is affected by the raging errors, by the geometrical arrangement of the beacons, and by the location of the mobile robot, it is necessary to select the optimal beacons to improve the localization accuracy in multiple blocks. As the beacon selecting method, one is to change the block and update the beacon information according to the robot position, and the other is to recognize the boundary between each block and to aware the new block. However, the case of above mentioned methods can cause the problem that the beacon information cannot be updated because of the block recognition failure at the boundary, or because beacons do not work well. Therefore, this paper proposes the efficient algorithm for adding new beacons or failure of block switching.

Beacon scheduling algorithm is based on the distance from the mobile robot to the beacon and geometrical arrangement of the beacons. In the case of iGS which uses threshold value, every beacon has the same detectable range. Three beacons at least are needed for localizing a mobile robot. Thus, it is possible to schedule beacons according to the position of the mobile robot if the mobile robot knows own position, position of beacons and beacon detectable range. Figure 4 shows the example of beacon scheduling.

When a mobile robot locates at A point, $b_1$, $b_3$ and $b_4$ are usable and the robot employs $b_1$, $b_2$ and $b_4$ after it moves into B point. And then, if the mobile robot moves to C point, it employs $b_2$, $b_4$ and $b_5$ to localize. Like the above case, it is possible to make the beacon schedule to select the usable beacons according to the position of the mobile robot. However, if the mobile robot moves to D point, $b_1$, $b_2$, $b_3$, $b_4$ and $b_5$ are able to obtain the distance data from every beacon. Since three distance data are needed for trilateration, the mobile robot should select three of five beacons because the more beacons it uses, the much time it needs. To select optimal beacon set, the DOP analysis [9] is adopted to determine which beacons can be used.

GDOP values are calculated from the positions of the mobile robot and usable beacons set. The best reliable beacons set have the lowest GDOP value and the beacon schedule uses it. At D point in Fig. 4, $b_1$, $b_3$ and $b_5$ beacons set or $b_2$, $b_3$ and $b_5$ beacons set have the lowest GDOP value. If there are GDOP values to be equal, a low beacon ID number has a priority. Therefore, $b_1$, $b_3$ and $b_5$ should be called at D point. Figure 5 shows beacon schedule with selected beacons set while it moves from A to D and Fig. 6 summarizes the beacon scheduling algorithm developed.

**Beacon Schedule**

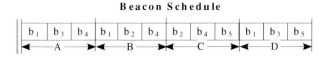

Fig. 5. Beacon Schedule

**Fig. 6.** Beacon scheduling algorithm

Coverage check is to make beacon list, B_List, which the mobile robot is able to utilize beacons which are obtained by using the position of the mobile robot and coverage of beacons. If there are more than three beacons, generating combination is carried out for making the combination of beacons set, which consist of three beacons. DOP Analysis is produced for calculating DOP values of the beacon combination. And then B_List is sorted in ascending order of DOP values. Finally, beacon schedule list, MBS_List, which has the optimal usable beacons set geometrically, is returned for precise localization.

## 4    Experiments

The mobile robot used in this paper is developed with DC motors having embedded encoders and the dsPIC30F4012 from Microchip for the control. The experimental iGS is composed of the localizer on the mobile robot and the beacons on the wall or ceiling shown. The localizer system uses the TMS320C2406A from TI for the system control, the rfPIC12F675F from Microchip for the RF signal control, and the AT40-10P (40 kHz) from Nippon Ceramic for the ultrasonic signal receiver. The beacon system uses the MSP403F1101A from TI for the system control and the AR40-10P (40 kHz) for the ultrasonic signal transmission. Estimating distance from beacon to receiver takes 43ms per a beacon and the average error in measuring the distance is 2.3mm. The experiments are implemented indoor environment, where eight beacons are deployed in the workspace by the vertex of (x, y, z)[unit : mm] with the mobile robot, to prove the algorithms in this paper. The monitoring programs for the user were developed on a PC using Visual C++ 6.0 which enables the real time monitoring of the robot motion on the two dimensional map. Figure 7 and Fig. 8 shows the experimental environments used in experiments.

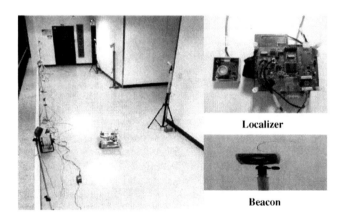

**Fig. 7.** The experimental environment

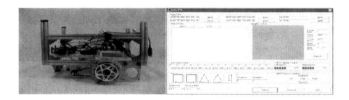

**Fig. 8.** The mobile robot and monitoring program

Figure 9 shows the deployment of the beacons and the route of the mobile robot. Eight beacons are deployed in the workspace with the mobile robot moving from point A to Point D.

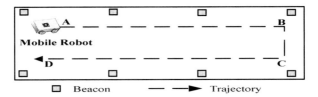

**Fig. 9.** The deployment of the beacons and the route of the mobile robot

Two different experiments are carried out to demonstrate the performance of the multi-block application and compare the trajectory of the mobile robot. Experiment 1, as shown in Fig. 10, uses the conventional multi-block system which beacon information is updated by using block switching algorithm at block boundary. The navigation result is seen to have different levels of error when the beacons change, because the system selected certain beacons without choosing the optimal beacons according to the positions of the mobile robot and beacons. As a result, there were several gaps in the route of the mobile robot when the block and the beacons are changing.

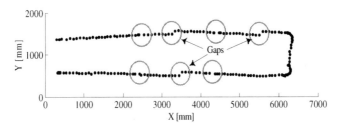

**Fig. 10.** Result of the navigation with the conventional multi-block system

Experiment 2 uses beacon scheduling algorithm proposed in this paper. Figure 11 illustrates the trajectory of the mobile robot. The system obtains a smoother trajectory for the mobile robot without route gaps than experiment 1, since the optimal beacons were selected from the positions of the robot and beacons.

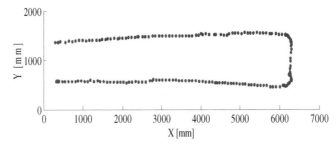

**Fig. 11.** Result of the navigation with the beacon scheduling algorithm

# 5    Conclusions

The ultrasonic sensor based localization system has been widely used since it is cheap, accurate and easy to control in indoor localization. However, on account of their decay phenomena when they are transmitted over a long distance, ultrasonic sensors are not suitable for application in large indoor environments. In this paper, to overcome these shortages of ultrasonic sensors while emphasizing their advantages, a new approach with multiple beacons has been proposed. For the real time localization of mobile robot, beacon scheduling algorithm without effecting beacons placement has been developed. The effectiveness of the localization system is verified through real experiments of mobile robot navigation. This localization system can be applied for the location based service in a various field as well as robot position system.

**Acknowledgments.** This research was supported by the MKE(The Ministry of Knowledge Economy), Korea, under the Special Navigation/Localization Robot Technology Research Center support program supervised by the NIPA (National IT Industry Promotion Agency)" (NIPA-2010-(C7000-1001-0004)).

# References

1. Myung, H., Lee, H.K., choi, K., Bang, S.W.: Mobile robot localization with gyroscope and constrained Kalman filter. International Journal of Control, Automation, and Systems 8(3), 667–676 (2010)
2. Borenstein, J., Feng, L.: Measurement and correction of systematic odometry errors in mobile robots. IEEE Transactions on Robotics and Automation 12, 869–880 (1996)
3. Tsai, C.C.: A Localization System of a Mobile Robot by Fusing Dead-reckoning and Ultrasonic Measurements. IEEE Transactions on Industrial Electronics 47(5), 1399–1404 (1998)
4. Abuhashim, T.S., Adbedl-Hagez, M.F., Al-Jarrah, M.A.: Building a Robust Integrity Monitoring Algorithm for a Low Cost GPS-aided-INS System. International Journal of Control, Automation, and Systems 8(5), 1108–1122 (2010)
5. Sooyong, L., Song, J.-B.: Mobile Robot Localization using Range Sensors: Consecutive Scanning and Cooperative Scanning. International Journal of Control, Automation, and Systems 3(1), 1–14 (2005)
6. Ngai, M.K., Quang, P.H., Shoudong, H., Gamini, D., Gu, F.: Mobile Robot Localization and Mapping using a Gaussian Sum Filter. International Journal of Control, Automation, and Systems 5(3), 251–268 (2007)
7. Lee, Y.J., Yim, B.D., Song, J.B.: Mobile Robot Localization based on Effective Combination of Vision and Range Sensors. International Journal of Control, Automation, and Systems 7(1), 97–104 (2007)
8. Han, S.S., Lim, H.S., Lee, J.M.: An Efficient Localization Scheme for a Differential-Driving Mobile Robot Based on RFID System. IEEE Trans. on Industrial Electronics 54(6), 1–8 (2007)
9. Park, J.H., Choi, M.G., Lee, J.M.: Indoor Localization System in a Multi-block Workspace. Robotica 28, 397–403 (2010)
10. Ching, C.T.: A Localization System of a Mobile Robot by Fusing Dead-reckoning and Ultrasonic. IEEE Trans. on Instrumentation and Measurement 47, 1399–1404 (1998)

11. Qinhe, W., Hashimoto, H.: Fast Localization of Multi-targets in the Intelligent Space. In: Annual Conf. SICE 2007, pp. 264–269 (2007)
12. Seo, D.G., Lee, J.M.: Localization Algorithm for a Mobile Robot Using iGS. In: The 17th International Federation of Automatic Control World Congress, pp. 742–747 (2008)
13. Manolakis, D.E.: Efficient Solution and Performance Analysis of 3D Position Estimation by Trilateration. IEEE Trans. on Aerospace and Electronic Systems 32, 1239–1248 (1996)
14. Thomas, F., Ros, L.: Revisiting Trilateration for Robot Localization. IEEE Trans. on Robotics 21, 93–101 (2005)
15. Barshan, B.: Fast Processing Techniques for Accurate Ultrasonic Range Measurements. IOP J. Meas. Sci. Technology 11, 45–50 (2000)
16. Eom, W.S., Lee, J.M.: Ubiquitous Positioning Network of a Mobile Robot with Active Beacon Sensors. In: Int. Conf. on Circuits/System, Computers and Communications, pp. 255–256 (2007)
17. Yi, S.Y., Choi, B.W.: Autonomous Navigation of Indoor Mobile Robots Using a Global Ultrasonic System. Robotica 22, 369–374 (2004)
18. Kim, S.B., Lee, J.M., Lee, I.O.: Precise Indoor Localization System For a Mobile Robot Using Auto Calibration Algorithm. In: The 13th International Conference on Advanced Robotics, pp. 635–640 (2007)
19. Eom, W.S., Park, J.H., Lee, J.M.: Hazardous Area Navigation with Temporary Beacons. International Journal of Control, Automation, and Systems 8(5), 1082–1090 (2010)

# Position Estimation Using Time Difference of Flight of the Multi-coded Ultrasonic

Woo-Jin Seo, Bong-Su Cho, Woo-Sung Moon, and Kwang-Ryul Baek

Department of Electrical Engineering,
Pusan National University,
Busan, Korea
seowoojin@gmail.com,
{mscho97,crenmoon,krbaek}@pusan.ac.kr

**Abstract.** The environment where mobile robots move is modeled as 2-dimensional space. Three ultrasonic receivers are in a line. The transmitters attached to the mobile robots transmit ultrasonic signals which contain different 9bit PR (pseudo-random) codes. The receiver calculates TDOFs (Time Difference of Flight) of each transmitted signals by CCF (Cross Correlation Function). According to TDOFs, the possible position of the mobile robot is represented by hyperbolic curves. The position of the mobile robot is an intersection of hyperbolic curves. The intersection is calculated by bisection method. The external device becomes simple compared to traditional method. The proposed system is verified experimentally.

**Keywords:** multi-coded ultrasonic, position estimation, TDOF, hyperbolic curve.

## 1    Introduction

Research for the autonomous mobile robot which recognizes environment and determines the situation by itself is being developed actively. To estimate the position of the mobile robot, there are absolute position estimation and relative position estimation [1]. This paper describes the method using TDOFs of ultrasonic signals which is one of the absolute position estimation methods.

One of the traditional methods using ultrasonic sensors is that four transmitters transmit ultrasonic signals sequentially and receivers calculate TOF (Time of Flight) of ultrasonic signals in the rectangular space. Another traditional method is that all the transmitters generate multi-coded ultrasonic at the same time and the receivers calculate the timing of the reception by CCF after binarization [1].

In this paper, the receivers are installed on one side of the space. The mobile robots move across a single plane that is modeled as 2-dimensional space. The positions of the mobile robots are estimated by the differences of distances using TDOFs. Therefore, sync signal is not needed and the external device becomes simple. The mobile robots transmit coded ultrasonic signals. 9-bit PR codes are assigned to each

S. Jeschke, H. Liu, and D. Schilberg (Eds.): ICIRA 2011, Part I, LNAI 7101, pp. 604–609, 2011.

mobile robot. The number of the mobile robots can be increased by adding the PR code. To calculate TDOFs from received signal, the receiver processes cross-correlation with the PR codes after binarization. The possible positions according to TDOFs are represented by two hyperbolic curves. The intersection of the hyperbolic curves is the position of the mobile robot. The intersection of the hyperbolic curves is calculated by bisection method [4]. The performance of this system is verified through experiment.

## 2     Signal Processing of Multi-coded Ultrasonic

9bit PR codes are assigned to each mobile robot [2]. The mobile robots transmit multi-coded ultrasonic signals. The bit interval, which is the minimum interval that each bit does not affect other bits, was experimentally defined to be 1ms. The receiver calculates TDOFs by CCFs after binarization. Sliding window is used to binarize received signal [3]. CCFs between a binarized signal and PR codes are calculated for TDOFs. The CCFs have the highest values at arrival time.

Fig. 1. shows sequences of the signal processing of the multi-coded ultrasonic. The first signal is raw data from ultrasonic receiver. The following signals show output according to steps of sliding window and CCF. The largest value of CCF shows TOAs (Time of Arrival) which is circled below.

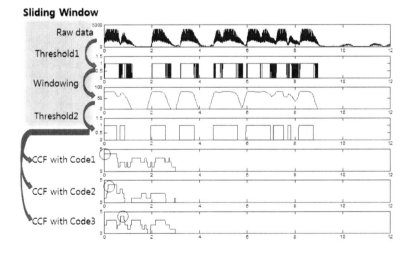

**Fig. 1.** The sequences of signal processing

## 3     Position Estimation Using TDOF

The system configuration to estimate the position of the mobile robot is shown in Fig. 2. The three ultrasonic sensors of an external device, which is shown at Fig. 2, are in a line at one side of the space. The mobile robots move within the space where ultrasonic signals can be received by all of the ultrasonic sensors. The mobile robots have ultrasonic transmitters in eight directions. The receiver estimates the position of the mobile robot by ultrasonic signals which are received from ultrasonic sensors.

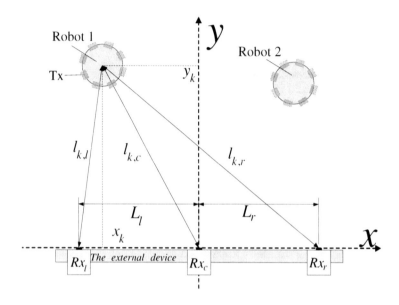

**Fig. 2.** The configuration of the system

$x_k$ and $y_k$ are the position at k-th sequence. $l_{k,l}$ is the distance between the mobile robot and the receiver $Rx_l$. $l_{k,c}$ is the distance between the mobile robot and the receiver $Rx_c$. $l_{k,r}$ is the distance between the mobile robot and the receiver $Rx_r$. $L_l$ is the distance between the receiver $Rx_l$ and the receiver $Rx_c$. $L_r$ is the distance between the receiver $Rx_c$ and the receiver $Rx_r$. The TDOF between $Rx_l$ and $Rx_c$ is denoted by $\Delta t_{k,cl}$. The TDOF between $Rx_c$ and $Rx_r$ is denoted by $\Delta t_{k,rc}$. The position of mobile robot is estimated from two TDOF $\Delta t_{k,cl}$ and $\Delta t_{k,rc}$ which are measured from the ultrasonic receiver.

The differences of distances between the mobile robot and the ultrasonic sensors can be calculated from TDOF. $d_{k,l}$ is the difference between distances from the central and left sensors to the mobile robot. $d_{k,r}$ is the difference between distances from the right and central sensors to the mobile robot. The velocity of ultrasonic is denoted by character c. The differences of distance between $l_{k,l}$ and $l_{k,c}$ and between $l_{k,c}$ and $l_{k,r}$ is the following.

$$d_{k,l} = l_{k,l} - l_{k,c} = c \cdot \Delta t_{cl}, \quad d_{k,r} = l_{k,c} - l_{k,r} = c \cdot \Delta t_{rc} \tag{1}$$

The locus of the points which has constant difference of distance from the two fixed points is a hyperbolic curve. A general form of hyperbolic curve is the following.

$$\frac{x^2}{a^2} - \frac{y^2}{b^2} = 1 \tag{2}$$

The two equations derived from the parameters of the proposed system are the following.

$$\frac{(x_{k,l}+\frac{L_l}{2})^2}{(\frac{d_{k,l}}{2})^2}-\frac{y_k^2}{\left(\sqrt{(\frac{L_l}{2})^2-(\frac{d_{k,l}}{2})^2}\right)^2}=1 \tag{3}$$

$$\frac{(x_{k,r}-\frac{L_r}{2})^2}{(\frac{d_{k,r}}{2})^2}-\frac{y_k^2}{\left(\sqrt{(\frac{L_r}{2})^2-(\frac{d_{k,r}}{2})^2}\right)^2}=1 \tag{4}$$

Each equation at equation (3) and (4) has two hyperbolic curves. The two unique hyperbolic curves can be selected according to the signs of $d_{k,l}$ and $d_{k,r}$. Therefore, the two hyperbolic equations can be calculated.

$$x_{k,l}=d_{k,l}\sqrt{\frac{y_k^2}{L_l^2-d_{k,l}^2}+\frac{1}{4}}-\frac{L_l}{2} \tag{5}$$

$$x_{k,r}=d_{k,r}\sqrt{\frac{y_k^2}{L_r^2-d_{k,r}^2}+\frac{1}{4}}+\frac{L_r}{2} \tag{6}$$

The possible position takes two hyperbolic traces when $d_{k,l}$ and $d_{k,2}$ are determined. The intersection of the two hyperbolic curves is the position of the mobile robot. The bisection method is applied to find the intersection of the two hyperbolic curves. The bisection method is a numerical root-finding method.

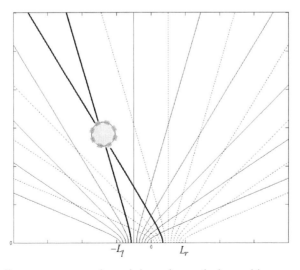

**Fig. 3.** Hyperbolic curves at some $d_{k,l}$ and $d_{k,r}$ and a particular position according to the two hyperbolic curves

Fig. 3. shows hyperbolic curves at several $d_{k,l}$ and $d_{k,r}$. The thin solid curves are hyperbolic curves according to several $d_{k,l}$. The dotted curves are hyperbolic curves according to several $d_{k,l}$. The thick solid curves show the curves at certain $d_{k,l}$ and $d_{k,r}$ measured from the receiver. The intersection of the two curves is the estimated position of the mobile robot.

To apply bisection method, the position of the mobile robot is assumed between $(x_k, y_{min})$ and $(x_k, y_{max})$. The initial values of $y_{k,l,0}$ and $y_{k,h,0}$ are the following.

$$y_{k,l,0} = y_{min}, \ y_{k,h,0} = y_{max} \tag{5}$$

To calculate $y_k$ following equation is applied.

$$y_{k,m,i} = \frac{y_{k,l,i} + y_{k,h,i}}{2} \tag{6}$$

$$y_{k,l,i+1} = y_{k,l,i}, \ y_{k,h,i+1} = y_{k,m,i} \ \ if \ \ x_{k,l}(y_{k,m,i}) > x_{k,r}(y_{k,m,i})$$
$$y_{k,l,i+1} = y_{k,m,i}, \ y_{k,h,i+1} = y_{k,h,i} \ \ if \ \ x_{k,l}(y_{k,m,i}) \le x_{k,r}(y_{k,m,i}) \tag{7}$$

$$y_k = y_{k,m,20} \tag{8}$$

$y_k$ is applied into the equation (5) or (6) to calculate $x_k$.

## 4     Experiment

The experiment system is configured as Fig. 2. The two mobile robots are placed at the predetermined positions. The mobile robots transmit ultrasonic signal with its own code at every 100ms. The experiments are performed a thousand times at each position. Fig. 4. shows the result of the experiment. The position errors are larger when the mobile robot is far from the central ultrasonic sensor. The x position and the y position are correlated according to the position of the mobile robot.

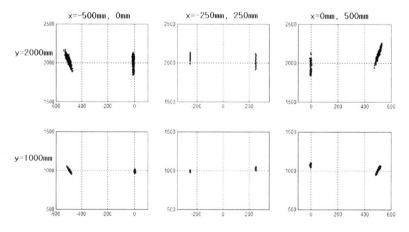

**Fig. 4.** The measured position of the mobile robot

## 5     Conclusion

In this paper, the position of the mobile robot is estimated by multi-coded ultrasonic. The three ultrasonic sensors of the receiver are in a line at one side of the space which is modeled as 2-dimension. The mobile robots transmit multi-coded ultrasonic signals. The receiver measures the TDOF from the received signal by CCF after binarization. The differences of distances are calculated from TDOF. When the differences of distance are determined, the possible positions are represented by hyperbolic curves. The position of the mobile robot is estimated from the hyperbolic curves by bisection algorithm.

The proposed method to estimate the position of the mobile robot uses simple external devices to receive the multi-coded ultrasonic. The result shows that the proposed method provides reliable data. The errors of measured data have a pattern according to the position of the mobile robot. To improve the performance of position estimation, the pattern of errors has to be studied.

**Acknowledgements.** This research was financially supported by the Ministry of Education, Science Technology (MEST) and Korea Industrial Technology Foundation (KOTEF) through the Human Resource Training Project for Regional Innovation.

## References

1. Cho, B.-S., Cho, S.-B., Yang, S.-O., Baek, K.-R.: Implementation of the ultrasonic local positioning system using dual frequencies and codes. Journal of Institute of Control, Robotics and Systems 14(7), 647–655 (2008)
2. Moon, W.-S., Cho, B.S., Jang, J.W., Baek, K.R.: A multi-robot positioning system using a multi-code ultrasonic sensor network and a kalman filter. International Journal of Control, Automation, and Systems 8(6), 1349–1355 (2010)
3. Barshan, B., Ayrulu, B.: Performance comparison of four time-of-flight estimation methods for sonar signals. IEEE Electronics Letter 34(4), 1616–1617 (1998)
4. Chapra, S.C.: Applied Numerical Methods with MATLAB for engineers and scientists. McGraw-Hill, New York (2005)

# Detecting Free Space and Obstacles
# in Omnidirectional Images

Luis Felipe Posada, Krishna Kumar Narayanan,
Frank Hoffmann, and Torsten Bertram

Institute of Control Theory and Systems Engineering, Technische Universität
Dortmund, 44227, Dortmund, Germany
felipe.posada@tu-dortmund.de

**Abstract.** This paper introduces a new approach for detecting free
space and obstacles in omnidirectional images that contributes to a
purely vision based robot navigation in indoor environments. Naive Bayes
classifiers fuse multiple visual cues and features generated from heterogeneous segmentation schemes that maintain separate appearance models
and seeds for floor and obstacles regions. Pixel-wise classifications are
aggregated across regions of homogeneous appearance to obtain a segmentation that is robust with respect to noise and outliers. The final
classification utilizes fuzzy preference structures that interpret the individual classification as fuzzy preference relations which distinguish the
uncertainty inherent to the classification in terms of conflict and ignorance. Ground truth data for training and testing the classifiers is obtained from the superposition of 3D scans captured by a photonic mixer
device camera. The results demonstrate that the classification error is
substantially reduced by rejecting those queries associated with a strong
degree of conflict and ignorance.

**Keywords:** Visual navigation, obstacle detection, free space estimation,
floor/obstacle classification.

## 1 Introduction

In recent years vision based navigation has gained increased interest in the
robotics community [3]. The motivation for using vision in robotics is attributed
to the increasing availability of powerful computer vision systems at affordable
costs, the passive behavior of vision sensors and the fact that vision in contrast
to proximity sensors enables the appearance based distinction of objects such as
ground floor, obstacles, people, doors, walls, cabinets and corridors.

Free space and obstacle detection is an important problem in mobile robotics
since it supports high level tasks such as localization, navigation and map building and in the context of mapless navigation, replaces or augments proximity
sensors supporting a direct mapping from visual cues onto actions characteristic
for reactive behaviors. The literature reports several schemes of robot free space
and obstacle detection, including approaches that: model the appearance of objects with histograms [19,11]; are based on motion or optical flow [10]; detect

S. Jeschke, H. Liu, and D. Schilberg (Eds.): ICIRA 2011, Part I, LNAI 7101, pp. 610–619, 2011.
© Springer-Verlag Berlin Heidelberg 2011

ground patches from planar homographies [14], use stereo vision and homographies [1,6]; mix color and texture [15,2]. Recently, self-supervised detection of traversable terrain gained increasing attention in outdoor robotics. The so called near-to-far online learning [4,7,9] extracts the ground truth about local flat drivable terrain from laser range sensors. A model is generated from the ground truth data in order to classify remote traversable areas of off-road terrain beyond the short range training region in front of the vehicle.

Although the role of uncertainty in the context of autonomous robot navigation has been long recognized in the robotic community [5], few approaches to estimate the local free space explicitly take uncertainty into consideration, even further, distinguishing among the causes of uncertainty, namely lack of evidence and conflicting evidence and utilize this information in the context of robot decision making. A fuzzy approach for map building and path planning is investigated in [13]. The authors in [12] demonstrate that in some scenarios the fuzzy fusion of sensor data is advantageous in comparison to probabilistic approaches for map building.

This paper presents an approach of free space and obstacle detection which is novel in several aspects: (i) Fusion of multiple classification generated from heterogeneous segmentation schemes maintaining separate apereance models and seeds for obstacles and floor and (ii) Explicit model of uncertainty in the classification by means of fuzzy preference structures [8].

## 2   System Architecture

The overall system architecture is shown in Fig. 1. The classification relies on four segmentations: Marker based watershed, histogram backprojection using the hue-saturation channel, histogram backprojection using the normalized red-green color space and region growing. In marker based watershed [17], the gradient image is interpreted as a landscape, as it is flooded from a set of initial seeds called markers such that homogeneous regions emerge separated by watershed lines. Histogram backprojection [18] compares the appearance of an image with the color histograms of reference models. Region growing is similar to clustering, it starts from a set of seeds and adds neighboring pixels to a growing region based on their similarity. A more detailed description of the segmentation methods is provided in section 3.

The scheme maintains separate appearance models for floor and obstacles, thus capturing the decision boundary between floor and obstacles in more refined manner compared to a floor versus rest classification. Two ensemble of classifiers combine the evidence of single segmentation experts for both models. The first ensemble called *obstacle classifier*, is intended to detect obstacles by fusing the segmentations arising from seeds and histogram models of obstacles. The second ensemble called *floor classifier*, attempts to recognize floor regions by combining the segmentations using seeds and histogram models of the floor. A detailed description of the ensemble of classifiers is provided in section 4.

Watershed operates in an unsupervised manner in that it does not consider the class label of the markers in advance. Rather markers are randomly distributed

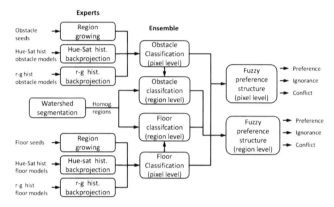

**Fig. 1.** System architecture

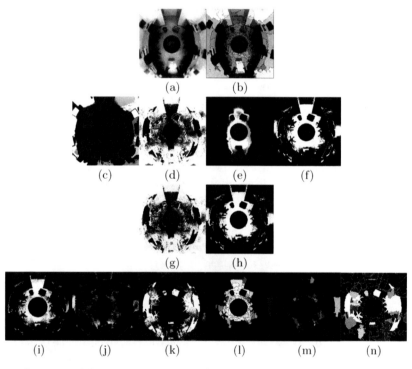

**Fig. 2.** Overview of the processing steps in the obstacle-floor detection: (a) Input image. (b) marker-based watershed. (c,d) Obstacle segmentations with region growing and histogram backprojection. (e,f) floor segmentations with region growing and histogram backprojection. (g,h) Obstacle and floor classifier (i,j,k) Pixel-wise preference,ignorance and conflict. (l,m,n) Preference,ignorance and conflict processed per watershed regions (watershed lines shown for visualization purposes).

across the image, albeit with a higher density near the image center to achieve a finer tessellation in the robots immediate vicinity which is most relevant for local navigation. Given the unsupervised nature of watershed segmentation, it is not directly applicable for classification. However, it enables the partition of the image into homogeneous regions, of which the pixel-wise classifications belonging to the same region are aggregated to obtain a more robust classification of the entire region.

In order to resolve inconsistencies between the predictions of both ensemble classifiers, the classifications are decomposed into a preference structure that represents the uncertainty in terms of conflict and ignorance. Following the idea of fuzzy preference structures for classification introduced in [8], the classifications are mapped into the domain of decision making under fuzzy preferences. The authors in [8] establish a relationship between classification learning and fuzzy preference modeling and decision making. The resulting structure is a fuzzy relation which for every pair of class labels $\lambda_i, \lambda_j$ defines a degree of

- preference: which determines the degree to which the classification $\lambda_i$ is preferred over $\lambda_j$
- indifference: the degree to which both labels are in conflict in the sense that both classification are supported by training data
- incomparability: reflects the degree of ignorance, in other words the lack of information supporting either classification

Figure 2 illustrates the pivotal processing steps to generate an obstacle floor classification from the original image of a typical indoor scene.

## 3   Image Segmentation

This section describes in detail the segmentation schemes that provide the features for subsequent classification. Histogram Backprojection [18] identifies regions in the image which match with a reference model in appearance. The normalized histogram reference model $M$ in a 2D color space, is compared with the normalized histogram $H$ of the current frame $I$ and the backprojection image $B$ computed by,

$$B(u,v) = min\left(\frac{M(c(u,v))}{H(c(u,v))}, 1\right),\tag{1}$$

where $c(u,v)$ denotes the 2D color of pixel $(u,v)$. The backprojection image $B(u,v) \in [0,1]$ is interpreted as the degree of similarity between the region and the reference model. Our scheme maintains multiple models $M_k(c(u,v))$ for the classes floor $\lambda_f$, obstacle $\lambda_o$ and background $\lambda_b$. The similarity of the current histogram with a class is given by the maximum similarity with any of its representing models:

$$B_i(u,v) = \max_{k \in \lambda_i} min\left(\frac{M_k(c(u,v))}{H(c(u,v))}, 1\right).\tag{2}$$

Region growing starts with a set of seed points and neighboring pixels are added to the region in an incremental fashion based on their similarity. Each segmentation originates from a single seed of known class label. The region growing segmentation is repeated $N_i$ times with different seeds. $N_i(u, v)$ counts how often the pixel $(u, v)$ belongs to the final region, thus indicating the similarity of that pixel with prototype pixels of class $\lambda_i$. It is important to notice that a pixel which is not captured by a particular region growing instantiation might still belong to the corresponding class, as region growing is a local method and only expands to those pixels that are connected with the original seed. In particular the obstacle regions are often fragmented due to the multitude of objects. Therefore, it is essential to relate the absolute counts to the average number of pixels $< M_{ki} >$ in a single region growing segmentation. A pixel has a membership degree to class $\lambda_i$ given by

$$\mu_i(u, v) = \max\{\frac{N_i(u, v)}{N_i} \frac{\cap M_i}{\overline{M_i}}, 1\}. \tag{3}$$

The relative frequency $N_i(u, v)/N_i$ is scaled by the ratio between the size of the union of all segmentations $\cap M_i$ of class $\lambda_i$ and the average size $\overline{M_i}$ of a single segmented region. The ratio is a coarse estimate of the number of fragmented segments of a class. Therefore the score of a fragmented class is weighted more strongly in comparison to a class that forms a connected region.

## 4    Classification

The classification is based on the ensemble of experts paradigm [16]. The key aspect behind ensemble based classification is to benefit from the combination of multiple, possibly diverse opinions to come up with a more informed decision. Diversity is one of the cornerstones of ensemble systems where heterogeneous segmentations based on different cues and features ensure that the segmentations exhibit different errors at specific instances. This heterogeneity is a fundamental property in order to reduce the generalization error beyond the individual segmentation error rates. The combination of evidence in the *floor, obstacle classifier* is accomplished by a Naive Bayes classifier that predicts the posterior probability of the class of a single pixel as either belonging to a class obstacle $\lambda_o$ or floor $\lambda_f$. The likelihood $p(f_i|C_j)$ of a feature $f_i$ given the class $C_j$ is modeled by a Gaussian distribution. The likelihoods of the data and the class priors are estimated from the observed frequencies of classes and features in the training data. The naive Bayes classifier computes the posteriori probability of the classes according to the likelihood of the conditionally independent features:

$$p(C_j|f_i) = \frac{1}{Z} p(C_j) \prod_{i=1}^{n} p(f_i|C_j) \tag{4}$$

in which the normalization factor $Z$ is the evidence of the features $f_i$.

## 4.1   Fuzzy Preference Structures

The fuzzy preference structures for classification, reduce the problem of classification to one of decision making. The idea is to interpret the output of a binary classifier $r_{i,j} = M_{i,j}(x)$ for a query $x$ as a preference of class label $\lambda_i$ in comparison with $\lambda_j$. In this sense, the value $r_{i,j} \in [0,1]$ can be interpreted as the degree to which classification $\lambda_i$ is preferred over $\lambda_j$. Denoting $r_{i,j} = \mathcal{R}(\lambda_i, \lambda_j)$, the matrix

$$\mathcal{R} = \begin{bmatrix} 1 & r_{1,2} & \cdots & r_{1,m} \\ r_{2,1} & 1 & \cdots & r_{2,m} \\ \vdots & & & \vdots \\ r_{m,1} & r_{m,2} & \cdots & 1 \end{bmatrix} \tag{5}$$

is obtained by merging the binary fuzzy classifiers for each possible combination of class labels into a fuzzy preference relation.

We are interested in decomposing the weak preference relation $\mathcal{R}$ into a fuzzy preference structure that describes the strict preference relation $\mathcal{P}$, the indifference relation $\mathcal{I}$ and an incomparability relation $\mathcal{J}$. In principle any fuzzy t-norm and its dual t-conorm are suitable to obtain preference structure $(\mathcal{P}, \mathcal{I}, \mathcal{J})$ [8]. The employed decomposition is given by:

$$\mathcal{P}(\lambda_i, \lambda_j) = r_{i,j}(1 - r_{j,i}) \tag{6}$$
$$\mathcal{I}(\lambda_i, \lambda_j) = r_{i,j} r_{j,i} \tag{7}$$
$$\mathcal{J}(\lambda_i, \lambda_j) = 1 - (r_{i,j} + r_{j,i}) \tag{8}$$

Notice that this definition of incomparability coincides with the width of the distribution. At the extreme values $r_{i,j} = 1 - r_{j,i} \in \{0,1\}$ of the weak preference we obtain a strict strong preference $\mathcal{J}(\lambda_i, \lambda_j) \in \{0,1\}$. Finally, the degree of indifference assumes its maximum for $r_{i,j} = r_{j,i} = 0.5$, in that all classifiers have no preference of either class.

The ensemble classifiers outputs are interpreted as a score $s_{i,j}^k \in [0,1]$. In order to improve the statistics we consider weak preferences across an entire region rather than on the basis of single pixels. The minimum of the scores in a region denote the weak preference for $\lambda_i$ in comparison with $\lambda_j$ for a region $R_n$ segmented by unsupervised watershed and is defined as

$$r_{R_n}(i,j) = \min_{(u,v) \in R_n} s_{i,j}(u,v) \tag{9}$$

As the min operator is rather sensitive to noise and outliers, it is advisable to replace it by the $\alpha$-quantile of the distribution. In our case the 20% lowest scores are ignored and the weak preference is given by the $\alpha = 0.15$. Fig. 2(l,m,n) illustrate $\mathcal{P}, \mathcal{I}, \mathcal{J}$ computed for each watershed region. Fig. 2(i,j,k) with pixelwise computation of $\mathcal{P}, \mathcal{I}, \mathcal{J}$ is also shown for comparison purposes.

## 5   Experimental Results

A photonic mixer device camera (PMD) generates the labeled instances for validation of the image segmentation based classifier. The training and validation data consists of about one million pixels captured from 30 images of which the true class label is established from the PMD depth information and 3D segmentation. Half of the images are used for training and the other half for testing.

The ground truth labeled data is generated by means of a PMD camera which captures 3D range data at a 204 x 204 pixel resolution across a 40° × 40° field of view. The depth image of different scenes such as corridors, open rooms and confined spaces is obtained by rotating the robot and PMD camera by 360° and capturing scans at each pose. The 3D data from the PMD is subsequently fitted to planar surfaces by means of random sampling consensus (RANSAC). Surface normal orientation, distance to the camera and connected components determine whether a pixel and its associated 3D point are labeled as obstacle or floor. The process is ilustrated in Fig. 3.

(a)          (b)          (c)          (d)

**Fig. 3.** Seeds projection: (a) Range image, (b) Planes fitted from the 3D data with RANSAC, (c) Seeds projected into the omnidirectional view, (d) Ground truth data after 360° scan-matching and considering points over the horizon

Fig. 4 illustrate the fuzzy preference structure for omnidirectional images of prototypical indoor scenes. The first scenario illustrate a situation in which the robot encounters isolated obstacles which exhibit high level of ignorance reflecting the lack of data to distinguish those novel objects into either floor or obstacle. The second scenario illustrates a scene of ambigious appearance, which exhibits a substantial amount of conflict due to the similar color of floor and background. The following scenarios depict different levels of texture, illumination and shadows.

Table 1 report the classification error rate after decomposing the *floor classifier* and *obstacle classifier* using fuzzy preference structures. The analysis assumes that the classifier is allowed to reject a certain fraction of queries with highest ignorance or conflict. The results shows the pixel-wise classification and the region-wise classification where pixels belonging to watershed regions are aggregated using equation 9. The results confirm the supposed improvement: computing statistics across a region improves the classification accuracy as the error is substantially reduced by rejecting those queries associated with a strong degree of conflict and ignorance.

Table 2 present the results in order to assess the performance of the proposed method in comparison to standard approaches such as a naive Bayes classifier that uses all features. The results demonstrate that maintaining two separate models for floor and obstacle is cleary superior to one versus rest approaches. Combining heterogeneous segmentations is better than to rely on a

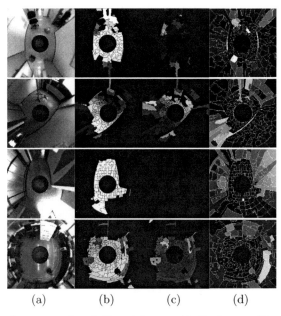

(a)             (b)             (c)             (d)

**Fig. 4.** Classification examples: (a)Input image, b) Preference $\mathcal{P}$, c) Conflict $\mathcal{I}$, d) Ignorance $\mathcal{J}$ (watershed lines shown for visualization purposes)

**Table 1.** Classification error based on rejection of queries according to conflict and ignorance

| | Pixel-wise | | |
|---|---|---|---|
| Rejection rate | Ignorance 0% | Ignorance 10% | Ignorance 20% |
| Conflict 0% | 0.152 | 0.140 | 0.133 |
| Conflict 10% | 0.134 | 0.118 | 0.107 |
| Conflict 20% | 0.128 | 0.109 | 0.102 |
| | Region-wise | | |
| Rejection rate | Ignorance 0% | Ignorance 10% | Ignorance 20% |
| Conflict 0% | 0.122 | 0.109 | 0.091 |
| Conflict 10% | 0.111 | 0.095 | 0.072 |
| Conflict 20% | 0.106 | 0.086 | 0.065 |

**Table 2.** Classification Error of Other Methods

| | |
|---|---|
| Histogram backprojection (Only Floor model) | 0.129 |
| Region growing (Only floor seeds) | 0.194 |
| Histogram backprojection (Floor & Obstacle model) | 0.126 |
| Region growing (Floor & Obstacle model) | 0.178 |
| Naive Bayes all features | 0.116 |

single segmentation. Although, the Naive Bayes classifier reports similar error rate compared to the fuzzy structure approach using watershed regions, it is not able to distinguish among the causes of the uncertainty. This ability is of vital importance in robot decision making as previously unobserved obstacles or detection of novel terrain are detected in areas of high ignorance. The true class of these regions might reveal itself upon closer inspection. In contrast, in areas that exhibit a high conflict, it is unlikely that further data reduces the uncertainty which is attributed to the inherent ambiguous appearance. In the context of robot navigation areas of high conflict should be avoided in any case, whereas regions of high ignorance do not need to be excluded for traversal a priori unless they constitute a risk of immediate collision.

## 6   Conclusion

This paper introduced a novel approach for free space and obstacle detection in omnidirectional immages. The approach pursues the ensemble of experts paradigm to fuse heterogeneous segmentations schemes maintaining separate models for floor and obstacles. Pixel-wise classifications belonging to homogeneous regions are processed together to improve the statistics and achieve a classification that is more robust with respect to noise and outliers. The uncertainty of the classifications is explicitly expressed in terms of preference, conflict and ignorance utilizing fuzzy preference structures. The experimental results confirm the initial hypothesis that multiple diverse visual cues in conjunction with an explicit representation of uncertainty attributed to ignorance and conflict is of paramount benefit to vision based robot local navigation. Future work is concerned with incorporating additional geometric features and domain specific knowledge to further improve the distinction of novel terrain and obstacles.

## References

1. Batavia, P., Singh, S.: Obstacle detection using adaptive color segmentation and color stereo homography. In: IEEE Int. Conf. on Robotics and Automation (2001)
2. Blas, M.R., Agrawal, M., Sundaresan, A., Konolige, K.: Fast color/texture segmentation for outdoor robots. In: IEEE/RSJ Int. Conf. on Intelligent Robots and Systems, pp. 4078–4085 (2008)
3. Bonin-Font, F., Ortiz, A., Oliver, G.: Visual navigation for mobile robots: A survey. Journal of Intelligent Robotics System 53(3), 263–296 (2008)
4. Dahlkamp, H., Kaehler, A., Stavens, D., Thrun, S., Bradski, G.: Self-supervised monocular road detection in desert terrain. In: Proc. of the Robotics Science and Systems Conference (2006)
5. Driankov, D., Saffiotti, A.: Fuzzy Logic Techniques for Autonomous Vehicle Navigation. Studies in Fuzziness and Soft Computing. Springer, Heidelberg (2001)
6. Fazl-Ersi, E., Tsotsos, J.K.: Region Classification for Robust Floor Detection in Indoor Environments. In: Kamel, M., Campilho, A. (eds.) ICIAR 2009. LNCS, vol. 5627, pp. 717–726. Springer, Heidelberg (2009)

 7. Grudic, G., Mulligan, J., Otte, M., Bates, A.: Online learning of multiple perceptual models for navigation in unknown terrain. In: 6th International Conference on Field and Service Robotics (2007)
 8. Hüllermeier, E., Brinker, K.: Learning valued preference structures for solving classification problems. Fuzzy Sets and Systems 159, 2337–2352 (2008)
 9. Kim, D., Sun, J., Min, S., James, O., Rehg, M., Bobick, A.F.: Traversability classification using unsupervised on-line visual learning for outdoor robot navigation. In: Int. Conf. on Robotics and Automation, ICRA (2006)
10. Kim, Y., Kim, H.: Layered ground floor detection for vision-based mobile robot navigation. In: IEEE Int. Conf. on Robotics and Automation, vol. 1 (2004)
11. Lenser, S., Veloso, M.: Visual sonar: fast obstacle avoidance using monocular vision. In: IEEE/RSJ Int. Conf. on Intelligent Robots and Systems (2003)
12. Noykov, S., Roumenin, C.: Occupancy grids building by sonar and mobile robot. Robotics and Autonomous Systems 55, 162–175 (2007)
13. Oriolo, G., Ulivi, G., Vendittelli, M.: Real-time map building and navigation for autonomous robots in unknown environments. IEEE Transactions on Systems, Man and Cybernetics Part B 28, 316–333 (1998)
14. Pears, N., Liang, B.: Ground plane segmentation for mobile robot visual navigation. In: IEEE/RSJ Int. Conf. on Intelligent Robots and Systems (2001)
15. Plagemann, C., Endres, F., Hess, J., Stachniss, C., Burgard, W.: Monocular range sensing: A non-parametric learning approach. In: IEEE Int. Conf. on Robotics and Automation (May 2008)
16. Polikar, R.: Ensemble based systems in decision making. IEEE Circuits and Systems Magazine 6(3), 21–45 (2006)
17. Roerdink, J.B.T.M., Meijster, A.: The watershed transform: Definitions, algorithms and parallelization strategies. Fundamenta Informaticae 41(1-2), 187–228 (2001)
18. Swain, M.J., Ballard, D.H.: Color indexing. International Journal of Computer Vision 7, 11–32 (1991)
19. Ulrich, I., Nourbakhsh, I.: Appearance-based obstacle detection with monocular color vision. In: Proc. AAAI 2000, Austin, TX (2000)

# A Composite Random Walk
## for Facing Environmental Uncertainty
## and Reduced Perceptual Capabilities

C.A. Pina-Garcia, Dongbing Gu, and Huosheng Hu

School of Computer Science and Electronic Engineering, University of Essex,
Colchester, UK
{capina,dgu,hhu}@essex.ac.uk

**Abstract.** Theoretical and empirical studies in Biology have showed
that strategies based on different random walks, such as: Brownian random walk and Lévy random walk are the best option when there is some
degree of environmental uncertainty and there is a lack of perceptual
capabilities.

When a random walker has no information about where targets are
located, different systematic or random searches may provide different
chances to find them. However, when time consumption, energy cost and
malfunction risks are determinants, an adaptive search strategy becomes
necessary in order to improve the performance of the strategy. Thus, we
can use a practical methodology to combine a systematic search with a
random search through a biological fluctuation.

We demonstrate that, in certain environments it is possible to combine
a systematic search with a random search to optimally cover a given area.
Besides, this work improves the search performance in comparison with
pure random walks such as Brownian walk and Lévy walk. We show these
theoretical results using computer simulations.

# 1 Introduction

Several studies suggest that Brownian walks and Lévy walks are commonly used
models to fit animal movement [1,2,3,4,5], these strategies represent the standard
methods for exploring a given area where there is not available information about
where targets are located; a target may be an abstraction from any particular
object that must be collected by a random walker (in this study we will refer a
random walker as a robotic agent).

A fast searching with reduced perceptual capabilities and some degree of uncertainty is commonly seen on exploration tasks that are carried on by mobile
robots or synthetic agents [4,6]. In addition, the major aim is to maximize the
chance of finding as many targets as possible.

Random walks have become a necessary tool for exploration tasks in robotics
field, where researches try to mimic strategies based on animal behavior to face
search uncertainties and environmental changes [4].

S. Jeschke, H. Liu, and D. Schilberg (Eds.): ICIRA 2011, Part I, LNAI 7101, pp. 620–629, 2011.

Plank and Codling [7] argue that "Lévy walks can be optimal strategies for searching randomly located targets in complex environments [2,3]. However, the assertion that the Lévy searching model is superior to other movement processes (such as composite random walks) is being questioned".

In this paper, we show how a simulated composite random walk can cope with environmental uncertainty with reduced perceptual capabilities. Thus, this approach also presents an acceptable performance compared with others random searches (i.e. Brownian walk, Lévy walk and intermittent strategies).

The remainder of this paper is organized as follows. Section 2 describes two main types of search strategies: random searches and systematic searches. Section 3 explains our composite random walk using a ballistic motion strategy and sequences of knots. Subsequently, in section 4 we present preliminary experiments about our assumption. Results from these experiments are compared in section 5. Finally, section 6 concludes the paper.

## 2   Methods

According to the inherent properties of the searching mechanism, it is possible to find two main types of searching strategies: *random searches* and *systematic searches*. In random searches, these rules rely on stochastic processes (i.e. the sampling of probability distributions), while, in systematic searches, the rules to optimally cover a given area are based on deterministic algorithms (i.e. fixed and organized plans) [3].

### 2.1   Random Searches

A random walk consists of a series of steps (possibly of different size) in randomly chosen directions [8]. Bearing this in mind, Viswanathan *et al.* [2] define a Lévy walk as a distribution function $P(l_j) \sim l_j^{-\mu}$ with $1 < \mu \leq 3$ where $l_j$ is the flight length. The $\mu$ exponent is the Lévy index and controls the range of correlations in the movement. Thus, Lévy models comprise a rich variety of paths ranging from Brownian motion ($\mu > 3$) to straight-line paths ($\mu \to 1$) [3].

**Brownian Walk.** This random search is derived from the probability distribution that is specified in a Lévy walk, when the Lévy index ($\mu > 3$). The Gaussian is the stable distribution for the special case $\mu \geq 3$ owing to the central limit theorem. Where its behavior does not present a heavy tailed distribution. some remarkable features presented by a Brownian walk are as follows: explorations over short distances can be made in much shorter times than explorations over long distances, the random walker tends to explore a given region of space rather thoroughly, it tends to return to the same point many times before finally wandering away. It chooses new regions to explore blindly. The random walker has no any tendency to move toward regions that it has not occupied before; it has absolutely no inkling of the past and lastly,its track does not fill up the space uniformly [5,4]. A Brownian walk plotted in our simulator tool is depicted in Figure 1a.

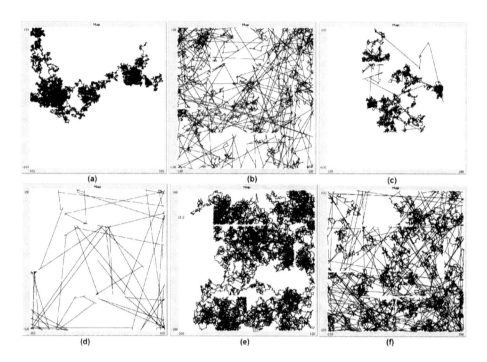

**Fig. 1.** Plots showing simulated random walks: (a) Brownian walk ($\mu = 3$); (b) Lévy walk ($\mu = 2$); (c) Adaptive switching behavior between Lévy walk and Brownian walk; (d) Intermittent strategy using regime 1; (e) Sequence of knots as a random walk; (f) Composite random walk

**Lévy Walk.** A Lévy movement pattern is generally assumed to be a "scale-invariant," i.e., it has the fractal property that the sampling scale used by the observer should not affect the observed properties [7]. In particular, a Lévy walk is known to be a super diffusive at all scales [2]. The trajectory of a Lévy walk comprises short walks with a turning angle step, $\phi_n = \theta_n - \theta_{n-1}$, is drawn from a uniform distribution on $[-\pi, \pi]$ [7].

A Lévy distribution is advantageous when target sites are sparsely and randomly distributed, irrespective of the value of $\mu$ chosen, because the probability of returning to a previously visited site is smaller than for a Gaussian distribution [2]. Theoretical arguments and numerical simulations suggest that ($\mu \approx 2$) is the optimal value for a search in any dimension and the solution to certain optimal foraging problems [1,2,3,4]. Figure 1b shows a plot of a simulated Lévy walk.

**Adaptive Switching Behavior between Lévy Walk and Brownian Walk.**
Nurzaman *et al.* [4] compare the efficiency of a Lévy walk ($\mu = 2$), a Brownian walk ($\mu = 3$) with an adaptive switching between Lévy and Brownian walk based on biological fluctuation.

The biological fluctuation allows the robot can adaptively adjust its random search property based on encounters with targets in the environment. Nurzaman et al. [4] designed a model for representing the switching probability through a simple unimodal potential function $U(z(t)) = (z(t) - h)^2$ where $z(t)$ is a variable characterizing biological fluctuation given by

$$\dot{z}(t) = -\frac{dU(z(t))}{dz}A(t) + \epsilon(t) \tag{1}$$

$$= -2(z(t) - h)A(t) + \epsilon(t) \ . \tag{2}$$

Where $h$ is the position of the attractor, $A(t)$ is the activity parameter and $\epsilon(t)$ is the noise term (white noise), representing the stochastic driving force. Thus, the switching probability at time $t$ from Lévy random walk to Brownian random walk is given by

$$P(t) = \exp(-z(t)) \ . \tag{3}$$

The fitness of the environment is defined by the activity parameter $A(t)$ given by

$$A(t) = \begin{cases} A_{min}, & \text{if } \alpha(t) \leq A_{min} \\ \alpha(t), & \text{if } \alpha(t) > A_{min} \ . \end{cases} \tag{4}$$

$$\alpha(t) = C\alpha(t-1) + K_F F(t) \ . \tag{5}$$

$$F(t) = \begin{cases} 1, & \text{if one or more targets are found at time t} \\ 0, & \text{if no targets are found at time t} \ . \end{cases} \tag{6}$$

with $0 < C < 1$ and $K_F$ is a constant with a large value with respect to $A_{min}$. Figure 1c shows a plot of a simulated adaptive switching behavior between Lévy walk and Brownian walk.

**Intermittent Strategy or "Saltatory".** Bénichou et al. [9] showed that the search strategy is optimal when the average duration of "motion phases" varies as the power either 3/5 or 2/3 of the average duration of "search phases," depending on the regime. The intermittent strategy, often referred to as "saltatory" [11], can be understood intuitively when the targets are difficult to detect and sparsely distributed. In this strategy the random walker presents two distinct phases: (1) a search phase, during which the searcher explores its immediate vicinity using its sensors. This scanning is modeled as a "slow" diffusive movement. (2) a motion phase, referred to during which the searcher moves "fast" and is unable to detect a target.

Bénichou et al. [9] assumed that the searcher randomly switches from phase 1 (respectively, 2) to phase 2 (respectively, 1) with a rate per unit time $f_1$ (respectively, $f_2$) and that the targets are immobile and randomly distributed with uniform density. The rates $f_1$ and $f_2$, which minimize the first passage time of the searcher at a target location, are given by two different regimes: First, if $f_{1max} \ll 1/\tau$, the optimal frequencies are such that $f_1 = f_{1max}$ and

$$f_2 = \left(\frac{4}{3\tau}\right)^{1/3} f_1^{2/3} . \tag{7}$$

Where $\tau = D/v^2$, $D$ is the diffusion coefficient and the velocity $v$. In this regime (R1), the random walker spends more time searching than moving.

Second, if $f_{1max} \gg 1/\tau$ the optimal frequencies are such that $f_1 = f_{1max}$ and

$$f_2 = \left(\frac{2\sqrt{2}}{\tau}\right)^{1/3} f_1^{3/5} . \tag{8}$$

In this regime (R2), the random walker spends more time moving than searching. Figure 1d shows a plot of a simulated intermittent strategy using regime 1.

## 2.2   Systematic Searches

Bartumeus *et al.* [3] argue that systematic search strategies only work when some a priori relevant (although partial) information about targets (deterministic algorithms fixed and organized plans).

**Using Sequences of Knots as a Random Search.** Knots could be considered as a sequence of movements or steps based on a set of simple rules, these rules can be projected on a square lattice following the axes with consecutive steps with the aim to form a stable structure [12].

Fink *et al.* [12,13] suggest six states: $R_\odot, R_\otimes, C_\odot, C_\otimes, L_\odot$ and $L_\otimes$. These states may be considered as movements, hence, a consecutive array of well structured steps on a square lattice represents a knot. $R$ for a right move, $L$ for a left move and $C$ for a centre move. A knot $K_i$ is formed by a finite number of vertices joined by a group of links with the aim to fit a topological structure.

Pina-Garcia and D. Gu [14] define $R$ and $L$ as follows: if $\alpha_i \leq \tau \leq \beta_i$ then $p_r(t+1) = p_r(t) + v$ and the robot turns to the right or to the left an amount of $\theta(t)$ from the normal distribution $N(0, 90)$, where $p_r$ is the robot position at time $t$, $v$ is the speed, $\theta$ is a random number between 0 and 90 degrees and $\tau$ is the time step between two limits $\alpha_i$ and $\beta_i$. Subsequently, $C$ is defined as a persistent direction with speed $v$. For implementation details see [14]. Figure 1e shows a plot of a simulated sequence of knots as a random search.

# 3   Composite Random Walk

In some cases when systematics search becomes less effective, the random walker must attempt to move in such a way so as to optimize their chances of locating targets by increasing the chances of covering a given area [3].

We propose a composite random walk that switches between a systematic strategy and a random search strategy. This switch is based on environmental changes (encounter rate) sensed by the robot, we use an adaptive switching behavior (biological fluctuation) defined by equations 1 to 6. Specifically, we compute $P(t) = \exp(-z(t))$ with a conditional function where if $P(t) = 1$, then a sequence of knots is triggered according to a deterministic algorithm with a finite time correlated to a decaying period of the environment activity $A(t)$. Otherwise, our random walker presents a ballistic motion as a default behavior defined as having $\mu \to 1$ from a Lévy walk (see algorithm 1).

This composite random walk uses a stochastic model for interacting with a patchy environment. Thus, depending of the value of the activity $A(t)$, a strong tendency to switch behavior will be displayed by the robot. Figure 1f shows a plot of a simulated composite random walk.

---

**Algorithm 1.** Composite random walk that switches between a systematic strategy and a random search strategy

---

**begin**

    $A_{min} \leftarrow 0.0001$ // *Minimum activity*
    $C \leftarrow 0.999$ // $0 < C < 1$
    $K_F \leftarrow 0.1$ // *A constant with a large value with respect to $A_{min}$*
    $h \leftarrow 0.7$ // *Position of the attractor*
    $\epsilon(t) \leftarrow 0.5$ // *White noise*

    // *Activity level for $\alpha(t)$*
    $\alpha(t) \leftarrow (C * \alpha(t-1)) + (K_F * F(t))$
    $\alpha(t-1) \leftarrow \alpha(t)$

    // *The fitness of the environment is defined by the activity parameter $A(t)$*
    **if** $\alpha(t) \leq A_{min}$ **then**
    |   $A(t) \leftarrow A_{min}$
    **else**
    └   $A(t) \leftarrow \alpha(t)$

    $z(t) \leftarrow ((-2) * (z(t) - h) * A(t) + \epsilon(t))$ // *Simple unimodal potential function*

    // *Switching probability at time t*
    **if** $z(t) < 5$ **then**
    └   $P(t) \leftarrow \exp(-z(t))$

    // *A sequence of knots or a ballistic motion is displayed according to $P(t)$*
    **if** $P(t) \geq 1$ **then**
    |   $F(t) \leftarrow 0$
    |   Start sequence of knots // *Systematic strategy*
    **else**
    └   Start ballistic motion // *Random search strategy*

---

## 4    Simulations

We devised a group of simulations in order to evaluate search efficiency of six strategies (i.e., Brownian, Lévy, adaptive, intermittent, knots and composite). All the experiments were run and programmed on a java based platform (Netlogo [15]). A screen view of the simulator is depicted in Figure 2.

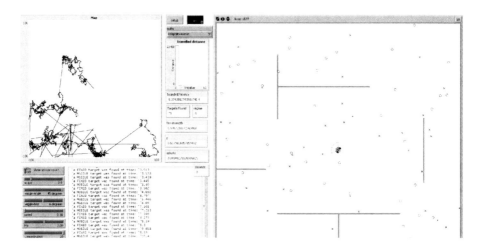

**Fig. 2.** Our simulator: on your right side, showing a robot searching inside a complex environment. On your left side, plotting the path followed by the robot.

In all our experiments, targets were considered mobile and non-mobile in accordance with a destructive foraging [3]. The right side scenario depicted in Figure 2 was used for running all the experiments. Initial conditions were defined as follows: the size of the area is $100 \times 100$ (Netlogo units), initial position of the robot is located at (0,0) on the plane, velocity has been defined with a value of 0.30. In addition, 80 targets divided in two types were deployed: 40 non-mobile targets distributed randomly inside the environment and 40 mobile targets provided with a Brownian motion as a default behavior.

Search efficiency function $S_{eff}$ is defined as follows

$$S_{eff} = \frac{\sum_{i=0}^{n} T_i}{d} \quad \text{where} \quad n \in \mathbb{N} \quad \text{and} \quad d \neq 0. \tag{9}$$

Where $T_i$ denotes the number of targets that were found at time $t$ and $d$ is the traveled distance.

Simulations were tested using different parameter values. Specifically, parameters related to the biological switching behavior: $\epsilon = 0.5$, $h = 0.7$, $A_{min} = 0.0001$, $K_F = 0.1$, $C = 0.9999$ for adaptive switching behavior strategy and $C = 0.999$ for our composite random walk strategy. A destructive encounter dynamics was considered in the efficiency simulations, i.e. the target found by the random walker becomes undetectable in subsequent displacements (destructive foraging) [3].

## 5   Results

We performed 10 trials per each strategy with an average duration of 2000 seconds each one. Intermittent strategy was divided in two regimes $R1$ and $R2$ for experimental purposes. In every experiment traveled distance, search efficiency and targets found, were registered for subsequent comparisons. Thus, the mean and the standard deviation of each metric were computed to get the statistical support for evaluating the performance between every strategy. Our collected results are shown in table 1; from left to right we present name of the strategy, Lévy index $\mu$, search efficiency, targets found and traveled distance.

**Table 1.** Performance of searching strategies. Ordered from left to right by name, Lévy index $\mu$, search efficiency, targets found and traveled distance.

| Name | $\mu$ | Search Efficiency | Targets Found | Traveled Distance |
|------|-------|-------------------|---------------|-------------------|
| Brownian | $\mu = 3$ | $1.56 \times 10^{-4}$ | $38.8 \pm 4.8$ | $2.4 \times 10^5$ |
| Lévy | $\mu = 2$ | $4.10 \times 10^{-4}$ | $79.3 \pm 1.0$ | $2.0 \times 10^5$ |
| Adaptive | $\mu = 2, \mu = 3$ | $1.54 \times 10^{-4}$ | $46.8 \pm 4.3$ | $3.0 \times 10^5$ |
| Intermittent R1 | $\mu = 1$ | $1.87 \times 10^{-4}$ | $59.6 \pm 3.9$ | $3.1 \times 10^5$ |
| Intermittent R2 | $\mu = 1$ | $2.87 \times 10^{-4}$ | $72.1 \pm 2.6$ | $2.5 \times 10^5$ |
| knots | N/A | $3.18 \times 10^{-4}$ | $57.2 \pm 7.2$ | $1.7 \times 10^5$ |
| Composite | $\mu = 1$ | $4.70 \times 10^{-4}$ | $80$ | $1.7 \times 10^5$ |

The Lévy walk was used as a base model for deriving strategies such as: Brownian walk, adaptive switching behavior, intermittent strategy and our composite random walk ($\mu$ ranging between 1 and 3). It should be noted that, for the particular case of using sequences of knots as a random search (see [14]), this strategy is considered as a systematic search and uses a deterministic algorithm.

Search efficiency ($SE$) is plotted in Figure 3, where preliminary results suggest that our composite random walk is slightly more efficient than the rest of the strategies ($SE = 4.70 \times 10^{-4}$). In addition, for all cases the Lévy index plays a relevant role in the strategy; specifically, in the Lévy walk case ($\mu = 2$ and $SE = 4.10 \times 10^{-4}$) where long steps and less backtracking than Brownian random walk ($\mu = 3$ and $SE = 1.56 \times 10^{-4}$) is observed [1].

In contrast, using a ballistic motion ($\mu \to 1$) not necessarily implies a better efficiency as intermittent strategy (R1 $SE = 1.87 \times 10^{-4}$ and R2 $SE = 2.87 \times 10^{-4}$) shows, this is because in motion phases there is not any sensing action. However, the composite random walk combines a ballistic motion with a systematic search (sequences of knots), resulting in a significant improvement due to a super-diffusive behavior, i.e., covering as much ground as possible.

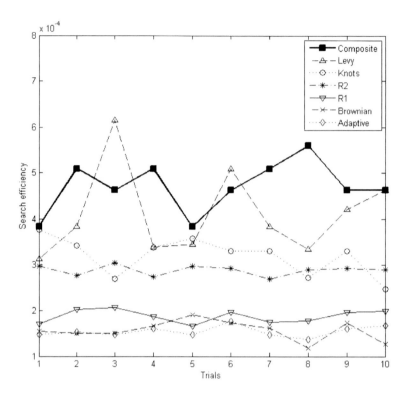

**Fig. 3.** Plot showing the search efficiency (*SE*) of six strategies: Brownian, Lévy, adaptive, intermittent (R1 and R2), knots and composite)

## 6   Conclusions and Future Work

Six different strategies were simulated, four random searches (Brownian, Lévy, adaptive and intermittent), one systematic search (sequences of knots) and our composite random walk. The resulting data obtained from experiments were analyzed by comparing the best search efficiency for each strategy.

Our results showed that combining a random search with a deterministic algorithm improved significantly a searching task where environmental uncertainty is unavoidable. In this study, we have proposed a composite random walk that switches from a failed strategy into a better strategy that optimizes encounter rates with the targets. In addition, our comparative results show that the search efficiency mainly depends on a scale invariant and super-diffusive phenomena. Thus, for each sort of environment, there might be a range of "original" strategies to speed up concrete search problems in robotics exploration.

Our results suggest that, a simple ballistic motion combined with a deterministic algorithm might optimize searching time of non-mobile and mobile targets, by filling up the search space uniformly.

**Acknowledgements.** The authors thank the reviewers of this paper for their useful comments. This research work is financially sponsored by European Union FP7 program, ICT-231646, SHOAL. Mr. Pina-Garcia has been partially supported by the Mexican National Council of Science and Technology (CONA-CYT), through the program "Becas para estudios de posgrado en el extranjero" (no. 213550).

# References

1. James, A., Plank, M.J., Brown, R.: Optimizing the encounter rate in biological interactions: ballistic versus Lévy versus Brownian strategies. Physical Review E 78(5), 51128 (2008)
2. Viswanathan, G.M., Buldyrev, S.V., Havlin, S., Da Luz, M.G.E., Raposo, E.P., Stanley, H.E.: Optimizing the success of random searches. Nature 401(6756), 911–914 (1999)
3. Bartumeus, F., Da Luz, M.G.E., Viswanathan, G.M., Catalan, J.: Animal search strategies: a quantitative random-walk analysis. Ecology 86(11), 3078–3087 (2005)
4. Nurzaman, S.G., Matsumoto, Y., Nakamura, Y., Shirai, K., Koizumi, S., Ishiguro, H.: An adaptive switching behavior between levy and Brownian random search in a mobile robot based on biological fluctuation. In: 2010 IEEE/RSJ International Conference on Intelligent Robots and Systems (IROS), pp. 1927–1934. IEEE (1927)
5. Berg, H.C.: Random walks in biology. Princeton Univ. Pr. (1993)
6. Vergassola, M., Villermaux, E., Shraiman, B.I.: 'Infotaxis' as a strategy for searching without gradients. Nature 445(7126), 406–409 (2007)
7. Plank, M.J., Codling, E.A.: Sampling rate and misidentification of Lévy and non-Lévy movement paths. Ecology 90(12), 3546–3553 (2009)
8. Codling, E.A., Bearon, R.N., Thorn, G.J.: Diffusion about the mean drift location in a biased random walk. Ecology 91(10), 3106–3113 (2010)
9. Bénichou, O., Coppey, M., Moreau, M., Suet, P.H., Voituriez, R.: Optimal search strategies for hidden targets. Physical review letters 94(19), 198101 (2005)
10. Bénichou, O., Coppey, M., Moreau, M., Voituriez, R.: Intermittent search strategies: When losing time becomes efficient. EPL (Europhysics Letters) 75, 349 (2006)
11. Bell, W.J.: Searching behaviour: the behavioural ecology of finding resources. Chapman and Hall Ltd. (1991)
12. Fink, T., Mao, Y.: Tie knots, random walks and topology. Physica A: Statistical Mechanics and its Applications 276(1-2), 109–121 (2000)
13. Fink, T.M., Mao, Y.: Designing tie knots by random walks. Nature 398(6722), 31–32 (1999)
14. Pina-Garcia, C.A., Gu, D.: Using Sequences of Knots as a Random Search. In: Groß, R., Alboul, L., Melhuish, C., Witkowski, M., Prescott, T.J., Penders, J. (eds.) TAROS 2011. LNCS, vol. 6856, pp. 426–427. Springer, Heidelberg (2011)
15. Wilensky, U.: NetLogo: Center for connected learning and computer-based modeling. Northwestern University (1999)

# Motion Design for Service Robots

Elias Xidias[1], Nikos A. Aspragathos[2], and Philip Azariadis[1]

[1] Department of Product and Systems Design Engineering,
University of the Aegean, Syros, Greece
[2] Department of Mechanical Engineering & Aeronautics, University of Patras, Greece,
{xidias,azar}@aegean.gr, asprag@mech.upatras.gr

**Abstract.** This paper considers the motion design problem for a service robot which is moving and manipulating objects in a partly known indoor environment such as stores and libraries. A service robot is requested to serve a set of work-stations in the environment providing transport and delivery tasks. The objective is to determine the optimum sequence of the work-stations visited by the service robot exactly once assuring that the robot's path through the work-station is collision free. In addition, a time optimal algorithm is presented for motion planning of the manipulator for pick and place objects at the work-stations. Simulation examples are presented to show the effectiveness of the proposed approach.

**Keywords:** service robot, indoor environment, multi-goal, motion planning, bump-surface.

## 1    Introduction

In recent years, service robots (SRs) are of immense interest due to their capability to perform complex tasks in many fields such as automated transportation systems in offices, hospitals and libraries [1]. The purposes of automation are both to save time and manpower and to improve the service quality. In a market store or a library, several stations should be visited by a service robot distributing goods or books to the shelves. An optimal route is required for saving time and expenses.

Yamamoto and Yun [2] studied the problem of navigating a mobile manipulator among obstacles by simultaneously considering the obstacle avoidance problem and the coordination problem. They assume that only the manipulator and not the platform may encounter the obstacle. The proposed controller allows the system to retain optimal or sub-optimal configurations while the manipulator avoids obstacles using potential functions. Tanner and Kyriakopoulos studied the problem of obstacle avoidance by the entire mobile manipulator system [3]. Their non-holonomic motion planner is based on a discontinuous feedback law under the influence of a potential field.

Recently attempts appeared to study the robot characteristics or to develop robots for transportation and/or distribution of goods in professional environments. Gurcan et al. [4] investigated the need for automated transportation systems in hospitals. They found that among other alternatives, mobile robots stand out as the most prominent

S. Jeschke, H. Liu, and D. Schilberg (Eds.): ICIRA 2011, Part I, LNAI 7101, pp. 630–638, 2011.

means of automation of transportation tasks in hospitals. An autonomous mobile robotic system with manipulator has been developed to retrieve items from bookshelves and carry them to scanning stations located in the off-site shelving facility [5]. In that work the control is considered for navigation as well as for pickup books using the manipulator with high efficiency.

In this paper, we present an integrated approach which combines some of the positive characteristics of several previous approaches with new ideas to generate an approach that provides an effective solution to the problem of motion design of a SR moving in a partly known indoor environment.

## 2    Motion Design Problem: General Assumptions and Notations

Consider a SR moving in a library environment, in which obstacles (either static or moving) exist. Here, moving obstacles correspond to customers, employees and to any other moving object such as another SR, in the library environment. The set of predetermined stations $\hat{S} = \{S_1, ..., S_m, ..., S_M\}$, $M \geq 1$, represents the desk and the bookshelves where the SR should pick up or place books. The overall requirements that must be taken into account are: (i) In order to simplify the representation of the SR's environment, we construct a 2D environment $W$ by the projection of the initial 3D environment in the $u_1u_2$-plane. (ii) The SR is a mobile manipulator, where the mobile platform is represented by a rectangular-shaped body with two rear wheels and two directional front wheels with a limited steering angle [8] and a PUMA 560 is mounted in the center of the top of the mobile platform. (iii) The SR it is equipped with range-sensors encircled around it. The set of sensors defines a region $RS$, which is encircled by a circle of radius $r_s$ located in the middle of the robot's body. (iv) The SR is moving only forward with variable velocity in the interval $(0, v_{max}]$, in all our examples we set $v_{max} = 0.5$. (v) A SR's path always starts from the library desk (depot), goes through all the stations (each station should be served only once) and terminates at the library desk. (vi) Each station $S_m$ is associated with a feasible region, which is represented by a circle, in which the mobile platform can be located to perform a pick and place task without violating the constraints of the manipulator and of the environment. (vii) The moving entities are represented by circular disks and are moving with constant velocities $|v_{obs}| = 0.5$. (viii) The dynamic constraints of the SR are ignored. (ix) The static obstacles, such as walls and bookshelves, have fixed and known geometry and location.

### 2.1    The Workspace Model

For the representation of the SR's workspace we adopt the method based on the Bump-Surface introduced by Azariadis and Aspragathos [6]. The Bump-Surface concept is a method that represents the entire workspace by using a B-Spline surface embedded in a higher dimension Euclidean Space. The construction of the

Bump-Surface $S$ is based on a control-points net with variable density depending on the required path-planning accuracy, i.e., denser the grid, higher the accuracy. In addition, due to the flexibility of the B-Spline surfaces we can capture the desired accuracy by taking advantage of their ability for local and global control [9].

# 3    Optimal Motion Design

In this section an integrated approach is presented for optimal multi-target motion planning of a mobile platform in partly known environments cluttered with known static obstacles and unknown moving ones, as well as the motion planning of a manipulator mounted on the platform and performing manipulations at the target locations.

## 3.1    Motion Design in Static Environment

The main objective of this Section is to simultaneously determine the schedule and the path for a SR taking into account only the static obstacles of the environment and the dimensions of the mobile platform. The mathematical representation of the SR path should be able to provide simplicity, in order to avoid extensive mathematical formulations and derive fast and stable computational algorithms, flexibility and local control, in order to allow for movements within complex environments and narrow passages, accuracy, in order to make sure that the SR will pass through the work stations, and so on. For these reasons we adopt NURBS [9] to represent the SR's path, namely $\mathbf{R}(s)$, in this paper. A second degree NURBS curve is utilized to represent $\mathbf{R}(s)$ as

$$\mathbf{R}(s) = \frac{\displaystyle\sum_{i=0}^{N_c-1} N_i^2(s) w_i \mathbf{p}_i}{\displaystyle\sum_{i=0}^{N_c-1} N_i^2(s) w_i}, \quad s \in [0,1] \tag{1}$$

Here, $N_i^2(s)$ is the B-Spline basis function, $w_i$ are the weight factors and $\mathbf{p}_i$ are the $N_c$ control points of $\mathbf{R}(s)$ defined as in the following: (i) $\mathbf{p}_0 = \mathbf{p}_{N_c-1}$ denoting the depot location of SR and (ii) $\{\mathbf{p}_1,...,\mathbf{p}_{N_c-2}\} = (\{\hat{\boldsymbol{S}}\} \cup \{\boldsymbol{g}_\omega, \omega=1,...,N_b\})$ defined in $\mathcal{W}$, where $\boldsymbol{g}_\omega$ are intermediate points. The number $N_b$ is given by $N_b = r(M+1)$ where $r$ being the number (user-defined) of the points between each sequential pair of $\boldsymbol{S}_m$. Furthermore, the control points which correspond to the work stations $\hat{\boldsymbol{S}}$ are located to the centre of the associated circles.

A feasible path $\mathbf{R}(s)$ is one that, firstly, does not collide with the static obstacles and secondly, its curvature $k(s)$ never exceeds an upper-bounded curvature $k_{max}$ in order to satisfy the kinematic constraints and force the platform velocity in the interval $(0, v_{max}]$. Following the results from [6] the arc length of $\mathbf{R}(s)$ approximates the length $L$ of its image $\mathbf{S}(\mathbf{R}(s))$ on $S$ as long as $\mathbf{R}(s)$ lies onto the flat areas of $S$.

In order to take into account the geometry of the mobile platform we select the vertices $\mathbf{a}_\kappa$, $\kappa = 1,...,4$, on the perimeter of the platform. Thus, similarly with the midpoint $\mathbf{R}$, each point $\mathbf{a}_\kappa$ follows a curve $\mathbf{a}_\kappa = \mathbf{a}_\kappa(s)$ in $\mathcal{W}$. Then following the results from [6], we measure the "flatness" $H_\kappa$ of the image $\mathbf{S}_z(\mathbf{a}_\kappa(s))$ of $\mathbf{a}_\kappa(s)$ on $S$.

Let $E = e^{\left(\sum_{\kappa=1}^{4} H_\kappa\right)} * L$, be a penalized length function corresponding to $\mathbf{S}(\mathbf{R}(s))$. $E$ takes a value in the interval $(L, +\infty)$, if the platform collides with the obstacles and the value $L$, otherwise. Then, the requirement for a collision-free path for the mobile platform can be described as an optimization sub-problem with respect to control points $\mathbf{p}_i$, written as

$$\min E \tag{2}$$

Furthermore, in order to ensure that the curvature $k_i(s), i = 1,...,N_c + 1$ at every point $\mathbf{R}_i$ never exceeds $k_{max}$ the following condition should also hold:

$$k_i(s) \le k_{max}, \ s \in [0,1] \tag{3}$$

An optimum velocity profile must be generated for the platform to travel along an assigned path $\mathbf{R}(s)$ whose length function onto $S$ is $E$. Since the main constraint is planning forward motions only, the velocity $v(s)$ is constrained by the relation,

$$0 < v(s) \le v_{max} \tag{4}$$

The velocity $v(s)$ can never become negative and can be equal to zero only at the depot locations. Since $\mathbf{R}(s)$ is discretized, the measurement of the velocity $v_i$ at every point $\mathbf{R}_i$ is defined by [8],

$$v_i = \begin{cases} v_{max}, \ if \ k_i = 0 \\ \min\left(v_{max}, \sqrt{\dfrac{\tau_0}{k_i}}\right), \ if \ k_i \ne 0 \end{cases} \tag{5}$$

where, $\tau_0$ is a constant which depends on the friction between the wheels and the ground, and the gravity constant $g$.

Let $\mathbf{R}_i$ and $\mathbf{R}_{i+1}$ be two sequential points on $\mathbf{R}(s)$. Furthermore, it is assumed that the platform is moving from the point $\mathbf{R}_i$ to the point $\mathbf{R}_{i+1}$ in an infinitesimal time $\Delta t_i$, and $\Delta E_i$ is the corresponding displacement along $\mathbf{R}(s)$. The average velocity of the platform during this period is represented by $\Delta v_i$. The travel time $\Delta t_i$ from point $\mathbf{R}_i$ to point $\mathbf{R}_{i+1}$ is given by,

$$\Delta t_i = \frac{\Delta E_i}{\Delta v_i} \tag{6}$$

Then, the overall time required for the platform to travel along $\mathbf{R}(s)$ is calculated by

$$t_p = \sum_{i=0}^{N_c-2} \Delta t_i = \sum_{i=0}^{N_c-2} \frac{\Delta E_i}{\Delta v_i} \tag{7}$$

Taking the above analysis into consideration, the motion planning problem for the static environment is formulated as an optimization problem given by

$$\min(t_p) \text{ subject to } k_i \leq k_{max}, \ i = 1,...,N_c \tag{8}$$

The minimization of problem (8) with respect to the control points $\mathbf{p}_i$ leads to a collision-free path for the platform, which satisfies all the requirements. A modified GA has been implemented to resolve the problem depicted by eq.(8). A mixed integer and floating-point representation was selected for the encoding of the variables [10].

## 3.2    Avoiding Moving Obstacles

Once the global path $\mathbf{R}(s)$ has been created, the robot starts to move along this path in order to serve the stations. If the SR detects a moving obstacle entering in the $RS$ region another algorithm is activated to modify the initial trajectory. In this part of the paper the algorithm introduced in [11] for the deviation from the initial path is presented in brief.

At every point $\mathbf{R}_i, i = 1,...,N_c$ (which correspond to the time instance $t_i$) of $\mathbf{R}(s)$, the SR using the set of the onboard range-sensors checks if any of the moving obstacles are entered in the region $RS$. If there are no moving obstacles in the region $RS$, then the robot moves to the next point $\mathbf{R}_{i+1}$ of $\mathbf{R}(s)$ without modifying its motion. If SR detects a moving obstacle then, taking into account the necessary information of the onboard sensors, it is able to compute the relative velocity $v_{ro}(t_i)$ between the SR and the moving obstacle. By computing the $v_{ro}(t_i)$ we can determine if a collision occurs (for details see [11]). If $v_{ro}(t_i) \leq 0$, the SR is moving away from the moving obstacle and no maneuvers are needed. If $v_{ro}(t_i) > 0$, the SR is moving towards to the moving obstacle. In this case, the SR motion should deviate from the initial path in order to avoid collision with the moving obstacle.

Suppose that at time $t_i$ the SR is moving towards the moving obstacle, i.e., $v_{ro}(t_i) > 0$, then, in order for the SR to avoid getting trapped in obstacles' concave regions and bypass any blocking obstacle, the geometry of the moving obstacle should be modified. The modified obstacle derived from the union of its traces, at the time interval $[t_i, t_{i+M}]$, where $t_{i+M}$ is the time instance where the SR collides with the obstacle. Then, the Bump-Surface is used in order to determine a "new" path $\mathbf{R}'(s)$ for the SR where the initial point is $\mathbf{R}_i$ and the final point is $\mathbf{R}_{N_c}$. The local path planning problem is solved using a GA [7]. Finally, the SR is moving to the point $\mathbf{R}'_1(s)$, which corresponds to the time instance $t_{i+1}$, and repeats the above procedure.

It must be noticed that in order to ensure that the SR has a smooth motion the following condition is incorporated:

$$\min(\theta(t_{i+1}) - \theta(t_i))$$ (9)

where $\theta(t_i)$ is the SR's orientation at time $t_i$ and $\theta(t_{i+1})$ is the SR's orientation at time $t_{i+1}$.

## 3.3   Manipulator Motion Planning

This section presents a method for solving the motion-planning problem for the onboard manipulator operating in a 3D environment. When the platform arrives to a station $\mathcal{S}_m, m = 1,...,M$ stops and starts to execute a predefined task.

Using the Bump-Surface, the manipulator's workspace is represented by a 3D surface embedded in $\mathfrak{R}^4$. A global optimization problem is then formulated considering simultaneously the task-scheduling and the collision-free motion planning of the manipulator among the obstacles. The optimization problem is solved using a Genetic Algorithm (GA) with a special encoding that considers the multiplicity of the Inverse Kinematics [12].

In order to take into account the shape of the manipulator a set of probabilistic points $a_v^n, v = 1,...,N$, defined in the initial 3D environment, is selected on the surface of each $n$-link ($n=2,...,6$) according to the requested accuracy (e.g., higher accuracy is achieved using a big number of $N$), where $N$ is the overall number of probabilistic points. Thus, following the results from [10] the minimization of the following objective function,

$$Flat = \sum_{\mu=1}^{2+\mathcal{R}+\tau} H_\mu$$ (10)

with respect to the joint variables $\theta_\mu \in \mathfrak{R}^6, \mu = 1,...,2+\mathcal{R}+\tau$, satisfies the requirement for collision-free robot's configurations, where $H_\mu$ is the "flatness" of the image $a_v^n(s)$ on $S$ (see [12]), $2+\mathcal{R}+\tau$ is the total number of configurations between the initial and final configuration, $\mu$ is a robot configuration, $\tau$ corresponds to the configurations between the successive configurations resulting from linear interpolation of the joint variables and the number $\mathcal{R}$ is the intermediate configurations between two successive task-points specifies the trajectory of the robot while moving between the initial and final configuration.

The total travel time $t_{total}$ needed to move the manipulator from the book pick-point to the book place-point through the intermediate configurations is given by

$$t_{total} = t_A + t_\mathcal{R} + t_B$$ (11)

where $t_A$ is the time spent by the manipulator to travel from the pick configuration to the first intermediate configuration, $t_\mathcal{R}$ is the time spent by the manipulator to travel from one intermediate configuration to another one and $t_B$ is the time spent by the manipulator to travel from the last intermediate configuration to the final configuration corresponding to the book place-point (for details see [12]).

Thus, the multi-objective function given by

$$E_M(\boldsymbol{\theta}) = w_1\, t_{\text{total}}(\boldsymbol{\theta}) + w_2\, Flat(\boldsymbol{\theta}), \text{ with } w_1 + w_2 = 1 \tag{12}$$

expresses the total cycle time. For the optimization of the multi-goal motion planning problem a modified Genetic Algorithm is selected [12].

## 4    Experiments

Due to space limits, we present in this section only one representative experiment.

*Test case*: The experiment corresponds to a library scenario shown in Fig.1, which is cluttered with narrow corridors, static obstacles and one circular moving obstacle. The SR has to travel between a depot and 4 work stations. The number of the unknown control points between the stations is set equal to 5. The solution path is shown in Fig. 1(a). The magenta dashed curve shows the final path and the black curve shows the initial path, i.e., the path derived by taking into account only the static obstacles and the dimension of the platform. The SR passes through the stations depot-$\mathcal{S}_1$- $\mathcal{S}_3$- $\mathcal{S}_4$- $\mathcal{S}_2$-depot. Fig. 1(b), shows a time instance of the proposed motion of the SR. The rectangular object (grey color) presents the mobile platform where the black dot represents the onboard manipulator and the red circular disk represent the moving object. The black circle represents the *RS* area. Fig. 2 shows the SR in front of the bookshelf (station $\mathcal{S}_1$) where the manipulator gets a book from the box and put it in the bookshelf.

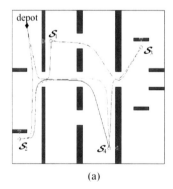
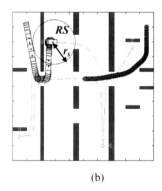

(a)                                    (b)

**Fig. 1.** (a): The solution path (magenta) and the initial path (black). (b) A time instance of the SR's motion and the obstacle's motion.

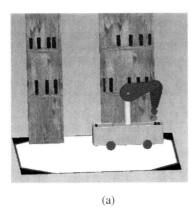

(a)                                                    (b)

**Fig. 2.** (a) The manipulator taking a book from the box. (b) The manipulator putting a book on the bookshelf.

As can be seen from the above example the proposed method is able to schedule the motion of a SR and simultaneously to produce collision-free motion for the onboard manipulator in complicated environments with narrow corridors and rooms. The generated solution path satisfies (in a near optimum way) all the established motion design criteria and constraints.

## 5    Conclusions

An integrated approach for motion design of a SR in a partly indoor environment has been presented in this paper. The overall problem has been resolved be applying the Bump-Surfaces methodology in order to represent the entire environment with a single mathematical entity. With this representation one is able to formulate the current motion design problem as a constrained global optimization problem in order to compute a valid path for both the mobile platform and the manipulator.

## References

[1]  Schmidt, G., Hanebeck, U.D., Fischer, C.: A mobile service robot for the hospital and home environment. In: Proceedings of the IARP Second International Workshop; Smith, T.F., Waterman, M.S.: Identification of Common Molecular Subsequences. J. Mol. Biol. 147, 195–197 (1981)

[2]  Yamamoto, Y., Yun, X.: Coordinated Obstacle Avoidance of a Mobile Manipulator. In: Proc. of the IEEE Int. Conf. on Robotics and Automation, pp. 2255–2260 (1995)

[3]  Tanner, H., Kyriakopoulos, K.: Nonholonomic Motion Planning for Mobile Manipulators. In: Proc. of the IEEE Int. Conf. on Robotics and Automation, pp. 1233–1238 (April 2000)

[4]  Özkil, A.G., Zhun Fan, S.D., Aanæs, H., Kristensen, J.K., Christensen, K.H.: Service Robots for Hospitals: A Case Study of Transportation Tasks in a Hospital. In: Proceedings of the IEEE International Conference on Automation and Logistics, Shenyang, China (August 2009)

[5]   Suthakorn, J., Sangyoon, L., Yu, Z., Choudhury, S., Chirikjian, G.S.: An Enhanced Robotic Library System for an Off-Site Shelving Facility. In: Yuta, S., et al. (eds.) Field and Service Robotics, STAR, vol. 24, pp. 437–446. Springer, Heidelberg (2006)

[6]   Azariadis, P.N., Aspragathos, N.A.: Obstacle representation by Bump-surfaces for optimal motion-planning. Robotics and Autonomous Systems 51(2-3), 129–150 (2005)

[7]   Goldberg, D.E.: Genetic Algorithms in Search, Optimization and Machine. Learning. Addison Wesley Publishing Company (1989)

[8]   LaValle, M.S.: Planning Algorithms. University of Illinois (2004)

[9]   Piegl, L., Tiller, W.: The NURBS Book. Springer, Heidelberg (1997)

[10]  Xidias, E.K., Azariadis, P.N.: Mission design for a group of autonomous guided vehicles. Robotics and Autonomous Systems 59(1), 34–43 (2011)

[11]  Xidias, E., Aspragathos, N.: Dynamic Motion Planning for Mobile Robots Using the Bump-Surface Concept. In: Proceeding of the 2nd European Conference on Mobile Robots, Ancona, Italy, September 7-10 (2005)

[12]  Xidias, E.K., Zacharia, P.T., Aspragathos, N.A.: Time-optimal task scheduling for articulated manipulators in environments cluttered with obstacles. Robotica 28(3), 427–440 (2010)

# Author Index

Aach, Til   I-553
Abu-Dakka, Fares J.   I-83
Agarwal, Manoj   I-346
Aguilar, Mario F.   I-300
Aiying, Chee   I-324
Alfraheed, Mohammad   II-589
Al Khawli, Toufik   II-199
Aloulou, Amira   II-251
Alpen, Mirco   I-1
An, Jinung   II-536
Andaluz, Victor H.   I-563
Andersen, Knud A.   II-430
Annighöfer, Björn   I-312
Arena, Paolo   II-46
Aspragathos, Nikos A.   I-486, I-509, I-630
Assad, Iyad F.   I-83
Atorf, Linus   I-553
Auerbach, Thomas   II-199
Azariadis, Philip   I-630

Baddeley, Bart   II-75
Badreddin, Essameddin   I-192
Baek, Kwang-Ryul   I-575, I-604
Barroso, Giovanni C.   I-300
Bartenbach, Volker   II-548
Baumgartner, Tobias   II-348
Beckers, Marion   II-199
Behnke, Sven   I-33, II-145, II-157
Behrens, Alexander   I-553
Bellot, Delphine   II-389
Berg, Christian   II-56
Bertram, Torsten   I-172, I-610
Besari, Adnan Rachmat Anom   II-599
Bhat, Rama B.   I-376
Bhattacharya, Sambit   II-317
Bi, Qingzhen   II-465
Bilberg, Arne   II-12
Bocanegra, Juanjo   I-416
Bodenhagen, Leon   II-430
Bongardt, Bertold   I-465
Boubaker, Olfa   II-251
Brandl, Christopher   I-542
Brecher, Christian   II-179, II-189

Bremer, Hartmut   II-569
Brenken, Benedikt   I-542
Buchholz, Guido   II-199
Buescher, Christian   II-168
Burger, Wolfgang   II-548
Busch, Felix   I-112

Cannan, James A.R.   I-202
Carbone, Giuseppe   I-122
Carelli, Ricardo   I-563
Casillas, Jorge   II-525
Ceccarelli, Marco   I-122
Chang, Zongyu   I-270
Chen, Guimin   I-291
Chen, Shengyong   II-85
Chen, Wenbin   I-183
Chen, Xiang   I-250
Chen, Xinpu   I-162
Chen, Xubing   II-487
Chen, YuShan   II-378
Cheng, Hongkai   I-22
Cheng, Xuegang   II-378
Cheng, Yongzhi   I-22
Cho, Bong-Su   I-575, I-604
Choi, Sunghee   I-594
Corves, Burkhard   I-132, I-152, I-240, II-179
Cruse, Holk   II-65
Czejdo, Bogdan   II-317

de B. Serra, Antonio   I-300
de la Cruz, Jesus M.   II-579
Deng, Jiaming   I-436
Deuse, Jochen   I-112
Dietrich, Franz   I-142
Ding, Han   I-445, II-465, II-477
Ding, Hao   I-520
Ding, Ming   I-221
Ding, Ye   II-452
Dong, Haiwei   II-558
Drimus, Alin   II-12
Droeschel, David   II-157
Dröge, Alicia   II-589

Du, Yingkui    II-95
Du, Zhengchun    I-281
Dürr, Volker    II-24

Eppelt, Urs    II-199
Ercan, M. Fikret    II-495
Esakki, Balasubramanian    I-376
Esser, Martin    I-93, II-179

Falkenberg, Ole    I-312
Feng, Ying    II-263
Ferrein, Alexander    II-241
Fjerdingen, Sigurd Aksnes    II-525
Florescu, Mihaela    II-275
Florez, Juan Manuel    II-389
Floros, Georgios    II-105
Frick, Klaus    I-1
Fritz, Peter    II-199
Fu, Zhuang    II-505
Fugl, Andreas R.    II-430

Ganapathy, Velappa    I-324
Ganesan, Thayabaren    II-358
Gao, Lixin    II-85
Gattringer, Hubert    II-569
Geppert, Tim    I-397
Gloy, Yves-Simon    II-199
Gosselin, Clément    I-152
Graham, Paul    II-75
Gries, Thomas    II-199
Groh, Konrad    I-73
Gropengießer, Willem    I-12
Groß, Horst-Michael    II-328, II-368
Gu, Dawei    II-579
Gu, Dongbing    I-620, II-287
Gu, Guo-Ying    II-263
Guan, Enguang    II-505
Gunura, Keith    I-416

Haag, Sebastian    II-179, II-189
Hägele, Martin    I-542
Han, Shubo    II-317
Hänsch, Paul    II-297
Hauck, Eckart    I-335, I-366
Hellbach, Sven    II-24
Herman, Przemyslaw    I-53
Hild, Manfred    I-388, I-397
Hirai, Shinichi    I-496
Hiwada, Eriko    II-210
Hoffmann, Frank    I-172, I-610

Hopmann, Christian    II-199
Horn, Joachim    I-1
Hourani, Hamido    I-335, I-366
Hu, Huosheng    I-202, I-620, II-287
Huan, Ruohong    II-116
Huang, Gan    II-135
Huang, Qiang    I-122
Huang, Ruining    I-260
Huang, Xiaolin    I-183
Huptych, Marcel    I-73
Husbands, Philip    II-75
Hüsing, Mathias    I-152
Hüttner, Stefan    I-102

Iftikhar, Muhammad    II-358
Iida, Fumiya    I-416
Iida, Tomohiro    I-221
Ishibuchi, Hisao    II-515
Ivanescu, Mircea    II-275

Janssen, Markus    I-93
Jeschke, Sabina    I-335, I-366, II-168, II-589
Jiang, Dongsheng    II-505
Jordt, Andreas    II-430

Karimi, Hamid Reza    II-401
Kataoka, Yuuki    I-496
Kessler, Jens    II-368
Khanal, Bishesh    II-609
Khosravi, Mohammad A.    I-455
Kiriazov, Petko    II-307
Klingender, Max    II-589
Klocke, Fritz    II-199
Koch, Reinhard    II-430
Komatsu, Rikako    II-220
Kong, Dong-Uck    II-536
Kordasz, Marta    I-53
Koustoumpardis, Panagiotis N.    I-486
Kowalewski, Stefan    II-297
Kratz, Stephan    II-199
Krause, Tammo    II-56
Krug, Stefan    I-102
Krüger, Norbert    II-430
Kubota, Naoyuki    II-210, II-220
Kuhlenkoetter, Bernd    I-112
Kumar, Naveen    I-346

Lakemeyer, Gerhard    II-241, II-348
Lee, Jangmyung    I-594

Lei, Min    I-212
Leibe, Bastian    II-105
Lenac, Kristijan    I-584
Li, Hui    I-122
Li, Xiang    II-495
Li, Zexiang    I-260
Lin, Hua    I-478
Liu, Honghai    I-478
Liu, PinKuan    I-445
Liu, Xin-Jun    I-250
Löchte, Christian    I-142
Lose, Juliane    II-199
Lou, Yunjiang    I-260
Lüdtke, Mathias    I-542
Luo, Zhiwei    II-558

Ma, Lvzhong    I-426
Ma, Zhenghua    I-436
Madonski, Rafal    I-53
Mannheim, Tom    I-132
Mariappan, Muralindran    II-358
Marín, Francisco Javier    II-525
Masuta, Hiroyuki    II-210
Mata, Vicente    I-83
Mateos, Luis A.    I-406
Maycock, Jonathan    II-34
Mayer, Marcel    II-168
Mayr, Johannes    II-569
Md Palil, Md Dan    II-599
Meng, Guang    I-212
Meng, Jianjun    II-135
Mertens, Alexander    I-542
Michaeli, Walter    II-199
Mitzel, Dennis    II-105
Mizoguchi, Hiroshi    I-221
Mladenova, Clementina    II-420
Molitor, Thomas    II-199
Moon, Woo-Sung    I-575, I-604
Morel, Guillaume    II-389
Mucientes, Manuel    II-525
Müller, Rainer    I-93, II-179
Müller, Steffen    II-328
Mumolo, Enzo    I-584
Mustafa, Mahmoud    II-338

Narayanan, Krishna Kumar    I-172, I-610
Nefzi, Marwène    I-152
Nieuwenhuisen, Matthias    I-33
Nikolova, Gergana    II-307

Nojima, Yusuke    II-515
Nolich, Massimiliano    I-584

Obo, Takenori    II-220
Oehler, Bastian    II-145
Olsen, Martin M.    II-430
Otto, Marc    II-24
Oyekan, John    II-287

Pajares, Gonzalo    II-579
Pan, Tongqing    I-270
Pan, Yun    II-116
Park, Jaehyun    I-594
Paskarbeit, Jan    II-1
Patané, Luca    II-46
Payandeh, Shahram    I-230
Petersen, Henrik G.    II-430
Philippides, Andrew    II-75
Pilz, Ulf    I-12
Pina-Garcia, C.A.    I-620
Popescu, Nirvana    II-275
Posada, Luis-Felipe    I-172, I-610
Prabuwono, Anton Satria    II-599
Pryor, Mitch    II-442
Przybyla, Mateusz    I-53
Pyschny, Nicolas    II-189

Raatz, Annika    I-142, I-366
Ragavan, S. Veera    I-324
Ramirez-Serrano, Alex    II-338
Ramu, Vigneswaran    II-358
Reinhart, Gunther    I-102
Reiser, Ulrich    I-542
Reisgen, Uwe    II-199
Reißig, Gunther    I-520
Ren, Cheng    II-125
Reßmann, Axel    II-199
Riedel, Martin    I-132, I-152, II-179
Ritter, Helge    II-34
Roberti, Flavio    I-563
Röck, Sascha    I-73
Rossmann, Jürgen    II-229

Sanchez-Benitez, David    II-579
Santos, Vitor A.    I-300
Schäffersmann, Mattias    II-1
Schiffer, Stefan    II-241, II-348
Schilberg, Daniel    II-168, II-589
Schjølberg, Ingrid    II-525
Schlette, Christian    II-229

Schlick, Christopher     I-542
Schmitt, Robert     II-199
Schmitz, Josef     II-1
Schneider, Axel     II-1
Schneider, Dorian     I-553
Schommer, John     II-297
Schroeder, Kyle     II-442
Schröter, Christof     II-328, II-368
Schulz, Dirk     I-33, II-145
Seo, Woo-Jin     I-575, I-604
Shen, Huiping     I-426, I-436
Shen, Xiong     II-412
Siddique, Mohammad     II-317
Sidibé, Désiré     II-609
Siedel, Torsten     I-388, I-397
Soares, Jose M.     I-300
Song, Lin     I-63
Steffen, Jan     II-34
Stein, Thorsten     II-548
Strauss, Roland     II-46, II-56
Stueckler, Joerg     II-145
Stursberg, Olaf     I-520
Su, Chun-Yi     I-376
Sudowe, Patrick     II-105
Sun, Ronglei     I-183
Szewczyk, Jérôme     II-389
Szkodny, Tadeusz     I-44

Taghirad, Hamid D.     I-455
Tahboub, Karim A.     I-192
Takemura, Hiroshi     I-221
Tang, Dalai     II-220
Tang, Guoyuan     II-412
Tang, Xiaomei     II-116
Tang, Yandong     II-95
Tang, Zhouming     I-230
Tao, Shaobin     I-426
Taufik,     II-599
Termini, Pietro Savio     II-46
Thomas, Carsten     I-112
Thombansen, Ulrich     II-199
Toibero, Juan Marcos     I-563
Transeth, Aksel Andreas     II-525
Triantafyllou, Dimitra     I-509

Vafaei, Alaleh     I-455
Valero, Francisco     I-83
van der Zander, Benito     II-105
Veneva, Ivanka     II-307
Verl, Alexander     I-542

Veselovac, Dražen     II-199
Vette, Matthias     II-179
Vig, Lovekesh     I-346
Vincze, Markus     I-406
Vitanza, Alessandra     II-46
Volkhardt, Michael     II-328

Wagner, Bernardo     I-563
Wahle, Martin     I-240
Walder, Florian     I-12
Wang, Dangxiao     I-532
Wang, Hao     I-281
Wang, Jinbo     II-487
Wang, Jinsong     I-250
Wang, Wei     I-436
Wang, Xin     II-125
Wang, Ying     I-162
Wang, Yuhan     II-465
Wang, Zhehu     II-116
Wehner, Rüdiger     II-65
Weidner, Mario     I-388
Welle, Jochen     II-145
Weltin, Uwe     I-312
Werner, Herbert     I-12
Wijaya, Kurniawan     I-520
Wilging, Klaus     II-548
Willatzen, Morten     II-430
Willms, Konrad     II-199
Witt, Jonas     I-12, I-312
Wolters, Philipp     I-335, I-366
Wu, Jianhua     I-356
Wu, Jun     I-532

Xidias, Elias     I-630
Xie, Fugui     I-250
Xiong, Caihua     I-22, I-183, II-452
Xiong, Youlun     II-487
Xiong, Zhenhua     I-356, II-477
Xu, Fei     I-162
Xu, GuoHua     II-412
Xu, Lixin     I-270
Xu, Xiaolong     II-412
Xu, Xiong     I-356
Xue, Changyu     I-436

Yan, Weixin     II-505
Yang, Suixian     I-63
Yang, Tingli     I-426
Yang, Wenyu     II-378
Yang, Yuhu     I-270

Yao, Zhenqiang    I-281
Ye, Shuai    II-125
Ye, Tao    I-22
Yu, Haidong    I-281
Yu, Kun    II-412

Zamri, Ruzaidi    II-599
Zäpf, Bianca    II-56
Zhang, Dingguo    I-162, II-135
Zhang, Gang    I-445
Zhang, Pu    I-281
Zhang, Shouyin    I-291

Zhang, XiaoJian    II-452
Zhang, Xiaoping    II-378
Zhang, Xiaoqin    II-85
Zhang, Yongsheng    I-260
Zhang, Yuru    I-532
Zhao, Ge    II-95
Zhao, Huan    II-477
Zhao, Li    II-85
Zhao, Yanzheng    II-505
Zheng, Zhongqiang    I-270
Zhu, Limin    II-263, II-465, II-477
Zhu, Xiangyang    I-356, II-135